Routledge Handbook of Chinese Security

Located in the center of Asia with one of the largest land frontiers in the world and 14 neighbors whose dispositions could not easily be predicted, China has long been obsessed with security. In this Handbook, an internationally renowned team of contributors provide a comprehensive and systematic analysis of contemporary thinking about Chinese national security. Chapters cover the PRC's historical, ideological and doctrinal heritage related to security, its security arrangements and policies targeting key regions and nations of the world, the security aspects of the PRC's ground, air, sea, space and cyber forces, as well as the changing and expanding definition and scope of China's security theory and practice.

The Handbook is divided into three thematic parts:

Part I focuses on national security, covering traditional views of security and the impact of China's historical experience on current security dispositions as well as non-traditional security.

Part II looks at China's relations with the great powers, regional security and China's involvement with collective security organizations.

Part III provides an overview of China's institutionalized security forces; looking at the army, navy, air force and Second Artillery (strategic nuclear forces) and offering analysis of China's recent interest in space as a security concern and cybersecurity.

This volume is essential reading for all students of Asian Security, Chinese Politics and International Relations.

Lowell Dittmer is Professor in the Department of Political Science at the University of California, Berkeley, USA.

Maochun Yu is Professor of East Asia and Military History at the United States Naval Academy.

Routledge Handbook of Chinese Security

Edited by
Lowell Dittmer and Maochun Yu

LONDON AND NEW YORK

First published 2015
by Routledge
2 Park Square, Milton Park, Abingdon, Oxon OX14 4RN

and by Routledge
711 Third Avenue, New York, NY 10017

Routledge is an imprint of the Taylor & Francis Group, an informa business

© 2015 selection and editorial material, Lowell Dittmer and Maochun Yu; individual chapters, the contributors

The right of Lowell Dittmer and Maochun Yu to be identified as authors of the editorial material, and of the individual authors as authors of their contributions, has been asserted by them in accordance with sections 77 and 78 of the Copyright, Designs and Patents Act 1988.

All rights reserved. No part of this book may be reprinted or reproduced or utilized in any form or by any electronic, mechanical, or other means, now known or hereafter invented, including photocopying and recording, or in any information storage or retrieval system, without permission in writing from the publishers.

Trademark notice: Product or corporate names may be trademarks or registered trademarks, and are used only for identification and explanation without intent to infringe.

British Library Cataloguing in Publication Data
A catalogue record for this book is available from the British Library

Library of Congress Cataloging-in-Publication Data
Routledge handbook of Chinese security / edited by Lowell Dittmer and
  Maochun Yu.
    pages cm
  1. National security—China.   2. China—Military policy.   3. China—Strategic aspects.   4. China—Armed Forces.   5. Geopolitics—China.
  6. China—Foreign relations.   7. Security, International.   I. Dittmer, Lowell, editor.   II. Yu, Maochun, editor.
   UA835.R58 2015
   355'.033051—dc23
   2014043222

ISBN: 978-0-415-85543-3 (hbk)
ISBN: 978-1-315-71297-0 (ebk)

Typeset in Bembo
by Apex CoVantage, LLC

Printed and bound in the United States of America by Publishers Graphics, LLC on sustainably sourced paper.

Contents

List of figures	ix
List of tables	xi
List of contributors	xiii
Editors' note and acknowledgements	xv
Introduction: China's security perspective *Lowell Dittmer*	1

PART I
Chinese national security   19

  1 The historical legacy of Chinese security policy   21
     Yuan-kang Wang

  2 Marxist ideology, revolutionary legacy and their impact
     on China's security policy   34
     Maochun Yu

  3 Economics and security in China   49
     Marc Lanteigne

  4 China's non-traditional security   64
     Patricia Thornton

PART II
Geostrategic perspectives   79

Section A: The great powers   80

  5 China and the United States: common and contested interests   81
     Christopher Twomey

  6 Russia and Chinese security   90
     Yu-Shan Wu

Contents

7   Security dimensions of China's relations with Japan — 104
    June Teufel Dreyer

8   China as "offshore balancer" and South Asia's regional
    security complex — 123
    Enze Han and Lawrence Saez

Section B: Regional security — 137

9   Courting the LDCs: how partnerships with post-colonial governments
    became a top CCP security interest — 138
    Edward Friedman

10 China's security and the Arctic — 155
    Linda Jakobson

11 Security dimensions of China's relations with the Korean Peninsula — 167
    Jinwook Choi

12 Taiwan and Chinese security — 181
    Jean-Pierre Cabestan

Section C: Collective security — 200

13 The United Nations in Chinese security — 201
    Liselotte Odgaard

14 The paper partnership: security in Sino-European relations — 217
    Jonathan Holslag

15 Central Asia and China's security policy — 229
    Niklas Swanström

16 China's securitization of the South China Sea dispute — 241
    Daniel Lynch

PART III
China's security forces — 255

Section A: The PLA Army — 256

17 The PLA Army — 257
    Dennis J. Blasko

18	The Chinese Air Force and Chinese security *Kenneth Allen and Jana Allen*	275
19	China's "fortress fleet" comes of age *James R. Holmes*	306
20	The Second Artillery and nuclear forces in 2014 *Richard D. Fisher, Jr.*	321

Section B: China's evolving space capabilities — 333

21	China's evolving space capabilities: implications for US interests *Mark Stokes and Ian Easton*	334

Section C: China's security in the information age — 354

22	China's security in the information age *Greg Austin*	355

Index — *371*

Figures

11.1	Trade volume between North Korea and China, 1990–2013	170
11.2	Share of North Korea's trade with China, 1990–2012	171
14.1	Chinese academic interest in EU military and EU foreign policy	224
17.1	Military region structure	262
17.2	Group army structure	265
18.1	PLAAF branches and subordinate units	278
19.1	China's fortress-fleet zone	308

Tables

11.1	North Korea's trade with China, 2007–13	170
14.1	Overview of security priorities in the joint statements following Sino-European summits	219
17.1	Army maneuver (infantry, armored, helicopter, and SOF) units	260
21.1	Known or suspected Chinese ground-launched ASAT tests	350

Contributors

Jana Allen is Senior Research Analyst at Defense Group Inc. (DGI), USA.

Kenneth Allen is Senior China Analyst at Defense Group Inc. (DGI), USA.

Greg Austin is Senior Visiting Research Fellow at King's College, London, and a Professorial Fellow at EastWest Institute, USA.

Dennis J. Blasko is an Asia analyst in CNA's China Security Affairs Group, USA.

Jean-Pierre Cabestan is Professor in Political Science at Hong Kong Baptist University, Hong Kong.

Lowell Dittmer is Professor in the Department of Political Science at the University of California, Berkeley, USA.

June Teufel Dreyer is Professor of Political Science at the University of Miami, USA.

Ian Easton is a research fellow at the Project 2049 Institute, USA.

Richard D. Fisher, Jr. is Senior Fellow on Asian Military Affairs at the International Assessment and Strategy Center, USA.

Edward Friedman is Professor Emeritus in the Department of Political Science, University of Wisconsin–Madison, USA.

Enze Han is Associate Professor of International Security of East Asia at SOAS, University of London, UK.

James R. Holmes is Professor of Strategy at the Naval War College, USA.

Jonathan Holslag is Research Fellow at the Brussels Institute of Contemporary China Studies (BICCS), Belgium.

Linda Jakobson is Nonresident Fellow at the Lowy Institute for International Policy, Australia.

Jinwook Choi is Senior Fellow and Director at the Center for North Korean Studies, Korea Institute for National Unification (KINU), Korea.

Contributors

Marc Lanteigne is Senior Research Fellow at New Zealand Contemporary China Research Centre, New Zealand, and Senior Research Fellow at Norwegian Institute of International Affairs (NUPI), Norway.

Daniel Lynch is Associate Professor of International Relations at the University of Southern California, USA.

Liselotte Odgaard is Associate Professor at the Institute for Strategy, Royal Danish Defence College, Copenhagen, Denmark.

Lawrence Saez is Professor in the Political Economy of Asia at SOAS, University of London, UK.

Mark Stokes is Executive Director of the Project 2049 Institute, USA.

Niklas Swanström is Director of the Institute for Security and Development Policy, Sweden.

Patricia Thornton is Associate Professor of Chinese Politics at the University of Oxford, UK.

Christopher Twomey is Associate Professor at the Naval Postgraduate School, USA.

Maochun Yu is Professor of East Asia and Military History at the United States Naval Academy.

Yuan-kang Wang is Associate Professor at Western Michigan University, USA.

Yu-Shan Wu is Director and Distinguished Research Fellow at the Institute of Political Science, Academia Sinica, Taiwan.

Editors' note and acknowledgements

This Handbook is the product of a collective endeavor to bring together the most salient and up-to-date developments in Chinese security studies in one single volume for both specialists and new students of the field.

While issues related to Chinese security have multiplied exponentially in recent years, due to rapid increases in Chinese military capabilities and dramatic changes in international and regional security dynamics that have greatly affected China's security posture and re-organization, it has become imperative to bring up to date the key new developments of Chinese security studies, to include some new frontiers such as cyber warfare into consideration. We thank Routledge publishing house for its recognition of such an important need, and for its trust in us to edit the volume.

This is also a production by the world's renowned and accomplished scholars who have already shouldered a considerable amount of research and service missions in their own specialties. We would like to thank all the contributors for their devotion to the specific assignments, for their diligence in drafting and correcting the texts, and for the grace and good humor with which they responded to our critiques and suggestions. Some topics, especially those related to cyber and non-traditional security dimensions, are so new that there are not significant bodies of work on them in existence. We thank those colleagues for having chosen this book to debut their fresh research. Our gratitude also goes to Namson Ngo-Le who helped us with the index.

Routledge's editorial team has been helpful and supportive throughout the process. In particular, Ms. Helena Hurd has been our main interlocutor in the UK. We would like to extend our special thanks for her patience, professionalism and undying faith in us to get the job done.

Where possible and practical, Chinese is transliterated using pinyin.

Lowell Dittmer, Maochun Yu

Introduction
China's security perspective

Lowell Dittmer

What follows is an attempt to collect, in a single volume, a reasonably comprehensive and systematic analysis of contemporary Chinese thinking about Chinese national security in all its aspects, as represented by outstanding scholarly authorities in their respective fields of specialization. It is organized into three main parts (although the divisions are somewhat arbitrary, with many overlaps): Part I is concerned with national security, which is to say with those aspects of security that impinge on the nation-state as a whole. The first two chapters, on traditional views of security and on the impact of the Chinese revolution, are concerned with the impact of China's historical experience on current security dispositions. This is followed by chapters on the political-economic dimension of security and on the impact, only recently academically recognized, of "non-traditional" security. Part II is focused on the security dimension as broken down into discrete geographic areas. This section is in turn subdivided into a first subsection focused on the great powers, a second dealing with regional security (including two chronic trouble spots with tie-ins to great power dynamics), and a third dealing with China's experience with collective security organizations. Part III encompasses China's institutionalized security forces; i.e., with the People's Liberation Army, as subdivided into army, navy, air force, and second artillery (strategic nuclear forces). This is followed by chapters on China's more recent interest in space as a security concern and in cybersecurity.

National security

China is currently the third largest country in the world in terms of land mass, just slightly larger than the United States. This has not always been so, for China in its long history has contracted, fragmented, or expanded on the basis of the internal or external balance of power. At present it identifies with the generous territorial expanse of the last Chinese imperial dynasty, the Qing, relinquishing claim only on Outer Mongolia (now Mongolia) and certain territorial concessions made in the border settlement with Russia (the Republic of China in Taiwan has not made these concessions). It has one of the longest land boundaries in the world, some 13,743 miles, greater than that of the Roman Empire during the reign of Augustus, sharing land borders with 14 states and maritime boundaries with eight other states (in the sense that China's maritime sovereignty claims abut theirs).[1,2] These boundaries have been perpetually insecure. To the west and the north China confronted a host of mostly nomadic "barbarian" forces, which always threatened and sometimes succeeded in overthrowing and displacing Han Chinese governments. In the nineteenth and the beginning of the twentieth centuries the chief threat to Chinese national security came from the east, along the coast that the Chinese imperial leadership had sealed off in the late Ming. China has throughout its long history had many wars (3,756 between 770 BCE and 1912), both civil and external, and security has perforce always ranked very high on the agenda. Yet the Chinese have historically also had a very strong moral sense. From a moral perspective this history of violence has been problematic, even repugnant. This is the basic dilemma Yuan-kang Wang confronts in his chapter on the traditional legacy.

China's recorded "tradition" lasts more than three thousand years with a great many vicissitudes, in the course of which a number of stratagems were devised to reconcile the concern for morally upright behavior with the perpetually looming threat of violence and chaos. Among the most fundamental was to identify righteousness and harmony with the Chinese community and wickedness with the enemy menacing the frontier. The Chinese community was based on righteousness, a moral hierarchy of officials trained in classic Confucian prescripts and led by the Son of Heaven who alone was capable of regulating the community in accord with the order of the universe. If either the people or their bureaucratic or hereditary leadership should fail to perform satisfactorily, a "rectification of names" [*zheng ming*] would be in order, meaning deviants would be disciplined to act properly in accord with their roles. The Son of Heaven or emperor was a special case given his key function: if he failed to mediate properly between universal order and the community, for example by taking the "hegemonic road" [*ba dao*] of despotism and wanton cruelty (instead of the *wang dao*, or princely road of justice), he was no longer an emperor but an ordinary man who could be assassinated with impunity, according to Mencius. Outside this moral order were two types of people: "barbarians," who were ill-acquainted with the proper moral order and embodied the forces of chaotic violence, and tributaries, who acknowledged their moral inferiority via tribute to the Son of Heaven and paid obeisance to his (mercifully vague) moral precepts. If either of these groups, but particularly the former, should commit some moral outrage such as invading the realm, the emperor was entitled to lead "punitive" expeditions to subdue them. These were by definition wars of defense and therefore "just" wars. Inasmuch as the very existence of such forces on the frontier was an implicit threat the emperor was also justified in launching preventive offensives. This was a form of "active defense" that was by definition also just. Hence what Wang calls the "cult of the defense" [*ziwei fanji*]: all of China's wars are inherently defensive and hence just, even if fought in Korea or Burma (now Myanmar). Thus the brief February 1979 attack on Vietnam was a "defensive counterattack" intended to teach this former colony a "lesson."

Yet just war was a blanket category cloaking all manner of amorality. Although (or because) all Chinese wars were defensive and just, those who fought them were entitled to be very flexible in formulating a strategy, of which the top priority was winning. Within the Confucian culture of harmony and righteousness is a subculture of warfare, with a canon of "Seven Military Classics" including Sun Zi's famous *Art of War*, according to which the ends of survival and victory justify any effective means. This tradition justifies total war, total conquest, according to Shi Yinhong. Deception is particularly prominent. To be sure, there is also a rationale of economy of force—subduing the enemy without fighting or with minimal losses is always preferred—but winning is the ultimate. This martial subculture, framed in what Johnston calls a parabellum premise (peace by preparing for war), is focused mainly on land warfare, as most security threats historically came from the land (and China was less successful in formulating a strategy to deal with those emanating from the sea). This too became a part of China's cultural legacy. But it is of course important not to essentialize Chinese culture. After all, political culture governs only the symbolic order, from which actual human behavior could deviate considerably.

China's revolutionary legacy illustrates both a dramatic attempt to smash tradition as well as its underlying elasticity and tenacity. Mao's thought, "Marxism-Leninism with Chinese characteristics," represented a complete transvaluation of traditional values. A child of the May Fourth era, Mao Zedong once said he hated Confucius from the age of eight. He led campaigns against both Confucius and the Duke of Zhou in the Great Proletarian Cultural Revolution, Mao's late-life campaign to revive revolutionary values among the younger generation. Whereas traditional morality was based on hierarchy, revolutionary morality was egalitarian. Traditional morality relegated women and workers to lower status, Maoist morality ennobled them. Tradition revered the old, revolution esteemed the new, the young. The despised commoners should be not only respected, but served: "Serve the people." While Confucius thought any man could become a *junzi* (gentleman) through sincere self-cultivation, Mao turned this upside down: "The people, and only the people, are the makers of world history." "The lowly are the most intelligent, the elite are the most ignorant." Confucian morality emphasized order, harmony, and moderation: "The gentleman avoids the absolute, avoids the extreme." Mao Zedong's consistent focus was on "contradictions," "class struggle" was the "key link." In one of his theoretical innovations Mao said that struggle would continue even in the Communist utopia. Yet although Mao's thought essentially contradicts Chinese tradition, there are some continuities. For both, the public interest supersedes private interests. And Mao borrowed liberally from China's martial subculture, particularly from such popular novels as *Water Margins* and *Romance of the Three Kingdoms*. Ultimately, the post-Mao leadership forged a synthesis of Mao's thought with a revived traditional morality (including Confucius) that leaves little of the former intact: the revolution itself is still sacrosanct, but the Cultural Revolution (or any notion of "continuing revolution") is now repudiated.

The revolution has had at least three significant effects on China's security disposition. First, the miraculous survival and ultimate victory of the Red Army over seeming vastly superior adversaries after several times being on the brink of extinction reinforced Marxist historical determinism to infuse a sanguine confidence in China's inevitable victory that has skewed their battlefield estimates ever since, leading the PRC to plunge into ventures that more realistic estimates might have eschewed. Perhaps most dramatically articulated in Mao's poetry, this optimism was also systematically built into the Chinese media apparatus and emerges in contemporaneous Chinese security policies. Thus only one year after surviving the civil war and before that a Japanese invasion, both costing millions of lives and extensive damage, China plunged into the Korean War against the strongest military in the world, which China (and North Korea) survived at the cost of a million casualties. Second, for the next three decades the Maoist conception of "people's war" remained the default defense strategy for defense of the Chinese mainland, augmented by the advent of nuclear weaponry in the mid-1960s. The basic concept is to maintain the support of the population and draw the enemy deep into the interior where the population (a benign "sea" in which the Red Army could "swim") could help bleed them dry in a mix of mobile and guerrilla warfare, thence proceeding to "surround the cities from the countryside." First introduced in Mao's writings during the Sino-Japanese War, this strategy was first fully utilized against the Nationalist Government in the Chinese Civil War. During the Sino-Japanese War the CCP prioritized husbanding its forces for an expected later conflict with Nationalist (*Guomindang*) forces, implementing a "united front" that has also become part of the Party's strategic repertory. This involves temporary collaboration with a lesser foe (the GMD) against a greater one (Imperial Japan), after which the former can be disposed of. Another novel feature was the Maoist approach to peace talks, which might be conducted while still fighting (*da da, tan tan*—fight

fight, talk talk). "People's war" was employed not only in defense of the mainland but with some alterations in the First Indochina War and in guerrilla actions in Laos, Myanmar, the Philippines, India and Nepal. Third, in a radical departure from China's traditionally defensive "Great Wall" security orientation the CCP promptly launched a wholesale propagation of revolution that could hardly be called defensive. These were still "just wars" in that they were conceived as part of an international class war and hence no longer based on "selfish" national interests; though this claim has been viewed skeptically, particularly after Sino-Soviet friction arose over the direction of proletarian internationalism, it does seem to have had an effect on Chinese security policy. At a time when China was cutting itself off economically from the rest of the world (including the Soviet Union and other "socialist revisionists"), it became intensely engaged in fomenting international class struggle. Based on Yu's formidable collection of primary sources this effort was far more than ideological. There was a vast outflow of military weaponry in the 1960s in support of China-endorsed national liberation wars, as Mao scorned Khrushchev's "peaceful coexistence" and decreed that revolution could succeed only by violence. By 1978, over 68 countries had received Chinese military aid—guns, ships, tanks, aircraft, cannons, missiles, ammunition. Over a thousand PLA personnel died serving in Vietnam, where they assisted in taking Dienbienphu and later shot down 1,707 American aircraft. Although China was the poorest country in the world to provide foreign aid (mostly via loans, which it was quick to write off), Chinese aid was the highest as a percentage of the donor country's per capita income. The two leading Communist powers initially agreed with a division of revolutionary labor consigning Asian developing countries to China, but ideological disagreements emerged in the early 1960s and China became more internationally ambitious, which led Moscow to compete with Beijing for leadership of the world revolution. This competition drove revolutionary efforts in an increasingly violent and radical direction, which Christensen deemed "worse than a monolith."[3] While the American foreign policy establishment took it very seriously at the time,[4] in retrospect the impact seems to have been quite modest, as lasting revolutionary transformations occurred in only a few countries, due partly to stultifying rivalry between the two revolutionary enablers.

Since the death of Mao and Deng Xiaoping's introduction of "reform and opening to the outside world" at the Third Plenum of the Eleventh Party Congress in December 1978, much of the Maoist legacy has been discarded or drastically revised. Captivated by the concept of a "revolution in military affairs," the PLA has reduced its numbers (though remaining the largest armed force in the world) and launched an ambitious modernization program, focusing on professional training of officers and acquiring (and now manufacturing) highly sophisticated weaponry. Discrete parts of the Maoist repertoire have survived: the United Front, the identification with the developing world, the interleaving of coercion and diplomacy, the continuing suspicion of the United States. But the Maoist form of world-transforming ambition seems to have completely given way to an intense and increasingly militant nationalism. The Maoist dream of leading a world revolution seems to have been displaced by Xi Jinping's "Chinese dream" envisaging expansion only along China's maritime periphery—at least for now.

The place of the economy in China's security picture has evolved fundamentally, as Marc Lanteigne makes plain. During the Maoist period the focus was split between increasing economic production and socialist transformation, under the premise that the two were mutually complementary. This complementarity seemed initially to be borne out by the evidence, though as China turned away from the Soviet model and began experimenting with its own political-economic innovations under Maoist assumptions of "politics in command" and the historical priority of relations of production, this assumption became untenable. The international role of the economy was deeply influenced by Lenin's theory of imperialism, leading to a suspicion of trade and investment flows and ultimately to an attempt to cut off any form of economic dependency and "stand on two legs." Here Deng's "opening to the outside world" marked a dramatic departure. China seemed to discard imperialist suspicions with surprising ease and open itself to trade and investment from all sources of capital, and to adjust foreign and defense policies to minimize friction with the economic requirements of rapid modernization. At this point the engagement in international class war became an embarrassment and China's revolutionary clients were cut loose. In the 1980s China proclaimed itself a "socialist market economy" (though this has been disputed by socialists), justifying this by repositioning Chinese development at the "primary stage of socialism." This hybrid model retained the Leninist political apparatus largely intact, along with all the institutions of command planning (five-year plans, economic ministries, central bank), while permitting the retail market to develop and eventually conducting "property reform" legitimating private ownership of assets (particularly housing). When the rapid growth of the private sector led to a boom and bust cycle in the 1980s culminating in mass protests in 1989 the political economy was adjusted to facilitate greater central financial control and strengthen Party leadership. Externally China adopted the "NIC" (newly industrialized country) model of export-oriented growth (although it was considerably more open to foreign direct investment (FDI) than some of the NICs), and in 1994 pegged its currency to the US dollar, its biggest export market, to keep export prices low. This soon resulted in a large balance of payments surplus with the US and the EU, much of which it proceeded to invest in US treasury bills, becoming the largest foreign holder of American debt. This lowered US interest rates and maintained a favorable bilateral exchange rate but created what Lawrence Summers called a balance of financial terror. But the Maoist split focus was resolved in favor of production alone with record results. With a three-decade annual average growth rate of nearly 10 percent China's GDP surpassed that of Canada in 1993, Italy in 2000, France in 2005, UK in 2006, Germany in 2008, and Japan in 2010. In 2011 it became the world's leading manufacturing power and in 2012 it surpassed the US as the world's biggest trading nation. At the advent of reform, China's total trade value was only $20.6 billion, ranking thirty-second among all trading nations. Since then, China's economy has grown more than a hundred-fold. By early 2014, China's foreign exchange reserve cache exceeded US$4 trillion, the largest ever accumulated.

China's rapid economic growth has had at least three effects on its security, one direct, the others indirect and more speculative. The direct impact is that military spending increases commensurate with overall GDP growth even if it remains a constant percentage of the budget, and in China's case it seems to have outpaced an already very rapid GDP growth. From the mid-1990s to the late 2000s China's share of global wealth doubled while its military budget grew around six-fold. According to SIPRI, a Swedish research institute, annual defense spending rose from over $30 billion in 2000 to almost $120 billion in 2010, second only to the US and larger than any other Asian country. America still spends many times as much on defense, but China's rate of increase is faster, so if spending trends continue China will achieve military parity within 15–30 years. The pace of China's development of technologically advanced weapons has continued to surprise intelligence analysts, with the development of anti-ship ballistic missiles and fifth generation stealth fighters and now hypersonic glide missiles. One indirect effect is that of power transition theory, which assumes that if and when a rising power surpasses a hegemonic power insecurity is heightened, thus increasing the risk of war. This is by no means an iron law but at best a propensity the conditions for which require further study. But both American and Chinese defense thinkers are quite aware of China's approaching convergence and it remains to be seen whether this will intensify their competition.

The third effect has to do with economic statecraft; that is, China's government may use its new power to wield political influence. This possibility has made China's neighbors and economic partners increasingly worried not only because China is suddenly so big, creating asymmetrical relations in which China would suffer less than its partners from any application of sanctions; but also because China's "people's democratic dictatorship" has greater control over its economy than non-authoritarian regimes. During the first three decades of its rise China has however made very little use of economic statecraft. As a socialist interloper in an otherwise largely capitalist international economy with a previous reputation of attempting to wreck that economy and still upholding divergent ideological and human rights standards, Beijing was quite sensitive, particularly after the Tiananmen crackdown. China was careful to keep politics and economics separate and Deng's *taoguang yanghui* (hide brilliance and keep a low profile) ruled the day. But since around 2008, when Chinese consumers boycotted the French supermarket Carrefour in response to French demonstrations against the Chinese Olympic torch run, the PRC has been willing to wield economic power with greater frequency and assurance. Amid the uproar over China's territorial claims in the South China Sea it often escapes notice that China has since the signing of the ASEAN-China FTA in 2010 become Southeast Asia's biggest trade partner. In a replay of *da da, tan tan*, Beijing has accompanied the use of salami tactics to expand its territorial holdings in its near seas with a "smile campaign" of high-level diplomacy, loans, infrastructure investments (a new Infrastructure Investment Bank), friendship treaties (with ASEAN) and trade promotion (two "new silk roads" through Central and Southeast Asia). As Lanteigne notes, there is an increasing overlap of economics and security in Asia, and while Beijing has learned to exploit this it also remains concerned lest others do so as well, in a conspiracy to "encircle" or "contain" the PRC (as in the Trans Pacific Partnership, or TPP, which excludes China).

Many hoped the end of the Cold War confrontation between capitalism and communism would inaugurate a new era of peace and prosperity. In a sense, that has been true: there have been very few inter-state wars since the end of the Cold War. But as Patricia Thornton points out, this has been accompanied by an upsurge in intra-national troubles: civil wars, epidemics, earthquakes, tsunamis, famines, and floods. Such disasters also have an impact on national security, conceptually "securitized" to comprise "non-traditional security." Beijing was quick to recognize the importance of nontraditional threats, partly because of its own experience (SARS in 2003, the "color revolutions" in Central Asia in 2004–2005, the Wenchuan earthquake in 2008, the Arab or Jasmine Spring in 2010, ongoing violence in Xinjiang by supporters of Eastern Turkestan independence), and partly because "traditional" threats to China virtually disappeared at the end of the Cold War with the dissolution of the Soviet Union. China has spent more on "nontraditional" or domestic security than on traditional security every year since 2010. As Thornton details, China's definition of this still elliptical term has focused on anti-regime violence and specifically on the "three evils" of separatism, terrorism, and religious fundamentalism (as notably encountered lately in the Xinjiang-Uighur and Tibetan Autonomous National Minority Regions). But as land confiscations, inadequate health care, environmental pollution and other maladies have aroused popular protest and taken a toll on the economy, the state has become increasingly willing to "securitize" them as well. Beijing seems to have moderated its regulation of nongovernmental organizations/civic associations, for example, in hopes of enlisting them in the fight against nontraditional insecurity. Hoping to ameliorate its image in Southeast Asia, Beijing has also proposed (in a keynote speech by Li Keqiang at the Boao Forum in April 2014) a regional security cooperation framework to tackle nontraditional security challenges.

Geostrategic dimensions

Beijing has periodically reshuffled its ranking of significant international others over the last six decades. While rhetorically identifying with the "Third World," China has always considered itself a player in global power politics and soon persuaded others to accept this. The United States has always topped Beijing's list of important interlocutors, initially as enemy number one, later as strategic quasi-ally, now as leading trade partner and conditional strategic partner. China and the US share many broad strategic interests, Christopher Twomey points out, including stability in the Asian region (including the suppression of terrorist movements) and opposition to proliferation of weapons of mass destruction (WMDs), particularly those in China's ally North Korea. China as now the world's leading trading power and the US as second biggest share an interest in maintaining the global commons and promoting the continuation of globalization, though with regard to bilateral trade the relationship is encumbered by China's large trade imbalance, often attributed to a deliberately undervalued currency. The economic relationship has raised the issues of absolute vs. relative gains and power transition theory. Other tension areas include the American alliance network in the Asia-Pacific: the US has five bilateral security alliances, with Japan, South Korea, the Philippines, Thailand and Australia; China welcomed these during the Cold War when they were deemed a useful bulwark against the USSR, but now that the USSR is no more, China considers them an outdated "relic of the Cold War." Instead China advocates a "new security concept" (updated in 2014 as the "new Asian security concept") based on peaceful coexistence, mutual cooperation ("win-win") and noninterference. The underlying issue is whether China is a "revisionist" power with expansionist ambitions (the "China threat theory") or committed to the international status quo, a debate Beijing tried to defuse in the 2000s with its endorsement of "peaceful development" only to revive in the 2010s with its arms buildup and maritime claims. Like many of China's Asian neighbors the US under Barack Obama has attempted to "hedge," cooperating when mutually beneficial (e.g., nuclear proliferation in North Korea and Iran) while elsewhere engaging in a controlled form of competition. While the US has no maritime claims of its own, the two disagree over the somewhat technical issues of the security aspect of the Exclusive Economic Zone (EEZ) and right of free passage, and the US security commitments to its five Asian partners may entail defense of conflicting territorial claims. Although both have frequently averred their commitment to a peaceful relationship (which Xi Jinping calls a "new type of relation among major powers"), these unresolved underlying issues have stimulated China's rapid arms buildup along its eastern coastline ("anti-access, area denial"), apparently aimed to deter US air and naval forces; this in turn stimulated a US commitment to strengthen the Seventh Fleet and build an "Air-Sea Battle Plan," notwithstanding its own tight budget constraints. Despite ongoing attempts at military exchanges and joint maneuvers both nations' military establishments view the other as a possible future adversary and are engaged in preparations for that contingency.

China's longest land border has always been with Russia, and relations between the two have historically been characterized by deep ambivalence, from the Mongol invasion in the fourteenth century to Tsarist territorial encroachment in the nineteenth century. Even indispensable Soviet support for the Communist Revolution was counterbalanced by aid for and even in 1945 a mutual defense treaty with the Nationalist government. Though accompanied by florid attestations of undying friendship, the 30-year Sino-Soviet mutual defense alliance had by the mid-1960s degenerated into incendiary ideological polemics, a public dispute over the direction of the world revolution, and border clashes over conflicting territorial claims. Hardly had the two Communist leaderships laboriously reconstructed a cordial relationship in 1989 than the Soviet Union began to fall apart, dissolving in December 1991 into 15 independent republics. Though the two neighbors initially moved in ideologically orthogonal directions they opted not to relinquish their hard-earned and strategically useful reconciliation after the Cold War, and they demilitarized their long border and successfully completed border demarcation (China also amicably settled with the three bordering former Soviet republics in Central Asia). In 1994 they proclaimed a "strategic partnership" (the first and still the closest of China's 54) and in

2001 a 20-year friendship treaty. Since that long and carefully staged reconciliation the two have maintained a cordial and mutually beneficial security relationship despite recurrent friction over such issues as Chinese immigration, natural resource exploitation in Central Asia, and declining Chinese weapons purchases. Carefully tracing the vicissitudes of their strategic relationship since the end of the Cold War Yu-Shan Wu argues that its warmth (and hence its relevance to Asian security) is contingent on the relationship of each nation to the US, which alone has the power to block their respective "core interests." The core interests of Russia and China are not shared but analogous: Beijing desires sovereign control of its near seas at least up to the "first island chain" (and then up to the second); Moscow would like ideally to reintegrate the former constituents of the USSR, especially the three independent states considered to be Russia's primary sphere of influence, Belarus, Kazakhstan and Ukraine, into a "customs union," or at least prevent them from joining NATO or the EU. (Even the Chinese-organized Shanghai Cooperation Organization, of which Russia is a full member, is looked on with some suspicion.) In sum, both countries wish to consolidate their peripheral security, and since Washington has opted to block the efforts of both their current relationship has grown very close (and alienated from the US). As their core interests are geographically distinct and non-overlapping there has been little apparent cooperation on strategic offensives (or what Wu calls "issue linkage") so far. But apparently coordinated timing does split US containment efforts, and there has been discussion in China of a moving to a mutual security alliance.[5]

Japan and China are geographically fated to be close neighbors and Japan was culturally influenced by China with its language, architecture, culture, religion, philosophy, and law, but relations have since been up and down, contingent on relations with other powers. During the heyday of the Sino-Soviet alliance Japan was a common threat; the Sino-Soviet Treaty explicitly pledged immediate military assistance if either were attacked by "Japan and any state which might directly or indirectly join with it," June Dreyer reminds us. China was definitely upset by the use of Japan as the principal American base during the Korean War, and by the Japan-US Security Treaty signed in 1951. But during the Sino-Soviet dispute, and particularly after the US opening to China in 1972, relations improved considerably. Japan was among the first to recognize China after the Nixon visit and in 1978 the two signed a mutual friendship treaty. During this period Beijing was so keen for reconciliation that the terms of recognition did not impose war reparations on Japan, Zhou Enlai (1972) and Deng Xiaoping (1978) agreed to defer the issue of sovereignty over the Senkaku islets to "later generations," Zhou Enlai (1972) said China no longer opposed the Japan-US Strategic Treaty, and Deng Xiaoping (1978) even claimed to favor strengthening Japan's Self-Defense Forces (SDF). In return, Japan agreed to an "anti-hegemony" clause in the friendship treaty implicitly critical of the Soviet Union, the shelf life of which would prove limited. While the 1980s are generally considered the "golden age" of Sino-Japanese friendship the first inklings of mutual suspicion appeared in the wake of the Tiananmen crackdown, and Chinese criticism of an increase in Japanese arms spending in 1987–1991, briefly exceeding the tacit 1 percent (of GDP) limit. In 1995–1996 the Taiwan Strait crisis threatening Japan's former colony Taiwan and its own strategic lines of communication (SLOCs) upset the Japanese, helping stimulate Japanese accession to US pressure to revise the range of application of the mutual security treaty to include "adjacent waters," which Beijing feared would include Taiwan. In the early 2000s Koizumi's six visits to Yasukuni Shrine revived once more the "historical issue" of Japan's inadequate apologies for war atrocities, and in 2005 spontaneous anti-Japanese demonstrations in China (plus the threat of Chinese Security Council veto) helped squelch a proposed reorganization of the UN Security Council that might have included Japan. Prime Ministers Abe and Fukuda contributed to "ice-breaking" in the wake of the five-year Koizumi freeze in 2006–2008, culminating in a joint venture for development of one specific subsurface natural gas field near the putative maritime boundary (Chunxiao, now operational) while suspending the issue of sovereignty. But since 2010 relations have worsened rapidly, largely over the territorial (Senkaku/Diaoyu) issue, beginning with a Chinese fishing boat collision with Japanese coast guard vessels near Senkaku/Diaoyu in 2010, followed in 2012 by the purchase of three of the five islets by the Japanese government, which aroused violent protests in some 200 Chinese cities. In November 2013 China unilaterally declared an Air Defense Identification Zone including the Senkaku/Diaoyus, over international protests. All this has culminated in an increasingly tense relationship between the ships, planes and drones of the two nations patrolling their claimed sovereign territory and trying to chase each other away. One effect has been to boost Japanese defense spending after an 11-year decline (but still below 1 percent of GDP).

Sino-Indian relations, like Sino-Soviet relations and unlike Sino-American or Sino-Japanese relations, began with high hopes, only to decline—at about the same time as Sino-Soviet relations but for different reasons. In 1950 India was among the first countries to end formal ties with the Republic of China on Taiwan and recognize the PRC, and with the signing of the Panch Shila by Nehru and Zhou Enlai in 1954 the two countries became pioneering leaders of what would become the nonaligned bloc. But India's accommodation of the Dalai Lama and his followers fleeing Tibet following the Chinese crackdown in 1958 soured the relationship. A territorial dispute then arose in the late 1950s, which China resolved with a preemptive attack in 1962: further border incidents followed in 1967 and 1987. India emerged with a loss of territory and an enduring enmity. Both nations have since established heavy military infrastructure along border areas, but India continues to complain of Chinese border incursions. Despite the Indian loss in the western sector (in and near Kashmir) China still claims territory in Arunachal Pradesh in the east. Border talks and confidence-building measures were initiated in 1993 but the territorial issues remain unresolved. Yet beginning with Rajiv Gandhi's visit to China in 1988 both countries have attempted to restore diplomatic and economic ties. In 2008, China emerged as India's largest trading partner and the two countries have also attempted to extend their strategic and military relations. But though bilateral trade has grown by some 50 percent per year, India faces a steep trade imbalance. Both of these nuclear weapon states seem to be engaged in maneuvers to outflank each other: in the 1990s India launched a "Look East" policy to cultivate economic, cultural, and security ties with Southeast Asia, gaining membership in the Asian Regional Forum and the East Asian Summit and reaching oil and gas deals with Vietnam and Myanmar. China's corresponding effort in South Asia, as Han and Saez make clear has been even more successful. China has been Pakistan's "all-weather friend" since the 1960s and contributed significantly to that nation's nuclear and missile armament, much to Delhi's chagrin. While the expression "string of pearls" was coined not in Beijing but by a Western ad man, the idea is not too far from Chinese strategy as the country has engaged in building ports and infrastructure in Pakistan, Bangladesh, Sri Lanka, and Myanmar. India's neighbors welcome these investments to balance against the South Asian hegemon, helping Beijing gain observer status in the South Asian Association for Regional Cooperation (SAARC)—Delhi has thus far blocked Beijing's efforts to gain full membership. Many of India's neighbors now have more trade with China than with India. Despite this strategic rivalry Washington may have difficulty enlisting a proudly autonomous Delhi in any so called encirclement campaign. In fact the two have many interests in common on climate change and other issues involving the developing world, and India has with China's approval gained candidate membership in the Shanghai Cooperation Organization (SCO) and membership in the BRICS.

China has since the early 1950s identified with what was then called the Third World of newly independent developing nations as a primary reference group, though as Edward Friedman points out this identification was compromised from the beginning by an unresolved tension between joining this group and sponsoring Communist revolution within it.[6] Chinese policy toward the Third World went through a "freeze-thaw" cycle largely geared to relations with the Soviet Union: during a freeze Beijing focused on national liberation wars and revolutionary militancy, while during thaws it emphasized the "five principles of peaceful coexistence" and constructive solidarity with the poor, the colored, the wretched of the earth. An enduring symbol of the latter is the Tanzania-Zambia (TanZam) Railway, built from 1970 to 1975 as a turnkey project financed by China. The single longest railway in sub-Saharan Africa and Beijing's largest single foreign-aid project, it remains in operation (as TAZARA), albeit in the red. The contradiction between revolution and developmentalism of course quietly vanished with the advent of Deng's reform and opening policy. China's munificent financial support for the developing world however also flagged during the early reform period (as did PRC contributions to the UN) as the PRC focused on its own development, though rhetorical identification continued and China's votes in the UN General Assembly tallied closely with those of the developing bloc. Edward Friedman sees a sharp increase in support after Tiananmen when China was ostracized by much of the developed world. In the wake of the Asian Financial Crisis Beijing was able to synchronize its support of developing nations with its emerging critique of the existing international order by generously supporting Thailand and other afflicted countries. In the aftermath of the crisis Beijing supported the Chiang Mai Initiative, a regional alternative to the IMF. Beijing's enormous foreign exchange cache, accumulated largely since its admission to the WTO in 2001, has enabled a massive increase in outgoing subsidized loans, grants, and FDI—more loans than grants, however, and the latter are tied to the purchase of Chinese exports. Nevertheless the lack of conditionality and uncomplicated speed of Chinese deals are generally appreciated by recipients. China's ostentatious ties to the developing world are of little import in traditional security terms, except perhaps marginally in terms of "no strings attached" arms sales.[7] The major security impact is likely to be "nontraditional" in terms of a subtle and generally tacit competition between China and world financial institutions, which China has begun to critique as insufficiently accommodating of the developing world. The China Developmental Bank according to some estimates now gives more loans than the World Bank—even though China is still also a recipient of World Bank loans. China's challenge may eventuate in viable alternatives, as suggested not only by critiques of the old international financial order but the recent founding of an Infrastructure Investment Bank and a BRICS bank, both tailor made for developing economies. Yet China is still a long way from this, and in any event the dream of new solidarity between China and the developing world overlooks the incoherence of the latter—some developing countries are prospering, some are in turmoil and failing; some welcome Chinese turnkey investment, others prefer to employ their own work force; some fit smoothly into global production chains, others compete with Chinese product mixes; all are different. And China's unconditional friendliness with developmental authoritarianism can jeopardize material and reputational investment in such regimes when the "masses" overthrow them, as in Libya.

On July 11, 2014, Chinese icebreaker *Xue Long* ("Snow Dragon") embarked on the country's sixth Arctic expedition, with 65 scientists on board; in December 2013 a China-Nordic research center was opened in Shanghai. As a major contributor to global warming China is interested in taking advantage of the new freight opportunities opening along the Northern Sea Route (NSR) as the ice recedes.[8] Some climate models predict the Arctic Ocean could be ice-free in summer by the middle of this century. The NSR, now navigable only with the accompaniment of an icebreaker, cuts the freight distance between Rotterdam and Shanghai by 22 percent. Huang Nubo, a Chinese property magnate (and former propaganda ministry official), after failing to strike a deal in Iceland, purchased one million square meters of uninhabited prime north Norwegian real estate in September 2014; although both Huang and O.K. Giaever (the seller) claimed this was a private transaction to build a tourist resort it sparked speculation that it betokened some grand design to bolster Chinese interests in the Arctic. China became in 2013 an observer on the Arctic Council, and some Chinese even claim sovereignty over unclaimed territory on behalf of "the common interests of mankind," of which China is surely a part. But according to Linda Jakobson China is still more interested in budding opportunities in the Antarctic. Security implications of the poles are as yet unclear, but as they materialize the Chinese will not want to miss them.

The Korean Peninsula, a "minnow among whales" and convenient land bridge (and invasion route) between China and Japan, has long been deemed vital to the security interests of both countries. Stalin apparently encouraged Mao to enter the Korean War as a test of his commitment to internationalism when the DPRK was on the brink of being defeated and driven into exile in 1950. But in view of the threat to China's peripheral security Mao probably would have intervened anyhow. In any event the intervention saved the DPRK and became the blood seal for China's only security alliance that has endured. Beijing remained a loyal patron throughout the Maoist period despite Pyongyang's oscillation between Beijing and Moscow to improve its terms of trade during the Sino-Soviet dispute. But South Korea developed much more rapidly than the North under Park Chung Hee's developmental dictatorship, and when South Korean President Roh Tae-woo launched his "Nordpolitik" in 1988 both the Soviet Union (1990) and China (1992) abandoned their One Korea policies to recognize the South. This enhanced the strategic leverage of China and South Korea while isolating the North. The North responded by intensifying ongoing efforts to develop its own nuclear deterrent. When these efforts were brought to light by International Atomic Energy Agency (IAEA) inspectors in 1993 and Pyongyang, after first denying the report and kicking out the inspectors, threatened to withdraw from the Nuclear Nonproliferation Treaty (NPT), this precipitated a crisis in which the US briefly considered a preemptive strike on the nuclear reactors in Yongbyon. While a compromise called Agreed Framework was negotiated by Jimmy Carter and Kim Il Sung to resolve the crisis in 1994, this turned out to be but the first of several DPRK agreements that were made but then broken by the North in its continuing clandestine effort to develop nuclear weapons, disregarding a decade-long depression and famine in which hundreds of thousands perished. This goal was finally achieved with successful nuclear tests in 2006, 2009, and 2013, lending Pyongyang not only effective deterrence but the capability to threaten its neighbors with impunity, as it demonstrated in two lethal provocations against the South in 2010. In view of North Korea's economic dependency on the PRC, those threatened by the North's relentless self-strengthening have entreated Beijing to use its economic leverage to coerce Pyongyang to relinquish its nuclear weapons and normalize its foreign relations. Beijing's top priority is however stability rather than eliminating nuclear weapons that will never threaten Beijing, and it has pursued a delicate balance between constraining the North not to provoke its Western neighbors and enabling it to survive economically. The result thus far has been favorable to Beijing, strengthening North Korean deterrence against absorption by the South while still enjoying Western gratitude as the sole live link to Pyongyang. Thus, although Jinwook Choi observes that Beijing now regards the DPRK as a bit of a liability to its political-economic courtship of the South, he doubts Beijing will make any high-stakes effort to coerce it to renounce nuclear weapons.

Taiwan, though also a nation divided by civil war and the Cold War, poses different problems for Chinese security. As Beijing still firmly believes it is "part of China" despite over a century's separation, it is a "core interest" with which reunification is imperative for China's legitimacy.

Thus while Beijing could recognize both North and South Korean sovereign membership in the UN, for example, the "one China principle" is sacrosanct. As such, Taiwan intimately affects the Party-state's vested ideal interests. Any reasonable reunification proposal would involve reciprocal political adjustments (as opposed to annexation, the German model), but the CCP's aversion to domestic political reform (e.g., democracy) makes any such concessions impossible; even Taiwan's impact as a democratic special administrative region (SAR) in a "two systems" setup is problematic. Certainly there are also parallels. As in the two Koreas, China continues to threaten the use of force, but in China's case the threat is conditional and has even resulted in a kind of moral hazard after a series of cross-Strait crises that were resolved peaceably. Yet in another sense the threat of force has gained credibility, as the more rapid economic growth of the mainland and the elimination of the Russian threat have enabled Beijing to strengthen and modernize the forces facing Taiwan disproportionately. Thus the military balance has in most estimates shifted to China's advantage. Even if the US were to intervene in such a scenario, as it did in the 1995–1996 missile crisis, the mainland has developed anti-access area denial (A2/AD) weaponry that would make intervention far more costly. According to Jean-Pierre Cabestan, one plausible PLA battle plan would be a blitzkrieg, using massive air bombardment to neutralize Taiwan's air cover and navy and "decapitating" the island's political-military leadership with a swift ground invasion before US forces can become engaged (other options include a blockade, or simply a devastating missile attack followed by peace talks). Still, it is generally assumed that China would prefer to "win without fighting" rather than risk an invasion or some other kinetic scenario. Especially since 2005, when Beijing struck a deal with Taiwan's KMT leadership to accept the "1992 consensus" (one China, different interpretations) as a basis for talks, Beijing has emphasized its preference for peaceful reunification and attempted to use the thriving trade relationship and cordial political ties to integrate the high-tech island economically and then politically, as in the formula successfully pursued in the return of Hong Kong. This might plausibly avoid the prospect of US military intervention, which is contingent on the use of force and not in principle against reunification per se. Under current conditions of political détente China's tactics, according to Cabestan, focus on "carrots," reserving force for outright "secession" (independence). Specifically, China aims to win over a politically decisive coalition in the business community by enhancing their economic stake in the status quo, reviving the CCP-KMT united front (already a significant nongovernmental pilot organization), and neutralizing the military via espionage, cultivation of retired officers, and other blandishments (the core of Taiwan's military is still KMT).

Despite a promising beginning marked by PRC participation in the Korean War in the name of revolutionary solidarity, China during the Maoist period had a disappointing experience with collective security, owing to strategic disagreements with the leadership of the Communist bloc that led to a collapse of trust in the credibility of extended deterrence, as illustrated in the 1958 Taiwan Strait crisis and the 1962 Sino-Indian border war. China thus withdrew not only from various Communist international organizations but from all collective security involvement during the Sino-Soviet dispute, remaining somewhat wary of multilateral organizations until the late 1990s. Its entry into the UN in 1971 however opened new opportunities for China to propound its vision of a multipolar world order (Deng Xiaoping espoused "three worlds" in a speech to the General Assembly in 1974) and North-South redistributive justice. China reliably votes with the developing world majority in the UN General Assembly, and has shown political skill both in staffing the Human Rights Commission with supporters to avoid embarrassing censure votes and in depicting this as a symbolic blow for developing countries; China has also convoked a like-minded group of developing countries in support of its position on climate control. In 2005 Hu Jintao presented China's four-point plan for a "harmonious world" that could tolerate varying political values. In short, China has been able to use the UN to make the world safe for socialism with Chinese characteristics. While the consensus on China's early UN participation was that Beijing was "free riding" the institutional status quo, Beijing has more recently taken a more active and independent role in UN decision-making. Consistent with its strict views on sovereignty Beijing (together with Russia) on four occasions vetoed UN resolutions to intervene in the Syrian civil war, for example. Yet although Beijing's support can generally be relied on in such cases, Liselotte Odgaard contends that in its skilled use of parliamentary procedures to get its way Beijing may also become socialized in procedural democracy. And despite Beijing's principled aversion to intervention in internal affairs China has approved and is now a major contributor to UN peace-keeping operations.

China's view of the European Union is ambivalent: the EU is on the one hand respected as a major trade partner (currently China's largest) and useful counterbalance to US "hegemony," on the other hand there is a certain contempt for its disunity, military weakness, and political dependency on the US. As a pole in global multipolarity the EU earns PRC support, *mutatis mutandis*—but not as a model for Asian integration, given China's fundamentalist views on sovereignty. However, the still incompletely integrated EU gives Beijing ample opportunity to play part of the community against the other, or to opt instead for bilateral deals and use them as leverage. The two powers have been able to pool influence on some issues of shared concern (e.g., opposition to the 2003 invasion of Iraq), while on other issues vital to European security their interests diverge (e.g., sanctions on Iran, support for the Hezbollah, Ukraine). But Beijing's detailed comprehension of most issues in the EU's geographical sphere of interest is limited. As for security, "Europe and China exchange more and more, but seem to become less and less able to identify which specific common security it serves in the long run," writes Jonathan Holslag (p. 218). There has been some successful cooperation of PLAN ships with EU security forces in controlling piracy off the African coast. Although EU sanctions on weapons sales is still an irritant, the EU remains a major contributor to the technological modernization of China's security apparatus. China-EU trade frictions are redolent of those with the US on smaller scale; China would like Europe to grant China market economy status (meaning lower tariffs) and refrain from the use of anti-dumping actions against Chinese exports (as in the recent solar panel dispute), but Europe will find that politically difficult given the current large imbalance of payments and Europe's long recession.

The SCO is the first collective security organization organized by China. It is an institutionalized continuation of the Group of Five (China, Russia, and the three former Soviet Republics Kazakhstan, Kyrgyzstan and Tajikistan bordering China in Central Asia) that formed a team (under Russian leadership) to negotiate boundary issues after the disintegration of the Soviet Union in 1991. That collapse left a temporary vacuum in the 1990s as the Russian Federation became absorbed in domestic affairs, which the PRC was keen to fill after being shut out of Central Asia for two centuries. China had two reasons for founding the SCO: one was to fill the economic vacuum, specifically by extracting the region's energy resources and other raw materials in exchange for Chinese light manufactures. This has worked out very successfully, according to Niklas Swanström: trade has boomed, and Chinese investment grew from US$1 to $46 billion from 2000–2012; in Xi Jinping's September 2013 tour of the region he signed energy deals worth $100 billion, some 10 percent of China's total imports.

The second goal was security: the formation of independent republics in Central Asia provided ethnic nationalism with states, which China worried might have an attraction or demonstration effect on its own community of ethnic Uighurs in the Xinjiang Autonomous Region, which borders three Central Asian republics (there are some 300,000 ethnic Uighur refugees from Xinjiang in Central Asia, comprising a sort of irredenta). Indeed it seems that the disintegration of the USSR provided a fillip for militant ethnic nationalists hoping to revive the short-lived post-World War II East Turkestan Republic in Xinjiang, and some of these groups have resorted to violence, resulting in some 2000 deaths since 2007 according to state media. Inasmuch as Xinjiang has been declared one of China's "core interests" the PRC has adjured the leaderships of the adjoining Central Asian republics to help fight the "three evils" of "separatism, terrorism, and religious extremism," which they have duly pledged to do; the SCO has also formed an anti-terrorism institute in Uzbekistan. Yet Beijing must tread lightly in pursuing its security interests as Russia still has a strong military presence in the region and has discouraged Chinese military engagement. As the other leading power in the region Russia views the SCO with some ambivalence as a vehicle of Chinese penetration, preferring to coordinate arrangements through organizations linked to the Commonwealth of Independent States (of which China is not a member), but the Central Asian republics seem to prefer an organization in which they can play the two big powers off against each other. The SCO is an "anarchic" organization in which any member can veto any proposal (as one might expect given China's views on sovereignty), putting its political efficacy in doubt. What seems to hold it together amid the tacit conflict of interest between its two founding leaders is two things: shared opposition to US liberal penetration, and an aversion to "color revolutions." But this is by no means the end of the troubles afflicting the SCO, Swanström makes clear: some of the observers (there are now more observers than there are member states) complicate things for the organization—74 percent of the world's opium is now grown in (observer state) Afghanistan, and heroin trade and criminal gangs are thus penetrating China. Depending how the counterinsurgency fares after NATO withdrawal Afghanistan may also be a source of terrorism. As elsewhere, there is some resentment of Chinese commercial penetration for undercutting domestic labor or commerce.

ASEAN, founded in 1967 by five countries but since grown to embrace all ten Southeast Asian nations, is probably the leading multilateral governmental organization in Asia, which has also organized several larger spinoffs: the ASEAN Regional Forum (ARF), the East Asian Summit, the ASEAN-EU Meetings (ASEM), the ASEAN Defense Ministers Plus (ADMM+, a meeting of defense ministers of ASEAN plus eight dialogue partners) to discuss mutual political, economic and security issues. The organization is a veto-group based on consensus, and thus discussion is easy but decisions are hard, and implementation still harder. To the extent that China aspires to be the leader of Asia there is a latent competition between the two, which ASEAN has attempted to bridge by including China (often balanced by Japan and India) in its regional extended forums. But China's territorial claims to the South China Sea pose a direct challenge to ASEAN as an impartial arbiter of regional justice, Daniel Lynch makes clear, so including China in discussions of how to settle such claims has been frustrating, especially inasmuch as China prefers to negotiate these disputes bilaterally. ASEAN has attempted to formulate a code of conduct but progress has been glacial, so far resulting only in the 1992 nonbinding Declaration on Conduct. Meanwhile China has attempted to isolate those states that dispute its claims while launching a "smile campaign" (including generous loans and investment projects) to propitiate those who do not, rendering ASEAN impotent and reducing the issue to a set of bilateral deals. On the one hand China has made clear it does not intend its subtle aggression to result in war, but on the other its ultimate objectives appear to be divisive and far-reaching.

China's security forces

The rise of reform and opening was heralded by a decline in Chinese defense spending as Beijing focused on economic construction. But since Tiananmen the military has enjoyed higher budgetary priority: increases in military spending have consistently exceeded already impressive GDP growth, and from 2002 to 2012 the PLA budget grew by 175 percent. To become a great power, China has concluded, a strong military is *sine qua non*.

Introduction

Historically the threats to China's security have emanated from land frontiers—from nomadic tribes in Central Asia, from the north (Mongolia, Manchuria, Russia), or from Japan through Korea—and China has therefore always been a land power first and foremost. And it is likely to remain so, according to Dennis Blasko, even though the army has been downsized and the navy and air force have received bigger shares of recent budgets. Even after a 25 percent cut of its 1997 size, the PLAA at 1.6 million remains the largest standing army in the world, making up 70 percent of all Chinese military personnel. The army's deployment reflects a traditional continental defense orientation against possible land invasion, apt to play little role in China's expansive strategic ambitions (unless, of course, an invasion of Taiwan comes into play). In November 2013 a major reform in the army was announced to make it smaller and more technologically advanced, with "new-type units" including special forces and other more mechanized, "informationalized" forces.

The PLA Air Force (PLAAF) is according to Kenneth and Jana Allen now committed to an "active defense" policy, granting it somewhat more tactical flexibility. With the acquisition since 2001 of advanced Russian aircraft and air defense systems and, since around 2007, equally advanced indigenously constructed aircraft, the air force has displayed considerable panache in occasional encounters with American or Japanese pilots. China's emergence as the world's leading trading power has allowed Chinese interests to be engaged in sometimes hazardous corners of the world and the air force has undertaken to protect them, for example flying 1,655 Chinese personnel out of Libya during that country's civil war. Besides developing Chinese stealth jets and other advanced aircraft China boasts one of the largest and most sophisticated surface to air missile systems (SAMs) in the world.

The PLA Navy has been at the forefront of China's ambition to rise to great power status at least since naval strategist Liu Huaqing's elevation to the vice-chairmanship of the Party's Central Military Commission in 1989 (later to the Politburo Standing Committee). Implicit in James R. Holmes's analysis is the assumption that Liu's ambitious timetable for naval expansion beyond the two "island chains" will be deferred to allow China to first consolidate control of the "near seas" within the first island chain: i.e., the East and South China Seas and the Yellow Sea. To achieve this the PLAN plans to construct a "fortress fleet" that, with the help of land-based fire support, can provide an "active defense" against American intervention. Although earlier strategists such as Mahan discounted the fortress concept as too passive, Holmes argues that with the help of such technological advances as the DF21D anti-ship ballistic missile (ASBM), capable of hitting an American aircraft carrier up to 1,700 miles away, plus China's large submarine fleet, Sovremenny-class destroyers, and its own aircraft carrier, this strategy becomes more plausible. Chinese maritime strategy thus appears to be to continue its sausage-slicing, islet-hopping takeover of the near seas (carefully avoiding any *casus belli* and using aid, loans and investment to propitiate or divide rival claimants to the territory) while deploying a formidable fortress fleet to deter outside "interference."

China's nuclear rocket forces, under the command of the Second Artillery Corps, will no doubt bolster that deterrence in the event of frontier conflict, as military spokespersons such as General Xiong Guangkai have already intimated. China's nuclear missiles seem to have entered a period of rapid growth. The recent introduction of the DF41 mobile, solid-fueled ICBM (which can be launched instantaneously, as opposed to previous liquid-fueled models), and the JL2 submarine-launched ballistic missile (SLBM) to be borne in the second generation 094 or third generation 069 ballistic missile submarines (SSBNs), both armed with multiple independently targeted reentry vehicles (MIRVs), will assure China a second-strike deterrent capability. Great secrecy surrounds Chinese nuclear strategy and capability, but according to Richard D. Fisher their numbers may exceed previous estimates as many are stored in a cavernous "underground Great

Wall." China also boasts perhaps the world's largest arsenal of short-range ballistic missiles capable of a first strike against Taiwan as well as contributing to A2/AD capability.

"The PRC is emerging as a world leader in space," according to Mark Stokes and Ian Easton. Space is on the frontier for all advanced security forces, not having figured in any previous war. The bulk of the Chinese enterprise is under the command of the General Armaments Department (GAD), which takes charge of navigation satellites, communication satellites, data relay stations, and mapping satellites, though the Second Artillery and the Air Force are also interested. Despite having joined Russia in protesting alleged American weaponization of space and urging extension of the nonproliferation treaty to space, China has joined the race to develop anti-ballistic missile and anti-satellite capabilities.

Another recently emerging area on the frontier of Chinese security interests is cyberwarfare. Xi Jinping has appointed himself chair of a recently created leading small group on cybersecurity and informationization, underlining China's determination to become a "cyberpower." Greg Austin divides Chinese efforts in this realm into internal "stability maintenance" measures on the domestic internet on the one hand and international cyberwarfare on the other. Whereas he considers Chinese cyberwar efforts to still be lagging far behind analogous US efforts and in a "catchup" mode, the "great Chinese firewall" is comprehensive and highly competent, boasting a huge internet police force as well as mercenary internet opinion leaders. In the cat-and-mouse game between the internet police and the world's largest online population various forms of communication cycle opportunistically; for a while the microblog (Sina Weibo) seemed invincible, but if a seditious posting appears—even a bad word—it can now be predicted to disappear within minutes. And in the views of Mandiant and other cyber authorities Chinese estimates of their cyberwar gap may be far too modest. Edward Snowden testified that the American National Security Agency had spied on the Chinese telecommunications giant Huawei, a company suspected by US defense officials of having ties to the People's Liberation Army. On the other hand the American Justice Department in May 2014 made great show of indicting five officers in Unit 61398 of the PLA for "serious cyber security breaches against six American victim entities" (viz., Westinghouse, Alcoa, US Steel Corp., the United Steel Workers Union, Allegheny Technologies, and SolarWorld), all of which had to "provide hard evidence of their hacking that could stand up in court." To be sure, in such a secretive world in which national pride is heavily invested such an exchange of accusations and denials is not very meaningful.

Conclusions

Located in the center of Asia with one of the largest land frontiers in the world and 14 neighbors whose dispositions could not easily be predicted (not to mention an equally vulnerable maritime frontier), China has long been obsessed with security. Despite a dominant ideology apotheosizing "harmony," the country has been afflicted by a great many invasions, civil wars, peasant rebellions, imperial punitive expeditions, and Western imperialist depredations. The post-revolutionary regime has attempted to reclaim that image, but the legacy of the past is not unmixed, nor is the record to date of the PRC. Since the end of the Cold War, Beijing has gained the country's greatest level of conventional security since the hundred years of humiliation. The Soviet Union has been succeeded by a weaker and more complaisant state, Central Asia has opened to Chinese commerce, Southeast Asia has welcomed the locomotive of the Asian network of commodity chains, and even true believers must strain to see the US or Japan as security threats in conventional terms. Beijing has responded so far to this position of diminished security threats in two ways. First, by turning its attention to the issue of nontraditional internal security: terrorism and dissidence are at the top of Beijing's list, but pollution, health and welfare provision, and inequality are also targeted. Second, viewing the first decades of the twenty-first century as a "time of opportunity" China has raised the ante in its definition of external security. The definition of "core interests" has been interpreted to include claims on territories not visible on most nineteenth century maps, and China has emerged as a more self-assured and formidable claimant of most of them. Is it conceivable that this, along with the quite un-Confucian drive for world power, represents some eerie reincarnation of the Maoist spirit?

Notes

1 Taiwan must be included as a state in any realistic analysis of Chinese security.
2 Assuming in this (security) context that Taiwan is a state, as it insists.
3 Thomas J. Christensen, *Worse than a monolith: alliance politics and problems of coercive diplomacy in Asia* (Princeton, NJ: Princeton University Press, 2011).
4 See Gordon H. Chang, *Friends and enemies: the United States, China, and the Soviet Union, 1948–1972* (Stanford, CA: Stanford University Press, 1990).
5 See Dingding Chen, "Are China and Russia moving toward a formal alliance?" *The Diplomat*, May 30, 2014. Available online at http://thediplomat.com/2014/05/are-china-and-russia-moving-toward-a-formal-alliance.
6 Many leaders of the new nations (perhaps Zhou Enlai himself) were embarrassed by Zhou's announcement during a 1964 tour of the continent that "Africa is ripe for revolution."
7 China has become the world's fourth biggest supplier in major weapons over the past five years, replacing France, according to a report released by the Stockholm International Peace Research Institute (SIPRI). Zhang Yiwei, "China No. 4 in global arms sales," *Global Times*, March 18, 2014.
8 Cf. Information Office of the State Council of the People's Republic of China, "China's policies and actions for addressing climate change," Beijing, October 2008. Available online at www.ccchina.gov.cn/WebSite/CCChina/UpFile/File419.pdf (accessed September 29, 2014).

Part I
Chinese national security

1
The historical legacy of Chinese security policy

Yuan-kang Wang

China has a rich tradition of military writings and a long history of warfare for over two thousand years. In ancient China during the Warring States period, the Military School (*bing jia*) contended for influence on policymakers with other schools of thought including Confucianism, Legalism, Daoism, and Moism. The military corpus continued to grow as subsequent dynasties confronted various security threats. Thousands of military treatises were written over the centuries, many of which were lost, but some survived the test of time. In the eleventh century, the Song Dynasty compiled the *Seven Military Classics*, including Sun Zi's famous *Art of War*. These canonized texts are still widely read today.[1] Military writings aside, official dynastic histories preserved numerous accounts of Chinese warfare. Each of these accounts presented a Chinese perspective—though not necessarily that of China's adversary—of what had transpired in the war, including the cause of war, the number of troops, war aims, logistics, conduct of war, and casualties. Given the enormous size of the literature, it is not possible to present a comprehensive account of Chinese strategic thought and practice in the space available here. This limitation notwithstanding, we can still identify important recurrent themes in the traditional military writings and actual strategic behaviors.

There are five themes that characterize the historical legacy of Chinese security policy. First, Sinocentrism puts China at the center of the known world, manifested in the hierarchical tribute system. Second, Confucian pacifism affects China's perception of itself as a peaceful, defensive, and nonaggressive nation and infuses morality into its foreign policy rhetoric. Third, Chinese realism guides actual strategic behavior and shows amoral pragmatism in the conduct of military affairs. Fourth, stratagems based on historical anecdotes may inform Chinese tactical maneuvers to deceive and outsmart the opponent. Finally, geography, along with the historical change in military technology, has a profound effect on resource allocation in Chinese defense planning, affecting the development of land power and sea power. These five themes reveal a diverse tradition in Chinese security policy, which I discuss below.

Sinocentrism

Historically, the Chinese saw themselves not as an empire or as a nation-state but as the center of civilization. The Chinese term for "China," *Zhongguo*, literally means "the country at the center" or "the central states." In this worldview, China stood at the center of the known world, or all-under-Heaven (*tianxia*). Foreigners, attracted by the splendor and superiority of the Chinese civilization, came to the Chinese court to pay tribute to the Son of Heaven and accepted their status as a vassal of the Chinese emperor. The Chinese way of diplomacy was hierarchical and non-egalitarian. Foreign relations were arranged in a concentric circle with China at the center, surrounded by tributary states and then by barbarians. The farther away from China, the less civilized the region. Unlike the Westphalian nation-state system, the concept of sovereign equality between states did not exist in the Chinese world order.

This Sinocentrism affected how traditional China conducted its frontier policy. John Fairbank popularized the notion of the "tribute system" to describe the Chinese world order. Non-Chinese rulers participated in the tribute system by observing appropriate rituals and ceremonies and were given a patent of appointment for their rulership as well as a seal for use in official communications. Leaders of tributary states could address themselves only as "king" (*wang*); the term "emperor" (*huangdi*) was reserved exclusively for the ruler of China. Tributary states adopted the Chinese calendar and dynastic reign-title. Their envoys periodically brought local products as tribute and performed appropriate ceremonies, including the full kowtow (kneeling three times, each time tapping their head to the ground for another three times, for a total of nine taps), in the Chinese court and received lavish gifts in return. The Chinese court granted tributary states with trading privileges at the capital and at the frontier. Polities that embraced Chinese culture and writing, such as Korea and Vietnam, were considered civilized and received a higher status in the tribute system, while those that did not, such as nomadic polities, were viewed as uncivilized and received a lower status. In Confucian thinking, the influx of tribute-paying foreign envoys strengthened the legitimacy of the Chinese throne, because the tribute symbolized his status as the accepted ruler of all-under-Heaven. For tributaries, Chinese recognition and investiture had the effect of enhancing the legitimacy of the local rulers, a process similar to diplomatic recognition of states today.[2]

The tribute system took shape in the Han Dynasty (206 BC–AD 220) and waxed and waned throughout the ages until its collapse in the nineteenth century under European gunboats. Material power was indispensable in creating and sustaining the tribute system.[3] Chinese rulers used the tribute system to organize foreign relations in a way that helped the country achieve its security objectives. By obliging foreigners to pay tribute, it was hoped, China would transform them into civilized and unthreatening peoples. Tributary states could call for Chinese help if attacked. China, as the leader of all tributaries, provided the public good of security. Trading privileges were granted as reward to those who accepted the tribute system or were withheld as punishment to those who refused to obey. Preponderant material capacity enabled China to set the "rules of the game" and to dictate the boundaries of appropriate behavior.

Sinocentrism does not mean that China was always the hegemonic power in Asia. Although there are periods in Asian history when China was predominant, there are also substantial periods when China was the weaker state or was divided into several competing ones. An oft neglected fact is that China was unified for less than 50 percent of the time in the last two thousand years,[4] which means that for the majority of Asian history there was no single hegemon. It is historically inaccurate to assume that the Asian state system was always hierarchic with China at the center. Sinocentrism is mainly a civilizational concept.[5]

Sinocentrism gave rise to a Chinese tendency to give paternalistic advice to others. As the leader of the civilized world, Chinese rulers were obliged to admonish deficient behavior on the part of their tributary states and to guide them into good governance. For instance, on hearing from his envoy that Korea lacked sufficient fortifications against Japanese pirates (which were also a threat to China), Ming Emperor Hongwu sent a rescript in 1369 to the Korean king stating that "we cannot neglect to counsel you of the ways of avoiding danger and protecting your kingdom." He went on to instruct the Korean king in the proper way to beef up defense, replenish food supply, and construct buildings to conduct government affairs.[6] Along with the tendency to give out advice was a moralistic approach to foreign policy announcements. Communications to foreign polities were often couched in moralistic language. As the superior culture, Sinocentrism placed China on the moral high ground when it reprimanded foreign rulers for insubordinate behavior or when it launched a punitive war against an allegedly immoral regime. Imperial China demanded respect, sincerity, and submission on the part of tributary states, and when those demands were not met, it put the blame entirely on the offending party.

The legacy of Sinocentrism did not disappear after China adopted the modern Westphalian system of sovereign equality. We still observe a Chinese tendency to give advice to foreign visitors. During the Cold War, leaders of pro-Mao Communist parties from around the world traveled to Beijing to pay symbolic tribute and to hear from the teachings of Mao Zedong.[7] Official photographs and television footage frequently show foreign dignitaries listening attentively and nodding appreciatively as Chinese leaders lecture them. PRC foreign policy announcements are frequently couched in moralistic language. Chinese leaders have employed the Five Principles of Peaceful Coexistence (mutual respect for sovereignty and territorial integrity, mutual nonaggression, noninterference in internal affairs, equality and mutual benefit, and peaceful coexistence) as an alternative to the US-dominated international order that limits the rights of sovereign states to pursue policies inconsistent with US interests and values. Chinese propaganda sharply criticized US imperialism and Soviet expansionism during the Cold War, accusing them of pursuing a policy of hegemony. Today, by saying that it will "never seek hegemony," Beijing attempts to stake out a morally superior foreign policy to the alleged US policy of pursuing "sole hegemony." The sloganeering of "peaceful rise" (later "peaceful development") and "harmonious world" taps into the human desire for peace and cooperation. It goes without saying that China's relatively weaker power position in the international system makes it easier to make these moralistic proclamations, which are consistent with its national interests.[8]

Confucian pacifism

Since Chinese culture is distinct, it is tempting to essentialize Chinese military writings and contrast them with the Western style of warfare. A popular view holds that the Chinese have traditionally prioritized defense, used war as a last resort, preferred an indirect approach, and shunned wars of total annihilation, while the West emphasized all of the opposite. The Great Wall of China is frequently cited as a symbol of this alleged preoccupation with defense and denigration of offensive use of force. This essentialized version of Chinese military tradition is often traced back to Confucianism. In the seventeenth century, the Jesuits who came to China were struck by a bureaucracy dominated by Confucian scholar-officials and its seemingly anti-militarist orientation. The Jesuit accounts of China later influenced Enlightenment thinkers such as Voltaire who wrote about the moral superiority of a benevolent China and praised its laws for rewarding moral behavior.[9] Max Weber was so impressed with the "pacifist character of Confucianism" that he wrote about how the Confucianists "faced military powers with aversion."[10] John K. Fairbank highlighted the "pacifist bias" of Confucianism that forbade expansion through brute force and conquest.[11]

Confucianism was the state ideology of Imperial China. Through its emphasis on the ruler's cultivation of virtue, Confucianism provided an important source of legitimacy for Chinese emperors. Learning Confucian classics was an essential element of the emperor's early education. For career-aspiring young Chinese, mastery of the Confucian classics was crucial to success in the imperial civil service examination. As a result, virtually all Chinese officials were well versed in the Confucian precepts. In matters of national security, Confucianism downplayed the efficacy of military force and instead prioritized the cultivation of virtue and morality. A virtuous ruler, like a shining city on the hill, will attract the submission of adversaries and face no threat around the world. Chaos and disobedience arise when the ruler is morally corrupt. Military conquests undermine the legitimacy of the ruler and are therefore counterproductive and self-defeating. A virtuous ruler should avoid wars of conquest. The Confucian literature is replete with passages that denigrate warfare and military expansion. This emphasis on moral virtue at the expense of the martial spirit produced a disdain for the military in Imperial China. "Disparagement of the soldier," writes Fairbank, "is deeply ingrained in the old Chinese system of values."[12]

The antimilitarism of Confucianism does not rule out war in certain situations. Confucius himself was in favor of military preparedness, but ranked its importance behind people's livelihood and trust in government. For the Confucians, war must serve a higher moral purpose in the form of a "righteous war" (*yizhan*). A state can use force only when reasons for doing so are morally justifiable. Once a righteous war is launched, the conduct of war must follow the principle of benevolence and justice, for instance, not attacking civilians and withdrawing after the just cause is served. There are two morally justifiable reasons for using force: self-defense and punitive war. If a state that practices moral statecraft is invaded by another state, then the victim can justifiably mobilize the country for war in self-defense. Alternatively, if the ruler of a state is found to be unjust or abusing its people, a punitive expedition can be launched to punish the abusive ruler and rescue the suffering people. This principle still holds even if the abusive state is stronger in power. For Confucians, moral and ethical principles override the sovereignty of another state and take precedence over the reality of power balance.[13]

But who gets to launch a punitive war? Confucius holds that only a sage-ruler has the right to launch punitive expeditions: "When the Way prevails in all-under-Heaven, the rites and music and punitive expeditions are initiated by the Son of Heaven" (*Confucius* 12:7, 16:2). Mencius develops the idea further, suggesting that when the ruler of a state is morally depraved, a punitive expedition is permissible to "rescue the people from the torments of water and fire" (*Mencius* 1.B.11). Like Confucius, Mencius insists that only the Son of Heaven can launch a punitive expedition; such a war is not aggression but rather punishment to correct unjust behavior. In practice, as whoever assumed the Chinese throne by definition had the Mandate of Heaven, and was thus virtuous, any military attack by the Chinese emperor could be morally justified. Those who refused to submit could easily be branded as bandits and criminals and deserving a punitive campaign. Conversely, since fighting a war will put strain on the people, a ruler's strategic restraint can be justified on the grounds of showing benevolence and caring for the people. Hence, Confucian rhetoric can be adapted to justify both attack and retreat. The Confucian conception of righteous war can be used to justify military attacks as punishments of those who lack virtue, or to justify strategic restraint by dismissing the utility of force and emphasizing the need to let the war-torn people rest.[14]

Thus, despite its antimilitarism, Confucianism is not entirely anti-war. This may sound paradoxical, but it raises questions about the use of morality to justify launching wars. In the history of human warfare, it is not difficult to find examples of conflict initiators using moral reasons to justify their military attacks. For instance, when the Ming Dynasty attacked the Mongols, it accused them of morally depraved behaviors and insubordination to the Son of Heaven. One finds similar moral justification in the 2003 US invasion of Iraq, that Saddam Hussein was abusing his own people and developing weapons of mass destruction. Conflict initiators often dress their military actions in moral terms.

The merging of morality and authority in the Son of Heaven gives rise to the idea of the Kingly Way (*wang dao*) in the Confucian conception of international order. According to Confucianism, there are two types of international order: the Kingly Way and the Hegemonic Way (*ba dao*). The Kingly Way is rule by benevolence, whereas the Hegemonic Way is rule by force. In the benevolent order, the dominant power follows the rules of virtue, humaneness, and compassion toward lesser states even though it is the most powerful state in the system. This Kingly Way preserves peace and stability in the system. In the hegemonic order, the dominant power takes advantages of its overwhelming military strength to conquer or subdue lesser states and force their compliance. This Hegemonic Way is the source of international instability. These two types of international order are frequently used to highlight the differences between China and the West. In this view, historical China emphasized moral leadership, whereas the West traditionally ruled by force. Morality and international order are thus directly related. A benevolent, humane Chinese world order is juxtaposed against the malevolent, ruthless power politics in the West. Some scholars even argue that balance of power politics in the West have resulted in numerous wars, whereas East Asia's hierarchical tribute system was relatively peaceful and stable.[15] Put in the context of contemporary international relations, Chinese scholar Yan Xuetong suggests that the United States has behaved irresponsibly in the Hegemonic Way, citing the 2003 Iraq War and other offenses; a rising China today should strive to follow the Kingly Way (which he calls "humane authority") and "provide a better model for society than that given by the United States."[16]

The assertion that China practiced the Kingly Way conflates political thought with history. Lofty Confucian ideals might not be reflected in actual practice. Rule by brute force is not alien to the Chinese tradition. Chinese dynasties have practiced wars of total conquest and wars of annihilation. Most Chinese are familiar with the conquests of the Qin First Emperor (r. 246–210 BC), the Han Emperor Wu (r. 141–87 BC), the Tang Emperor Taizong (r. 626–49), and the Ming Emperor Yongle (r. 1402–24). Chinese historian Shi Yinhong notes that this military tradition of total conquest is "more Napoleonic than Napoleon and more Clausewitzian than Clausewitz."[17] Chinese history has been at least as violent as Europe's.[18]

These ancient Chinese thoughts were vilified during the Mao years for being feudal and backward. But as Chinese power increases, confidence in historical traditions rises as well. Officers and analysts of the People's Liberation Army (PLA) have begun to embrace a cultural approach to Chinese strategy. Military researchers scour historical writings to find strategic inspirations and justifications for China's military buildup. They argue that Chinese strategic culture is defensive and pacifist. Lt. General Li Jijun of the Academy of Military Science asserts that "the defensive character of China's strategic culture is widely recognized in the world."[19] General Xu Xin, former deputy chief of staff of the People's Liberation Army, argues that "The Chinese nation has a long tradition of honoring peace. As early as two thousand years ago, Confucius emphasized that 'peace should be cherished.'"[20]

In its attempt to wrest the moral high ground, modern China has a tendency to justify its military actions as either self-defense or punitive expedition. Many members of China's elites believe that China fights only "just wars" and that China goes to war only in self-defense. Andrew Scobell aptly calls this widespread view "The Cult of Defense."[21] Beijing officially describes the border conflicts with India in 1962 and with the Soviet Union in 1969 as "self-defense counterattacks" (*ziwei fanji*). After Vietnam invaded Cambodia, a Chinese ally, China decided to use force against Vietnam to teach it "a lesson." The 1979 punitive expedition against Vietnam was described as a "self-defense counterattack" even though China initiated the war.[22] Other military actions, such as the Korean War (1950–53) and the two Taiwan Strait crises (1954–55 and 1958), were also described as defensive acts against US intervention. In Chinese eyes, Beijing's use of offensive military force was triggered by the opponent's aggressive acts and was thus self-defense in nature. It goes without saying that the other party to the same conflict saw Chinese aggression, not self-defense.

Chinese realism

If Chinese security policy was guided by Confucian pacifism, then wars should have been relatively rare in historical China. But that is not the case. Wars were common in Chinese history. A chronology of warfare compiled by the military historians of the Chinese Academy of Military Science shows that from 770 BC (Spring and Autumn) to 1912 (Qing Dynasty), China engaged in a total of 3,756 internal and external wars, averaging 1.4 wars per year.[23] The Chinese were no less warlike than other peoples of the world. The empirical record does not support the assertion that the Chinese world order was peaceful and stable.

Aside from the idealized Confucian pacifism, the Chinese also have a tradition of pragmatism and realism. As Confucian ideals were difficult to put into practice, Legalism (*fa jia*) provided a toolkit of administrative methods that were more useful in actual governance. Legalism, in contrast to the Confucian emphasis on virtue, prescribes severe punishment to correct bad behaviors and rewards for doing good deeds. The Legalist believes that virtue is born out of power. Ever since the adoption of Confucianism as the state ideology in the Han Dynasty, Chinese officials have been pragmatic by incorporating Legalist techniques in the administration of their vast country. As Fairbank notes, rewards and punishments could keep the common people in line, but Chinese officials needed something more inspiring to motivate the people. The emperor's observance of Confucian rituals and ceremonies gave him a certain virtue and an aura of legitimacy that drew people to accept and venerate his rule.[24] Government policies were written in the Confucian vocabulary of benevolence, virtue, and humaneness, but the policy substance was essentially Legalist. Commentators describe this millennium-old practice as "Legalism with a Confucian façade."[25] The clever fusion of the two opposing schools of thought reflects a high level of pragmatism in Chinese statecraft and remains a salient feature in later dynasties.

In Chinese military writings, we find a similar amalgam of idealism and realism. In the canonical *Seven Military Classics*, passages are strewn with the precepts of benevolence and humaneness on the one hand and the hard realpolitik of power and force on the other. The concept of righteous war fuses both morality and war and opens up possibilities to brand the enemy as unrighteous and thus deserving destruction and extermination. When a war is launched in the name of upholding a moral cause, any level of violence—ranging from capturing or killing the aggressor, annexation of the violator's territory, to extermination and total destruction of the enemy—becomes moral and just. In this way, the moral ends justify the violent means. This ends-means relationship reflects Chinese realism in the prosecution of warfare. The Confucian disdain for violence gave way to a realistic appreciation of the correlates of war. Studies have shown that Confucian China has been a practitioner of realpolitik for centuries.[26]

Sun Zi's adages of "subduing the enemy without fighting is the acme of skill" and "the best strategy is to attack the enemy's strategy, next best is to attack his alliances, next best is to attack his army, and the worst is to besiege his cities" are often used to demonstrate the Chinese proclivity for minimal violence, but this view ignores the numerous wars of annihilation in Chinese history. It also essentializes what may not be uniquely Chinese: military strategists across culture and across time invariably favor winning without having to fight for it. If military success could be achieved with minimal cost, who would not be in favor? Alastair Iain Johnston uses a strategic cultural approach to analyze Chinese military writings and identifies a realpolitik strategic culture that significantly influences Chinese grand strategic choice. He argues that the Confucian elements in the *Seven Military Classics* are largely symbolic and have no influence on actual Chinese strategic behavior. Because of this operative strategic culture of realpolitik, China has viewed conflict as inevitable, held a zero-sum view of the adversary, and valued the utility of force in resolving interstate disputes. In times of superior strength, China has preferred to pursue an offensive, expansionist grand strategy (e.g., extended campaigns beyond the borders, annexation of territories, and total annihilation of adversaries). In times of relative weakness, China would adopt a defensive grand strategy (e.g., static defense and deterrence) or even an accommodationist grand strategy (e.g., territorial concessions, economic incentives, and peace treaties).[27]

The cultural approach to Chinese strategy has its appeal, but it again risks essentializing a type of strategic thinking that may not be uniquely Chinese. Chinese realpolitik may have nothing to do with culture but with a deeper cause that lies in the anarchic structure of the system in which no central authority exists to enforce order. The realpolitik that we observe in Chinese strategic behavior may be universal, not culture-specific. There is no a priori reason to assume that the Chinese have a distinctive style of warfare. In fact, studies have shown that Western and Chinese military writings share similar logic about warfare. For instance, Michael I. Handel's textual analysis of the works by Sun Zi, Mao Zedong, Clausewitz, Jomini, and Machiavelli has shown that "the logic of strategy and waging war is universal rather than parochial, cultural, or regional."[28] Chinese realpolitik behavior shows no significant difference from realpolitik in the West, or elsewhere. Chinese realpolitik is best understood through international relations theory. The anarchic structure of the international system pushes states of various cultures to think and act in a similar fashion. Structural realism, an international relations theory, can explain Chinese realpolitik without resorting to an extra layer of cultural variables.[29]

An important source of confusion in the literature on Chinese strategic culture is the different definitions of culture adopted by analysts. A common method of defining culture is to include *both* beliefs and behaviors: "military culture refers to a discrete, bounded system of conduct and behavior to which members of the military are supposed to adhere, made of written and unwritten rules and conventions as well as distinctive beliefs and symbols."[30] A key drawback of this type of definition is that, by subsuming both thought and action within the concept of culture, it runs the risk of being mechanically deterministic and tautological.[31] Culture determines behavior, which is then read back into culture. It does not allow for the possibility of a disconnect between thought and action. A more useful definition, one that allows for social science-type testing, is to separate thought from action in the conceptualization of culture: "shared ideas, beliefs, and values collectively held within a society or by its elites that are transmitted from one generation to the next through a process of socialization."[32] Behaviors and practices are not included in this definition because whether a cultural norm influences actual behavior is something to be tested, not assumed. It is possible that some beliefs and values (such as Confucian ideals) may not be reflected in actual practices.

Regardless of how one approaches the issue of culture, it is clear that the old popular way of juxtaposing a Chinese style of warfare with a Western style of warfare is problematic. There are more commonalities than dissimilarities in Chinese and non-Chinese security policy. The idea that the Chinese world order has been more peaceful than that in the West has been resoundingly discredited. Wars were common in Chinese history. At the strategic level, the historical legacy of Chinese security policy is one of realpolitik based on rational assessments of relative power between China and its competitors.

Stratagems and deception

Even though Chinese realpolitik is not *sui generis*, Chinese history is rich with stories of using clever stratagems and deception to defeat adversaries. These stratagems are embedded in Chinese history and may inform Chinese tactical maneuvers. The use of stratagems does not necessarily imply a preference for nonviolence but rather it is considered a cost-effective way of achieving one's strategic goals. For the Chinese, outsmarting the opponent is the most celebrated trait of the strategist. As Sun Zi's *The Art of War* states, "Warfare is the Way of deception." Deception is using unorthodox methods to outwit and defeat the rival. Sun Zi explains: "Thus although capable, display incapability. When committed to employing your forces, feign inactivity. When your objective is nearby, make it appear as if distant; when far away, create the illusion of being nearby."[33] Once your armies become formless (*wu xing*) and thus unfathomable, the opponent will be in a disadvantageous position that you can exploit to your advantage.

A popular source of stratagems and deception is the *Romance of the Three Kingdoms* (*san guo yan yi*), a fourteenth-century novel by Luo Guanzhong about the ancient three kingdoms of Wei, Wu, and Shu (168–265 BC). Stories of the Three Kingdoms are well known to the Chinese through village storytellers, operas, movies and TV series. Some of the heroes such as Guan Yu are even worshipped as a Daoist deity in temples. Chinese strategists, diplomats, and military officers often use these stories to describe their maneuvers.[34] The book is full of tales and anecdotes that illustrate the use of clever stratagems to outsmart one's opponent. For instance, in the "empty fort stratagem," the stronger contestant led an army to attack a city defended by the weaker. Not having enough troops to defend itself, the weaker one feigned strength by opening the city gate, with its chief strategist Zhuge Liang, known to be a risk-averse person, calmly playing a musical instrument atop the wide open gate. Seeing this, the opponent feared walking into a trap set up by a well defended army and decided to withdraw. In the "sow discord stratagem," the Wei kingdom recruited two admirals to help rebuild its navy after its defeat by Wu. Alarmed by the Wei's move, Wu forged secret correspondence with the admirals and maneuvered to have Wei discover the papers. This deceptive stratagem tricked Wei into executing the two admirals for colluding with the enemy, thereby relieving Wu of a potential threat.

The use of stratagems is evident in today's China. Sinologist Perry Link uses the *Romance of the Three Kingdoms* to illustrate China's methods to control dissent. After a series of reports uncovering the spectacular wealth of Chinese leaders, in late 2013 China delayed the processing of visas for journalists from the *New York Times* and Bloomberg News without giving an explanation. Although most were issued a visa at the last minute, this tactic effectively instilled an atmosphere of fear among foreign journalists that might have led them to self-censor their reporting in the future. Similarly, scholars working on China face the risk of being denied a visa if they are critical of Chinese policies; losing access to China could jeopardize academic careers. Link concludes: "When US policymakers use terms like 'strategic partner' and 'responsible stakeholder' for the people at the top in Beijing, they are out of their depth."[35] In the security realm, China also employed stratagems to develop its Beidou Navigation System to achieve independence on satellite navigation for its military hardware including missiles, warships, and aircraft. When the US blocked Chinese access to satellite technology in the late 1990s, China turned to Europe by contributing 200 million euros (US$228 million at the time) to join the European Union's Galileo program. Through this partnership, China was able to acquire and develop a wide range of dual-use satellite technology that eventually helped it achieve strategic independence in satellite navigation, to the chagrin of EU officials who found out afterwards. The Beidou became operational well ahead of the Galileo system.[36]

Geography

Geography and security are closely related. Historically, China's main security threats came from the Asian continent, not from the ocean. The Chinese heartland, fertile and well irrigated, was an attractive target for foreign attacks. For more than two thousand years, Chinese dynasties competed for security with mobile nomadic polities skilled in horsemanship such as Xiongnu,

Khitans, Jurchens and Mongols. The Mongols and the Manchus even conquered China and established the Yuan (1279–1369) and the Qing (1644–1912) dynasties, respectively. Aside from continental threats, there had been sporadic threats from the maritime frontier, such as during the Ming Dynasty (1368–1644) when it faced *wokou* piracy along the coast and confronted a Japanese invasion of Korea in 1592–98. For most of history, however, the focus of Chinese security planners remained on the Asian continent. It was not until after the Opium War (1839–42) that the maritime frontier became a key source of security threat. Chinese strategists started to seriously consider the merits of frontier defense versus maritime defense.

The issue of frontier and maritime defense inevitably rests on resource allocation. When Chinese power was preponderant, the country could afford expansion on both fronts. The early Ming was able to launch several military expeditions against the Mongols and yet at the same time build the world's most powerful navy. The Mongolian campaigns involved as many as half a million Chinese soldiers, according to Ming records. The Ming fleet boasted about 27,000 crews on 250 ships and sailed as far as East Africa in the early fifteenth century. At the height of Ming naval power, there were 3,500 ships in operation along the coast of China. For overseas countries, "the very name of the Ming navy was sufficient to inspire awe."[37] The early Ming was able to simultaneously maintain both a powerful army and a strong navy because it had the material resources to do so. In comparison, the resource-strapped late Qing Dynasty faced a stark choice between frontier defense and maritime defense when Russia started to encroach on Xinjiang on the western frontier and when the Japanese invasion of Formosa (Taiwan) exposed China's inadequate coastal defense. In 1874, an intense policy debate erupted in the Qing court about whether to shift military funds from the inland Xinjiang to the maritime frontier. The Qing court, accustomed to a steppe-oriented strategy, was unable to adapt to the age of sea power and decided in favor of the frontier defense. In the end, a total of 51 million taels were allocated to support the military expenses in Xinjiang from 1875 to 1881, but only one million taels were actually appropriated for the navy every year. The prioritization of frontier defense was a debilitating blow to China's naval program. Immanuel C.Y. Hsu suggests that had the Xinjiang funds been invested in the naval program, China might have had a powerful navy and might not have lost to Japan in the humiliating Sino-Japanese War of 1895.[38] The Qing's failure to allocate sufficient resources to the maritime frontier contributed to its downfall.

Hence, China's geographical environment is a major factor affecting its military resource allocation and defense planning. China today has the longest land borders (13,743 miles) in the world, with 14 contiguous countries. During the Cold War, China faced security threats from both the Asian continent and the seacoast. On the land frontier, as many as 1.5 million troops were deployed along the two sides of the Sino-Soviet border.[39] Both countries fought a border conflict in 1969. On the maritime frontier, Chiang Kai-shek on Taiwan attempted to recover the mainland he lost in the Chinese civil war and concluded a mutual defense treaty with the United States. The Soviet threat, coupled with US escalation of the Vietnam War, created fear among PRC leaders about being drawn into a war. As the concentration of industry in coastal urban regions made the country vulnerable to attack, from 1964 to 1971 Mao Zedong and other Chinese leaders embarked on a massive program, called the Third Front, to move coastal industries inland and create an entire industrial structure in the inland provinces of Sichuan, Guizhou, Yunnan, and others. The Third Front was an extremely costly program, using up about 30 to 40 percent of national investment.[40] Defense concerns introduced inefficiency into China's industrialization program.

China is now the world's second largest economy and is expected to surpass the United States in the next decade or so. With rising economic capabilities, China will be able to allocate more resources to increase its military power. In addition to maintaining a large army, PRC leaders have made plans to turn China into a maritime power. Given China's expanding interests abroad and reliance on energy imports from overseas, such reallocation of resources toward the maritime frontier is to be expected. If history is any guide, whether China can become a maritime power will depend on its ability to maintain peace on the land borders.

Aside from influencing resource allocation, the geographical legacy of Qing conquests also affects Chinese defense planning today. The present territorial size of China is larger than most of the dynastic boundaries of the past. China's territorial boundaries waxed and waned throughout history. The Central Plain surrounding the Yellow River constituted the traditional Chinese heartland. The Ming Dynasty (1368–1644) did not directly administer the areas known today as Xinjiang, Tibet, Mongolia, and Manchuria. That China is so big today is a result of Qing conquest, which doubled the territorial size of Ming China. The Manchus of the Qing Dynasty spent nearly eighty years trying to defeat the Zunghars, conquering Mongolia, Xinjiang, and Tibet in the process. Through a series of expansions from 1683 to 1759, the Qing Empire became the largest continental empire in the world and a regional hegemon in East Asia. Its territorial size dwarfed that of any European country, its population was three times the size of Europe's total population, and its economy was estimated to be at least four times larger than that of Great Britain.[41] The Qing's westward expansion destroyed the nomadic confederations that had dominated the history of east and central Eurasia for two thousand years.

When the Qing Dynasty was overthrown in 1912, the Republic of China inherited its territorial boundaries. Mongolia soon declared independence and fell under Soviet sway. Over the centuries, the Manchu homeland in northeastern China has been fully integrated into the Chinese nation, with the Manchu language in danger of becoming extinct. The People's Republic of China continues to administer Inner Mongolia, Xinjiang, and Tibet. There are important strategic reasons for such control. Both Xinjiang and Tibet serve as buffer zones between the Chinese heartland on the one hand and Russia, India, and other nearby states on the other. Nonetheless, nationalist movements in Xinjiang and Tibet complicate security planning by the Chinese government and are now becoming a new source of domestic security concern.

Conclusion and future research

In studying Chinese strategic thought and military practice, it behooves us to be aware of the pitfalls of essentializing the Chinese tradition. The popular way of contrasting a Chinese style of warfare with a Western style of warfare does more to obscure than illuminate. Empirical studies of Chinese warfare show that the Chinese were as capable of total war as the Europeans. China has been a practitioner of realpolitik for centuries, often dressing its pursuit of power with a Confucian facade of benevolence. Sinocentrism deeply affected China's perception of its Century of Humiliation at the hands of Western powers and Japan and strengthened the resolve of Chinese leaders to pursue power and realize the so called China Dream. Despite the foreign policy rhetoric of harmony and peace, there is no reason to believe that China will behave differently from other great powers in history.

Yet the tendency to essentialize the Chinese tradition remains strong within China today. Civilian and military strategists established academic associations to promote the study of Chinese strategic culture and published monographs and articles on China's military cultural traditions. The content of Chinese strategic culture that they have identified is still Confucian pacifism: Chinese cultural tradition emphasizes harmony and peace, giving rise to a strategic culture that is defensive and nonaggressive. This revival of strategic culture seems to serve a political purpose as the Chinese leadership attempts to develop a peaceful rise discourse to ease international concerns over China's rising power. Its popularity notwithstanding, the strategic cultural approach adopted by the Chinese analysts risks falling into the trap of cultural determinism. As noted earlier, the empirical evidence does not support the Confucian strategic culture that they advocate.

Chinese security policy is an exciting field that has plenty of room for growth. First, unlike European security, the study of Chinese security policy remains under-theorized. Chinese military history, including the PRC period, is a fertile ground to build new theories or to test existing ones. Second, although structural realism can explain Chinese security policy at the strategic level, more studies need to be conducted on the use of stratagems in tactical maneuvers. What are the roles of historical anecdotes and ancient stratagems in Chinese defense planning and how do they supplement Chinese realpolitik? Third, more research is needed on the relationship between resource allocation and the simultaneous development of land power and sea power. China developed naval power during the Song, Yuan, and Ming dynasties, but for the majority of the time it has been a continental power. Only the Ming Dynasty was able to develop both land power and sea power in the early fifteenth century, but the rise of Mongol threat effectively pulled the seagoing Chinese back onto the Asian continent. Given its continental legacy, can the PRC become a full-scale maritime power? If so, will it exacerbate security competition with the United States?

Glossary

ba dao　霸道
bing jia　兵家
fa jia　法家
san guo yan yi　三國演義
tianxia　天下
wang dao　王道
wokou　倭寇
wu xing　無形
yizhan　義戰
zhongguo　中國
ziwei fanji　自衛反擊

Notes

1 The seven classics are *Taigong Six Secret Teachings, The Methods of the Sima, Sun Zi's Art of War, Wuzi, Wei Liaozi, Three Strategies of Huang Shigong*, and *Questions and Replies Between Tang Taizong and Li Weigong*. For an English translation of the seven military classics, see Ralph D. Sawyer and Mei-chün Sawyer, *The Tao of Deception: Unorthodox Warfare in Historic and Modern China* (New York: Basic Books, 2007).
2 John K. Fairbank, *Trade and Diplomacy on the China Coast: The Opening of the Treaty Ports, 1842–1854* (Cambridge, MA: Harvard University Press, 1953), 30.
3 Yuan-kang Wang, "Explaining the Tribute System: Power, Confucianism, and War in Medieval East Asia," *Journal of East Asian Studies* 13, no. 2 (2013): 207–32.
4 Quoted in Victoria Tin-bor Hui, "How China Was Ruled," *The American Interest* 3, no. 4 (2008): 53–65.
5 The idea of a hierarchical Asia is widespread. For instance, Samuel Huntington asserts that "Asians generally are willing to 'accept hierarchy' in international relations." David Kang writes, "East Asian regional relations have historically been hierarchic, more peaceful, and more stable than those in the West." Samuel P. Huntington, *The Clash of Civilizations and the Remaking of World Order* (New York: Simon & Schuster, 1996), 234–8; David C. Kang, "Getting Asia Wrong: The Need for New Analytical Frameworks," *International Security* 27, no. 4 (spring 2003): 57–85.

6 Feng Zhang, *Chinese Hegemony: Grand Strategy and International Institutions in East Asian History* (Stanford, CA: Stanford University Press, forthcoming).
7 Andrew J. Nathan and Robert S. Ross, *The Great Wall and the Empty Fortress: China's Search for Security* (New York: W.W. Norton, 1997), 23.
8 Andrew J. Nathan and Andrew Scobell, *China's Search for Security* (New York: Columbia University Press, 2012), 27–31.
9 Hans J. Van de Ven, *Warfare in Chinese History*, Sinica Leidensia (Leiden; Boston, MA: Brill, 2000), 4–5; Jonathan Spence, "Looking East: The Long View," in *China Roundabout: Essays in History and Culture*, ed. J. Spence (New York: W.W. Norton, 1992).
10 Max Weber, *The Religion of China: Confucianism and Taoism*, trans. Hans H. Gerth (Glencoe, IL: The Free Press, 1951), 140, 169.
11 John K. Fairbank, "Varieties of the Chinese Military Experience," in *Chinese Ways in Warfare*, ed. Frank A. Kierman Jr. and John K. Fairbank (Cambridge, MA: Harvard University Press, 1974), 7–9.
12 John K. Fairbank, *The United States and China*, fourth edn (Cambridge, MA: Harvard University Press, 1983), 68.
13 Cho-yun Hsu, "Applying Confucian Ethics to International Relations," *Journal of Ethics and International Affairs* 5 (1991): 15–31.
14 Victoria Tin-bor Hui, "Confucianism and Peacemaking in Chinese History," in *Peacemaking: From Practice to Theory*, ed. Susan Allen Nan, Andrea Bartoli, and Zacharia Mampilly (Santa Barbara, CA: Praeger, 2011).
15 Huntington, *The Clash of Civilizations and the Remaking of World Order*, 234–8; David C. Kang, *China Rising: Peace, Power, and Order in East Asia* (New York: Columbia University Press, 2007); David C. Kang, *East Asia before the West: Five Centuries of Trade and Tribute* (New York: Columbia University Press, 2010).
16 Xuetong Yan, *Ancient Chinese Thought, Modern Chinese Power*, ed. Daniel Bell and Zhe Sun, trans. Edmund Ryden (Princeton, NJ: Princeton University Press, 2011), 66, 99.
17 Victoria Tin-bor Hui, "History and Thought in China's Traditions," *Journal of Chinese Political Science* 17 (2012): 125–41.
18 Van de Ven, *Warfare in Chinese History*.
19 Li Jijun, "Lun Zhanlue Wenhua [On Strategic Culture]," *Zhongguo Junshi Kexue [China Military Science]*, no. 1 (1997): 8–15.
20 Xu Xin, "Daodi Shui Weixie Shui? [Who's Threatening Whom?]," *Liaowang [Outlook]*, no. 8–9 (1996): Reported by Fang Zhi, 48–9.
21 Andrew Scobell, *China's Use of Military Force: Beyond the Great Wall and the Long March* (New York: Cambridge University Press, 2003), 27–32
22 Ibid.
23 Fu Zhongxia et al., eds, *Zhongguo Lidai Zhanzheng Nianbiao [Chronology of Warfare in the Dynasties of China]* (Beijing: Jiefangjun chubanshe, 2002).
24 John K. Fairbank, *China: A New History* (Cambridge, MA: Harvard University Press, Belknap Press, 1992), 62.
25 Hui, "Confucianism and Peacemaking in Chinese History."
26 Alastair Iain Johnston, *Cultural Realism: Strategic Culture and Grand Strategy in Chinese History* (Princeton, NJ: Princeton University Press, 1995); Yuan-kang Wang, *Harmony and War: Confucian Culture and Chinese Power Politics* (New York: Columbia University Press, 2011).
27 Johnston, *Cultural Realism*.
28 Michael I. Handel, *Masters of War: Classical Strategic Thought*, third edn (London: Frank Cass, 2001), xxiv.
29 Wang, *Harmony and War*.
30 Nicola Di Cosmo, ed. *Military Culture in Imperial China* (Cambridge, MA: Harvard University Press, 2009), 3.
31 Johnston, *Cultural Realism*, 5–15.
32 Wang, *Harmony and War*, 12; Johnston, *Cultural Realism*, 37–9.
33 Sawyer and Sawyer, *The Tao of Deception*, 58.
34 Nathan and Scobell, *China's Search for Security*, 25.
35 Perry Link, "Paying a Price to Cross China's Border," *Washington Post*, December 20, 2013.
36 David Lague, "Special Report—In Satellite Tech Race, China Hitched a Ride from Europe," *Reuters*, December 22, 2013.
37 Jung-pang Lo, "The Decline of the Early Ming Navy," *Oriens Extremus* 5 (1958): 149–68.

38 Immanuel C.Y. Hsu, "The Great Policy Debate in China, 1874: Maritime Defense vs. Frontier Defense," *Harvard Journal of Asiatic Studies* 25 (1964): 212–28.
39 Nathan and Scobell, *China's Search for Security*, 15.
40 Barry Naughton, "The Third Front: Defence Industrialization in the Chinese Interior," *China Quarterly*, no. 115 (1988): 351–86.
41 Mark C. Elliott, *Emperor Qianlong: Son of Heaven, Man of the World* (New York: Pearson Longman, 2009), 141; James Louis Hevia, *Cherishing Men from Afar: Qing Guest Ritual and the Macartney Embassy of 1793* (Durham, NC: Duke University Press, 1995), 31.

2

Marxist ideology, revolutionary legacy and their impact on China's security policy

Maochun Yu

When one thinks of China, a binary image usually emerges. On the one hand, China is viewed as a nation of rich historical heritage and tradition, with a civilizational bloc of its own in East Asia that centers on an integral set of Confucian values and moral codes, an imperial management system supported and sustained by a mature and sophisticated civil service selection and maintenance scheme, and a self-awareness of Sino-centralism that best manifests itself in the tributary system. On the other hand, China is also a modern, socialist country of twentieth-century political and ideological ethos, with a communist party that is the direct product of Marxism-Leninism, whose historical mission is to reject traditional—or, in Marxist parlance, feudal—traits that have molded the Chinese culture, in order to create a socialist new nation based upon the basic designs mapped out by the Communist Party's various ideological ancestors, from Marx and Lenin to Mao Zedong and Deng Xiaoping.

Such binary, often contradictory, strands of China are also reflected in the accumulative body of Chinese security studies, with one school of thought stressing the historical China while the other sees a symbiosis between contemporary China and its avowed ideological commitment to communism. But frequently, these two stands are not mutually exclusive. This is partly because China's past does provide the communist government in Beijing a practical utility, i.e. an order of imperial grandeur and geopolitical hegemony that China's leaders would like to restore. Much of today's political agenda under the Communist Party's General Secretary Xi Jinping rests on the grand objective of realizing a "Chinese Dream" that is basically a historic revival of the nation's past greatness, albeit under the firm leadership of a Marxist-Leninist political party. In fact, many of today's leading security experts in China often draw their intellectual inspirations from Chinese traditional texts and political tenets to interpret and articulate China's contemporary national security strategies and approaches. Yet, the core of China's security considerations, strategic orientations and modus operandi is undoubtedly guided by the modern ethos of a revolutionary China, fundamentally affected by the nation's founding principles of Marxism, Leninism, and China's own revised or adapted versions of these principles. While the impact of China's traditional culture on today's Chinese security is explored in greater detail in Chapter 1, this chapter will focus on the evolution of China's revolutionary legacy and its ideological impact upon the formulation and development of China's security policies and practices that are reshaping today's global security environment.[1]

Normatively speaking, security is intrinsically related to a nation state, which is perhaps why both the words "nation" and "state" are often coupled with "security" to produce the formulaic phrases "national security" or "state security." In the context of today's China, the two phrases are in fact interchangeable, both serving to define a primary motivation of security policy as a nation's parochial self-interest. A good national security policy is therefore a contribution to patriotism.

But historically, that has not always been the case in communist China, because for decades security policy has not been primarily motivated by "patriotism" in the normal sense. It is highly ideological and reflective of the basic tenets of its founding philosophy of Marxism, Leninism and Mao's communist theories that go far beyond the realm of a Chinese patriotism. The PRC security policy, as guided by communist ideology, also has a distinctive operational method that makes the traditional modus operandi of conceptualizing and practicing "national security" often irrelevant.

Understanding this ideological strand of PRC diplomacy is of significant contemporary relevance. For many years, the belief that the PRC leadership conducts its diplomacy and security matters just like everybody else, with a nationalistic world view and a quest for the commonly defined national security, has been prevalent in the capitals of the non-Chinese world. While this understanding of the PRC national security may have been normatively useful, it has been proven practically insufficient.

The ideological origins of Chinese security

The Chinese Communist Party (CCP) was founded in 1921 as an Asian branch of the Third Communist Internationale, or the Comintern, which was founded by Vladimir Lenin in 1919 as an organizational hub of global communist revolution. From the very beginning, the CCP regarded its mission as part of the worldwide communist takeover. Mao Zedong concisely stated in the 1920s that "the Chinese revolution is an integral part of the world proletarian revolution."[2] In the late 1930s and early 1940s, Mao believed that the Chinese revolution had entered the more advanced stage of the so called "new democratic revolution," which of course remained "a part of the worldwide proletarian socialist revolution." According to Mao, the main target of this Chinese revolution had now become imperialism, also known as "international capitalism."[3]

Yet the prerequisite for a national security policy is the existence of an internationally recognized government. Before the proclamation of the PRC in October 1949, the CCP had only foreign policy but not much security policy. As the Communist troops swept across China and the Nationalist government retreated to Taiwan, the CCP leaders began to formulate the foundations of a national security doctrine and diplomatic policy for the soon-to-be-established regime. In the spring of 1949, Mao Zedong put his theory of "the new democratic revolution" in practice by formulating three basic principles of security and strategic orientations for the new Communist government. These strategic principles matched closely the foremost mission of the communist revolution at the time: the resolute struggle against imperialism led by the United States.

First, as Mao laid out in his writings and orders, the new regime would not recognize the diplomatic legitimacy of any countries that had maintained diplomatic relations with the Nationalist government, a "running dog" of the American global hegemony. As such, all foreign diplomats still in China would be treated not as diplomats but as expatriates; all treaties reached between all previous Chinese governments and other countries would be void. Mao called this policy "building a brand new stove," meaning a complete break with "the Old China."[4]

Secondly, the new Communist regime would "purify" China of all traces of "imperialist countries" and would not tolerate any official or non-governmental ties any Western countries had left after the Communist takeover. This was called "the house cleansing" policy. In late January and early February of 1949, Anastas Mikoyan, Stalin's special envoy, was sent to the CCP headquarters on a secret mission. Mao elaborated on his house cleansing policy, calling imperialist influences in China "trash, dirt, lice, bedbugs, and fleas" that needed to be purified.[5]

Thirdly, Mao announced the policy of "Leaning to One Side" [*yibiandao*]. As early as 1947, Mao had fully accepted the "Two Camps Theory" that originated with Stalin's ideological czar Andrei Zhdanov in 1946. Guided by the Zhdanov Doctrine, Mao believed that the Soviet Union and the United States led two ideologically opposite—socialist and capitalist, respectively—camps of nations. These two camps were mutually exclusive and intended to destroy each other. Mao further pointed out that with the CCP-led Communist Revolution China had thus become a solid member of the Soviet-centered camp of socialism and communist revolution,[6] and that any hope of maintaining a neutral position between the two camps had become fantasy and should in fact be seriously purged from within the CCP. In the article "On People's Democratic Dictatorship," written on the occasion of the 28th anniversary of the founding of the CCP, Mao finalized the policy of completely leaning toward the Soviet Union against international capitalism led by the United States.

These three principles of the PRC's strategic and security outlook have a symbiotic relationship with the proletarian revolutionary ideology. Once the party calls, the government immediately follows. The General Program [*gongtong gangling*], the de facto constitution of the new regime, adopted them in toto and made them the statutory foreign policy and national security foundations. Article Eleven of Part One of the General Program states that "The People's Republic of China is united with all the peace-loving, freedom-loving nations and peoples. But first and foremost, the PRC stands resolutely on the side of the international camp of peace and democracy composed of the Soviet Union, and all other people's democratic countries and oppressed peoples. We together struggle against invasions of imperialism, for a long lasting world peace." Article 55 of the General Program reaffirms the policy of "building a brand new stove." Article 56 incorporates Mao's "house cleansing" policy.

After openly joining the camp as a governmental entity, the PRC was immediately embraced by all the "happy campers" of the Soviet-led communist bloc. On October 3, 1949, the USSR became the first country to recognize and establish diplomatic relationship with the PRC, followed by Bulgaria, Romania, Yugoslavia, Hungary, North Korea, Czechoslovakia, Mongolia, East Germany, and Albania. The only non-communist country that established diplomatic relationship with the PRC in the immediate aftermath of the proclamation of the PRC was Burma.

The ideological practice of Chinese security in the first decade

The three ideologically driven principles of PRC security and diplomacy, especially "Leaning to One Side" diplomatic principle, were carried out with revolutionary vigor, and dominated the security practice of the new communist nation. First targeted were the diplomatic officials of "imperialist countries" still in China. When the CCP troops were sweeping across China proper and seemed militarily unstoppable, some Western governments, notably the Truman Administration of the United States, still remained hopeful of maintaining certain kinds of governmental ties with the Communists, who, during Roosevelt's presidency, had been painted by many influential US military and security officials as "agrarian reformers" in straw hats. Witnessing the imminent Communist victory, the Truman Administration decided to stay in China until repelled by force. In accord with the principle of "Two Camps," American officials in China were handled with resolute harshness. The US Consul General at Peiping (Peking) sent a letter to the newly created CCP diplomatic agency to seek official relationship of engagement. His letter was returned unopened by the Communists, who refused to recognize his official status as a diplomat. The US Consul General at Shenyang was arrested for espionage.[7]

The new regime also moved quickly to control foreign owned companies in China. By 1952, virtually all American operated enterprises and financial firms in China, including Texaco and American Standard, were either confiscated, frozen or destroyed by the new regime. The British did not fare any better either, although they officially recognized China in January 1950. In 1952, London decided that the 40 airplanes previously operated by the Central Airline, stationed in Hong Kong at the time, should be given back to the company under the World War II air force legend Clair Chennault. This enraged Beijing because the Communist underground and intelligence agents had already gained operational control of these planes in Hong Kong. In retaliation, the CCP confiscated all assets of major British firms left in Shanghai, Tianjin and Wuhan. Similarly, all foreign operated news agencies, hospitals, schools, relief and charitable organizations were forced to close their offices in China. All religious activities, often a major conduit of foreign connections, were put under strict CCP control.[8]

By far the most important principle of PRC security strategy and diplomacy was "Leaning to One Side." Mao was eager to form the strongest alliance with the Soviet Union for reasons primarily of ideological symbiosis. For three months, from December 16, 1949 to February 17, 1950, Mao Zedong visited Moscow for the first time. The big entourage led by Mao concluded various treaties with the Soviet Union, cementing the prevailing image of two communist giants joining hands in a worldwide communist expansion. But Mao's trip to Moscow was mostly a journey in search of ideological unity between Stalin and him.

For years, Stalin and Mao were rivals for Marxist ideological correctness. Stalin had grown profoundly distrustful of Mao's version of communism and had been doubtful of Mao's judgment in the prior Stalin-Trotsky controversy over the nature and strategies of the Chinese revolution. While Stalin wanted a CCP-KMT United Front against Japan, Mao doubted the utility and ideological correctness of forming an alliance with the reactionary KMT under Chiang Kai-shek, a view that closely echoed that of Leon Trotsky. Mao had long felt Stalin's distrust and was eager to straighten out any remaining differences while he was in Moscow. The timing couldn't be better now that Mao appeared in Moscow as the ultimate winner of the revolution in China, vindicated by his uncompromising ferocity against and victory over Chiang Kai-shek's Chinese Nationalist Party. He badly needed Stalin's recognition of his ideological correctness. This recognition was important because Mao was determined to convince Stalin that Mao himself was a genuine communist and that the two great leaders of communist countries should now forget internal ideological bickering and forge ahead to face the common enemy, the imperialism headed by the United States.[9]

Yet Mao's thirst for ideological recognition was not entirely quenched by Stalin. Upon the initial welcoming meeting, Stalin praised Mao's phenomenal victory in China but avoided directly offering a *mea culpa* for the past distrust of Mao's ideological purity. Mao was instantly annoyed and opined with awkward seriousness, "No, no. I have been the target of a prolonged attack and an isolation campaign. I have had nowhere to register my complaints," thus explicitly demanding recognition of his ideological correctness from Stalin, who never obliged wholeheartedly. Throughout Mao's visit to Moscow, Stalin addressed him as "Mister" Mao instead of the more proletarian title of "comrade."[10]

This episode epitomizes the drive behind the PRC's many international behaviors. It indicates the importance of being seen to be pure believers in communism within the Soviet-led socialist camp. The success or failure of the PRC lay in its ability to find tangible ways to prove its own faith in the cause in order 1) to dissipate Stalin's remaining suspicion that Mao might be another Tito, and thus 2) to prove the CCP's worthiness to be an integral member of the camp, and 3), perhaps more importantly, to eliminate any misunderstandings among all communist parties and to enhance the grand alliance of the worldwide communist movement. It is imperative for us to keep this in mind because the CCP's security moves and international behavior have often been directed by such motives. To Mao, the first chance to present tangible proof of his ideological correctness came in June 1950 when the Korean War broke out.

It would be incorrect to assume that Mao actively pursued the outbreak of the Korean War, as old and new evidence seems to have confirmed. Mao and the CCP had a much larger scheme of revolution for East Asia. Among many things discussed with Stalin while in Moscow during Mao's long stay in the USSR was the bigger role the CCP could now play in East Asia. Stalin was of the opinion that the center of world revolution was moving to China after the Chinese Communist takeover and that China would play a central role in promoting revolutions in Asia. Accordingly Stalin offered China a large amount of WWII surplus weapons that the Soviets no longer needed.[11]

To beef up this new Chinese role in promoting communist revolutions in Asia, Ho Chi Minh of Vietnam was invited to Moscow to join the Mao-Stalin talks. At the meeting, several issues were settled. First, China would use part of the surplus Soviet military equipment Stalin had generously promised to help the Vietnamese communists in their fight against the French. Second, China would send a military advisory mission to Ho's headquarters. And in April and May 1950—before the outbreak of the Korean War—a Chinese military mission entered Vietnam to fulfill "the duty of the proletarian internationalism."[12]

In its overall strategy, however, the CCP regarded "the liberation of Taiwan" as its top priority. The CCP therefore saw the outbreak of the Korean War as both a surprise, for it could serve as a diversion from "the liberation of Taiwan," and a piece of good news, since this was indeed a good opportunity to provide tangible proof of China's ideological correctness. Chen Jian's path-breaking work indicates that Mao was indeed eager to enter the war in Korea once it broke out to fulfill its own revolutionary vision of an uncompromising struggle against the US-led international imperialism and that "there is little possibility that China's entrance into the Korean War could have been averted," regardless of whether MacArthur decided to stop at the 38th parallel or to push toward the bank of the Yalu River.[13] In other words, China's entrance into the Korean War was not motivated by a traditional security concern caused by the UN troops' military advance toward the Yalu River but by a communist ideological commitment to deal a blow to international capitalism.

When Stalin refused to provide air force to accompany the 300,000 Chinese People's Volunteers in Korea, Mao looked at this as a slap in the face of proletarian internationalism and as a sign of Stalin's lack of determination to fight against the top imperial nation. Mao confidently ordered his troops into Korea to prove his ideological fidelity. This function of the Korean War was well summed up by Zhou Enlai: "Stalin is ready to change his view on things when reality proves he is wrong. For example, he used to doubt whether we (the CCP) were real Marxists, whether we dare fight imperialism. But when we started the Resist Americans and Assist the Koreans Campaign [the PRC's name for China's military involvement in the Korean War], such views of his on us changed. So, Stalin was open minded after all."[14]

Much has been said about the tension between the CPSU and the CCP. While there is certainly truth in this assumption, one ought to remember also that in the first decade of the PRC regime, the relationship between the CPSU and the CCP was for the most part close. As late as 1959, Zhou Enlai said the following in a speech delivered in Moscow: "The Soviet Union and China are brotherly countries of socialist nature. Marxism and Leninism tightly unite our two countries and all other socialist countries. Our two nations are closest comrades-in-arms and our comradery has experienced enduring tests. Our destiny is the same and our interests are inseparable{ . . . }the Soviet Union and the People's Republic of China and all other socialist countries will forever be united as one entity, striding forward in heroic steps, marching along a wide road toward communism!"[15] Even on issues such as the Soviet suppression of the 1956 Poland and Hungary uprisings, the CCP and the CPSU were in agreement. Liu Shaoqi and Deng Xiaoping led a CCP delegation to Moscow most directly voicing Beijing's unwavering support for the Soviet military actions in Poland and Hungary.[16]

In November 1957, Mao Zedong visited Moscow for the second time, on the occasion of the global communist camp's celebration of the fortieth anniversary of the Bolshevik Revolution. Ideologically intoxicated, Mao delivered his passionate speeches in the Soviet Union to communist leaders from all over the world. In these speeches, Mao claimed that the international balance of power between the socialist camp and the capitalist camp had fundamentally shifted in the communists' favor. Mao announced that imperialists and all other reactionaries were mere paper tigers and that "the east wind has overpowered the west wind."[17] At a rally of Chinese students in Moscow, Mao radiated boundless enthusiasm for the cause of communism and declared that "there must be a leader for the socialist camp. That leader is the Soviet Union. Communist and workers' parties of all countries should have a leader. That leader is the Communist Party of the Soviet Union (CPSU)!"[18] The problem was whether the Soviet Union and Khrushchev would take on that leadership role heroically and smash international capitalism with gallantry and nuclear blasts, as Mao had expressed a desire for, and vociferously urged, in his open speeches in Moscow.

The limits of ideology

The escalation of communist ideological fervor in CCP diplomacy and international relations, and the perpetual search for proof of Mao's ideological correctness in international military and political arenas, could also be dangerous to the communist cause itself. At the twentieth CPSU Congress, convened in February 1956, Khrushchev did two things that caused the beginning of the Sino-Soviet tension. First, Khrushchev proposed a new Soviet policy of "three peacefuls" on world revolution. It included peaceful co-existence with the capitalist countries, peaceful competition with the capitalist countries, and peaceful transition from capitalism to socialism through parliamentary elections. Second, Khrushchev delivered a scathing secret report on the crimes Stalin had committed.

Deeply shaken by Khrushchev's moves, a month later the CCP convened a Politburo meeting responding to Khrushchev's extraordinary new policy and his de-Stalinization. The CCP came to the conclusion that Khrushchev's new policy of "three peacefuls" constituted a denial of the legacy of the Bolshevik October Revolution that emphasized violent takeover of the capitalist governments; that Stalin was still a "great Marxist," despite his mistakes; and that to denounce Stalin was to deny the "Dictatorship of the Proletariat," the cornerstone of Marxist-Leninist state theory and doctrine. Subsequently, Mao ordered the *People's Daily* to run an editorial entitled "On the Historical Lessons of the Dictatorship of the Proletariat," which began a long series of articles attacking the CPSU positions on war, peace, and Marxist theories.

To counter the CPSU's ideological heresy of peaceful co-existence with world capitalism, Mao showed his defiance by going further in the dangerous game of escalating belligerence against "the decaying imperialism." On August 23, 1958, in order to rebuke Khrushchev's "capitulationism" to the capitalist camp, in a display of the CCP's proletarian internationalism Mao seized on the opportunity of the US Marines' landing in Lebanon to order the sudden shelling of the KMT-occupied off-shore islands of Quemoy and Matsu. This was meant as a retaliation against the US military move in the Middle East and to embarrass Moscow.[19] Mao's private doctor, who was with Mao when he made the decision, commented, "It was Mao's challenge to Khrushchev's bid to reduce tensions between the Soviet Union and the United States{. . .}. For Mao, the shelling of Quemoy and Matsu was pure show, a game to demonstrate to both Khrushchev and Eisenhower that he could not be controlled and to undermine Khrushchev in his new quest for peace. The game was a terrible gamble, threatening the world with atomic war and risking the lives of tens of millions of ordinary Chinese."[20]

To Khrushchev, Mao's adventurism was indeed dangerous. In June 1959, Khrushchev decided to rescind an earlier agreement to provide China with prototype atomic bombs and the related technical data. While Khrushchev was preparing for his trip to the United States to meet with Eisenhower, China and India clashed on their shared border in August 1959. Khrushchev regarded this as Mao's deliberate effort to create international tension to dampen his peace effort with the United States. Weeks later, the Soviet Union agreed to provide India with a $375 million loan. Mao was outraged. In late September, Khrushchev went to Beijing to join the fanfare of the tenth anniversary celebration of the founding of the PRC. But Khrushchev went to Tiananmen Square by way of Camp David and carried straightforward messages pressuring Mao to give up the idea of an imminent armed struggle with international capitalism.[21]

China's view on the world situation remained Leninistic when the 1960s began. It believed that monopoly capitalism was structured in such a way that a new round of world war was imminent and inevitable. As such, true communists should not be afraid of new world war. Rather, they should take advantage of the world war to bury the capitalist system altogether. In February 1960, the Warsaw Pact member countries met and issued a declaration stating that a new world war would be catastrophic to the lives of hundreds of millions of people and should be avoided at any cost. China was invited as an observer, but the Chinese delegation at the meeting dissented on such ideological deviation from Lenin's strident stress on the necessity of a violent worldwide communist revolution. Two months later, the *Red Flag* journal and the *People's Daily*, both official organs of the CCP, carried an editorial entitled "Long Live Leninism!" It was a rehash of Mao's repeated theory of all imperialists being paper tigers. But it had more astonishing statements such as "although an imperialist war could bring people of all nations great sacrifice, the people who survive this war shall create a civilization and a bright, beautiful future upon the debris of shattered imperialism that will be thousands of times better."[22]

By the end of 1960, the bitter quarrel between the Soviet bloc and the CCP on ideological issues had escalated to such a degree that the Soviet Union decided to pull all of its expert advisers out of China in retaliation. Yet it was over the issue of Soviet-American negotiations on nuclear arms control that finally split up the Sino-Soviet alliance. Mao's strategic view on the world situation was to a large degree based upon the Soviet Union's advancement in nuclear and space technologies, especially the satellite advantage of the socialist camp since the launch of Sputnik. When the Soviets and the Americans joined hands in Washington to limit or ban nuclear tests in various areas (excluding underground), Mao believed Khrushchev had given up the communist advantage in key nuclear strike powers, thus betraying the cause of communism and indeed becoming a "revisionist." Mao vowed to develop China's own nuclear program.

By 1963, the CCP's ultra-radical views could no longer be regarded by the Soviets as reasonable and Mao had been categorized as a madman and warmonger. To sum up the CCP's differing ideological view at the time, the Central Committee in Beijing delivered to Moscow what it considered to be the "right" path for the communist camp to follow: "The proletarians of the world, unite; the proletariat and all the oppressed peoples and nations, unite against imperialism and reactionaries in all countries, struggling for world peace, national liberation, people's democracy and socialism. Let us safeguard and expand the socialist camp, gradually reach the complete victory of world revolution; establish a new world without imperialism, without capitalism, and without exploitative systems."[23] This is indeed ideological intoxication.

The two middle areas: Mao's new doctrine of international security and strategy

With the Sino-Soviet ideological split, the PRC had opted out of the Soviet camp and could find only one small "socialist beacon" to ally with in all of Europe: Albania. The overwhelming majority of communist countries took the side of the CPSU. Only a handful of them tried to remain neutral. Ho Chi Minh was the heartbroken comrade who tried to mediate the quarrels between the two big brothers. He even developed a charming theory of the origin of the Sino-Soviet split. According to Ho, it had much to do with a personal style of expression, or something of a cultural misunderstanding between an Asian party and a European party, and he earnestly told Mao so on his special patch-up trip to see him in August 1960.[24]

To Mao, however, the tide was irreversible. He now saw not only ideological deviation in the CPSU but gradually came to feel the imposing presence of an imperialist Russia along the extended borders between the two countries. So now there were two kinds of imperialisms to the CCP: the capitalist imperialism led by the United States, and the socialist imperialism led by the Soviet Union. And only socialist China could save the world from a capitalist victory in the epic global ideological battle.

Around 1963, Mao Zedong developed a new strategic philosophy of the world revolutions. This is the theory of "Two Middle Areas [*liangge zhongjian didai*]." According to this theory, Mao believed that between the two super powers were two vast middle areas. The first middle area would include those countries in Asia, Africa and Latin America that were either already independent or were fighting for independence. The second middle area included the developed countries of Western Europe, Canada and so on. However, Mao believed that the first middle area was the area of fierce contention and of "concentrated contradictions." This area was also the source of the global revolutionary whirlwind. Accordingly, the national liberation movements in this area constituted the most important strike against the forces of imperialism.[25]

Guided by this theory of world revolution, PRC diplomacy emerged out of the much exalted Soviet-centered "socialist camp" of the 1950s and began to wage a war on imperialism on its own, a war based upon Mao's new revolutionary ideology. Mao's deputy and Defense Minister Lin Biao went even further and creatively applied Mao's strategy of "Encirclement of the Cities through the Countryside" to the international struggle against imperialism. In his famous article September 3, 1965, "Long Live the Victory of the People's War," Lin Biao stated that the center of world revolution had shifted to China; that as long as China did not deviate from the right course of Marxism, there was hope for the world; that Europe and North America were the world's cities, and Asia, Africa, and Latin America were the world's countryside; and that it was now the time to utilize Mao's tested strategy to stage a worldwide revolution by encircling imperialism (the cities) from the world's countryside.

Therefore, starting from 1964, the PRC invested heavily in the first middle area. Mao sent extensive military aid to many countries in the first middle area to stage revolutions against imperialism. Until 1964, the PRC had been providing military hardware to some revolutionary countries, especially North Korea and North Vietnam. But there was a great jump in military hardware outflow from 1964. Between 1964 and 1968, the number of countries receiving military aid from the PRC increased from a dozen to more than 60. From December 1963 to January 1964, Zhou Enlai visited 14 Asian and African countries considered to be in Mao's first middle area. During this trip, Zhou announced a most generous, no-strings-attached policy of giving out military aid and providing military training to these countries. Within one year, nine countries, including Pakistan, Tanzania, Mali, Burundi, Guinea-Bissau, and Congo, requested and received the PLA's free military hardware. By the end of 1978, over 60 countries, including Bangladesh, Nepal, Sri Lanka, Egypt, Zimbabwe, Gabon, Sudan, Uganda, Zambia, and Somalia, had received PRC military aid. Between 1964 and 1978, China provided the following to boost revolutions in countries of the first middle area: 4.20 million guns of various types, 90,000 cannons, 3,620 tanks and armored carriers, 1,430 war planes, 352 war ships, 15 sets of guided missile systems, 449 missiles, 4.3 billion units of ammunition, and 51.30 million shells.[26]

The first significant investment of Mao's revolutionary cause was in Vietnam, where the US troops were fighting the Vietnamese communist insurgents in the south and the Hanoi government in the north was staunchly organizing and supporting the insurgents in the south. According to a senior Hanoi official, between October 1965 and July 1970 the PRC dispatched to North Vietnam over 300,000 troops, whose specialties ranged from anti-aircraft artillery force, military engineering, and railroad construction to military logistics and signal intelligence. Many American war planes were shot down by the Chinese troops.

North Vietnam received the most generous PRC assistance of all countries helped thus. This aid included heavy and light weapons, ammunition and other military gear, enough to equip two million soldiers of the North Vietnamese army, navy, air force and militia. It also included hundreds of factories and repair shops, 300 million meters of cloth, 30,000 trucks, 5 million tons of food, 2 million tons of gasoline, hundreds of millions of cash in US dollars, and a 3,000 mile long oil pipeline that extended Chinese supply of gasoline to South Vietnam.[27] During the same period, 4,300 PLA officers and soldiers were wounded and nearly 1,100 PLA officers and soldiers were killed and buried in Vietnam.[28] To ship the vast amount of war materials to Viet Cong in South Vietnam, the Chinese created a secret coastal shipping line connecting Chinese Hainan Island, where the cargo ships disembarked, with several islands off the coast of Central Vietnam, where goods were picked up by Viet Cong in South Vietnam.[29]

Throughout the Vietnam War, China's military engagement with the US forces, mainly in the area of anti-aircraft artillery support, and its consequences were substantial. Official Chinese documents have revealed that between 1965 and 1969, the period covering the peak of military actions in Vietnam, the PLA's AAA batteries inside Vietnam engaged the US combat aircraft 2,153 times, shooting down 1,707 US war planes and damaging a further 1,608 American military aircraft.[30]

The second largest single sum of military aid to one country was given to Albania, China's only hope of a Maoist revolution in Europe and Mao's "countryside stronghold" closest to "the cities." Due to Mao's ideological obsession with war and revolutions, there was no limit to the assistance given to meet Albania's needs. In the 18 years between 1961 and 1978, a staggering amount of military aid, worth 1.5 billion Chinese yuan, was provided to Albania. This included 752,000 guns, 11,000 cannons, 890 tanks and armored carriers, 180 war planes, 46 war ships, 2 complete sets of surface to air missile systems, 224 missiles, 196 torpedoes, 4,230 military trucks, 1.56 billion bullets, 8.22 million shells and various other military items.[31]

In addition to Vietnam, China also provided a massive amount of military aid to communist forces in Laos. In Africa, the country at the top of Mao's revolutionary priority was Tanzania (and Zanzibar before the two united in 1967). From 1964, Mao provided the Tanzanian government with a generous package of military aid, including large sums of light weapons, tanks, war planes, and a complete air force security system.[32] Military training for the countries in the first middle area was also important in Mao's revolutionary strategy. Between 1964 and 1978, the PLA trained military personnel for over 40 countries in Asia, Africa and Latin America. Over 6,400

Chinese military experts were dispatched abroad and they trained over 8,000 trainees from these countries, including such well known figures as Laurent Kabila of the Democratic Republic of the Congo and Abu Nidal of the Palestinian Liberation Organization.[33]

It is important to point out that while the tumultuous Cultural Revolution created a paralyzing interregnum in the PRC's domestic operations, the PRC's revolutionary warfare and ideological diplomacy in the first middle area never was seriously affected. On the contrary, it enjoyed a remarkable constancy. Comparatively speaking, the PRC's international security practices suffered far less interruption from the chaotic Cultural Revolution.[34] China's massive military aid programs for the first middle area countries remained very steady in the 14 years between 1964 and 1978.

Throughout the entire history of the PRC, Taiwan has remained a focal point of China's international security and military strategy considerations. While it would be inaccurate to say that the Taiwan issue is not one of national reunification, it would definitely be wrong to argue that national reunification is the PRC's only consideration in the matter. Since its founding in 1949, the Chinese Communist government has on numerous occasions been willing to negotiate territorial issues with governments or nations deemed friendly and ideologically acceptable. These have led to land cessions to those nations, most of which belonged to the "socialist camp," such as Mongolia, Burma and Kazakhstan. The sizes of these cessions were many times bigger than Taiwan.

On the contrary, the core of the Taiwan issue has always been ideological. To "liberate Taiwan" fits perfectly well with CCP's proletarian sanctimony of being the ultimate savior of the entire Chinese population. To get rid of the KMT regime in Taiwan was, in the eyes of Mao, essentially a matter of wiping out "reactionary forces," not necessarily only for national reunification. The reactionary nature of the KMT regime to Mao was made most obvious when the Americans became heavily involved, which also testified to the ideological correctness of Mao's theory of the imperialist domination of the Chinese through its "running dogs" such as Chiang Kai-shek.

If national reunification and maintaining nationalistic pride was the primary driving force of China's foreign policy and security practice, Hong Kong, an almost perfect case to shore up nationalism, would have been easily taken over by the PLA in late 1949 and early 1950. Nevertheless, the CCP's policy toward Hong Kong remained uncharacteristically conciliatory. The momentous PLA military offensive suddenly stopped just 25 miles from Hong Kong in 1949. In this regard, a nationalist interpretation of the PRC's security motivation would not suffice. It has even been reported that the CCP and the British did strike a nine-point secret deal as early as August 1945 on the future of Hong Kong. Under this deal, the Communists promised not to try to re-take Hong Kong in exchange for the rights of legal presence of the CCP representatives and propaganda in Hong Kong. A result of the mutual secret communications, some historians note, was Britain's recognition of the PRC in 1950.[35]

Despite constant claims by the PRC over the decades, Taiwan may not even be the key issue between the United States and the PRC. It may well be just a footnote in Mao's overall ideological scheme of world revolution and his obsessive campaign against communist revisionists for perpetual ideological correctness. As Mao explained to his personal physician in 1958 regarding why he decided to bombard the islands of Quemoy and Matsu but not to launch an invasion, "If we take them over, we lose our link." Mao reasoned, "Doesn't everyone have two hands? If we lose our two hands, then Taiwan is no longer in our grip. We let it slip away. The islands are two batons that keep Khrushchev and Eisenhower dancing, scurrying this way and that way. Don't you see how wonderful they are?"[36] The instrumental value of maintaining Taiwan as a problem between the US and the PRC but not attempting to have it solved can also be great. As Mao intimated to his personal physician in 1958:

> Khrushchev just doesn't know what he's talking about. He wants to improve relations with the United States? Good, we'll congratulate him with our guns.{ . . . }Let's get the United States involved, too. Maybe we can get the United States to drop an atom bomb on Fujian. Maybe ten or twenty million people will be killed. Chiang Kai-shek wants the United States to use the bomb against us. Let them use it (to prove their imperialist nature of aggression). Let's see what Khrushchev says then.{ . . . }Some of our comrades don't understand the situation. They want us to cross the sea and take over Taiwan. I don't agree. Let's leave Taiwan alone. Taiwan keeps the pressure on us. It helps maintain our internal unity. Once the pressure is off, internal disputes might break out.[37]

The legacies of ideological commitment affecting China's security: 1979–2014

Mao's ideological fanaticism did not begin to fade until 1978 when Deng Xiaoping began to re-evaluate Mao's obsession with war and revolution. While still a die-hard communist as a lifelong commissar and party secretary, Deng Xiaoping was more pragmatic and less of a romantic ideologue intoxicated with revolutionary ferment. Deng believed that international strategy and security based solely upon ideological obsession were no longer practical because the world had entered a new age. Instead, he advocated a policy of "Beyond Ideology and Social Systems" as the new guideline for the PRC's diplomacy worldwide.[38]

But Deng by no means intended to jettison communist ideology. He only meant to scale down Mao's ideological and military romanticism in order to save the world's only true socialist country—in Deng's view—from total economic and social collapse as a result of Mao's ruinous policies. That is to say, unlike Mao, Deng now believed that world war was not inevitable; that factors for world peace at that moment outweighed the factors for war; and that it was possible to achieve a relatively long-lasting world peace. As for China, Deng believed that the CCP ought to take full advantage of this long-lasting peace to concentrate on building China's economy and defense: by the time international peace collapsed, which Deng believed it surely would, China would be in a winning position.[39]

But we should not overestimate the degree to which Deng Xiaoping changed China's ideological commitment. Fundamentally, the PRC since Deng Xiaoping has remained a communist regime. Many basic tenets and practices of Mao's era still dominate China's basic understanding of national and international security and strategy in the post-Cold-War world. One example is China's understanding of international alignment, which is still based on the old Maoist concept of imperialist conspiracy to undermine the superior socialist system of China. The vocabulary may have changed, but the language is still communistic, which explains why Deng Xiaoping believed that the momentous Tiananmen pro-democracy movement of 1989 took place precisely because of an international plot to change China's socialism and the Dictatorship of the Proletariat through a sinister, well-planned "Peaceful Evolution." After the crackdown, Deng spoke of the mysterious interplay of an "international mega-climate" [*guoji da qihou*] and a hidden "domestic minor climate" [*guonei xiao qihou*].

The legacy of Mao's ideological diplomacy is also easily found in today's PRC exercise in "enemy politics," which embodies the constant vigilance against omnipresent international enemies, real or imagined. This prevalent method of ideological consciousness-raising at home and abroad is best illustrated in the Sino-US relationship since the Tiananmen Massacre. Despite the outrage of the American people toward the massacre, the overwhelming majority of US government agencies, from the administrations of George H.W. Bush to Barack Obama, have strongly advocated a policy of "constructive engagement" with the PRC. In terms of politics and rights, China may not be right, but it is huge and the market is tempting. The preponderance of such a sentiment toward post-Tiananmen PRC is not difficult to find if one stays in Washington for only a few days.

Yet to sustain a communist system such as the PRC's and to enhance internal unity under the CCP, Chinese supreme leaders after Mao Zedong, from Deng Xiaoping and Jiang Zemin to Hu Jintao and Xi Jinping, have all diligently campaigned to create an image of the US government as the monstrous superpower determined to "contain" China in each and every way, despite the White House's continuous hobnobbing with Zhongnanhai. There is a remarkable consistency among Chinese supreme leaders in the use of this theory of a US-led capitalist conspiracy to destroy socialist China as the most potent justification for, under Mao, the maintenance of a draconian totalitarian social order, and an increasingly technologically sophisticated, authoritarian and omnipotent national security state under Deng Xiaoping, Hu Jintao and Xi Jinping. In 1949, Mao claimed that "for a very long period, US imperialism laid greater stress than other imperialist countries on activities in the sphere of spiritual aggression, extending from religious to 'philanthropic' and cultural undertakings{ . . . }and [has organized] a US fifth column{ . . . } [to] overthrow the people's government led by the Communist Party of China."[40]

In 1990, Deng Xiaoping got more specific: "There is a proposal in the United States now: to fight a world war without gun smoke.{ . . . }Capitalism hopes to declare a final victory over socialism. In the past, it used weapons, including atomic bombs, hydrogen bombs, which was opposed by people of the world. But now it is engaged in the peaceful evolution."[41] Deng saw this as only a part of the worldwide struggle against socialism, of which China had become the only representative after the collapse of the Soviet Union and the democratic uprisings that overthrew communist rule in Eastern Europe. "The Western world does indeed hope to see unrest in China. It hopes to see disturbances not only in China, but also in the Soviet Union and Eastern Europe. The Unites States, other Western countries, are engaged in a peaceful evolution targeting socialist countries."[42]

Deng's successor Jiang Zemin was an even more devout believer in this US-led capitalist conspiracy against socialist China. "For a longer period of time in the future," Jiang wrote in 1993, "the United States will still be our main opponent in diplomatic dealings.{ . . . }US policy toward China has always had two sides. A peaceful evolution against China is the long-term strategic goal of some people in the United States."[43] Hu Jintao, Jiang Zemin's successor, echoed his predecessors closely. "The ideological field has always been the important battle front, fiercely fought over between our enemies and us," Mr. Hu was quoted in the PLA-produced documentary *Silent Struggle* as saying. "If trouble appears in this battle front, it may well lead to social turmoil or even the loss of our political rule. To create chaos in a society, to overthrow a government, our enemies usually start with piercing a hole in our ideological system, that is, to first focus on confusing people's minds."[44]

Yet it is the current Chinese supreme leader Xi Jinping who has emerged as the most earnest inheritor of Mao Zedong when it comes to stressing the purity of Marxist-Leninist ideology and a global ideological and political struggle between the two camps of socialism, now led by China, and capitalism, now led by the waning but still fierce United States. "Western countries' strategic calculation to contain our country's development will never change," Xi was quoted in *Silent Struggle* as saying. "They will never want a socialist country like ours to carry out a smooth peaceful development."[45] Since his ascendance to the supreme leadership position in late 2012, Xi Jinping, who obtained a doctoral degree in scientific socialism from Tsinghua University, has intensified a nationwide ideological re-indoctrination, re-installing Mao-era heroes such as the good cadre Jiao Yulu, the model communist soldier Lei Feng, and a myriad of other symbols of Maoism.

Much like Mao in the 1950s, 1960s and early 1970s, today's CCP is in dire need of a hostile enemy like the United States and has deliberately exaggerated the extent to which Americans are anti-China. However, this is not to say that there are no ideological heretics within China's security policy circles who do not follow exactly the stringent guidelines from the supreme leadership. There are indeed many Chinese scholars who have deviated from the PRC's ideological constancy in security studies, but there is little, if any, market share of their ideas, let alone career enhancement opportunities for them; they are often regarded by the state security and Party disciplinary apparatchiks as traitors infiltrated and controlled by foreign, mainly US, anti-China forces.[46]

Overall, the continuing longevity of China's communist revolutionary legacy and communist ideological commitment has left indelible imprints in the Chinese security establishment. The only difference, perhaps, is that in the Mao era the ideological rivalry between socialism and capitalism was openly confrontational and boisterous while the post Mao-era ideological contest is equally epic and of equal intensity and lethality but, for the most part, a silent struggle, as the recent Chinese ideologically laden educational documentary aptly phrases it.[47]

Notes

1 I would like to thank the *Washington Journal of Modern China* for allowing me to use some material from an article I authored for its fall 1999 issue.
2 Mao Zedong, "Who Can Lead the Revolution? [Sheineng lingdao geming?]," February 1927, *Mao Zedong Selected Works*, Volume 2, 2nd ed., p. 666.
3 Ibid., p. 647.
4 Mao Zedong, "On the People's Democratic Dictatorship (Lun Renmin Mingzhu Zhuanzheng)," June 30, 1949, in *Mao Zedong Selected Works*, Volume 4, 2nd ed., p. 1434.
5 Shi Zhe, *Zai lishi juren shengbian: Shi Zhe huiyilu [Alongside the Great Men in History: Memoir of Shi Zhe]*, Beijing: Central Documents Press, 1991, p. 379.
6 He Di, "On the Evolution of the CCP's Policy toward the United States, 1944–1949," in Yuan Ming, Harry Harding eds., *Sino-American Relations, 1945–1955: A Collaborative Reassessment of a Troubled Time*, Beijing: Beijing University Press, 1989, p.93.
7 Shi Zhifu, *Zhonghua renmin gongheguo duiwai guanxi shi [Diplomatic History of the PRC]*, Beijing: Beijing University Press, 1994, pp. 24–6.
8 Ibid., pp. 26–9.
9 Liu Jiecheng, *Mao Zedong he Sidalin [Mao Zedong and Stalin]*, Beijing: Central Party School Press, 1993, p. 14.
10 Ibid., pp. 43, 63.
11 Qian Jiang, *Zai shenmi de zhanzheng zhong: Zhongguo junshi guwen tuan fu Yuenan zhengzhan ji [In the Secret War: The History of Chinese Military Advisers in Vietnam]*, Henan: People's Press, 1994, pp. 17–18.
12 Ibid., p. 18.
13 Chen Jian, "China's Road to the Korean War," in *The Cold War in Asia, The Cold War International History Project Bulletin*, Issues 6–7, Winter 1995/1996, p. 85.
14 *Selected Works of Zhou Enlai*, Volume 2, Beijing: People's Press, 1984, p. 302.
15 Zhou Enlai, "Speech at the Twenty-first CPSU Party Congress, 28 January, 1959," in *Selected Works of Zhou Enlai (1898–1976)*, ed. Chinese Communism Research Group, Hong Kong: Yishan Books Inc., 1976, p. 497.
16 Shi Zhifu, op. cit., pp. 46–7.
17 Mao Zedong, "All Reactionaries Are Paper Tigers," in *Mao Zedong Selected Works*, Volume 5, pp. 499–500.
18 Shi Zhifu, op. cit., p. 367.
19 Ibid., pp. 86–7.
20 Li Zhisui, *The Private Life of Chairman Mao: The Memoirs of Mao's Personal Physician*, New York: Random House, 1994, pp. 270–1.

21 Shi Zhifu, op. cit., pp. 157–8.
22 Ibid., p. 159.
23 Ibid., pp. 166–7.
24 Zhang Yi, Wen Yong, "Comrades and Brothers: Mao Zedong and Hu Zhiming," in Liu Wanzheng et al., eds., *Mao Zedong guoji jiaowang lu [Record of Mao Zedong's Encounters with Foreign Leaders]*, Beijing: Central Party School Press, 1995, pp. 57–9.
25 *The Red Flag*, issues 3 and 4, 1963.
26 Han Huaizhi et al., eds., *Dangdai Zhongguo jundui de junshi gongzuo [Military Work of Chinese Armed Forces in Contemporary China]*, Volume 2, Beijing: Chinese Social Science Academy Press, 1989, pp. 578–80.
27 Zhang Yi, Wen Yong, op. cit., pp. 62–3.
28 Han Huaizhi, et al., op. cit., p. 557.
29 Qiang Zhai, "Beijing and the Vietnam Conflict, 1964–1965," in *Woodrow Wilson Center Conference on the Cold War History, Hong Kong*, January 9–12, 1996, p. 20.
30 Han Huaizhi, et al., op. cit., p. 552.
31 Ibid., pp. 581–2.
32 Ibid., pp. 583–4.
33 Ibid., pp. 585–6.
34 Shi Zhifu, op. cit., p. 194.
35 Tan Lumei, "The Secret Sino-British Agreement of Hong Kong, 1945," in *Bungei Shunji Monthly* (Japan), as reported by Reuters, June 11, 1997.
36 Li Zhisui, op. cit., p. 270.
37 Ibid., p. 262.
38 Tian Zengpei, ed., *Gaige Kaifang yilai de Zhongguo waijiao [China's Diplomacy Since Reform and Opening]*, Beijing: World Knowledge Press, 1993, p. 6.
39 Ibid., pp. 1–4.
40 Mao Zedong, "Farewell, John Leighton Stuart!" in *Selected Works of Mao Zedong*, pp. 365–6.
41 Deng Xiaoping, "We Are Confident that We Can Do Things Better in China," September 16, 1989, in *Selected Works of Deng Xiaoping*, Volume 3, p. 102.
42 Ibid.
43 Jiang Zemin, "We Must Never Deviate from Maintaining Our Nation and State's Utmost Interest in Foreign Affairs," July 12, 1993, in *Selected Works of Jiang Zemin*, Volume 1, p. 325.
44 *Jiaoliang Wushen [*较量无声; *Silent Struggle]*, produced by the Chinese National Defense University, the PLA General Political Department, the PLA General Staff, and CASS, June 2013. The entire 90-minute documentary can be viewed on YouTube at: www.youtube.com/watch?v=M_8lSjcoSW8.
45 Ibid.
46 A good example is the recent hunt by the Party establishment for "conspirators and trouble makers" directly controlled by foreign forces among the scholars at the Chinese Academy of Social Sciences. See "Inspector Questions CASS Ideology," *The Global Times* [English], June 16, 2014. Available online at http://epaper.globaltimes.cn/2014–06–16/54796.htm.
47 See note 44.

Select bibliography

Deng Xiaoping, *Selected Works of Deng Xiaoping*, Volume 3, Beijing: People's Press, 2001.
Han Huaizhi, et al., eds., *Dangdai Zhongguo jundui de junshi gongzuo [Military Work of Chinese Armed Forces in Contemporary China]*, Volume 2, Beijing: Chinese Social Science Academy Press, 1989.
Jiang Zemin, *Selected Works of Jiang Zemin*, Volume 1, Beijing: People's Press, 2006.
Li Zhisui, *The Private Life of Chairman Mao: The Memoirs of Mao's Personal Physician*, New York: Random House, 1994.
Liu Jiecheng, *Mao Zedong he Sidalin [Mao Zedong and Stalin]*, Beijing: Central Party School Press, 1993.
Liu Wanzheng, et al., eds., *Mao Zedong guoji jiaowang lu [Record of Mao Zedong's Encounters with Foreign Leaders]*, Beijing: Central Party School Press, 1995.
Mao Zedong, *Selected Works of Mao Zedong*, Volume 2, Beijing: People's Press, 1952.
———, *Selected Works of Mao Zedong*, Volume 4, Beijing: People's Press, 1960.
———, *Selected Works of Mao Zedong*, Volume 5, Beijing: People's Press, 1977.
Qian Jiang, *Zai shenmi de zhanzheng zhong: Zhongguo junshi guwen tuan fu Yuenan zhengzhan ji [In the Secret War: The History of Chinese Military Advisers in Vietnam]*, Henan: People's Press, 1994.

Shi Zhe, *Zai lishi juren shengbian: Shi Zhe huiyilu [Alongside the Great Men in History: Memoir of Shi Zhe]*, Beijing: Central Documents Press, 1991.

Shi Zhifu, *Zhonghua renmin gongheguo duiwai guanxi shi [Diplomatic History of the PRC]*, Beijing: Beijing University Press, 1994.

Tian Zengpei, ed., *Gaige kaifang yilai de Zhongguo waijiao [China's Diplomacy since Reform and Opening]*, Beijing: World Knowledge Press, 1993.

Yuan Ming, Harry Harding, eds., *Sino-American Relations, 1945–1955: A Collaborative Reassessment of A Troubled Time*, Beijing: Beijing University Press, 1989.

3
Economics and security in China

Marc Lanteigne

The convergence of economics and security in China's strategic thinking

One of the most visible changes to China's security policies since the period of the Deng Xiaoping reforms of the late 1970s has been the increasing overlap between Beijing's growing economic interests and its strategic concerns. China's economic power has continued to mature on an international scale since the 1990s, with the country achieving the status of second largest global economy behind the United States as of early 2011, with some studies suggesting that the Chinese economy may surpass the total GDP of the United States in 2016 or shortly thereafter.[1] While some analysts have even suggested that China has already surpassed American economic power at least from certain viewpoints (such as purchasing power parity (PPP)),[2] others have noted that China's economy still faces a long period of continuing reform with many domestic challenges yet to be overcome. A 2013 book on China's international power acknowledged the country's great economic gains of the past three decades, but noted that the Chinese economy remained overly dependent on exports at the expense of domestic development, and with its lack of multinational corporations and global brands, the study concluded, China is a 'partial economic power'.[3]

Although China's economic growth remains impressive, there is still a host of considerable economic challenges facing the country's policymakers. China's large population presents a unique set of challenges to Beijing's economic policies. As Chinese political analyst Zheng Bijian noted, China faces a 'multiplication/division' conundrum, namely that any socio-economic problems, even small ones, have the potential of being multiplied by 1.3 billion, China's current population, and any economic gains, regardless of size, must be divided among those same 1.3 billion Chinese citizens.[4] Despite China's impressive overall growth, per capita income remains low by Western standards, estimated by the World Bank to be approximately US$6,560 in 2013.[5] Other socio-economic issues, including corruption and mismanagement, the challenges of developing a welfare state, reforming the country's large agricultural sector, growing urbanization (estimated to be at 53.7 per cent of the population in early 2014),[6] and income inequality, especially between coast and interior, continue to challenge the Chinese government. Deng's suggestion that the country should 'let some people get rich first' did assist with the reform process by opening the doors to more robust economic growth, but also created widening income gaps between richer and poorer citizens that are still major policy concerns today. According to a January 2014 report by China's National Bureau of Statistics, the Gini Coefficient in China stood at 0.47 in 2013, up from 0.42 per cent in 2009.[7] As any figure above 0.4 is seen as an indicator of potential public unrest, it has been a priority for Beijing since the start of the reform era to better address underdevelopment levels, especially in the country's interior.

There is also an increasing environmental cost of China's decades of rapid economic growth, namely air, water and land pollution caused by industrialization, coal-burning, construction and vehicle emissions, with pollution levels in major Chinese cities frequently surpassing minimum safe global standards by a wide margin since 2008. As environmental damage rarely respects borders, this situation is seen as a serious issue not only for China but also the surrounding regions.[8] In addition to long-term health concerns, there is the question in China of the 'Green GDP',[9] the income of a given country minus the costs of environmental damage. The Chinese government intends to get tougher on the causes of pollution, both for health reasons and to prevent future socio-economic problems, a policy underscored in a March 2014 Chinese parliamentary session by Premier Li Keqiang, who called for 'war against pollution' (*xiang wuran xuanzhan*) in the country as popular discontent over air and water quality began to solidify.[10] Beijing has increasingly been more open to the idea of combating pollution on a variety of levels, and has made mention of the benefits of a 'circular economy' (*xunhuan jingji*)[11] that combines environmental protection policies with sustainable development. Nonetheless, the government wishes to be at the forefront of any 'green movement'.

Globally, China's economic growth has had an increasing impact as the country has developed greater confidence in its dealings with countries and regions beyond Asia. As of early 2014, the United States was China's top trading partner (with volume estimated at US$521 billion), followed by Hong Kong, Japan, South Korea and Taiwan.[12] As a result of China's overall economic growth and steady integration into the global market, and the country's ongoing support for globalization and economic institutions, the links between economics and security in Chinese policymaking have increased and become more distinct. This phenomenon can be explained in several ways.

What is economic security?

Following the death of Mao Zedong in 1976, when China gradually abandoned its reliance on command economics along Soviet lines, the country has increased its engagement with the global economy through a series of phases and initiatives. This has produced great economic benefits but with considerable risks to Chinese security, especially considering the political capital that the Chinese government has placed on ensuring stability and growth as the country continued its process of 'deep reform' (*shenhua gaige*) in the 1990s and afterwards under the governments of Jiang Zemin and Hu Jintao.[13] China's strategic thinking must increasingly focus on the problems of 'economic security' (*jingji anquan*) with the understanding that many of the country's economic and strategic interests have become internationalized. It was also during this decade that China's own policy version of 'comprehensive security' (*quanmian anquan*) began to coalesce,[14] reflecting Beijing's growing view that military security was increasingly entwined with issues that had traditionally been considered 'low political' matters, including economics, trade and the environment. Although 'hard' security issues such as border and maritime disputes remain at the forefront of Beijing's strategic concerns, these areas are becoming more visibly merged with economics.

'Economic security' has been defined as the necessity of access to resources, finance and markets that is required to maintain a sustainable level of welfare and state power.[15] Market access frequently requires extensive engagement of the international economy on a variety of levels. Security in this sense involves preventing internal and external threats to economic stability and future prosperity, a challenge that economic interdependence and globalization have further complicated. The Asian Financial Crisis of 1997–8 was arguably Beijing's first serious exposure to the risks of globalized markets. China's move away from a closed economic system and toward greater globalization has required a corresponding number of material and financial resources needed to maintain high levels of growth. Although China's size and increasing economic 'weight' in the international system have prevented the same degree of internal and external pressures faced both by smaller economies and by states that were also emerging from a communist or command economic system, the government remains wary of an erosion of the role of the Chinese Communist Party (CCP) due to 'peaceful evolution' (*heping yanbian*),[16] ideas and policies brought from the West, such as differing views on human rights and democratization that are viewed as an anathema to Chinese governance. Although peaceful evolution concerns are hardly new to the Chinese government, economic interdependence and the rise of mass communications have resulted in greater sensitivity to perceived challenges to the CCP via outside actors and influences.

From a military viewpoint, economic security has also been defined as economic activities, such as trade, designed to assist in a given country's defence, the use of economic means for offensive or defensive strategic purposes (sanctions, embargoes, travel restrictions, and, in extreme cases, blockades), and the prevention of economic weaknesses that could undermine a state's ability to project or maintain military power. Many components of military power, such as energy or raw materials, are currently available only through international transactions, exposing states to vulnerability due to price swings and potential international-level economic shocks outside of their control, as the post-2008 credit crunch (*jinsuo*) and subsequent global financial crises demonstrated. In a broader sense, there is the concern that economic instability on a regional or global level could have a significant impact on state security.[17]

Modern great powers are not immune to the problems of economic insecurity. China is seeking to further develop its domestic economy and maintain internal stability while increasingly being forced to rely on market forces outside of its supervision or control. As one paper argued, during the first stages of China's reforms the country had the luxury of treating economic development and security concerns as largely separate issues. The country chose to avoid military confrontations with its neighbours following the brief border conflict with Vietnam in 1979, to instead pursue complex and painful economic restructuring. Under Deng, a focus on building economic strength was seen as the best defence against future international challenges.[18]

The ability to maintain the division between economics and security changed abruptly in the 1990s as the post-Cold War order began to take shape. The Iraq/Kuwait Gulf War in 1991 demonstrated not only the growing magnitude of American military power and technology but also the strengthened link between economic power and military capabilities.[19] At the same time, with Beijing focusing on the difficult first stages of the reform process, it was a policy priority for the Jiang government to avoid regional disputes in favour of concentrating on domestic reforms. As noted above, the 1997–8 Asian Financial Crisis also underscored the shared vulnerability of the international economic system when several East Asian economies faced rapid currency devaluations and financial chaos due to a spillover effect from Thailand's ill-fated policy of allowing its currency value to float on global markets despite severe structural problems.[20] Beijing, which was at an earlier stage of economic reform, and at that point still maintained tight currency controls, was one of the few regional economies largely untouched by the crash. Beijing did have to intervene in Hong Kong, which had just reverted to Chinese administration, to prevent the former colony's stock market from collapsing and the peg between the HK dollar and the American dollar from dissolving. Although China was praised for being an island of stability as other Asian economies faltered, the events shook Chinese confidence in its own economic stability.

The government of Jiang Zemin took from those chaotic events a better understanding of growing linkages that comprised economic security thinking, as well as the growing 'economics-security nexus'[21] that was developing in East Asia. The interconnectedness of Asian economies meant both potential shared prosperity and mutual economic risks capable of negatively impacting the delicate Chinese reform process. While Beijing took steps to ensure the continuing stability of its domestic reforms, the country also sought methods of ensuring ongoing growth while minimising potential economic security threats.

Rewards and risks in China's economic rise

Following the Dengist policies of 'reform and opening up' (*gaige kaifang*), Beijing discarded its staunch policies of self-sufficiency (*zijizizu*) and accepted international aid and assistance to help rebuild its economy after the ravages of the Cultural Revolution of the late 1960s that had greatly isolated China politically and financially. The country then began to develop trade with Asian partners and eventually the West, taking advantage of a large and greatly untapped consumer market, requiring Beijing to quickly amass a great deal of information about markets in Asia and beyond, as well as the economic structure of various trading partners on domestic and regional levels. For example, as China was expanding its economic interests in the West in the 1990s, both North America and Europe were establishing large-scale economic communities, namely the North American Free Trade Agreement (created in 1994) and the European Community (formalized as the European Union in 1993). This prompted the need for even more information-gathering on a larger scale and within a very short time. The main focus of Chinese economic interests was building stronger links with the Pacific Rim, including supporting regional economic institutions such as the Asia-Pacific Economic Cooperation forum (APEC), created in 1989, and later the ASEAN-Plus-Three (APT) mechanism (1996) and the East Asian Summit (EAS) (2005), while improving economic ties with the United States and Europe, as both were seen as important sources of more varied goods and technologies.

After the turn of the century, China began to expand its economic concerns, engaging in 'cross-regional' diplomacy in Africa, Latin America, the Middle East and the South Pacific. China's admission to the World Trade Organization (WTO) in December 2001, after fifteen difficult years of negotiations, enabled the country to better benefit from liberalized trading, gave it more say in the process of making trade rules, and removed the possibility of China being denied 'most-favoured nation' (MFN) preferential status by the United States in the future.[22] This also provided a boost of confidence that China could manage itself successfully in a rarely predictable global financial system.

These initiatives were greatly assisted by what was termed a 'charm offensive' (*meili gongshi*) as well as 'smile diplomacy' (*weixiao waijiao*), with China stressing the need for economic partnerships and cooperation based on mutual interests. China's focus on separating economic agreements from political and governance issues and not placing 'conditionality' on aid partners, often referred to as a 'no strings' approach to economic cooperation, contrasted with Western policies and gained much attention among developing states seeking an alternative partner to the United States and Europe.[23] This economic diplomacy also contributed to the perception of the country's soft power (*ruan shili*), referring to the power of attraction, with features and attributes that are considered prepossessing rather than positive or negative coercion (hard power). The rapid growth of China's economy as well as its ability to withstand internal and external market shocks, including the Asian Financial Crisis and the global financial crash a decade later, further brought China's economic capabilities to international attention. Discussion of an alternative Chinese model of development, a 'Beijing Consensus' (*Beijing gongshi*),[24] swiftly evolved from thought experiment to serious policy debate worldwide, which would later be affected by concerns about the United States' long-term financial health following a recession and a torpid recovery process after late-2008.

China's economic foreign policy has gained influence in many regions, and this has resulted in Beijing's competition with the United States and Europe for diplomatic influence, especially in developing regions such as sub-Saharan Africa, Eurasia and Latin America. The position of China in the BRICS grouping of large emerging economies, which was formalized in 2009 and includes Brazil, Russia, India and South Africa, further suggests Beijing's growing confidence both in its own economic power and in its ability to engage economies outside of the Asia-Pacific. Springing originally from an abstract policy concept, the BRICS have slowly developed as an alternative bloc to Western economic policies, and have started to create more formal institutions, including a development bank along the lines of the World Bank/International Monetary Fund.[25]

Between 1978 and 2004, China's total GDP increased fourfold to approximately US$1.4 trillion, while at the same time the country's international trade levels grew from a negligible level to one where China had unseated the United States to become the largest global goods trader, with total exports and imports totalling approximately US$4.16 trillion by the end of 2013.[26] At that time, China's GDP was estimated at approximately US$9.4 trillion despite pressures from the economic downturn after 2008, and maintaining high levels of GDP increases became more difficult during the global recession. When the reform process took root, the Chinese government had traditionally viewed an average GDP growth rate of 8 per cent to be the minimum required for the country to maintain its socio-economic stability and job-creation targets, but when Western global markets began to experience debt crises, Chinese Premier Li Keqiang suggested in late 2013 that China would still be in a position to meet the necessary job-creation conditions, especially in urban areas, while maintaining unemployment at 4 per cent, as long as Chinese growth stabilized at approximately 7.2 per cent. This demonstrated a significant change from the 'protect the eight' (*bao ba*) governmental policies of the turn of the century, meaning that China's growth rate needed to be kept above 8 per cent to maintain stability.[27] By mid-2014, Beijing appeared to be having some success in keeping growth rates in the 7 per cent range,[28] but future financial health would depend on both Chinese policies and the durability of the global economic recovery. The Xi government and the Chinese media have begun to commonly use the term 'the new normal' (*xin changtai*) to describe a more modest Chinese economy with slower growth rates.[29]

At the onset of the global financial crisis, Chinese first-quarter GDP growth in March 2008 stood at 11.3 per cent, but fell to 6.6 per cent by March of the following year as the global crisis became more acute. By the last quarter of 2013, GDP growth stood at 7.7 per cent,[30] generating debates regarding China's economic vulnerability in the future and whether the country was headed for a 'soft landing' (*ruan zhuolu*), a slowdown of growth to levels not as severe as a recession but also not high enough to trigger price inflation. This had been a serious problem in China during the previous boom years of the late 1980s and early 1990s. Following the financial crisis, Beijing was one of the few major economies still posting robust growth, as the United States and European Union began a long recovery, and Japan also sought economic stability after a series of recessions. While other Pacific Rim states, including Australia, India, Indonesia and South Korea, also managed to avoid recession after 2008, China nonetheless found itself as both a metaphorical tent pole and a weather vane for the global economy.

The debate over the degree to which China should continue to open itself to the international economy dominated much of the final years of the Hu Jintao government (2002–12) and the opening years of the administration of Xi Jinping thereafter. The origins of the debate could be traced to previous attempts by the Chinese government to promote economic growth while maintaining a level of control and stability, referred to as a 'vigour/chaos cycle' (*yifang jiuhuo, yihuo jiuluan, yiluan jiuzhua, yizhua jiusu, yusuzai fang*).[31] In short, reforms commonly and beneficially lead to greater economic vigour but also to heightened risk and greater potential for disorder. The 'chaos' leads to an economic retrenchment by the state, possibly resulting in stagnation, which eventually prompts another attempt at reform in the name of 'reinvigorating'. This retrenchment, for example, was viewed during the latter half of the Hu Jintao government as Beijing began to slow down various liberalization processes.[32]

The debate over the degree to which the Chinese state should maintain oversight in key economic sectors has persisted since the start of the reform era. During the economic reforms of the 1990s, the Party sought to reduce state oversight of state-owned enterprises, focusing on developing the largest SOEs in sectors considered vital to the economy and/or essential for China's engagement with the global market, a process termed 'grasp the big, drop the small' (*zhuada fangxiao*), but a further reduction in the role of the state in the economy has remained problematic. In February 2012, the World Bank published a paper, in conjunction with the Development Research Centre of China's State Council, entitled *China 2030*.[33] The report advocated further market liberalization and the reform of state-owned enterprises to prevent a slowdown of the Chinese economy and reduce the risk of China falling into a 'middle income trap' (*zhongdeng shouru xianjing*), whereby a given economy grows to a certain degree and then is unable to progress further due to a lack of productivity and innovation. The need for greater attention to market forces was confirmed at the November 2013 Third Plenum of the Chinese Communist Party. After the event, the 'decisive' role of market forces in developing the Chinese economy was confirmed, along with greater income rights for farmers and the loosening of restrictions on investment.[34]

Manufacturing for export remains the cornerstone of the Chinese economy. In 1990, China's share of global output of manufactured goods stood at only 3 per cent, but by 2011 China had taken first position with 19.8 per cent, just ahead of the United States at 19.4 per cent.[35] At the same time, Beijing has also sought to diversify its service and high-technology sectors to further distance itself from the heavy industry- and agriculture-dominated economics of the previous century. However, a reliance on manufacturing was also dependent on developing global markets for Chinese goods, which became more complicated after the financial crisis.

Beijing's strategies of 'inviting in' (*qing jindai*) foreign interests and companies were matched later in the 1990s reform period by encouraging Chinese firms to 'go out' (*zouchuqu*) and develop international brands. Examples have included Lenovo (computers), Haier (white goods) and Xiaomi (mobile phones). These policies further enabled China to move from a regional to a global economic power, but also resulted in increased risks to the country's still-reforming economy. Greater economic 'interdependence', the establishment of inter-state links including via economics and companies, may promote prosperity and even peaceful relations but also presents the problems of sensitivity and vulnerability to open markets.[36] The former refers to heightened awareness of economic-political policies of trading partners, usually a neutral effect, while the latter refers to exposure to the effects of changes in policy from trading partners, which could potentially be negative. For example, after China ceased to be an exporter of oil in 1993, Beijing needed to import greater percentages of oil as its economy continued to boom, and in October 2013 it was announced that China had become the world's topmost petroleum importer, surpassing the United States. China remains the second largest consumer of oil after the US, with the percentage of oil Beijing needed to import in 2014 estimated at 58 per cent of total petroleum consumed.[37] While importing oil and gas has offset, somewhat, China's reliance on inefficient and polluting coal, it has also rendered the country more vulnerable to international energy prices and crises in areas of the world, such as the Middle East, Africa or Eurasia, that are major fossil fuel producers. It remained to be seen whether the dramatic drop in global oil prices at the end of 2014 would be a longer-term phenomenon and if so how that would affect Chinese growth.

It has also been argued that the problems of economic vulnerability leading to state insecurity are more acute when there is an asymmetric trading relationship.[38] China has had a very short time to adjust to global markets and trade in relation to other modern economic powers, and the country's leadership has a long memory regarding the late Qing Dynasty (1735–1911) and Republican eras (1911–49) when China was exploited both politically and economically by stronger colonial powers. Thus, despite China's rapid economic growth and resiliency there remains a degree of wariness toward being vulnerable either to the chaos of market forces or to exploitation by other large economic powers.[39] This concern became magnified after the onset of the global financial crisis, when China's exports came under increasing strain as Western economies could no longer afford to purchase the same amounts of Chinese goods.

By the middle of 2014, China held approximately US$3.95 trillion in foreign exchange reserves, primarily as a hedge against domestic or international economic crises, the largest amount of funds ever managed by a single state.[40] The majority of these reserves are in American dollars, and are viewed as a major part of what has been called China's increasing 'symbiosis' with the American economy, meaning that successes or failures on one side would inevitably affect the other greatly.[41] The depth of China's integration into the global economy was well illustrated in February 2008 when the Shanghai stock market dropped nearly 9 per cent in value on a single day, creating a backlash in Western and Asian markets. The event was an early sign of how China's economic health can have a butterfly effect (*hudie xiaoying*) on global markets. In addition, China's trade surplus has been a sensitive political issue with the United States and Europe as the West seeks to emerge from the crisis and is wary of perceived protectionism by Beijing. However, due to the post-2008 recession and lower demand for Chinese goods, this surplus began to decrease in value, from US$296 billion in 2008 to US$155 billion three years later.[42]

Differences between Washington and Beijing were noted in economic circles even before the global recession began, as Washington criticized Beijing for unfair trading practices benefiting Chinese manufacturers and questioned the increasing amount of American currency purchased by Beijing in recent years. China's currency still lacks a flexible exchange rate and remains subject to government controls. Until 2005 the value of China's currency, the renminbi, was pegged directly to the value of the US dollar. However, the peg was *de facto* reinstated in 2008–10 due to concerns about the global financial crisis, and there have been ongoing calls in the West for the renminbi to be allowed to appreciate higher.[43] After 2005, and especially since the financial crisis, Beijing has been sensitive to relinquishing too much control over its currency value despite outside protests. China's currency has been enmeshed in a 'managed' or 'dirty' float policy, with the government making adjustments to ensure a high degree of control over the renminbi's value. There are other potential sources of Chinese/American rivalry over natural resources, including energy, as China increases its purchases of international oil and gas supplies. Policymakers in Beijing remain sensitive to any 'China Threat' (*Zhongguo weixie*) policies emanating from Washington that would seek to curtail Chinese economic growth,[44] especially in light of questions over the United States' own future economic health.

Despite these considerable challenges to China's economic security, there remain some signs of optimism within the upper echelons of the Chinese government, as evidenced by the emerging policies of President Xi Jinping after 2012 regarding the development of a 'Chinese Dream'

(*Zhongguo meng*). While this somewhat ambiguous concept, not new in Chinese governance, is open to interpretation from both within China and without, its theories have been linked by Xi to the concept of Chinese 'rejuvenation' (*fuxing*), suggesting increased confidence in the economic future of the country.[45] It stands in marked contrast to the much more guarded statements of Xi's predecessor, Hu Jintao, which included a muted focus on the 'scientific outlook of development' (*kexue fazhanguan*) and building China into a 'moderately prosperous society' (*xiaokang shehui*).

Access to resources and trade

Probably the most visible aspect of China's developing economic security policies has centred on access to raw materials. In addition to fossil fuels, China's economy, and more specifically its minimum acceptable rate of economic growth, requires many other external raw materials ranging from construction materials to foodstuffs, from consumer goods to base and precious metals. These needs have had a profound effect on the global economy, with positive effects on states with a high degree of dependency on resource exports, since prices have risen due to Chinese demand.[46] As China's population becomes richer and a 'middle class' or 'stratum' (*zhongchan jieji / zhongchan jieceng*) becomes more pronounced, there is increasing need for international resources to help build the Chinese economy.[47] As a result, resource diplomacy (*ziyuan waijiao*) has taken a more prominent position in Chinese foreign relations, especially in parts of the developing world. Beijing's primary strategic concern in this area has been that of economic restraint by the West, which is a variation of previous concerns in Beijing about security containment or 'strategic encirclement' (*zhanlue baowei*), to use the Chinese term. These concepts refer to Western or US-led policies to prevent Beijing from gaining access to necessary resources, capital, or transportation routes.[48] With China's economic interests now spread over a much wider global area, debates about 'containment' are not limited to the traditional definition of having its own territory encircled by adversaries, but also of having its overseas economic commitments challenged or even thwarted by the West.[49] Although a physical interdiction of Chinese trade is unlikely and unviable, there are possibilities for friction between China and the United States and its allies in economic areas. Potential examples include more overt competition for commodities and fossil fuels between China and Western actors, and exclusion from Western-dominated trade regimes such as the embryonic Trans-Pacific Partnership (TPP).

Beijing faces several challenges as it seeks to maintain a steady energy supply. This has led to a re-thinking about the issues and problems of energy security (*nengyuan anquan*), defined as the need to obtain satisfactory and stable supplies of energy at viable prices and under conditions that do not endanger 'national values and objectives'.[50] Energy security has been a longstanding concern of other large energy consuming states, including the United States and Europe, at least as far back as the energy shocks in the Middle East in the 1970s, but China must now examine the same policy choices within an international milieu, one much more susceptible to energy competition. In addition, China, a relative newcomer to the politics of international energy trade, must often engage regions that have been heavily dominated by Western interests and firms, such as the Middle East. Beijing has been criticized in the West for signing gas and oil deals with states such as Iran and Sudan, and later South Sudan when that country became independent in 2011. When South Sudan achieved independence, Beijing was placed in the awkward position of trying to maintain good economic-political relations with both sides despite ongoing border tensions.[51]

The Gulf region in the Middle East, including Saudi Arabia, is a key source of China's imported oil and gas, but Beijing has also been striking deals for joint oil and gas development with Central Asia (especially the Caspian Sea region), Russia, Latin America, sub-Saharan Africa and Canada. While Beijing has been willing to make use of its expanding economic resources to secure foreign oil and gas supplies, it has been wary of Western concerns about how China's need for imported fossil fuels affects global prices and access to these resources, raising the question of whether heightened international competition for oil and gas may occur as a result of Beijing's entrance into global energy markets.

Additionally, part of escalating tensions between China and Japan regarding demarcation of the East China Sea (ECS) and deteriorating Chinese relations with the Philippines and Vietnam over the South China Sea (SCS) in 2011–12 involved the question of whether there were substantial oil and gas deposits in the disputed zones. Despite other factors to which these two ongoing disputes can be attributed, including nationalism among the major actors involved, the legal and historical claims to the small islands in the two regions (mainly the Diaoyu/Senkaku Islands in the ECS and the Spratly and Paracel Islands in the SCS), and the desire for China to develop sovereign home waters, referred to in policy circles as 'blue national soil' (*lanse guotu*),[52] energy also plays a role in the disagreements. For example, after a diplomatic cooling-off period between China and Vietnam, tensions were raised again in May 2014 when the Chinese National Offshore Oil Corporation (CNOOC) unilaterally moved an oil platform, the *Haiyang Shiyou 981*, into disputed waters in the SCS close to the Paracel Islands, leading to anti-Chinese protests in Vietnam and condemnation of China's actions from Hanoi. Ships from both China and Vietnam moved into the area, leading to tense standoffs while Beijing reiterated that the platform was within Chinese waters (based on Chinese claims to the Paracels that Vietnam does not recognize).[53]

Moving beyond strictly energy concerns, economic sensitivities surrounding the ECS region were further illustrated in September 2010 when a Chinese fishing vessel was challenged by Japanese Coast Guard vessels in disputed waters in the East China Sea, resulting in the fishing boat colliding with two of the Japanese ships and the Chinese crew being taken into custody.[54] However, diplomatic pressure from China, along with an oddly timed temporary suspension of rare earth mineral shipments, necessary for high-technology manufacturing, from China to Japan during the diplomatic standoff prompted a policy reversal and the trawler captain was eventually released without trial.[55] Since that time, the war of words between the two states over the East China Sea and the disputed islands has become more rancorous.

China has also encountered challenges in its resource diplomacy on other fronts. There has been much debate about China's economic engagement of Africa and whether a low-level competition for resources and diplomatic power has resulted from increased Chinese economic interest. In addition to the Sudan example, China's trade relations with controversial regimes in Uganda and Zimbabwe prompted some international scrutiny, while there was also a public backlash against Chinese investment that has dominated domestic political debate in Zambia.[56] Beijing has sought to downplay its interest in joint resource development in Africa by stressing its aid policies there as well as its support for peacebuilding activities. For example, in 2013, China agreed to send a detachment of between five and six hundred personnel,[57] an exceptional number, to participate in a United Nations peacekeeping operation in the western African nation of Mali in the wake of that country's tenuous security situation following its 2012 civil war. Mali had little in the way of resources sought by Beijing and the mission illustrated China's growing commitment to improving peace and combating poverty on the continent. However, there remain concerns in the West that Africa could be a focal point for economic competition in the future.

Another example of China's economic interests getting caught in international security concerns can be found in the 2014 crisis between Russia and Ukraine over the status of the Crimean

Peninsula. In September 2013, Beijing and Kiev signed a deal that would see China invest in 3 million hectares of Ukrainian land, representing 5 per cent of the country's total land area and 9 per cent of its total farmland, in order to supply foods to Chinese consumers.[58] However, when anti-government protests in Ukraine intensified in early 2014, leading to the ousting of the country's president, Viktor Yanukovych, in February of that year, Russia responded with the forced seizure of the Crimean Peninsula the following month, drawing international condemnation and placing Beijing in a difficult diplomatic position. China did not want to jeopardize its economic interests in Ukraine, nor support an action that essentially violated the sovereignty of another state, especially given China's own history along those lines.

However, Beijing was reluctant to jeopardize its relations with Moscow, relations that are dominated by oil and gas trade, including the China segment of the Eastern Siberia–Pacific Ocean (ESPO) oil pipeline completed in late 2012, and an ambitious fossil fuel joint venture in eastern Siberia signed by Chinese and Russian officials in October 2013.[59] The Sino-Russian bilateral energy partnership deepened further in May 2014 when a joint natural gas development deal, worth an unprecedented US$400 billion, was signed, giving Beijing preferential access to Russian gas for 30 years.[60] Thus, in this case China opted for a middle course, abstaining rather than exercising a veto during a United Nations Security Council vote that would have condemned a March 2014 Crimean independence referendum supported by the Russian government of Vladimir Putin,[61] while calling for diplomatic solutions and disagreeing with Western calls for sanctions on Moscow.

Another factor in China's desire for access to resources has been the role of maritime trade routes that China has increasingly been using as a result of its resource diplomacy. Since the Chinese People's Liberation Army Navy (PLAN) began to be expanded and modernized in the 1990s, including the purchase and refurbishing of an aircraft carrier, one of the emerging mandates of Chinese naval forces has been to defend the integrity of vital sea lanes of communication (*haishang jiaotongxian*), or SLoCs, especially as China became more economically dependent on imported raw materials and energy, including from across the Indian Ocean in the Middle East and Africa.[62] Since 2003, Beijing had been warning of the potential for economic and strategic harm, possibly resulting from China not assuming more direct military oversight of key waterways used by Chinese commerce, especially the Malacca Strait, which in Beijing's view were vulnerable to piracy, terrorism and third-party interdiction, a situation Chinese policymakers subsequently named the 'Malacca Dilemma' (*Maliujia kunju*).[63] Although piracy has largely abated in the Malacca region due to increased patrols and enforcement, the region remains a strategic priority for Beijing. In early 2013, China announced the formation of a unified Coast Guard (*Zhongguo haijing*), overseen by the State Oceanic Administration, mandated to patrol Chinese waters and combat smuggling, illicit fishing, and other illegal economic activities, including in disputed waters.[64]

During 2014, the Chinese government announced a series of new trade initiatives under the concept of 'one belt and one road' (*yidai yilu*), a strategy of developing new land and sea links with vital markets in Europe. These linkages, often referred to as a revival of the traditional 'Silk Road' trading routes during the imperial eras, would include overland transportation via Central Asia as well as greater use of the Indian Ocean to link Chinese markets with South Asia, Eastern Africa, the Middle East and Southern Europe. These links would be augmented with Chinese infrastructure spending worth approximately US$16 billion.[65]

Economic cooperation as strategy

China's concern over the longer-term health of the global economy as well as the end result of the most recent set of WTO international trade talks, otherwise known as the Doha Round, has been illustrated by its more open and accepting views on preferential trade talks on a bilateral and regional level.⁶⁶ The Doha Round, begun in 2001, has produced few results in the wake of sharp divisions both among developed economies and between developed and developing actors. Larger regional organizations such as APEC were increasingly viewed by regional governments as too large and unwieldy to produce short-term results. China's accession to the WTO, coupled with this uncertainty, encouraged the country to actively pursue alternative preferential trade agreements (PTAs), both for improved access to different economies and to demonstrate Chinese commitments to the overall global trade system. One outstanding question that has affected China along with other Asian economies that have sought out free trade agreements is whether these deals will buttress the global trade infrastructure or create a 'noodle bowl' scenario involving lost revenue due to chaotic and overlapping micro-agreements.⁶⁷

China's early PTAs included deals with Hong Kong and Macau as well as developing states including Chile, Costa Rica, Peru, and Pakistan. The Asia-China Free Trade Agreement (ACFTA) of 2010 further strengthened diplomatic ties between Beijing and the ASEAN states in the wake of the Asian Financial Crisis. By the middle of the 2000s, Beijing had shifted its attention to signing PTAs with developed economies, with New Zealand being the first OECD country to sign a preferential trade agreement with Beijing in 2008, followed in 2013 by Iceland and Switzerland and in 2014 by Australia.⁶⁸ Other similar negotiations were less successful, such as talks with Norway that were suspended indefinitely after the Nobel Peace Prize was awarded to a Chinese dissident in 2010.⁶⁹

PTA talks have now assumed an important foreign policy role for Beijing in its pursuit of what has been termed 'commercial diplomacy' (*shangwu waijiao*), referring to the use of commercial power, including potential market access, that Beijing is swiftly developing to influence decisions related to economics but also related to diplomacy and even strategic affairs. All manner of international commerce issues, including tariffs, services, competition policies and privatization, may factor into the application of commercial diplomacy. In addition, while much strategic-related diplomacy often involves zero sum (*linghe*) outcomes, commercial diplomacy is based on a preference for win-win (*gongying*) results, well in keeping with current Chinese economic diplomacy, which stresses improving bilateral relations and which has encouraged Beijing to make many economic and strategic policy inroads internationally as well as regionally.

Some of China's PTAs have developed more pronounced strategic dimensions. For example, the Iceland agreement was notable as the first such deal with a European economy, important given that Chinese attempts to commence preferential trade talks with the European Union in the early 2000s were largely unsuccessful. Since the Iceland and Switzerland PTAs have illustrated Beijing's success in finalizing deals with European economies (neither Iceland nor Switzerland are EU members), this may place pressure on the EU to rethink its economic strategies toward China.

The Iceland deal also served to further bolster China's economic presence and visibility in the Arctic region. With the melting of the ice cap, the Far North has generated increasing interest to Chinese policymakers due to the greater accessibility of raw materials. In addition to joint Sino-Russian energy development in Siberia, China has also signed energy agreements with Canada (2012) and Iceland (2013), and is regarded as a major potential investor in Greenland's emerging mining sector.⁷⁰ China is also seeking increased access to Arctic sea routes, which have become more viable due to climate change. The PTA with Iceland is an important component of Beijing's policy of ensuring that it is not excluded from potential economic goods in the Arctic and further certifying that China is viewed regionally and internationally as a 'near-Arctic state' (*jin beiji guojia*).⁷¹

Another example of how Chinese free trade policy has developed strategic overtones would be the Economic Cooperation Framework Agreement (ECFA) signed by Beijing and Taipei in

2010. The agreement permitted reductions of tariffs on cross-Strait trade and allowed Taiwan to belatedly enter into the free trade process that had been underway across Asia since the end of the 1990s. The agreement also acted as a cornerstone of the warming relations between the two sides following the ascension to power of Ma Ying-jeou, leader of the Kuomintang (Nationalists), or KMT, in Taiwan in 2008, on a platform of improving Chinese relations after 8 years of near-toxic cross-Strait affairs under the previous Taiwanese government of Chen Shui-bian of the Democratic Progressive Party (DPP).

In addition to improving economic and political ties across the Taiwan Strait, the ECFA provided the opportunity for Taipei's pursuit of bilateral free trade agreements of its own, and the first two such deals with economies that do not formally recognize Taiwan, namely New Zealand and Singapore, were completed in 2013. However, the ECFA has its detractors in Taiwan who have voiced concerns that the agreement ties the two economies together too closely and gives China too much decision-making power over the Taiwanese economy. In late 2013, the Ma government sought to expand liberalized trade with Beijing via the Cross-Strait Service Trade Agreement (CSSTA), which resulted in student protests in Taipei in March 2014 amid worries that further deepening economic links across the Strait would eventually allow China to absorb the island economically.[72] Much will depend on the outcome of the next Taiwanese presidential elections, scheduled for March 2016, and whether the post-2008 cross-Strait détente is maintained following that vote, especially should the more mainland-sceptic DPP return to power.

Finally, there is the ongoing debate over China and the Trans-Pacific Partnership, a free trade deal designed to deepen trade liberalization in the Asia-Pacific region, going much further than the original APEC process. Although strictly an economic mechanism, the TPP has become enmeshed in security concerns in the Pacific Rim. The TPP began humbly in 2005 as an understated preferential trade agreement between four small states that together possessed a long resume of such deals, Brunei, Chile, New Zealand, and Singapore. However, the TPP then captured international attention when the United States sought to join the group after 2010 and attempted to more directly set the agenda of the negotiations. The US was followed by several other larger economies, including Australia, Canada, Japan, Mexico and Vietnam. South Korea and Taiwan also expressed interest in joining the group given the potential of developing a truly comprehensive cross-Pacific free trade pact, a goal that had largely eluded APEC. However, China was not invited to join the TPP, and the United States had little enthusiasm for including Beijing in the short term.[73] This exclusion led to some concerns in China that it was being subject to economic containment with the TPP a tacit economic arm of the American pivot/rebalancing policy in the Asia-Pacific that was announced by the Obama Administration in late 2011, a move that many Chinese policymakers also viewed as an undeclared form of containment. The Xi government has proposed alternatives to the TPP, including the Regional Comprehensive Economic Partnership (RCEP) talks, which do not include the United States, as well as a possible revival of the 'Free Trade Area of the Asia-Pacific' (FTAAP) concept that has been discussed within APEC for over a decade.[74]

Conclusions

Although China remains a developing state, with an extensive list of potential economic reforms, the country's rise as an economic power has not only had significant effects on an international scale, but also resulted in the inclusion of economic issues into Beijing's growing strategic agenda. Since China's economic interests have expanded to play a crucial part in its foreign policy, there is a greater degree of sensitivity in the country toward maintaining access to the goods, services and transportation routes that have become crucial for further growth and the continuation of the Chinese reform process. Since the Chinese government has placed a great deal of emphasis on maintaining sufficiently high levels of economic growth to combat poverty, underdevelopment and social disorder, a greater amount of Beijing's economic interests have become securitized. At the same time, several 'hard' security issues that China is facing, including maritime frontier disputes, also have developed significant economic dimensions. Therefore, the main question in examining China's growing concerns about economic security is whether the country's deepening economic interests will be a source of greater cooperation or conflict.

The author wishes to thank Li Dongkun and Jason Young for their comments on a previous draft of this chapter.

Notes

1 'Balance of Economic Power Will Shift Dramatically over the Next 50 Years, Says OECD', *Organisation for Economic Cooperation and Development*, November 9, 2012. Available online at www.oecd.org/newsroom/balanceofeconomicpowerwillshiftdramaticallyoverthenext50yearssaysoecd.htm.
2 Arvind Subramanian, *Eclipse: Living in the Shadow of China's Economic Dominance* (Washington, DC: Peterson Institute for International Economics, 2011).
3 David Shambaugh, *China Goes Global: The Partial Power* (Oxford and New York: Oxford University Press, 2013), 156–7.
4 Bijian Zheng, *China's Peaceful Rise: Speeches of Zheng Bijian, 1997–2005* (Washington, DC: Brookings, 2005), 20.
5 'China', *The World Bank*, 2014. Available online at http://data.worldbank.org/country/china#cp_wdi.
6 'China Plans Investment and Reform to Ease Urbanization Drive', *Reuters*, March 16, 2014.
7 Liyan Qi, 'China Official 2013 Gini Coefficient Edged Down from 2012', *Reuters*, January 20, 2014. For example, according to the World Bank, some countries, including Brazil and South Africa, have Gini Coefficients at over 0.5. See figures at http://data.worldbank.org/indicator/SI.POV.GINI.
8 Judith Shapiro, *China's Environmental Challenges* (Cambridge and Malden, MA: Polity Press, 2012), 1–12; Ross Garnaut, Frank Jotzo and Stephen Howes, 'China's Rapid Emissions Growth and Global Climate Change Policy', *China's Dilemma: Economic Growth, the Environment and Climate Change*, ed. Ligang Song and Wing Thye Woo (Washington, DC: Brookings, 2008), 170–89.
9 Vic Li and Graeme Lang, 'China's "Green GDP" Experiment and the Struggle for Ecological Modernisation', *Journal of Contemporary Asia* 40(1) (February 2010): 44–62.
10 'China to "Declare War" on Pollution, Premier Says', *Reuters*, March 4, 2014.
11 Alexander Collot d'Escury, 'Can China Kickstart Its Circular Economy and Kick Its Smog?' *The Guardian*, January 15, 2014.
12 'Top 10 Trading Partners of the Chinese Mainland', *China Daily*, February 19, 2014.
13 Guoli Liu and Lowell Dittmer, 'Introduction: The Dynamics of Deep Reform', *China's Deep Reform: Domestic Politics in Transition*, ed. Guoli Liu and Lowell Dittmer (Lanham and Boulder: Rowman & Littlefield, 2006), 1–24.
14 Russell Ong, *China's Security Interests in the Twenty-First Century* (London and New York: Routledge, 2007), 12.
15 Barry Buzan, 'New Patterns of Global Security in the Twenty-First Century', *International Affairs* (London) 67(3) (July 1991): 431–51, 445–6.
16 Russell Ong, '"Peaceful Evolution", "Regime Change" and China's Political Security', *Journal of Contemporary China* 16(53) (2007): 717–27.
17 Vincent Cable, 'What Is International Economic Security?' *International Affairs* (London) 71(2) (April 1995): 305–32; Beverly Crawford, 'The New Security Dilemma under International Economic Interdependence', *Millennium: Journal of International Studies* 23(1) (March 1994): 25–55.
18 Zhao Quansheng, *Interpreting Chinese Foreign Policy* (Hong Kong: Oxford University Press, 1996), 51.
19 Daojiong Zha, 'Chinese Considerations of "Economic Security"', *Journal of Chinese Political Science* 5(1) (spring 1999): 69–87, 76.
20 Wang Zhengyi, 'Conceptualizing Economic Security and Governance: China Confronts Globalization', *Pacific Review* 17(4) (2004): 523–45.

21 T. J. Pempel, 'Soft Balancing, Hedging, and Institutional Darwinism: The Economic-Security Nexus and East Asian Regionalism', *Journal of East Asian Studies* 10 (2010): 209–38.
22 Christopher Edmonds, Sumner J. La Croix and Yao Li, 'China's Rise as a Trading Power', *China's Emergent Political Economy: Capitalism in the Dragon's Lair*, ed. Christopher A. McNally (New York and London: Routledge, 2008), 169–89, 172–3.
23 Elizabeth C. Economy and Michael Levi, *By All Means Necessary: How China's Resource Quest is Changing the World* (Oxford and New York: Oxford University Press, 2014), 72–5.
24 Joshua Cooper Ramo, *The Beijing Consensus: Notes on the New Physics of Chinese Power* (London: Foreign Policy Centre, 2004).
25 Stephanie Nolen, 'BRICS Nations Rally around Russia', *Globe and Mail*, July 11, 2014.
26 Jamil Anderlini and Lucy Hornby, 'China Overtakes US as World's Largest Goods Trader', *Financial Times*, January 10, 2014.
27 Grace Zhu and Yajun Zhang, 'China Needs 7.2 per cent Growth to Ensure Employment', *Reuters*, November 5, 2013; Eve Cary, 'Goodbye Bao Ba', *The Diplomat*, April 3, 2012.
28 Xiaoyi Shao and Koh Gui Qing, 'China Second Quarter GDP Seen Steady at 7.4 per cent, Recovery in Sight', *Reuters*, July 7, 2014.
29 Mark Magnier, 'China Faces Tough Adjustments as It Adapts to "New Normal" in 2015', *Wall Street Journal*, December 30, 2014.
30 'China's GDP Up 7.7 per cent in 2013', *Xinhua*, January 20, 2014.
31 Justin Yifu Lin, Fang Cai and Zhou Li, *The China Miracle: Development Strategy and Economic Reform*, third edn (Hong Kong: The Chinese University Press, 2008), 205.
32 Derek Scissors, 'Deng Undone? The Costs of Halting Market Reform in China', *Foreign Affairs* 88(3) (May/June 2009): 24–39.
33 *China 2030: Building a Modern, Harmonious, and Creative High-Income Society*, World Bank (2012). Available online at www.worldbank.org/content/dam/Worldbank/document/China-2030-complete.pdf.
34 'Market to Play "Decisive" Role in Allocating Resources: Communiqué', *Xinhua*, November 12, 2013.
35 Peter Marsh, 'China Noses ahead as Top Good Producer', *Financial Times*, March 13, 2011.
36 Mark Gasiorowski, 'Economic Interdependence and International Conflict: Some Cross-National Evidence', *International Studies Quarterly* 30(1) (March 1986): 23–8, 24; Robert Keohane and Joseph Nye, *Power and Interdependence: World Politics in Transition* (Boston, MA: Little, Brown, 1977), 12–13; Katherine Barbieri, 'Economic Interdependence: A Path to Peace or a Source of Interstate Conflict?' *Journal of Peace Research* 33(1) (February 1996): 29–49, 33.
37 Lucy Hornby, 'Record Imports Make China World's Top Importer of Crude Oil', *Financial Times*, October 12, 2013; 'China's 2014 Oil Demand, Imports to Grow Faster – CNPC Research', *Reuters*, January 15, 2014.
38 Barbieri, 'Economic Interdependence', 32.
39 Justin Yifu Lin, *Demystifying the Chinese Economy* (Cambridge and New York: Cambridge University Press, 2012), 57–60.
40 'China Focus: Fast Growth in China's Forex Reserves Unlikely to Continue', *Xinhua*, January 15, 2014; Grace Zhu, 'China's Forex Reserve Returns "Relatively Good"', *Wall Street Journal*, June 12, 2014.
41 Susan Shirk, *China: Fragile Superpower* (Oxford and New York: Oxford University Press, 2007), 25–8.
42 Nick Edwards, 'China Surprises with Export-led Trade Surplus', *Reuters*, April 10, 2012.
43 Eswar S. Prasad, *The Dollar Trap: How the US Dollar Tightened Its Grip on Global Finance* (Princeton, NJ, and Oxford: Princeton University Press, 2014), 229–33.
44 For example, see Andrew J. Nathan and Andrew Scobell, 'How China Sees America: The Sum of Beijing's Fears', *Foreign Affairs* 91(5) (September/October 2012): 32–47.
45 Zheng Wang, 'The Chinese Dream: Concept and Context', *Journal of Chinese Political Science* 19(1) (2014): 1–13.
46 Clifford Krauss, 'Chinese and US Demand Drives Commodities Surge', *New York Times*, January 15, 2008.
47 Yingjie Guo, 'Class, Stratum and Group: The Politics of Description and Prescription', *The New Rich in China: Future Rulers, Present Lives*, ed. David S. G. Goodman (New York and London: Routledge, 2008), 38–52.
48 John W. Garver and Fei-ling Wang, 'China's Anti-Encirclement Struggle', *Asian Security* 6(3) (2010): 238–61.
49 For example, see Steve Chan, 'Geography and International Relations Theorizing: Their Implications for China', *Eurasian Geography and Economics* 54(4) (2014): 363–85.
50 Daniel Yergin, 'Energy Security in the 1990s', *Foreign Affairs* 67(1) (fall 1988): 111.

51 Luke Patey, *The New Kings of Crude: China, India and the Global Struggle for Oil in Sudan and South Sudan* (London: Hurst, 2014), 101–20, 239–43.
52 James R. Holmes, 'The Commons: Beijing's "Blue National Soil"', *The Diplomat*, January 3, 2013. Available online at http://thediplomat.com/2013/01/a-threat-to-the-commons-blue-national-soil/.
53 Vu Trong Khanh and Nguyen Anh Thu, 'Vietnam, China Trade Accusations of Vessel-Ramming Near Oil Rig', *Wall Street Journal*, June 24, 2014.
54 Suk Kyoon Kim, 'China and Japan Maritime Disputes in the East China Sea: A Note on Recent Developments', *Ocean Development and International Law* 43 (2012): 296–308.
55 Chien-peng Chung, 'China-Japan Relations in the Post-Koizumi Era: A Brightening Half-Decade?' *Asia-Pacific Review* 19(1) (2012): 88–107.
56 Ian Taylor, *China's New Role in Africa* (Boulder and London: Lynne Rienner, 2009), 166–7.
57 Tim Witcher, 'China Offers 500 Troops to UN Mali Force: Envoys', *Agence France-Presse*, May 23, 2013.
58 'China to Invest in 3 Million Hectares of Ukrainian Farmland – Media', *Reuters*, September 22, 2013.
59 Wayne Ma and Lukas Alpert, 'Russia Lets Down Guard on China', *Wall Street Journal*, October 18, 2013; Andrew C. Kuchins, 'Russia and the CIS in 2013: Russia's Pivot to Asia', *Asian Survey* (January/February 2014): 129–37, 132.
60 Jane Perlez, 'China and Russia Reach 30-Year Gas Deal', *New York Times*, May 21, 2014.
61 'Foreign Ministry Spokesperson Qin Gang's Remarks on the UN Security Council's Vote on the Draft Resolution on the Referendum in Crimea, 2014/03/16', *Foreign Ministry of the People's Republic of China*, March 16, 2014.
62 Gabriel B. Collins, 'China's Dependence on the Global Maritime Commons', *China, the United States and Twenty-First Century Sea Power: Defining a Maritime Security Relationship*, ed. Andrew S. Erickson, Lyle J. Goldstein and Nan Li (Annapolis, MA: Naval Institute Press, 2010), 14–37.
63 Marc Lanteigne, 'China's Maritime Security and the "Malacca Dilemma"', *Asian Security* 4(2) (2008): 143–61.
64 Andrew Erickson and Gabe Collins, 'New Fleet on the Block: China's Coast Guard Comes Together', *Wall Street Journal*, March 11, 2013.
65 Tang Danlu, 'Xi Suggests China, C. Asia Build Silk Road Economic Belt', *Xinhua*, September 7, 2013; 'China Planning $16.3 Billion Fund for "New Silk Road"', *Bloomberg*, November 4, 2014.
66 Guoyu Song and Wen Jin Yuan, 'China's Free Trade Agreement Strategies', *Washington Quarterly* 35(4) (fall 2012): 107–119; Yang Jiang, 'China's Pursuit of Free Trade Agreements: Is China Exceptional?' *Review of International Political Economy* 17(2) (2010): 238–61.
67 Jayant Menon, 'Dealing with the Proliferation of Bilateral Free Trade Agreements', *The World Economy* 32(10) (October 2009): 1381–2.
68 Marc Lanteigne, 'Northern Exposure: Cross-Regionalism and the China-Iceland Preferential Trade Negotiations', *China Quarterly* 202 (June 2010): 362–80; Marc Lanteigne, 'The Sino-Swiss Free Trade Agreement', *CSS Analyses in Security Policy* 147 (February 2014): 1–4.
69 Angus Grigg, 'China Cools on Australia Free Trade Deal', *Financial Review*, February 19, 2014.
70 Mads Fuglede, Johannes Kidmose, Gary Schaub Jr. and Marc Lanteigne, 'Kina, Grønland, Danmark – konsekvenser og muligheder i kinesisk Arktispolitik [China, Greenland, Denmark – Impacts and Opportunities in China's Arctic Policy]', *University of Copenhagen Centre for Military Studies*, January 2004. Available online at http://cms.polsci.ku.dk/cms/kina-i-arktis/Kina__Gr_nland__Danmark_-_Konsekvenser_og_muligheder_i_kinesisk_Arktispolitik.pdf/.
71 Nathan Vanderklippe, 'For China, North is a New Way to Go West', *Globe and Mail*, January 19, 2014; Joseph Chinyong Liow, 'Arctic Summer: Who Should Benefit from Global Warming?' *Foreign Affairs Snapshot*, June 21, 2014.
72 Jenny Hsu, 'Taiwan Police Evict Protesters from Cabinet Building', *Wall Street Journal*, March 21, 2014.
73 Jason Lange, 'US Sees Hurdles to China Joining Pacific Trade Pact', *Reuters*, January 23, 2014.
74 'China Eyes Asia-Pacific FTA at APEC Meeting, Says Foreign Minister', *Xinhua*, October 29, 2014.

4
China's non-traditional security

Patricia Thornton

Introduction

Although the concept of "non-traditional" security remains outside the mainstream in Western security studies, it enjoys considerable popularity in China. Both scholars and policy makers in the PRC quickly embraced the key tenet that defining national security primarily in military terms is potentially misleading, and could, over the long term, serve to increase global insecurity.[1] One recent example of China's warmer reception of non-traditional security is the announcement, following the Third Plenary Session of the Eighteenth Party Congress in November 2013, that China plans to establish a "National Security Committee" (*Guojia anquan weiyuanhui*) in order to coordinate national security efforts across a full spectrum of both traditional and non-traditional security issues. Although the idea of creating such a body was initially floated at least 15 years earlier under the leadership of Jiang Zemin, resistance from within the bureaucracy as well as the Chinese military slowed implementation. In the interim, coordination and decision making have been overseen since September 2000 by the Party Central Committee's National Security Leading Small Group (*Guojia anquan lingdao xiaozu*).[2] However, the appearance of new multifaceted challenges in more recent times has served to highlight the need for a centralized formal advisory body at the upper echelons of the Party-state with manpower and resources sufficient to formulate, coordinate and execute national security policy, particularly with non-traditional security threats currently on the rise. In explaining the Party Congress's resolution to establish the committee, current Party General Secretary Xi Jinping observed, "Our nation is facing pressures both to safeguard its sovereignty, security, and development interests externally, and to uphold its political security and social stability internally, and a rising number of dangers of all sorts that are foreseeable as well as some that are difficult to anticipate."[3] Accordingly, unlike the National Security Council, the Washington, DC counterpart after which it is partially modeled, the new Chinese organization is tasked with broadly defined responsibilities over both foreign policy and domestic security, including relations with Tibet and unrest in non-Han majority areas such as Xinjiang Province; however, like the Department of Homeland Security, the US agency created after the September 2001 attacks, China's new National Security Committee will also coordinate anti-terrorism efforts and monitor cybersecurity threats, calling in the Public Security Bureau to participate on the committee when it discusses matters of domestic stability.[4] As Major General Li Shengquan of China's National Defense University explained in *Study Times*, the official journal of the Central Party School, insofar as national integration remains incompletely realized in the People's Republic, the new committee would of necessity draw no distinction between traditional and non-traditional threats in the protection of Chinese political security, territorial sovereignty, and social stability against the three rising dangers of terrorism, separatism, and extremism.[5] Indeed, in his address to the initial meeting of China's National Security Committee, Xi emphasized that the newly formed group would "pay attention not only to external security, but to internal security" and "emphasize not only traditional security, but non-traditional security," and would view "political, territorial, military, economic, cultural, social, technological, information, ecological, natural resource, nuclear and other forms of security equally within the overall system of national security."[6] The resulting decision-making body thus represents an ambitious new organizational hybrid designed to redress China's persistent problems with inter-agency cooperation in the security sector, including bureaucratic "stove-piping" and jurisdictional conflicts characteristic of policy making within a "fragmented authoritarian" system,[7] with an expansive remit with respect to national security.

What accounts for the relatively higher resonance of the concept of "non-traditional security" in China? Dali Yang recently observed that the implementation of significant governance reforms in post-Deng China has been driven largely by the response of the leadership to a series of non-military crises that began with the Tiananmen Square demonstrations in 1989, the fall of the Soviet Union in 1991, the Asian Financial Crisis in 1997, and the rise of new sectarian groups against which the state cracked down in 1999, all against the background rising levels of social unrest that continued through the next decade. Within 3 years, Chinese leaders scrambled to cope with the outbreak and spread of the Severe Acute Respiratory Syndrome (SARS) epidemic in 2002–3. In 2004, the so called "color revolutions" that swept Eastern Europe raised alarms for the Hu-Wen regime, and, only four years later, the disastrous Wenchuan earthquake struck, followed by a national scandal over adulterated milk powder that poisoned a staggering 94,000 infants across the country, and the global financial meltdown. Violent demonstrations likewise ignited in Tibet, followed by unrest in Xinjiang the following year, with separatists carrying out knife and bomb attacks in 2010 and failing in an attempted plane hijacking in 2011. Later that year, the so called Arab Spring ignited a brief flurry of urban protests from would-be Jasmine revolutionaries in the PRC, which met with a swift and overwhelming response from police. Yet, surprising both critics and skeptics, Yang points out that the post-Dengist leadership not only weathered these challenges, but rose above them, by increasing intra-government discipline, heeding constitutional constraints, and largely honoring its international engagements and obligations.[8] "Crisis," Yang concluded, "has been the midwife of reform. Faced with multiple challenges, the country's leaders have been on a perpetual drive since the late 1980s to improve governance and rebuild the fiscal prowess and institutional sinews of the central state." In Yang's view, the post-Deng leadership has succeeded in producing a "more efficient, more service-oriented, more disciplined" bureaucracy in responding to a full range of "non-traditional" challenges to China's security, "often themselves invoking the rhetoric of crisis in the process."[9]

As Yang suggests, periodic crises have thus played a dual role in shaping China's response to non-traditional security issues, in the sense of spurring both policy learning and institutional reform from within the bureaucracy.[10] Institution building and governance reforms in response to particular crises are much in evidence in the field of non-traditional security studies in China. As one noted scholar at the Shanghai Institute for International Studies observed,

> China's vulnerability to non-traditional threats may be attributable to its insufficient institutional and physical preparedness. Since the 1990s, China has been frequently hit

by non-traditional security threats; in particular those effecting economic security (for instance, the East Asian financial crisis), health security (for example, SARS, bird flu, AIDS), environmental security threat (for instance, floods, sand storms, droughts). Terrorism and transnational crime have already damaged China's security, and the degree of damage will only increase. Disease and environmental degradation are not new for China, but they have increased remarkably as a result of globalization and economic liberalization.[11]

However, as others have pointed out, the dynamics of crisis have a particular utility to political leaders as well, often in terms of providing windows of opportunity for Party leaders to redefine issues, strike at political opponents, and further particularistic agendas.[12] A key driver behind the relatively more enthusiastic adoption of the concept of non-traditional security in China is likely the utility of a broader conception of security in supporting the Party-state's interest in suppressing domestic political rivals, preventing social opposition, and controlling potentially restive segments of the domestic population. As Ayoob points out, "the security predicament" faced by countries undergoing rapid development stems in large part from the pressing need to telescope the state-making process into a single "mammoth state-building enterprise" to meet simultaneous internal and external challenges.[13]

Thus, although the detection and surveillance of internal threats also plays a role in the development of non-traditional security measures in liberal democracies,[14] security in nations still undergoing development is usually "inextricably intertwined with domestic issues of state making, state breaking, and regime legitimacy."[15] Crisis has proved a key driver of the Chinese state-making process in recent decades, triggering capacity building not only in response to non-traditional security threats, but also in honing the ability of the state's repressive apparatus in order to identify and defend against potential challengers.[16] Perhaps unsurprisingly, whereas most Chinese scholars and policy makers either reject outright or downplay elements of the United Nations-defined concept of "human security" as an attempt to impose liberal values on China's domestic governance agenda, they embrace non-traditional security concerns in other realms, frequently linking these to broader "social management" measures pursued domestically.[17] Chinese scholarly and policy discussions of non-traditional security issues emphasize the principles of state sovereignty and non-interference, while steering clear of human rights, humanitarian intervention and democracy. Another noteworthy difference is the embracing of "soft power" as a part of "comprehensive national power" in Chinese security discourse. Non-traditional security issues have therefore emerged largely as a vehicle for strengthening state interests and maintaining social stability in China, nominally unassociated with the concept of universal human rights.

China and the concept of non-traditional security

Non-traditional security studies challenge the undergirding propositions of the neorealist orthodoxy in security studies in the Western tradition, including its privileging of a rational, state-centric worldview based on the primacy of military power in an anarchic environment, and the assumption that international politics is fundamentally ahistorical, recurrent, and non-contextual. Advocates of broadening traditional security studies have argued that the analysis of threats to security should not be confined to statist, military challenges, but should be extended to include economic, societal, environmental, and human security challenges. Scholars associated with the Copenhagen Peace Research Institute and, later, the Copenhagen School have been particularly influential in bringing discussions of societal and human security into the field. Buzan, in his landmark book, made the case that the security of society—defined as the cultural and linguistic survival of a social identity group—should be regarded as a logical extension of state security;[18] Buzan's erstwhile coauthor Wæver defines societal security as "the sustainability, within acceptable conditions for evolution, of traditional patterns of language, culture, association, and religious and national identity and custom."[19] In addition, Buzan and Wæver have argued that the post-Cold War global security order is increasingly defined by regional dynamics, and comprehensive and cooperative security arrangements that do not target any third power, many of which are oriented around non-traditional security concerns such as pollution, food safety, piracy, and natural disaster preparedness and response.[20]

The interest of Chinese scholars and policy makers in non-traditional security dates back at least as far as 1994, when Wang Yong of Beijing University's Department of International Relations addressed the importance of expanding Chinese cooperation with other international organizations, particularly on issues pertaining to the environment, illegal drugs, and refugees.[21] Two years later, in 1996, then Foreign Minister Qian Qichen introduced China's so called "new security concept" (NSC), which incorporated both traditional and non-traditional elements, at the Asian Regional Forum meeting. Qian described the NSC as a comprehensive approach to security emphasizing non-interference, abstention from the use of force, peace through dialogue and cooperation, and economic development as integral aspects of security. The concept was subsequently incorporated into China's 1997 Defense White Paper.[22] A 1998 article on the related concept of "comprehensive security" (*zonghe anquan*) by Wang Yizhou of the Institute of World Economics and Politics at the Chinese Academy of Social Sciences enumerated a series of non-traditional security concerns including economic, information, cultural, and ecological threats that demanded new response measures. Wang concluded that "the concept of comprehensive security demands that we take traditional security interests, which have the military as their center, and place them alongside those of human, collective, global and other forms of non-traditional security and interests, and maintain them in a state of balance."[23] Writing on China's "new security concept" less than a year later, Beijing University's Wang Yong returned to some of the ground covered in his earlier article, but also invoked the case of the 1997 Asian Financial Crisis to argue that in an era of globalization, "a non-traditional security problem is capable of causing as much damage as a traditional security issue: it can take [a country's] wealth accumulated over a very long period of time and, through currency devaluation and a stock market crash, destroy it as utterly and completely as a war might."[24]

The impact of the September 11 attacks on the United States in 2001 brought an enhanced level of urgency to the discussions surrounding non-traditional security issues in China. Having signed the United Nations Convention against Transnational Organized Crime in December 2000, and The Shanghai Convention on Combating Terrorism, Separatism and Extremism in June 2011, in May 2002, China issued a further position paper on enhanced cooperation in the field of non-traditional security issues. The 2002 position paper, while calling for an expansion of transnational cooperation and closer coordination of regional cooperation in combating non-traditional security threats, reasserted the principles of mutual respect for sovereignty and non-interference in internal affairs; the paper also appealed for what it called a shared "new security concept featuring mutual trust, mutual benefit, equality and coordination."[25] Two months later, in July 2002, the Ministry of Foreign Affairs released a position paper further elaborating China's new approach to security, emphasizing "non-traditional security areas such as combating terrorism and transnational crimes, in addition to the traditional security areas like preventing foreign invasion and safeguarding territorial integrity."[26] At the Sixth ASEAN-China Summit in Phnom Penh in November, the Joint Declaration of ASEAN and China on Cooperation in the Field of Non-Traditional Security Issues was released, calling for the strengthening of both practical cooperation and joint research on non-traditional security issues among member states, particularly targeting illegal drug and human trafficking, piracy, terrorism, arms smuggling, money laundering, and international economic and cyber crime.[27] After the outbreak of the SARS epidemic the following year, China and ASEAN organized a special summit in Bangkok to discuss cooperation on SARS and other public health threats—an issue that had been overlooked during the previous summit—and saw the agreement of member nations to hold scheduled meetings every three years specifically to address collective non-traditional security concerns. In addition, annual ministerial meetings were scheduled to discuss financial, public health and environmental challenges, and a special working group of experts and high-ranking officials was formed in order to advise on matters of non-traditional security policy implementation within the ASEAN bloc.[28] As Aris has argued, in recent years, ASEAN members are increasingly relying on the ASEAN Way in the ASEAN Regional Forum (ARF)—a high-level mode of international exchange that takes principles of mutual non-interference and non-intervention as its heart and in which decisions are taken by consensus rather than by majority vote—in order to "constitute an informal regional security community." Inter-sessional meetings, which generate proposals for the superordinate inter-governmental level and culminate in agreements at the ARF ministerial meetings, focus on a wide range of non-traditional security measures, such as confidence building and preventive diplomacy, counter-terrorism and transnational crime, disaster relief, maritime security, and non-proliferation and disarmament. The 2003 China-ASEAN summit produced a Joint Declaration on ASEAN-China Strategic Partnership for Peace and Prosperity that included formal provisions for cooperation in the realm of non-traditional security targeting counter-terrorism, illicit drug trafficking, trafficking in persons, illegal migration, sea piracy, and international economic crimes, and to enhance competence in criminal technology, forensic sciences, immigration, road transport management, and investigation into cyber crimes.[29]

Northeast Asia has likewise emerged as a site of extensive regional cooperation, particularly on environmental concerns. Since the foundation in 1999 of the Tripartite Environment Ministers Meeting (TEMM), China, Japan and South Korea have institutionalized trilateral cooperation to combat pollution, stem environmental degradation, and foster joint action to protect both air quality and the marine environment regionally. The Northeast Asian Conference on Environmental Concerns (NEAC), the Northeast Asia Subregional Program on Environmental Cooperation (NEASPEC), and the Asian Development Bank's Global Environment Facility project on the prevention and control of yellow dust and sandstorms have likewise become important fora for the dissemination of ecological research, and the promotion of collaboration on non-traditional security concerns in northeast Asia.[30]

Another key regional organization designed to address non-traditional security issues is the Shanghai Cooperation Organization (SCO), which originated in the 1990s as a framework designed to facilitate the settlement of border issues between China and the Central Asian republics with Russian involvement. At the initial 1996 and 1997 meetings of its precursor, the Shanghai Five, representatives of China, Russia, Kazakhstan, Kyrgyzstan, and Tajikistan signed treaties to demilitarize the border regions and foster cooperation between member states. Subsequent meetings deepened economic integration in the region, and took steps to revive "Silk Road" trade. In 2001, when the organization admitted Uzbekistan as its sixth member, it renamed itself the Shanghai Cooperation Organization. Mongolia was granted observer status in 2004, and Iran, Pakistan, and India likewise became observers the following year. While the current focus of the SCO covers both traditional and non-traditional security cooperation, ongoing efforts to combat the "three evils" of terrorism, extremism, and separatism in the region have emerged as the centerpiece of contemporary collaboration, with the SCO's Regional Anti-Terrorist Structure

(RATS) taking the lead in facilitating the collection of information and, theoretically, the coordination of joint action.[31]

However, since the mid-1990s, China's deepening engagement with non-traditional security issues on an international level has been paired with strenuous internal measures aiming to safeguard domestic stability. The CCP's powerful Central Political-Legal Committee, reestablished in the wake of the 1989 Tiananmen demonstrations, resumed and progressively tightened central control over the Ministries of Public Security and State Security, the Procuratorate and the courts, the people's militia and the People's Armed Police (PAP) over the course of the 1990s. By the middle of the decade, domestic capacities of detection, surveillance, and repression targeting particular ethnic or socio-economic groups that are viewed as problematic for the maintenance of social stability had been greatly enhanced, and particularly those seen as potential challengers to the continued rule of the Party-state. Central spending on internal security is substantial and continues to escalate: Ministry of Finance figures reveal that in 2010 spending on public security outpaced the official national defense budget for the first time, a trend that has continued for three years.[32] Chief among the externalities of economic reform is the mounting "security predicament" for the Party-state, which in scaling back somewhat on centralized economic control to boost production and innovation has undermined some of its traditional levers of social control. New sources of instability have emerged from within society and relative inequality levels have soared, fueling social conflict. So called "mass incidents" of social protest have notably risen from 8,700 in 1994 to 90,000 in 2006,[33] prompting a recent admission by the chairman of the National People's Congress Wu Bangguo that "it is possible that the state could sink into the abyss of internal disorder."[34] As Tanner has noted, the official response to rising social unrest and crime has been "campaign-style policing": "concentrated, fixed-term, special targeting of particular categories of crime for arrest and severe punishment" featuring sporadic but intense mobilizations of vast police and public security personnel to carry out "stern blows" against particular targets. Despite widespread criticism of this approach, "campaign-style policing" survives in large part as an organizational response to relatively low police/citizen ratios, forcing Chinese police to rely heavily on the active participation of grassroots volunteers, Party activists, and ordinary citizens to maintain social order.[35] In addition, local authorities frequently blend national "strike hard" targets with their own local security agendas.[36] In practice, in part due to the persistence of "campaign-style policing" over the course of the reform era, new institutional building to address non-traditional security issues on a transnational level has been combined with domestic "strike hard" campaigns designed to weaken social opposition, repress potential political rivals, or increase control over potentially restive groups.

China's "security predicament"

China's increasing attention to non-traditional security issues has therefore coincided with a heightened sense among central elites of looming crises, both at home and abroad; official responses have frequently combined international institution building with domestic "strike hard" measures against internal targets. For example, early discussion of non-traditional security in China took place against the backdrop of the still unfolding Asian Financial Crisis. The Fifteenth Party Congress decision in September 1997 to deepen state-owned enterprise reform resulted in the furloughing of some six million workers in 1997, more than seven million in 1998, and almost eight million by 1999.[37] By 1998, the real unemployment rate had skyrocketed to between 7.9 and 8.5 percent, the highest in the history of the People's Republic.[38] In addition, economic growth stalled: whereas exports in 1997 had increased 17.3 percent over the previous year, 1998 saw a mere 0.5 percent increase, due to market contraction in Japan and South Korea.

At the same time, Chinese exports lost their competitive advantage due to currency devaluation in Southeast Asia, fueling further economic malaise. Sporadic and uncoordinated instances of social unrest increased in 1998 and 1999, largely in response to proposed plant closures or enterprise mergers, unpaid welfare payments due to laid-off workers, unpaid pension benefits from shuttered or loss-making enterprises, and due to widespread popular suspicion that official corruption was at least partially to blame.[39] April 1999 saw by far the largest public demonstration in the capital since the suppression of the student protests in Tiananmen Square a decade before, when more than ten thousand followers of a spiritual group known as Falun Dafa staged a non-violent sit-in before the gates of Zhongnanhai, the central leadership compound in downtown Beijing, which the participants had planned in part on the internet. Although the group's popularity and discipline had taken both the central leadership and the police by surprise, the rise of new spiritual and charitable groups as well as alternative health care practices in fact represented a natural response to mounting economic pressures and the disappearance of a social welfare net in China's major cities. The earlier dismantling of the commune system and privatization of state-owned enterprises had seriously compromised the access of many reform-era citizens to reliable health care and other services; and newly relaxed restrictions on rural-urban migration had given rise to a new underclass with an urgent need for social services.[40]

In his 1999 work addressing non-traditional security threats in the People's Republic, Fu called attention to the interrelated nature of the danger posed by the Asian Financial Crisis to China's economic security, and the "ethnic and religious conflicts" liable to arise in periods of social unrest. One consequence of globalization, Fu warned, was the escalating influence of non-state actors, with which the existing security system was ill-equipped to deal.[41] As Yang noted, to safeguard economic security in the wake of the Asian Financial Crisis, the central government undertook a wave of institution building, moving quickly to secure its regulatory control over stock markets and securities. It furthermore promulgated a new and unified legal framework for the domestic securities market, reformed the IPO process, and strengthened supervision over share underwriting, and corporate governance and disclosure in order to delimit the scope for insider trading and other wrong-doing. Under the guise of ensuring market order and national economic security, central authorities undertook ambitious and sweeping regulatory reforms, reorganizing the State Administrations of Quality and Technical Supervision, Environmental Protection and Drug Administration. Armed with new administrative muscle, stiffer punishments for infractions, and bold legislative mandates, China's new regulatory agencies began a widely publicized nationwide quality inspection drive that ultimately folded into a unified national campaign-style effort in 2001 to "rectify market economic order" that mobilized local and municipal police to engage in broad sweeps targeting counterfeit and substandard goods, fake and pirated products, and unsafe places of business. However, also targeted in the large-scale raids were popular points of access for low-income consumers, including street stalls, market fairs, and internet cafes. In 2001, authorities closed half a million workshops for producing fake products, confiscated 158 million illegal publications, and 4.2 million copies of pirated software. Over the next few months, during the first half of 2002, central authorities likewise closed a total of 36,424 street stalls for selling fake or substandard products; and, in the summer of 2002, Beijing municipal authorities suspended the operation of all internet cafes.[42]

Central authorities likewise moved to increase control over domestic social order in the wake of increasing mobilization at the social grassroots, particularly targeting social and civic groups with possible international links. The provisional regulations adopted in the aftermath of the Tiananmen student demonstrations that required all social organizations to locate official sponsors were strengthened. Nearly a decade later, the 1998 "Regulations on the Registration and Management of Social Organizations" specifically required official sponsors to first determine that the social organization seeking affiliation corresponded to an actual social need of some sort, and to ascertain that the organization in question was not in some way redundant, overlapping in function with a pre-existing group. Sponsoring government departments or official arms of the Party-state were furthermore deemed liable for ensuring the legal compliance of subordinate social organizations, and were held legally responsible for any infractions of law. One popular strategy for circumventing the new regulations had social organizations registering as businesses under relevant commercial or industrial bureaus. In addition, in 1999 the Ministry of Public Security promulgated a series of "Regulations on Public Order in Mass Cultural and Sport Activities," stipulating that groups sponsoring cultural or sports activities involving more than 200 people file a written application with the local public security office.[43] Falun Dafa, the spiritual group that had organized the April 1999 demonstration near Tiananmen, was officially branded a "heretical and superstitious cult" and banned in July; the organization's assets were confiscated, its offices and practice sites—including 39 branches nationwide, 1,900 subunits, and some 23,000 places where it purportedly held gatherings—were sealed and placed under heavy police surveillance. These measures were repeated with similar groups that had likewise fallen under suspicion, often because of alleged links to "hostile forces both inside and outside the country" intent on endangering national security by conspiring with "pro-democratic" and "anti-China" forces overseas.[44] The resources of the powerful Political-Legal Committee, which oversees the work of the Ministries of Public Security and of State Security, the Procuratorate, the courts, the people's militia, and the PAP, were substantially beefed up in 1999 in order to cope with the campaign against "evil heretical sects" like Falun Dafa. In 2002, the leader of that *xitong* (系统) (Zhou Yongkang, now under attack) was for the first time given a chair on the Politburo Standing Committee. In addition, a new organization was established at the center—the Leading Small Group for Stability Maintenance Work (*Zhongyang weiwen gongzuo lingdao xiaozu*), with subordinate offices to oversee "stability maintenance" (*weiwen*) at every level of the Party-state, all the way down to the level of the township.[45]

The crisis triggered by the SARS outbreak of 2002–3, characterized by Fidler as a "political pathology of the first post-Westphalian pathogen" by virtue of the challenge it posed to a global health policy environment still defined by state-centric institutions,[46] unfolded against the backdrop of a power succession within the Party. Outgoing General Secretary Jiang Zemin's efforts to "strengthen the ruling capacity" of the Party had long been laced with dire warnings and repeated exhortations that cadres remain vigilant against impending threats to both internal and external security. Yet, whereas most epidemiologists agree that the earliest case of SARS probably occurred in mid-November 2002 in Foshan, a city in Guangdong Province, Chinese officials attempted to suppress information regarding the scale of the epidemic. Although the World Health Organization's Global Network had been alerted to the outbreak in the PRC via unofficial sources by the end of November 2002, its first official approach to the Chinese government apparently occurred on February 10, 2003, when two unrelated sources reported that the disease was raging through southern China.[47] The following day, Guangdong health officials finally admitted during a brief press conference that a total of 305 cases had been reported in the province, five of which had proved fatal. Following a series of similarly terse announcements that aimed to reassure the public and quell panic, official silence resumed on February 23 on the orders of the Guangdong Party secretary, and continued through the meeting of National People's Congress in March that oversaw the official transfer of political power from Jiang Zemin to Hu Jintao. During the NPC meeting, the WHO issued its first global warning about SARS. After dispatching a team of experts to China on March 22, the WHO issued the first travel advisory in its history. By mid-April, newly installed Premier Wen Jiabao was warning officials that the situation was "extremely grave," and the new Hu-Wen team hastily established a new task force involving top military and civilian officials to oversee the struggle against SARS.[48]

Invoking a biopolitical discourse of national security, the new Hu-Wen Administration put in place a series of emergency measures that centralized political power while disproportionately targeting already disadvantaged groups in society for enhanced surveillance and control, in hopes of minimizing resistance from potentially unruly social forces. Calling for a "people's war" against SARS, the propaganda machine ramped up to extol the nation's efforts against SARS, and to laud Chinese health personnel as new "SARS heroes" and "angels in white," while the less fortunate substrata of the citizenry were targeted for special handling. Fearing that migrant laborers in China's major cities might return home and spread SARS into the hinterland, China's vast "floating population" was put under travel restrictions. Known Falun Dafa practitioners were likewise arrested and accused of spreading rumors that the epidemic was a form of divine retribution against the Communist Party. Itinerant peddlers and street vendors were subject to close monitoring and heavy-handed repression because of their mobility and the potentially substandard quality of the goods they might hawk as prophylactics or cures. Large numbers of poor peasant farmers in Beijing to petition the central government for redress on any number of issues were also rounded up by police and either threatened with arrest or quarantined.[49]

By the end of 2004, the so called "color revolutions" sweeping Eastern Europe triggered a new sense of urgency as Chinese leaders scrambled to assess the potential threat to regime security. Hu Jintao directed research institutes and think tanks connected to the Party-state to examine thoroughly the process of political change in formerly socialist countries. As a result, the Chinese Academy of Social Sciences and several of its provincial equivalents dispatched a series of fact-finding missions and organized at least seven national, cross-departmental conferences and symposia between 2004 and 2006 addressing the causes and processes behind the color revolutions. The consensus that emerged as a result of these crisis-driven investigations portrayed an ominous scenario of collaboration between liberalizing media, increasingly activist civil society forces and Western agencies for political change. The domestic policy result was, as Chen characterized it, "low-intensity coercion": intensified campaigns for ideology reinforcement, and enhanced restrictions over liberal media, political activism, public interest advocacy, and Sino-Western civil cooperation. State outlays on internal security grew 36 percent during the 2007 fiscal year: government spending on the police, prosecutor's offices, and the judiciary rose nearly 60 percent, while spending on the PAP grew nearly 51 percent. A series of new directives attempting to reign in independent journalism and police loyalty among media professionals were quickly implemented in 2005 and 2006; and in March 2005, the Ministry of Civil Affairs, which oversees social and civic organizations, issued new directives mandating annual inspections of legally registered NGOs operating in China that paid particular attention to the documentation of sources of NGO funding, and the connections of Chinese NGOs to Western foundations. Control over the internet was likewise tightened: in April 2006, administrators of 14 major portals in Chinese cyberspace were called on to cooperate voluntarily with government officials to filter out social and political content deemed inappropriate for China's internet users.[50] These controls were tightened again in 2011 during the so called Arab Spring when a group of Chinese activists attempted to use social media and the internet to spark off a homegrown "Jasmine Revolution" in China's major cities: searches for the words "Egypt" and "jasmine" on the micro-blog functions of major Chinese web portals such as Sina.com and Sohu.com, and on Sina Weibo, the Chinese version of Twitter, were quickly blocked, and many mainland Chinese users who rely on virtual private network connections (VPNs) reported that they were unable to access the internet as they had in the past.[51] Cybersecurity has continued to loom large in both scholarly and policy discussions of China's non-traditional security agenda, with surveillance and censorship efforts continuing to keep pace with new developments in social media, including the explosion of Chinese social media such as microblogging sites (i.e., Sina Weibo) and mobile chat applications (i.e., Weixin, or WeChat). For example, recent speculation has traced a March 2014 crackdown on some of the most popular liberal-leaning WeChat public accounts to the workings of another Party Central Committee leading small group also chaired by Party General Secretary Xi Jinping, which met for the first time only two weeks before.[52]

In March 2008, a series of peaceful demonstrations took place in Lhasa to mark the anniversary of the Tibetan uprisings against Communist Party rule in 1959. Within about a week's time, the demonstrations turned violent, involving attacks on Han and Hui immigrants, and the looting and destruction of property. The rapid escalation of widespread ethnic violence overlapping with the meeting of the National People's Congress and in the run-up to the Olympics in Beijing signaled a new political crisis for Beijing. The PAP were called in by the local government, and the area was placed under martial law. Just over a year later, in July 2009, violent protests rocked Urumqi, the capital city of the Xinjiang Uighur Autonomous Region in China. These two waves of ethnic uprisings, taking place in borderland regions that are considered core national security interests, were quickly defined by central leaders as threats to China's sovereignty, territorial integrity and national unity, interests secondary only to that of preserving the CCP leadership. A November 2009 *People's Daily* editorial announced that China's sovereignty claims over Taiwan, Xinjiang, and Tibet were within the scope of China's core interests, a message that was repeated in spirit by then Vice President Xi Jinping during a February 2012 visit to Washington, DC, when he stressed the need for the US to demonstrate respect for China's core interests, including Tibet. The 2008 and 2009 waves of ethnic unrest sparked the adoption of "Regulations on Emergency Command in Handling Emergencies by the Armed Forces" in November 2010, which permitted a wider margin for using force without the permission of central authorities, including automatic approval to local governments for the unrestricted use of force in the event of local riots. The *Regulations* placed the collection and dissemination of intelligence at the center of decision making in such cases, and a premium was likewise placed on the cooperation of neighboring states' attempts to address insurgency. Over the longer term, since the twin crises of unrest in Xinjiang and Tibet, Chinese leaders have advocated a combination of traditional hard power use of force and non-traditional socio-economic development in order to safeguard stability in the border regions. In 2011, Xinjiang hosted a joint anti-terrorist SCO exercise organized by Chinese intelligence in the Tianshan Mountains, a traditional safe haven for Uighur insurgents, with India, Pakistan, and Mongolia serving as observer states for the drills. In 2013, the first ever PAP joint exercise with foreign counterparts took place in China when the Snow Leopard Commandoes, an elite anti-terrorism force organized under the PAP, took part with Russia in Beijing.[53]

Although some observers have emphasized the importance of external developments in generating outbursts of ethnic violence in recent years, it is clear that Chinese policy has also played a key role in this regard. For example, although the establishment of political, economic, and cultural linkages with Central Asia has been described as vital to the Party-state's strategy of development and integration for Xinjiang, they are simultaneously viewed as a potential source of threat to state security due to the history of trans-border ethno-religious movements. Although China's struggle against those it has labeled "splittists" and "separatists" in border regions pre-dates the events of 9/11, Chinese leaders quickly fastened onto the securitizing potential of the global "war on terror" in order to justify its ongoing repression of Uighur opposition, making avid use of post-9/11 amendments to its criminal law to intensify its crackdown on Uighur dissent and opposition. The widespread human rights violations that took place in Xinjiang throughout the 1990s during the series of "Strike Hard" campaigns have escalated: Uighur émigré organizations, Amnesty International, and Human Rights Watch have voiced their concerns regarding the "thousands" of Uighurs who were arrested or detained under the new amendments between 2001 and 2005, and Xinjiang's *People's Daily* confirmed in early 2006 that authorities had arrested 18,227 people in Xinjiang for "endangering national security" over the previous 12 months alone.[54] According to some observers, the rapid "securitization" of ethnic tensions and the frequent deployment of crisis governance in handling ethnic unrest in China's border regions have resulted in a new "insecurity dilemma," defined as a "self-defeating strategic interaction [in which] insecure states{...}embark on state-building to mitigate their insecurities" and in which the search for national security paradoxically ends in rising insecurity for all parties.[55]

Conclusion

The broad fusion of traditional and non-traditional security concerns in Chinese foreign policy-making practice, as evidenced by the scope of issues to be addressed by its newly created National Security Committee as well as its championing of its "new security concept," is closely linked to its still unfolding state-building process. According to a top Party journal, with the current General Secretary of the Chinese Communist Party Xi Jinping at its head, the committee will specifically target five types of "unconventional security threats," including extremists, online agitators and the ideological challenges to the Chinese culture posed by Western nations. However, it is unclear whether its ambitious remit, designed to address the "highly intertwined and complicated" nature of contemporary security threats across the broadest possible range of potential challenges to social stability, national unity, and state sovereignty, should be read as a sign of China's increasing strength or weakness in the wake of its continuing rise on the global stage.[56] Some analysts have warned that the rising importance of non-traditional security challenges in the wake of the September 11, 2001 attacks in the US may give rise to a "boomerang effect" in which foreign policy decision makers, in China as elsewhere, must engage in a precision balancing act weighing both traditional and non-traditional security issues; yet also remain mindful that an excessive focus on one form of security at the expense of the other might potentially provoke new threats or give rise to new vulnerabilities as a result of the poor balancing of ends and means in a radically altered security environment across the globe.[57]

However, on the other hand, China's increasingly powerful contemporary "security state" apparatus has deep historical roots that can be traced at least as far back as the early communist movement.[58] Although there is ample evidence of both the institutionalization and professionalization of the state security apparatus over the course of the reform era, unlike in democratic regimes in which the depoliticization of security and intelligence functions is ensured through relatively open and transparent legal and institutional means, the contemporary Chinese state continues to shape its security apparatus around an expansive palette that includes both foreign and domestic, traditional and non-traditional security issue areas that ultimately secure the consolidation of the Party's power and ensure its continued survival. What we may in fact be seeing in the post-Mao security state is "not simply the replacement of an outmoded revolutionary style of politics with a modern technocratic mode, but rather a complex amalgam of the two."[59] The contemporary leadership's increasing attention to the realm of non-traditional security concerns likewise bears the hallmarks of the long arc of its state-making process over time and its traditional strategic culture, both of which exert some influence on the ways in which security threats are defined today.[60] Yet, as in the past, China's contemporary involvement with non-traditional security has tended to serve, first and foremost, its internal security agenda. Nevertheless, the continuing fear of dissent from within constrains its cooperation with non-state actors, as well as its neighbors, perhaps most clearly seen in its responses to recent upsurges in ethnic unrest. Farther afield, whereas non-traditional security discussions at the international level often focus on climate change, water, food, and energy security—arguably where China's influence on the world stage has its greatest impact—China's decidedly state-centric approach may ultimately undercut the legitimacy of its cooperative and diplomatic efforts, as well as its image as a responsible stakeholder in global politics in the years to come.

Glossary

ASEAN   Association of Southeast Asian Nations
Falun Dafa   法轮大法
Leading Small Group for Stability Maintenance Work   中央维稳工作领导小组
National Security Committee   国家安全委员会
National Security Leading Small Group   国家安全领导小组
NEAC   Northeast Asian Conference on Environmental Concerns
NEASPEC   Northeast Asia Subregional Program on Environmental Cooperation
New Security Concept   新安全观
RATS   Regional Anti-Terrorist Structure
Social management   社会管理
Stability maintenance   维稳
WHO   World Health Organization

Notes

1 R. Ullman, "Redefining security," *International Security* 8:1, 1983, 129.
2 A. L. Miller, "The CCP Central Committee's Leading Small Groups," *China Leadership Monitor* 26, 2008, 2–21.
3 F. Gong, "Guojia anquan weiyuanhui sheli hou de anquan guanli [Security Management after the Establishment of the National Security Committee]," *Xuexi Shibao* [*Study Times*], 13 January 2013.
4 K. MacLoughlin, "Chinese Power Play: Xi Jinping Creates a National Security Council," *The Christian Science Monitor*, 13 November 2013; J. Perlez, "Chinese Security Panel Given Foreign and Domestic Role," *The New York Times* [International Edition], 14 November 2013, 4.
5 S. Li, "Tongchou guojia anquan de zhanlüe zhiju [The Raising of the Comprehensive National Security Strategy]," *Xuexi Shibao* [*Study Times*], 18 November 2013, 7.
6 Xinhua she [New China News Agency], "Xi Jinping: Jianchi zongti guojia anquan guan, zou Zhongguo tese guojia anquan daolu [Xi Jinping: Keeping to the Totality of the National Security Concept, Walking the Road of Chinese National Security with Chinese Characteristics]," 15 April 2014.
7 A. Mertha, "Fragmented Authoritarianism 2.0," *The China Quarterly* 200, December 2009, 995–1012.
8 D. Yang, *Remaking the Chinese Leviathan: Market Transition and the Politics of Governance in China*, Stanford, CA: Stanford University Press, 2004.
9 D. Yang, "State Capacity on the Rebound," *Journal of Democracy* 14:1, 2003, 49.
10 P. M. Haas and E. B. Haas, "Learning to Learn: Improving International Governance," *Global Governance* 225, 1995, 255–85.
11 X. Yu, "Understanding and Preventing New Conflicts and Wars: China's Peaceful Rise as a Strategic Choice," *Global Change, Peace & Security* 17:3, 2005, 283.
12 J. T. S. Keeler, "Opening the Window for Reform Mandates, Crises, and Extraordinary Policy-Making," *Comparative Political Studies* 25:4, 1993, 433–86.
13 M. Ayoob, *The Third World Security Predicament: State Making, Regional Conflict, and the International System*, London: Lynne Rienner, 1995, 31–47.
14 C. Bell, "Surveillance Strategies and Populations at Risk: Biopolitical Governance in Canada's National Security Policy," *Security Dialogue* 37:2, 2006, 147–65.
15 Ayoob, op. cit., 49.
16 P. M. Thornton, "Crisis and Governance: SARS and the Resilience of the Chinese Body Politic," *The China Journal* 61, January 2009, 23–48.

17 A. Acharya, "Human Security: East versus West," *International Journal: Canada's Journal of Global Policy Analysis* 56:3, 2001, 442–60.
18 B. Buzan, O. Wæver, and J. De Wilde (eds), *Security: A New Framework for Analysis*, London: Lynne Rienner Publishers, 1998.
19 O. Wæver, "'Societal Security': The Concept," in O. Wæver, B. Buzan, M. Kelstrup, and M. Barnett (eds), *Identity, Migration, and the New Security Agenda in Europe*, New York: St. Martin's Press, 23.
20 B. Buzan, and O. Wæver, *Regions and Powers: The Structure of International Security*, Cambridge: Cambridge University Press, 2003.
21 Y. Wang, "Lun xianghu yicun dui woguo guojia anquan de yingxiang [On the Influence of Reciprocity and Co-existence on Our National Security]," *Shijie Jingji yu Zhengzhi* [*World Economics and Politics*] 6, 1994, 62–7.
22 D. Arase, "Non-Traditional Security in China–ASEAN Cooperation: The Institutionalization of Regional Security Cooperation and the Evolution of East Asian Regionalism," *Asian Survey* 50:4, 2010, 818.
23 Y. Wang, "Lun zonghe anquan [Theorizing Comprehensive Security]," *Shijie Jingji yu Zhengzhi* [*World Economics and Politics*] 4, 1998, 6.
24 Y. Wang, "Lun Zhongguo de xin anquan guan [Theorizing China's New Security Concept]," *Shijie Jingji yu Zhengzhi* [*World Economics and Politics*] 1, 1999, 45.
25 Ministry of Foreign Affairs, "Guanyu jiaqiang feichuantong anquan lingyu hezuo de zhongfang lichang wenjian [Position Paper on Enhanced Cooperation in the Field of Non-Traditional Security Issues]," 29 May 2002.
26 Xinhua she [New China News Agency], "Zhongguo guanyu xinanquan de lichang wenjian [China's Position Paper on the New Security Concept]," 31 July 2002.
27 Association of Southeast Asian Nations [ASEAN], "Joint Declaration of ASEAN and China on Cooperation in the Field of Non-Traditional Security Issues Sixth ASEAN-China Summit Phnom Penh, 4 November 2002."
28 J. Tang and G. Zhang, "Cong 'feidan' fenghui kan xingcheng zhongde Zhongguo Dongmeng feichuantong anquan lingyu hezuo jizhi [A View on the Formation of China–ASEAN Cooperation Mechanisms in the Field of Non-traditional Security from the SARS Summit]," *Dongnanya Zongheng* [*Southeast Asia Review*], 12, 2003, 13–14.
29 S. Aris, "The Shanghai Cooperation Organisation: 'Tackling the Three Evils,'" *Europe-Asia Studies* 61:3, May 2010, 818–20.
30 Cui, Shunji, "Beyond History: Non-traditional Security Cooperation and the Construction of Northeast Asian International Society," *Journal of Contemporary China* 22:83, 2013, 868–86 at 870–2.
31 Ibid.
32 C. Buckley, "China Internal Security Spending Jumps Past Army Budget," *Reuters*, 5 March 2011; B. Blanchard and J. Ruwitch, "China Hikes Defense Budget, to Spend More on Internal Security," *Reuters*, 5 March 2013.
33 Y. Tong and S. Lei, "Large-Scale Mass Incidents in China," *East Asia Policy*, 2:2, 2010, 487–508.
34 M. Bristow, "Chinese Leader Rules Out Democracy," *BBC News Online*, 10 March 2011.
35 M. S. Tanner, "Campaign-Style Policing in China and Its Critics," in B. Bakken (ed.), *Crime, Punishment, and Policing in China*, London: Rowman & Littlefield, 2005, 171–2.
36 S. Trevaskes, *Policing Serious Crime in China: From "Strike Hard" to "Kill Fewer,"* London: Routledge, 2010, 86–9.
37 B. Naughton, *The Chinese Economy: Transitions and Growth*, Cambridge, MA: The MIT Press, 2007, 186–7.
38 A. Hu, "Zhongguo jingji zengzhang de xianzhuang duanqi qianjing ji changqi qushi [Current Situation, Short-Term Prospects and Long-Term Trends in Chinese Economic Growth]," *Zhanlüe yu Guanli* [*Strategy and Management*] 3, 1999, 33–4.
39 S. Breslin, "The Politics of Chinese Trade and the Asian Financial Crises: Questioning the Wisdom of Export-Led Growth," *Third World Quarterly* 20:6, 1999, 1194–6.
40 P. Thornton, "The New Cybersects: Popular Religion, Repression, and Resistance," in Elizabeth J. Perry and Mark Selden (eds), *Chinese Society: Change, Conflict and Resistance*, London and New York: Routledge, 2010, 254–64.
41 M. Fu, "Cong jingji anquan jiaodu tan dui 'Fei chuantong anquan' de kanfa [Some Views on Non-Traditional Security from the Perspective of Economic Security]," *Xiandai Guoji Guanxi* [*Contemporary International Relations*] 3, 1999, 1–5.

42 Yang, 2004, op. cit., 92–106.
43 A. Saich, "Negotiating the State: The Development of Social Organizations in China," *The China Quarterly* 161, March, 124–41.
44 M. Xia and S. Hua, "The Battle between the Chinese Government and the Falun Gong," *Chinese Law and Government*, 32:5, September/October 1999, 105; K. A. Thomas, "Falun Gong: An Analysis of China's National Security Concerns," *Pacific Rim Law & Policy Journal* 10, 2000, 471; P. M. Thornton, "Manufacturing Sectarian Divides: The Chinese State, Identities, and Collective Violence," in J. L. Peacock, P. M. Thornton, and P. B. Inman (eds), *Identity Matters: Ethnic and Sectarian Conflict*, Oxford and New York: Berghahn Books, 171, 180.
45 K. Kan, "Whither Weiwen? Stability Maintenance in the Eighteenth Party Congress Era," *China Perspectives* 1, 2013, 88.
46 D. P. Fidler, "SARS: Political Pathology of the First post Westphalian Pathogen," *The Journal of Law, Medicine & Ethics* 31:4, 2003, 485.
47 Ibid., 491.
48 P. M. Thornton, "Crisis and Governance: SARS and the Resilience of the Chinese Body Politic," *The China Journal* 61, January 2009, 31–3.
49 Ibid., 40–1.
50 T. C. Chen, "China's Reaction to the Color Revolutions: Adaptive Authoritarianism in Full Swing," *Asian Perspective* 34:2, 2010, 5–51.
51 J. D. Goodman, "Trying to Stir Up a Popular Protest in China, from a Bedroom in Manhattan," *The New York Times*, 29 April 2010, 10.
52 D. Wertime, "Surprising Crackdown on China's Hottest Social Media Platform," *Foreign Policy.com*, 13 March 2014.
53 L. Odgaard and T. G. Nielsen, "China's Counterinsurgency Strategy in Tibet and Xinjiang," *Journal of Contemporary China*, ahead-of-print, 2014, 1–21.
54 M. Clarke, "Widening the Net: China's Anti-terror Laws and Human Rights in the Xinjiang Uyghur Autonomous Region," *The International Journal of Human Rights* 14:4, 2010, 542–58.
55 T. Topygal, "Insecurity Dilemma and the Tibetan Uprising in 2008," *Journal of Contemporary China* 20:69, 2011, 184.
56 T. Ng, "'Cultural threats' among Five Focuses of New National Security Panel, Colonel Says," *South China Morning Post*, 14 January 2014.
57 P. H. Liotta, 'Boomerang Effect: The Convergence of National and Human Security," *Security Dialogue* 33:4, 2002, 473–4.
58 X. Guo, *China's Security State: Philosophy, Evolution, Politics*, Cambridge: Cambridge University Press, 2012.
59 E. J. Perry, "From Mass Campaigns to Managed Campaigns: 'Constructing a New Socialist Countryside,'" in S. Heilmann and E. J. Perry, *Mao's Invisible Hand: The Political Foundations of Adaptive Governance in China*, Cambridge, MA: Harvard University Press, 49.
60 A. I. Johnston, *Cultural Realism: Strategic Culture and Grand Strategy in Chinese History*, Princeton, NJ: Princeton University Press, 1988.

Select bibliography

Ayoob, M. (1995) *The Third World Security Predicament: State Making, Regional Conflict, and the International System*. London and Boulder: Lynne Rienner.
Buzan, B. (1984) *People, States and Fear*. Cambridge: Cambridge University Press.
Buzan, B. and Wæver, O. (2003) *Regions and Powers: The Structure of International Security*. Cambridge: Cambridge University Press.
Guo, X. (2012) *China's Security State: Philosophy, Evolution, Politics*. Cambridge: Cambridge University Press.
Johnston, A. I. (1998) *Cultural Realism: Strategic Culture and Grand Strategy in Chinese History*. Princeton, NJ: Princeton University Press.
Naughton, B. (2007) *The Chinese Economy: Transitions and Growth*. Cambridge, MA: The MIT Press.
Trevaskes, S. (2010) *Policing Serious Crime in China: From "Strike Hard" to "Kill Fewer."* London: Routledge.

Part II
Geostrategic perspectives

Section A
The great powers

5

China and the United States
Common and contested interests

Christopher Twomey[1]

Nations use power to advance their national security interests. The United States and China share some important security interests. However, there are also a significant number of conflictual security interests that separate them as well. This chapter's survey of these issues is decidedly pessimistic. It should be noted at the outset, however, that this does not represent an accurate, comprehensive perspective on the bilateral relationship. Economic, and to a lesser extent social and political, ties serve to greatly dampen these security tensions. Nevertheless, it is critical to have an accurate understanding of those contested security issues.

This chapter will proceed as follows. First, those common interests, both global and regional, will be surveyed. Then a range of contested issues in Sino-American relations that are fundamentally derived from relations with third parties will be highlighted. These serve as the primary drivers of any potential conflict, and the role of third parties adds to their complexity. There are, additionally, a range of more direct, narrowly bilateral issues that might come between the two powers, and these serve as the final substantive section of this chapter.

Common interests

Even in the security realm, the situation is not entirely bleak. Both the United States and China benefit from—and actively pursue—a broad based stability in the Asia-Pacific. Economic development is a critical goal for both, and this requires an extensive geopolitical stability. In the absence of a credible threat of major great power war involving either, maintenance of this stability is a paramount goal for both. This has a tremendous dampening effect on the various bilateral and trilateral (i.e., those including a third party) tensions as discussed below. China regards regional stability as key, and continues to view the international situation as favorable for its stated policy of peaceful development, as a "period of strategic opportunities."[2]

For China, access to international markets and commodity suppliers is extremely important. China depends on international trade more extensively than do most other large economies, making it highly vulnerable to any threat to international trade stability. For instance, China's proportion of trade (exports plus imports) to GDP is 53 percent, as compared with 30 percent in the United States or 26 percent in Brazil.[3] Economic growth—important for all countries—is critical for legitimacy-challenged communist party dictatorships such as the PRC. Given the importance of trade to China's economy, maintaining access to that becomes an issue of security, at least for the regime ruling China.

While China's trade is heavily weighted towards its Asian neighbors, China also depends on other regions. The United States and Europe are key locations for final exports of its manufactured goods. The Middle East is a vital source of imported energy. Latin America and Africa are important sources of other natural resources. This diversified (by virtue of the scale of China's economy, if nothing else) set of international economic relations means that China has significant interest in political stability across the globe, a perspective that the United States broadly shares.

Both powers similarly share an interest in generally reducing the role of non-state actors, especially those in terrorist movements. As major states, both have an interest in delegitimizing such behavior, in general. Specifically, of course, each has somewhat different interests. The United States is most concerned with Al Qaeda-like movements that challenge established orders in the Middle East. On the other hand, China is more concerned with Central Asian groups that might complicate its rule over its western province of Xinjiang, such as the East Turkmenistan Independence Movement. Still, neither side's particular emphasis does anything to detract from their shared interests on this issue.[4]

Both Beijing and Washington have a shared interest in avoiding the further proliferation of weapons of mass destruction, particularly nuclear weaponry and technology. Both have robust nuclear arsenals. Both benefit from being part of the global nuclear-armed oligarchy. While each has specific concerns and different priorities (in North Korea, Iran, and South Asia, specifically), at a general level avoiding further proliferation enhances each side's security. Interestingly, it is in this area that China's traditional advocacy of developing nations' interests more generally is most challenged. Increasingly, China sides with the "nuclear haves" in non-proliferation fora. Related to this, China has been an active participant in the Nuclear Security Summit process that the United States has promoted.[5]

Finally, and most tentatively, the two sides share some interests with regard to maintaining open access to global commons. China's participation in anti-piracy patrols in the Gulf of Aden has been the most positive and tangible sign of this.[6] Active diplomacy on limiting the militarization of space suggests the beginnings of an evolution in China's conception of its interests there as well (although this has to be balanced—perhaps outweighed—by continuation of PLA anti-satellite tests).[7] On other global commons issues, such as the Arctic and broader environmental issues, there are important distributional issues that may divide the two, but some shared long-term interests also exist.

These are all real, tangible national security interests for each side. The two independently (and at times, jointly) engage in policies to advance their interests in these areas that serve to enhance the interests of the other. While other contested interests dominate the remainder of this chapter, these areas of aligned security interests should not be ignored or characterized solely as "soft" security interests.

Sources of tension beyond the bilateral relationship

The United States has a great number of alliances and other partnerships in East Asia that complicate the bilateral Sino-American relationship. To a lesser extent, the same can be said of selected Chinese partnerships with her neighbors (i.e., North Korea, Russia, and Pakistan). While each of these other relationships that the US has—Taiwan, Japan, Korea, and the South China Sea—is treated separately in a chapter in this volume, they will be discussed briefly here through the lens of the Beijing-Washington interaction.

Although the situation across the Taiwan Strait in 2014 is more stable than at any time in the past seven decades, it will likely remain an enduring concern for Sino-American relations. The United States, for reasons of domestic politics and international interests, has supported the democratic government in Taipei. While opposing provocative moves to change the *status quo* (which generally would consist of moves towards *de jure* independence), the United States has viewed Taiwan as a friend and partner in the region. Taiwan's political and economic structure mean that it is likely to continue to be viewed as such by large swaths of the American foreign policy elite. Furthermore, the Taiwan Relations Act and the momentum of traditional US-Taiwan relations have established a practice of arms sales and military support from the United States to Taiwan.

China views Taiwan's continued political separation from the mainland as a reminder of the "Century of Humiliations" and, in particular, a result of US interference in its own domestic affairs. Taiwan's existence as a separate sovereign entity, with a significant military capability of its own, also complicates China's ability to project maritime power into the Pacific Ocean. As such, continued US support for Taipei—militarily, or even politically—is viewed as inimical to Beijing's interest in ensuring the territorial integrity of the state of China as the CCP defines it. Taiwan, and ensuring its eventual reunification with the PRC, is routinely included in Beijing's list of "core interests."

Today, the current KMT administration of President Ma Ying-jeou has dampened tensions with Beijing. However, given long-term trends in Taiwanese social identity as distinct from that in the PRC, this policy does not represent an immutable political consensus in Taiwan. It is quite possible that a future DPP, or even a different KMT, leadership will construe Taiwan's interests *vis-à-vis* the PRC differently. Similarly, PRC policy elsewhere in the region may dampen Taiwan's interest in the current warm economic relationship. In such a situation, Taiwan would again re-emerge as an important area of conflict for the United States.

Given the evolving balance of power over the Taiwan Strait, a revitalization of the Taiwan issue in the Sino-American relationship would be problematic. Increasingly, the PLA possesses the capability to dominate the waters around and the air above Taiwan in the absence of US intervention.[8] Such military dynamics would require more active US contributions in the case of an eruption of military conflict, and deeper US-Taiwan ties in any tense peace across the strait. Such would feed negative spirals in broader US-China relations.

US ties to Japan are even stronger, as befits a 60-year ally that hosts major US combat forces in the region. Given Japanese-Chinese tensions over a wide range of issues—historic animosity, geo-strategic situation, contested territorial disputes—this triangular relationship is rife with tension. In the absence of underlying Sino-Japanese tensions, the US-Japan alliance would play an ambiguous role for China. On the one hand, by reducing the propensity for Japan to develop a military commensurate with its economic and geopolitical status, China welcomes this treaty. China has—at times—spoken positively of this "cork in the bottle" role for the alliance, particularly as it pertains to reducing Japanese demands for nuclear weapons given the provision of an umbrella of extended deterrence for Tokyo. However, as the US-Japan alliance has increasingly evolved to take on broader roles, within which Japanese military capabilities have been encouraged to grow and play a larger regional role, China expresses concerns about the alliance. Shifts in the declared goals of the alliance, now to include strong hints at a regional role and repudiation of Japan's former restrictions against collective defense, are viewed as threatening to Beijing.

Japanese bases house major American combat elements in the region. The Seventh Fleet is home-ported in Yokosuka and Sasebo; it includes the only forward deployed carrier in the US Navy. That and the combat support vessels that are part of the carrier strike battle group, plus a separate destroyer squadron (recently increased in size as part of the "pivot" discussed below), are the most capable naval assets in the region. The Fifth Air Force includes squadrons of F-15 and

F-16 as well as tactical airlift craft and C2ISR support craft. Modern American F-22 squadrons have also rotated through Japanese bases. Although a partial redeployment to Guam is underway, the Third Marine Division will retain important capabilities deployed in Okinawa. This very large set of US forces represents the first forces that would be used in the context of any US-China conflict in the region, and its presence shapes Chinese perceptions of both Japan and the United States.

One specific area of concern for Beijing is US-Japanese collaboration on missile defense systems. This raises several concerns. One, it deepens the integration between the two militaries at an operational level. Integrated missile defense operations require synthesized pictures of the battle space for both navies, which requires deep connections between the C2ISR (command, control, intelligence, surveillance, and reconnaissance) systems. Two, missile defenses reduce one of the key areas of asymmetric advantage that Beijing has militarily over Japan. Three, missile defense technology development may potentially lead to reductions in Japanese prohibitions on exporting weapons, which might enhance Japan's ability to play a role in developing military capabilities elsewhere in the region. There are already nascent moves in this regard (arms sales of naval vessels) between Japan and the Philippines, and to a lesser extent Vietnam.

Since 2010, the most prominent flashpoint in Sino-Japanese relations has been the Senkaku Island dispute (called the Diaoyu Islands in Chinese).[9] The United States is enmeshed in this dispute for two reasons. First, Washington gave Japan administrative control over the islands when it returned Okinawa and other Ryukyu islands to Tokyo in 1972. Second, with increasing prominence, the United States has reiterated that the Senkaku Islands are covered by the US-Japan treaty, even if the United States takes no stand on the ultimate disposition of their sovereignty. As tensions between Japan and China heated up following an incident caused by a drunken Chinese fishing ship captain ramming a Japanese coast guard vessel in 2010, Washington has been drawn into that crisis.

The United States has had to balance competing pressures from China and Japan over this issue. In response to the escalation of tensions, and particularly dramatically increased Chinese government and military patrols around the Senkakus, increasingly senior US leaders have reiterated long-standing US policy positions regarding the status of the islands in international law and with regard to the treaty (most recently at the presidential level in May 2014). Some Japanese actions, particularly those suggesting a desire to revise past apologies or acceptance of responsibility for transgressions during WWII, have met with formal US complaints and vigorous protests from China. These have apparently served to appease domestic constituencies in Japan clamoring for a stronger response to Chinese provocations over the islands. The complex triangular interrelations over this issue are a grave and unpredictable element in Sino-American security relations.

The Korean Peninsula is the most likely source of war in Asia; while American and Chinese interests are far from diametrically opposed, neither are they perfectly aligned. If the most important issue for the United States today is the denuclearization of a state that behaves erratically, for China the issues posed are more disparate. North Korea has proven a challenge for Beijing to deal with. Proliferation—particularly that which provokes regional reactions China finds problematic—is something Beijing wishes to avoid.[10] Avoiding the migration outflows that would accompany any major conflict is also a high priority, particularly given that the neighboring region is a relatively backward industrial rustbelt that already suffers from high unemployment and the risk of associated social discontent. More problematically, however, China welcomes the existence of a buffer state to a staunch US ally.

South Korea hosts another set of forward deployed US military forces. The US capabilities in the ROK consist of several squadrons of tactical fighters and important parts of a mechanized division. More importantly, a history of joint command with the ROK military exemplifies a degree of integration that the US–Japan alliance is only beginning to move towards. Any collapse or conquest of North Korea that led to the reunification of the peninsula on the South's terms would bode danger from Beijing's perspective. Without credible commitments from the United States to avoid continuing that alliance, such an outcome brings the only possible peer competitor for Beijing to its doorstep. Such credible commitments are hard to envision, in Beijing, Seoul, or Washington.

Absent such an extreme outcome as reunification, continued statecraft aimed to denuclearize North Korea will also put China and the United States at odds. Clearly, there are some signs of evolution in China's posture on the issue, but they only go so far. Even in 2010, in the context of a series of extreme North Korean provocations (the sinking of the ROK Navy frigate, the *Cheonan*, and the shelling of ROK marines and civilians on Yeonpyeong), China vociferously opposed US moves to signal military support of its attacked ally. The moribund Six Party Talks diplomatic forum shows no sign of significant progress on resolving the issue. Instead, continued North Korean weapons developments are leading to further US-ROK missile defense cooperation, delay in shifting responsibilities in the alliance to the ROK military, and, generally, heightened calls for tightening of alliances with the United States from both Seoul and Tokyo. This strains US-China relations, even if the moves are not necessarily aimed at Beijing.

The South China Sea presents a final area of indirect security contention between the United States and China. There, China and five other claimants vie for control over the Spratly and Paracel Islands, extending as far as a thousand miles from continental China. Driven in part by recent deadlines to register claims under the United Nations Convention on the Law of the Sea, but also by rising Chinese military power, recent events have raised the prospect of renewal of military conflict in this region.[11] Given the existence of US treaty commitments to the Philippines, renewed engagement with Indonesia, and burgeoning cooperation with Vietnam, this is another area that brings the United States and China into competition.

As with the Senkaku Islands, the issue is not contested sovereignty between the United States and China, but rather how disagreements between China and third parties will be resolved. The United States takes no stand on who owns these islands in the region. However, Washington does advocate resolution both without recourse to violence and in accordance with established international law. The Chinese position, ambiguous in nature but with regular reference to "historic claims," suggests alternate foundations.[12]

Militarized conflict over South China Sea formations in the modern era dates at least to the PRC's attack on South Vietnamese-held features in 1974. Chinese consolidation over the Paracels was completed in 1988, and important instances of further expansion occurred in 1994, as noted in Chapter 16. The United States' role in these conflicts was minimal. However—beginning with the Chinese expulsion of the Philippines from Mischief Reef in 1994 and the bolstering of Chinese facilities there in 1998—the Philippines has increasingly looked to its alliance with the United States as a bulwark against further expansion. Desultory US diplomacy did not prevent Chinese consolidation of control over Scarborough Shoal in 2012. Contemporary People's Liberation Army-Navy and Chinese coast guard pressure over the Philippine-held Second Thomas Reef further south has yet, as of writing, to lead to further expansion of Chinese control in the region. But this series of Chinese and regional spirals has involved the United States in these territorial disputes to a degree not previously seen.

A final wrinkle on the South China Sea is the presence of a major Chinese naval base in Hainan Island, at the north edge of the sea. It is a major base for one of China's three naval fleets, and potentially for the emerging Chinese nuclear missile armed submarine force (Jin-class, Type-95 SSBNs). Additionally, the new Chinese aircraft carrier, the *Liaoning*, is engaging in trial operations there. Given those military developments, the region has drawn particular interest from US intelligence-gathering platforms. This has at times led to military confrontations at sea.[13] While to some extent this final aspect of the SCS serves as a transition to the more purely bilateral aspects of the potential rivalry, it too is exacerbated by US alliance and partnership links in the region.

The issues listed above do challenge the United States and China even if they are not direct sources of contestation between them. Indeed, in many cases the presence of an unpredictable third player complicates the situation. The prospect for misperceptions, miscommunications and unintentional consequences increases with additional players. Indeed, identifying an outcome that represents a fair "social" preference for three or more actors is impossible in many cases, as expressed in Arrow's theorem.[14]

Direct sources of tension in Sino-American relations

There is a range of direct problems in Sino-American relations as well. At the broadest level, there are hints of tension over the traditional US role in East Asia. As China grows and deploys into the Pacific well beyond her coastal waters, some worry whether the Pacific Ocean is large enough for the two powers.[15] China has referred to "near seas" and "far seas," or alternatively, regions beyond the first and second island chains.[16] The United States has long forward deployed in those seas, and routinely patrols there as well. Any hint of a Chinese equivalent of a "Monroe Doctrine" would bring the two into direct conflict. In general, however, China has eschewed such expansive declarations of its interests. A recent US media emphasis on China's "new assertiveness" lacks neither careful historic analysis nor careful evaluation of the purported changes in Chinese policy.[17] Still, this area is constantly evolving and issues such as the ADIZ declaration in 2013 and the oil exploration in waters contested by Vietnam in 2014 are less ambiguous.

In the wake of extensive military conflicts in Iraq and Afghanistan, the United States is engaged in rebalancing its security commitments towards East Asia. While never entirely absent from the region, those wars—and indeed the cold war centered in Europe—have impelled the United States to focus its attentions elsewhere. Although presaged in the George W. Bush Administration, the "Pivot" policy was instituted by President Obama in 2010.[18] While it includes important economic and diplomatic components—most prominently, the Trans-Pacific Partnership trade pact proposal—most of the attention on it has centered on its security implications. While abjuring containment of China, important elements of the policy include substantial increases in US military capabilities deployed near China and a reinvigoration of US alliances at China's periphery.[19]

Above, these specific concerns with US alliances were raised, one by one. More broadly, this web of relations suggests to some in China a broader goal of containment by the United States.[20] Indeed, during the height of the US war in Afghanistan, when US basing in Central Asia expanded quickly, "encirclement" appeared rather comprehensive. Any moves towards multilateralizing the US treaty relationships with South Korea, Japan, and the Philippines would greatly exacerbate this. Expansion of that group to include others in the region such as Malaysia, Vietnam, and Indonesia would be similarly problematic. Taiwan is a case all its own, with any development of a security "alliance" being grounds for war from Beijing's perspective. Although not currently developed institutionally, these concepts do get discussed at times. Former Prime Minister Shinzo Abe of Japan floated proposals for a "concert of democracies" to stabilize security relations in Asia in 2006, including the United States, Australia, India, and Japan. Ongoing developments of missile defense early warning systems in Japan and, potentially, South Korea, Taiwan, and the Philippines might serve to provide operational advantages by creating a network of sensors.[21] There are, however, reasons to temper such concerns. Abe's proposals did not meet with wide support in Australia and elsewhere. There are limited long-range missile defense capabilities outside of Japan. At a broader level, there are impediments for a multilateral alignment for a variety of strategic reasons.[22]

More pessimistically, however, there are some signs of nascent arms race spirals between the United States and China. The term "race" here might be a bit too strong; for over 20 years an "arms stroll" has characterized Asia more generally.[23] There are interactive dynamics in the modernization of the United States and China. Both militaries look at the other as a potential enemy and develop capabilities with the other in mind. This is most readily apparent in the development of capabilities in China that serve area denial and anti-access operational concepts (A2/AD)[24] and the development of AirSea Battle (ASB) operational concepts in the United States. China seeks to deny the US Navy freedom of movement in the seas near to its shores through the deployment of advanced submarines, anti-ship missiles (both cruise and ballistic) and advanced tactical aircraft. The US military seeks to maintain the freedom to deploy in the region through maintaining antisubmarine warfare expertise, developing missile defense capabilities, and ensuring networks of sensors can withstand piecemeal attack. Developing advanced strike capabilities as part of this US response will further heighten Chinese threat perceptions, perpetuating the spiral.[25]

Nuclear weapons and strategic systems present a specific area of concern given the extreme risks that they pose. Again, there is no evidence of any significant arms race between the two. But it is clear that there is a synergy between US missile defense systems and Chinese nuclear modernization. China views even modest quantities of US missile defense interceptors as threatening to its ability to credibly threaten retaliation against any American nuclear escalation.[26] Given the modest size of China's nuclear arsenal (relative to the nearly 5,000 warheads the United States possesses, China is thought to have approximately 240),[27] such concerns are reasonable. Dealing with such a threat through countermeasures should be viable for China, if somewhat uncertain and difficult to assess given classification issues. Similarly, China has concerns regarding advanced precision strike capabilities that might be used to winnow China's strategic arsenal without the United States having to cross the nuclear threshold (at least by some definitions). This, too, serves to challenge China's ability to pose a retaliatory threat to the United States.

The United States avers that its missile defense systems are not aimed to affect the "strategic balance" with either Beijing or Moscow,[28] but are instead intended to reduce the prospects of irrational attacks or coercive threats from North Korea or other so called "rogue" states. In order to do so, however, early warning and other surveillance systems must be forward deployed in the East Asian region. This requires deeper alliance ties with South Korea and Japan, furthering Beijing's sense of encirclement and being subjected to a US-led containment policy.

There are important Sino-American tensions in other strategic realms as well. In space there are clear signs of Chinese development of anti-satellite weaponry (ASAT).[29] Given the relatively large US dependence on space-based systems, Beijing may regard this as a source of comparative military advantage. Both the United States and China possess latent capabilities for such weapons in their missile defense systems. Thankfully, dueling kinetic ASAT tests in 2007–8 have not been repeated as the two sides have avoided the most provocative spirals here. Given the offense-dominant nature of that environment, the militarization of the space environment is inherently unstable.[30] On the positive side, there is some recognition of this on both sides, and the beginnings of some discussions between the two on possible arms control or confidence-building measures. Most attainable in the near term is some international code of conduct derived from the European Union proposals along such lines. Beyond that, Beijing has continued to work with Moscow to hone a Treaty on the Prevention of the Placement of Weapons in Outer Space, the Threat or Use of Force against Outer Space Objects (PPWT). The initial proposals made in 2008 were not viewed particularly favorably by the United States in the absence of verification specifics and with consensus regarding what is and what is not a "weapon" under the provisions of the threat. Ongoing deliberations in China suggest an awareness of these concerns and the prospect of future engagement on these dangerous issues.

A final strategic arena worth noting is the emerging area of cyber security. Given the potential for conflict in this realm to compromise strategic communications systems, to say nothing of directly injuring civilian societies on either side, it merits consideration in any discussion of strategic issues. Both sides have engaged in espionage against the other through such means, and such operations highlight vulnerabilities prone to attack as well as to espionage. There has been substantial concern in the United States regarding Chinese behavior in this regard.[31] The revelations in the United States over the substantial capabilities of the National Security Agency's cyber operations have shown that both sides are engaged in such activities.[32] This too serves to deepen the security rivalry between the two, and it exists in an area where "red lines" are unclear and tangled with those in other realms as well.

Conclusion

As this brief survey shows, Sino-American security relations are likely to be strained in the future. The dynamics listed above, both bilateral and multilateral, highlight a number of areas where security tensions might erupt into violence. Background conditions of arms buildups and strategic developments aimed at the other side increase the prospects for misperceptions and miscalculations.

While there is a wide range of open channels for military diplomacy between the two, these have often lacked substance. In the strategic realm in particular, there is no official channel for such discussions despite approval at the presidential level for such in 2008. In terms of other military engagements, these have often been used as bargaining chips to be offered or rescinded in response to other political agendas. Even with deeper discussions, these will not "solve" any of the deeper problems highlighted above (although they do reduce the prospects for unintentional escalation of problems in any one of them).

As noted at the outset of this chapter, however, it is to other areas in the US–China relationship that we must look for grounds for optimism. Vibrant economic ties put this relationship in a very different category than either the US–USSR or the UK–German relations in the twentieth century. It is on the power of such factors to influence policymakers that our hopes must rest for ensuring the stability in the relationship.

Notes

1 This chapter represents the author's own views and does not officially represent any US government policy.
2 See consistent White Paper language on this point over a sustained period. Most recently, in Information Office of the State Council of the People's Republic of China, "China's National Defense in 2012" (Beijing, 2013).
3 "Trading Up," *The Economist*, January 18, 2014. Data for 2012. Available online at www.economist.com/news/finance-and-economics/21594343-which-country-gets-most-out-international-commerce-trading-up.
4 Miwa Hirono and Manshu Xu, "China's Military Operations Other Than War," *The RUSI Journal* 158, no. 6 (December, 2013): 74–82.
5 Christopher P. Twomey, "After the Summit: Investing in Nuclear Materials Security" (NBR Issue Brief, National Bureau of Asian Research, Seattle, WA, April, 2012).
6 Andrew S. Erickson and Austin M. Strange, "Learning the Ropes in Blue Water," *Proceedings* (United States Naval Institute) 139, no. 4 (April, 2013): 34–8.
7 Brian Weeden, "Through a Glass, Darkly: Chinese, American, and Russian Anti-satellite Testing in Space" (Secure World Foundation, Washington, DC, March 17, 2014); Colin Clark, "'Landmark' Space Policy Shift as China, Others Agree to Space Code of Conduct Talks," *Breaking Defense* (July 23, 2013).
8 David A. Shlapak et al., "A Question of Balance: Political Context and Military Aspects of the China–Taiwan Dispute" (MG-888, RAND, Santa Monica, CA, 2009).

9 Other issues, such as the extent of continental shelf claims for China and the resulting EEZ boundaries between Japan and China are also problematic, but do not involve the United States quite as deeply.
10 Christopher P. Twomey, "Explaining Chinese Foreign Policy toward North Korea: Navigating between the Scylla and Charybdis of Proliferation and Instability," *Journal of Contemporary China* 17, no. 56 (2008): 401–23; Thomas Plant and Ben Rhode, "China, North Korea and the Spread of Nuclear Weapons," *Survival* 55, no. 2 (April, 2013): 61–80.
11 For the best dissection of these issues see the series of assessments in the *China Leadership Monitor*, co-authored by Michael Swaine and various co-authors. Michael D. Swaine, "Perceptions of an Assertive China," *China Leadership Monitor* 32 (2010); Michael D. Swaine, "China's Assertive Behavior, Part One: On 'Core Interests,'" *China Leadership Monitor* 34 (2011): 1–25; Michael D. Swaine and M. Taylor Fravel, "China's Assertive Behavior Part Two: The Maritime Periphery," *China Leadership Monitor* 35 (2011).
12 M. Taylor Fravel, "China's Strategy in the South China Sea," *Contemporary Southeast Asia* 33, no. 3 (2011): 292–319.
13 See for instance Raul Pedrozo, "Close Encounters at Sea: The USNS Impeccable Incident," *Naval War College Review* 62, no. 3 (June, 2009): 101–11.
14 Kenneth Arrow, "A Difficulty in the Concept of Social Welfare," *Journal of Political Economy* 58, no. 4 (August, 1950): 328–46.
15 John J. Mearsheimer, "The Gathering Storm: China's Challenge to US Power in Asia," *The Chinese Journal of International Politics* 3, no. 4 (2010): 381.
16 Nan Li, "The Evolution of China's Naval Strategy and Capabilities: From 'Near Coast' and 'Near Seas' to 'Far Seas,'" in *The Chinese Navy: Expanding Capabilities, Evolving Roles*, ed. Philip Saunders, Christopher Yung, Michael Swain, and Andrew Yang (Washington, DC: National Defense University, 2011).
17 Alastair Iain Johnston, "How New and Assertive Is China's New Assertiveness?" *International Security* 37, no. 4 (2013): 7–48.
18 Robert S. Ross, "The Problem with the Pivot: Obama's New Asia Policy Is Unnecessary and Counterproductive," *Foreign Affairs* 91 (2012): 83.
19 Kurt M. Campbell and Ely Ratner, "Far Eastern Promises: Why Washington Should Focus on Asia," *Foreign Affairs* 93, no. 3 (May/June, 2014).
20 Andrew J. Nathan and Andrew Scobell, "How China Sees America: The Sum of Beijing's Fears," *Foreign Affairs* 91, no. 5 (September/October, 2012): 32–47.
21 See recent congressional attention to the issue.
22 John Duffield, "Asia-Pacific Security Institutions in Comparative Perspective," in *International Relations Theory and the Asia-Pacific*, ed. G. John Ikenberry and Michael Mastanduno (New York: Columbia University Press, 2003).
23 As far as this author can tell, the term was first used in William Branigin, "As China Builds Arsenal and Bases, Asians Wary of 'Rogue in the Region,'" *Washington Post* (March 31, 1993), p. A21.
24 That term, however, is not used in China, and it is unclear what the appropriate concept is for the PLA. Christopher P. Twomey, "Tailoring A2/D2 Equivalents: Counterintervention, Assassin's Mace, System of Systems, and the Three Non's—Non-linear, Non-contact, Asymmetric," in *Assessing the PLA under Hu Jintao*, ed. David Lai, Roy Kamphausen, and Travis Tanner (Carlisle, PA: Strategic Studies Institute, 2014).
25 Indeed, there is already clear evidence that the Chinese watch such US developments very closely. Acton's report was closely read in Beijing: James M. Acton, "Silver Bullet?: Asking the Right Questions about Conventional Prompt Global Strike" (Carnegie Endowment for International Peace, Washington, DC, 2013).
26 Michael Chase and Christopher P. Twomey, "Chinese Views on Missile Defense," in *Missile Defense: The Fourth Wave and Beyond*, ed. Catherine M. Kelleher and Peter J. Dombrowski (Palo Alto, CA: Stanford University Press, 2015, forthcoming).
27 Robert. S. Norris and Hans. M. Kristensen, "Chinese Nuclear Forces, 2010," *Bulletin of the Atomic Scientists* 66, no. 6 (November 1, 2010): 134–41.
28 "Ballistic Missile Defense Review Report" (Department of Defense, Washington, DC, February, 2010).
29 Weeden, "Through a Glass, Darkly"; Clark, "'Landmark' Space Policy Shift."
30 James C. Moltz, *Asia's Space Race: National Motivations, Regional Dynamics, and Global Implications* (New York: Columbia University Press, 2011).
31 Nicole Perlroth, "Electronic Security a Worry in an Age of Digital Espionage," *The New York Times* (February 10, 2012).
32 David D. E. Sanger and Nicole Perlroth, "NSA Breached Chinese Servers Seen as Security Threat," *The New York Times* (March 22, 2014).

6
Russia and Chinese security

Yu-Shan Wu

The Soviet Union was the staunchest supporter of the communist movement in China since the founding of the Chinese Communist Party (CCP) in 1921. Twenty-eight years later, the CCP defeated the ruling Kuomintang (KMT) in the Chinese Civil War and conquered mainland China, driving the KMT government to the island of Taiwan. The People's Republic of China (PRC) was established with the blessing of its Soviet comrades. However, the fraternal relationship between the two communist behemoths gave way in the 1950s to ferocious ideological debate and open armed conflict in the 1960s, as China steered away from Russia's grip in pursuit of its own version of socialist development, and competed with Moscow for leadership of the world communist movement. The Zhenbao Dao border conflict in 1969 was the climax of Sino-Soviet antagonism.

Before its ultimate collapse, the Soviet Union attempted to improve its relation with the PRC by addressing Beijing's security concerns. Normalization of bilateral relations was announced when the general secretary of the Communist Party of the Soviet Union Mikhail Gorbachev visited China in May 1989, immediately before the Tiananmen crackdown. After the collapse of the Soviet Union, and the reorientation of Russia towards the West under Boris Yeltsin, it seemed that the divergent development of Russia and China might put an end to the short rapprochement between Beijing and Moscow. The opposite turned out to be true.

Ideology never determines international relations. During the Cold War period a similar ideological stance did not bring Beijing and Moscow together. After the Cold War was over, different domestic systems did not drive China and Russia apart. In the early 1990s, it took only two years for Boris Yeltsin and the Russian Atlanticists to realize that the West would never accept Russia as one of their own members, and would always guard against it. NATO would not only survive the end of the Cold War, it would expand eastward to the Russian border. As Yeltsin turned to Beijing for support, he was embraced by a post-Tiananmen Communist leadership that had successfully defied Western prediction of imminent regime collapse, and yet still found itself greatly isolated internationally. The rapprochement between the two great continental powers resumed. In the following years, as the US continued to put pressure on China and Russia, their relationship warmed up and gradually developed into a quasi-alliance.

Although the post-Cold War international system has been the prime mover of Sino-Russian relations, there are other forces bearing on the relationship. The two sides have complementary needs in arms sales and energy cooperation. These are the positive factors. However, the history of border disputes, a fear of "yellow peril" on the Russian part, a power transition that favors China, and other disagreements tend to limit Russo-Chinese collaboration. These are the negative factors. However, it turned out that under the overall international structure, namely with the US putting pressure on both China and Russia, proactively or in reaction to the behaviors of the two countries, the positive factors overwhelmed the negative factors, and the Sino-Russian relationship consolidated as time went by. Whether this "axis of convenience" can withstand the inherent rivalry between the two great continental powers remains an issue of academic debate.[1]

This chapter is divided into five parts. The first discusses the overall strategic picture that has shaped the Sino-Russian relation to this date. The second focuses on how the border issue was put to rest. The third touches on energy cooperation. The fourth deals with arms sales between the two continental military powers. The fifth section asks where the Sino-Russian relation is going.

The strategic picture

There was a short period of time after the birth of the Russian Federation as an independent state when Moscow decisively tilted to the West. This was the heyday of Atlanticism. However, Yeltsin failed to receive the promised support from Western countries, and his shock therapy reform sent the Russian economy into a tailspin. The Russian president decisively shifted to Eurasianism in 1994. As Yeltsin turned to Beijing for support, he was embraced by the post-Tiananmen Communist leadership that had successfully defied Western predictions of imminent regime collapse after the nationwide Tiananmen protests and the fall of European communism, and now found itself greatly isolated internationally. The delinking of China's MFN status from its human rights performance in 1994 offered little comfort, for the US continued to view the PRC as the last bastion of international communism in the new world order under American hegemony. In September 1994, Yeltsin and his Chinese counterpart Jiang Zemin met in Moscow and declared that China and Russia had forged a "constructive partnership." Two years later, at a Shanghai summit, Russia and China announced the formation of a "partnership of strategic coordination" (*zhanlue xiezuo huoban guanxi*), since enshrined as a "comprehensive strategic collaborative partnership," the most important of all 54 formal Chinese "partnerships." Yeltsin's strategic turn became most obvious when he sacked his pro-West Foreign Minister Andrei Kozyrev and replaced him with the Eurasia-centered pragmatist Yevgenii Primakov in January 1996.[2] However, it should be noted that Russia ultimately yielded to the overwhelming power of the West during this period of time, despite its call for a multipolar world and an anti-hegemonic coalition.[3]

In the latter half of the 1990s, the volatile relations between the US and the two great continental powers boosted Beijing-Moscow relations. The 1995–6 missile crisis in the Taiwan Strait and the 1999 bombing of the PRC's embassy in Belgrade by NATO's air force bruised US-PRC relations, while NATO's eastward expansion to include former Soviet bloc countries and military operation in Kosovo pushed Russia into a corner.[4] No wonder China and Russia signed the Sino-Russian Treaty of Good-Neighborly and Friendly Cooperation, and upgraded the Shanghai Five group with the Declaration of Shanghai Cooperation Organization in the summer of 2001.[5] These acts can be viewed as "soft balancing" or "quasi-alliance formation" against the US.[6] The intention of Russia and China can be clearly seen in their championship of "a multipolar world," and the rejection of "a one-dimensional model dominated by the group of most developed countries and backed up by the economic and military might of the US and NATO."[7]

This strategic picture took a turn in the early 2000s. The September 11, 2001 attacks on US domestic targets by al-Qaeda and the resultant "war on terror" greatly reduced American pressure on Moscow and Beijing. Washington's criticism of Russia's suppression of Chechen separatists and China's stifling of Uyghur independence movements rapidly died down. This had to do with the ostensibly common roots of the three movements that were plaguing the three countries. Furthermore, both Russia and China were forthcoming in offering help to counter international terrorism. Moscow shared with the US intelligence about Islamist terrorist activities in Afghanistan and the Middle East and raised no objection when Washington sought to establish military bases in Kyrgyzstan and Uzbekistan.[8] Later on, Russia only meekly objected to the American invasion of Iraq. Even the three "color revolutions" in Georgia (November 2003), Ukraine (November 2004), and Kyrgyzstan (March 2005) and NATO's second eastward expansion into former Soviet satellites and ex-Soviet republics in March 2004 did not arouse strong reaction from Moscow.[9] For Vladimir Putin, Yeltsin's successor, Russia simply did not have the capabilities to pursue foreign policy goals in defiance of the West at the time.[10] Russia had to turn inward, implement economic reform, gain strength, and then come back at a later time. This can be characterized as the "economization of foreign policy."[11] There were striking similarities between Russia's foreign policy in the early Putin period and China's post-Tiananmen posture as embodied in Deng Xiaoping's motto of "keep a cool head, maintain a low profile, never take the lead, and prepare for major actions."[12] In the early 2000s, both Beijing and Moscow adopted a low-profile foreign policy towards the West. This, together with Washington's preoccupation with fighting international terrorism, goes a long way in explaining the relative tranquility in the East-West relations.

The "truce" did not last long. In mid-2006 Russia dramatically changed its foreign policy stance towards the West. Putin began vigorously criticizing US unilateralism and obsession with the use of force, the planned deployment of missile defense systems in Central Europe, the eastward expansion of NATO, the imposition of the West's development models on unwilling countries, and the "archaic, undemocratic, and awkward" international economic system that was under the control of a small number of developed countries.[13] The relationship became so bad that hours after Barack Obama won the presidential race in November 2008, President Dmitri Medvedev threatened to place Russian missiles in Kaliningrad to counter the US missile defense system in Eastern Europe.[14]

The negative trend was temporarily halted when Obama "reset" the US-Russian relationship, suspended the plan to deploy anti-missile systems in the Czech Republic and Poland, and stopped the process of expanding NATO to include Ukraine and Georgia. The personal relation between Obama and his Russian counterpart Medvedev, a protégé of Prime Minister Putin, was much better than that between their two predecessors. However, the Russo-Georgian War in the summer of 2008 dealt a serious blow to this reset relation. On the Sino-American front, the relationship deteriorated rapidly, with the US backing its Southeast Asian and Japanese allies in their territorial disputes with China since 2009. The sinking of a South Korean frigate by the North and the shelling of an offshore Korean island prompted the US to send naval forces to the area, which again antagonized Beijing. Finally, Obama declared a US strategic "pivot" to Asia, with China the obvious (albeit officially denied) target. The latter half of the 2000s thus looked like a replay of the latter half of the 1990s, only this time the US was facing a reinvigorated Russia and a rising China that was about to overtake Japan as the world's second largest economy. The mechanism of the US and the West pressurizing the two continental powers and prompting their collaboration shifted into high gear.

This pattern of relations continued into the early 2010s. Faced with a more assertive China, Japan responded with electing into office a reborn Shinzo Abe, who championed military buildup, visited Yasukuni Shrine, and intended to rewrite Japan's "Peace Constitution" and restore the country's right to wage war in "collective defense." The US was dragged by Japan into a more conflictual position with China. On the European front, the election of a pro-Russia president

Viktor Yanukovych intensified the competition between Europe and Russia for Ukraine. The abrupt turnabout of Yanukovych's policy away from Europe prompted massive and sustained demonstrations in the Maidan Square of the capital Kyiv, which ended with the toppling of the government and the fleeing of Yanukovych. Russia responded by annexing Crimea and Sevastopol, which have Russian majorities. Eastern Ukraine was embroiled in Russia-aided separatism. The US and Europe vehemently contested Russia's move. Towards the middle of the 2010s, in both East Asia and Eastern Europe, one finds geopolitical conflicts between the Eurasian continental powers and the US-led maritime alliances. It is only natural that China and Russia would scratch each other's backs when faced with Western pressure. This includes Russia's harsh attitude towards Japan, and China's "understanding" of the complex historical situation in the annexation of Crimea.[15] A pattern had been established firmly for China and Russia to help each other whenever there is trouble between either of them and the Western world. The West-induced collaboration between the two countries remained a prominent phenomenon. After the visit by China's newly elected president Xi Jinping to Russia in March 2013, the first state visit for the Chinese leader, discussion of elevating the Sino-Russian strategic partnership to a formal alliance abounded. It is obvious that political synchronization between the two countries has been increasing.

The border issue: put to rest

The expansion of the Russian Empire into the Far East touched off a series of conflicts between Russia and the Qing Dynasty in the eighteenth and nineteenth centuries. Through the Treaty of Aigun (1858) and the Convention of Peking (1860), Qing China ceded huge areas of territories to Russia.[16] These "unequal treaties" were never formally recognized by the succeeding Republic of China or the People's Republic of China governments. The 1968–9 border conflict between China and the Soviet Union added to the historical animosity between the two countries over the disputed lands. After Gorbachev extended an olive branch to China in his Vladivostok speech in 1986, bilateral relations began to thaw, culminating in Gorbachev's state visit to Beijing in 1989. In the aftermath of the Tiananmen crackdown, a besieged China sought friendship from Moscow by showing willingness to recognize the existing border between the two countries. This resulted in two demarcation agreements (1991, 1994) on the eastern and western sections of the border, with the first signed hurriedly between China and the Soviet Union before the latter's collapse. It is clear that the need to elicit Russian support at the difficult time of international isolation brought Jiang to the conclusion that the border issue should be cast aside to facilitate bilateral relations with Russia.[17] Here one clearly sees the impact of external threats to the development of Sino-Russian relations.

With the basic principle laid down, namely to recognize the border status quo, the two sides moved to the operational level, and signed various executive agreements on detailed demarcation (1997, 1999), border cooperation (1995), and common economic usage of islets in the border river (1999). The climax of this process was the Sino-Russian Treaty of Good-Neighborly and Friendly Cooperation signed in July 2001. Article Six of the Treaty states that neither party has "territorial claim on the other," and that both are resolved to build "the border between the two countries into one where ever-lasting peace and friendship prevail" (*yongjiu heping shidai youhao*). The sincerity to reach a genuine rapprochement and cast the border issue off the road towards Sino-Russian cooperation is beyond doubt. The momentum reflects the need for the countries to cooperate when facing mounting pressure from the West.

After 2001, only two border issues remained between Russia and China, accounting for 2 percent of the 4,195-kilometer borderline. The Abagaitu Islet (ostrov Bol'shoi) in the Argun River and the Heixiazi-Yinlong Dao (ostrov Bol'shoi Ussuriiskii and ostrov Tarabarov) at the confluence of the Ussuri and Amur Rivers. The latter was particularly controversial because it lies south of the main navigation route of the Amur and thus should be, and was, Chinese territory according to the Peking Treaty, despite a map attached to the treaty that indicated otherwise.[18] The Soviet Union occupied Heixiazi-Yinlong in 1929 during the height of the conflict over the Manchurian Chinese Eastern Railway (*zhong donglu shijian*). This was never accepted by China. By the time Russia and China were settling their border issues in the 1990s, the Ussuriiskii-Tarabarov Island had long been integrated into Kharbarovsk and Russia's local authorities were vehemently opposed to giving any territorial concessions to the Chinese.[19] This was one of the major reasons why the border issue was not completely solved in the 1990s.

Russia's local governments were worried about other issues. The far eastern area of Russia was sparsely populated (with a rapidly diminishing population) and resource rich, while the adjacent Chinese territories were much more densely populated and lacking natural resources. This drove fear among Russians of a "Yellow Peril," as shown in the influx of a large number of illegal Chinese immigrants into the Russian Far East.[20] Rising Russian nationalism was yet another factor that grew under the semi-competitive political system of the country. Russians held stereotypes of the Chinese people that were much more unfavorable than the stereotypes held by the Chinese about the Russians.[21] These factors mitigated against territorial concessions to China.

Solution to the remaining territorial issues came at a time when Moscow contemplated a change of an oil pipeline project originally designed to provide Russian crude to China exclusively. As the route was shifted away from China and moved to the Pacific coast under energetic lobbying by the Japanese, Russia compensated China on the border issue. Initially Moscow refused to give an inch of land under its control (June 2001). Later it agreed to make only marginal concessions (roughly 80 square kilometers of Heixiazi). A breakthrough was made in January 2002 when both sides showed some flexibility in their territorial demands. Finally an even division of Heixiazi was accepted as the principle, with Yinlong completely ceded to China. According to a complementary agreement on the eastern section of the Sino-Russian border signed in October 2004, the PRC gained a total of 337 square kilometers of land previously under Russian administration.[22]

From the way the border issue between China and Russia was solved, one notices the working of two major factors: the international environment and the linkage of issues. The pressure from the West and the need to elicit Russian support led post-Tiananmen China to recognize the historical territorial losses in the border negotiations of the 1990s, while the linkage between the pipeline and the border issues led Russia to make territorial concessions to China on Heixiazi-Yinlong (Ussuriiskii-Tarabarov). Even in the 2004 case, one still finds the international factor looming large in the background, prompting Russia and China to solve their border issues and develop their relations in the face of external pressure.[23]

Energy cooperation: intensified

Russia is the world's second largest exporter of petroleum, while by October 2013 China had become the biggest oil importer by surpassing the US. Russia seeks a reliable buyer who can pay on schedule, and China needs to diversify its imports and reduce dependence on the Middle East and Africa where politics has always been turbulent and supply unstable. China can provide Russia with both market and capital, equipment and exploratory capabilities. The long border means oil can be transported much more conveniently than by sea. There are no political differences that can hinder the trade between the two. China has grown its economy much more quickly than any other major economy in the world, increasing its needs for oil rapidly; for its part, Russia is determined to use its energy resources to build a high profile not only in energy but in the international system in general. It is true that there is a dispute over price: China seeks a replacement cost for coal, which is abundant and cheap, while Russia seeks a replacement cost from Europe, which pays top dollar. Nevertheless, supply and demand find their equilibrium. In short, Russia and China are natural companions in energy cooperation. It would be odd if the two did not develop a close relationship in energy.[24] However, if we look into the actual development of this relationship, we find the overall strategic structure playing a vital role that goes beyond economic calculations.

The Sino-Russian energy relationship developed through four stages.[25] During the first stage, because Russia heavily tilted towards the West and China was still self-sufficient in oil, there was a lack of interest in building up energy relations between the two. In 1996, the Sino-Russian energy relationship moved into the second stage. In that year Yeltsin shifted to Eurasianism while China had (since 1993) become a net oil importer, hence the intensified interest in exploring the possibility of building a pipeline from Angarsk to China's northeast.[26] In 2000, the election of Putin to the presidency ushered in a new era. Putin intended to develop Russia into a "super energy power," use energy sector growth as the engine for overall economic growth, transform Russia from an energy exporter to a rule maker on the international energy market, and regain the country's international influence and prestige.[27] His government laid out a grand plan in "Energy Strategy of Russia until 2020" to realize these production goals. The Far East was considered a vital area for the fulfillment of Putin's vision. The Angarsk-Daqing pipeline was adopted for priority consideration, with an expected yearly transport volume of 20 to 30 million tones. However, because of very active Japanese lobbying and recalculation of costs and benefits by the Russian government, the Angarsk-Daqing line was first replaced by the Angarsk-Nakhodka line that veered north and ended at Nakhodka, a port on the Russian Pacific Coast, instead of Daqing in northeast China, and then by the Taishet-Nakhodka line that branched out at Skovorodino to connect to Daqing. Its main route nevertheless still ended at Nakhodka to supply oil to the whole East Asian region (East Siberia-Pacific Ocean Oil Pipeline, ESPO).[28] In order to accommodate China's needs, Russia promised to supply oil from West Siberia to Xinjiang. The Skovorodino-Daqing spur was completed in 2010, reported to be operational in 2012. Also, it was at this time that Russia made territorial concessions on Heixiazi-Yinlong.

The fourth stage started with Putin being reelected as president, and his ambitious energy plan reaffirmed. During this latest period of time, because of quarrels between Russia and Ukraine, and between Russia and Belarus, over gas prices and delays in payments, energy supplies to Europe via these countries were disturbed, causing great inconvenience and an acute sense of uncertainty among Europeans. Later on, the Russo-Georgian War in 2008 and the Euromaidan Revolution in Ukraine in 2014 caused great tension between Russia and Europe, making both sides worried about security in energy supply and demand. This situation prompted not only the Europeans to seek an alternative source of energy, but also the Russians to shift to more reliable customers in Asia.[29] From stage one through four, both the demand and supply side of Sino-Russian energy relations became increasingly more interested in this relationship, because of either intrinsic needs or the overall strategic condition. Mutual benefits and Western pressure drove China and Russia ever closer.

There remain limits to the energy relation between Russia and China. For one thing, Europe remains Russia's main energy export market. Both economic and strategic considerations require Russia to keep hold of it. On the Chinese side, Russia is a good supplement to the Middle East as a source of imports, but not as a replacement. Russia is interested in linking export of energy to the export of its electricity and nuclear power facilities, energy equipment, and industrial technology, while China is only interested in importing energy and diversifying sources. Russia furthermore intends to solicit Chinese capital to develop an integrated energy supply system in East Siberia, and grow the local economy, a goal not shared by the Chinese.[30] It is also doubtful whether Chinese energy imports will grow incessantly, as Beijing is most interested in developing its own resources. As a major portion of the oil demand is for power generation, it can be satisfied by nuclear power and other energy sources. Furthermore, the increase in the demand for oil is distributed unevenly across China's regions. The fastest demand growth comes from south-east China, which is very difficult for Russian pipelines to reach. As in territorial disputes, "China threat" also haunts Russian policy makers in energy. East Siberia and the Russian Far East are the areas that provide and transport Russian energy to China. Presumably these areas can benefit from the energy trade. However, they are also most vulnerable to "Chinese irredentism" and "overflow of surplus population from China."[31] There remains a deep fear, particularly among Russia's local elite, of the "China threat."

Despite the limits and constraints, energy cooperation between Russia and China has grown in leaps and bounds. In 2013, Russia accounted for 9 percent of China's imports of crude oil.[32] It had risen to an unprecedented 12 percent in early 2014. During Xi Jinping's visit to Moscow in March 2013, a series of energy deals were signed that included a pledge by Rosneft to triple its oil deliveries to China from 300,000 barrels per day (b/d) to as much as one million b/d, which is the amount that Saudi Arabia, China's top crude oil supplier, delivered in 2012. In June 2014, the two countries came to an agreement on a $400 billion deal for the delivery of 38 billion cubic meters of natural gas from Russia to China starting in 2018. The driving force behind these energy deals is obviously mutual economic needs, but the two countries are also attracted to each other due to the realization that alternative suppliers and markets are less reliable. Russia's precarious relation with Europe, and China's fear of turbulence in the Middle East, provide powerful incentives for the two to cling ever closer in energy, the differences in policy goals, deep-rooted cultural prejudices and myths, and historical suspicions notwithstanding.

Arms sales: locked to each other

Russia is the largest supplier of sophisticated weapon systems to China, accounting for the majority of China's arms import throughout the years since the early 1990s. The volume of arms sales fluctuated over time, basically in sync with the overall strategic relationship between the two countries and their mutual needs. As in energy, one finds four stages of arms sales, which roughly correspond to the first and second terms of Yeltsin, the first term of Putin, and his second term and thereafter. At the first stage Russia tilted decisively to the West, and put arms sales to China on the backburner. Yeltsin and Kozyrev were less interested in honoring a Soviet-era deal with China than impressing the US and the West, which had imposed an arms embargo on China in the aftermath of the Tiananmen crackdown. Although the arms sales that involved 72 Su-27SK fighters went through eventually, there was much disgruntlement on the Chinese side. Following the improvement of overall relations between the two countries from constructive to strategic partnership, arms sales to China accelerated. In 1995, China agreed to pay $1.4 billion for the technology and licenses to manufacture the Su-27s in Shenyang.[33] With the blessing of Yeltsin, Russia sold large-scale sophisticated weapon systems to China in 1999 that included Su-30MKK multi-role fighters, S-300PMU-2 surface-to-air missile systems, and Tor-M1field anti-air missiles.[34] In the 1990s the Russian economy was experiencing a prolonged period of traumatic transition, and the government ran huge budget deficits. Arms exports constituted the largest source of government revenue, and China and India were the two most important buyers. Economic necessities dictated Russia's arms export policy and its arms relation with China.

After Putin was elected president, Russia continued selling large amounts of weapons to China at the annual volume of $2 billion to $3.5 billion.[35] In 2007 there was a dramatic drop of arms sales, reflecting a shorter list of sophisticated weapons that Russia was able to sell and China willing to buy, a series of disputes over property rights violations and technology transfer issues, and China's shift to self-reliance.[36] After making substantial purchases from Russia, China began to reverse engineer a host of Russian weapons such as the Su-27 fighter and the NORINCO T-90 tank. Some of the products were sold on the international market, to the chagrin of the Russians. China also launched its indigenous submarine program that produced diesel- and nuclear-powered attack submarines, as well as ballistic missile submarines. As the Chinese defense industry had matched Soviet-era technologies, while Russia refused to sell China its most advanced weapons, the arms transfer between the two countries was stranded. For the Chinese, it seemed that large purchases of Russian weapon systems were no longer necessary or desirable.

Finally, there came a surge of weapons sales in 2013, as Russian manufacturers figured they needed large orders from the Chinese side to sustain the necessary level of R&D activities to explore higher-end products, and the Chinese apparently ran into technical difficulties with their jet engines. The 2013 sale included four Lada-class attack submarines and 24 Su-35 fighter jets. These were the most sophisticated weapons that the Russians were able to offer, and their Chinese customers were eager to buy. This line of weapons was developed with funds from the sale of less advanced systems and their production licenses in an earlier period. Without the Su-27 sale there would be no Su-35, and no Lada-class submarine would be produced without the Chinese procurement of the Kilo-class. Thus Russia found no alternative to selling its most sophisticated weapon systems to China for funds necessary to sustain its arms industry. As India was equally interested in the Russian arms and apparently less keen to reproduce them, and would need weapons at the same level to compete with the Chinese, Russia was in a good position to make similar sales to India. However, as China, the principal buyer, has significantly developed its own capabilities in designing and producing sophisticated weapon systems, and would want nothing less than the best Russia can offer, the arms transfer relationship between the two countries cannot continue as in the 1990s and early 2000s.[37] With Russia no longer capable, and the West not willing, to supply state-of-the-art systems, self-reliance will be China's main strategy in the future, as in its successful space program.

It seems that the arms transfer relation between Russia and China reflects basic economic factors and strategic rivalry between the two countries. Russia needs to sustain its arms industry and finance its government budget while China desperately wants to modernize its military. The inherent suspicion between the two countries prevented the sale of state-of-the-art weapons by Russia to the Chinese, as was the case between 2007 and 2013. However, such a view overlooks the big strategic picture. The fact that the two potential adversaries are locked in an arms transfer relationship owes much to the working of the overall strategic structure: both China and Russia are shunned by the West. Russia has been considered a military threat in decline, and China a threat on rapid rise. There could be no close military collaboration or sale of sophisticated weapon systems between the West and either of the two continental powers. This being the case, arms sales can only be conducted between Russia and China. It is within this framework that one finds the economic needs, drive for modernization, and inherent suspicion between the two countries at work. Arms sales, like all other security relations between China and Russia, is embedded in an international system in which the West exerts great pressure on the two continental powers and pushes them together. The fact that the arms sale between Russia and China could develop to such a high level of quantity and quality speaks volumes about the strategic structure in which the two countries find themselves.

Where is the Sino-Russian relation going?

The above analysis argues that despite geopolitical rivalry, historical mistrust, cultural prejudices, and Russia's fear of Chinese irredentism and population overflow, Sino-Russian relations have grown steadily since the 1990s, and the primary reason for this has been Western pressure that propelled the two continental powers together. But will this situation last? For those who see the weaknesses in the Sino-Russian bilateral relation, their strategic partnership is fragile and prone to disruption. For those who see the strengths in the relation, however, the partnership is robust.

Doubters of the "robustness theme" argue that the Sino-Russian relation has not reached the level the two countries' geographical proximity and economic complementarity might imply, and that the forces driving China and Russia apart outweigh the forces propelling them together.[38] The relation between the two countries is characterized as "strategic parallelism without partnership or passion."[39] The arms sale is shown to be a case of economic interest dictating policy against Russia's national interest and the Russian views on this are ambivalent at best.[40] In an edited volume that provides comprehensive review of all important aspects of the Sino-Russian relationship, *The Future of China-Russia Relations: Asia in the New Millennium*, the contributors tend to agree that the Sino-Russian partnership has conspicuously lacked strategic cohesiveness and ideological affinity; that it is plagued by mutual suspicion and mistrust; that it increasingly favors China at the expense of Russia; and that it will be undermined by the rapid rise of Chinese power and the relegation of Russia to the role of a junior partner.[41] There is a similar theme in Bobo Lo's *Axis of Convenience: Moscow, Beijing and the New Geopolitics*. In short, many observers in the West question the validity of official claims by China and Russia about the robustness of their strategic partnership.[42]

Believers of the "robustness theme" typically emphasize the importance of the US factor, as shown in the book title of *The Next Great Clash: China and Russia vs. the United States*.[43] The Sino-Russian partnership is understood in the context of an international system in which the US attempts to exert hegemonic control and impose its political values on the world. The partnership is intended to remedy this situation.[44] It is emphasized that Russia and China are equal partners in their pursuit of a multipolar world and in their defiance of unipolar hegemony.[45] For some Russian scholars, the Russo-Chinese partnership can even be seen as a powerful response to the US's pivot to Asia, and to the lack of appreciation by American leaders of Russia's role in the Asia-Pacific.[46] It is also emphasized that for many Russian policy makers an alliance with China would bring about control of both heartland and rim, both Eurasia and Asia-Pacific, and hence the chance for Russia to reassert its claim to be a great power.[47] The usefulness of a closer relationship with Beijing is testified to by the consistent policy of all the top leaders in Moscow: Gorbachev, Yeltsin, and Putin, apart from a brief period in the early 1990s.[48] On the Chinese side, not only is the robustness of the Sino-Russian partnership affirmed, there is even lively discussion of elevating the partnership to a formal alliance against the US.[49]

Both the doubters and believers of the robustness theme point out important aspects of Sino-Russian relations. Although up to this point, the partnership has remained robust, whether it will remain so hinges to a large extent on the ability of the two countries to handle the shifting balance of power between them, and on the policy by the West. China, as the major challenger to US hegemony and prime target of America's pivot, will stick to its special relation with Russia, so the robustness of the Sino-Russian partnership hinges on Moscow. Until now Russia has felt much greater pressure from the US than from China, hence its quasi-alliance with the latter against the former. If China is gradually catching up with the US in economic power and becoming stronger militarily, Russia will face a different situation. A destabilizing factor in horizontal alliance is the rapid growth of a member *vis-à-vis* other member(s). China's rise would fulfill that condition, and Russia may hence shift to oppose the rising giant on its border. For this really to happen, Moscow has to feel much less pressured by the US and NATO, so that comparatively speaking China would become a greater threat, and a shift of strategy is warranted.[50] As the US is increasingly aware of the threat posed by a rising China, it might be willing to sacrifice certain interests in Eastern Europe and the former Soviet Union (such as Ukraine and Georgia) in order to induce Moscow to think the hitherto unthinkable. One thing is clear, though: if Washington insists on expanding NATO into former Soviet territories, no Russian leader would be able to extricate the country from the ready partnership offered by Beijing. Russia's relation with the US thus hinges on Washington's willingness to accommodate Moscow's core needs.

After Russia's annexation of Crimea in March 2014, the prospect of an amicable relation between the West and Russia seems as remote as can be imagined. The background of the Ukrainian crisis is intensified competition between Europe and Russia to integrate Ukraine into their respective systems: the EU and the Eurasian Union. When Ukrainian President Yanukovych made an abrupt turnabout on his previous decision to sign an Association Agreement with the EU, the Maidan Revolution began. As it is unthinkable for a post-Soviet republic to join both the EU and the Eurasian Union, the West and Russia are trapped in a zero-sum game. The deep East–West divide in Ukraine and the history of bitter rivalry between the two political camps in the country set the stage for confrontation. While the EU finds it totally unacceptable that an independent sovereign nation in Europe was forced to side with Russia and amputated territorially when it refused to do so, Russia views Europe's move to take Ukraine away as encroaching on not only Russia's security, but its history, culture, and identity. The inability for the two sides to compromise beforehand and their indulgence in supporting proxies to fight an ugly political battle not only ruin the chances of peace and security in the region, but engulf all the nations on the two sides of the divide in Europe. This being the case, Russia would find absolutely no reason to turn away from China, no matter how strong the latter grows economically and militarily, for Moscow is being besieged by the West, and the premise of Russia's strategy reorientation is conspicuously absent.

China benefits from the tension between Russia and the West, for it produces a loyal ally on the Chinese side whenever there is any conflict between China and the West. This situation would add to the pressure on the US in East Asia. At a time of economic difficulty and shrinking military budget, it is unlikely that the US would be able to sustain a double-front confrontation with both Russia on the European theater and China on the Asia-Pacific theater. Historically China benefitted from the conflict between the West and the Soviet Union: that is how it got to play pivot in the great strategic triangle. The surge of international terrorism against the US was a functional equivalent to the Soviet Union for Beijing during a time when it was steaming ahead with rapid economic growth and gaining the potential to challenge the US hegemony. Preoccupation with the war on terror on the part of the US exempted China from direct American pressure for a precious decade. The eruption of the Russo-West conflict over Ukraine later served the same function, acting to cement the quasi-alliance between China and Russia, and providing leverage for Beijing in its competition with the US. The chances of Russia's strategic reorientation from the East to the West would have to wait much longer, as anxiety in Moscow over the rise of China dissipates amid fear of Russia's siege by the West.

Glossary

Abagaitu Islet 阿巴该图洲渚
Aigun Treaty 瑷珲条约
Argun River 额尔古纳河
Daqing 大庆
Heixiazi Dao 黑瞎子岛
Kuomintang 国民党
Yinlong Dao 银龙岛
Yongjiu heping, shidai youhao 永久和平，世代友好
Zhanlue xiezuo huoban guanxi 战略协作伙伴关系
Zhenbao Dao 珍宝岛
Zhongdonglu shijian 中东路事件

Notes

1 For the characterization of the Russo-Chinese relation as "axis of convenience," see Bobo Lo, *Axis of Convenience: Moscow, Beijing and the New Geopolitics*, Washington, DC: Brookings Institution Press, 2008.
2 Robert Legvold, "Introduction," in Robert Legvold (ed.), *Russian Foreign Policy in the Twenty-First Century and the Shadow of the Past*, New York: Columbia University Press, 2007, pp. 3–34; Tom Casier, "Putin's Policy towards the West: Reflections on the Nature of Russian Foreign Policy," *International Politics* 43, no. 3, July 2006, pp. 386–7.
3 The height of Russia's protest against the West came during the Kosovo crisis, when in June 1999 Russian troops dashed into Kosovo and occupied Pristina Airport, in violation of international agreements. However, this move did not alter the overall picture in Kosovo, as NATO kept control of the province and ultimately watched it declare independence. For Russia, Kosovo was the prelude to Crimea.
4 Christopher Williams, "Russia's Closer Ties with China: The Geo-Politics of Energy and the Implications for the European Union," *European Studies* 27, 2009, p. 153.
5 The 2001 Sino-Russian Treaty unmistakably targets the US, despite the official insistence that it is based on "no alliance, no confrontation, and not geared towards a third party" (*bu jiemeng, bu duikang, bu zhendui disanguo*).
6 For a discussion of whether the 2001 Treaty constitutes a Sino-Russian alliance, see Robert H. Donaldson, "The Arms Trade in Russian-Chinese Relations: Identity, Domestic Politics, and Geopolitical Positioning," *International Studies Quarterly* 47, 2003, 710.
7 See the 1997 Russo-Chinese "Joint Declaration on a Multipolar World and the Formation of a New International Order," and Igor Ivanov's interpretation of the issue. Bobo Lo, *Russian Foreign Policy in the Post-Soviet Era: Reality, Illusion and Mythmaking*, New York: Palgrave Macmillan, 2002, p. 25.
8 Marshall I. Goldman, "Russia and the West: Mutually Assured Distrust," *Current History* 106, no. 702, October 2007, p. 314.
9 This was the second honeymoon of US-Russia relations. See Andrew Kuchins, "Russia and China: The Ambivalent Embrace," *Current History* 106, no. 702, October 2007, pp. 321–7.
10 In Putin's address to the Russian parliament in 2000, he frankly admitted that, "The growing gap between leading nations and Russia pushes us towards becoming a third world country," and so he would pursue a foreign policy of "pragmatism, economic effectiveness, and the priority of national tasks." See Vladimir Putin, "Annual Address to the Federal Assembly of the Russian Federation," July 8, 2000. Available online at www.kremlin.ru/eng/speeches/2000/07/08/0000_type70029type82912_70658.shtml (accessed July 20, 2008).
11 Tom Casier, "Putin's Policy towards the West," p. 389.
12 Liu Xinli and Cui Weifeng, "Eluosi jueqi de fengxiangbiao—buduan qiangying de dui Mei taidu [An Indicator of Russia's Rise—Ever Hardening Attitude towards the United States]," *Fazhiyushehui* [*Legal System and Society*] (Kunming) 7 (first part), March 2008, p. 280.
13 Huang Dengxue, "Cong tuirang dao kangzheng—shi xilun Eluosi dui Meiguo waijiao zhengce de xin bianhua [From Retreat to Resistance: An Analysis of the Latest Change of Russia's Foreign Policy towards the United States]," *Guoji zhengzhi yanjiu* [*Studies of International Politics*] 2, 2008, pp. 159–73.

14 For a discussion of the causes of Russia's foreign policy surge, and the importance of domestic political competition and electoral cycles, see Yu-shan Wu, "Russia's Foreign Policy Surge: Causes and Implications," *Issues & Studies* 45, no. 1, March 2009, pp. 117–62.
15 For this Putin particularly thanked China in his historical address to the Russian Parliament immediately before the signing of an agreement with the leaders of Crimea and Sevastopol to annex the two territories to Russia on March 19, 2014. Putin said, "we are grateful to the people of China, whose leaders have always considered the situation in Ukraine and Crimea taking into account the full historical and political context." President Putin's address to Parliament over Crimea, RT. Available online at http://rt.com/politics/official-word/vladimir-putin-crimea-address-658/ (accessed March 20, 2014).
16 The total area of ceded territories amounted to 1.4 million square kilometers, including those in the northeast and northwest parts of China. See Huang Yao-yuan, "Zhong-E bianjie wenti zhi yanjiu—shen shi Putin fang Zhongguo Dalu jiejue Zhong-E bianjie wenti zhi zhengyi [A Study of Sino-Russian Border Problems—Reviewing the Issue of Putin's Visit to Mainland China to Solve the Sion-Russian Border Problems]," *Guofang zazhi* [*Defense Journal*] 20, no. 4, April 2005, p. 42.
17 There was opposition to the Chinese "concessions" to Russia over the border issue both in and outside mainland China. Some argued that although it is hardly conceivable that China could retake the lost territories at the moment, it could wait until the balance of power between the two countries shifted more to the Chinese side in the future and then make claims on the territories. To sign a border deal with Russia would perpetuate the territorial losses that were imposed on China when the country was weak and vulnerable. See Jiang Yi, "Zhong-E bianjie wenti de youlai jiqi jiejue de zhongda yiyi [The Origins of the Sino-Russian Border Problem and the Significance of Its Solution]," *Ouzhou yanjiu* [*Chinese Journal of European Studies*], 7, 2006, pp. 106–7.
18 Jiang Yi, "Zhong-E bianjie wenti de youlai jiqi jiejue de zhongda yiyi," p. 104.
19 Huang Yao-yuan, "Zhong-E bianjie wenti zhiyan jiu," pp. 46–8.
20 For a discussion of the "Yellow Peril," see Mikhail A. Alexseev and C. Richard Hofstetter, "Russia, China, and the Immigration Security Dilemma," *Political Science Quarterly* 121, no. 1, spring 2006, pp. 1–32.
21 Thus for example a survey of stereotypes conducted jointly by Harbin Academy of Social Sciences and Amur National University found that Chinese respondents thought Russians brave (40 percent), kind and passionate (35 percent), and patriotic (34 percent), while the main characteristics of the Chinese in the minds of the Russian respondents were diligent (20 percent), insolent (13.4 percent), untidy (9.4 percent), and shrewd (8.6 percent). See Li Chuanxun, "Jinnianlai Zhong-E pilin diqu zhengzhi guanxi fenxi [An Analysis of the Political Relation in the Sino-Russian Border Areas in Recent Years]," *Eluosi Zhongya dongou yanjiu* [*Russian Central Asian and East European Studies*] 3, 2003, pp. 12–18.
22 For a detailed account of the negotiation process that led to the 2004 agreement, see Tang Jiaxuan, "Zhong-E Heixiazi Dao wenti tanpan neimu [The Inside Story of the Sino-Russian Negotiation over the Heixiazi Dao]," *Xiangchao* [*Hunan Tide*] 3, 2011, pp. 51–6.
23 According to Tang Jiaxuan, the PRC's foreign minister in the early stages of the Sino-Russian negotiation over the border issue, Putin told Jiang in the Kremlin on July 16 that, "Some external forces often 'remind' us of the outstanding border issues whenever they can, in an attempt to sabotage the normal development of Sino-Russian relations." See Tang Jiaxuan, "Zhong-E Heixiazi dao wenti tanpan neimu," p. 53.
24 For a discussion of the complementarity of Russia and China in their energy relation, see Yuan Xinhua, "Zhong-E shiyou hezuo tanxi [An Exploration into the Sino-Russian Petro Cooperation]," *Dongnanya zongheng* [*Around Southeast Asia*] 10, 2007, pp. 74–9.
25 Yuan Xinhua, "Zhong-E shiyou hezuo de jichu ji fazhan qianjing [The Base of the Sino-Russian Petro Cooperation and Its Prospects]," *Shanghai xingzheng xueyuan xuebao* [*Journal of Shanghai Administration Institute*] 8, no. 4, 2007, pp. 69–78.
26 Yuan Xinhua, "Zhong-E shiyou hezuo tanxi."
27 See Feng Yujun, "Guoji shiyou zhanlue geju yu Zhong-E nengyuan hezuo qianjing [The International Petro Strategic Structure and the Prospect of Sino-Russian Energy Cooperation]," *Xiandai guoji guanxi* [*Contemporary International Relations*] 5, 2004, p. 25.
28 In February 2009 a deal was reached between Russia and China. Under its terms, the Russian oil company Rosneft and oil pipeline monopoly Transneft would receive $25 billion from the China Development Bank for supplying China with 300,000 b/d from 2011 to 2030, a total of 2.2 trillion barrels. The money will underwrite the completion of the Taishet-Nakhodka line with its offshoot to Daqing. In addition to that, Transneft also agreed to send an additional 140,000 b/d of Western Siberian oil to

China through an oil pipeline from Kazakhstan to Western China. The ESPO spur began operation in 2011. For a discussion of the ESPO pipeline controversy, see Hong-yi Lien, "Zhongguo dui Eluosi shiyou nengyuan zhanlue yu waijiao [PRC's Oil-Energy Strategy and Diplomacy to China]," *Guoji guanxi xuebao* [*The Journal of International Relations*] 24, July 2007, pp. 51–86.

29 Thus for example the proposed Trans-Caspian Gas Pipeline would run under the Caspian Sea and transport gas from Turkmenistan, or even Kazakhstan, via Azerbaijan and Turkey, to Central Europe, circumventing Russia. On the Russian side, its "Energy Strategy of Russia until 2030" promulgated in 2009 states as its goal the increase of the Asia-Pacific's share of Russia's energy export to 26 percent by 2030. See Zhang Xuekun, "Zhong-E nengyuan hezuo de xian zhuang, yingxiang yinsu ji yiyi fenxi [An analysis of the state, factors of impact, and meaning of the Sino-Russian energy cooperation]," *Heping yu fazhan* [*Peace and Development*] 4, 2013, pp. 81–2.

30 Xu Xiaojie, Cheng Jian, and Wang Yeqi, "Eluosi nengyuan zhanlue tiaozheng yu Zhong-E youqi zhanlue hezuo [Adjustment of Russia's Energy Strategy and the Sino-Russian Strategic Cooperation in Oil and Gas]," *Eluosi yanjiu* [*Russian Studies*] 2, 2007, pp. 56–7.

31 Yuan Xinhua, "Zhong-E shi you hezuo de jichu ji fazhan qianjing," pp. 75–6.

32 Besides oil, the two sides have cooperated in electricity export, hydropower, natural gas supplies, coal export, and other energy sectors, but the most important is still Russian supply of crude oil to China. For a full survey of energy cooperation between the two countries, see Bin-win Peng, "The Challenges and Opportunities of China's Energy Cooperation with Russia," *Journal of Russian Studies* 10, January 2012, pp. 49–64.

33 Some observers argue that the sale of the Su-27 production license was caused by Russian protests over China's alleged illegal incorporation of Su-27 technologies into China's J-10 fighter; some note that China bought licensed production of the Su-27 after it failed to successfully reverse engineer it; others claimed that it was a deal made by Russia's arms industry without government authorization, hence jeopardizing Russian national security. See Loro Horta, "From Russia without Love: Russia Resumes Weapons Sales to China," *Pac Net*, no. 89, December 12, 2013. Available online at https://csis.org/files/publication/Pac1389.pdf (accessed March 20, 2014), and Stephen J. Blank, "The Dynamics of Russian Weapon Sales to China," Strategic Studies Institute, US Army War College, 1997. Available online at www.strategicstudiesinstitute.army.mil/pubs/display.cfm?pubID=83 (accessed January 20, 2014).

34 One main reason for Russia to sell arms to China was obviously the need to buttress its defense industry at a time when there was a dramatic decline in the world market for arms. Between 1991 and 1995, 2.5 million of 6.1 million employees left the defense sector; in 1996, only 10 percent of the industry's capability was being utilized; and at the beginning of 1998, the government owed 18.5 trillion rubles to defense enterprises. See Robert H. Donaldson, "The Arms Trade in Russian-Chinese Relations," p. 713.

35 China purchased some $15 billion of Russian weapons from 1992 to 2005, representing about 40 percent of Moscow's overall arms sales. Between 2001 and 2006 the average arms sales from Russia to China was $2.7 billion, an unprecedented high. On China's side, 95 percent of arms imports were from Russia during the period 2000 to 2005.

36 Russia claimed that the Chinese J-11B was a reverse-engineered copy of the Su-27SK equipped with Chinese avionics and engines, and thus cancelled the 1995 production-licensing agreement that allowed China to manufacture 200 Su-27s.

37 For an analysis of Russian arms sales to China, see Horta, "From Russia without Love."

38 Erica S. Downs, "Sino-Russian Energy Relations: An Uncertain Courtship," in James A. Bellacqua (ed.), *The Future of China-Russia Relations*, Lexington: University Press of Kentucky, 2010, p. 146.

39 Richard Weitz, *China-Russia Security Relations: Strategic Parallelism without Partnership or Passion*, Strategic Studies Institute, US Army War College, 2008. Available online at www.strategicstudiesinstitute.army.mil/pubs/display.cfm?pubID=868> (accessed January 20, 2014).

40 Paradorn Rangsimaporn, "Russia's Debate on Military-Technological Cooperation with China," *Asian Survey* 46, no. 3, May/June 2006, pp. 477–95.

41 Bellacqua, *The Future of China-Russia Relations*.

42 Bobo Lo, *Axis of Convenience*.

43 Michael Levine, *The Next Great Clash: China and Russia vs. the United States*, Westport, CT: Praeger Security International, 2007.

44 M.L. Titarenko, "Zhong-E zhanlue xiezuo huoban guanxi de lishi [A History of the Sino-Russian Partnership of Strategic Cooperation]," *Dangdai Zhongguoshi yanjiu* [*Contemporary China History Studies*] 13, no. 6, 2006, pp. 69–74.

45 L. P. Delyusin, "Shiji zhijiao de E-Zhong guanxi [The Russo-Chinese Relation at the Turn of the Century]," *Guowai shehuikexue* [*Social Sciences Abroad*] 3, 2003, pp. 77–81.
46 C.G. Luzyanin, "Xinshiqi E-Zhong guanxi de fazhan yu zhanwang [The Development and Prospect of the Russo-Chinese Relation in the New Time]," *Dongbeiya xuekan* [*Journal of Northeast Asia Studies*] 2, 2013, pp. 3–4.
47 Natasha Kuhrt, *Russian Policy towards China and Japan*, New York: Routledge, 2007.
48 Alexander Lukin, "The Russian Approach to China under Gorbachev, Yeltsin, and Putin," in Gilbert Rozman, Kazuhiko Togo, and Joseph P. Fergusson (eds), *Russian Strategic Thought toward Asia*, New York: Palgrave Macmillan, 2006.
49 Wang Shuchun and Wan Qingsong, "Lun xinxing Zhong-E guanxi de weilai zouxiang: jieban haishi jiemeng? [On the Direction for the New-type Sino-Russian Relation: Forming a Companionship or an Alliance?]," *Dangdai yatai* [*Journal of Contemporary Asia-Pacific Studies*] 4, 2013. Available online at www.cctb.net/llyj/lldt/qqzl/201401/t20140126_300956.htm (accessed April 1, 2014).
50 For a discussion of the impact of the "American factor" in the Sino-Russian relation, see Zhao Huasheng, He Ming, and Shi Yajun, "Wending tuijin de Zhong-E guanxi [The Sino-Russian Relation in Steady Progress]," in Feng Shaolei and Xiang Lanqin (eds), *Eluosi yu daguo ji zhoubian guanxi* [*The Relation between Russia and Great Powers and Its Neighbors*], Shanghai: Renmin chubanshe, 2005, pp. 112–13.

Suggested further reading

Bellacqua, James A. (ed.), *The Future of China-Russia Relations*, Lexington: University Press of Kentucky, 2010.
Kuhrt, Natasha, *Russian Policy towards China and Japan*, New York: Routledge, 2007.
Legvold, Robert (ed.), *Russian Foreign Policy in the Twenty-First Century and the Shadow of the Past*, New York: Columbia University Press, 2007.
Lo, Bobo, *Russian Foreign Policy in the Post-Soviet Era: Reality, Illusion and Mythmaking*, New York: Palgrave Macmillan, 2002.
Lo, Bobo, *Axis of Convenience: Moscow, Beijing and the New Geopolitics*, Washington, DC: Brookings Institution Press, 2008.
Lukin, Alexander, *The Bear Watches the Dragon: Russia's Perceptions of China and the Evolution of Russian-Chinese Relations since the Eighteenth Century*, Armonk, NY: M. E. Sharpe, 2003.
Rozman, Gilbert, Kazuhiko Togo, and Joseph P. Fergusson (eds), *Russian Strategic Thought toward Asia*, New York: Palgrave Macmillan, 2006.
Wilson, Jeanne, *Strategic Partners: Russian-Chinese Relations in the Post-Soviet Era*, Armonk, NY: M. E. Sharpe, 2004.

7

Security dimensions of China's relations with Japan

June Teufel Dreyer

Following the economic and psychological devastation of World War II, Japan began a spectacular rise, soon becoming the world's second largest economy. Three decades later, assisted in no small part by Japanese aid, China began an even more spectacular climb from an economy that had stagnated under socialism, to a gross national product that surpassed Japan's in 2011. At the same time, it began an impressive military buildup. The change in the two nations' relative strength exacerbated pre-existing tensions that include, but are not limited to, territorial disputes. A classic security dilemma has evolved in which each side, claiming provocation by the other, rationalizes improvements in its military capabilities.

Post-war separate development: 1945–72

With China humiliated by Japan in two successive wars, that of 1894–5 and World War II, the government of the People's Republic of China (PRC) has from its inception been acutely sensitive to any development that might indicate Japan's intent to pursue an aggressive policy toward it. Although denouncing the Treaty of San Francisco of 1951, to which the PRC was not invited since the Republic of China was at that time more widely recognized as the legitimate government, the Beijing leadership must have looked on with favor as Japan agreed to divest itself of all territories acquired through conquest.

It must likewise have been pleased at the promulgation of the new Japanese constitution, with its declaration in article nine that Japan would henceforth abstain from militant actions and that to that end it would "forever renounce war as a sovereign right of the nation and the threat or use of force as means of settling international disputes. In order to accomplish the aim of the preceding paragraph, land, sea, and air forces, as well as other war potential, will never be maintained. The right of belligerency of the state will not be recognized."[1]

How sensitive Chinese analysts were to the nuances of the discussions between Japanese and American drafters on the wording of the constitution is not known. What is relevant here is that, at Japanese insistence, the apparently innocuous phrase "in order to accomplish the aim of the preceding paragraph" was a later addition to the final draft of the constitution, which had prohibited offensive warfare, using forces in self-defense, and maintaining *any* type of military establishment. Inserting this clause allowed an interpretation of the constitution that permits Japan, consonant with its status as a sovereign nation, to exercise the right of *individual* self-defense and to maintain a Self Defense Force (SDF) for that purpose, as long as they were not designed to settle *international* disputes, i.e., collective defense.

Although apparently not cognizant of the implications of this addition, the Chinese nonetheless denounced the treaty as having created an anti-communist US-Japanese alliance. In return for Japan agreeing not to defend itself, Washington had put Japan under its nuclear umbrella, receiving permission to place its troops and military assets in Japan to that end. By this time, the Korean War had broken out and, with China having entered the war on the side of North Korea, the United States belatedly began to rethink the wisdom of having a non-militarized Japan. The Japanese government proved recalcitrant on the issue of rearmament, declaring its unswerving commitment to its peace constitution. Yoshida Shigeru, its formidable prime minister, announced what came to be called the Yoshida Doctrine: Japan would concentrate on economic development while simultaneously keeping a low diplomatic profile.

Develop it did, helped significantly by generous American aid in rebuilding factories destroyed by wartime bombing and purchases occasioned by the need for Japanese products in order to pursue the war in Korea as well as heavy use of Japanese bases pursuant to that endeavor. This was clearly detrimental to the PRC's military efforts in support of its North Korean ally.

Other ominous signs existed as well. After the Japanese surrender in 1945, Chiang Kai-shek, almost certainly with the encouragement of Washington, ordered the imperial army to stay at its post in order to use it as a bulwark against communist expansion. As US President Harry Truman wrote in his memoirs,

> It was perfectly clear to us that if we told the Japanese to lay down their arms immediately and march to the seaboard, the entire country would be taken over by the communists. We therefore had to take the unusual step of using the enemy as a garrison until we could airlift Chinese National troops to South China and send marines to guard the seaports.[2]

Shortly thereafter, an estimated 20,000 troops of the imperial army helped Chiang Kai-shek fight the communist Red Army in the Chinese civil war.[3]

Chinese leaders viewed the re-creation of the zaibatsu, large corporations with interlocking directorates and close ties to the Japanese government and now known, in a somewhat different form, as keiretsu, as a further sign that Japan was about to return to its aggressive past. The rehabilitation and return to power of several individuals who had been accused, though not convicted, of war crimes provided further confirmation of this view. Prominent among these was Kishi Nobusuke, who had been Minister of Munitions in the cabinet of the notorious Prime Minister Tōjō Hideki and became prime minister himself in 1957. Moreover, as Japanese businesses expanded throughout Asia, it began to seem to Chinese leaders that the country was intent on re-establishing the Greater East Asia Co-Prosperity Sphere that had made much of the rest of the area an economic colony of the Empire of the Rising Sun. In addition, the Japanese seemed to have developed a collective amnesia on the matter of the war. History books tended to skirt lightly over the war years or stop their narrative before it began. Demands for compensation from those who had been pressed into servitude in mines or brothels received short shrift, it being declared that the affected parties had "volunteered" their services. A staple of Japan's thriving film industry was films such as *Battle for the Japan Sea* and *Admiral Yamamoto* that Chinese interpreted as glorifying war.[4] China's concerns about Japan were mirrored on the other side of the Yellow Sea. Japan saw a huge, hostile neighbor closely allied with the Soviet Union and dedicated to spreading communism throughout the world. The 1950 Sino-Soviet Treaty of Friendship, Alliance, and Mutual Assistance explicitly bound the two states to take all measures to prevent a repetition of aggression "by Japan and any state which might directly or indirectly join with it, pledging immediate military and other assistance with all the means at its disposal."[5] The PRC had a large, if ill-equipped, military that was receiving Soviet help in its modernization process. In 1964, China would become a nuclear power, which was particularly upsetting to Japan as the only country that nuclear weapons had ever been used against in war. Chinese films, too, tended to glorify the alleged deeds of its own military. And an entire reworking of history took place in which the heroic Red Army had conquered the Japanese with no mention of the role of the United States or Chiang Kai-shek's KMT. In the mid-1950s, as part of a literary effort to abolish what was called the doctrine of the wavering middle, all Japanese soldiers had to be portrayed as viciously cruel. In 2002, the Chinese Censorship Bureau refused to allow the screening of a Chinese film about the war against Japan: Chinese civilians looking after a Japanese prisoner were not depicted as hating him.[6]

Conveniently ignored in this reworked narrative was any mention of the extent of wartime collaboration between Chinese and the Japanese occupiers. Nor was there acknowledgement of the existence of a significant number of Japanese anti-war films like *Harp of Burma*, in which a former imperial army soldier refuses repatriation to Japan, preferring to stay in Burma to do penance as a mendicant monk.

Although Chinese accounts of the Korean War claimed stunning victories over US/NATO forces, the leadership was aware of the deficiencies of its force and set about remedying them with Soviet help. Meanwhile, under American pressure, euphemistically referred to as *gaiatsu*, or foreign pressure, the Japanese government created a 75,000-man National Police Reserve, carefully described as a non-military territorial defense police force. In 1954, it became known as a Self Defense Force. These decisions were not popular with Japan's opposition parties, particularly the Japanese Socialist Party and Japanese Communist Party, the left-wing labor unions who supported them, and vocal segments of the electorate who had suffered grievously during the war and were determined to make sure militarism did not reassert itself. Japanese police were aware that some of these groups received funding from China, but did not disclose, and perhaps did not know, the amounts.[7] Chinese suspicions about Japanese remilitarization were ongoing, the Sino-Soviet split that became obvious in the late 1950s all but isolated the PRC in the communist world, and both Beijing and Moscow courted Tokyo's favor. China easily gained the upper hand: the Soviet Union refused Japan's demands for the return of four island groups (Habomai, Shikotan, Etorofu, and Kunashiri) referred to in Japan as the Northern Territories, while Beijing supported Japan's claim. The famine that resulted from the PRC's disastrous Great Leap Forward of 1958 temporarily diminished the lure of the Chinese market for Japanese business—the country had little ability to purchase anything beyond food—but grew again as the PRC's economy recovered. For Japan, the Sino-Soviet split allayed concerns about an invasion by monolithic international communism. The anti-Japanese clause of the Sino-Soviet treaty became irrelevant since the treaty itself was no longer meaningful.

China's reduced concerns about the revival of Japanese militarism did not prevent its media from railing against the existence of the Self Defense Force or any of its activities. It reported regularly on opposition to the SDF within Japan, reiterating the Japan Socialist Party's repeated claims that the very existence of the organization was unconstitutional. When right-wing writer Mishima Yukio committed ritual suicide in 1970 after an abortive effort to emphasize the need for Japan to have a normal military, the PRC issued a barrage of denunciation against what it termed remilitarization. This conveniently overlooked Mishima's real message, which was to restore traditional Japanese culture's balance between aesthetics, symbolized by the chrysanthemum, and the martial, with the sword as its iconic image. He advocated not remilitarization but something akin to the Swiss system of military service. And, as Chinese policymakers no doubt noticed but did not choose to publicly comment on, SDF members openly ridiculed his ideas, while the Japanese government prosecuted those who had aided his efforts.[8]

As the Mishima drama played out, an issue of more enduring contention had begun. In May 1969, a survey conducted under the auspices of the United Nations Economic Commission for Asia and the Far East (ECAFE) reported that "a high probability exists that the continental shelf between Taiwan and Japan may be one of the most prolific oil reservoirs in the world," adding, however, that the area remained untested.[9] Although a *New York Times* reporter predicted that both China and Taiwan might claim rights if a major strike were reported,[10] this did not immediately happen. The Japanese government (GOJ) commissioned its own survey, occasioning a claim by Taiwan and discussions between Tokyo and Taipei on possible joint development. At this point, the government of China weighed in. American analysts at the time opined that, in addition to territorial issues, Beijing wished to prevent a strengthening of ties between the two that would work to the disadvantage of China's claims to Taiwan.[11] In any case, Beijing was soon claiming the islands therein, called the Diaoyu in China and the Senkaku in Japan, as China's sacred territory and railing against the fraud of the reversion of Okinawa "in an attempt to include the Diaoyu and other islands{. . .}within its own territory."[12]

The islands passed from American control back to Japan when Okinawa, from which they had been administered prior to the war, reverted.[13] The GOJ owned one of the five islands outright and collected taxes from the Japanese owners of the others; the American government leased one of these for use in bombing practice. During discussions about normalization between China and Japan in 1972, Premier Zhou Enlai suggested that the disposition of sovereignty be postponed, thereby temporarily removing the issue from contention. There were sporadic incidents involving Chinese fishing boats thereafter, some more worrisome than others.

The most serious occurred in April 1978 when between 80 and 120 vessels[14] bearing banners and signs declaring the islands to be Chinese appeared off their shores, with some of the fishermen holding machine guns. The incident was puzzling in that Beijing was trying to get the GOJ to sign a treaty of peace and friendship that, since it included an anti-hegemony clause clearly directed against the Soviet Union, Tokyo was reluctant to agree to. The intrusion of the fishing boats was the antithesis of peace and friendship.

After the Chinese agreed to the inclusion of a sentence saying that the anti-hegemony clause was not directed against any third country, and after paramount leader Deng Xiaoping stated that the disposition of the islands should be put off for future generations, the Japanese government accepted Beijing's unconvincing explanation that the boats had accidentally entered the area while pursuing a school of fish.[15] The treaty was duly signed, with the Japanese government seeming to construe Deng Xiaoping's statement about shelving the islands dispute to mean that the issue had been settled.

Chinese sources expressed periodic concern throughout this period about perceived moves toward remilitarization. The ambitious plan for defense of the sea lanes out to the Strait of Malacca announced by then head of the Japan Defense Agency (JDA) Nakasone Yasuhiro in 1970 was treated with particular vituperation, although Nakasone had made clear that the enemy he had in mind was the Soviet Union.[16] In the end, Nakasone's plans were defeated by internal Japanese resistance. China continued to express concern about any Japanese actions, even low-level exercises or small increments in the SDF force structure, although the tone was ritualistic. While the PRC media regularly railed against the US-Japan Mutual Security Treaty as a Washington-Tokyo axis designed to contain China, officials privately seemed to regard the partnership—which the GOJ adamantly refused to call an alliance—as a force restraining the revival of Japanese militarism. In Japan, there were strong suspicions that the constant harping on the alleged lack of Japanese remorse for World War II or minor weapons upgrades were being used to persuade the GOJ to offer more economic assistance. Enjoying better relations with both the United States and Japan during the 1970s and early 1980s, Chinese leaders did not fear that the Japanese-American partnership was directed against the PRC. Moreover, at this time all three had poor relations with the Soviet Union.

In discussions at the time of the normalization of Sino-Japanese relations, Zhou Enlai stated that China no longer opposed the security treaty. And in September 1978, Deng Xiaoping told a Japanese delegation that he was in favor of an SDF buildup.[17] In May 1980, on the first state visit of a PRC leader to Japan, Hua Guofeng told a press conference that "[a]n independent and sovereign state should have the right to maintain its own defense so as to safeguard its independence and sovereignty. As to what Japan will do, we do not interfere in its internal affairs."[18]

Mutual insecurities mount

By the mid-1980s, several developments began to change the Chinese leadership's relative lack of concern with Japanese defense issues. Sino-Soviet ties began to thaw, and Beijing backed away from supporting Japan's claims to the Northern Territories. After the previously mentioned Nakasone Yasuhiro became prime minister, he expanded the SDF and, in 1983, eased the ban on weapons exports to allow the forwarding of weapons technology to the United States. Japanese defense spending increased by between 5 and 8 percent between 1987 and 1991, even briefly exceeding the informal 1 percent of GDP limit in 1987, though only barely. The Chinese media reacted sharply: a red line had been crossed from which, they predicted erroneously, there would be no retreat: "the change can be summarized in one word: the break. Given the first break, it is unavoidable that the second and the third breaks and more breaks will follow, and the state of affairs will get out of control."[19]

Within the PRC, resentment was building against Japan's commanding economic presence in China: in 1985, there were anti-Japanese demonstrations protesting Tokyo's alleged plan to recreate the much resented Greater East Asia Co-Prosperity Sphere. There were strong hints that at least some of the demonstrators thought their government had been too accommodating to Japanese capitalism, arousing concern within the leadership that the demonstrations could turn against them. In the following year, Hu Yaobang, regarded as pro-Japanese, was deposed after student demonstrations in favor of more democracy.

The much larger pre-democracy demonstrations of 1989 had no meaningful effect on Sino-Japanese relations. Although the government's brutal suppression of the demonstrators left the Japanese public with a bad impression, the GOJ argued against sanctions, saying that isolating China would do more harm than good. Businessmen returned to China as soon as their government told them it was safe. The Japanese government's willingness to accommodate the PRC's post-Tiananmen leadership's harder line did not, however, result in a more benign view of Japan by Beijing. Already by 1990, criticisms were being voiced. A Chinese naval strategist's 1990 article on maritime threats to his country included among them:

- American encouragement to Japan to take more responsibility for the defense of sea lines of communication
- Japan's naval expansion exceeding the PRC's ability to counter it
- Japan's claim to the Diaoyu/Senkaku islands
- Japan agreeing with South Korea to jointly exploit the sea beds in areas the PRC believed to be within its territorial waters[20]

The disintegration of the communist world that followed soon after removed the Soviet Union as the *raison d'être* of the US-Japanese security partnership, though not the partnership itself. With the USSR no longer extant, it also removed the initial impetus for the normalization of US-PRC relations: common fear of the Soviet Union. Already uncomfortable with the United States having become the sole superpower, Beijing opposed the American-led United Nations intervention to reverse Iraq's conquest of Kuwait, fearing its ramifications for a similar action against China.

Elsewhere, Tokyo was much criticized for its meager efforts to help the UN effort, and responded by agreeing to take more responsibility in peacekeeping efforts and in supporting its US treaty partner. These were unpopular with the Japanese public for a number of reasons. Financial concerns were added to ongoing ideologically based opposition from left-wing and pacifist groups: Japan's property bubble had burst in 1990, with what was expected to be a temporary period of readjustment slipping into two decades of economic malaise. In addition, the Japanese were leery of being drawn into a Sino-American confrontation.

Post-Cold War tensions accumulate

After the Tiananmen incident, the Chinese leadership, aware that it was unpopular in significant domestic constituencies, encouraged the growth of nationalism and found that it resonated with large numbers of citizens. Japan was a handy target. Rallies were staged during anniversaries of events leading up to and during World War II and museums were opened with great publicity, becoming part of school trips as well as staples of tourist itineraries for all nationalities. Any action by Japan that could be construed as a return to militarism was magnified in the Chinese press.

While encouraging nationalism was popular, it had the disadvantage of creating a force that might prove difficult to control. When Mao Zedong and Zhou Enlai determined that, for the sake of a greater threat from the Soviet Union the PRC must change abruptly from a position of denouncing the United States to cooperating with it, they had little difficulty doing so, although even Mao told Nixon that, for the sake of appearances, it would be acceptable for the two to denounce each other for a while. Nor, at a later date, had Deng Xiaoping experienced great obstacles to his policy of the open door to the capitalist world:[21] their nationalist credentials as icons of the revolution were unassailable. Jiang Zemin and his successors did not have this luxury. In what a former State Department official called an echo chamber of nationalism,[22] government actions created public pressure for tougher policies regardless of whether these were conducive to solving problems between the two sides. Being accused of being too conciliatory to Japan, as indeed Hu Yaobang had been, could prove dangerous to one's continued presence in office. Unfortunately, such strident denunciations caused alarm in Japan, and calls to take countermeasures. Nationalism was rekindled in Japan as well, albeit in the face of some resistance, as in the case of teachers who refused to attend daily flag-raisings and sing the national anthem at their schools.

Moves to enhance Japan's defense posture were loudly denounced in Beijing. In February 1992, the country's National People's Congress passed a law unilaterally claiming ownership of the many disputed islands in the South and East China seas, including the Diaoyu/Senkaku group. A strong protest by Tokyo was rebuffed as "meaningless." Although Prime Minister Miyazawa said that his country could not accept Chinese law, both sides agreed that they did not want the law to affect bilateral ties.[23] A planned visit by the imperial couple, greatly desired by the Chinese side since it wanted a more strongly worded apology for Japanese actions in World War II than it had received from the GOJ thus far, did take place. However, the language of the apology was less than desired.

In the following year, the North Korean government launched a missile into the Sea of Japan. SDF officials noted that that a portion of western Japan was within range of the missile, a Nodong-1, and revealed that North Korea was developing newer versions with the capability to reach all of Japan, which was incapable of defending itself against such an attack. There were also fears that terrorists could enter the country and, among other scenarios, sabotage its nuclear plants. Voices began to argue that Japan should become a "normal country," *futsu no kuni*, capable of both defending itself and contributing to the security of the international community.

In a development that surprised foreign analysts, Japan's Democratic Socialist Party agreed to drop its opposition to the constitutionality of the SDF in order to become a coalition partner of the more conservative ruling party. This enabled Japan to take part in international peacekeeping operations (PKOs) despite ongoing concerns about the constitutionality of such participation. The official position has been that, as a sovereign state, Japan has the right of collective self-defense, but that the country's constitution means that it cannot do so. The government finessed that issue by ruling that PKOs do not constitute collective action to settle international disputes (see the beginning of this chapter) but are, by definition, collective peacekeeping.

Beijing media denounced the innocuous-sounding decision as darkly motivated and, when SDF members were sent to a PKO in Cambodia, deemed that it had been undertaken with the motive of re-establishing Japan's military power in Southeast Asia. *Beijing Review* stated, erroneously in view of Washington's continual prodding, that "Tokyo no longer seeks Washington's approval before taking steps{. . .}[and has] advanced its own version of a new world order."[24] *Guoji Wenti Yanjiu*[25] (*International Issues Research*), house journal of the China Institute of Contemporary International Relations (CICIR), termed the action an effort to fill the military vacuum in Asia left by the withdrawal of the USSR from Vietnam and the United States from the Philippines. It cited a 1991 article in the Japanese journal *Gunji Kenkyu* (*Military Research*) opining that, if the SDF received a direct order from the PKO commander, it would be obliged to use force. Another red line had been crossed, the CICIR article claimed.

Japan moves closer to the United States

Meanwhile, Chinese ships began to appear more frequently in what Japan considered its territorial waters, raising anxieties in Tokyo. A classic security dilemma was evolving in which each side profoundly distrusted any actions by the other and felt the need to take countermeasures. This took on a larger dimension when, in 1995–6, in response to Beijing's anger at Taiwan's president paying an unofficial visit to the United States, the PLA began a year of war games that looked like preparation for an assault on Taiwan and included missile firings that disrupted Japanese shipping through the Taiwan Strait. Tokyo became alarmed not only for its shipping interests in the strait and its extensive investments in Taiwan but because, should China absorb the island, the PRC's territorial waters would closely abut those of Japan. In fall 1995, the Japan Defense Agency prepared an internal document for the Japan-US Security Consultative Committee, also known as the Two-Plus-Two, suggesting an upgraded security relationship between the two states.[26] This included better intelligence gathering and investigation of the prospect of joint anti-missile research, which was understood to include Japan's participation in the US Theater Missile Defense (TMD). Beijing reacted strongly against Japan's inclusion in TMD, as it suspected such efforts were aimed not at North Korea but the PRC.

The Japan-US Joint Declaration on Security Alliance for the Twenty-First Century that was signed on April 17, 1996 took note of the existence of instability and uncertainty in the Asia-Pacific region, mentioning "heavy concentrations of military force, including nuclear arsenals," "unresolved territorial disputes," and "potential regional conflicts."[27] Behind the bland wording on the need to maintain a stable and prosperous environment was an important shift in the Japan–US relationship—now explicitly referred to as an alliance for the first time—from a focus on the defense of Japan to one whose goal was the maintenance of peace in Asia, with Japan considered an active partner therein. In a related document signed two days before that underscored Tokyo's new role, Japan agreed to provide logistics support in contingencies involving *shuhen jitai*, the areas surrounding Japan.[28] Beijing insisted on, but did not receive, guarantees that the phrase did not cover the Taiwan Strait. Whereas in the past at least some Chinese leaders had quietly approved of the Japan–US security relationship, reasoning that it provided a "cork in the bottle" of a revival of Japanese militarism, the new guidelines seemed to indicate that Japanese right-wing pressure had forced the cork out of the bottle: Washington and Tokyo had united in an effort to contain China. Indeed, it would have been difficult for the Chinese leadership not to see the documents as an effort at containment of the PRC.

Nor was it difficult to see why other powers might wish to contain the PRC. As the correspondent for a leading Hong Kong magazine pointed out,

> Who in Asia has the largest nuclear arsenal? Answer China. Where in the region are there unresolved territorial disputes? Answer the South China Sea, where China's claims are disputed by a handful of other countries. As for potential regional conflicts, there is none more destabilizing than China's insistence that Taiwan is one of its provinces. And, of course, the Chinese have been accused by the U.S. on more than one occasion of being guilty of actions that could cause the proliferation of weapons of mass destruction, as well as their means of delivery.[29]

If the Chinese leadership was aware that its actions in the Taiwan Strait in 1995–6 were influential in the strengthened US–Japan relationship, there was no public acknowledgement thereof. The two sides continued sniping at each other with, for example, the Chinese media railing against the Japanese participating in TMD and conservative Japanese politicians riposting that the system was essentially a burglar alarm that no one but a would-be thief would object to his neighbor installing. What Japanese statements did not address, and a matter of considerable concern to the Chinese leadership, was that TMD could be used to defend Taiwan from attack by China.

Not all Japanese were happy about the new arrangements. The center-left Mainichi Shimbun worried that the agreement "effectively pushes China out of a previously fairly balanced triangular relationship," while the pro-China Asahi Shimbun expressed fears of entrapment, arguing that the foreign ministry might not have been aware of the danger it had put itself into by pledging to review defense cooperation guidelines with regard to contingencies in "the areas surrounding Japan."[30] The net result of the April 1996 agreements was, Asahi asserted, to change the nature of the security treaty system into one obliging Japan to assist the United States.[31] Other sources argued that it was childish to think that security agreements were not reciprocal: if Japan refused to help the United States, then the United States would have no reason to continue to protect Japan. In this analysis, the danger of Japan being abandoned by the US was greater than the risk of Japan being trapped by the US into hostility to China.

Two events in 1998 pushed the two sides into a still more confrontational mode. First, on August 31, North Korea launched its more advanced Taepodong missile over Japan to an eventual landing in the Pacific Ocean. Second, in late November, then-president Jiang Zemin paid a state visit to Japan in which he angered both government and public opinion by ordering the GOJ, in less than diplomatic language, to issue a statement on Taiwan that he had previously been told privately that it would not.

With regard to the first, an embarrassed Japanese government admitted it had not detected the launch, nor would it have been able to protect the country against the missile if it had been detected. This prompted calls for a stronger defense posture, specifically including TMD. One critic compared the SDF to a fire department that could not put out fires but only try to see whether fires could be prevented. With Sino-Japanese relations already tense, Beijing did not believe that fear of North Korea was the reason behind discussions about building up Japan's missile defenses. *Shijie Zhishi (World Knowledge)* accused Tokyo of "behaving like Xiang Zhuang performing the sword dance as a cover for his attempt on Liu Bang's life."[32] Readers familiar with Chinese history would understand this as an allusion to an incident that took place in 206 BC, when the founder of the Han Dynasty narrowly survived an assassination attempt. Beijing was accusing Tokyo of using North Korea as a surrogate for China in order to persuade the Japanese public to back a stronger defense policy.

Beijing's misgivings were further magnified when, in mid-October 1999, a Japanese vice-minister of defense said he thought that the Diet, the country's parliament, should consider abandoning the country's self-imposed ban on nuclear weapons. His resignation a few days later did not stanch an outpouring of criticism from Chinese media. Although the PRC has had nuclear capability since 1964, it regards Japan's possession of such weapons as unconstitutional; Japanese supporters of acquiring the weapons reply that, first, the constitution does not mention nuclear weapons and, second, that, just as Beijing has always maintained that its nuclear force exists for defensive purposes alone, Japan's would as well.

China's interpretation of Japan's true motive as being itself rather than North Korea was later confirmed in a series of not-for-attribution interviews conducted by an American congressional commission with high-ranking members of the Japanese defense and foreign ministries. For example, a JDA official expressed the view that, although North Korea was capable of doing great harm to Japan, he believed that the problems between them could be dealt with so that this worst case scenario would not happen. The official characterized North Korea as a failed state and a short-term problem. China, on the other hand, was a rising power and a long-term threat to Japan's security.[33]

Then-premier Zhu Rongji's 2000 visit to Tokyo succeeded in smoothing the feathers ruffled by Jiang Zemin's peremptory behavior 2 years before, and included an agreement to exchange ship visits. However, in what is unlikely to have been accidental, and might have reflected a split in the top leadership, Beijing released a White Paper during the visit that attacked the US–Japan defense relationship, warning that the peace and stability of the Asia-Pacific Region would be imperiled by their cooperation in TMD development.[34] The Chinese military also took note of the Japanese Defense Agency's announced shift of emphasis from the north (i.e. the Soviet Union) to the west (China).[35]

Post-9/11 developments

The following year brought two more irritants to Sino-Japanese relations: the accession of a strong prime minister, Koizumi Junichiro, to office in April, and the al Qaeda attacks on New York's Twin Towers and the Pentagon in September. Koizumi, though repeatedly professing to want better relations with Beijing, irritated it with yearly visits to Yasukuni Shrine. The shrine is dedicated to the spirits of all Japanese who have died in the country's wars, and includes tablets commemorating fourteen individuals who were declared Class A war criminals by a post-World War II Allied tribunal. While those who attend maintain that they are honoring the sacrifices of those who have fallen in battle and that they pray only for peace, Beijing contends that they pay homage to criminals and harbor thoughts of re-creating a militarized state. Tokyo, pointing out that Japanese prime ministers visited Yasukuni at least ten times after the war criminals' tablets were added to the shrine with no protests from China, implies that some other, unspecified, factor must be involved.

Koizumi also dispatched the SDF to Iraq, albeit in non-combat roles and in response to Washington's prodding. Unarmed, they had to be guarded by US forces. Beijing suggested, probably correctly, that Koizumi would have wanted to take this action regardless of pressure from the United States, and expressed its opposition. Even before Koizumi visited the shrine, a forum of Beijing experts had convened to discuss whether Tokyo had the conditions for creating a powerful armed force. As reported by *Zhongguo Qingnian*, the newspaper of the Communist Youth League, the answer was an unqualified yes. Japan could, said the paper, produce nuclear weapons within 3 to 6 months, and between one and two thousand medium- and long-range missiles within a year. Its military technology was already on a par with that of the United States, and Japan had actually taken the lead in software, radar, communications network control microelectronics, and data storage.[36]

In 2002, a confrontation erupted over the Chinese police entering the Japanese Consulate-General in Shenyang to remove North Koreans who had sought asylum there. The Chinese side maintained, with some evidence, that the Japanese had given permission for them to enter.[37] A Japanese Ministry of Foreign Affairs investigation cleared the personnel involved of blame, though there were suspicions that the incident was used to discredit the so called China School of MOFA, which had been accused of practicing a *dogeza gaik* (a ketou foreign policy) of excessive accommodation to Chinese wishes.[38] Beijing media noted that Japan's 2004 National Defense Program Outline (NDPO) had for the first time mentioned China by name, as opposed to using the threat of North Korea as a surrogate. *Renmin Ribao*, observing the Japanese move away from saying North Korea when it meant China, opined that the NDPO indicated a fundamental shift away from Japan's previous defensive policy and an indication of its desire to play a more active role internationally as a "normal" country, meaning one with a military.[39]

At the same time, Japan became concerned by yet another increase in the intrusion of Chinese vessels into areas Japan considered its territorial waters, suspecting that they were designed to show Japan that the PRC intended to control the entire East China Sea. Tokyo issued a formal protest against the illegal passage of a submerged Han-class submarine through its waters in November 2004. Five days after receiving it, the Chinese government expressed regret, saying that the submarine had accidentally strayed. While some analysts were inclined to accept this explanation, others believed that the delay in issuing a statement indicated that it was intentional, with the navy not informing the central government of what it was doing. The latter explanation raised a more worrisome question: whether, to use Mao Zedong's phrase, the Chinese party still controlled the gun.[40]

In 2005, anti-Japanese riots broke out in several Chinese cities with considerable damage to Japanese diplomatic and commercial properties. Participants denounced Koizumi's visit to Yasukuni Shrine, the Japanese government's approval of a textbook that minimized the country's actions during World War II, and Japan's application for permanent membership in the United Nations Security Council in a reorganization of the council proposed by then–secretary-general Kofi Annan. All had been heavily publicized in the Chinese press. At first, leaders seemed to support the students, responding to official protests by saying that it was Japan who owed China an apology, not vice-versa. Chinese Vice Premier Wu Yi abruptly canceled her meeting with Koizumi when, at a Diet committee meeting, he defended his right to visit the shrine. The Japanese public was offended by this insult to their leader even as the vice premier became a heroine in China and anti-Japanese protests escalated. When unrest began to target other grievances, as when an estimated 2,000 retired PLA men from 20 provinces converged on military headquarters in Beijing to demand pension increases, 30,000 people protested against pollution in northeast China, factory workers in the southeastern special economic zone of Shenzhen demanded unions, and anti-corruption signs appeared in Shanghai, the PRC leadership moved to quell the demonstrations.[41]

After a meeting of foreign ministers, the PRC agreed to repair damage to Japanese diplomatic buildings but not to provide any other compensation or apologize. Two former prime ministers, including Nakasone, urged an end to visits to Yasukuni, and a supra-partisan group of Diet members began to discuss building a new war memorial that would not be freighted with association with war criminals. Collaborative activities continued as, for example, when Japan offered its expertise on what the head of the PRC's environmental protection agency described to a United Nations conference as "the god of death in the air."[42]

Issues were not so much forgotten as downplayed. Hu Jintao warned that Sino-Japanese ties could go cold "in an instant,"[43] the two sides could not agree on a joint declaration over the form of a future East Asian community that proponents hoped would resemble the European Union,[44] and the head of the Democratic Party of Japan (DPJ) took issue with his own party when he criticized the country's leaders for "chanting that we should be friendly with China while avoiding the real issues."[45] A telecommunications specialist at the Japanese consulate in Shanghai committed suicide, leaving a note explaining that he had been coerced into providing secret information to a PRC operative on his country's policies on the island disputes between them.[46]

Even as economic relations remained good, the two sides continued to snipe at each other. Summed up in the phrase "hot economy, cold politics," trade between the two expanded. While Chinese officials decried any Japanese move that could be construed as evidence of remilitarization, Japanese complained regularly about the implications of annual double-digit increases in the PRC's defense budget and each new weapon acquired, such as the PLA destroying one of its own satellites in low-earth orbit in January 2007. In the same month, the Japanese Defense Agency was raised to ministry status, providing Chinese media with yet another piece of evidence for their contention that Japan was returning to its pre-World War II militancy. It seemed that the stronger China became, the more it sought to avenge itself against past humiliation by Japan, while in Japan nationalism was stimulated by the weakening of the country's economic primacy as the PRC rose in stature both economically and militarily.

A hopeful sign

Nevertheless, by 2008, the two sides reached agreement in principle on the exploitation of a disputed oil and gas field in the East China Sea called Chunxiao in Chinese and Shirakaba by Japan. Each side declared that, although it had not surrendered its claims to sovereignty over the disputed area, joint development would proceed. While Western media treated the agreement as an impressive breakthrough—the generally circumspect *Economist*, for example, describing it as "profit before patriotism"[47]—reaction from the parties involved was more nuanced. Japan's *Nikkei Weekly* pointed out that the agreement was "riddled with compromises" and left important details for future negotiations.[48] Despite the PRC's controlled media, many politically aware Chinese citizens expressed strong negative feelings about the pact. A Chinese journalist for an influential Singapore paper summarized his objections as being, first, that the agreement had tacitly endorsed Japan's position on the median line; second, that Japan had made no reciprocal gesture for this concession with regard to the disputed Diaoyu/Senkaku islands; and third, that Japan's "unreasonable" claim to a stake in Chunxiao had been partially met.[49]

Chinese official sources attempted to deflect criticism by arguing that what had been agreed on was not joint development but cooperative development: in the former, the two sides would participate as equal partners, each bound by its own laws and paying taxes to its own government, while under the latter arrangement, Japan would be bound by Chinese law and pay taxes to China.[50] PRC critics were not satisfied with these statements. Chinese official sources had several times used the word "joint" rather than cooperative.[51] And, while a Japanese official agreed that Japan might pay taxes to China, he added that the details had yet to be finalized. References to the project ceased: patriotism had prevailed over profit.

Sino-Japanese relations under Hu Jintao and the DPJ

With both sides apparently eager to downplay the ill feelings resulting from the collapse of the agreement, Sino-Japanese relations resumed a familiar pattern of easing followed by tensions. Jiang Zemin, regarded as hostile to Japan, had been replaced by Hu Jintao in 2002 but had had prickly relations not only with Koizumi but the three Liberal Democratic Party (LDP) prime ministers who followed him in rapid succession, all of whom had vowed to improve Sino-Japanese ties.[52] The election of a prime minister from the opposition DPJ in September 2009 gave hope of an improvement in relations: Hatoyama Yukio had campaigned on the issue, promising to establish an equilateral triangular relationship among China, Japan, and the United States and remove American bases from Okinawa. Chinese media noted approvingly that when Hatoyama's grandfather had been prime minister, he had tried hard to normalize relations with the PRC but was prevented from doing so by US pressure, and that his father as foreign minister had held talks with China on concluding a Peace and Friendship Treaty. Moreover, Hatoyama had promised not to visit Yasukuni while in office. In a highly symbolic act, his first foreign trip as prime minister was to Beijing, not Washington. He announced a *yu-ai* (friendship) policy whose cornerstone was to be an East Asian Community (EAC) that pointedly did not include America. Another attempt at writing a joint history of World War II was begun, and cultural exchanges of ancient artifacts were made.

However, Beijing appeared disinclined to offer reciprocal gestures. Chinese ships continued to intrude into waters the Japanese considered theirs. Responding to Japanese complaints, a spokesperson for the PRC's ministry of defense stated curtly that Tokyo's efforts to play up a Chinese military threat and strengthen the Japanese-American relationship to counter it would result in a deterioration in Beijing's trust.[53] In March 2010, after a Chinese helicopter flew dangerously close to an MSDF ship, according to Japanese sources, retired general Xu Guangyu responded that China's neighbors had better get used to the Chinese navy (PLAN)'s presence: it was just protecting its national interests.[54] Hatoyama's critics charged that his policy of appeasement had emboldened China. Widely regarded as inept, he was quickly succeeded by fellow DPJ party member Kan Naoto, who had even worse luck. In September 2010, less than 3 months after assuming the prime ministership, a Chinese fishing boat collided with two Japanese coast guard (JCG) ships who were trying to steer it away from the Diaoyu/Senkaku islands. The captain was arrested rather than deported, as had been the case in previous issues, although this incident, since it involved damage to Japanese government ships, was more serious. Beijing argued that, since the islands rightfully belonged to China, the fishing boat's presence there was legal; the fault lay with the JCG: the captain should be released immediately.

The Japanese government, arguing that the country's legal procedures required that he be put on trial, declined to do so. Beijing announced that it would halt shipments of rare earths to Japan (crucial to the country's auto industry),[55] began an excruciatingly time-consuming inspection of all Japanese products being imported into China, advised travel agencies not to book their clients to Japan, and charged several Japanese nationals with spying. It also declared its intention thenceforth to have Chinese vessels patrol the area, and has done so. There were anti-Japanese demonstrations in some 200 Chinese cities. Albeit carefully controlled so that they did not spill over into anti-Chinese government protests, they nonetheless resulted in great damage to property and calls to boycott Japanese-made products. Japanese restaurants and cars, most of them owned by Chinese, were destroyed.

The captain was released, in what was widely regarded as a political disaster for Kan. The prime minister's misfortunes were multiplied by the triple disaster of earthquake, tsunami, and nuclear meltdown of March 2011. In September, Kan was succeeded by a third DPJ prime minister, Noda Yoshihiko. Noda fared no better, facing numerous financial problems attendant on the triple disaster and a right wing that had been energized by the fishing boat incident. When the conservative mayor of Tokyo, Ishihara Shintaro, announced his intention to purchase the islands from their Japanese owners on behalf of Tokyo municipality, Beijing responded angrily. Noda, hoping to calm the situation and believing that Ishihara meant to erect structures on the island to further solidify Japanese control, announced that he intended to buy them[56] on behalf of the national government and would not put structures on them. Although Beijing warned that this would not suffice, Noda chose what he thought would be the less provocative option and proceeded with the purchase.

Not placated, Beijing sent additional ships to the area and increased its overflights many times over.[57] Several thousand demonstrators threw eggs and plastic bottles at the Japanese embassy in Beijing, with other demonstrations reported from a total of 85 cities. A Dutch observer of the scene in Beijing commented that the dynamics of ultra-nationalism on both sides had been unleashed, creating a situation that would do severe damage to bilateral economic relations and stability in the region and beyond.[58] Vice Chair of the Central Military Commission Xu Caihou said that the PLA should be prepared for combat.[59]

At a Beijing symposium on the islands issue, China Institute of Contemporary International Affairs expert Ji Zhiye opined that Japan's decision to purchase the islands reflected its weakening national strength: it was intended to distract Japanese citizens from the country's poor economic situation and increase public support for increased military spending. Chinese Academy of Social Sciences analyst Feng Zhaokui described the purchase as a key step toward ultra-rightism.[60]

The eighty-first anniversary of the Mukden Incident on September 18, which had triggered the Japanese invasion of Manchuria, provided fresh impetus for more anti-Japanese demonstrations. In what seemed to be a plea for peace, the Beijing-published *Global Times* editorialized that, although China could easily destroy Japan, it had no need to do so: demonstrations were one way that China dealt with invasion and provocations by other countries when it was weak. Having become more powerful, perhaps it was time to leave such means behind.[61] As Japanese factories closed and announced plans to move production facilities to other countries, some netizens expressed concern that job losses could hurt China, and that unemployed workers meant a greater probability of social instability.[62] To Tokyo's surprise, the Chinese government informed it that ceremonial events to mark the fortieth anniversary of the normalization of Sino-Japanese relations would proceed, albeit on a somewhat smaller scale than originally planned.[63] Trade declined in 2012, but began to recover in 2013.

Although a wider confrontation was avoided, Chinese ships stepped up their patrols of the disputed waters, and China's two highest delegates canceled their plans to attend the International Monetary Fund-World Bank meeting in Tokyo.[64] In Japan, public opinion shifted to the right. While Okinawans continued to demand the removal of American bases from their prefecture, most Japanese felt a greater need for US protection. The economy continued to suffer from the effects of the 3/11 disaster, with citizens demanding an end to nuclear power generation as well as, perversely, opposition to paying higher prices for the import of fossil fuels. Many held the DPJ and its lack of experience in governance responsible. In September 2012, the LDP was returned to power with hard line advocate Abe Shinzo re-assuming the prime ministership.

Speculations on why Beijing did not better accommodate a Japanese government that had tried to improve bilateral relations ranged from a hawkish faction within the PLA and a China that had grown arrogant due to its rapid rise to power to a party and government that needed to divert its population's attention away from domestic problems by creating a foreign enemy. Those who argued the first pointed out that certain generals, many of them retired or not in command positions, who the government was careful to explain spoke only for themselves, made incendiary statements, with one of them apparently calling for bombing Tokyo and bathing it in blood. Although the general later dissociated himself from the statement, it nonetheless became popular with anti-Japanese demonstrators who regarded the general as the source.[65]

Proponents of the second view noted that references to a Japan that did not matter anymore had become standard comments on social media, and that Japanese players at sports events were taunted with comments like "little Japan." A *Renmin Ribao* commentator urged Abe to abandon hope of getting Washington's support for Japan's ownership of the Diaoyu/Senkaku islands since it was folly to think that the US would choose to support Japan at the cost of its relations with China. Japan's over-dependence on the US in terms of its own relationship with China, he continued, meant missing "strategic opportunities" to establish long-term relations with China. To extricate itself from this dilemma, Japan should show its sincerity through unspecified "practical actions."[66] *Global Times* announced that, given the frequency of Chinese maritime and air overflights of the disputed islands, "Japan's 'actual control' over the islands has gone."[67]

As for the third hypothesis, Chinese analysts themselves have discussed their leadership's use of Japan as a diversion from domestic concerns. Military expert Ni Lexiong has stated that "the navy's aggressive presence will help Beijing win more support from the public amid the current worsening social unrest."[68]

While Beijing stated that it was willing to negotiate the issue of the disputed islands, it added that it would never sacrifice its sovereign rights over them. Japan refused to admit there was a dispute, since the islands clearly belonged to Japan. Each side was disinclined to accept mediation. Chinese defense budgets continued to rise by double digits. Japan's defense budget began to rise, albeit by exceedingly modest increments—0.8 percent in 2013 and 2.2 percent in 2014, after 11 years of actual decline.[69] A tortured debate is taking place about whether the constitution can be interpreted to allow the right of collective self-defense, with Abe's advisers favoring it while a recent poll indicated that almost twice as many people opposed the re-interpretation as supported it.[70]

Nonetheless, coast guard ships continue to warn off Chinese vessels from waters around the disputed islands and fighter planes are scrambled against Chinese overflights; the Self Defense Force trains to protect unnamed remote islands and retake unnamed islands if they are captured. Observers became concerned that the continual confrontations between Chinese and Japanese air and maritime patrols could lead to war. Others believe that, although the PRC is no longer dependent on Japanese help to develop its economy, the Sino-Japanese trade relationship is too valuable to both sides to resort to war.

The current situation

After Abe took office, the US and China agreed to expand Japan's role in their security alliance while maintaining an American military presence. Under the agreement, a new missile-defense radar system would be constructed in Japan, American drone aircraft deployed there for the first time, and joint efforts undertaken to combat cyberterror threats.[71] When, in November 2013, Beijing declared an Air Defense Identification Zone (ADIZ) that included the disputed islands, as well as part of previously declared ADIZs by Korea and Japan, Vice President Biden, in a meeting with Abe, announced that the United States was deeply concerned by the attempt to unilaterally change the status quo in the East China Sea, and assured Abe that America would "remain steadfast in our alliance commitments."[72]

Exactly what this last statement means is a subject of intense interest in both Tokyo and Beijing. According to article five of the US-Japan Mutual Security Treaty,

> Each party recognizes that an armed attack against either party in the territories under the administration of Japan would be dangerous to its own peace and safety and declares that it would act to meet the common danger in accordance with its constitutional provisions and processes. Any such armed attack and all measures taken as a result thereof shall be immediately reported to the Security Council of the United Nations in accordance with the provisions of Article 51 of the Charter. Such measures shall be terminated when the Security Council has taken the measures necessary to restore and maintain international peace and security.[73]

Given the PRC's veto in the Security Council, this last sentence is singularly un-reassuring. Moreover, contrast this article 5 with article 5 of the North Atlantic Treaty Organization's agreement that

> The parties agree that an armed attack against one of them in Europe or North America shall be considered an attack against them all and consequently they agree that, if such an armed attack occurs, each of them, in exercise of the right of individual or collective self-defense recognized by Article 51 of the Charter of the United Nations, will assist the party or parties so attacked by taking forthwith individually and in concert with the other parties, such action as it deems necessary, including the use of arms force, to restore and maintain the security of the North Atlantic area.[74]

The much looser wording of the former, the fact that the US pointedly takes no position on the ownership of the islands, and the frequent iteration by American officials that "The security treaty between the United States and Japan applies to any provocative set of circumstances. However, we are encouraging all sides to take appropriate steps so that there will be no misunderstandings, no miscalculations that could trigger an environment that would be antithetical to peace and stability,"[75] understandably cause many Japanese to doubt the strength of the American commitment to their defense.

Such statements are interpreted as urging Japan to exercise caution without the expectation of reciprocal caution by China. Hence, many Japanese do not believe that the United States will in fact defend Japan. In such an analysis, should America ever be forced to choose between Japan and China, the more pragmatic choice would be to choose China, and hence the security treaty is a treaty in name only.[76] Since the PRC has in fact not attacked the Diaoyu/Senkaku islands but simply surrounded them, typically with fishing boats and maritime surveillance vessels rather than the navy, the provisions of the security treaty have not been violated. The definition of provocative circumstances is open to a wide variety of interpretations, some of them applicable to Japan: for example, Washington expressed its displeasure to Abe for his visit to Yasukuni in December 2013 as jeopardizing stability in Asia.[77] Only a few months earlier, US Pacific Commander Admiral Samuel Locklear had stated that the major threat to Asian regional security was climate change, a singularly un-reassuring statement to Japanese defense planners.[78]

The situation at present is a diplomatic impasse while Beijing continues cautiously but actively to consolidate its position and Japan moves glacially to defend its claims. Although the possibility of a forceful confrontation cannot be ruled it, it seems unlikely. If current trends persist, Beijing is likely to quietly assume control of the islands even as Japan continues to assert its sovereignty over them. Something similar may be taking place in the South China Sea, as the PRC turns its claim for control of the area inside its nine-dashed line into a reality. Whether this will assuage Beijing's security concerns with regard to Japan remains to be seen. If, through some unforeseen but not entirely impossible set of circumstances, Beijing does not assert its primacy over Japan, the insecurity, whether genuine or an excuse for a further expansionist agenda, will assuredly continue.

Conclusions

A classic security dilemma has evolved in which each side regards the other's military and diplomatic activities with suspicion. China launched its first aircraft carrier in 2012; a year later, Japan commissioned its largest naval vessel since World War II. Though the ship is officially classified a helicopter destroyer, Chinese sources argue that it could easily be modified for use as an aircraft carrier.[79] In summer 2014, Japan's Cabinet Legislation Bureau issued a decision allowing the SDF to engage in collective self-defense, albeit under highly restrictive conditions.[80] Prime Minister Abe has reached out to other Asian nations who fear Chinese expansionism, China complains of a plot to encircle and contain it. Neither country's military has recent combat experience. While the PLA is by far the larger in both personnel and number of weapons and is a nuclear power, Japan's Self Defense-Forces are better trained and are backed by the United States.

Neither side seems inclined to back away from their conflicting claims. While pessimists believe that conflict is imminent, optimists believe that the obvious economic gains to both sides from peaceful relations will mitigate current frictions.

Glossary

ADIZ   Air Defense Identification Zone
DPJ   Democratic Party of Japan
EAC   East Asian Community
ECAFE   United Nations Economic Commission for Asia and the Far East
GOJ   Government of Japan
LDP   Liberal Democratic Party
MSDF   Maritime Self-Defense Force
NDPO   National Defense Program Outline
PKO   United Nations Peacekeeping Operation
PLA   People's Liberation Army
PLAN   People's Liberation Army Navy
PRC   People's Republic of China
SDF   Self Defense Forces
TMD   Theater Missile Defense

Notes

1   www.mod.go.jp/e/d_act/d_policy/dp01.html.
2   Harry S. Truman, *Memoirs*, Vol. 2, *Years of Trial and Hope, 1946–53* (New York: Doubleday, 1956), p. 66.

3 Donald G. Gillin, *Warlord: Yen Hsi-shan in Shansi Province, 1911–1949* (Princeton, NJ: Princeton University Press, 1967), p. 285.
4 Ti-wen Tao, "Striking Revelation of Japanese Militarism's Ambitions for Aggression: On the Reactionary Japanese Film, *Battle of the Japan Sea*," *Beijing Review*, February 5, 1971, pp. 13–17.
5 www.foia.cia.gov/sites/default/files/document_conversions/89801/DOC_0001086032.pdf
6 Peter Hays Gries, *China's New Nationalism: Pride, Politics, and Diplomacy* (Berkeley: University of California Press, 2004), p. 835.
7 The Japan Communist Party was estimated to have received four to five hundred million yen from the PRC before the JCP split with China in 1966. Additionally, Japanese "friendly firms" doing business in China were granted a standard subsidy of 1 percent, known to have risen to 20 percent in one case. Friendly firms that attended the Canton (Guangzhou) trade fair were accorded an additional 2 percent to "cover their expenses," leading observers to conclude that China was "buying trade," Koito Chugo, "The JCP and Red Chinese Funds," *Japan Times*, February 3, 1962, p. 12.
8 See e.g. John Nathan, *Mishima: A Biography* (Boston: Little, Brown, 1974) *passim*, and Henry Scott-Stokes, *The Life and Death of Yukio Mishima* (New York: Farrar, Straus, and Giroux) *passim*.
9 "Technical Bulletin Vol. 2, Economic Commission for Asia and the Far East Committee for Co-ordination of Joint Prospecting for Mineral Resources in Asian Offshore Areas" (New York: United Nations, May 1969), p. 41.
10 Philip Shabecoff, "Japan's Oil Find off Taiwan Poses Title Problems," *New York Times*, August 28, 1960, p. 1.
11 US Central Intelligence Agency, Directorate of Intelligence, "The Senkaku Islands Dispute: Oil under Troubled Waters," CIA-RDP79R00987A000300030008-8, May 1971, declassified May 2, 2007, p. 14.
12 *Japan Times*, March 5, 1972, p. 1.
13 The governments of both the Republic of China on Taiwan and the People's Republic of China maintain that the islands were administered by Taiwan, and should therefore have reverted to Chinese control after World War II, but no evidence to support this claim has been discovered.
14 These are estimates of the high and low periods for the period. Some vessels stayed, others arrived and left, with new boats entering the area as they did.
15 Diplomats privately speculated that factional disputes within the Chinese leadership had been the motivating force for the intrusion.
16 No author, "Japanese Reactionaries Step Up Naval Expansion," *Beijing Review*, October 29, 1971, pp. 18–19.
17 *Kyodo*, September 6, 1978.
18 No author, "Premier Hua Addresses Japanese Press," *Xinhua*, May 26, 1980; see also Victor Cha, *Alignment Despite Antagonism: The US-Korea-Japan Security Triangle* (Stanford, CA: Stanford University Press), p. 105.
19 No author, *Xinhua*, February 12, 1987.
20 Shengzhu Lu, "Liangqian Nianqian de Zhongguo Haiyang Huanjing [Two Thousand Years of China's Maritime Environment]," *Junshi Zhanwang* [*Military Prospects*], Beijing, pp. 33–4.
21 There was opposition, as a brief campaign to denounce Deng through association with Li Hongzhang, the official who had negotiated an end to the Sino-Japanese War of 1894–5, albeit only after the Chinese side had been resoundingly defeated.
22 Susan Shirk, *China: The Fragile Superpower* (New York: Oxford University Press, 2007), pp. 78–104.
23 *Yomiuri*, February 17, 1992.
24 *Beijing Review*, February 3–16, 1992, pp. 10–12.
25 *Guoji Wenti Yanjiu* [*International Issues Research*], April 13, 1992, pp. 18–24.
26 *Sankei Shimbun*, September 16, 1995.
27 www.mofa.go.jp/region/n-america/us/security/security.html.
28 www.mofa.go.jp/region/n-america/us/security/guideline.html.
29 Frank Ching, "US-Japan Ties Reinvigorated," *Far Eastern Economic Review*, May 2, 1996, p. 40.
30 A summary of press comments from several Japanese newspapers was published by *Kyodo*, April 18, 1996.
31 Ibid.
32 Xiangqing Meng, "A Strategic Measure with Ulterior Motives: Background and Attempt of Japan's Participation in the Theater Missile Defense System," *Shijie Zhishi* [*World Knowledge*], Beijing, April 1, 1999, pp. 18–19.
33 Author's interviews, March 2003.
34 China Defense White Paper 2000, *Xinhua*, October 16, 2000, p. 3. Available online at www.xinhuanet.com.
35 *Jiefang Junbao* [*PLA Daily*], June 21, 2000.
36 *Zhongguo Qingnian Bao*, July 7, 2001.

37 A video camera showed a consulate guard handing a Chinese soldier his cap after it had fallen off; and a Japanese consular official shaking hands with the squad leader of the Chinese police before they entered the consular premises. The consular official and squad leader were said to have dined together previously. *Kyodo*, May 17, 2002.
38 Author's interviews.
39 *Renmin Ribao*, December 14, 2004.
40 Peter Dutton's, *Scouting, Signaling, and Gatekeeping: Chinese Naval Operations in Japanese Waters and the International Law Implications* (Annapolis, MD: US Naval War College China Maritime Studies No. 2, 2009) analyzes this incident in detail.
41 Shirk, p. 175.
42 *Xinhua*, May 12, 2005; *Yomiuri*, May 12, 2005.
43 *Xinhua*, May 23, 2005
44 *Asahi*, November 25, 2005.
45 *Yomiuri*, December 15, 2005.
46 *Yomiuri*, December 30, 2005.
47 *Economist,* June 21, 2008.
48 *Nikkei Weekly*, June 23, 2008.
49 Ching Cheong, "Tokyo Seen as Having the Upper Hand," *Straits Times*, June 21, 2008.
50 *South China Morning Post*, June 28, 2008.
51 See, inter alia, *China Daily*, June 20, 2008; transcript of Ministry of Foreign Affairs statement June 18, 2008. Available online at http://news.xinhuanet.com/english/2008–06/18/content_8394206.htm (accessed February 3, 2012).
52 For a summary of Sino-Japanese relations in this period see June Teufel Dreyer, "China Up, Japan Down? Implications for US Policy," *Orbis*, Vol. 57, Iss. 1 (winter 2013): 83–100.
53 *China Daily*, February 26, 2010.
54 *South China Morning Post*, May 6, 2010.
55 Keith Bradsher, "Amid Tension, China Blocks Vital Exports to Japan," *New York Times*, September 22, 2010. Available online at www.nytimes.com/2010/09/23/business/global/23rare.html?pagewanted=all&_r=0.
56 Of the five Diaoyu/Senkaku islands, one was owned outright by the Japanese government and the other four by three members of the Kurihara family, who had in turn bought the islands decades before from the Koga family and paid taxes to the central government on them. The two brothers agreed to sell their three islands, the sister declined.
57 *Xinhua*, September 11, 2012.
58 Willem van Kemenade, personal communication to the author, September 15, 2012.
59 *Xinhua*, September 14, 2012.
60 *Xinhua*, September 15, 2012.
61 *Global Times*, September 18, 2012.
62 *Global Times*, September 20, 2012.
63 *Jiji*, September 21, 2013.
64 *Wall Street Journal*, October 11, 2012.
65 For examples of these, see http://chimericanews.com/2013/01/a-list-of-protest-slogans-from-recent-anti-japanese-protests-in-china/.
66 *Renmin Ribao*, October 23, 2012.
67 *Global Times*, December 14, 1012.
68 Cited in *South China Morning Post*, May 6, 2010.
69 Ministry of Defense, Government of Japan, "Plan for Defense Programs and Budget of Japan: Overview of FY 2014 Budget" (unpaginated). Available online at www.mod.go.jp/e/d_budget/pdf/251009.pdf.
70 A joint poll conducted by major daily newspaper *Mainichi Shimbun* and Saitama University at the end of 2013 showed 54 percent against and 28 percent in favor. *Mainichi Shimbun*, February 12, 2014. Available online at http://mainichi.jp/english/perspectives/news/20140212p2a001000c.html.
71 *Kyodo*, October 3, 2013.
72 www.tealeafnation.com/2013/02/chinese-generals-angry-online-rant-has-japanese-laughing-and-many-chinese-cheering/#sthash.87MHgWFo.dpuf; www.whitehouse.gov/the-press-office/2013/12/03/remarks-press-vice-president-joe-biden-and-prime-minister-shinzo-abe-jap.
73 www.mofa.go.jp/region/n-america/us/q&a/ref/1.html.
74 www.nato.int/cps/en/natolive/official_texts_17120.htm.

75 A standard comment, this one from then-assistant secretary of state Kurt Campbell in Kuala Lumpur, December 13, 2012. Available online at www.state/gov/p/eap/rls/rm/2012/12/201682.htm.
76 See e.g. Susumu Yabuki, "China-Japan Territorial Conflicts and the US-Japan-China Relations: Historical and Contemporary Perspective," *The Asia-Pacific Journal*, Vol. 11, Iss. 9, No. 2, March 4, 2013. Available online at http://japanfocus.org/Yabuki-Susumu/3906?rand=1363092477&type=print&print=1.
77 *Wall Street Journal*, December 26, 2013. Available online at http://online.wsj.com/news/articles/SB10001424052702304483804579281103015121712.
78 Bryan Bender, "Chief of US Pacific Forces Calls Climate Biggest Worry," *The Boston Globe*, March 9, 2013. Available online at www.bostonglobe.com/news/nation/2013/03/09/admiral-samuel-locklear-commander-pacific-forces-warns-that-climate-change-top-threat/BHdPVCLrWEMxRe9IXJZcHL/story.html.
79 Using short take-off vertical landing (STOVL) aircraft such as the as yet un-deployed US-developed F-35 B. No author, "Japan Unveils Largest Warship since World War II," *Associated Press*, August 6, 2013.
80 The situation must pose a clear threat to Japan, not only to an ally; the action must be undertaken only as a last resort; and the use of force is limited to the minimum necessary to protect the Japanese people. Nonetheless, a number of Japanese are concerned that the decision assumed that the constitution can be interpreted if not amended by the highest executive body rather than the supreme court. Michyo Ishida, "Japan's Parliament Begins Collective Self Defence Debate," *Channel News Asia*, July 15, 2014.

Select bibliography

Richard Bush, *The Perils of Proximity: China-Japan Security Relations* (Washington, DC: Brookings Institution, 2010).

Reinhard Drifte, *Japan's Security Relations with China Since 1989: From Balancing to Bandwagoning?* (London: RoutledgeCurzon, 2002).

Christopher W. Hughes, *Japan's Remilitarisation* (London: Routledge, 2009).

James Manicom, *Bridging Troubled Waters: China, Japan, and Maritime Order in the East China Sea* (Washington, DC: Georgetown University Press, 2014).

Caroline Rose, *Sino-Japanese Relations: Facing the Past, Looking to the Future?* (New York: RoutledgeCurzon, 2004).

8

China as "offshore balancer" and South Asia's regional security complex

Enze Han and Lawrence Saez

Introduction

Conventional studies on South Asian regional security tend to look at China's long-term strategic agenda from the viewpoint of India, namely the way in which India perceives its position of primacy within the South Asian regional security complex as being challenged by China.[1] Specifically, China's so called "string of pearls" strategy has generated great anxiety in India about China's intention in the Indian Ocean and the subcontinent.[2] In these frameworks of analysis, China and India are potential military adversaries and China seeks to develop a relationship with individual South Asian countries in order to offset India's presence in the region. However, what has been missing in the literature is how China is being actively utilized by other regional states in South Asia, such as Pakistan, Bangladesh, Nepal, Bhutan, and Sri Lanka, to balance against India's hegemonic position.

This chapter analyzes recent developments in China's long-term strategic agenda, particularly since the publication of its White Paper on Peaceful Development in 2011 and the recent re-orientation of China's foreign policy emphasis to neighbor countries since President Xi Jinping came to power in late 2012. Focusing on China's recent economic and strategic engagement with South Asian countries, the chapter will demonstrate that India's position of primacy within the South Asian regional security complex is increasingly being eroded and challenged. However, this erosion of India's position of primacy can also be seen through the lens of how other South Asian countries are strategically using China as a counterbalance against India, the *de facto* regional hegemon in South Asia. The chapter depicts China as the 'offshore-balance' for its engagement with other South Asian countries, and how such engagement generates a competitive dynamic that increases the bargaining power of these countries in their efforts to undermine India's regional hegemonic position within South Asia.

This chapter starts with a theoretical discussion of foreign policy choices of small states in the international system, and how great power competition can create greater bargaining range for small states. Rather than dismissing smaller states as irrelevant pushovers in international relations, this chapter discusses the scenarios in which great powers are outplayed and taken advantage of by the former. Keeping this theoretical focus in mind, the chapter reviews recent developments in China's grand strategy and its particular relevance for our understanding of the changing security dynamic in South Asia. The chapter then provides an overview of Pakistan's, Bangladesh's, Sri Lanka's, Nepal's and Bhutan's strategic engagements with China for the last decade, and examines how such engagements have been undertaken to increase their bargaining power relative to India. The chapter thus contributes to the literature on alliance behavior of smaller states in international relations in the context of rising powers.

Small states and the balance of power

The mainstream literature in international relations (IR) tends to have a big-power bias and has overlooked profound changes in the international system, particularly with the rise of Asian powers.[3] Certainly big powers, particularly the superpowers, have a preponderant influence at the international system level; and their foreign policies towards small states can also significantly constrain and shape both the small states' foreign policy as well as their domestic politics. However, this does not mean that small states are inconsequential in international relations. Of particular interest for this chapter is the phenomenon whereby small states take advantage of the competition among big powers to play them off against one another. Conventional neorealist theory suggests that big powers use smaller regional powers as offshore balancers against potential rivals in the international system.[4] Because of the competitive need for influence, the big powers' courting of small states inadvertently gives the latter more room to maneuver in their foreign policy. The key necessary condition for such a dynamic is competition among bigger powers. In situations where a big power has an unchallenged sphere of influence, the small states often have little foreign policy choice other than bandwagoning with it. However, in situations where there are at least two big powers competing for influence, the bargaining dynamic between the small states and the big powers would change quite significantly by bestowing more leverage to the small states. For example, during the Cold War period, many poor small states played the superpowers off against one another, notably in postcolonial Africa.[5] Such dynamics can also been seen in the competition over smaller Third World countries between China and Taiwan for diplomatic recognition before 2008, when both countries carried out so called "dollar diplomacy" by throwing money at many Caribbean and African states. Such competitive dynamics inevitably led to some courted countries, such as Liberia, Gambia and El Salvador, switching diplomatic recognition between the two sides several times so as to maximize their economic gain.[6]

The role of India in the South Asian regional security complex

In South Asia, India has historically enjoyed a position of hegemony over many of its surrounding countries. This hegemonic presence is a result of India's geographic and population size as well as on the basis of its economic and military assets compared with other South Asian countries. Smaller South Asian countries' perceptions or evaluations of their material and security relations are inevitably intertwined with those of India. However, in recent years such hegemony has been increasingly challenged by the engagement of China in South Asia. The involvement of China has thus created a competitive dynamic that smaller states in South Asia have started to take advantage of in dealing with India. Pakistan, one of India's direct military rivals, has had a long-standing strategic partnership with China, particularly after the signing of the 1963 Sino-Pakistan Frontier Agreement.

In recent years, China has cultivated strong trade and commercial relationships with most South Asian countries. Relations have deepened with the assistance of Chinese state-owned companies in the construction of physical infrastructure projects throughout the subcontinent, notably the ongoing construction by the China Overseas Port Holding Company of a deep sea port in Gwadar, Pakistan. Once completed, the port will feature seven berths and one bulk cargo terminal. Phase I of the project (which incorporated three multipurpose berths) was completed in December 2006, at an estimated cost of $248 million, of which China provided nearly 80 percent of the initial development costs.[7] Phase II of the project started in 2007 and aims on completion to include four container berths and a bulk cargo terminal, at an estimated cost of $932 million. The worsening insurgency-led turmoil in Balochistan and other operational challenges have prevented the completion of Phase II of the Gwadar Port, and thus in January 2014 the China Overseas Port Holding Company took full operational control of the project.[8]

In a similar way, the China Merchants Holding International company has participated in the proposed development of a deep sea water port on the island of Sonadia, near Cox's Bazaar, Bangladesh. Chinese state-owned companies have also spearheaded a number of ambitious infrastructure projects in Sri Lanka, such as the development of the Hambantota Port and Export Zone, the modernization of the Sri Lankan railway system, and the construction of an international container terminal in Colombo. Finally, by the end of 2014, China is expected to finalize the extension of the high altitude Qinghai-Tibet railway line that will link Lhasa to Xigase, near the China-Nepal border.

Since the signing of the 2004 South Asia Free Trade Agreement (SAFTA), there has been an increase of intraregional South Asia trade.[9] However, Chinese commercial engagement with South Asian states has provided an outlet for new commercial and trade partnerships beyond trade in traditional goods and services. Having to choose between China and India as a trade partner, some smaller South Asian countries have opted to enhance their trade links with China (relative to India), particularly by becoming a destination for Chinese weapons exports. For instance, in 2004 (the year of the signing of the SAFTA), Bangladesh imported $1.7 billion from India and $1.4 billion from China. By 2012 the balance of trade had reversed, with Bangladesh importing $6.1 billion from China and $4.7 billion from India. Moreover, there is some evidence that smaller South Asian countries are re-routing their exports to China. For instance, Sri Lanka's exports to India peaked in 2005 (the year in which Sri Lanka's civil war ended) and plummeted by 56.7 percent by 2009. In contrast, Sri Lanka's exports to China increased by 89.8 percent during the same time period.[10] Combined with China's participation in the development of large infrastructure projects in Pakistan, Bangladesh and Sri Lanka, India's hegemonic position in South Asia has been diluted.

Recent developments of China's grand strategy

Chinese foreign policy during the past few years has often been described as assertive.[11] The 2007–8 financial crisis in the West, China's hosting of the Olympic Games in 2008, and its continual robust economic growth to replace Japan as the second largest economy in the world in 2010 have all allegedly boosted the confidence of the Chinese government. At the same time, such developments have raised hopes and expectations among both the CCP elite and the Chinese masses about China's growing international profile and the "rightful" status China deserves as a great power. From much of the nationalist Chinese masses' point of view, the CCP has often been too weak to stand firm and protect China's core national interests, particularly on issues of territorial integrity such as Taiwan, Tibet, and increasingly the disputes in the East and South China Seas.[12] This domestic nationalist pressure thus propelled the Chinese State Councilor Dai Bingguo to summarize China's core national interests as preserving 1) China's basic political system and national security; 2) state sovereignty and territorial integrity; and 3) stable and continual socio-economic growth.[13]

Such definition of core national interests certainly is a bit elusive. Together with the continual economic growth and military build-up, they have all led to increased anxieties from both the reigning superpower—the US—and other regional states about the implications of China's "rise." Facing the 'China Threat' theory, the Chinese government in 2011 published a White Paper on Peaceful Development, in order, as the title implies, to portray its development as peaceful. In the White Paper it is stated that China "takes a path of peaceful development and is committed to upholding world peace and promoting common development prosperity for all countries."[14] The White Paper further clarifies that China's core national interests include "state sovereignty, national security, territorial integrity and national reunification, China's political system established by the constitution and overall social stability, and the basic safeguards for ensuring sustainable economic and social development."[15] Certainly, this emphasis on territorial integrity would not ease tension with some of the neighboring countries; however, the White Paper tries to re-assure other countries that China's rise will be peaceful and mutually beneficial. It particularly emphasizes a cooperative approach towards common development whereby China wishes to "ensure that its own development and the development of other countries are mutually reinforcing."[16]

Despite such "re-assuring" tactics, the international environment China has found itself in during the past few years has changed quite significantly, particularly with the United States' re-orientation of its foreign policy in its "pivot" to Asia. Coinciding with the American repositioning to the Asia Pacific region, several hotspots of territorial disputes between China and neighboring countries have flared up (i.e., the territorial disputes in the South China Sea, primarily between China, Vietnam and the Philippines, and between China and Japan over the Senkaku/Diaoyu Islands). Such a changing international environment has thus generated a tremendous amount of pressure on the Chinese government in terms of an appropriate response. It is in this context that on October 25, 2013, President Xi gave a foreign policy speech on the focus of China's diplomatic work. In this speech, he particularly emphasized that China's strategic goal is to have "good neighborly" relations with countries around China, to make them more politically friendly and economically integrated, and to seek deeper security cooperation and closer people-to-people ties.[17]

This emphasis on neighbor countries perhaps signals some rethinking in the current Chinese government's approach to foreign policy. According to Yan Xuetong, this means that in the future Chinese foreign policy is likely to switch from its current focus on the US to neighbor countries. Instead of trying to "appease" the US, which according to Yan is not "appeaseable" due to structural tensions between the existing superpower and a rising challenger, China should focus its energy on building a truly friendly and stable international environment around China.[18] Certainly China is involved in several territorial disputes with neighboring states, particularly with regard to its maritime boundary, but there are many countries in the region that do not have such major conflicts of interest. Thus, with this new orientation towards building good relations with neighbor countries, we can easily envision China putting South Asia in a prominent position on its foreign policy agenda. The following section will discuss China's engagement with South Asia and some recent developments with regard to this new emphasis on neighbor countries.

China's engagement with South Asia

It has been argued that China has historically undertaken three disaggregated foreign policy approaches in dealing with South Asian countries. These three strategies included what they referred to as *ambivalent competition, contingent cooperation* and *secretive cooptation*.[19] Saez and Chang argued that China's relations with India—which involve complex economic and military interactions—were characteristic of ambivalent competition. Clearly a defining factor in the nature of India's competition with China was the 1962 India-China border war. Although a relatively minor episode in contemporary Chinese history, the 1962 war was a humiliating defeat for India's armed forces, one that has marked India's subsequent strategic thinking. On the other hand, India and China have, in recent years, understood the potentially beneficial outcomes from bilateral trade. Nevertheless, although the total volume of trade between India and China has increased dramatically, India's trade deficit with China has also grown, reaching $37.5 billion in 2012.[20]

In contrast, China's relations with Pakistan, Bangladesh and Sri Lanka were identified as being motivated by contingent cooperation, meaning that the bilateral relationship is guided by the attainment of very specific goals for China. As Saez and Chang note, the "nature of this relationship is often cordial and cooperative, but only driven unilaterally and not based on reciprocity."[21] Finally, Saez and Chang posited that China's relations with Nepal, the Maldives and Myanmar exemplified secretive cooptation. In relation to these last three countries, China exerted its power covertly, without making use of overt policy instruments to assert its power.[22] However, it should be noted that in recent years, it is apparent that China has exercised its power overtly in Myanmar. For instance, the direct Chinese involvement in peace negotiations between ethnic Kachin rebel groups and the Myanmar government is emblematic of China's increasing assertiveness in the region.

Over the last few years, however, China's engagement with South Asia has increasingly shown a shift towards a more interactive and mutually beneficial bilateral relationship between China and those smaller South Asian countries with which it has traditionally maintained a contingent cooperative engagement. Although it appears that China's relationship with Pakistan, Bangladesh, Sri Lanka and Nepal is asymmetrical in terms of expected gains, with the balance falling to China in terms of ability to make inroads into South Asia, these South Asian countries also benefit from engaging with China by using China as an "offshore balancer" against the regional hegemon (i.e., India). By virtue of its inherent relative economic and military strength, India has historically exerted a strong influence in South Asia. In some of these smaller South Asian countries, India inevitably has a strong influence, yet it lacks complete dominance and control. The strategy pursued by Pakistan, Bangladesh, Sri Lanka, Nepal and Bhutan is to offset India's hegemonic presence in South Asia by deepening their relationship with China. This approach solidifies the expected unilateral gains that China obtains from Pakistan, Bangladesh and Sri Lanka, but at the same time it serves to stave off India's more immediate threats regionally. As will be shown in the brief country case studies below, China has utilized a number of tools, notably weapons supply, asymmetric trade and development assistance, and other forms of strategic engagement to deepen its presence in South Asia. In a sense, it could be argued that in the absence of complete hegemonic control by Indian in the South Asian security complex, China is attempting to establish its position of dominance in the region.

China's strategic engagement with India

India is South Asia's largest and economically most powerful nation. As such the nature of China's relationship with India is singular and complex. During India's early post-independence, relations with China were cordial and it became the first non-socialist country to establish diplomatic relations with the PRC.[23] The two countries shared an outward-looking internationalist foreign policy based on a set of broad principles encapsulated by the Five Principles of Peaceful Coexistence introduced with the signing of the 1954 agreement on trade and communications between the Chinese region of Tibet and India. These principles, which were mutual respect for sovereignty and territorial integrity, mutual non-aggression, non-interference in each other's affairs, equality and mutual benefit, and peaceful coexistence, formed part of the ten-point declaration signed at the 1954 Bandung Conference of Asian and African states.

Tensions between China and India arose as a result of unresolved boundary claims between post-independence India and Tibet. These tensions were aggravated when India's prime minister, Jawaharlal Nehru, decided to grant asylum to the Dalai Lama during the revolts in Tibet in the late 1950s. The conflicting territorial claims by China and India led to a one-month border war in October 1962 that resulted in a substantial loss of Indian territory to Chinese forces. Having clearly asserted its battlefield superiority, China declared a unilateral ceasefire and withdrew its troops behind the contested line of control. According to Sidhu and Yuan, "India had lost the war and was forced to accept both territorial loss and national humiliation on a grand scale."[24]

The 1962 border war has been the most important event to define Sino-Indian relations. Although the two countries did not formally cease diplomatic relations, such relations were characterized by low-intensity hostility. It was not until December 1998, on the occasion of Indian Prime Minister Rajiv Gandhi's official visit to China, that a thaw began. The visit, the first by an Indian prime minister since 1954, "was a definitive moment in Sino-Indian relations."[25] The two countries gradually shifted away from diplomatic hostility and began to explore avenues for commercial and institutional cooperation.

The most notable aspect of China's improved relationship with India has been in terms of a sharp increase in bilateral trade. In 1990, bilateral trade was $270 million, a decade later it increased to $2.8 billion. Official visits to India by Chinese Prime Minister Wen Jiabao in April 2005 and Chinese President Hu Jintao in November 2006 set the tone for a dramatic upswing in bilateral trade. President Hu is credited with putting forward an ambitious five-point proposal to increase Sino-Indian economic cooperation.[26] One of the outcomes of these visits was that the Nathu La pass connecting India's state of Sikkim and Tibet was opened to bolster bilateral trade. This mountain pass had been the site of a border skirmish in 1967, so at a symbolic level it represented a new approach to bilateral relations. More importantly, President Hu proposed that bilateral trade increase to $40 billion by 2010. By 2010, though, Chinese exports to India exceeded $40 billion and bilateral trade had reached $61.4 billion. The latest available figures show that bilateral trade between India and China exceeded $66.5 billion in 2012.[27] Nevertheless, the increased volume of trade disguises the fact that China is increasing its trade surplus with India. By 2012, India's trade deficit with China stood at $28.9 billion.[28]

At present, it appears that China's relations with India have moved away from hostility and "are increasingly based upon principles of 'engaged balance.'"[29] A big part is due to the fact that China would like to rely on India's cooperation in changing the current international order to one of multipolarity. As emphasized most recently by President Xi in the Indian newspaper *The Hindu*, China would like to work together with India to "make the international order more fair and reasonable."[30] Thus, in order to counter the perceived hegemony of the US and the West in the international system, it seems China and India, as the two most populous and rapidly developing countries, do share certain common interests in making themselves better represented and heard in various international organizations, particularly the IMF and the World Bank. At the same time, China and India, together with the other BRICS countries, have most recently made an effort to create a New Development Bank, which many have labeled a potential competitor for the Bretton Woods institutions.[31]

China's strategic engagement with Pakistan

Although China's relationship with Pakistan has been identified as being one of contingent cooperation, it is undoubtedly the most robust and long-lasting of China's diplomatic and strategic interactions in South Asia. Pakistan was one of the first non-Soviet bloc countries to cease diplomatic relations with the Republic of China and to recognize the PRC. At a strategic level, China's relations with Pakistan were initially motivated by an effort to limit Soviet influence in the region during the second phase of the Cold War (1962–79). Pakistan was a member state of the Central Treaty Organization (CENTO), so formally it formed part of the US encirclement strategy in Central Asia and the Middle East against the USSR. At the same time, China offered support to Pakistan during the Soviet invasion of Afghanistan.

Sino-Pakistani relations were also solidified in the aftermath of the 1962 border war between India and China. During the 1962 border war, China launched a two-pronged offensive, in Aksai Chin in the northeastern section of the Ladakh region of Jammu and Kashmir and in the North Eastern Frontier Agency, and was able to briefly capture thousands of square kilometers of territory claimed by India. The border war resulted from the lack of clarity in the border between China and India, particularly along parts of the Kashmir area held by Pakistan but claimed by India. In order to resolve any lingering border disputes, China and Pakistan agreed to formally delimit and demarcate the Xinjiang and the contiguous border areas by signing the 1963 Sino-Pakistan Frontier Agreement. According to the conditions of the agreement, China ceded nearly 2,000 square kilometers of captured Indian territory to Pakistan, while Pakistan recognized Chinese sovereignty over hundreds of square kilometers along Ladakh and northern Kashmir, northeast of the Siachen Glacier. The implications of this exchange of land between China and Pakistan are important, as they would inhibit any resolution of the conflict in Kashmir without the involvement of China.

From the Soviet invasion of Afghanistan in 1979 until the collapse of the Soviet Union in1991, China attempted to maintain peripheral stability by enhancing its economic and military assistance to Pakistan. It also sought to defuse tensions between Pakistan and India, particularly after both countries carried out underground nuclear tests in 1998. Although Pakistan has served as a frontline state during periods of conflict in Afghanistan, China's assistance to Pakistan co-existed with American military and economic involvement in the country. As a result, the level of trade between China and Pakistan increased dramatically. In 2000, the total volume of trade between China and Pakistan was $1.2 billion; by 2012 their bilateral trade had increased tenfold to $12.4 billion. During the same period, the trade volume between China and Pakistan also skyrocketed. In 2000, the total volume of trade between China and India was $2.8 billion, by 2012 their bilateral trade was $66.5 billion.[32] It should be noted, however, that in 2012 India had a $28.9 billion trade deficit with China, whereas Pakistan sustained a $6.2 billion trade deficit with China.

China's strategic interests in Pakistan are substantial. At a commercial level, Pakistan is a major recipient of Chinese weapons exports, while India does not purchase weapons from that country. At present, Pakistan is the world's largest recipient of Chinese weapons transfers. In 2012, for instance, Pakistan received 47.8 percent of Chinese global arms exports.[33] Viewed from the perspective of the recipient country, Pakistan has become increasingly reliant on Chinese weaponry as China provides 54 percent of Pakistan's weapons imports. Pakistan has invested heavily in conventional weaponry, which will enhance its defensive capabilities against a potential attack from India. To that effect, Pakistan has imported Chinese tanks, fighter jets and patrol boats. In addition, Pakistan has purchased Chinese radar and communications equipment. Pakistan's engagement with China has thus appeased Pakistan's concerns about dependence on US military assistance and weapons transfers.

In the past, particularly with passage of the Pressler and the Glenn Amendments to the US Arms Export Control Act, the US has undermined Pakistan's military security by imposing strong economic sanctions and forbidding the transfer of US military weaponry unless it could be certified that Pakistan was not developing a nuclear weapons program. Following the economic sanctions imposed on Pakistan after it carried out underground nuclear tests in 1998, Pakistan sought assistance from China to develop its nuclear weapons program. Pakistan's early generation Hatf-1 and Hatf-2 missiles were designed and produced indigenously. However, according to the Federation of American Scientists, the newer Shaheen series of solid-propellant short-range ballistic missiles are imports from China.[34] In addition to Chinese assistance in the development of Pakistan's missile program, China has also pledged to assist in the construction of nuclear power plants in Pakistan. For instance, in 2013, China and Pakistan signed an agreement that will lead to the construction of a 1,000 megawatt CHASNUPP-5 nuclear power reactor in the Chashma nuclear power complex. Moreover, China and Pakistan are negotiating the construction of two nuclear power reactors to be constructed at Paradise Point, near Karachi.

China's strategic engagement with Bangladesh

Following Bangladesh's secession from Pakistan, India was Bangladesh's closest ally in South Asia. India's involvement in Bangladesh's nationalist movement was instrumental in making possible that country's independence. For instance, India's Lieutenant General Jagjit Singh Aurora, the commander of the joint Bangladesh-India allied forces, was one of the signatories to Pakistan's agreement of surrender in 1971. India's relations with Bangladesh were strongest during the rule of Sheikh Mujibur Rahman (1971–5), but began to deteriorate once Bangladesh suffered a string of coups d'état.

Starting with General Ziaur Rahman (1977–81, no relation) and continuing with General Hossain Mohammad Ershad (1982–90), Bangladesh began to distance itself from India due to a number of bilateral irritants. These included disagreements over the diversion of water from the Farakka Barrage, conflicting sovereignty claims over the New Moore (or South Talpatti) offshore sandbar, and the illegal crossing by Bangladeshi nationals into Indian territory.[35] On the diplomatic front, for instance, Bangladesh sought to take the lead regionally by promoting regional cooperation through multilateral institutions. Bangladesh's leadership prompted the formation of the South Asian Association for Regional Cooperation (SAARC) in 1985.[36] The Association was structured in a way so as to provide equal voice to all SAARC members, thus limiting the exercise of India's regional leadership.

Since China was a strong ally of Pakistan, China did not support the Mukti Bahini (the insurgent group that led Bangladesh's independence from Pakistan). Once Bangladesh became an independent country, China exercised its veto in the UN Security Council to try to prevent Bangladesh from joining the United Nations. Nevertheless, China's relations with Bangladesh have evolved towards closer economic and military cooperation since 1977. On the other hand, Bangladesh's relations with India began to deteriorate over a number of issues, including the controversy over Bangladeshi refugee camps in India and well as lingering border disputes and disagreements about the sharing of water and energy resources.

During Bangladesh's tumultuous transition to democracy, the country's highly polarized political parties were unanimous in expressing their desire to maintain political and diplomatic independence from India. In contrast, successive Bangladeshi governments continued to foster closer relations with China in an effort to offset Indian influence. The result of this relationship has been a dramatic increase in Chinese exports to Bangladesh and a corresponding bilateral trade deficit with that country. In 1990, the year when Bangladesh began its transition to parliamentary democracy, China's exports to Bangladesh were $149 million. They increased to $899 million in 2000 and skyrocketed to $7.9 billion in 2012. In contrast, Bangladesh's exports to China increased timidly from $23.9 million in 1990 to $478.9 million in 2012.[37]

In recent years, China has provided Bangladesh with important military logistical support. For instance, in 2008, China assisted Bangladesh in the construction of an anti-ship missile launch pad. Mirroring China's assistance in the construction of costly deep sea water ports elsewhere,

China has been in negotiations to begin assisting Bangladesh in the construction of a deep sea port on the island of Sonadia, near Cox's Bazaar. China is also assisting Bangladesh in the construction of a motorway linking China and Bangladesh via Myanmar. According to one analyst, the transport of cargo from Kunming, China, to the deep sea water port at Sonadia would reduce transport distances to Europe by 4,000 kilometers.[38]

More recently, Bangladesh has increasingly become an important destination for Chinese weapons exports. In 2012, Bangladesh displaced Myanmar as the world's second largest destination for Chinese weapons exports. According to SIPRI, Bangladesh received 16.8 percent of China's total arms exports in 2012.[39] Chinese weapons exports accounted for 82 percent of Bangladesh's weapon imports.

Chinese military assistance has emboldened the government of Bangladesh to distance itself further from India at the diplomatic level. For instance, Bangladesh spearheaded China's inclusion as an observer to SAARC, South Asia's most important regional institution.[40] The inclusion of China in SAARC as an observer is a direct challenge to India's wish not to allow membership expansion of this regional body. Although India and Bangladesh are not military rivals, they have had an uneasy relationship due to a number of border, water sharing and illegal migration issues. As such, Bangladesh has also asserted its independence from Indian positions on a number of energy trading schemes and water sharing arrangements.

China's strategic engagement with Sri Lanka

Sri Lanka's economy is heavily reliant on exports. As such, Sri Lanka's foreign policy has traditionally been motivated by an effort to strengthen trade and commercial relations with other nations. China has maintained cordial relations with Sri Lanka, mostly guided on the basis of a commercial maritime agreement signed in 1963. A decade later, China had become Sri Lanka's largest destination for its exports.[41]

Internal political considerations have distanced Sri Lanka's diplomatic engagement with India. The discriminatory government policies favoring the Sinhalese majority and the perceived mistreatment of the Tamil minority population became one of India's most important foreign policy concerns during the period from the 1970s through the 1990s. Sri Lanka's civil war (1983–2009) has been, without a doubt, the most complex political event in the island's history. During the initial stages of the conflict, India did not directly support the Liberation Tigers of Tamil Eelam (LTTE) rebel group, but it did provide humanitarian assistance, mostly in the form of food and medicine. Following an accord between the Indian and Sri Lankan governments, India pledged to send the Indian Peace Keeping Force (IPKF) in order to participate in peacekeeping operations in northern Sri Lanka. Although initially welcomed as potential saviors by the Tamil population, the IPKF began to fight off attacks from the LTTE forces. India's ill-fated attempt (from 1987 until 1990) to act as an intermediary between the Sri Lankan government and the LTTE rebel group resulted in a humiliating withdrawal of the IPKF starting in 1989. A few years later, an LTTE suicide bomber assassinated Rajiv Gandhi as he was campaigning in Tamil Nadu on the eve of the national parliamentary election in 1991.

Although China maintained a policy of non-interference during most of Sri Lanka's long running civil war (1983–2009), China's relationship with Sri Lanka has evolved in recent years, particularly after the presidential election of Mahinda Rajapaksa in 2005. A year after the 2004 tsunami, China became Sri Lanka's largest financer of economic development programs, amounting to a quarter of all economic development projects financed on the island.[42] Since 2005, there has been a notable increase in Chinese economic and military influence in Sri Lanka.

China's relationship with Sri Lanka led to a dramatic bilateral increase in trade in goods and services. The volume of trade between China and Sri Lanka tripled between 2005 and 2012, from $977 million to $3.1 billion.[43] More significantly, by 2008, China also became Sri Lanka's largest source of arms imports.[44] The substantial increase in Chinese arms exports to Sri Lanka, tripling Sri Lanka's arms imports in 2007, represented an important boost in the ability of the Sri Lankan armed forces to overcome Tamil Tiger insurgent forces. According to Wheeler, "it is undeniable that Chinese weapons played a significant role in the final stages of the civil war."[45]

Since the end of the civil war, China has remained Sri Lanka's most important ally and the key international player in the island's post-conflict reconstruction. Mirroring its involvement in Pakistan and Bangladesh, China has financed the construction of a deep sea water port at Hambantota. The construction of the port is being delivered by the China Harbor Engineering Company and Sinohydro Corporation. Phase I of the project, which included the construction of two multipurpose berths, was completed in 2010. According to the Sri Lanka Ports Authority, the estimated cost of Phase I of the project was $361 million, of which 85 percent was funded by China's Ex-Im Bank.[46] Phase II of the project (which will feature a container terminal) is expected to cost $750 million and will be completed by the end of 2014. It is projected that Phase III of the project will include a dockyard. On completion of all three phases of the project, the port at Hambantota (officially known as the Magampura Mahinda Rajapaksa Port) will be the largest port in South Asia.[47] China has also offered technical assistance to Sri Lanka in the modernization of Sri Lankan Railways and in the development of the Colombo International Container Terminal (CICT).

More importantly, Sri Lanka's relationship with China has served as a shield from efforts to investigate alleged atrocities committed by the Sri Lankan armed forces during the last stages of the civil war. Obtaining accurate information about probably grave violations of human rights in Sri Lanka has been a challenge. Sri Lanka's government has resolutely refused to facilitate any such investigation. China has been a strong supporter of the Sri Lankan government's efforts in this regard. For instance, the Chinese embassy released a sharply worded statement that condemned "any efforts that politicize or have double standards on human rights, as well as pressurize other countries using human rights as a tool." The statement added that "the international community, instead of taking measures that may complicate the issue, should respect the right of the Sri Lankan government and people to choose their own path of promoting human rights and create a favorable external environment for Sri Lanka to pursue stability and economic development."[48]

Sri Lanka has continued to benefit from China's economic involvement in the island's infrastructure development. In return, Sri Lanka has also enjoyed China's explicit support regarding its internal affairs. For instance, during his visit to Sri Lanka in September 2014, President Xi Jinping stated that China "resolutely opposes any move by any country to interfere in Sri Lanka's internal affairs under any excuse."[49] *The New York Times* interpreted these strongly worded statements as evidence that China "chips away at India's traditional dominance in the region."[50] On the basis of China's support, India has been hesitant to openly condemn the Sri Lankan government's lack of accountability on human rights issues and eventually abstained from voting on a US-led UN Human Rights Council (UNHRC) resolution calling for the Sri Lankan government to take measures to facilitate the reconciliation of the Tamil population.

China's strategic engagement with Nepal and Bhutan

By virtue of their geographic location, Nepal and Bhutan are the only two South Asian countries that exclusively share borders with India and China. They are also the only two landlocked countries in South Asia, naturally forcing them to pursue a clear strategy *vis-à-vis* their large neighbors. On the one hand, India and Nepal signed the 1950 Treaty of Peace and Friendship, which provided close cooperation on trade, defense and foreign policy issues. However, as argued by Rose (1971), Nepal's "strategy for survival" was to serve as a trade and cultural bridge between both countries.⁵¹ The policy of balancing out Nepal's position with India and China was pursued by Nepal's last two monarchs, King Mahendra (1955–72) and King Birendra (1972–2001). In contrast, Bhutan opted to develop strong economic and military relations with India, exemplified by the terms of the 1949 Indo-Bhutanese Treaty of Friendship, which established a joint engagement in foreign relations. It was not until the 2007 revisions to the Indo-Bhutanese Treaty of Friendship that Bhutan's independence from India in foreign policy was explicitly delineated.

China's primary strategic concerns with Nepal and Bhutan are related to their proximity to Tibet, one of China's most politically sensitive regions. One of the issues of mutual concern has been the presence of Tibetan refugees in Nepal. Since disruptions in Tibet in the 1950s, Nepal has become a gateway for Tibetan refugees. The UNHCR (2014) estimates that there are over 20,000 Tibetan refugees residing in Nepal.⁵² From Nepal's perspective, the large presence of refugees constitutes a significant economic drain, whereas China is concerned about any potential security risks that these refugees may pose inside its border.

In 1994, the United Communist Party of Nepal (Maoist) (UCPN-M) was founded and two years later sought to replace the Nepalese monarchy with a democratic republic. To that effect it launched what it called a "people's war" against the Nepalese monarchy.⁵³ Although the UCPN-M styled itself as a "Maoist" party, it has no direct operational link to China and it has developed its own indigenous political ideology under the direction of its chairman, Pushpa Kamal Dahal (aka Prachanda). Given these circumstances, China nominally maintained a position of neutrality during Nepal's civil war (1996–2006) between Maoist insurgents and government forces loyal to the monarchy. However, when an arms embargo was imposed on Nepal by the US, Britain and India in 2005, China provided some military supplies to King Gyanendra's forces. Curiously, once the civil war ended and Maoist leaders took charge of the government after the 2008 elections, Nepal's relations with China continued to improve. Nepal's first elected prime minister since the end of the civil war, Pushpa Kamal Dahal, sought to revoke the 1950 Treaty of Peace and Friendship with India and called for closer cooperation with China.

From the resignation of Prachanda in 2009 until the 2013 constituent assembly elections in Nepal, the country has lived in a state of political limbo as the constituent assembly failed to write a new constitution. The newly established Nepalese government, led by Prime Minister Sushil Koirala, has moved quickly to start trade negotiations with China with the expectation that new trade links can be developed for Nepalese exports. Although China's exports to Nepal continued to grow during the civil war, Nepal's exports to China stagnated because vast sections of Nepalese territory were under the control of Maoist insurgents, thus making it difficult to mobilize goods within the country towards the border access points. By 2009, the total value of Nepal's exports to China was \$5.2 million, the lowest since 2001. Since then, there has been a marked improvement in Nepalese exports to China, reaching \$29.5 million in 2012.⁵⁴ The end of the civil war enabled some Nepalese products, notably carpets, animal hides, and medicinal herbs, to be transported along the Araniko highway to the Nepal-China border at Kodari.

There have also been growing expectations about the extension of the high altitude Qinghai-Tibet railway line linking Lhasa to Xigase, which would facilitate the transportation of goods and services. It is unclear, however, whether this new trade route would help increase Nepalese exports to China or whether it would lead to a widening of Nepal's trade deficit with China. In 2012, Nepal exported \$29 million to China and imported \$1.9 billion from that country, resulting in a trade deficit for Nepal of \$1.7 billion, equivalent to 10 percent of Nepal's gross domestic product.⁵⁵ On the other hand, there is growing concern that China is pressuring Nepal to control the activities of Tibetan refugees in Nepal. For instance, a 2014 Human Rights Watch report noted that there has been closer monitoring of Tibetan refugees by Nepalese security forces and the repatriation of some refugees to China.⁵⁶ The Nepalese authorities have enacted stringent prohibitions on political protests by Tibetan refugees and have been accused by Human Rights Watch of using short-term preventative detentions to intimidate activists within the Tibetan community in Nepal.[57]

Implications of China's offshore balancer role

China's offshore balancer engagement in South Asia has several implications for the region. There appears to have been an important strategic shift in China's engagement with South Asia. China's engagement with various South Asian countries has helped expand the country's commercial and trade presence in the region. The economic cooperation between China and South Asian countries has also led in the direction of developmental assistance, typically with the provision of technical assistance for disaster relief and in the construction of large infrastructure projects. As has been noted here, South Asian countries have been an important destination for Chinese weapons exports.

Although China's trade and commercial engagement with South Asia has been of direct benefit to China, in turn smaller South Asian countries have begun to utilize their relations with China to provide a counterbalance to any possible expansion of Indian hegemony in the region. We have characterized this particular strategy adopted by South Asian countries as placing China as an offshore balancer to India. As we have shown here, with illustrations from Pakistan, Bangladesh, Sri Lanka and Nepal, smaller South Asian countries have been able to use China as an offshore balancer to India with varying degrees of success.

One of the implications of China's offshore balancer role has been to weaken the commitment of smaller South Asian countries to international human rights norms, as illustrated by the case of Sri Lanka's intransigence to calls to investigate alleged atrocities committed by government forces during the last stages of the civil war in that country. Another important implication of China's offshore balancer strategy has been the use by South Asian countries of Chinese influence as a bargaining tool in relation to India, particularly in asserting increasing independence from India in diplomatic issues. For instance, in this chapter we have highlighted how SAARC, South Asia's most important international organization, was structured in a way that prevented any assertion of regional hegemony by India. We have also shown how Bangladesh, much to the chagrin of India, sponsored China's presence as an observer in SAARC summits. Correspondingly, Bangladesh has increased its independence from India on a number of issues, including water sharing and energy trading proposals. The third implication of China's offshore balancer strategy *vis-à-vis* South Asia is the likelihood of greater military competition and friction between China and India. In a sense, China and India have an asymmetric relationship with smaller South Asian countries. On the one hand, India does not enjoy a network of strong regional allies, whereas China (through trade and infrastructure development assistance) has substantially strengthened its relations with smaller South Asian countries in recent years. As we have shown, China has now become the largest weapons supplier to Pakistan, Bangladesh and Sri Lanka. These military links in effect neutralize any potential hegemonic influence of India within a regional security complex.

Notes

An earlier version of this paper was presented at the ISA/FLACSO international conference held in Buenos Aires, Argentina, July 23–5, 2014. The authors would like to thank Hsin Chih Chen, Taeheok Lee, M. Matheswaran and David Mitchell for useful comments and suggestions.

1 M. Karim, *The Future of South Asian Security: Prospects for a Nontraditional Regional Security Architecture*, Seattle: National Bureau of Asian Research, 2013.
2 B. Chellaney, "Countering China's 'String of Pearls,'" *Washington Times*, May 6, 2013. Available online at: www.washingtontimes.com/news/2013/may/6/countering-chinas-string-of-pearls/; A. Townshend, "Unraveling China's 'String of Pearls,'" *Yale Global Online Magazine*, September 16, 2011. Available

online at http://yaleglobal.yale.edu/content/unraveling-chinas-string-pearls; A. Vines, "Mesmerised by Chinese String of Pearls Theory," *The World Today*, February/March, 2012: 33–4.
3 A. Florini, "Rising Asian Powers and Changing Global Governance," *International Studies Review*, Vol. 13, No. 1 (2011): 24–33.
4 C. Layne, "From Preponderance to Offshore Balancing: America's Future Grand Strategy," *International Security*, Vol. 22, No. 1 (summer 1997): 86–124; J. Mearsheimer, "A Return to Offshore Balancing," *Newsweek*, December 31, 2008. Available online at www.newsweek.com/return-offshore-balancing-82925?piano_t=1.
5 U. Ohaegbulam, "The United States and Africa after the Cold War," *Africa Today*, Vol. 39, No. 4 (1992): 19–34.
6 D. Erikson and J. Chen, "China, Taiwan, and the Battle for Latin America," *Fletcher Forum of World Affairs*, Vol. 31, No. 69 (summer 2007): 1–10; G. Bowley, "Cash Helped China Win Costa Rica's Recognition," *New York Times*, September 12, 2008. Available online at www.nytimes.com/2008/09/13/world/asia/13costa.html?_r=0 (accessed March 25, 2014).
7 S. Shahid, "Gwadar Port Inaugurated: Plan for Second Port in Balochistan at Sonmiani," *Dawn*, March 21, 2007. Available online at www.dawn.com/news/238494/gwadar-port-inaugurated-plan-for-second-port-in-balochistan-at-sonmiani.
8 S. Fazl-e-Haider, "Insurgency Stunts Gwadar Progress," *Asia Times*, May 9, 2014. Available online at www.atimes.com/atimes/South_Asia/SOU-01-090514.html.
9 L. Saez, *The South Asian Association for Regional Cooperation (SAARC): An Emerging Collaboration Architecture*, London: Routledge, 2011.
10 International Monetary Fund, *Direction of Trade Statistics*, Washington, DC: International Monetary Fund, 2014.
11 A. Friedberg, *A Contest for Supremacy: China, America, and the Struggle for Mastery in Asia*, New York: W. W. Norton & Company, 2012; M. Yahuda, "China's New Assertiveness in the South China Sea," *Journal of Contemporary China*, Vol. 22, No. 81 (2013): 446–59.
12 For a discussion on Chinese nationalism and foreign policy, see J. Weiss, *Powerful Patriots: Nationalist Protest in China's Foreign Relations*, New York: Oxford University Press, 2014.
13 See www.chinanews.com/gn/news/2009/07-29/1794984.shtml.
14 See http://english.gov.cn/official/2011-09/06/content_1941354.htm.
15 Ibid.
16 Ibid.
17 "Xi Jinping: China to Further Friendly Relations with Neighboring Countries," *Xinhua*, October 26, 2013. Available online at http://news.xinhuanet.com/english/china/2013-10/26/c_125601680.htm.
18 X. Yan, "Start of Full-Scale Reform of Chinese Foreign Policy," www.charhar.org.cn/newsinfo.aspx?newsid=6675; G. Zhao, "China: Periphery and Strategy," in Shanghai Institute for International Studies (ed.), *China and Asia's Security*, Singapore: Marshall Cavendish, 2005, p. 67.
19 L. Saez and C. Chang, "China and South Asia: Strategic Implications and Economic Imperatives," in Lowell Dittmer and George Yu (eds), *China, the Developing World, and the New Global Dynamic*, Boulder, CO: Lynne Rienner, 2010, p. 100.
20 IMF, 2014, op. cit.
21 Ibid, p. 101.
22 Ibid.
23 A. Athwal, *China-India Relations: Contemporary Dynamics*, London: Routledge, 2008.
24 W. Sidhu and J. Yuan, *China and India: Cooperation or Conflict?* Boulder, CO: Lynne Reinner, p. 15.
25 Athwal, 2008, op. cit., p. 25.
26 S. Sharma, *China and India in the Age of Globalization*, Cambridge: Cambridge University Press, 2009.
27 IMF, 2014, op. cit.
28 Ibid.
29 C. Ogden, *Indian Foreign Policy*, Cambridge: Polity Press, p. 124.
30 J. Xi, "Toward an Asian Century of Prosperity," *The Hindu*, September 17, 2014. Available online at: www.thehindu.com/opinion/op-ed/towards-an-asian-century-of-prosperity/article6416553.ece#comments.
31 R. M. Desai and J. R. Vreeland, "What the New Bank of BRICS Is All About," *The Washington Post*, July 17, 2014. Available online at www.washingtonpost.com/blogs/monkey-cage/wp/2014/07/17/what-the-new-bank-of-brics-is-all-about/.
32 IMF, 2014, op. cit.
33 SIPRI, "Importer/Exporter TIV Tables." Available online at http://armstrade.sipri.org/armstrade/page/values.php.

34 Federation of American Scientists, "WMD around the World: Pakistan." Available online at http://fas.org/nuke/guide/pakistan/missile/.
35 N. Jayapalan, *India and Her Neighbours*, New Delhi: Atlantic Publishers, 2000, pp. 133–69.
36 Saez, 2011, op. cit.
37 IMF, 2014, op. cit.
38 A. K. M. Shafiqullah, "Deep Sea Port in Sonadia: A Unique Opportunity for Bangladesh," *The Daily Star*, March 20, 2013. Available online at www.thedailystar.net/beta2/news/deep-sea-port-in-sonadia-a-unique-opportunity-for-bangladesh/.
39 SIPRI, 2013, op. cit.
40 Saez, 2011, op. cit.
41 T. Wheeler, *China and Conflict-Affected States: Sri Lanka*, London: Saferworld, 2012.
42 Ibid.
43 IMF, 2014, op. cit.
44 SIPRI, 2013, op. cit.; Wheeler, 2012, op. cit.
45 Wheeler, 2012, op. cit., p. 18.
46 Sri Lanka Ports Authority, "Development of Port in Hambantota." Available online at www.slpa.lk/port_hambantota.asp?chk=4.
47 S. Sirimane, "Hambantota Port, Gateway to World," *The Sunday Observer*, February 21, 2010. Available online at www.sundayobserver.lk/2010/02/21/fea20.asp.
48 Embassy of the People's Republic of China in Sri Lanka, "China's Position on Sri Lanka's Human Rights Related Issues," November 28, 2013. Available online at http://lk.china-embassy.org/eng/xwdt/t1103383.htm.
49 D. Bastians and G. Harris, "Chinese Leader Visits Sri Lanka, Challenging India's Sway," *The New York Times*, September 16, 2014. Available online at www.nytimes.com/2014/09/17/world/asia/chinese-leader-visits-sri-lanka-chipping-away-at-indias-sway.html?_r=0.
50 Ibid.
51 L. Rose, *Nepal: Strategy for Survival*, Berkeley: University of California Press, 1971.
52 UNHRC, "UNHCR Regional Operations Profile: South Asia," 2014. Available online at www.unhcr.org/cgi-bin/texis/vtx/page?page=49e487856.
53 See M. Hutt (ed.), *Himalayan "People's War": Maoist Rebellion*, London: Hurst, 2004.
54 IMF, 2014, op. cit.
55 Ibid.
56 Human Rights Watch, "Under China's Shadow: Treatment of Tibetans in Nepal," 2014. Available online at www.hrw.org/sites/default/files/reports/nepal0314_ForUpload_2.pdf.
57 Ibid.

Select bibliography

Friedberg, Aaron (2012). *A Contest for Supremacy: China, America, and the Struggle for Mastery in Asia* (New York: W. W. Norton & Company).
Hutt, Michael, ed. (2004). *Himalayan "People's War": Maoist Rebellion* (London: Hurst).
Jayapalan, N. (2000). *India and Her Neighbours* (New Delhi: Atlantic Publishers).
Karim, Mahin (2013). *The Future of South Asian Security: Prospects for a Nontraditional Regional Security Architecture* (Seattle: National Bureau of Asian Research).
Khurana, Gurpreet (2008). "China's 'String of Pearls' in the Indian Ocean and Its Security Implications," *Strategic Analysis*, Vol. 32, No. 1: 1–39.
Ong, Russell (2002). *China's Security Interests in the Post-Cold War Era* (London: Curzon).
Rose, Leo (1971). *Nepal: Strategy for Survival* (Berkeley: University of California Press).
Saez, Lawrence (2011). *The South Asian Association for Regional Cooperation (SAARC): An Emerging Collaboration Architecture* (London: Routledge).
Weiss, Jessica (2014). *Powerful Patriots: Nationalist Protest in China's Foreign Relations* (New York: Oxford University Press, 2014).
Wheeler, Thomas (2012). *China and Conflict-Affected States: Sri Lanka* (London: Saferworld).
Zhao Gancheng (2005). "China: Periphery and Strategy," in Shanghai Institute for International Studies (ed.), *China and Asia's Security* (Singapore: Marshall Cavendish).

Section B
Regional security

9

Courting the LDCs

How partnerships with post-colonial governments became a top CCP security interest

Edward Friedman

Overview

Why China would court post-colonial less developed countries (LDCs) may seem superficially obvious. At the founding of the People's Republic of China (PRC) by the Chinese Communist Party (CCP) in 1949, China was itself a post-colonial LDC. It had suffered invasion and partial occupation by Hirohito's imperial military. General Tojo's Japan had exploited the resources of northeast China. It is natural to expect that the CCP would identify with all similar governments. The PRC therefore would seek to cooperate with other post-colonial governments in promoting international organizations (IOs) that would help the LDC overcome the negative consequences of exploitation by colonialism. Indeed, in the 1950s, India and other non-aligned LDCs reached out to the PRC, assuming they would find a like-minded government in it. And the CCP government has in fact continually invoked a rhetoric of support to post-colonial, LDC, Third World governments and a non-industrialized south.

The only problem with this logic of why the CCP would of course court LDCs is that the PRC has in actual practice, rather than courting post-colonial governments, privileged PRC domestic politics and international interests. In fact, the CCP government attacked the non-aligned movement and, in 1962, invaded India, a non-aligned movement leader. The PRC only began seriously courting LDCs in general after certain events of 1989 to 1991 changed the CCP leadership's understanding of what foreign policies would best protect their core interest, the preservation and legitimation of the CCP political system, a single-party dictatorship.

By that time, post-colonial Third Worldism had lost its coherence. Before the CCP re-imagined its core security interests in 1989 to court LDCs to defeat so called Western democracies, the CCP government's core regime security concern, despite zigs and zags on who was its enemy, was never understood in ways that would legitimate a general courting of the LDCs. The PRC turned towards post-colonial governments at a time when Third Worldism no longer described how former colonial states actually behaved. That is, instead of seeing the world market as exploitation to be avoided, they have come to see the world market as an opportunity for growth. By this time, a world power PRC was becoming the world's largest economy, an economic superpower. It was certainly not a less developed country. It was a market-maker.

Not courting the Third World

After seizing state power by winning a civil war, PRC leader Mao signed a military pact with Stalin's USSR on February 14, 1950. Moscow and Beijing became allies in a Cold War against a camp led from Washington. The PRC focused on deterring the US military, which was temporarily occupying and democratizing a defeated militarist Japan. In this Cold War atmosphere, with the CCP anxious that America might invade China as had Japan, Mao mistrusted and would not aid LDC governments that were either friendly to the US camp, as were the Philippines and Pakistan, or were neutral governments not joining the anti-US camp, as was the case, in the 1950s, with non-aligned governments such as Nehru's India and Tito's Yugoslavia. The CCP's top security interest was taken to be winning Soviet economic assistance and military backing. Courting LDCs was not a core security interest.

After Stalin died in 1953, Mao concluded that the PRC, imagined as a world power, should become—indeed, given its long revolutionary history, deserved to be—the leader of the world's anti-imperialist movement. The Soviet Union, hitherto the leader of this camp, was then re-imagined by the CCP as the major obstacle to the PRC becoming a proper world power and replacing the USSR. Relations with Moscow therefore deteriorated. Mao's anti-Soviet fixation led to deadly military clashes with the Soviet Union by 1969. During that post-Stalin period of worsening PRC relations with the USSR, CCP ruling groups turned increasingly against governments and movements among LDCs friendly to the Soviet Union, such as Vietnam and Cuba. The PRC instead backed murderous armed fundamentalist insurgents, as long as they were anti-Soviet. The CCP helped armed movements such as Sendero Luminoso in Peru, the Khmer Rouge in Cambodia, and the White Flags in Burma, not LDC governments. LDCs such as Thailand or Malaysia were considered enemies. The PRC helped groups hoping to topple those LDC governments by offering insurgents friendly to the CCP a safe base, guerrilla training, and radio stations in the PRC.

Mao's assault on Soviet interests persuaded Moscow that Beijing was a security threat. Moscow considered turning its military against the PRC. The core security interest of Mao's China then changed yet again. Self-isolated and threatened by Brezhnev's militarist USSR by 1969, Mao concluded that his political interest and China's security required entente with the American side of the Cold War, the world's only reliable anti-Soviet force. Security for the PRC had first meant balancing against the USA. Next the PRC balanced against the USSR. Either way, courting post-colonial LDCs was not a major CCP interest.

By 1970, Mao's PRC would ally with any and all anti-Soviet forces. This included the military dictatorship of Pinochet in Chile and Holden Roberto's group in Angola, which allied with Apartheid South Africa against a Soviet-backed popular liberation movement. Mao's attempts to topple post-colonial African leaders friendly to Moscow became so odious among Africa nationalists that the Tanzanian President, Julius Nyerere, flew to Beijing to tell Mao that the CCP had to stop such behavior for China to have any credibility in Africa.

The PRC obviously was not courting LDCs. As realist IR would predict, the PRC instead balanced against its number one enemy, first the USA, then the USSR. In the anti-Soviet era the PRC did, however, spend a large amount of Chinese revenues on trying to keep some LDC governments from backing the USSR and to aid some post-colonial regimes and movements already opposed to the USSR.

Anti-imperialism had an ambiguous quality. It was interpreted in the PRC to serve CCP domestic politics and balance of power security interests. Mao eventually explained his anti-imperialism to harmonize with his anti-Soviet agenda. In Mao's nationalist narrative, all Sinicized areas and regions that were culturally Han that had been conquered by prior empires in Asia were now all Chinese, part of Mao's PRC. Since an expanding Tsarist Russia, starting in the seventeenth century, had pushed back against the Manchu military conquests of the Qing Empire whose subject population was largely Han, and since the Soviet Union, after its establishment in 1917, incorporated the territories of prior Tsarist Russian conquests, the Leninist USSR was dubbed by Mao, after Beijing turned against Moscow, to be a continuation of the old Russian Empire, new tsars. Chinese students had to know, for the college entrance exam, the exact number of square kilometers supposedly stolen from China by Russia. The worst imperialist country was said to be the USSR, led by the CPSU. Discussing the PRC's similar inheritance and incorporation of Qing Empire territorial conquests, however, was and is taboo in the CCP. Nationalistic anti-imperialism has undergone many mutations in China.

Rather than acknowledge that the original Chinese nationalism from 1895 to 1912 was anti-Manchu, the CCP treats Manchus as if they were Chinese in order to legitimate the large territory of the PRC as virtually congruent with the territorial conquests of Manchu Qing expansionism. PRC policy on anti-imperialism changed yet again after Mao died in 1976, but the CCP still did not opt to court post-colonial governments, although CCP rhetoric remained pro-Third World. Instead, an economic reform group whose paramount leader was Deng Xiaoping in the 1977–81 period decided to (1) abandon Mao's anti-Soviet obsession, and (2) focus on modernizing China, investing in the PRC's future rather than in anti-Soviet fundamentalist groups. Security for the PRC, to Deng's CCP, meant ending material backwardness and making the state strong.

Prior aid to post-colonial LDCs therefore was treated as a waste. LDC aid from the PRC plummeted because it seemed to have little to do with the CCP's security preoccupation of growth at any price. Continuing government funding for scholarships to Africans to study in China was after Mao's death broadly seen as a waste of precious and scarce Chinese resources that should go to needy Chinese. To grow and to grow strong, CCP ruling groups in the early Deng era reached out to the International Monetary Fund (IMF), the World Bank, Japan, etc. for advice on how to modernize. The post-colonial world did not exist as a security concern for CCP reform leaders during the 1980s. Security meant ending backwardness and becoming strong.

Clearly, the PRC since its founding in 1949 has not had a consistent policy of courting post-colonial governments. However, starting in 1989, unexpected events led CCP ruling groups to re-imagine where the core threat to the survival of the CCP system was located. As a result, the core interest of the authoritarian CCP was re-imagined as defeating the alleged international source of the global democratization of communist party governments. Because of traumas from 1989 to 1991, as a previously Leninist East Europe democratized, the PRC, for the first time, began to consider courting post-colonial governments. CCP ruling groups began to rethink authoritarian Chinese security such that the CCP's single-party dictatorship needed to partner with LDCs, especially authoritarian regimes that shared the CCP's opposition to the spread of democracy.

In short, what has been decisive for Chinese policy priorities *vis-à-vis* the post-colonial world since 1949 is not some supposed preternatural identity of China as a Third World county, but changes in the security environment of the PRC that altered the preoccupations of changing ruling groups. To survive, after confronting and crushing a nationwide democracy movement in 1989 and then being sanctioned by the industrialized democracies for human rights violations, the CCP concluded it needed LDC friends and partners.

Reaching out to the post-colonial LDCs

The CCP's security situation changed completely in the 1989–91 period. In spring 1989, there were pro-democracy movements all over the PRC. The CCP leadership was split over how to respond. The winning group, led by Deng, decided to not conciliate the popular movement. He chose instead to dispatch the PRC military on June 3–4, 1989, to end the nationwide movement's occupation of Tiananmen Square in the center of Beijing. The CCP bloodily crushed Chinese supporters of democracy with a rapid and ruthless march by the PLA from the outskirts of Beijing to the square.

The CCP was then purged of leading liberal reformers. The ruling coalition became more hard line and chauvinist. The security forces became weightier. The CCP did not want to end up toppled as had been the fate of Leninist party dictatorships from Mongolia to Mozambique. CCP leaders therefore re-imagined the major threat to their system's survival. In a post-Cold War era in which the military superpower USSR had imploded and the communist party of the Soviet Union had lost power, in an era in which the CCP was confronting economic, political and weapons sanctions by the industrialized democracies of the Organization for Economic Cooperation and Development (OECD) responding to the June 4, 1989 massacre of pro-democracy Chinese, paramount leader Deng's PRC could no longer use the USA to balance against the USSR, especially since Gorbachev had pulled invading Soviet troops out of Afghanistan in 1989, thereby removing a common enemy, a threatening USSR that hitherto had provided the glue for Beijing-Washington entente.

Suddenly, to CCP ruling groups, movements for democratization and for secession, both supposedly promoted by "the West," seemed enemy number one. The big question among PRC ruling groups was how to preserve the CCP's single-party dictatorship and avoid state implosion or regime democratization. Who would stand with the CCP authorities against Chinese democrats and against ethno-religious resisters to communalist oppression?

Unexpectedly, post-colonial African governments approached the anxious CCP government with promises to pay no attention to OECD sanctions. The LDCs sought friendship with the CCP government. They did not support the agendas of the European democracies. Suddenly, CCP rulers realized that the LDCs could help legitimate the CCP. Supporting LDCs became a major security interest of an otherwise isolated and authoritarian, Han CCP government. Post-colonial Third Worldism could contribute to CCP security, the core interest of the PRC state.

A new security agenda

The overtures from post-colonial governments to the CCP in the wake of post-June 4 OECD sanctions such as banning lethal weapons sales to the PRC reflected a long history of support for the PRC from LDCs, especially from governments in Africa. When Mao's China moved towards testing a nuclear weapon in the early 1960s, governments in Moscow and Washington were made nervous. But LDC governments celebrated a post-colonial (colored?) China breaking the nuclear monopoly of the old (white?) world powers. To the LDCs, China was one of them. Similarly, in 1971, when post-colonial governments' votes helped win the PRC its membership of the UN Security Council as one of the P-5, the five powers with the right to veto resolutions, once again Africans celebrated the PRC's success.

Despite the vicissitudes of CCP policy towards post-colonial LDCs since the founding of the PRC, many anti-imperialist LDC leaders saw post-colonial China as a natural partner.

In the 1990s, the CCP concluded that LDC support could preserve PRC dignity and security by voting down OECD efforts in IOs, such as the UN Human Rights Commission, to investigate and condemn the systemic violations of fundamental human rights by the CCP's single-party dictatorship, efforts that otherwise could delegitimize CCP power. Post-colonial governments could serve a new security priority of the CCP.

As a result of the PRC's new security interest in LDCs, the aid spigot to post-colonial governments was re-opened. China's top leaders began to visit LDCs far more than did OECD leaders. To make the PRC seem at one with the LDCs, the CCP presented China, a rising world power PRC, not as a rising world power that was a new member of a global ruling class, but as the world's most successful developing country, an LDC promoting south-south cooperation.

Despite this positive general re-orientation towards post-colonial governments, the CCP did not yet have a set of pro-LDC policies to offer. These evolved gradually in response to events and in harmony with a CCP interpretive framework of cooperating with post-colonial governments to perpetuate the CCP's monopoly of unaccountable power at home and internationally to make the PRC the center of world power. CCP self-interest and realism guided PRC policy, not post-colonial consciousness.

The post-colonial world is complicated by regional forces. Geography is not quite destiny, but it does have a very large impact on international security relations. Whereas a number of China's neighbors in Asia have deeply scarred historical memories of Chinese invaders, plunderers, and murderers that inform wary contemporary views among governments in Asia of today's modern, assertive, superpower PRC, people in Latin America, Africa, the Middle East, South Asia, and much of Central Asia are different. They were never threatened in pre-modern times by the military of an imperial China. They have no bad historical memories of a dangerous China. The PRC, to those post-colonial governments and peoples who do not have unhappy memories of earlier entanglements with imperial China, is considered a contributor to LDC independence, dignity, and prosperity. These nationals welcome China to their region.

In fact, the CCP can and does help post-colonial governments balance against historically threatening would-be regional hegemons, the USA in Latin America, Europe in Africa, Russia in Central Asia, and India in South Asia. In short, geography and history have given the post-Mao economic tiger of a reform-era PRC tremendous advantages in much of the post-colonial world. Therefore, post-colonial governments have real reasons for welcoming close ties to the PRC. But it was not obvious to CCP leaders, in the wake of OECD sanctions in response to the CCP's June 4 massacre of Chinese supporters of constitutionalism, how to respond to the opportunity offered by LDC friendship to strengthen CCP security.

The new PRC security policy of favoring post-colonial governments became more fully formed after the Asian Financial Crisis (AFC) of 1997–8. In 1997, economic bubbles burst in three Asian countries, Thailand, Indonesia, and South Korea, for very different internal reasons. All three economies had been recently inflated by Japanese investments seeking alternatives to the wounded Japanese economy, which had stagnated since a Japanese financial bubble had burst in 1991. All three Asian economies went bust around the same time. The negative impact was region-wide. Money—especially that of Japanese investors and ethnic Chinese—quickly fled from the bubble economy countries, intensifying their plight and portending an ever-deepening crisis.

The IMF took its job to include bailing out distressed LDCs in order to limit the international impact of financial crises such as the AFC. In return for the bailout, the IMF required that the troubled post-colonial governments agree to a set of conditions that would supposedly make the economy of the wounded country solvent and able to earn foreign exchange again. The government of Japan found that the IMF conditionalities for the AFC sufferers, known as a structural adjustment program (SAP), were not suited to these Asian countries that had been, and remained, export powerhouses. Japan therefore offered to help create a monetary fund to stimulate these Asian economies that would quickly get them back on a growth trajectory. The government of Japan believed that putting these highly competitive Asian developing economies through an economic wringer, the IMF SAP, would unintentionally exacerbate their plight, thereby wounding much of Asia.

The US government disagreed. The Clinton Administration intervened to block the Japanese initiative. The Clinton Administration strongly urged Japan to back off and to let the IMF do its work. Tokyo did as Washington requested.

The CCP government learned from these events. PRC ruling groups did not like the US support of the IMF SAP. It seemed in part responsible for the de-legitimation of the authoritarian government of Indonesia, hitherto understood as an Asian developmental state. The AFC crisis and IMF SAP facilitated an Indonesian transition to democracy. The authoritarian CCP felt threatened by policies that led to democratization. The AFC/IMF nexus taught CCP leaders that the legitimacy and security of their authoritarian single-party dictatorship could be threatened by the hegemony of US-centered IOs. These IOs were created by the US at the end of World War II. They were very useful to PRC economic growth, but they also seemed to endanger authoritarianism, as in Indonesia. Politics was privileged in the CCP, and the CCP began to ponder alternate IOs that would better serve its interests.

The Tokyo alternative to the US-backed IMF, which the PRC initially criticized, eventually made sense to the CCP. The Japanese initiative, an Asian monetary fund to bail out Asian governments, suggested that China could join in multilateral IOs that could serve the CCP interest of preserving authoritarianism instead of serving an American interest of promoting democracy. The PRC therefore could join with others in Asia, and exclude the United States, to create an IO, in this case an Asian Financial Mechanism (AFM), which could prevent crises, transitions to democracy, and imperatives imposed by IOs friendly to the US government and democratization. For the first time, the CCP could see a way to build and use multilateral organizations that were not dominated by America, IOs that could serve CCP security interests and also be welcome by authoritarian post-colonial regimes. This orientation became central to PRC security policy. Helping LDC ruling groups survive and prosper would help the CCP. The PRC found a security stake in the stability and persistence of post-colonial governments.

The reform-era CCP well understood that growth premised on deep involvement with the world market, the antithesis of a post-colonial agenda, required that the PRC join the major IOs that helped structure the international economic system, the IMF, World Bank, and GATT (General Agreement on Trade and Tariffs), which in 1995 became the World Trade Organization (WTO), a facilitator of global trade. But the CCP suspected that this set of organizations, known as the Bretton Woods (BW) System (because these IOs were, in large part, the result of 1944 agreements made at Bretton Woods in New Hampshire by the World War II Allies who had joined to fight against fascist aggression), promoted policies that were not at one with the authoritarian CCP's most basic political interest, its entrenchment in power.

To the CCP, from a political perspective, the BW IOs were tools of American, European or democratic interests. They were therefore a threat to the security of the authoritarian CCP. The PRC, in response, began to try to create IOs in which the CCP government would join with LDC governments to de-Americanize the world, that is, to create alternative IOs that would better serve the core interest of the authoritarian CCP.

The CCP government did not try to overthrow and replace the BW IOs. The PRC was not revisionist; the CCP government actually tried to use those BW IOs to serve China's economic growth purposes, a policy in conflict with the conventional agenda of post-colonial governments. Indeed, the PRC sought to join the WTO so as to get better access to the markets of the world. But the CCP also mistrusted BW IOs, fearing they contained a hidden political agenda of promoting democracy and human rights. Therefore, the CCP tried to join, create or strengthen

IOs not centered on America and the democracies, but instead centered on the PRC and on post-colonial governments friendly to the PRC.

After the AFC, as with the creation of the AFM, the CCP could imagine a way out of the IO policy dilemma of only having IOs centered on the democracies of the OECD. Therefore, the CCP would promote an alternative world order, one meant also to be attractive to LDCs, based on IOs not dominated by the US government and its democratic allies. The AFM, a response to the AFC, proved it was possible to do so. The goal for the CCP became an alternative system of China-centered IOs joining the PRC with post-colonial governments, IOs that would become a center of the world economy for China and the LDCs.

Much of CCP security policy with LDCs since the AFC has been premised on this new turn in PRC security policy. In Northeast Asia, the PRC would join IOs with Japan and South Korea. In Southeast Asia, China would join with ASEAN (ten nations of Southeast Asia) in the APT (ASEAN Plus Three) (ASEAN plus China, Japan, and South Korea; no USA), and CAFTA (China-ASEAN Free Trade Association). These IOs seemed preferable in the CCP to US-centered institutions such as APEC (Asia Pacific Economic Cooperation) or TPP (Trans Pacific Partnership). The CCP would court the LDCs to join its alternative IO world, one centered on China.

Since the AFC and the AFM, the PRC has grown ever more committed to building alternative IOs that are, as far as possible, China-centered, rather than America-centered. As realist IR theory predicts, a quest for security turns into a quest for ever more power. The CCP is trying to create a new world order that is China-centered, that helps the PRC become the world's dominant nation. LDCs are central to this CCP project, imagined as a security agenda, but actually a recipe for maximizing the PRC's power in the world, not promoting Third Worldism

From a historical point of view, the post-colonial world lost its coherence by the end of the 1970s. The concept of a Third World could no longer usefully guide policy. Petro-states had risen. Post-colonial states that would need foreign exchange to buy oil were in trouble. The hope for a New International Economic Order (NIEO) that would help LDCs get rich using a commodity cartel as had OPEC (Organization of Petroleum Exporting Countries) imploded in the LDC bankruptcies of the Third World debt crisis of 1982. Mexico then sought to rise by joining a North American Free Trade Agreement (NAFTA). East European countries sought to rise by joining a European common market. The PRC dived into the world market and rose spectacularly. Soon, India, Brazil, and others followed.

The rapid rise of former LDCs re-shaped the contours of world power. Reaching out to Africa for energy, mineral resources, and food, China and India became competitors in an Indian Ocean region that included East Africa. Brazil came to Africa from the west as part of a South Atlantic region. The large wealth and power differences among LDCs and the competitiveness of some former LDCs made the notion of an NIEO or post-colonial order almost meaningless. The notion of PRC-LDC cooperation on common south-south interests hid the real economic challenges to all LDC states of world market growth in their diverse and rapidly changing regions.

Nonetheless, in India, Brazil, and South Africa, there remained post-colonial passions. Political leaders and influentials tend to mistrust Europe and America. They often scapegoat this "West" for their own economic tribulations. They imagine freedom and dignity as requiring a search for alternatives to "the West." As a result, authoritarian China's quest for power to defeat or marginalize the democracies of the so called West is attractive to and resonates with some popular post-colonial passions. These ideological tendencies facilitate acceptance of the CCP government's alternate IO agenda.

Post-colonialism continues to be an important political force long after its economic rationale of de-linking from the world market has discredited post-colonial economic policies and long after world politics has been transformed by the awesome rise of emerging market economies that turn nations that were once part of a Third World into major competitors for world power. In this era, the PRC is the leader and the major beneficiary of continuing post-colonial passions.

Central Asia and other regions

Given the CCP's agenda for courting post-colonial governments in Central Asia, the PRC has fostered a minilateral IO, the Shanghai Cooperation Organization (SCO). The US is excluded. The SCO includes China, Russia, and a number of Central Asian Muslim republics. They serve China's most basic security interest in at least two ways beyond its members voting in IOs to protect authoritarian China from censure or criticism by human rights IOs. First, member states turn over to the CCP government persons the PRC identifies as splitists, such as Turkic Muslim Uighurs who resist discriminatory Chinese policies against Uighurs. In ASEAN, Cambodia and Vietnam have likewise turned over to the PRC personages the CCP has identified as threats to their authoritarian regime, including a leading Chinese democrat in exile.

Another way the SCO serves core PRC security interests is by helping it deal with energy dilemmas. Since 1993, the PRC has had to import ever more oil to fuel rapid industrialization and vehicle usage. This growing need made the CCP regime focus on the question of where imported oil comes from. After the militarily strong USSR imploded in 1991, with China's northern and western borders now secure from military threats, the CCP focused on neighboring maritime territories and the sea lanes of communication (SLOC) across the Indian Ocean to petro-states such as Saudi Arabia, Iran, and Iraq, which became the leading sources of China's energy imports. From a Beijing perspective, the PRC was marching west. But oil tankers from the petro-states heading for China had to pass through waterways dominated by the US Navy, symbolized by a narrow choke point, the Strait of Malacca, between Singapore and Sumatra in Indonesia.

The CCP leadership was anxious that China could be made insecure by a need to import oil from West Asia. That is, China's energy imports might become hostage to the good will of the US Navy, which good will could be lost should the PRC attack Taiwan, Japan or the Philippines, allies and friends of America. The imperatives of PRC security led to three policy conclusions by CCP ruling groups: (1) China had to dominate what it dubbed its near seas, the energy-rich SLOCs of the South China Sea in Southeast Asia and the East China Sea in Northeast Asia. (2) China had to build a blue water navy strong enough that China's oil imports would not forever be hostage to the US Navy. This agenda was not a Third Worldist program. It would require courting regional LDC help for Chinese port access to Myanmar, Bangladesh, Pakistan, and Sri Lanka. The PRC would act as had other world powers and not as a post-colonial agenda would dictate. (3) China had to diversify its sources of energy throughout the various regions of the world. Security interests dictated that the PRC not be dependent on oil from petro-states whose energy exports had to cross oceans controlled by the US Navy. This security project was called solving the Malacca Strait Dilemma, although very little oil bound for the PRC actually goes through the strait.

As a result of the Malacca Dilemma, the CCP would court the energy-rich states of Central Asia and build pipelines to carry the oil and natural gas from Central Asia overland into China. The PRC offered loans and investments to drill for it and to build pipelines to carry it into China. CCP petro SOEs (state owned enterprises) were subsidized by the PRC government to defeat competitors for contracts on the basis of price or bribery. The CCP sees itself as offering good deals to LDCs so they will choose China.

Central Asian LDCs and the minilateral SCO have been most helpful in advancing the PRC's security interests of obtaining energy and avoiding the Malacca Strait Dilemma, as well as advancing China's great power interest in promoting a de-Americanized world, an international system not rewarding democratizers. When the dictator in Uzbekistan had peaceful, pro-democracy demonstrators gunned down, he was immediately invited to and fêted in the PRC. Certain kinds of LDCs were most helpful in meeting the CCP's understanding of security.

Post-colonial countries are ordinarily imagined as Africa and Latin America. Such a shriveled notion of the post-colonial ignores the popular backlash against Russian imperial expansion in Central Asia, Japanese militarist conquest in Korea, and Han Chinese expansion in Southeast Asia. That is, there are also deep post-colonial experiences in East and Central Europe, Central Asia and Mongolia, and South and Southeast Asia. Nations in Asia, anxious about Han CCP power expansion, have worries that Africans and Latin Americans lack. Consequently, the PRC's security options are structured by regional particulars.

Regional specifics

Clearly, regions are different. Regions, superficially merely a geographic given, should be thought of as both mutable and theoretical categories. It is important to clarify how the PRC's LDC security imperative leads to different policy choices by the CCP in the diverse LDC regions of the world—Latin America, Africa, Central Asia, South Asia, Southeast Asia, and the Pacific islands. Let's first look at Southeast Asia, home to the Malacca Strait and the energy-rich South China Sea.

Economic reformers in the CCP government had a policy proposal for the South China Sea and the East China Sea that would solve the Malacca Strait Dilemma and serve Chinese security interests. They would agree with neighboring Asian LDCs to bracket territorial disputes. The PRC and each of its neighbors would then share the energy. The relation could be win-win. Finding China acting as a partner, the LDCs would not be anxious about PRC territorial aggrandizement. The LDCs would have no reason to seek help from the USA to balance against the PRC since China would be a partner, not a threat to these LDCs.

But in regions where CCP claims to maritime territories clashed with the far more legitimate claims of China's Asian neighbors, the post-June 4 hardline leadership of the CCP refused to compromise on sovereignty, in contrast to Mao who compromised on territorial disputes with neighbors for the sake of political ties. Instead, post-Deng leaders, Jiang Zemin, Hu Jintao, and Xi Jinping, were ever more strongly committed to the notion that unless the PRC dominated its so called near seas, unless it were the predominant power in Asia, then China could not be what it supposedly always had been until momentarily interrupted, humiliated and weakened by so called capitalist imperialism, that is, a natural international number one, a uniquely magnanimous leader of the civilized world. The PRC's rise to global centrality was meant to be good both for China and also all LDCs.

Yet serious tensions have intensified between the PRC and neighboring Asian LDCs. In short, there is a disconnect between the CCP policy of courting the LDC world and a revanchiste CCP nationalism that imagines less powerful, less wealthy, and supposedly less cultured LDC nations as naturally submitting to the purportedly benign leadership of a large, wealthy, powerful and still rising PRC. From this CCP perspective, LDCs whose understanding of their independence requires balancing against the PRC are betraying the best interests of their people.

By the second decade of the twenty-first century, this was the reality for many Asian LDCs that bordered the PRC, from India to Mongolia. Their sovereignty interests, the core of post-colonial consciousness, were understood by an expansive world power PRC as challenges to CCP security. The CCP hopes it can throw enough money at these Asian governments and people to convince them to acquiesce to PRC leadership and interests.

But, outside of Asia, LDCs did not border or fear China. They had no problematic historical memories generated by imperial Chinese expansion. They had no worries of a territorially expansionist Chinese neighbor. Instead, they could imagine good ties to the PRC as strengthening their independence by serving as a balancer against prior regional hegemons—from Russia in Central Asia to Australia in the South Pacific. Whereas in India, Southeast Asia, and East Asia, America was welcomed by post-colonial governments to balance against world power China, everywhere else, except Europe, the PRC was welcomed in to balance against other regional hegemons. Region is a key geo-historical variable shaping China's LDC security policies. Realist interests trumped post-colonial consciousness.

Africa as a model

In IOs, the CCP, for its security, courts African LDC votes against proposed investigations of the CCP's systemic abuses of fundamental human rights and obtains energy (and other primary products) needed to sustain the Chinese economy. At first, the PRC's petro SOEs were welcome in the Sudan because OECD sanctions against Sudanese ruling groups for facilitating mass murder in the Darfur area kept OECD oil giants out of the Sudan.

In 2007–8, some international human rights activists proposed launching a campaign against the CCP government and its petro SOEs for supporting the Sudanese ruling groups, seen as war criminals, by branding the 2008 Beijing Olympics the genocide Olympics. The CCP, in response, created a small group to explore how to defeat the campaign. Eventually, the CCP supported an African Union force sent to the Sudan. The PRC investigative team also learned that the oil that Chinese SOEs exported from the Sudan mostly went to Japan rather than to China. The PRC's petro SOEs, from the Gulf of Guinea to Venezuela, sold oil on the world market to maximize firm profits. They did not sell the oil to a more distant China paying less.

In Africa, therefore, Chinese petro SOEs do not actually promote PRC security interests. Central Asia is a unique region in that the oil and natural gas from that area are piped into China. Otherwise the CCP's petro SOEs worked for themselves. They increasingly sought safe oil and natural gas deals in OECD regions such as Canada and Europe rather than in risky LDCs. They are not driven by post-colonial priorities.

As with the AFM in Southeast Asia and the SCO in Central Asia, China in Africa established a minilateral IO, FOCAC (Forum on Cooperation between Africa and China). Excluding the USA, it courted African leaders with aid, loans, investment, infrastructure, scholarships, and Confucian Institutes to teach Chinese language and respect for Chinese culture, as interpreted by the CCP to serve the CCP. The PRC promoted its aid as superior to the European variety because PRC aid supposedly had no strings attached to it. That is, its aid came without human rights or good governance conditionality.

Of course, PRC monies did in fact come with strings attached. The LDC recipients of these monies would "respect" CCP "sensitivities." That is, these post-colonial governments would act in IOs such as the UN's Human Rights Commission or International Labor Organization so as not to embarrass the CCP. They would block any attempt to investigate and report critically on the CCP's systemic abuses of human rights. The LDCs would also not have state-to-state relations with Taiwan, a democratic island with a population of 23 million north of the Philippines, which is claimed by the PRC to be part of China.

These PRC political conditions were not overly onerous for LDCs. Their governments did not much concern themselves with the plight of Taiwanese who sought a dignified position in the international community. In addition, LDC anti-imperialist nationalism and/or authoritarian self-interest worked against following a European lead on promoting human rights in the LDCs. Governments with a post-colonial consciousness were attuned to the CCP rhetoric on absolute sovereignty and non-interference.

The paradigmatic case was Angola. In 2006 the European Union (EU) was finalizing negotiations with the corrupt, authoritarian government in Angola. Europe offered a financial bailout, with the Angolan government, in return, agreeing not to crush Angolan societal groups promoting good governance. But then the PRC offered Angolan ruling groups financial support without conditionality. The Angolan government swiftly accepted the PRC alternative. In return, CCP SOEs received rights to Angolan energy. For its part, the CCP government bailed out the Luanda government and built needed infrastructure. Under these contracts, however, PRC aid, in contrast to most EU aid, was "tied" aid. That is, the African side agreed to PRC firms managing the projects, supplying the equipment from PRC sources, and providing Chinese laborers to do the building. Soon there were more Chinese in Angola than Portuguese, although Angola had been a Portuguese colony for some 500 years.

The PRC's Angola Model has been replicated throughout Africa. World Bank statistics suggest that China's deep economic involvement has sped African growth. But CCP practices worried European nations and, eventually, more and more Africans. Europe found that the PRC was keeping corrupt rulers in power. PRC money was being wasted in too many corrupt rip-offs. Instead of stable growth, more African states would fail to solve their domestic problems, leading to an emigrant outflow into Europe and increasing instability in Africa that could facilitate the growth of criminality and Islamist terrorist groups. While PRC monies stimulated African growth, development was more questionable. After all, North Korea's ruling groups survived and prospered using the earnings from commodity exports to the PRC. But development requires re-investing export earnings in education, infrastructure, and upgrading, as petro-states have done since they stopped wasting export earnings on European luxuries and, instead, invested in airlines, airport hubs, alternative energy, sovereign wealth funds, and high-end tourism.

In short, PRC investment in the global south was not all good. Africans found Chinese workers often displacing African workers and Africa regularly being de-industrialized by cheap Chinese industrial imports while Africa became a mere supplier of raw materials to the PRC and an importer of industrial products from the PRC. To many anti-imperialist African nationalists, this meant that China in Africa practiced neo-colonialism. That is, PRC policies led to similar results as had European colonialism, preventing indigenous industrialization. In fact, the CCP's version of the Asian variety of capitalism that privileged state subsidization of industrial exports not only de-industrialized LDCs from South Africa to Brazil but also undercut industry in OECD countries such as Spain and Italy.

African critics of Chinese neo-colonialism found that the Angola Model, which the PRC followed all over the region, led the Chinese to take out primary product riches from Africa and to find means to price the product in ways that benefitted the Chinese far more than it did Africans. African nations were thereby losing their future in return for, too often, sub-standard infrastructure that served the corrupted and not the nation. PRC aid fixated on infrastructure, ignoring poverty alleviation, social safety nets and vulnerable communities.

Whatever truth there is in the neo-colonial critique of CCP policy, China remains very popular in Africa, where post-colonial consciousness persists. Therefore African governments continue to support the PRC's security interest by their votes on the UN Human Rights Council and International Labor Organization. China in Africa is experienced as helping Africa by investing, building infrastructure, and keeping the prices for African raw materials higher than they otherwise would be, thereby enriching African nations. Africans are further benefitting as India, Malaysia, South Korea and Japan come more deeply into the region in order to compete with China. Such world market benefits for Africa, however, have little to do with a PRC post-colonial policy agenda.

Still, Europeans tend to believe that, in the long run, because the PRC backs narrowly self-interested ruling groups, the opportunity offered to Africa by the huge economic surge of Chinese loans, investments and imports will be wasted, that Africa will, like North Korea, stagnate or even suffer new debt crises. The CCP dismisses the European critique as the sour grapes of colonial oppressors who are losing their hold over African economies. While there is disagreement about how to understand colonialism and neo-colonialism, to be discussed below, the CCP experiences PRC security as much strengthened and CCP SOEs (tied to ruling groups in the PRC) much enriched by the PRC government's general application of the Angola Model to Africa and other world regions.

The content of anti-imperialism

China's appeal to post-colonial regimes is shaped not only by regional particulars but also by an understanding of imperialism as exploitation by the industrial democracies from across the seas. This focus on nineteenth century European behavior ignores a historical reality—that agrarian empires all over the world from ancient times into the twentieth century have tended throughout history to expand as far as their power permitted. Since the fourteenth century, Ming China expanded as far as it could until conquered by Manchus in the seventeenth century. The Manchu homeland was to the northeast of the Great Wall of China. The Manchus' multicultural Qing Khanate invaded and incorporated, besides the lands of Sinicized Han, the territories of communities of Mongols, Turkic-speaking Muslims, Tibetans, hill nations north of Burma, Thailand and Laos, and some of the Austronesian nations of coastal Taiwan. Manchu military expansion during the Qing Dynasty also clashed with the imperial expansion of the Russian tsars. A backward Europe was long an economic laggard and came late to large-scale imperial expansion.

Internal dynamics, not European behaviors, have long been decisive in the territory known as China. As exemplified by the White Lotus Rebellion of the 1790s, the Manchus' powerful and expansionist Qing Dynasty eventually decayed internally and therefore declined. When it was defeated in an 1894–5 war with the Meiji Empire of Japan, there rose in China an anti-Manchu racist nationalism the purpose of which was to topple the Manchus and, with Japanese aid, to put Han Chinese in power so as to end humiliating rule over Han by a Manchu minority backed by Tsarist Russia. In the 1911–12 republican revolution that ended the ancient monarchy, Han carried out racist pogroms against Manchus.

Eventually, the new Republic of China was ruled by Chiang Kai-shek's Nationalist Party (KMT). Its anti-imperialism took a militaristic and expansionist Japan as enemy number one. Mao did not. After a US-led coalition defeated Imperial Japan in World War II, Chiang's forces lost power in 1949 in a civil war to a communist armed force whose political leader was Mao. He dismissed anti-Japan nationalism as mere bourgeois ideology. Mao would not execute Japanese war criminals, rejected reparations from Japan, brushed off Japanese apologies as unnecessary, and, by 1972, banned negative portrayals of Japan in the PRC.

In Mao's class struggle perspective, which targeted Chinese reactionaries, ordinary Japanese people also were the victims of Japan's capitalist imperialists. For Mao, in his final years, enemy number one was a supposedly anti-socialist USSR, portrayed as continuing to control the huge Manchu Qing territories supposedly stolen by the military of the Russian tsars. The Soviet Union, territorial successor to the tsars, was deemed by Mao to be the imperialist (social imperialism) enemy of the people of the world.

To build an autarkic society with virtually no role for trade, money, market or household property, Mao embraced an anti-imperialist narrative in which the British-initiated Opium War of 1839–42 revealed the exploitative evils of the world market. Mao down-played the prior decay of the Manchu rulership that made the Qing Empire so weak that even distant, little Britain could defeat the once formidable Qing military. Mao ignored the social decay in the Qing Empire that had led to an opium plague and the banning of opium in the 1720s by the Qing Dynasty, more than a century before the British narcotraffickers initiated a war to get a chunk of the huge Chinese opium market of the Qing Empire. Imperialism and social imperialism, that is, the world market and Russia, were treated as Mao's enemies.

When Mao died in 1976 and Deng Xiaoping became paramount leader, Deng, looking to East Asian economic dynamism initiated by the neo-mercantilist Japanese variety of capitalism, found that subsidizing and promoting industrial exports in the world market was a way to rise. Therefore, for Deng, Mao's Opium War narrative legitimating economic autarky misled. Deng described China's decline as having begun following the fifteenth century death of Ming Emperor Zhu Di who had promoted international ocean trade and power. His successor outlawed China's great ocean commerce, burnt the shipyards, and tore up the blueprints for ships. For Deng, Mao's self-sequestration, like the Ming in the fifteenth century, was self-wounding for China, denying the nation the many benefits of international exchange. For Deng, as for Chiang Kai-shek, Japanese imperialism would be played up as China's enemy, but for Deng this was only in order to create hatred of Japan to legitimate the CCP as the patriots who supposedly fought and defeated a militarist Japan. Deng had no interest in a post-colonial agenda of de-linking from the world market.

In short, post-colonialism was understood in the reform-era PRC to serve changing CCP ruling group interests. The trauma of imperialism has been differently interpreted since 1949 by the diverse and mutable interests and policies of ruling groups in the PRC. At different times, post-colonial anti-imperialism in China has targeted Manchus, Japanese, class enemies, Russians and British. There is no "natural" policy response to ever changing notions of imperialism. LDC leaders who, like Mao, understood the world market as a plague to be avoided also ended up promoting autarkic policies that kept their peoples miserably poor. They slighted the opportunities the world market offered for wealth creation.

After the CCP crushed a nationwide democracy movement in 1989 and the Soviet Union imploded in 1991 into many ethno-religious states, Chinese nationalism was once again re-imagined by the CCP. This time the CCP's enemies were (1) Han people who might seek to democratize the authoritarian PRC, (2) ethno-religious communities that might split China, and (3) international forces (first and foremost the USA) that might support these domestic Chinese forces that were unhappy with the repressive consequences of Han CCP authoritarianism.

Looking at the formation of a number of Muslim republics in Central Asia when the USSR imploded, the CCP worried that Turkic-speaking Muslim Uighurs in the PRC would seek to secede from the atheistic, Han PRC as Kazakhs, Tajiks, Uzbeks, Kyrgyz etc. seceded from the USSR. The CCP therefore abandoned the Leninist-Stalinist policy of cultural autonomy for ethnic communities and instead imposed on Tibetans and Uighurs alienating policies of cultural fusion, forced assimilation and religious repression. Post-June 4 Chinese nationalism that legitimated the repression of these Buddhist and Muslim communities in the PRC did not, however, much impact the presuppositional framings of post-colonial governments that, focused on their own political independence and economic wellbeing, assumed that China still, of course, was one of them.

Latin America and other regions

In general, in most LDC regions, PRC policies advance CCP security interests. Latin America, on the other side of the Pacific Ocean from China, never had any deep experiences with China in pre-modern times. There are no conflicting territorial claims. There are no large Muslim or Buddhist communities to empathize with the sufferings imposed on Uighurs or Tibetans in the PRC by the CCP. In contrast to Asia, there are, in short, no forces in Latin America to take China to be an unwelcome presence.

Anti-US governments in Cuba, Venezuela etc. imagine the PRC as sharing their anti-US preoccupation. Although the PRC actually displays little interest in wounding its beneficial economic ties with the USA, the PRC has become deeply involved with these Latin American anti-Yankee regimes. But China does not offer philanthropy. As with the Angola Model, China's state firms are profiting greatly from their business deals with Venezuela.

More important, even Latin American democracies welcome PRC economic involvement as a source of economic growth and as a political balancer for maximizing independence from the USA. Governments in the region, therefore, to serve their own core interests, tend to respect CCP security interests on issues such as no state-to-state relations with the democracy in Taiwan and no support for human rights activities that would call attention to the CCP's systemic abuses of fundamental rights.

Divisions within Latin America, however, have kept the CCP from organizing a region-wide, minilateral IO excluding the US, although the PRC tries to join the many sub-regional IOs of Latin America. Regions shape the PRC's opportunity structure. The CCP got the Middle East to agree to a minilateral IO similar to FOCAC in Africa, but the Middle East already is pervaded by a slew of meaningful regional organizations that serve real regional interests such that the China-centered minilateral IO seems superfluous. It is without substance in the Middle East, which has its own strong organizations. The CCP government's preferences, in addition, are deflected by the region's strong divisions—Israeli/Arab, Sunni/Shia, Iran/Saudi etc. But PRC realism has made courting Israel for militarily useful high technology a CCP policy preference.

In contrast to the Middle East, Africa was primed for the PRC's growth agenda. The timing was fortuitous. In politics, timing can be everything. By 1995, ever more African countries were abandoning self-wounding autarkic statist policies, ending civil wars, and conciliating clashing forces. Growth occurred at 5+ percent a year. When the PRC arrived soon after the OECD countries imposed sanctions on the CCP government for its June 4, 1989 massacre of democracy supporters in Beijing, Africa was already looking outward for economic partners. Africans therefore embraced China.

In the South Pacific islands, mainly democracies, it is anti-democratic forces in Tonga and Fiji that have been most welcoming of the authoritarian PRC, as with Cuba and Venezuela in Latin America. They seek to balance democratic "interference" by Australia and New Zealand. The PRC may support friendly authoritarian regimes, but the CCP has not yet tried to topple democratic governments. CCP policy succeeds with LDC governments when local ruling groups see cooperation with the PRC as in their own real interest, as something to be desired.

For Latin America, as for most of the LDC world with no security clashes with China, the PRC's positives far outweigh the negatives. To be sure, China's Asian variety of capitalism unbalances international economic relations so that Brazil, Mexico, Argentina etc. experience the PRC as a source of de-industrialization. In addition, Chinese SOEs tend to be bad for the environment. CCP firm insensitivities also result in clashes with workers and citizens all over the post-colonial world.

But to post-colonial governments, it is a far weightier factor that the PRC since 1978 has been the world's fastest growing economy. Soon it will be the world's largest economy. It already adds more wealth to the world each year than does the USA. Plugging into Chinese economic dynamism seems so advantageous to emerging market economies that Brazil, on the Atlantic Ocean, already does more trade with China, which is on the Pacific Ocean, than with the nearby USA. China is an economic powerhouse.

As part of its attempt to de-Americanize the world and make the PRC the world economic center, PRC firms are building infrastructure to the west coast of South America and talk about, in Central America, building a wide canal through Nicaragua to accelerate and deepen the economic integration of Atlantic Ocean Latin American states with the PRC on the Pacific Ocean. In sum, the CCP security strategy of making the world safe for authoritarianism under an economic superpower China is furthered by the PRC's economic policies to the LDCs, including Latin America, policies which make sense to Latin Americans. Therefore, the PRC is most welcome in the region.

The governments of the region are merely trying to serve their own interests. Latin American governments were largely disappointed by their growth rates in response to what they thought of as carrying out the prescriptions of the US government's neo-liberal Washington Consensus in the 1980s and 1990s. As a result, Argentina and others in the region agreed to treat the PRC as a market economy for WTO purposes, a self-wounding concession that made it more difficult for Argentina *et al.* subsequently to win disputes at the WTO over the PRC's market-distorting, statist privileging of CCP SOEs and their industrial exports.

The most important country in Latin America for the PRC is Brazil, not the anti-US governments of Cuba or Venezuela. Brazil is central to the CCP effort to de-Americanize the world by building alternative minilateral IOs, in this case the BRICS (Brazil, Russia, India, China and South Africa). These countries aligned with the CCP government at the 2009 Copenhagen conference on climate change to resist the European agenda of broad-ranging action to greatly limit pollution. LDCs tend to want to grow as rapidly as possible and not to be slowed in their efforts to catch up to the more advanced by the restrictions favored by OECD environmentalists. Therefore, despite a discrediting of the post-colonial economic agenda, shared post-colonial orientations continue to help make PRC initiatives attractive to LDCs.

Even India, an Asian neighbor of the PRC, sees cooperation with China in the BRICS as a positive, despite India experiencing the PRC as a major security threat. Although India is on its way to becoming the most populous nation and the world's fourth largest economy, CCP ruling groups treat India with disdain, a second class power, whereas India imagines itself as a re-emerging root civilization, China's rival for leadership in Asia and the post-colonial world. India finds the CCP's military sitting on its northern border. It finds a threatening PRC state insisting that India's northeastern province of Arunachal Pradesh is somehow actually part of the PRC because it was once part of a Tibetan empire. India also experiences itself as being surrounded in its own Indian Ocean by Chinese-built port facilities in neighboring Myanmar, Bangladesh, Sri Lanka and Pakistan, a so called string of pearls that is encircling and choking India.

If this India, involved in realist rivalries and territorial clashes over sovereignty with a world power PRC, still finds it useful to cooperate with the CCP in the BRICS, Brazil, which has no security conflicts with the PRC, has no reason not to be enthusiastic about the BRICS IO. The

CCP in 2014 used China's enormous accumulation of foreign exchange to lead the BRICS to create a development bank more useful to LDCs than are the IMF and World Bank. That is, LDCs, already beneficiaries of PRC trade, investments and loans, may yet find themselves to be even greater beneficiaries of CCP policies meant to court post-colonial governments to serve PRC security interests.

Despite the PRC's neo-colonial tendencies sketched above, CCP ruling groups want their relations with LDCs to be experienced as a win/win relationship. They are trying to institutionalize that policy goal in minilateral IOs that exclude the USA such as BRICS. In sum, with Brazil in particular, as in general with post-colonial governments, CCP policies have evolved since 1989 to court LDCs to help build a de-Americanized world system that would create a new international order, with the PRC as its economic center, a system that would make the world safe for China's single-party dictatorship, the CCP's top security interest. PRC policies, such as minilateral IOs that exclude America and offer alternatives to BW IOs, are succeeding in courting LDC governments. The LDCs respond to Chinese political and economic policies (trade, investment, infrastructure, loans etc.) to serve their own interests of more rapid growth and an independence made more secure from the intervention of prior regional hegemons. The PRC helps post-colonial governments with job creation and patriotic pride, which help keep ruling groups in power. For the CCP, the courting of LDCs serves the security interests of the PRC.

While securing energy resources and crushing secessionist forces have been top security concerns for the PRC since the early 1990s, the authoritarian CCP dictatorship has, since that turning point, experienced its core interest as preserving its authoritarian single-party system. The events of 1989 to 1991 in which Leninist tyrannies were confronted by popular movements persuaded the CCP ruling group that the major threat to CCP regime security was the democratizing and splitist efforts of dissatisfied groups in the PRC. These Chinese are depicted by the CCP as people manipulated by the United States in order to weaken the PRC so as to assure US hegemony.

Actually, the major IO promoting democratization and human rights was the EU, not the USA. The international headquarters of the Uighur movement was in Europe, in Germany. But Chinese leaders saw a fractured EU as incapable of strong action on behalf of a common foreign policy. When Germany wanted to end ethnic cleansing by Serbs against Muslim Kosovars in the former Yugoslavia, it could not do it on its own. It had to press the Clinton Administration to do the job for Europe. Therefore, the CCP experiences the USA as its top foreign policy challenge.

Whether it was the democratization of Yugoslavia, the subsequent Color Revolutions in Central Asia or the later Arab Spring movements, since the democratization movements of 1989–91 that toppled Leninist dictatorships, the CCP's core security concern has been to roll back the global tide of democracy and human rights so that the PRC's authoritarian order will persist. As a result of this preoccupation, CCP leaders concluded that they had a security priority in courting post-colonial LDCs to defeat democratization and make the world safe for CCP authoritarianism. This CCP security imperative was called "democratizing international relations." The goal of courting post-colonial governments by the CCP was that governments everywhere should imagine the PRC's single-party dictatorship not as a violator of fundamental human rights but as an embodiment of good governance, a promoter of stability and prosperity. LDCs came to be seen by the CCP as crucial to this PRC security agenda, which by the twenty-first century included promoting regional post-colonial minilateral IOs that would help de-Americanize the world and re-center the world economy on a purportedly magnanimous China, a PRC delivering win/win outcomes.

The goal of the CCP, starting in the 1990s, was to restore the greatness and global centrality of ancient China through an economic rise stimulated by industrial exports as pioneered in Bismark's Germany and Meiji Japan, not by LDC unity or by post-colonial policies treating the world market as an exploitative evil. The government of the PRC promised the LDCs that China's rise would be better for them than would siding with democratic world powers, portrayed as alien, selfish and greedy. PRC hegemony, not a Third World agenda, was presented as uniquely beneficent because it was the result of a deep and persistent Chinese culture, which supposedly taught Chinese, and only Chinese, the virtues of magnanimous paternalism.

That CCP ideology masks the complexities, sketched above, of what some in Africa and LDC peoples in other regions experience as PRC neo-colonialism. However, the negative consequences of deep economic interactions with the policies of the reform-era PRC economy SOEs backed by the CCP state could yet be addressed and corrected by future Chinese governments. The past need not be prologue. To serve its own interest, the CCP can learn and change. Or perhaps the CCP cannot change because vested ruling interests are too much enriched by PRC neo-colonial policies.

Of course, the PRC security interest addressed in this chapter is embraced by African and other LDC governments for their own reasons, not to serve the CCP, let alone its neo-colonial tendencies. Post-colonial governments use the PRC approach to them to win more independence from prior hegemons, to obtain faster growth, and to benefit from the prestige of partnership with a world power China, imagined as the most successful of all LDCs. The PRC is able to advance its security by partnering with LDC governments mainly because LDC governments find that partnership with the CCP advances their own most vital post-colonial interests.

While the future remains contingent on events and policy choices that cannot be known or predicted with any certainty, thus far the CCP government has gone from success to yet greater success in courting post-colonial LDCs in ways that are advancing the highest priority security interests of the PRC. Despite real negatives, such as the de-industrialization of many trading partners, the CCP government promotes policies that most LDCs, on balance, find to be very much in their own priority interests. PRC security, understood as CCP security, is thus far therefore well served by the PRC's post-1989 courting of post-colonial governments in all the many diverse regions of the world that do not experience an existential challenge from China's world power ambitions that China's Asian neighbors do experience. But in an era in which a world power, post-colonial China clashes with a world power, post-colonial India (or Iran with Turkey in Syria), the courting of LDCs is far more a tactic of a great or middle power's self-interest than it is a matter of post-colonial cooperation.

10
China's security and the Arctic

Linda Jakobson

Introduction: a melting Arctic

Climatic changes in the Arctic region are giving rise to new opportunities but also bringing about challenges for Arctic states and the broader international community alike. China is one of several non-Arctic states that over the past decade has become aware of the evolving Arctic environment's impact on its security. Not only will China's economic security, climate security and food security be affected by the melting ice, but possibly even the country's domestic security. Consequently China has taken several measures to enable it to take advantage of the opportunities and counter adverse repercussions of the challenges and threats.

The prospect of new, seasonally ice-free sea lanes emerging as a result of the melting Arctic ice is the most imminent, identifiable opportunity in the changing Arctic. No nation dependent on foreign trade can ignore the possibility that at some stage during the 2020s shipping could increase substantially along the Arctic sea routes. Economic prosperity in a globalized world, after all, relies heavily on the global maritime transport system.

According to World Meteorological Organization estimates, the Arctic reached its lowest annual sea ice level during September 2012. As of 2013, the September monthly decreasing average trend was -13.7 percent per decade relative to the 1981–2010 average, which in real terms means that between March and September 2013 there was a loss of 9.69 million square kilometers of sea ice.[1] This decrease in surface area has been accompanied by a reduction in the thickness of the ice, leading to predictions of "ice-free summers" in the Arctic.[2] Recent estimates predict that the Arctic will be free of ice during the three summer months by between 2020 and 2040.[3]

The Northern Sea Route (NSR) across the northern coast of Russia is expected to become commercially viable before the Northwest Passage through the Canadian archipelago because the ice is on average receding more quickly off Siberia than across the North American Arctic. This has direct relevance for East Asian countries, all of which have flourishing trade ties with Europe.

Another opportunity that the melting Arctic ice could provide is new fishing grounds, while yet a third is the possibility of extracting hydrocarbons and minerals. According to the US National Oceanic and Atmospheric Administration, new Arctic and sub-Arctic fish species have been reported from several areas.[4] Additionally, warming waters are attracting some species.[5] The 2008 US Geological Survey estimates that the Arctic contains up to 30 percent of the world's undiscovered gas and 13 percent of the world's undiscovered oil resources.[6] Crucial, however, from the viewpoint of assessing the possibility of conflict in the Arctic region is the estimate that over 84 percent of these resources are located within littoral states' Exclusive Economic Zones (EEZ) and continental shelves. The shelves of the United States, Canada and Greenland are the most likely to hold oil, while Russia's and Norway's shelves have the best prospects for gas.[7] Additionally, the region is presumed to contain vast amounts of coal, nickel, copper, tungsten, lead, zinc, gold, silver, diamonds, manganese, chromium and titanium.

As for the foreseeable challenges brought about by the changing Arctic environment, they are climatic changes, which will affect food production, extreme weather patterns, and sea-levels far beyond the Arctic region.

These opportunities and challenges impinge on China's security from several perspectives. This chapter will first describe thinking within China regarding the changing Arctic environment. It will then discuss the implications of the melting ice for China's security. Lastly, it will assess China's ambitions in the Arctic in light of the policy measures taken thus far by the Chinese Government.

Chinese views on the changing Arctic

China's polar research capabilities have developed considerably over the last two decades. Since 1994 Chinese researchers have had *Xuelong* (*Sea Dragon*), the world's largest non-nuclear powered scientific polar icebreaker, at their disposal. In 1999 *Xuelong* made its first expedition to the Arctic. In 2013 *Xuelong* for the first time traversed the Northern Sea Route along the Russian coast from the Pacific to the Atlantic. In 2015 China expects to launch a second polar research vessel, which is being built in China in cooperation with a Finnish company. Despite the increased attention by outsiders to China's growing interest in the Arctic, it is worth bearing in mind that Antarctica has been and remains the overwhelming focus of China's polar research. As of early 2014 China had made a total of 30 expeditions to the Antarctic and only five to the Arctic. This ratio of approximately six to one still holds true today when assessing allocation of human and monetary resources in China toward Antarctic and Arctic research.[8]

While natural scientists and environmental experts in China have studied the Arctic for years, among social scientists the Arctic is a new field. When the Stockholm International Peace Research Institute in March 2010 published one of the first English-language reports about China and the Arctic, only a handful of Chinese researchers focused solely on Arctic geopolitics or studied the United Nations Convention on the Law of the Sea (UNCLOS) from the viewpoint of the changing Arctic environment.[9] Today there are dozens of Chinese researchers within the social sciences who contemplate the Arctic future from a legal, geopolitical, military, commercial, and logistics standpoint. There are also numerous English-language articles assessing China's growing interest in the Arctic.[10]

A common theme in scholarly work worldwide is that the prospect of longer ice-free periods could have momentous implications for the Arctic's commercial development. In China as elsewhere there are differing estimates on how quickly the ice will melt and, for example, when a seasonally navigable Northern Sea Route will materialize. Likewise, predictions regarding the accessibility and commercial viability of resource extraction vary widely. Chinese researchers do not differ from their foreign counterparts in their assessments of the difficulties due to extremely harsh conditions that currently make any operation in the Arctic—including fishing—commercially non-viable.[11]

Views among the Chinese expert community of the strategic implications of the melting Arctic ice can roughly be characterized as following the same contours as views of experts worldwide. One view is that the ice will lead to increasing competition among states, which in turn will give way to inter-state tensions, and possibly even military clashes as nations clamor to extract minerals and hydrocarbons.[12] In a rare open-source article about the Arctic by an officer of the People's Liberation Army, Senior Colonel Han Xudong in 2008 warned that the possibility of use of force cannot be ruled out in the Arctic due to complex sovereignty disputes.[13]

Among those outside China who view the Arctic as geostrategically volatile and a possible battleground it is generally common to perceive China as a potentially assertive actor in the Arctic. Media headlines often promote alarmist thinking. Within China those who foresee strife emerging in the Arctic usually advocate that China take a more robust stance to safeguard its interests in the Arctic. In 2009 one of the earliest vocal advocates of China's polar rights, Guo Peiqing of the Ocean University of China, urged the Chinese Government to protect its legitimate rights in the Arctic. Guo stated that being distant from the Arctic should not be a reason for China to be inattentive.[14] Retired rear admiral Yin Zhuo created a stir in 2010 by stating that "the North Pole and the sea area around the North Pole belong to all the people of the world." Yin also said that "China must play an indispensable role in Arctic exploration as we have one-fifth of the world's population."[15]

Another view both outside and within China is that the Arctic has the potential to develop into a sphere of cooperation.[16] Among those that hold this view it is common to underline the numerous difficulties and uncertainties related to the prospective economic advantages of a melting Arctic. Unsurprisingly, in the few existing statements made by Chinese officials about the Arctic, the Chinese Government has emphasized the benefits of and the need to increase cooperation. China has not published an Arctic strategy and is unlikely to do so for at least another 10 years. The highest ranking Ministry of Foreign Affairs official with responsibility for the Arctic is an assistant minister, one level in rank above a department head but below a half-dozen vice-ministers and the foreign minister.

Two Chinese assistant ministers have made speeches (in 2009 and 2010) on China's views of the Arctic. Their remarks about the International Seabed Area being the common heritage of mankind have in several instances been misinterpreted by others to mean that China might regard the Arctic in its entirety as international waters (which there is no indication of). Nevertheless both assistant ministers expressed the need to "balance the rights and interests of the coastal states with the common interests of the international community," which clearly reflects China's concern that non-Arctic states will be not be able to fully take advantage of the transformed Arctic's potential opportunities.[17]

Implications of the melting ice

From China's viewpoint, regardless of whether one predicts cooperation or competition, the Arctic transformation is of fundamental importance because of its impact on China's food security. On the one hand, potential new fishing grounds are characterized in positive terms. In a paper published by the Foreign Ministry's research institute Tang Guoqiang, former PRC Ambassador to Oslo, called the Arctic a "major biological protein bank in the world."[18] On the other hand, the melting Arctic poses a threat to China's food production and economic development because of the impact that climatic changes stemming from the melting ice are having and will continue to have on agriculture. Naturally, for a nation of over 1.3 billion people food security is vital. Any disruptions of agricultural output could have dire consequences. For example, changes in the Arctic climate are believed to pose direct flood threats to agricultural production as well as to Chinese coastal cities. It is also linked to extreme weather. According to Ma Deyi, the chief scientist on China's fifth Arctic expedition in 2012, research shows that the increase of melting ice in September 2007, which at the time set a new record, caused a historically harsh winter storm in southern China with freezing temperatures in early 2008.[19] When in 2014 China's southern city of Guangzhou recorded the coldest winter since 1984 (measured by the period from 1 December 2013 to 28 February 2014), Chinese experts attributed it to the warming of the Arctic.[20]

According to several Chinese researchers, the Arctic is discussed by senior officials nearly exclusively in the context of climate change and the possible consequences for either food production fluctuations or social instability that floods, drought and extreme weather can give rise to.[21] China is particularly vulnerable, not only geographically because of existing water shortages and climate variations across its huge land mass, but also because weak political institutions are regarded by some Chinese experts to be a factor behind the weak crisis management capabilities of Chinese authorities.[22] These researchers have—among others—highlighted the havoc caused by the above-mentioned extreme winter storm in southern China during the Chinese New Year holiday in 2008, when the collapse of infrastructure and the inability of officials to coordinate rescue efforts left millions of travelers stranded in harsh conditions. These researchers warn that this was merely the beginning of China's encounters with climate threats. The Chinese authorities were quite successful in shaping the public narrative in the aftermath of the 2008 winter storm catastrophe. Everyone's attention was focused on this historically harsh storm, with the emphasis being placed on the "historical" and "unique" natural disaster, not on the authorities' incompetence in responding to it.

Ever since the United States National Intelligence Council (NIC) in June 2008 published parts of a 58-page confidential report on security threats posed by climate change, Chinese security analysts have started to approach the notion of climate security more seriously.[23] Before the NIC 2008 report the link between climate change and national security was hardly ever made in China.[24] Instead, Chinese leaders insisted that climate change be regarded solely as a development issue. Consequently, climate change was approached by Chinese officials on the basis of the environmental challenges it poses to the development of Chinese society and wellbeing of the Chinese people and mankind at large rather than as a possible or probable national security threat. For example, in the White Paper that China published on climate change in 2008, the term "climate security" is not even mentioned. Food security has been—and still is—the main focus of any analysis describing the threats China faces from climate change. But after the United States NIC report and especially after publication of the China-specific report commissioned by the NIC in April 2009 the relevance of climate change for national security has started to be acknowledged in China. A *China National Defense News* article published in December 2009 states that climate change is no longer a simple question of environmental protection and economics, but has transformed into a political and strategic question seriously affecting international peace and stability.[25]

The NIC reports have been described by Chinese analysts as a useful "reference for China for its own climate change studies."[26] As in so many other instances, Chinese analysts closely follow American trends and focuses.

While the 2008 NIC assessment itself is confidential, some analyses used as raw material have been published. Countries were ranked in terms of three climate risks: sea-level rise, increased water scarcity, and an aggregate measure of vulnerability based on projected temperature change compared with nations' ability to adapt. On all three fronts China faces severe challenges. The greatest number of people exposed to sea-level rise are in China, the Philippines, Egypt and Indonesia. China and the Philippines alone have 64 million people in the lowest elevation zones (1 meter above sea level). According to the 2008 posture statement of the US Army, "climate change will compound already difficult conditions in many developing countries. These trends will increase the likelihood of humanitarian crises, the potential for epidemic diseases, and regionally destabilizing population migrations."[27] In China the resettlement of millions of people will undoubtedly cause social tensions and threaten the social fabric that is vital for economic development. The 2009 follow-up NIC report on China highlighted the adverse impact of climate change on water resources, which could lead to a water crisis potentially impacting China's social, economic and political stability "to a great extent."[28]

According to research interviews, Chinese policymakers paid particular attention to the following two sentences in the public parts of the NIC report: "Climate change acts as a threat multiplier for instability" and "climate change *alone* is unlikely to trigger state failure in any state before 2030, but the impacts will worsen existing problems—such as poverty, social tensions, environmental degradation, ineffectual leadership, and weak political institutions."[29] In off-the-record discussions as well as in commentary published in China, Chinese observers noted the fact that the report was endorsed by all 16 US intelligence agencies and several retired American generals.

Following the publication of parts of the NIC report, the National Defense University in China was commissioned in 2009 by the State Council to write a detailed internal report about climate change from the perspective of the security threats it poses to China. At the same time the General Staff Headquarters of the PLA set up the Military Climatic Change Expert Committee that included academics and experts from inside and outside of the military.[30] This committee was asked to research the impact of climate change on military struggle and military capacity-building, so as to provide political and technical support to the PLA in response to the problems of climate change.

The challenges that the transformation of the Arctic gives rise to are at least partially offset by opportunities. Chinese experts who study the changing Arctic in the context of economic security see obvious benefits from the melting ice. A seasonally ice-free Arctic could become an important shipping route for a trade-dependent country such as China. The trip from Shanghai to Hamburg via the Northern Sea Route, which runs along the north coast of Russia from the Bering Strait in the east to Novaya Zemlya in the west, is 5,200 kilometers shorter than the route via the Strait of Malacca and the Suez Canal.[31] If the Northern Sea Route becomes commercially viable it would also be advantageous politically, as China would prefer to decrease its reliance on the Malacca Strait.

Moreover, although the vast majority of known natural resources lie within the EEZ of the coastal Arctic states and a non-Arctic state such as China therefore does not exercise rights over them, several Chinese specialists point to energy security in particular as a driver of China's interests in the Arctic.[32] Chinese Government officials are aware that China's interest in resource exploration sets off alarm bells abroad and are circumspect about mentioning resources.[33] In late 2013, a deputy-director general of the Ministry of Foreign Affairs gingerly stated in a Xinhua news agency interview that resource development in the Arctic was a "possibility, but not a priority for China."[34] Probably as a result of this awareness of the sensitivities related to resource exploration several Chinese researchers have recommended that climate change be prioritized in China's Arctic agenda so as to avoid controversy.[35] Climate change cooperation provides China with opportunities to partner with other states on the Arctic agenda.

China's Arctic ambitions

The Arctic is not high on the foreign policy agenda of the Chinese Government. Nevertheless, in recent years the Chinese Government has increased funding of Arctic research to be better prepared to protect what it perceives as its key interests in the Arctic. These key interests are, first, to strengthen China's capacity to respond appropriately to the effects that climatic changes in the Arctic will have on food production and extreme weather in China; second, to secure access at reasonable cost for Chinese shipping companies to Arctic shipping routes in the event the routes become a viable option during summer months; and third, to strengthen China's ability as a non-Arctic state to access resources and fishing waters.

From the ten Arctic-related projects chosen to be funded 2008–13 by the National Social Science Fund it is evident that the government wants to deepen its understanding of China's interests along the Northern Sea Route from a legal and strategic perspective. Research was conducted on "the legal issues of NSR from China's interest perspective"; "the international legal order and the expansion of China's interests in the Arctic"; "China's Arctic resource development strategy against the backdrop of NSR"; "China's NSR strategy and establishing maritime power"; "China's NSR strategy from the perspective of international law"; "legal channels to strengthen China's actual presence in the Arctic"; and "safeguarding China's Arctic route safety and strategy plan."[36]

Because of its three key interests China wants its voice to be heard when decisions are made on how the Arctic should be governed despite the fact that it is not an Arctic littoral state. The Chinese Government does not object to its officials expressing the stance that China does not want to be excluded. For example, Gou Haibo of the Department of Treaty and Law at the Ministry of Foreign Affairs wrote in 2011:

> The Arctic states have generally expanded their sovereign and jurisdictional rights within the Arctic. ... Inter-regional issues like shipping, resource exploration, and environmental protection have required cooperation between Arctic and non-Arctic states, which could potentially lead to the weakening of Arctic states' monopolistic position within the region. Given that cooperation is required with non-Arctic states, it is impossible for non-Arctic states to simply be the passive users of Arctic sea routes. Nor can non-Arctic states simply be the end consumers of the region's energy and resources. Rather, they need to actively participate in the decision-making processes and governance regimes within the Arctic region.[37]

China is already a part of the general framework of Arctic governance. Most importantly, China is a veto-wielding member of the United Nations Security Council, the ultimate authority of the 1982 UNCLOS, which China ratified in 1996. China is also represented in numerous international organizations and is party to other international agreements that pertain directly or indirectly to Arctic governance. For example, China is, along with 41 other countries, a signatory of the 1920 Svalbard Treaty, which grants all members equal rights to access Svalbard while recognizing Norway's absolute sovereignty. It is also a member in the International Maritime Organization (IMO), a UN agency responsible for adopting measures to secure international shipping and to prevent marine pollution from ships.

However, China remains an outsider when it comes to the Arctic Council, the key regional body specifically devoted to the Arctic, albeit one without decision-making powers and restricted from discussing military-security matters. Chinese officials have clearly stated that they regard the Arctic Council as the most influential international institution for developing Arctic governance and cooperation. As a non-circumpolar state China is not eligible to be a full member of the council.

In 2013, after active lobbying in the capitals of the eight member states of the Arctic Council, China's application to become a permanent observer was approved. At the same time four other Asian nations—India, Japan, the Republic of Korea and Singapore—became new permanent observers, a reflection of the growing interest across Asia toward the Arctic. Permanent observers have no voting rights in the Arctic Council. Only member states can vote.

Before the 2013 Arctic Council ministerial meeting, the permanent observer applications, and especially China's, were portrayed by media commentators as a controversial issue. The ministerial meeting had already twice (in 2009 and 2011) decided to push forward a decision about admitting new permanent observers. In the lead up to the 2013 meeting there was media speculation that it was China that was the elephant in the room. In private conversations several officials from Arctic states said that Russia was wary of allowing China into one of the last forums in which Russia is not overshadowed by its former "little brother."[38] Canada, in turn, was not eager to allow the European Union in as a permanent observer due to differing stances on seal hunting. All five Nordic nations expressed support for China's application, even Norway, which Beijing shunned diplomatically following the selection by the Nobel Peace Prize Committee of the imprisoned dissident Liu Xiaobo for the award.[39]

Why was China so adamant about becoming a permanent observer, considering that it still does not have voting rights? A number of reasons emerge. These include a concern that at some point in the future China would not be a desired *ad hoc* observer (permanent observers automatically receive an invitation to the council's meetings); China's hope that observers could over time attain more influence in the Arctic Council[40] (already today besides observing they have the right to propose projects, submit documents and express views); and the possibility that the differentiation between a member state and an observer is *de facto* quite symbolic as the "Council's authority is so limited" that in practice it functions as a "forum for friendly deliberation amongst states."[41]

How the relationship between Arctic Council member states and observers evolves in coming years will directly impact China's ability to influence decisions about the Arctic's future. Of particular relevance will be how China-Russia relations develop in general and on Arctic issues in particular. Russia has major economic, security and governance interests in the Arctic and is thus a key player in all decisions taken by the Arctic Council. Furthermore, in early 2014 Moscow announced plans to establish a new strategic military command in the Arctic, encompassing the Northern fleet, Arctic warfare brigades, and air force and air defense units.[42] This presumably has heightened concerns that China and many other nations already have of Moscow monopolizing decisions over the Northern Sea Route regarding tariffs to be applied by Russia for use of various necessary services, for example icebreaker assistance and a robust sea-and-rescue support system, in its coastal waters. Though senior leaders in both Beijing and Moscow glowingly describe the countries' present ties to be the best in history, the relationship is fraught with underlying suspicion and distrust due to historic grievances and the change in power balance between the two nations. To date there has been little interaction at the government level between China and Russia on geopolitical or legal issues pertaining specifically to the Arctic.

In the meantime, Chinese officials and scholars will continue to emphasize the global, rather than regional implications of the melting ice in an obvious attempt to legitimize China getting its voice heard in Arctic affairs. Chinese scholars have called China an "Arctic stakeholder" and a "near-Arctic state."[43] In a 2014 academic publication, Li Zhenfu, one of the first Chinese scholars to write about the Arctic's strategic value for China, linked China's strategy with regard to the Northern Sea Route to China's aspirations as a maritime power. Li went as far as to call the strategy an "important foundation to realizing the China Dream."[44]

Other non-Arctic states such as South Korea and Japan, which like China have increased expenditure in Arctic research, are also keen to be involved in discussions pertaining to Arctic governance and security mechanisms. Hence, China's "internationalizing of the Arctic issue" is welcomed by non-Arctic states.[45]

Conclusions

The uncertainty of the Arctic future, in the event that the ice continues to melt, and the uncertainty of how China will use its power, in the event that its economic rise continues, together constitute a powerful emotional backdrop for any analysis of China's intentions in the Arctic. Throughout history a rising power has caused jitters, and China is no exception. China's assertive behavior in recent years in its near seas has only increased anxiety about China's intentions everywhere. Meanwhile, the economic value of the Arctic remains unknown because the timing of accessibility of sea routes, fishing grounds and resources is uncertain and a reliable evaluation of what actually lies below the ice is not yet available.[46]

What kind of region the Arctic will develop into is as uncertain as the pace of the melting ice. On the one hand, there are numerous issues that could potentially give rise to inter-state tensions in the Arctic. A key concern of all nations aspiring to use the Northern Sea Route pertains to Russia's willingness to cooperate with others in a reasonable manner "without discrimination" and according to "good practices" developed by industry on several issues in its coastal waters.[47] Another major concern is the 1.1 million square-mile so called "donut hole" in the central Arctic Ocean that does not fall under any country's jurisdiction. Until a few years ago, this part of the Arctic Ocean was locked in ice for virtually the entire year. But in recent years when the ice cover has reached a record low during the summer months, about 40 percent of the "donut hole" has been open, with significant implications for fishing, for example. In sum, the need to establish governance and security mechanisms in the Arctic region is becoming more and more important.

On the other hand, the Arctic states have consistently declared their intent to develop the Arctic in a cooperative and peaceful manner. It is noteworthy that Russia, an instrumental actor in the development of all things Arctic from environmental protection and shipping logistics to resource exploration and fishing, has continuously emphasized the need and its willingness to cooperate on Arctic issues. No state currently perceives an immediate military threat in the region, nor expects one in the foreseeable future, as all territorial claims are being pursued under the terms allowed for by UNCLOS.

Nevertheless, the Arctic's untapped economic potential looms larger for every year the thickness of the ice recedes, raising the Arctic's strategic value in the minds of policymakers across the globe. Chinese officials are no exception. Despite the formal legal framework provided by UNCLOS, the melting ice has created a "new, essentially ungoverned space in the Arctic Ocean that governments are eager to secure."[48] Fear over China's potentially belligerent Arctic posture grows with every strident action its navy or maritime law enforcement agencies take in the South and East China Seas. Foreign observers one after the other deem China's Arctic actions part and parcel of an increasingly assertive maritime power.[49]

However, precisely because China is so insistent in its near seas that sovereignty is sacred and cannot be shared, it is unlikely that Beijing will challenge the coastal Arctic states' sovereign rights. In becoming a permanent observer of the Arctic Council, China committed to recognize the Arctic states' sovereign rights and jurisdiction in the Arctic. China can be expected to keep a low profile in the Arctic.

Amidst all hype about China's growing investment in the Arctic it is worth bearing in mind that China's investment in Arctic research constitutes about 0.1 percent of the total investment the government sets aside for scientific research.[50] Chinese research does indeed remain primarily focused on how the melting Arctic will affect China's continental and oceanic environment and how in turn such changes could affect domestic agricultural and economic development. As a nation that will be directly affected by the climatic changes brought about by the melting ice, China wants to prepare for the potential threats to its food security, climate security, and even domestic security, as well as the potential benefits for commerce and trade.

China is naturally also eager to explore ways to benefit from new fishing grounds and possibly natural resources, despite the fact that most of the known natural resources lie within the coastal states' EEZ. A foreseeable avenue for China would be to engage in co-development projects with one or more of the coastal states. China is trying to position itself as a possible partner for deep sea oil and gas exploration and other technically challenging projects.

As a rising major power China wants to ensure that it will not be excluded from discussions on new governance and security arrangements. No doubt China will persistently call itself a "near-Arctic state" and insist on recognition of the global, not merely regional implications of the melting Arctic ice. A comment by Qu Xing, who headed the Foreign Ministry-affiliated China Institute for International Studies, is indicative of China's Arctic aspirations. Qu said that being granted observer status shows that China's activities and opinions about the region have been recognized by all member states. China's official news agency Xinhua went further and stated: "Even without the power to vote, the Arctic Council's latest decision to grant observer status to China can guarantee the country's legitimate rights and activities in the region."[51]

China is not alone in its view that non-Arctic states have "legitimate interests and concerns" in the maritime Arctic related to commercial shipping, resource development and tourism.[52] Japan, South Korea and many other non-Arctic nations share this view.[53]

As for speculation that China might want a military presence in the Arctic by establishing a naval base, these concerns reflect a poor understanding of China's ambitions (which are very much focused on its near abroad) and, in the words of Canadian professor David Curtis Wright, are "overblown."[54]

Notes

1. D. Perovich et al. "Sea Ice," *Arctic Report Card: update for 2013*. National Oceanic and Atmospheric Administration, 2013. Available online at www.arctic.noaa.gov/reportcard/sea_ice.html (accessed 23 March 2014).
2. W.N. Meier et al. "Sea Ice," in M.S. Olsen et al. (eds), *Snow, Water, Ice and Permafrost in the Arctic: climate change and the cryosphere*, Oslo: Arctic Monitoring and Assessment Programme, 2012. Available online at http://amap.no/swipa/ (accessed 23 March 2014).
3. J. Astill, "The Melting North," *The Economist*, 16 June 2012. Available online at www.economist.com/node/21556798 (accessed 23 March 2014). See also Meier et al., "Sea Ice," Chapter 9, pp. 17–18; and National Oceanic and Atmospheric Administration, "Sea Ice: will the Arctic be free of ice in 30 years? The Future of Arctic Climate and Global Impacts." Available online at www.arctic.noaa.gov/future/sea_ice.html (accessed 23 March 2014).
4. F.J. Mueter et al., "Marine Fishes of the Arctic," *Arctic Report Card: update for 2013*. National Oceanic and Atmospheric Administration, 2013. Available online at www.arctic.noaa.gov/reportcard/marine_fish.html (accessed 23 March 2014).
5. R. Fujita, "The Arctic is Melting and the Fish are Moving In," *Ocean Science*, 4 April 2013. Available online at www.edf.org/blog/2013/04/04/arctic-melting-and-fish-are-moving (accessed 24 March 2014).
6. D. Gautier et al., "Assessment of Undiscovered Oil and Gas in the Arctic," *Science*, 29 May 2009.
7. "Hidden Treasure," *The Economist*, 16 June 2012.
8. Author's interview with senior official at State Oceanic Administration, Beijing, 21 March 2014. Ann-Marie Brady states that one-fifth of the Chinese Government's polar spending goes to the Arctic. A.-M. Brady, "Polar Stakes: China's polar activities as benchmark for intentions," *China Brief*, vol. 12, no. 14 (19 July 2012).
9. L. Jakobson, *China Prepares for an Ice-Free Arctic*, Stockholm: Stockholm International Peace Research Institute, SIPRI Insights on Peace and Security 2, 2010.
10. See e.g. D.C. Wright, *The Dragon Eyes the Top of the World: Arctic policy debate and discussion in China*, China Maritime Study 8, Newport, RI: Naval War College Press for the China Maritime Studies Institute,

August 2011; C. Campbell, "China and the Arctic: Objectives and Obstacles," US-China Economic and Security Review Commission Staff Research Report, 13 April 2012. Available online at www.uscc.gov/researchpapers/research_archive.php (accessed 4 April 2014); D.C. Wright, "China's Growing Interest in the Arctic," *Journal of Military and Strategic Studies*, vol. 15, iss. 2, 2013; S. Rainwater, "Race to the North: China's Arctic strategy and its implications," *Naval War College Review*, spring 2013, vol. 66, no. 2, 62–82.

11 See e.g. Yu, B. and Li, Y., "北方航线的综合评价研究 [Comprehensive Evaluation of the Northern Sea Route]," 大连海事大学学报, vol. 35 (June 2009), p. 228; Bai, C., Li, Z. and Yang, Z., "北极 航线探讨 [Research of Arctic Sea Routes]," 航海技术, no. 5 (2009), pp. 7–9; and Zhang, X. et al., "北极航线的海 经济潜力评估及其对我国经济发展的战略意义 [Assessment of the Economic Potential of Arctic Sea Routes and Its Strategic Significance for the Development of China's Economy]," 中国软科学, Supplementary issue 2, 2009, pp. 86–93.

12 "New Cold Wars over Arctic Wealth," *Global Times*, 27 July 2009.

13 Han, X., "备受关注的北极主权之争 [Closely Watched Dispute over Arctic Sovereignty]," 兵器知识·防务观察家, vol. 253, no. 9B (September 2008), pp. 16–19.

14 Quoted in L. Jakobson and J. Peng, *China's Arctic Aspirations*, Stockholm: Stockholm International Peace Research Institute, Policy Paper 34, 2012, p. 15.

15 Ibid.

16 See e.g. C. Le Miere and J. Mazo, *Arctic Opening: insecurity and opportunity*, London: International Institute of Strategic Studies. Adelphi series, December 2013, p. 78; and R. Huebert et al., *Climate Change and International Security: the Arctic as a bellwether*, Boston: Belfer Centre, Harvard University, May 2012, pp. 17–18.

17 Hu Zhengyue (Assistant Minister, Ministry of Foreign Affairs, PRC), "China's Arctic Policy," Presentation at High North Study Tour in Norway, 2 July 2009. See also Jakobson and Peng, *China's Arctic Aspirations*, pp. 11–15.

18 Tang Guoqiang, "Arctic Issues and China's Stance," China Institute of International Studies, 4 March 2013. Available online at www.ciis.org.cn/english/2013-03/04/content_5772842.htm (accessed 24 March 2014).

19 "北极科考团首席科学家马德毅谈科考 [Lead Arctic Expedition Scientist Ma Deyi Talks about the Expedition]," 半岛都市报, 3 July 2012. Ma Deyi is the director of the No. 1 Ocean Research Institute, the research institute for marine sciences and oceanology under the State Oceanic Administration.

20 "广州今冬30年来最冷 专家称与北极增暖有关 [Guangzhou Records the Coldest Winter in 30 Years. Experts Say it Has to Do with the Arctic Warming]," ifeng.com, 3 Mar 2014. Available online at http://news.ifeng.com/gundong/detail_2014_03/03/34373378_0.shtml (accessed 4 April 2014).

21 Author's research interviews with Chinese researchers focusing on Arctic issues, Beijing, September 2013; Shanghai, February 2014.

22 Ibid.

23 "Climate Change May Challenge National Security, Classified Report Warns," The Earth Institute, Columbia University, 2 July 2008. Available online at www.earth.columbia.edu/articles/view/2202.

24 For a thorough discussion of the development of approaches in China toward the securitization of climate change see D. Freeman, *The Missing Link: China, climate change and national security*, Brussels: Brussels Institute of Contemporary China Studies, BICCS Asia Paper, vol. 5, no. 8, December 2012, pp. 11–14. Available online at www.vub.ac.be/biccs/site/assets/files/apapers/Asia%20papers/201012%20-%20%20Climate%20Change%20Security.pdf (accessed 4 April 2014).

25 Ibid., pp. 20–1.

26 Author's research interviews 2009–2013 with Chinese academics and government analysts focusing on China's security in a broad sense as well as on climate change. See also H. Zhang, "解放军军队气候变化专家委员会在北京成立 [How Climate Change Impacts China's National Security]," 第一财经日报, 11 November 2009. Available online at http://finance.ifeng.com/news/20091130/1520788.shtml (accessed 5 April 2014).

27 US Army posture statement. Available online at www.arlingtoninstitute.org/fe-archive-volume-11-number-12 (accessed 4 April 2014).

28 *China: impact of climate change to 2030*, Washington, DC: National Intelligence Council. Special Report NIC 2009-02D, April 2009, pp. 4, 33.

29 Thomas Fingar, "National Intelligence Assessment on the National Security Implications of Global Climate Change to 2030," Office of the Director of National Intelligence, 25 June 2008.

30 Author's research interviews with a senior climate change official, 6 August 2008, and two PLA researchers, 3 March 2009, Beijing. See also "解放军军队气候变化专家委员会在北京成立 [People's

Liberation Army Military Climate Change Expert Commission Established in Beijing]," 解放军报, 28 November 2008.
31. T. Pettersen, "China Starts Commercial Use of Northern Sea Route," *Barents Observer*, 14 March 2013. Available online at http://barentsobserver.com/en/arctic/2013/03/china-starts-commercial-use-northern-sea-route-14-03 (accessed 6 April 2014).
32. 张胜军 李形 [S.J. Zhang and X. Li], "中国能源安全与中国北极战略定 [China's Energy Security and China's Arctic Strategy Orientation]," 国际政治经济研究, vol. 4, 2010; 孙凯 郭培清 [K. Sun and P.Q. Guo], "北极治理机制变迁及中国的参与战略研究 [The Evolution of the Arctic Governance System and China's Strategy of Participation]," 世界经济与政治论坛, no. 2, March 2012; and X. Li and R.G. Bertelsen, "The Drivers of China's Arctic Interests: political stability and transportation and energy security," in L. Heininen (ed.), *Arctic Yearbook 2013*, Ukureyri, Iceland: Northern Research Forum, 2013. Available online at www.arcticyearbook.com/images/Articles_2013/LIBERTLESON_AY13_FINAL.pdf (accessed 21 April 2014).
33. Jakobson and Peng, *China's Arctic Aspirations*, p. 15.
34. "Interview: China backs agenda of environment over development," English.news.cn, 23 October 2013. Available online at http://news.xinhuanet.com/english/indepth/2013-10/23/c_132824519.htm (accessed 21 April 2014).
35. Ibid., p. 16.
36. "国家社科基金项目数据库 [National Social Sciences Tuning Project Database]," with keyword "Arctic [北极]," Available online at http://gp.people.com.cn/yangshuo/skygb/sk/index.php/Index/seach (accessed 5 April 2014).
37. Gou, H., "中国参加北极事务涉及的国际法问题 [International Law and China's Participation in Arctic Affairs]," in Gao, Z. et al. (eds), 国际海洋法问题研究 [*Research of International Maritime Laws*], Beijing: Haiyang Chubanshe, 2011.
38. L. Jakobson, "China and the Arctic—what's the fuss?" *the interpreter*, 15 May 2013. Available online at www.lowyinterpreter.org/post/2013/05/15/Whats-the-fuss-about-China-and-the-Arctic.aspx.
39. Jakobson and Peng, *China's Arctic Aspirations*, p. 13. For more on the Arctic angle in China-Norway relations see p. 21.
40. Ibid.
41. Citations by O.S. Stokke of the Fridtjof Nansen Institute and T. Pedersen of the University of Tromsø in J. Vagadal Joensen, "A New Chinese Arctic Policy? An Analysis of China's Policies towards the Arctic in the Post-Cold War Period," Thesis, Aarhus University, 2013. Available online at www.academia.edu/4675427/A_New_Chinese_Arctic_Policy_An_Analysis_of_Chinas_Policies_towards_the_Arctic_in_the_Post-Cold_War_Period (accessed 4 April 2014).
42. Zachary Keck, "Russia to Establish Arctic Military Command," *The Diplomat*, 21 February 2014. Available online at http://thediplomat.com/2014/02/russia-to-establish-arctic-military-command/ (accessed 21 April 2014).
43. "China Defines Itself as a 'Near-Arctic State,' says SIPRI," Press release, Stockholm International Peace Research Institute, 10 May 2012. Available online at www.sipri.org/media/pressreleases/2012/arcticchinapr (accessed 5 April 2014).
44. 曾江, 郝欣 [H. Zeng and X. Hao], 北极航线战略研究进一步深化 [Deepening the Strategic Research on the Northern Sea Route], 中国科学报在线, 22 January 2014, Available online at www.csstoday.net/xueshuzixun/guoneixinwen/87381.html (accessed 6 April 2014).
45. A.-M. Brady, "China Playing a Long Game in Polar Governance," *World Politics Review*, 14 January 2014.
46. The line of thinking in this paragraph was inspired by "Debating the Fears of the Future: China and the Arctic," panel remarks by K.S. Kristensen, senior researcher, Centre for Military Studies, University of Copenhagen at a conference "China's Arctic Aspirations" in Copenhagen, 17 April 2013.
47. "Law of the Sea as Reflected in UNCLOS: the overarching legal framework" (from AMSA report 2009), ARCTIS Database. Available online at www.arctis-search.com/Law+of+the+Sea+as+Reflected+in+UNCLOS (accessed 22 April 2014).
48. Le Miere and Mazo, *Arctic Opening: insecurity and opportunity*, p. 77.
49. E. Economy, "Beijing's Arctic Play: just the tip of the iceberg," *The Diplomat*, 5 April 2014. Available online at http://thediplomat.com/2014/04/beijings-arctic-play-just-the-tip-of-the-iceberg/ (accessed 6 April 2014).
50. Jakobson and Peng, *China's Arctic Aspirations*, p. 19.
51. "China Granted Observer Status in Arctic Council," Xinhua, 15 May 2013.

52 O.R. Young, J.D. Kim and Y.H. Kim, "Introduction and Overview," in Young, Kim and Kim (eds), *The Arctic in World Affairs*, Seoul: Korea Maritime Institute; Honolulu: East-West Center, December 2012, p. 5.
53 L. Jakobson and S.H. Lee, "North East Asia Eyes the Arctic," in forthcoming volume edited by L. Jakobson and N. Melvin, Oxford: Oxford University Press, 2015.
54 D.C. Wright, "China's Growing Interest in the Arctic," p. 58.

Suggested further reading

C. Campbell, "China and the Arctic: objectives and obstacles," Washington, DC: US-China Economic and Security Review Commission Staff Research Report, 13 April 2012.

L. Jakobson and J.C. Peng, *China's Arctic Aspirations*, Stockholm: Stockholm International Peace Research Institute, Policy Paper 34, 2012.

X. Li and R.G. Bertelsen, "The Drivers of China's Arctic Interests: political stability and transportation and energy security," in L. Heininen (ed.), *Arctic Yearbook 2013*, Ukureyri, Iceland: Northern Research Forum, 2013.

S. Rainwater, "Race to the North: China's Arctic Strategy and Its Implications," *Naval War College Review*, vol. 66, no. 2, spring 2013.

G.Q. Tang, "Arctic Issues and China's Stance," Beijing: China Institute of International Studies, 4 March 2013. Available online at www.ciis.org.cn/english/2013-03/04/content_5772842.htm.

D.C. Wright, *The Dragon Eyes the Top of the World: Arctic Policy Debate and Discussion in China*, China Maritime Study 8, Newport, RI: Naval War College Press for the China Maritime Studies Institute, August 2011.

D.C. Wright, "China's Growing Interest in the Arctic," *Journal of Military and Strategic Studies*, vol. 15, iss. 2, 2013.

J. Yang, "China and Arctic Affairs," in L. Heininen (ed.), *Arctic Yearbook 2012*, Ukureyri, Iceland: Northern Research Forum, 2012.

O.R. Young, J.D. Kim and Y.H. Kim (eds), *The Arctic in World Affairs*, Seoul: Korea Maritime Institute; Honolulu: East-West Center, December 2012.

11
Security dimensions of China's relations with the Korean Peninsula

Jinwook Choi

Is China's policy towards the Korean Peninsula changing? This question was first raised in early 2013, when China took a strict position on North Korea's third nuclear test. China not only cooperated in adopting the UN Security Council Resolution 2094 but also placed substantial sanctions on the Chosun Trade Bank. Several months later, the Chinese Ministry of Commerce issued a list of items and technologies that could be misused in North Korea's missile, nuclear, chemical, and biological or other WMD programs. China also pressured North Korea by imposing administrative measures, banned tourism to North Korea, and placed a 20 kg limit on the commodities that each person can carry into North Korea.

It may be too early to say that the relationship between China and North Korea is at a turning point. However, increasing uncertainties concerning North Korea and changing security dynamism in Northeast Asia seem to be affecting China's relationship with the Korean Peninsula. There are a number of factors affecting China's policy towards the Korean Peninsula: the rise of China, the United States' pivot to Asia, Japan's collective self-defense, and Jang Sung Taek's execution and its consequences. The most important point is the sustainability of the structure of confrontation between the trilateral cooperation of the US, Japan, and South Korea *vis-à-vis* the China-North Korean alliance.

China takes into consideration the strategic value of North and South Korea. Both South and North Korea are crucial to China's interests. North Korea is a military buffer for China's security, while China is North Korea's most important benefactor. China provides half a million tons of crude oil to North Korea every year, and is North Korea's largest trade partner. The trade volume between the two accounts for more than 80 percent of North Korean trade. China also provides security and political support to North Korea.

The relationship between China and South Korea developed rapidly following normalization of relations in 1992. Sino-South Korea relations are most notable in terms of their economic relations. Since normalizing relations, the two have expanded their bilateral trade from a meager US$ 5 billion in 1992 to US$ 228.9 billion in 2013. China is already South Korea's largest export market and largest investment destination. In particular, South Korea's trade with China is larger than the sum of that with both the US and Japan. The relationship between the two is far weaker in the political and military area than in the economic sector. However, the value of South Korea increases when it comes to trilateral cooperation between the US, Japan, and South Korea, of which China perceives itself to be the target.

This chapter analyzes continuity and change in China's relations with the Korean Peninsula. Why is China so supportive of North Korea? What is the cost to China of maintaining North Korea as a buffer? What is the outlook for China's relationship with the Korean Peninsula?

A historical review of China's relationship with the Korean Peninsula

Historically, continental powers and Pacific Ocean powers have often clashed on the Korean Peninsula. China and Japan frequently invaded Korea and fought each other over who would dominate the Korean Peninsula until the late nineteenth century, when the United States, Russia, Germany, and France emerged as new stakeholders. As a result of victory in the Sino-Japanese War of 1894–5 and the Russo-Japanese War of 1904–5, Japan made the Korean Peninsula a protectorate in 1905 and a colony in 1910. The colonial rule ended in 1945, but it was divided into North and South along the thirty-eighth parallel, and two separate governments were established in 1948. When the PRC was established in 1949, its relationship with the Korean Peninsula was limited to its northern part until 1992, when China normalized its relationship with South Korea.

In the 1950s, China and North Korea both regarded their close alliance as sealed in blood. North Korea started an all-out war by invading South Korea on 25 June 1950, but it soon developed into a major conflict between the United States and China.[1] China had lost up to a million lives when the Korean War ended on 27 July 1953.[2] The relationship between China and North Korea once again turned out to be one of a bloody alliance, which began when the Chinese communists and Kim Il Sung's guerrilla units united to fight against Japanese colonialism and against the Kuomintang. A strong military alliance between South Korea and the United States was established to contain the communist threat in Northeast Asia.

The Korean War firmly embedded the roots of the Cold War in Northeast Asia. The Korean Peninsula became the frontline of the Cold War confrontation between the West and the East. This remains a big obstacle in transforming inter-Korean relations of confrontation and hostility into reconciliation and cooperation. It helped delay the normalization of relations between the United States and China until 1979. The northern part of the Korean Peninsula has remained as the most important buffer zone for China's security. To Pyongyang, China provided not only a security guarantee but also economic and political support. China and North Korea signed a Mutual Aid and Cooperation Friendship Treaty in 1961 that was renewed twice without alteration, in 1981 and 2001, remaining valid until 2021. It appears to have guaranteed China's automatic intervention in North Korea in case of invasion, although China denies it.

Nevertheless, the relationship between China and North Korea has not always been smooth. Domestic issues such as the August Factional Strife in 1956 and the Cultural Revolution made the relationship tense. Pro-Chinese factions and pro-Soviet factions led a failed attempt to dethrone Kim Il Sung from the position of chairman of the central committee of the party in August 1956, but purges of those rebels had to be delayed a few years because of prompt intervention by China and the Soviet Union.

Moreover, North Korea made an effort to maintain independent *juche* (self-reliance) ideologically, politically, militarily, and economically. North Korea tried not to depend on anyone, and kept a balance between the Soviet Union and China during the Soviet-Sino dispute of the 1960s.

From the 1960s to the 1980s, North Korea developed more self-reliance in the Beijing-Pyongyang bilateral relationship. However, China's Cultural Revolution in the late 1960s briefly weakened its relationship with North Korea because Chinese Red Guards criticized Kim Il Sung as a dictator. The Soviet-Sino conflict contributed to strengthening Sino-North Korean relations.

Khrushchev's advocacy for a peaceful coexistence between the West and East and criticism of the personality cult of Mao and Kim Il Sung was unacceptable to both countries. The Cuban Missile Crisis made the Soviet Union appear an unreliable coward. China and North Korea became ideologically united, criticizing Soviet revisionism. The personal ties between top leaders of the two sides also played a key role in stabilizing the relations between North Korea and China. Nevertheless, as China actively pursued reform and openness after 1978, the aspect of military obligation in the alliance was diluted.[3]

During the Cold War, Sino-DPRK relations faced their most important turning point, namely, the Sino-American rapprochement of the early 1970s. Interestingly, North Korea showed compliance when relations between China and the US were warming up, whereas countries such as North Vietnam and Albania demonstrated resentment. Nevertheless, this did not mean that Beijing would be willing to stand on Pyongyang's side on any matter that was important to the North Koreans. In 1975, Kim Il Sung visited Beijing in an attempt to elicit support from China for a military invasion of South Korea, but China demurred.

In the 1980s, Beijing demonstrated a willingness to accept the status quo and relented in its persistent efforts to bring revolutionary change to the Peninsula. This shift was particularly noticeable with Mao's death in September 1976, and continued with Deng Xiaoping's de-revolutionization process aimed to modernize all facets of China's development, including its agriculture, national defense, and industry. Its policy of "Reform and Opening to the Outside" indicated a makeover of China's policy line. In light of this, it can be understood that China's normalization with South Korea was undertaken as an extension of its willingness to accept the status quo.

Since the end of the Cold War in the early 1990s, relations between China and North Korea have been a little more complicated. First of all, normalization of relations between China and South Korea in 1992 was truly shocking to North Korea, even after the Soviet Union did the same thing 2 years before, and the relationship between the two was almost cut off. The stagnation of relations continued until 2000, when Kim Jong Il visited Beijing for summit talks with Jiang Zemin. It was not until 1996 that North Korea's trade with China became its largest, comprising 28.6 percent of its total. However, the trade volume was only US$ 566 million, slightly more than the trade with Japan (US$ 518 million) and never more than US$1 billion until 2003. More tellingly, China did not take systematic action at a central government level to salvage North Korea from its great famine between 1995 and 1997.

China's relationship with North Korea has begun to be restored incrementally since Kim Jong Il's visit to China in 2000. Trade volume increased 50 percent in 1 year from US$ 488 million in 2000 to US$ 738 million in 2001.

China began to play a more active role with regard to the Korean Peninsula from 2000. With China's rise, regional states expected China to take a more responsible role in the region and China also perceived that it should exercise a more constructive regional influence. Unlike a decade before, China was enthusiastic to resolve North Korea's nuclear problem. China convinced North Korea to participate in multilateral talks in spite of North Korea's insistence on bilateral talks with the United States. China has played a crucial role as a host country for the Six-Party Talks, which also included the two Koreas as well as the United States, Japan, and Russia. China has maintained a very clear position on North Korea's nuclear program: North Korea's nuclear weapons cannot be tolerated, and the North Korean nuclear crisis should be resolved by peaceful means. However, China does not want the North Korean regime to sustain too much pressure and become unstable.

It was a little surprising that during the 1990s, North Korea's survival was heavily dependent on the United States. The United States provided half a million tons of crude oil and hundreds of thousands of tons of grain to North Korea every year. It was not until 2008 that China became North Korea's lifesaver in a true sense. Kim Jong Il's health problems began, and the failure of North Korean currency reform in 2009 may have seemed a final blow to the regime's stability. As the relationship between Seoul and Pyongyang began to deteriorate in 2008 and tension between Washington and Pyongyang continued to brew over the North Korean nuclear program, the relationship between China and North Korea became more consolidated. In recent years, North Korea has depended on China for energy, food, and daily commodities, all of which are essential to the North Korean economy.

The total trade volume between North Korea and China more than tripled in 5 years, from US$ 1.9 billion in 2007 to US$ 6.0 billion in 2012. The rapid increase of trade between China and North Korea is attributed to North Korea's exports of strategic mineral resources such as

Table 11.1 North Korea's trade with China, 2007–13

	2007	2008	2009	2010	2011	2012	2013
Import	1,392	2,033	1,888	2,278	3,165	3,528	3,663
Export	582	754	793	1,188	2,464	2,485	2,911
Total trade	1,974	2,787	2,681	3,466	5,629	6,013	6,574
Balance	−810	−1,279	−1,095	−1,090	−701	−1,043	−751

Note: Unit: US$ million

Source: Korea Trade-Investment Promotion Agency (www.kotra.or.kr) for 2007–12; The Korea International Trade Association (www.kita.net) for 2013.

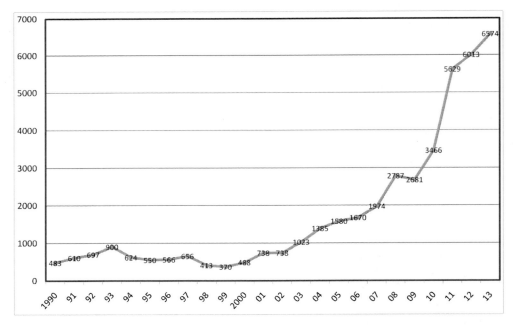

Figure 11.1 Trade volume between North Korea and China, 1990–2013 *(unit: US$ million)*

Source: Korea Trade-Investment Promotion Agency (www.kotra.or.kr) for 2007–12; The Korea International Trade Association (www.kita.net) for 2013.

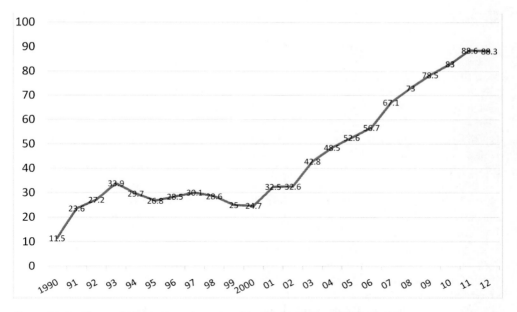

Figure 11.2 Share of North Korea's trade with China, 1990–2012 *(unit: %)*
Source: Korea Trade-Investment Promotion Agency (www.kotra.or.kr).

anthracite coal and iron to China, which resulted in severe electricity shortages and worsening economic problems. North Korea's mineral resource exports to China increased by 36 times in 9 years, from US$ 50 million in 2002 to US$ 1.8 billion in 2011. This accounts for 75.1 percent of North Korea's export volume to China. The total volume of mineral resources exports slightly declined to US$ 1.7 billion in 2012.[4]

With the end of the Cold War, relations between South Korea and China experienced dramatic improvements as their mutual economic involvement increased exponentially. In 1992, the Roh Tae-woo and Jiang Zemin governments established "friendly and cooperative relations." In 2003, the Roh Moo-hyun and Hu Jintao governments expanded the two states' relations by agreeing to a comprehensive cooperative partnership. In 2008, the Lee Myung-bak and Hu Jintao administrations established a strategic cooperative partnership, and the two states enjoyed strategic partnership not only on bilateral issues but also issues pertaining to regional and international affairs.

The two states have exchanged personnel in the field of military security, one of the most delicate areas of discussion, as well as exchanges in research and education programs. China-South Korea exchanges in human resources reached eight million people in 2013 and more than 740 flights a week take routes between China and South Korea. More than 800,000 South Koreans are resident in China, and Korea towns have been set up in Beijing, Shanghai, Qingdao, and other major cities. Korean students in China number approximately 63,000, and there are about 50,000 Chinese students in South Korea.[5]

However, China's lack of support in rebuking North Korea's actions during the 2010 *Cheonan* incident and the ensuing Yeonpyeong bombardment has given South Korea the impression that North Korea precedes South Korea in terms of China's strategic priority.[6] Although South Korea and China are strategic partners, the two seem to lack substantive trust with regard to problems concerning North Korea.

Jinwook Choi

North Korea: a strategic liability or asset to China?

There are two competing views on whether North Korea is an asset or strategic liability to China. According to the view that it is a strategic liability, the current Chinese policy towards North Korea is not logical. China's relationship with North Korea also comes at a cost. China's top policy goals towards the Korean Peninsula are "Stability, Peace, and Denuclearization." However, stability is far more important than the other two. It refers to the prospect of North Korea's implosion and a war between North and South Korea. If stability were to be compromised in North Korea, it would have devastating effects for China in terms of the massive inflow of North Korean refugees crossing the border. The numbers of such an influx would probably be much greater than that of the mid-1990s when the famine in North Korea pushed as many as three million North Koreans across the border into China. The question of North Korean refugees is a particularly sensitive one because of the 1.83 million Korean ethnic minority population in three northeastern provinces of China, including 799,000 people in the Yanbian Korean Autonomous Prefecture.[7]

In addition, China is concerned about the possible collapse of North Korea and its absorption by South Korea, which would lead to a stronger US-ROK alliance. North Korea is an important buffer for China's security. China has hesitated to put pressure on North Korea, which might cause instability in the region, in spite of nuclear tests or missile tests as well as the sinking of the *Cheonan* and shelling of Yeonpyeong Islands in 2010. China flexed its muscles to safeguard North Korea's response to the US military demonstration, and China does not even want to discuss North Korean contingency for fear of spurring Pyongyang to act out. In some ways, such reluctance on the part of China has encouraged North Korea's misbehavior.

This position as North Korea's reluctant enabler was fixed in 2008 and continued until February 2013, when North Korea conducted the third nuclear test. China's biased attitude towards North Korea's provocative threats and nuclear development contributes to strengthening North Korea-China relations. Some argue, however, that it has a negative impact on its own interests in many ways. In fact, its cost seemed to be grave. For liberal internationalists, China's position is somewhat difficult to accept; as a member of the international community, China would do better to utilize international institutions from which it can benefit.[8]

First, in terms of the costs, China's support for North Korea along with the US keenness to keep an eye on China's rise has led to the strengthening of the US-ROK alliance. It has also led to stronger trilateral military cooperation between the US, Japan, and South Korea. Such an arrangement not only serves to "jeopardize the security of the US and ROK but also China's own national interests."[9] It is ironic that China's efforts to keep North Korea stable out of fear of US pressure have actually increased US pressure in the form of a strengthened US-Japan-South Korea cooperation.

Second, neighboring nations concerned with China's military extension in the East and South China Seas in recent years have chosen to increase their reliance on the United States. This has had the effect of expanding the US network of alliances and partnerships not only in East Asia but also elsewhere in the Asia-Pacific.

Third, it gives the impression that China is not acting as a responsible state under international law. North Korea appears to be a blind spot for China; it has on occasions abstained from applying international law to North Korea's misbehavior. Providing immunity to and diluting the effect of sanctions against North Korea has promoted the view that China does not take international law seriously.[10]

In sum, the costs mentioned above are indicators of the reasons why China may adopt a different North Korea policy. According to these estimates, some inside China believe that China's

North Korea policy is illogical. As a result, there has been speculation that China is thinking about changing its diplomatic policy after North Korea's third nuclear test.[11]

Then why is China supportive of North Korea? While some believe that China's North Korea policy is illogical, others believe that, insofar as it is problematic to the US and South Korea, it is not. China suspects that the US cites the North Korean threat to justify strengthening its alliances and maintaining its military presence. Indeed, many argue that if the North Korea problem is resolved, there is no need for the US to stay on the Korean Peninsula.[12]

In other words, if the US is going to pressure China at any rate, China does not have any other option but to keep North Korea as a buffer. It is reasonable for China to back North Korea should it encounter a crisis with South Korea, the US, or Japan. Its economic ties with the US allies South Korea and Japan can act as additional leverage that the Soviet Union and the US did not have in the Cold War era. The West does not understand the vital importance of North Korea's geographic region to China's core national interest. Nothing can explain China's relationship with the Korean Peninsula better than its geopolitical significance. The Korean Peninsula (North Korea) is one of 14 neighboring countries with which China is faced. The length of the border between the two countries is 1,334 km,[13] and both sides of the border are among the respective countries' most populous border areas, including China's largest border city, Dandong. The distance from Beijing to this border is shorter than to any other border. Two Chinese PLA divisions are defending the border.

For many decades, China went to great lengths to keep the North Korean region close to its side. China's defeat in the Sino-Japanese War of 1894–5 resulted in the annexation of Korea by Japan, which also led on to the invasion of Manchuria in 1931. Subsequently, the heart of China was under threat. This is why China exerts much effort to keep North Korea near.

Indeed, it may be fair to say that China is as concerned about North Korea's nuclear weapons program as the US is. However, it is not left with many alternatives, because of North Korea's strategic value. In order to maintain its influence over Pyongyang, China cannot but provide economic and military aid to North Korea. While China tries to refrain from meeting all of North Korea's demands, North Korea is the biggest recipient of Chinese aid. China is particularly cautious about advanced weapons sales to North Korea.

The current policy is problematic, but there are no better options. China muddles through while continuing to hope that North Korea will reform. If the US sees that the rise of China will inevitably threaten its status as a superpower, then it would do China no good to abandon North Korea.

Changing dynamics in Northeast Asia

The security environment is changing dramatically in Northeast Asia. First of all, there is the US Pivot to Asia initiative. In the fall of 2011, the United States announced that it would be intensifying its role in the Asia-Pacific region in terms of military planning and foreign and economic policy. President Barack Obama stated in a November 2011 address to the Australian parliament, "the United States will play a larger and long-term role in shaping this region [the Asia-Pacific] and its future."[14]

On 10 November 2011, in a speech at the Center for East-West Studies at Hawaii University, US Secretary of State Hillary Clinton announced the new US "Pivot to Asia" strategy. Some people perceive it as the biggest change in the US Asia-Pacific strategy since the end of the Cold War. Particularly from the Chinese perspective, it means that the US will enhance its own military presence in the region rather than rely on Sino-US cooperation to deal with regional security issues. It may also mean that the US will contain China in a wider geographical area;

from alliance with Taiwan in the mid-1990s, efforts at perceived containment expanded to the South China Sea, East China Sea, and Yellow Sea. The US will prepare for possible direct military conflict with China rather than just watching and waiting and using deterrence. To this end, the US wants to establish a strong network of alliances and partners in the region.

The US appears to be concerned that in the restructuring of the Northeast Asian order, the strengthened cooperation between South Korea and China will have a negative effect on the US rebalancing strategy. In addition, it cannot be certain that inter-state cooperation for soft issues such as climate change will not expand or develop into cooperation for traditional hard issues. The same can be said for the responses of neighboring states, including Japan.

With regard to easing tensions on the Peninsula, the US supports dialogue. However, to this end, it is the view that dialogue must be preceded by North Korea's clear intent. After the February 29 Agreement was undermined by North Korea's long-range missile launch, the US requested that North Korea take steps beyond the agreement made on 29 February. This entails a nuclear and missile moratorium, suspension of the highly enriched uranium (HEU) program, implementation of the joint statement of 19 September 2005 and respect of the armistice agreement as prerequisites for the Six-Party Talks. Without such preceding steps, the US believes that dialogue with North Korea is meaningless, and that negotiations for denuclearization must be supported by strong deterrence. Moreover, the US is concerned that Chinese efforts to resume the Six-Party Talks are intended to weaken the US rebalancing strategy, as opposed to aiming at North Korea's denuclearization. Although it does agree that the Six-Party Talks is still a viable framework for negotiation, it is of the view that the international community's close cooperation must precede such talks.

One reason why the US cannot go beyond its position of "strategic patience" is because of the impact of its domestic politics. Decisions concerning North Korea are not left to the Secretary of Defense, but to the highest officials in the White House, who are very much preoccupied with domestic issues, and other international exigencies such as the Iranian problem. Therefore, rather than implementing a new security cooperation framework or system in Northeast Asia, it would rather commit to managing the status quo in a stable way.

There has also been a Chinese-proposed New Pattern of Great Power Relations, presented in response to the US rebalancing policy. This concept was somewhat ambiguous until June 2013 when it was clearly articulated by President Xi Jinping at the summit with President Obama. The core idea is that it seeks to free itself from the previous patterns of an emerging power challenging the existing power and the principal countries that defend the current international order, with heightened risks of hegemonic war.[15] It states that the US, the hegemonic power, and China, the emerging great power, can mutually cooperate and develop together. As a "developing state," China will respect the US leadership, rather than competing against it; and in return, it asks the US to respect China's core interests. President Xi Jinping's comment that the Pacific is large enough to be shared by the US and China well shows its symbolic meaning and vision. China has clearly shown its desire to keep Asia stable and peaceful through its New Pattern of Great Power Relations. However, President Xi's comments that Asian problems should be solved by Asian people at the Conference on Interaction and Confidence Building Measures in Asia (CICA) in May 2014 and China's initiative to establish the Asian Infrastructure Investment Bank (AIIB) at the BRICS meeting in Brazil of July 2014 may be suggestive of China's intentions to expand its influence in the region, weakening the strong US presence.

In the same light, China views the South Korea-US-Japan military cooperation as an important element of the US rebalancing policy, and that instability and nuclear brinksmanship in North Korea may provide another conduit through which to strengthen the US-led trilateral cooperation. To this end, China has responded to North Korea's provocations and nuclear tests with strong measures, displaying itself as a responsible power as well as South Korea's cooperative partner.

In addition, China believes that the core of peace and stability on the Peninsula lies in improvements in inter-Korean relations. To achieve this, it desires that the South Korean government promote a flexible North Korea policy. Many Korea-experts in China claim that one reason for heightened tensions during the Lee Myung-bak administration was South Korea's hardline North Korea policies. Therefore, China has high expectations for President Park Geun-hye's policy of trust-building on the Korean Peninsula. It officially stated in June 2013 during the South Korea-China Summit that China "welcomes the Trust-building Process on the Korean Peninsula, and it takes in high regard that South Korea has been making efforts to improve inter-Korean relations and ease tensions." On 18 November of the same year, the same position was articulated during the strategic dialogue between Chief of the National Security Office Kim Jang Soo and State Council Member Yang Jiechi.

As an important player in Northeast Asian security, Japan has been strengthening its alliance with the US as well as security cooperation in the backdrop of China's rise, territorial conflicts, and its corresponding efforts to mobilize the domestic public. This has, in effect, acted as an important factor strengthening the negative prospects in US-China relations. In China's view, Japan is taking advantage of the US rebalancing policy to readdress the 1978 Sino-Japanese Peace and Friendship Treaty, which mentions that the issue of territorial disputes will be shelved for later generations. It is also of the view that it is pursuing its right to exercise collective self-defense, through which it attempts to enforce its claimed territorial sovereignty. In other words, it can be said that stronger US-Japan alliance and worsening China-Japan relations could make the peaceful coexistence of the US and China far less likely.

During the Security Consultative Committee Meeting between the top foreign affairs and national security leaders of Japan and the US in Tokyo in October 2013 ("2+2 Meeting"), the US indicated that it "welcomes Japan's efforts such as the legal basis for issues concerning collective self-defense, increase in security budgets, etc.," and that "China must comply with international norms and establish military transparency." Such a warning tone is simultaneously indicative of its strengthened alliance with Japan and its provocative stance towards China.

Outlook for China's relationship with the Korean Peninsula

Recent dynamics in Northeast Asia have changed the environment in which China pursues its foreign policies, in particular its relationship with the Korean Peninsula. China has surpassed Japan in gross national product and has become the second largest economy in the world. Such performance becomes more notable when contrasted with the relative decline of the US, which recovered slowly after the 2008 global financial crisis. In addition, a long list of developments, including China's so called "New Pattern of Great Powers Relations," "peaceful rise," the US pivot to Asia or its "rebalancing" strategy, Japan's collective self-defense, and North Korea's nuclear weapons ambitions and recent missile tests, as well as the purge of Jang Sung Taek, have significant implications for Northeast Asia's balance of power.

To begin with, one of the major factors shaping China's policies on the Peninsula is the increasing uncertainty after the purge of Jang Sung Taek.[16] The fall of Jang Sung Taek may have served as a warning to North Korean elites. As a result, North Korean elites in the military, secret police, and the party may not quietly wait for Kim Jong Un's decision when faced with a political crisis like that surrounding Jang. Some may show their loyalty by making provocations towards South Korea or overreact in showing their loyalty to Kim Jong Un to survive the crisis.

Others may desperately challenge Kim Jong Un. Given the lack of resources to distribute even to powerful organizations and the collapse of the centrally planned economy, the struggle for economic interests may be repeated, although a power struggle like the case of Jang is not likely to happen again.

Another reason for the possibility of struggle for economic interests is the absence of institutions to coordinate conflicts and a control tower or leadership respected by competing organs. The sudden disappearance of a figure with absolute power causes a power vacuum in any political system and may threaten the stability of the regime. Change of a leader could be even more dangerous in an authoritarian country such as North Korea, where stability and leadership depend on an absolute leader. The Kim Jong Un regime may be even more unstable, particularly if Jang's execution was designed by a rival group of Jang's such as the Department of Organization and Guidance, rather than by Kim Jong Un.

The stability of the Kim Jong Un regime after the disappearance of Jang depends on how Kim handles whatever dilemma he faces. The "strong and prosperous nation" policy inherited from Kim Jong Il has certain self-contradictions. While building a strong economy, as Kim Jong Un proposes, is the utmost priority, this goal clashes directly with building a strong military. Domestically, building nuclear weapons and missiles takes resources from a regime prioritizing resource distribution to enhance the people's welfare. Externally, the nuclear and missile program constrains any inflow of foreign investment.

Another dilemma is the paradox of self-determination. Although North Korea asserts that nuclear weapons and satellites have made the country safer while surrounded by strong powers, the program has in fact led to further isolation from the international community and greater dependence on China for subsistence. While wary of China's rise and seeking improvement in relations with the US, South Korea, and Japan, the Pyongyang regime continues its nuclear and long-range missiles program, which serves to impede any fundamental breakthrough in these relationships. Thus ironically, the means adopted for self-determination effectively hampers North Korea's self-determination.

It remains to be seen whether North Korea can escape from its dilemma. However, current North Korean policies raise fears that they may only exacerbate the regime's dilemma in terms of both socio-economic and political instability in the long run. Jang's case shows the shortcomings of the military-first system without a control tower. Disappearance of an absolute-power control tower may make the decision-making process extremely unpredictable, uncertain and even dangerous. The weak grip of the central power over the military owing to Kim Jong Un's lack of experience makes the military even more autonomous.

North Korea's provocations as well as negative perceptions of North Korea on the part of the South Koreans after the execution of Jang have made the Korean Peninsula more uncertain than ever. Thus South Korea should make greater efforts to prepare for any contingency (possibility of implosion) by military coup or people's uprising, or military provocations by the North. However, such efforts should not discourage South Korea's long-term plan to make peace and gradually develop inter-Korean relations. The South should not de-emphasize any of these three agenda items, but all three agenda items should always be on the table.

The second factor shaping China's relations with the Peninsula is that the dividing line between, on the one hand, South Korea, the US, and Japan and, on the other, China and North Korea is perhaps becoming murkier than before. Leadership changes in the three leading Northeast Asian states have brought forward a fresh set of ideas and talking points. For example, China's Xi Jinping and South Korea's Park Geun-hye found much to discuss and agree on during their summit in June 2013. President Xi Jinping committed himself to supporting Korean unification and reaffirmed China's opposition to North Korea's nukes, probably expecting cooperation with South Korea regarding Japan's distortion of history.

China has been more than keen to weaken the trilateral cooperation between South Korea, Japan, and the United States, and drive a wedge between South Korea and the other two. It has taken full advantage of the discord between South Korea and Japan over Japan's historical revisionism on such issues as comfort women and rewriting textbooks. Such common concerns between China and South Korea have reinforced the strategic partnership, to the extent that both Japan and the US have expressed their discomfort. The establishment of a memorial hall for Ahn Joong Geun well exemplifies this point. Ahn Joong Geun was a symbol of the Korean independence movement who, in 1909 in Harbin, China, fatally shot Ito Hirobumi, the prime architect of Korea's colonization and former prime minister. Until recently, China was somewhat reluctant to associate itself with political activities commemorating Ahn Joong Geun. However, in early 2014, the memorial hall was opened in Harbin.

In terms of the relationship between South Korea and the United States, the US has shown a considerable level of concern about South Korea's worsening relations with Japan. For example, when President Park Geun-hye criticized Japanese leaders' perception of history and claimed that South Korea cannot support Japan's collective self-defense while US Secretary of Defense Chuck Hagel was visiting Seoul in September 2013, Hagel expressed his concerns over the possibility of a widening rift between the trilateral military cooperation between the US, Japan, and South Korea. Furthermore, he has explicitly stated to President Park Geun-hye that issues of history should not be mixed with security. This was a response to Seoul's concerns that Japan's collective self-defense would be exercised in issues on the Korean Peninsula, and that it is a geopolitical tool to shape Japan into a more muscular military.[17]

Japan's position is slightly more ambiguous, resulting from its inconsistent behavior. Japan's core security policy goal is to keep an eye on China; and to that end, it is important to maintain the trilateral military cooperation between the United States, Japan, and South Korea. However, Japanese political leaders' behavior on historical problems seems to conflict with its security goal. It aggravates relations between Japan and South Korea as well as between Japan and China. Prime Minister Abe deliberately visited Yasukuni Shrine in December 2013, thereby destroying the plan to organize a summit with South Korea.

It is difficult to understand exactly what Japan genuinely wants. To many in South Korea, Japanese behavior does not seem to contribute to its foreign policy goal of maintaining the trilateral military cooperation. China may believe that Japan benefits from the tensions in Northeast Asia, and that Japan is thus not serious about recovering relations. Such tensions with neighboring countries may help attract popular support for domestic purposes. More importantly, in this way Japan enhances its value as the only reliable ally of the United States in Northeast Asia.

At any rate, in gauging the vested interests South Korea and Japan respectively have in the trilateral military cooperation with the US, it is evident that Japan has much more to gain (and lose) than South Korea and thus it is actually Japan that should be making extra efforts to maintain the partnership. Therefore, if the trilateral cooperation is genuinely important to Japan, it should not highlight its historical quarrels, especially for the purpose of domestic public mobilization.

In such an environment, China cannot but make alterations in its relationship with North Korea. At the moment, China is faced with a strategic dilemma. Maintaining its relations with North Korea would damage its relations with South Korea and ultimately push it closer to the US and Japan. However, weakening ties with North Korea risks the possibility of implosion or unification, which would lead to a stronger US presence in the region. The lesser of the two evils would be to alter its relationship with North Korea to attract the South.

Conclusion

China's foremost concern on the Korean Peninsula is to maintain stability for its sustainable economic development. In this sense, it will not abandon North Korea because it serves as an effective buffer state. However, China has taken a stern approach to North Korea's third nuclear test conducted on 12 February 2013 because it wants to improve relations with South Korea. China perceives that this will contribute to the weakening of trilateral cooperation between South Korea, the US, and Japan, which it views as a major threat.

From Japan's point of view, it has claimed that South Korea has been pivoting from the US to China and has expressed concern regarding the worsening relations between the three Northeast Asian states. One question one has to ask is, which side has aggravated Chinese-Japanese relations and Korean-Japanese relations? In terms of the former, it could be argued that China is at fault, due to reasons such as territorial disputes on the Diaoyu/Senkaku Islets, and historical issues.

In the latter case, an interesting point may be related to Japan's efforts to improve relations with South Korea. The present situation is somewhat reminiscent of the Koizumi era of the mid-2000s when Japan claimed that closer ties between China and South Korea called for a strengthening of Japan-US relations. The US was suspicious of the Roh Moo-hyun Administration's efforts to improve relations with China, which could weaken the ROK-US alliance. However, such a Japanese strategy may or may not work in the Park Geun-hye Administration.

If seen optimistically, China's and Japan's policies have in fact worked in South Korea's favor. China's strategic support has been helpful in promoting its two goals of managing North Korea and unification. It is because of the strong relationship between South Korea, Japan, and the US that China has been attentive to South Korea. Therefore, it would not be wise for South Korea to weaken the trilateral military cooperation. In this respect, Japan's suspicions have perhaps led to a perception that South Korea's efforts to improve relations with China have been more extensive than has actually been the case. It is well known that South Korea needs China's cooperation for North Korea's denuclearization and unification. In the current state of affairs, such framing of the situation has not been detrimental to South Korea.

However, this may change depending on the US interpretation and understanding of the dynamics in the region. The US has clearly shown its intention to cooperate with China. The element of competition exists but there is much more to gain by cooperation. It also sees Japan and South Korea as critical partners for peace and stability in Northeast Asia.

In this respect, it is vital that the US understand clearly why these conflicts are emerging and being aggravated. The security dynamics in Northeast Asia have a long history. Northeast Asian states' rivalries have often been viewed as beginning as late as the 1990s with the emergence of the North Korean nuclear issue, or in the 1950s before and after the Korean War. However, historical rivalry extends much further and deeper, and cannot be easily understood simply by relying on international relations theories. Japan's concern over strengthening South Korea-China relations, China's intolerance of Japanese actions and South Korea's balancing of China on the one hand and the trilateral cooperation on the other makes far more sense in this respect. Given the geopolitical circumstances, the current South Korea-China relations are not cause for alarm. The US should not read too much into what does not exist on the basis of perceptions and misperceptions.

Notes

1 Though substantial, the role of the USSR was never visible during the Korean War. Stalin approved Kim Il Sung's plan to bring the whole Peninsula under communism, but did not anticipate the US intervention. The Soviet Union did not exercise its veto to block the UN Security Council's decision

to intervene in the war. The Soviet Union seemed to be afraid of getting involved in the war, and confrontation with the United States.
2 The Korean War technically never ended, because there has not been a peace treaty, but it had a great impact on China's security environment for many years to come. While the Chinese casualties were high, the actual numbers remain unavailable, with various estimates ranging from 400,000 to over one million. UN troops from 16 countries under the leadership of the United States immediately participated in the war to save South Korea, which lost Seoul in three days and as much as 90 percent of its territory at its peak. The UN forces and ROK army pushed North Korean forces back to the thirty-eighth parallel north 3 months after North Korea's invasion. They kept marching north and some of them reached the border with China, but faced heavy Chinese offensive. They were pushed back to the south of thirty-eighth parallel in 2 months, and the battle continued along the thirty-eighth parallel for two and a half more years.
3 J.H. Chung, "China-North Korea Relations in a New Era: Assessing Continuities and Changes," in J.W. Choi (ed.), *Korean Unification and a New East Asian Order*, Seoul: KINU, 2012, p. 52.
4 The Korea International Trade Association website. Available online at http://www.kita.net.
5 Ministry of Foreign Affairs, "Review of China," 11 March 2014. Available online at www.mofat.go.kr.
6 *Yonhap News*, 19 August 2012.
7 *Yonhap News*, 16 January 2014. Available online at http://news.naver.com/main/read.nhn?mode=LSD&mid=sec&sid1=102&oid=001&aid=0006703395> (accessed 14 March 2014).
8 According to liberal internationalists, the post-Cold War era has been marked by a set of rules and norms accepted by the international community, including market openness, nondiscrimination, etc. See G.J. Ikenberry, "The Rise of China and the Future of the West: Can the Liberal System Survive?" *Foreign Affairs*, January/February, 2008.
9 Y. Sun, "The Logic of China's North Korea Policy," Pacific Forum CSIS PacNet Newsletter, No. 39, 21 June 2012.
10 R.A. Cossa and B. Glosserman, "The Illogic of China's North Korea Policy," *Pacific Forum CSIS PacNet Newsletter*, No. 32, 17 May 2012.
11 It is presumed that the nuclear testing, ruthless military adventurism, and lack of communication of the Kim Jong Un regime led Beijing to have reservations about the risk of Kim Jong Un's nuclear weapons compared with the nuclear possession under Kim Jong Il.
12 Y. Sun, "The Logic of China's North Korea Policy," *Pacific Forum CSIS PacNet Newsletter*, No. 39, 21 June 2012.
13 The other 13 countries include Mongolia, Russia, Myanmar, India, Kazakhstan, Nepal, Vietnam, Kyrgyzstan, Bhutan, Pakistan, Laos, Tajikistan, and Afghanistan; S. Zhihua and X. Yafeng, "Contested Border: A Historical Investigation into the Sino-Korean Border Issue, 1950–1964," *Asian Perspective*, Vol. 37, No. 1, 2013, p. 21.
14 M.E. Manyin and S. Daggett, "Pivot to the Pacific? The Obama Administration's 'Rebalancing' Toward Asia," *CRS Report*, 28 March 2012, p. 1.
15 R. Bush, "Obama and Xi at Sunnylands: A New Pattern of Relations?" Available online at http://www.brookings.edu/blogs/up-front/posts/2013/06/04-obama-xi-new-pattern-relations-bush (accessed 20 March 2014)
16 This subsection is based on Dr. K.B. Han's unpublished thesis.
17 There is a deep distrust toward Japan. From South Korea's perspective, Japan has never repented of its colonization of Korea and the pain Koreans had to suffer for 36 years. Koreans were forced to change family names, not allowed to speak Korean, and were subject to extreme treatment unprecedented in the history of colonial imperialism.

Bibliography

Breslin, S., "China in the Asian Economy," in B. Buzan and R. Foot (eds), *Does China Matter? A Reassessment: Essays in Memory of Gerald Segal*, London: Routledge, 2004.
Chung, J.H., "China-North Korea Relations in a New Era: Assessing Continuities and Changes," in Jinwook Choi (ed.), *Korean Unification and a New East Asian Order*, Seoul: KINU, 2012.
Cossa, R.A. and Glosserman, B., "The Illogic of China's North Korea Policy," *Pacific Forum CSIS PacNet Newsletter*, No. 32, 17 May 2012.
Ikenberry, G.J., "The Rise of China and the Future of the West: Can the Liberal System Survive?" *Foreign Affairs*, January/February, 2008.

International Crisis Group, "Fire on the City Gate: Why China Keeps North Korea Close," *Asia Report*, No. 254, 9 December 2013.
Kaplan, R.D., "The Geography of Chinese Power: How Far Can Beijing Reach on Land and at Sea?" *Foreign Affairs*, May/June, 2010.
Korea International Trade Association, <http://www.kita.net>.
Korea Trade-Investment Promotion Agency, <http://www.kotra.or.kr>.
Manyin, M.E. and Daggett, S., "Pivot to the Pacific? The Obama Administration's 'Rebalancing' Toward Asia," *CRS Report*, 28 March 2012.
Nye, J.S., "The Future of American Power: Dominance and Decline in Perspective," *Foreign Affairs*, November/December, 2010.
Ross, R.S., "Comparative Deterrence: The Taiwan Strait and the Korean Peninsula," in A.I. Johnson and R.S. Ross (eds), *New Directions in the Study of China's Foreign Policy*, Stanford: Stanford University Press, 2006.
Roy, D., "North Korea: Bothersome Client State," in *Return of the Dragon: Rising China and Regional Security*, New York: Columbia University Press, 2013.
Roy, R.S., "Responses to the PacNet 32R—the Illogic of China's North Korea Policy," *Pacific Forum CSIS PacNet Newsletter*, No. 32R-A, 7 June 2012.
Snyder, S. and Byun, S.W., "China-Korea Relations: Seeking Alignment on North Korean Policy," *Comparative Connections*, Vol. 15, No. 1, 2013.
Sun, Y., "The Logic of China's North Korea Policy," *Pacific Forum CSIS PacNet Newsletter*, No. 39, June 21, 2012.
Sutter, R.G., "Relations with the Korean Peninsula," in *China's Rise in Asia: Promises and Perils*, Lanham, MD: Rowman & Littlefield, 2005.
———, "Relations with Japan and Korea," in *Chinese Foreign Relations Power and Policy since the Cold War*, Lanham, MD: Rowman & Littlefield, 2012.
Wang, F., "China's Search for a Grand Strategy: A Rising Great Power Finds Its Way," *Foreign Affairs*, Vol. 90, No. 2, March/April, 2011.
Wang, J.W., "From 'Strategic Competitors' to 'Stakeholders': US-China Relations during the Bush Administration," in G. Hauser and F. Kernic (eds), *China: The Rising Power*, New York: Peter Lang, 2009.

12
Taiwan and Chinese security

Jean-Pierre Cabestan

For a long time, Taiwan has been at the pinnacle of the People's Republic of China (PRC)'s security concerns and objectives. Today, the Beijing authorities still claim that Taiwan is a "sacred part of the PRC" and should in the future be reunified with the rest of the motherland. However, since 1979, the Chinese Communist Party (CCP) leadership has privileged "peaceful reunification" over "armed liberation." And, while refusing to formally renounce to the use of force, since the mid-2000s, it has quietly agreed to respect the status quo in the Strait, as long as Taiwan endorses the "one China" fiction and does not declare formal independence. The Kuomintang (KMT)'s return to power in Taiwan in 2008 has convinced the CCP to consolidate this strategy. As a result, while in the PRC's eyes reunification with Taiwan remains an important hard and soft security objective, the People's Liberation Army (PLA) has modified its order of priorities, putting more emphasis on such targets as the United States, Taiwan's unique security guarantor, particularly its forward military deployment in the Western Pacific and bases in Japan, and concentrating its attention on new objectives in the East and the South China Seas and beyond. The PRC is still aiming at imposing on Taiwan a military balance in the Strait that will gradually make the island more vulnerable. It also continues to put pressure on the US to stop or at least reduce its arms sales to Taiwan. But today Beijing thinks that its long-term security objective regarding Taiwan—moving the island step by step towards eventual unification by narrowing its options—can be achieved with the help of a much wider range of tools, not only military but also political, diplomatic, economic and cultural.

Can this strategy succeed, and if it can, why has Beijing not reduced its military pressure on Taiwan? In order to better understand China's security concerns towards Taiwan, it is useful to briefly present the background of its policy. We will also show that the island has remained an important military objective before evaluating the limits of the current strategy. We will conclude that, though the PRC does not need Taiwan back to rise and become a world power, reunifying the island will remain one of its "core national interests" and security objectives.

Historical background: Taiwan, a top political and security objective

Since the establishment of the PRC in 1949, Taiwan has constituted a major political and security challenge, and until today, Taiwan's reunification with the mainland has remained a top national objective. Its control by another, ideologically competitive Chinese regime, the Republic of China (ROC), which the PRC does not recognize, is taken to represent a threat to its territorial integrity as well as to CCP political legitimacy and, as a result, its comprehensive security. It is also perceived by Beijing as an obstacle to the PLA Navy's access to the high seas of the Western Pacific, and more generally to the restoration of China's great power status.[1]

Enacted in 1982, Beijing's state constitution illustrates in its preamble the importance of this mission: "Taiwan is part of the sacred territory of the People's Republic of China. It is the inviolable duty of all Chinese people, including our compatriots in Taiwan, to accomplish the great task of reunifying the motherland."[2] The strategy and tactics used by the CCP leadership to fulfill this task have deeply changed over the years, particularly since 1979 and even more so after the KMT's return to power in 2008, partly demilitarizing and de-ideologizing the issue. However, Taiwan has not only remained a key objective but since 2008–9 been elevated to the rank of China's "core national interests" (*guojia hexin liyi*), underscoring the long-term security and political importance of Taiwan's reunification.[3]

Mao Zedong's era: liberate Taiwan

We remember that in the spring of 1950, Mao Zedong's PLA was amassing forces in Fujian province and preparing an invasion of Taiwan, where Chiang Kai-shek and the remnant of the ROC government and Nationalist Army had taken refuge a few months earlier. We also recall that it was North Korean strongman Kim Il Sung's decision to invade South Korea in June of that year that compelled the PRC to abandon this plan. Threatened by the possible annihilation of Kim's regime, in October 1950, Mao decided to send his troops to the Korean Peninsula, pushing back the frontline to the thirty-eighth parallel. But as a result, the US Seventh Fleet was deployed in the Taiwan Strait, until today freezing up the split of China into two distinct and competitive polities, the PRC on the mainland and the ROC on Taiwan.[4]

Between 1950 and 1978, the Beijing authorities stuck to the well-known slogan: "We must absolutely liberate Taiwan!" (*women yiding yao jiefang Taiwan!*). However, they knew all too well that the PLA did not have the means to carry out this threat. And in the 1950s and 1960s what the PRC was most afraid of was Chiang's attempt to re-conquer the mainland, and more generally KMT espionage activity on its soil. In order to test the United States' alliance with the ROC and the Soviet Union's support of his policies, Mao triggered several crises with Taiwan, but did not actually try to directly challenge the US or the status quo in the Taiwan Strait, limiting his military offensives mainly to the bombing of some of the ROC's outer islands, located off the Fujian coast, such as Kinmen in 1958.[5] Conversely, on several occasions, Washington put strong pressure on Chiang to desist from ambitions for re-conquest. Moreover, before the Cultural Revolution, especially in the mid-1950s, with Mao's backing, Prime Minister Zhou Enlai tested a more accommodating policy of "peaceful liberation" or even "peaceful reunification," a policy that Deng Xiaoping would develop more systematically after 1979.[6] Nevertheless, until Nixon's trip to China in 1972 and, more importantly, the launching of the reforms and Sino-US normalization at the end of 1978, the PRC's Taiwan policy was both inflexible and aimed at challenging the US's containment strategy as well as the island's key role in this strategy. In other words, Taiwan was perceived as a crucial political, security and military issue.

Deng Xiaoping's era: peacefully reunify Taiwan

Since 1979, under Deng Xiaoping's recommendation, China has embarked on a "peaceful reunification" strategy towards Taiwan. It was clearly the establishment of diplomatic relations between Beijing and Washington as well as the political and the security assurances given by the latter to the former that made this new strategy possible.[7] As we know, the three key conditions set by the PRC to normalize relations with America were the US's adoption of a "one China policy," its "de-recognition" of the ROC and the closure of its military bases in Taiwan. Less than 3 years later, in September 1981, Beijing made an ambitious unification proposal to Taipei, granting the island the right to enjoy a large degree of autonomy as a "special administrative region" of the PRC, maintain its social and economic system, keep its military and being represented at the highest level in the PRC central government.[8] Favoring cross-Strait trade and people-to-people exchanges, including direct air and sea links, was a key feature of this policy. In December 1982, this "special administrative region" legal framework was enshrined under article 31 of the state constitution and became known as the "one country, two systems" formula. Though it was later to be introduced in Hong Kong (1997) and Macau (1999) with a less advantageous degree of autonomy, imagined by Deng himself, this recipe was first aimed at bringing Taiwan back into the womb of the motherland. Simultaneously, the PLA moved its troops away from the Fujian coast, contributing to demilitarizing the Taiwan Strait.

This new policy did not bear fruit overnight. Until the late 1980s, President Chiang Ching-kuo, Chiang's son, continued to ban contact with the PRC. It was only after Chiang had decided in 1986–7 to embark on an unprecedented democratization of the ROC political system that he initiated a change of policy towards the "Chinese communists" (*Zhonggong*): for instance, in late 1987, he allowed Taiwanese citizens to travel to the mainland and trade with it, through a third port. This policy was deepened in 1990–1 by his successor Lee Teng-hui who, while refusing to recognize the PRC, set up a non-official organization—the Strait Exchange Foundation (SEF)—and a channel of negotiation with the PRC, which did the same in establishing the Association for Relations across the Taiwan Straits (ARATS). In 1993, after having agreed in a verbal compromise that there was "one China," the SEF and the ARATS leaders met in Singapore in a historical summit.[9] As a result, trade and people-to-people travel across the Strait developed very rapidly, contributing to creating, if not a pro-China lobby, at least a class of Taiwanese business people pushing for a rapid relaxation of the barriers inherited from the Cold War era.

Beijing's more flexible policy did not however put an end to China's security concerns *vis-à-vis* the ex-"rebel island." As early as April 1979, the US Congress had adopted the Taiwan Relations Act (TRA), a law that perpetuated a loose security guarantee with "the people of Taiwan" and compelled the US administration to continue to provide "defensive weapons" to the island. The question of US arms sales to Taiwan had not been solved at the time of the US-China normalization, and Beijing was quick to denounce the TRA in the name of non-interference in other countries' internal affairs, forcing the US on 17 August 1982 to sign a third communiqué in which it agreed to "gradually reduce its sales of arms to Taiwan, leading, over a period of time, to a final resolution."[10] This agreement underscored China's long-term security objective: weakening step by step the Taiwanese military by preventing all foreign arm exporters from supplying arms to the island. In 1981, the Netherlands was ostracized for several years for having sold two diesel submarines to Taiwan and later, in the early 1990s, the French would be submitted to even stronger pressures after having delivered six La Fayette-class frigates and 60 Mirage-2000 fighters to the island. Paris was forced in 1994 to promise Beijing "not to participate anymore in the armament of Taiwan."[11]

Jiang Zemin's era: marry me or else{...}

This stronger reaction was motivated by the manifestation of additional new security concerns. Taiwan's democratization in the early 1990s and the emergence of a more visible distinct national identity on the island under the auspices of President Lee Teng-hui had convinced the Taiwanese government to adopt a more pragmatic and active foreign policy, aimed at increasing the number of its diplomatic allies and re-integrating the ROC into the United Nations while restraining as much as possible the surge of trade and economic exchanges across the Strait (go slow, or *jieji yongren*). Lee's non-official visit to the US in 1995 constituted the high tide of this offensive. The PLA's remilitarization of the Taiwan Strait had been initiated in the early 1990s after the end of the Cold War, the collapse of the Soviet Union and as a reaction to the Taiwanese military's modernization effort. Yet this visit triggered not only a serious rise of tension in the Strait, which came to be known as the 1995–6 missile crisis, but also a rapid increase of the PLA buildup along the coast facing the island. On two occasions, the PLA tested conventional missiles in the vicinity of Taiwan, notably in March 1996 on the eve of the ROC's presidential election, the first ever democratic election of a head of state in a Chinese society. As a result, the US dispatched two carrier groups to the Taiwan area and increased its arms sales to Taiwan, in effect freezing the implementation of the 1982 communiqué.[12] Although the ARATS and the SEF resumed talks in 1998, in Beijing's eyes, intensifying military pressure on the island had again become a key security objective. Since then the number of conventional missiles targeting the island has steadily increased to reach 1,100 heads by 2008 and, maybe more importantly, their accuracy and efficiency have also rapidly improved.

China's public objective was to disrupt the ROC's pragmatic diplomacy and its hope to be reintegrated as a normal nation-state into the international community. For example, when Lee Teng-hui announced in July 1999 that relations between the two sides of the Strait were "quasi-state to state relations," the PLA Air Force flew across the middle-line of the Strait, sending a clear signal to Taiwan, as well as the US. However, as Hong Kong (in 1997) and Macau (in 1999) were returning to China, Jiang Zemin, the then Chinese president, gave the strong impression that he wanted to accelerate Taiwan's reunification with China both through intimidation and seduction: "Marry me or else{…}." And while vehemently denouncing Lee and the Taiwanese "splittists," the PRC authorities also intensified their effort to stimulate Taiwanese companies' desire to trade with or relocate their production lines to the mainland.[13]

This strategy partly failed: in 2000, because the KMT was divided, Chen Shui-bian, the candidate of the Democratic Progressive Party (DPP), the major independence-leaning opposition grouping, was elected Taiwanese president. This major development convinced China to keep remilitarizing the Strait while increasing its pressure on the US to keep Chen on a tight leash.[14] But it also moderated its ambition: rather than hastening reunification, China's major security objective became preventing Taipei's formal independence from the Chinese nation. And at the same time, it took advantage of the KMT's defeat and disarray to reach out to this party in the hope of restoring relations with it. For instance, it rapidly endorsed Kuomintang (KMT) heavyweight Su Chi's so called "92 consensus" (*jiu-er gongshi*), a concept crafted in 2000 that refers to the verbal compromise reached in November 1992 in Hong Kong by the SEF and ARATS negotiators according to which there is "one China" (*yi ge Zhongguo*) but "both sides agree not to define it" (China) or "each side keeps its own definition" (*geze biaoshu*, Taiwan). While the Chen government refused to recognize the compromise reached then as a "consensus," the DPP-KMT rift was used by the PRC as leverage to weaken the former, strengthen the latter—which had kept control of the parliament—and woo the Taiwanese business community as well as the US to support a more accommodating mainland policy. As a result, the Chen Administration appeared more and more powerless *vis-à-vis* the unprecedented rise of cross-Strait trade and economic relations, forced for example as early as 2003 to gradually open "charter flights" and to relax its trade restrictions with the PRC. It was under Chen, in 2004, that China replaced the US as Taiwan's major trade partner.[15]

Hu Jintao's and Xi Jinping's eras: divide and rule Taiwan

Chen Shui-bian's various independence-leaning initiatives, such as the holding of a referendum on China's missile threat in 2004, and his re-election the same year convinced China to go further. In March 2005, it promulgated an "anti-secession law" (*fan fenlie guojia fa*) especially designed for (or against) Taiwan.[16] According to this piece of legislation, Beijing reserves the right to use "non-peaceful means" (*fei heping fangshi*) in three circumstances (art. 8): 1) Taiwanese independence "secessionist forces" prevail, 2) "major incidents entailing Taiwan's secession from China occur," and 3) "possibilities for a peaceful reunification should be completely exhausted." Although preventing independence remained Beijing's major objective, Taipei's anti-reunification procrastination was then formally elevated to the rank of *casus belli*, legalizing and widening China's options to use military force or intimidation to reach its goal. Echoing a threat made by Prime Minister Zhu Rongji in 2000 before Chen Shui-bian's election, this third cause of war underscored the extent to which reunification had remained the final objective of China's Taiwan policy.[17] In any event, in enacting this law, the PRC had clearly demonstrated that it was ready to use all the weapons at its disposal, not only military, economic, diplomatic or political but also legal ones, to achieve its security objective regarding Taiwan.

This important development did not disrupt the ongoing reconciliation between the CCP and the KMT: a month later, in April 2005, with the support of large segments of the Taiwanese business community, then-KMT chairman, Lien Chan, visited China, initiating the establishment of regular meetings between both parties that have intensified and stabilized after KMT candidate Ma Ying-jeou was elected ROC president in 2008. It was in that context that Hu Jintao, Jiang's successor, decided to tactically soften the PRC's position: in 2007, while keeping "peaceful reunification" as a final objective, Hu Jintao coined the new concept of "peaceful development" (*heping fazhan*) of cross-Strait relations, underscoring Beijing's apparent embrace of the status quo in the Strait and new priorities: deepening economic, cultural and people-to-people relations with Taiwan in order to make the island increasingly dependent on China, and as a result gradually "winning the hearts and minds" of the Taiwanese, hoping eventually to convince them to buy Beijing's "one country, two systems" formula. As we have seen, these objectives are far from new. And they did not put an end to the PLA buildup and its growing capability to threaten Taiwan. Actually, it was around 2005 that, according to most experts, the military balance in the Strait tilted definitely in favor of China. But China's discourse had softened and the PLA's actions around Taiwan became more discreet or subdued. Moreover, Chen Shui-bian's inability to move Taiwan towards independence, the US's growing frustration *vis-à-vis* the DPP government and the KMT's likely return to power had convinced Beijing to modify its order of priorities.[18]

Consequently, the Chen years also allowed China to convince the US more actively to contribute to the preservation of the status quo in the Strait. Although bringing Washington closer to its side has been Beijing's long-term objective, the DPP government and initiatives gave the occasion to China, if not to internationalize the Taiwan issue, at least to involve more directly the US in the stabilization of cross-Strait relations and more generally in what some analysts then called the US-China "co-management" of this question.[19]

Ma Ying-jeou's election and the KMT's return to power in 2008 have facilitated the success of China's new security strategy towards Taiwan. Abiding by the "92 consensus," Ma embarked on a "rapprochement policy" towards Beijing; soon after he came to power, direct scheduled air and sea links across the Strait were established and high level negotiations between the ARATS and the SEF resumed, allowing the signing of an ambitious Economic Cooperation Framework Agreement (ECFA) in June 2010 and many other technical accords before and after. A kind of "creeping normalization" between Beijing and Taipei governments has since then taken shape, which has eased direct contacts between the two sides' ministries.[20]

Simultaneously, Ma concluded a verbal diplomatic truce with the PRC, Taiwan being allowed under its official name (ROC) to keep its 23 diplomatic allies; later, he managed to convince China to accept the island's participation in the World Health Organization's Assembly and the International Civil Aviation Organization (ICAO) as an observer and under the name "Chinese Taipei."

As a result, in 2012, Ma was rather easily re-elected against Tsai Ying-wen, a DPP candidate who had not been able to convince Washington that she could keep relations across the Taiwan Strait stable and predictable. And since he succeeded Hu later that year, Xi Jinping has largely pursued his predecessor's "peaceful development" strategy towards Taiwan, playing the KMT and the business community off against the DPP and other anti-unification forces as well as pushing for the opening of political talks. He also deepened the quasi-normalization process: in February 2014, for the first time the PRC's Taiwan Affairs Office (TAO) director, Zhang Zhijun, and the ROC's Mainland Affairs Council (MAC) Chairman, Wang Yu-chi met in Nanjing and agreed to establish reciprocal SEF and ARATS representative offices.[21] And in June 2014, Zhang paid his first visit to Taiwan.

Having said that, since 2008, China's security policy towards Taiwan has only partly changed. Clearly, priority has now been given to the development of closer economic, political, cultural and people-to-people links with Taiwan. Beijing has mobilized to that end its usual united front tools. Nevertheless, the PLA's buildup on the other side of the Strait has not diminished, China's pressure on the US to stop arms sales to Taiwan has actually intensified, and, more importantly, its capability to complicate a US intervention in a Taiwan Strait armed conflict has continued to increase. Having elevated Taiwan to the status of "national core interest" in 2009, Beijing has simultaneously intensified its pressure on Washington as well as other capitals. Finally, preventing Taiwan from getting access to a full and internationally recognized statehood has remained crucial.

In other words, as we are going to see now, the PRC is likely to continue to "walk on two legs"—or use both military and political methods—to achieve its security objectives: preventing Taiwan's independence and inducing its unification.

Taiwan as a military objective

Since 2008, China has officially acknowledged that the danger of war with Taiwan has receded. Its January 2009 Defense White Paper clearly stated that the tension in the Taiwan Strait had been "greatly reduced."[22] And in its 2013 edition, the White Paper satisfactorily declared that, although "the 'Taiwan independence' separatist forces and their activities are still the biggest threat to the peaceful development of cross-Strait relations," "cross-Strait relations are sustaining a momentum of peaceful development."[23] Nevertheless, this very statement underscores the extent to which the demilitarization of the Taiwan issue is at best provisional and more probably an illusion. As the same document reiterated, "defending national sovereignty, security and territorial integrity" has remained Chinese defense policy's top objective. It also indicated that while developing new missions such as border security, "military operations other than war" (MOOTW) or the security of China's lanes of communication as well as the interests, companies and nationals abroad, the PLA's fundamental task was to empower the country to "resist foreign aggression and defend the motherland{…}to maintain peace, contain crises and win wars." In other words, if one of the three scenarios listed in the anti-secession law occurs, the PLA must be ready to use "non-peaceful means" to solve the Taiwan issue.

Deliberate uncertainties about the use of force

To be sure, the PRC government maintained much flexibility about the circumstances in which it would be forced to use these methods, as well as the actual content of these (see above). On the one hand, in all three scenarios, it is up to the Chinese authorities to evaluate the situation—the influence of the pro-independence forces, the magnitude of the domestic unrest or the determination of the Taiwanese government's opposition to open peaceful reunification negotiations—to conclude that only a military solution to the differences with Taiwan can be contemplated. While such a conclusion has seemed highly unlikely since the KMT's return to power in 2008, conversely, if after a certain amount of time the most accommodating Taiwanese government, under pressure from the society, still refuses to open political negotiations, a clear case of procrastination can be charged by the Chinese leadership or at least its most nationalistic or aggressive members. In addition, other causes of war, such as Taiwan's acquisition of nuclear weapons or a foreign intervention on the island, have been mentioned by Beijing earlier and must also be considered as possible *casus belli*.[24] In other words, Beijing's security strategy towards Taiwan is very much based on the uncertainty that the "anti-secession law" has introduced.

On the other hand, the Chinese government has refrained from defining what "non-peaceful means" would include in terms of actions. According to some Chinese analyses, these can go all the way from warning and intimidations to a blockade or a full-fledged invasion. And today, more and more PLA experts find in Sun Zi's *Art of War* (*Sunzi bingfa*) the best strategy to reunify Taiwan: a simple but clear show of force, since the best wars are the ones that do not need to be fought.[25] In any event, each of the three scenarios would require specific measures that by definition are impossible to predict since they would depend on circumstances that cannot be fully envisioned.

More importantly, there is no guarantee that in the future China would not be tempted again to exert military pressure in order not just to prevent a move towards formal independence but to speed up unification. As long as the KMT stays in power on Taiwan, this evolution appears unlikely. But the changing balance of power in the Strait as well as in the Western Pacific as a whole may convince CCP and PLA leaderships that resorting to non-peaceful methods can rapidly put a final end to a split in the Chinese nation that they never really accepted. Moreover, if the PRC takes control of Taiwan, it can better project its military power beyond the first island chain and put Japan as well as the US forward deployment at greater risk. In other words, for China, reunifying Taiwan would be a direct power multiplier.

In order to better comprehend what China may contemplate in terms of military action, the less speculative and most logical approach is to look at what policies, strategies and acts the CCP and the PLA leaderships have already adopted to prepare for such contingencies.

Beijing's major military objectives

Since the early 1990s, the PRC authorities have privileged the three following military objectives:

1) Develop capabilities to project military power across the Taiwan Strait or to militarily intimidate Taiwan.
2) Complicate any US military intervention with Japanese logistical support in a Taiwan war scenario.
3) Weaken Taiwan's military and will to fight by intensifying pressure on third-party countries, particularly the US, to stop or at least reduce their arms sales to Taiwan, as well as by multiplying contacts with retired Taiwanese military officers and increasing espionage activities on the island.

The first objective is a well-known one. While since Ma's election the PLA has given much more attention to the South and East China Sea territorial disputes, its modernization drive would allow its navy and air force to exert, if need be, very strong pressure on Taiwan.[26] These new capabilities are not clearly aimed at organizing a successful landing operation on the island, although the PLA will be in a position to implement this plan by 2020.[27] They rather give the PLA the means to destroy the ROC Air Force, take control of the airspace over the Strait and then impose a naval blockade on Taiwan.[28] The military usefulness of the 1,100–1,400 conventional missiles targeting Taiwan is not obvious either: they may destroy an equivalent number of military or civilian targets and, in conjunction with the PLA's expanding cruise missile arsenal, help prepare a blockade or a landing assault, but alone they cannot force Taiwan to surrender.[29] And while today the increasing but unspecified number of land-attack and anti-ship cruise missiles constitute both for Taiwan and the US a more meaningful threat,[30] the military added-value of these conventional ballistic missiles is arguably diminishing: these missiles rather constitute a weapon of intimidation capable of making a "warning strike";[31] and, as we will see, they more and more appear to be a bargaining chip with the US and Taiwan in exchange for some specific concessions: reduction of arms sales to the island for the former and opening political discussion or concluding a peace treaty for the latter.

The second objective is a more recent one,[32] but, in the eyes of the CCP and the PLA, it has become increasingly important because deterring the US from militarily intervening in the Strait would ease the success of any Sun Zi-inspired strategy of getting Taiwan back without a single shot. According to most scenarios drafted by the Taiwanese and the US military, the ROC armed forces can on their own resist a PLA offensive for only three to four weeks,[33] and they are organized and trained for that purpose. Consequently, a US intervention is vital for Taiwan, and preventing or thwarting it a crucial objective for the Chinese military.

The strategy and weapon systems that the PLA has developed since the early 2000s are therefore more and more aimed at deterring any US armed intervention in a Taiwan scenario.[34] For instance, its A2/AD (anti-access/area denial) strategy integrating land, sea, air, and space surveillance and strike capabilities can impose a far riskier environment on the US Seventh Fleet.[35] The PLA DF-21 missiles can target the US military bases in Japan or the Western Pacific (Guam). In addition to various types of cruise missiles, the PLA has also developed anti-ship missiles such as the DF-21D (range 1,500 km) and even hypersonic glide missiles that are intended to be able to badly damage or even sink a US aircraft carrier, forcing Washington to think twice before coming to Taiwan's help.[36] The PRC has in addition maintained an ambiguous position regarding the use of nuclear weapons in a Taiwan scenario: depending of the circumstances, the island can indeed easily be elevated by the Chinese leadership to the status of "vital national interest" and "sanctuarized," forcing the US to choose between a nuclearization of the conflict or disengagement.[37]

Of course, this strategy is based on the assumption that Taiwan would quickly surrender or accept Beijing's political conditions if abandoned by the US, which is likely but not certain. It is precisely for this reason that the PRC authorities are developing this capability hand in hand with its third objective: weakening Taiwan's military and will to fight.

One can object that these new weapon systems have little chance to be used in a war in the Taiwan Strait and are part of a strategy of empowerment *vis-à-vis* the United States or Japan and aimed particularly at better responding to the Obama Administration's "rebalancing" policy. But, in view of Taiwan's close security relations with the US, their use in other theaters, such as the South or the East China Seas, would also contribute to demonstrating the PLA's growing capabilities and indirectly weakening Taiwan's defense posture.

For obvious reasons, weakening the Taiwanese military has always been a key security objective of the PRC. In spite of its generous public statements (see above), Beijing's final aim clearly appears to be that of disarming Taiwan, allowing it, in case of reunification, to keep a police force, or at best a home guard. All the policies and actions taken by Beijing point in this direction. Among them, preventing arms sales to Taiwan has been one of the most important and constant objectives. Today, the US remains the only country that can still sell arms to Taiwan without being ostracized or sanctioned by China. Other weapon-exporting countries no longer dare take this risk, providing Taiwan only with small arms or minor military equipment, sales that remain in most cases under the radar. In 2009, taking advantage of the Obama Administration's softer (or perceived as such) China policy, Beijing tried to intensify its pressure on the US, openly threatening American companies that continued to sell weapons to Taiwan of being excluded from the Chinese market. This offensive targeted in particular Boeing. However, because of the US government's strong reaction, the PRC authorities refrained from carrying out their threat—thus far. But the pressure is clearly growing, even if for tactical reasons Beijing has never publicly criticized the Ma government for buying arms from the US.

In order to reduce or even stop US arms sales to Taiwan, China has also tried to trade this decision with the removal of its conventional missiles deployed against Taiwan. Raised for the first time by Jiang Zemin in his last meeting as PRC president with George W. Bush in October 2002, this proposal has more recently been revived by some American experts who are pushing for the acceptance of such a negotiation[38] or even a more accommodating policy towards China that would include a gradual disengagement from, if not an abandonment of Taiwan.[39] Although, in the foreseeable future, such a trade-off has little chance of succeeding, it is indicative of the new dimensions taken by the debate about Taiwan in the US.[40]

Finally, cultivating contacts with retired and, possibly, active Taiwanese military officers has increasingly been part of China's strategy. Aware of the pro-KMT or even unification inclinations of most Taiwanese generals and high-ranking officers, China is using them both as a pro-rapprochement or even disarmament lobby and as a source of classified information about the Taiwanese military. Although the number of local Taiwanese in the ROC officer corps has been growing steadily, it is still dominated by families of militaries who came from the mainland with Chiang Kai-shek and are much closer to the KMT than the DPP. Moreover, the ideology of the ROC armed forces is still guided by Sun Yat-sen's three principles of the people (nationalism, democracy and people's welfare), and particularly a greater-China nationalism that cannot reconcile with the society's growing Taiwanese identity (around two-thirds), let alone the pro-independence sentiments of some of its segments. Similarities with the Ukrainian officer corps before the partition of Crimea in 2014 are striking. In any event, the Taiwanese military's morale and will to fight have also clearly been weakened by a lack of investment in defense since the early 2000s by both the Chen and Ma governments. The ROC defense budget has stagnated at around US$10 million in the last decade and a half, representing only 2.2 percent of GDP in 2013 against 3.2 percent in 1999.[41] And as the Taiwanese military is moving towards a more costly all-volunteer force, a reform that should be completed at the end of 2017 (initially planned to be completed by 2014, its implementation has taken more time than expected), there is no indication that this budget will substantially increase.[42] Facing difficulties in recruiting and keeping good professional soldiers, NCOs and officers, the ROC armed forces are facing the danger of becoming less and less reliable as well as even more isolated from the society. The consequences of these trends are hard to assess, but most PLA experts have already publicly concluded that without US intervention, the Taiwanese would not fight but prefer to accept the conditions imposed by Beijing, whatever they may be. Or, to be more accurate, and in order to back up this strategy, China's military propaganda has been developing a very strong narrative aimed at weakening the morale of the Taiwanese and their will to fight, exaggerating the PLA's capabilities, including those *vis-à-vis* the US military, and understating the ROC armed forces' resolve.[43]

The PRC's increasing espionage activities on the island are also part of this strategy of affecting the morale of the Taiwanese. These activities are nothing new; but the deepening of economic and people-to-people exchanges, the rapid expansion of PRC tourism in Taiwan and the multiplication of family relations across the Strait have facilitated these activities. As expected, the PLA has particularly targeted ROC retired military officers or family members of active military officers who visit or decide to settle down on the mainland (since active members of the ROC military, like other civil servants, are banned from travelling to the PRC). In addition, quite a number of Taiwanese business people (*Taishang*) established on the mainland have been recruited by the PRC State Security to gather sensitive information. As a result, more and more cases have been reported by the Taiwanese media, underscoring an increasing and dangerous lack of security precautions among the Taiwanese military. This situation has developed to the extent that the US government and particularly the Pentagon is now seriously considering preventing its most sophisticated weapon systems and military equipment from being delivered to Taiwan.[44]

One can argue that China's military objectives focus on exerting strong psychological pressure on the Taiwanese military and society. One can also object that since 2008, and even before, the PLA has made a great effort to "neutralize" the Taiwan issue, in order to better go around it to reach more urgent or ambitious objectives—increasing its presence between the first and second island chain and in the Western Pacific as a whole. In addition, there may be conflicting views and strategies between PRC civilian and military leaders or within both groups. Unfortunately, we have no strong evidence of the existing or potential fault lines. In any event, China is clearly pursuing several strategies at the same time. As we will see, since it resumed its relations with the KMT, the CCP has privileged non-military methods to achieve its political goals. But imposing an advantageous military balance on Taiwan has always been part of the PRC's calculus, ready to be drawn on if required by the circumstances.

Taiwan as a political objective

To some extent, one can claim that since 1950, the PRC has never seriously envisaged unifying Taiwan by force, for a long time because it did not have the capability, and since 1979 (or even 1972) because it had concluded that time was on its side. Most countries' endorsement of the "one China policy" (including the US), the emergence of semi-direct and then direct contacts and trade relations across the Strait, and the asymmetry of the relation between the states have clearly facilitated the success of Deng's "peaceful reunification" strategy and favored what Hu has called the "peaceful development of cross-Strait relations." However, the Taiwanese have remained very reluctant to accept not only Beijing's "one country, two systems" formula but also the opening of political talks, let alone the negotiation of a "peace treaty" with the mainland. Protected by the TRA and praised by the US and the West for its democratic system, Taiwan feels that it can resist a political settlement and unification forever (DPP) or at least until mainland China democratizes (KMT).

Aware of this resistance, the PRC leadership has intensified peaceful efforts aimed at bridging the gap between the two sides. But instead of working out a middle ground with Taipei, Beijing has been keen to bring the Taiwanese closer to its view by using the following tools:

1) Deepening economic interdependence.
2) Multiplying people-to-people interactions as well as the number of cross-Strait agreements under the "one China" framework.

3) Using united front methods to soften the position of growing segments of the business, political, media and intellectual elites, and facilitate the conclusion of a political agreement favorable to China.

These "weapons" are far from being new: as we have seen, they go back to the launching of the "peaceful reunification" policy. Nevertheless, since 2008, the rapid expansion and diversification of cross-Strait relations and interactions have allowed the PRC to harvest the first substantial fruits produced by this strategy.[45]

Increasing dependence while giving the illusion of normalizing relations

There is no secret about the first two objectives, which, on the whole, Beijing has quite successfully reached, although probably at a slower pace than expected. In spite of Taipei's initial resistance, economic logic has gradually prevailed, particularly since the early 2000s: in 2013, cross-Strait trade reached US$197 billion, with a US$116 billion surplus (PRC imports: US$156.5 billion; PRC exports: US$40.5 billion) for Taiwan, according to China and US$165 billion, including Hong Kong, according to Taiwan; 40 percent of Taiwan's exports went to China (Hong Kong included), against 24 percent in 2000, while 63 percent of its stock of FDI is located there (US$134 billion). For a long time restricted, Taiwanese imports from the PRC have become more robust (16 percent of total imports). And although strict legal barriers have remained in place limiting their official amount (US$870 million in January 2014), Chinese FDI in Taiwan has actually increased to a much greater extent, coming through Hong Kong and more often the Caribbean fiscal paradises.[46]

These trade and economic flows have eased the emergence of people-to-people contacts and interactions across the Strait. Today, probably more than two million *Taishang* live on the mainland, including 500,000 in the Shanghai area. They enjoy a privileged legal status similar to other expatriates but that also now allows them to easily go back and forth, start business, bring Taiwanese cadres (*Taigan*) and pay limited taxes. The opening of scheduled direct flights across the Strait in 2008 and the sluggish state of the economy on the island have accelerated this major migration, as a growing number of young Taiwanese look for a better-paid job on the mainland.

Conversely, since the KMT's return to power in 2008, Chinese tourists have been allowed to visit Taiwan, their number growing rapidly from 1 million in 2009 to 2.85 million in 2013, providing much needed business to large segments of the service industry. In 2014, there were 118 daily flights directly crossing the Strait (Hong Kong and Macau excluded).

It is impossible to summarize both the density and the diversity of people-to-people interactions across the Strait. Since the early 1990s, they have included an increasing number of academic, educational, scientific and technical, and cultural exchanges. Sharing the same language (Mandarin, although most Taiwanese also speak Hokkien, a dialect from Southern Fujian) and cultural background (Confucianism), Chinese and Taiwanese can easily communicate and influence each other, preferring to stay away from politics and sensitive questions in order to move forward and cooperate.

There is however a double asymmetry in these interactions that has contributed to the success of Beijing's strategy: the first, the difference of size, has already been mentioned; the second is that, on the PRC side, people-to-people exchanges or agreements do not mean that the Party-state is not involved in one way or another. All exchanges with Taiwan, be they (semi-) official or nongovernmental, are coordinated by the CCP and State Council's TAO or its local ramifications. While the *Taishang* are organized on the mainland in Taiwanese business associations set up under the umbrella of the local TAO, PRC nationals living in Taiwan (in particular the 350,000 Chinese spouses married to ROC nationals) are not supervised by any government body. In other words, the difference of political system between China and Taiwan clearly favors the former's and its ability to reach its objective.

For Beijing, the multiplication of cross-Strait technical agreements consistent with the one China principle has also contributed to enhancing its security interests, not only because it has stabilized and somewhat normalized the relationship between both governments. Any normalization is likely to remain incomplete since the PRC cannot and will never recognize the ROC, but also, and more importantly, because all the agreements signed since 2008—to date 21, among them the 2010 ECFA—have directly narrowed Taiwan's room for maneuver and options for the future, rapidly increasing the cost of any return to the status quo ante.

Moreover, for Beijing, concluding these accords has been part of a strategy aimed at tackling the easy (economic) issues first and the hard (political) ones later. Although showing patience, China is to gradually increase its pressure on the KMT and Taiwan as a whole to sooner or later open political talks and, at a later stage, accept the negotiation of a peace agreement that would include the commitment of both sides to eventual reunification. And since his rise to power, president Xi has shown willingness to speed up this process by possibly linking the establishment of still undefined military confidence building measures (CBMs) to political discussions across the Strait.[47]

However, resistance on the island, both from the DPP-led opposition and within the KMT, to any move in that direction has complicated Beijing's plan. In that respect, the difficulties encountered by the Ma government in March 2014 to secure the ratification of the Cross-Strait Service Trade Agreement (CSSTA) signed by the SEF and the ARATS in June 2013 have underscored Taiwanese society's growing fear of seeing their island becoming too dependent on China. The peaceful occupation by the Sunflower Movement, a student-led organization, of the parliament for over 3 weeks in March–April 2014 and the support that it received from society as well as the opposition parties have forced the KMT, prior to any ratification of the CSSTA, to draft a law allowing the Legislative Yuan and the public to better scrutinize the development of cross-Strait relations. This development has also shown that Beijing's united front policy towards Taiwan, in spite of its recent activism, is far from having fulfilled its goals.

The limits of Beijing's united front strategy vis-à-vis *Taiwan*

Since 1949, Taiwan has been an important part of the CCP's united front policy and strategy. Reaching out to Taiwanese elites, isolating Chiang Kai-shek was for a long time the PRC's major objective. For that purpose, since 1949, among the eight small "democratic parties" working under the leadership of the CCP, there has been one representing the pro-unification Taiwanese politicians, the Taiwan Democratic Autonomous League (*Taiwan minzhu zizhi tongmeng*, 2,100 members in 2013) and another one, the KMT's Revolutionary Committee (*Guomintang geming weiyuanhui*, 81,000 members), gathering former opponents of Chiang. Reactivated after the Cultural Revolution, these groupings are represented in the Chinese Consultative People's Political Conference (CCPPC), a powerless second chamber that precisely symbolizes the united front between the CCP and forces that agree to cooperate with it under its leadership. These parties' role has been somewhat sidelined since the restoration of direct relations between the CCP and Taiwan's KMT. However, led at the national level by the CCPPC chairman (and number four of the CCP hierarchy), today Yu Zhengsheng, the CCP's united front policy towards Taiwan is still carried out both by its united front departments and the TAOs at each level.

The *Taishang* constitute an important and rather easy target of this policy, a growing number of them being invited to join the local CCPPCs or even people's congresses.[48] A trickier priority target has been the Taiwanese elites living on the island. Among them, reaching out to the Taiwanese entrepreneurs having business on the mainland was for a long time, particularly in the Lee and the Chen eras, Beijing's top objective. But since the early 2000s, the CCP has also managed to resume relations with Taiwan's anti-independence parties, first with smaller and more pro-unification political groupings such as the New Party, now marginalized, and in 2005, as we have seen, with the KMT. Since 2008, the CCP has also shown flexibility in establishing informal contacts with the DPP, in spite of this party's refusal to endorse the 92 consensus. Beyond these two types of elites, influential persons among the military, academic, cultural and media circles have also been targeted by China's united front strategy.

Has this strategy been successful? There is no doubt that it has made some inroads among the Taiwanese elites. The island business community is clearly more accommodating towards China than before: in 2012, quite a number of entrepreneurs known for their DPP inclinations supported Ma's re-election.[49] The KMT leadership, although more careful, at least publicly, not only supports Ma's "rapprochement policy" but now seems ready to open political talks with the PRC, its priority being the organization of a Xi Jinping-Ma Ying-jeou summit before the latter retires in 2016. While the DPP is opposed to any further political rapprochement with China, it is increasingly divided, some of its leaders, such as Frank Hsieh (Hsieh Chang-ting), being ready to endorse a softer version of the 92 consensus while others, such as party chairwoman Tsai Ying-wen or even her predecessor Su Tseng-chang, adopting a very pragmatic view on all the cross-Strait agreements already signed, privileging continuity over uncertainty. In the media world, the acquisition of the daily newspaper *China Times* (*Zhongguo shibao*) by Wang Eng-meng's Want Want group (*wangwang tuanti*) has been the most obvious illustration of the emergence of a pro-PRC and pro-unification media on the island.[50]

But can the CCP's united front policy achieve more than that? For one thing, the Taiwanese business and political elites want stability and predictability in their dealings with China. Richer and better connected to the business community, the PRC and, arguably, the US, the KMT machinery is much stronger than its main opponent, the DPP, and is likely to continue to privilege stability.. But, operating in a democratic environment and having to face a society that is more anxious about Taiwan's future, the political elite cannot move too close to Beijing, let alone sign any political accord without having it ratified by referendum by the Taiwanese. Increasing the DPP's chances of coming back to power in 2016, the KMT's humiliating defeat in the November 2014 local elections has clearly highlighted the political cost of a mainland policy that has been perceived as too accommodating by many Taiwanese.

Preventing Taiwan's democratic experience from influencing the PRC

This brings us to the PRC's final security concern regarding Taiwan: preventing the island's democratization precedent and democratic experience from influencing the CCP political reform and future. On several occasions, since 2005, some KMT leaders have tried to convince Beijing to allow its organization to again operate on the mainland, but, as expected, to no avail. And the Ma government has refrained from pushing too hard on this front, knowing too well that it may jeopardize the ongoing cross-Strait rapprochement.

However, one of the ironies of this amelioration has been the increasing interest, in PRC society, not only in the old mainland-based ROC but also in Taiwanese politics and democracy. Facilitated by the emergence of the internet and social networks as well as the surge of Chinese tourism to the island, each new major election in Taiwan has attracted a growing number of followers in the PRC and questions among these about their own political system's opaqueness, corruption and lack of democracy. This attention has already here and there led some PRC activists to run for local people's congress elections on Sun Yat-sen or KMT inspired platforms.[51]

Of course, these attempts have been rapidly repressed and have little chance of making a difference in the foreseeable future. But these new developments explain why the Beijing authorities have a vested security interest in closely monitoring cross-Strait people-to-people relations that may politically influence, or even destabilize, their regime and, consequently, stick to an understanding of reunification that would remain in any event very close to Hong Kong's "one country, two systems" formula. In other words, Taiwan's democratic influence on the mainland should be neutralized or contained.

Conclusion

Since 1949, the PRC has followed two concurrent security objectives regarding Taiwan. The first has been to exclude the ROC from the international community and to take its place as the sole official representative of China, while at the same time keeping Taiwan within the one China realm. That objective was secured in the United Nations and with the help of the US as early as 1971–2 and not challenged by the Taiwanese authorities, at least until the early 1990s. Also opposed by the US and the majority of the international community, Lee Teng-hui's and then Chen Shui-bian's attempts to bring the ROC-Taiwan out of its diplomatic isolation failed, easing the success and perpetuation of the one China principle and policy. And Deng Xiaoping's peaceful reunification strategy has opened the door to a multiplication of cross-Strait interactions and to a level of interdependence with Taiwan that has clearly narrowed Taiwan's options for the future. Deng's reforms have also accelerated the modernization of the PLA and dramatically modified the military balance in the Strait to the detriment of Taiwan. In other words, while it still seems as if the political status quo can be prolonged for a long time, the island's formal independence is today inconceivable.

Nevertheless the PRC has always had another security objective: Taiwan's reunification with the motherland. For basic strategic reasons, it was for a long time postponed to a more distant future. But the PRC cannot feel fully secure if this goal is not fulfilled and, in the first place, a clear path and negotiation process that would allow both sides of the Strait to move in this direction are not drawn up and gradually fleshed out. And today, Beijing appears to be in a stronger position to accelerate this evolution. The current Chinese leadership still sticks to Hu's "peaceful development" strategy. But it is far from certain that it believes that this strategy will allow this second objective to be reached by way of only the diplomatic, economic and united front methods described above. As we have seen, Jiang, Hu and Xi have all wished to keep strong military pressure on the island, even if this pressure has perpetuated there a sense of mistrust towards the PRC. While presented more and more today as a backup strategy, the use of non-peaceful means to "solve the Taiwan issue" cannot be totally dismissed if no progress is made for too long. The limits of the rapprochement that has taken place under the Ma Administration as well as the US rebalancing strategy (and its very ambiguities) may convince Beijing, probably not to start a war, but to revive military intimidations as a strategy to better secure long-term unification.

It is true that today tensions and short-term security priorities have moved to other theaters, such as the South or the East China Seas. The PLA is also busy with a much larger array of tasks and objectives. Besides, to reach the second island chain or high seas, the PLA can just go around Taiwan; it does not need to control every link in the chain. Put differently, Taiwan is not an obstacle to China's rise and growing influence in the world and particularly in the Asia-Pacific region. Actually, it never has been. However, symbolically and politically, Taiwan has remained the main and last hurdle to the Chinese nation's full reunification. Its control is perceived by the CCP and the PLA as a major power attribute. And the island's democratic experience may have a destabilizing impact on the mainland. While Taiwan's long-term security relationship with the US will probably continue to deter the PLA from embarking on adventurous operations, weakening this protection is likely to remain one of Beijing's key objectives, with the expectation being not to rapidly reunify with Taiwan but to gradually "neutralize" Taiwan and compel it to come to the political negotiation table. Because once the Taipei authorities have accepted a peace or an end of hostility accord, the next step will be easier to take, facilitating eventual unification. For all these reasons, Taiwan is likely to remain one of China's top security challenges and objectives in the future.

Notes

1. Alan M. Wachman, *Why Taiwan? Geostrategic Rationales for China's Territorial Integrity*, Stanford, CA: Stanford University Press, 2007; Office of Naval Intelligence, *The People's Liberation Army Navy: A Modern Navy with Chinese Characteristics*, Washington, DC: Navy Maritime Intelligence Center, August 2009.
2. "Constitution of the People's Republic of China," enacted on 4 December 1982. Available online at www.npc.gov.cn/englishnpc/Constitution/node_2824.htm.
3. "Senior Chinese Official Calls the US to Respect China's Core National Interests," *Renminwang*, 29 July 2009. Available online at http://english.people.com.cn/90001/90776/90883/6713167.html.
4. Richard C. Bush, *At Cross Purposes: US-Taiwan Relations since 1942*, Armonk, NY: M.E. Sharpe, 2004.
5. Michael Szonyi, *Cold War Island: Quemoy on the Front Line*, Cambridge and New York: Cambridge University Press, 2008.
6. Ministry of Foreign Affairs of the People's Republic of China, "A Policy of 'One Country, Two Systems' on Taiwan," 17 November 2000. Available online at www.fmprc.gov.cn/eng/ziliao/3602/3604/t18027.htm (accessed on 25 March 2014); Jing Huang, with Xiaoting Li, *Inseparable Separation: The Making of China's Taiwan Policy*, Singapore: World Scientific, 2010, pp. 32–43.
7. Conversely, it was the adoption by China of a peaceful reunification policy towards Taiwan that allowed the Sino-US normalization.
8. "PRC Leader Ye Jianying's Nine Point Proposal," 30 September 1981. Available online at http://csis.org/files/media/csis/programs/taiwan/timeline/sums/timeline_docs/CSI_19810930.htm (accessed 25 March 2014).
9. This compromise, later called by the KMT the 92 consensus, has always remained ambiguous since, for Beijing, "one China" is the PRC, and for Taipei, the ROC.
10. "Joint Communiqué of the United States of America and the People's Republic of China," 17 August 1982. Available online at www.taiwandocuments.org/communique03.htm.
11. Richard C. Bush, *Untying the Knot: Making Peace in the Taiwan Strait*, Washington, DC: Brookings Institution, 2005.
12. John W. Garver, *Face Off: China, the United States and Taiwan's Democratization*, Seattle and London: University of Washington Press, 1997.
13. Jean-Pierre Cabestan, "Taiwan in 1999: A Difficult Year for the Island and the KMT," *Asian Survey*, Vol. 40, No.1, January/February 2000, pp. 172–80.
14. Nancy Bernkopf Tucker, ed., *Dangerous Strait: The US-Taiwan-China Crisis*, New York: Columbia University Press, 2005.
15. Chi Su, *Taiwan's Relations with Mainland China: A Tail Wagging Two Dogs*, London and New York: Routledge, 2005.
16. "Anti-Secession Law adopted by NPC (full text)," 14 March 2005. Available online at www.gwytb.gov.cn/en/Special/OneChinaPrinciple/201103/t20110317_1790121.htm; 反分裂国家法, 14 March 2005. Available online at www.gwytb.gov.cn/gjstfg/xfl/201101/t20110123_1724057.htm.
17. Before this law was adopted, some PRC experts had favored the drafting of a "unification law" but they did not prevail; Jean-Pierre Cabestan & Benoît Vermander, *La Chine en quête de ses frontières. La confrontation Chine-Taiwan (China in Search of Its Frontiers: The Confrontation between China and Taiwan)*, Paris: Presses de Sciences Po, 2005, p. 144.

18 Jean-Pierre Cabestan, "The New Détente in the Taiwan Strait and Its Impact on Taiwan's Security and Future: More Questions than Answers," *China Perspectives*, No. 3, 2010, p. 22–33.
19 Nancy Bernkopf Tucker, *Strait Talk: United States-Taiwan Relations and the Crisis with China*, Cambridge, MA: Harvard University Press, 2009; Quansheng Zhao, "Managing the Challenge: Power Shift in US-China Relations" in Quansheng Zhao and Guoli Liu, eds., *Managing the China Challenge. Global Perspectives*, Abingdon and New York: Routledge, 2009, pp. 246–9.
20 Cabestan, "The New Détente in the Taiwan Strait," p. 22.
21 The official name of Taiwan, ROC, was however not mentioned by the PRC side; *Xinhua*, 12 February 2004; *Lianhebao* (*United Daily News*), 12 February 2014.
22 Information Office of the State Council, *China National Defense in 2008*, January 2009. Available online at http://english.gov.cn/official/2009–01/20/content_1210227.htm.
23 Information Office of the State Council, *A Diversified Employment of China's Armed Forces*, April 2013. Available online at http://news.xinhuanet.com/english/china/2013–04/16/c_132312681.htm.
24 Annual Report to Congress, *Military and Security Developments Involving the People's Republic of China 2013*, A Report to the Congress Pursuant to the FY2000 National Defense Authorization Act for Fiscal Year 2000, Washington, DC: Office of the Secretary of Defense, May 2013, p. 55.
25 John Wilson Lewis and Litai Xue, *Imagined Enemies: China Prepares for Uncertain War*, Palo Alto, CA: Stanford University Press, 2006.
26 Annual Report to Congress, op. cit., pp. 55–9.
27 Republic of China, *National Defense Report 2013*, Taipei: Ministry of National Defense, October 2013. Available online at http://report.mnd.gov.tw/m/minister.html.
28 David Shlapak, "Chinese Air Superiority in the Near Seas" in Peter Dutton, Andrew S. Erickson and Ryan Martinson, eds., *China's Near Seas Combat Capabilities*, Newport, RI: Naval War College, China Maritime Studies, No. 11, February 2014, pp. 63–4; Daniel J. Kostecka, "Aerospace Power and Counterstrike Doctrine in the Near Seas" in Dutton et al., *China's Near Seas Combat Capabilities*, op. cit., pp. 49–60.
29 Yitzhak Shichor, *Missiles Myths: China's Threat to Taiwan in a Comparative Perspective*, Taipei: CAPS Papers 45, August 2008. The number of short range ballistic missiles (SRBM) targeting Taiwan is over 1,100 according to US sources and around 1,400 according to Taiwanese sources; Annual Report to Congress, op. cit.; Republic of China, *National Defense Report 2013*, op. cit., Part 1, Ch. 2.
30 Annual Report to Congress, op. cit., p. 38; Michael S. Chase and Andrew S. Erickson, "The Conventional Missile Capabilities of China's Second Artillery Force: Cornerstone of Deterrence and Warfighting," *Asian Security*, Vol. 8, No. 2, 2012, pp. 115–37.
31 Ron Christman, "China's Second Artillery Force: Capabilities and Mission for the Near Seas" in Dutton et al., *China's Near Seas Combat Capabilities*, op. cit., p. 41.
32 David A. Shlapak, David T. Orletsky, Toy I. Reid, Murray Scot Tanner and Barry Wilson, *A Question of Balance: Political Context and Military Aspects of the China-Taiwan Dispute*, Washington, DC: RAND. 2009.
33 Roger Cliff, Phillip C. Saunders and Scott Harold, eds., *New Opportunities and Challenges for Taiwan's Security*, Washington, DC: RAND National Defense Research Institute, 2011. Available online at www.rand.org/content/dam/rand/pubs/conf_proceedings/2011/RAND_CF279.pdf.
34 Office of Naval Intelligence, *The People's Liberation Army Navy*, op. cit.
35 Timothy A. Walton and Brian McGrath, "China Surface Fleet Trajectory: Implications for the US Navy" in Dutton et al., *China's Near Seas Combat Capabilities*, op. cit., p. 125.
36 Annual Report to Congress, op. cit., pp. 5–6, 38.
37 The sanctuarization of what a nuclear power claims as its national territory implies that any conventional attack against this territory would automatically trigger a nuclear response, and this in spite of the PRC's principle of non-first use, a principle that has been highly debated and disputed since the mid-2000s; cf. James Rickard, "Sun Tzu, Nuclear Weapons and China's Grand Strategy," Monterey: Center for Contemporary Conflict, Naval Postgraduate School, July 2008. Available online at www.au.af.mil/au/awc/awcgate/nps/rickard_chin_grand_strat_jul08.pdf; Anthony H. Cordesman, Ashley Hess and Nicholas S. Yarosh, *Chinese Military Modernization and Force Development: A Western Perspective*. Washington, DC: CSIS, 23 August 2013.
38 Michael D. Swaine, *America's Challenge: Engaging a Rising China in the Twenty-First Century*, Washington, DC: Carnegie Endowment for International Peace, 2011, p. 360.
39 Bruce Gilley, "Not So Dire Straits: How the Finlandization of Taiwan Benefits US Security," *Foreign Affairs*, Vol. 89, No. 1, January/February 2010, pp. 44–56, 58–60; Charles Glaser, "Will China's Rise Lead to War?" *Foreign Affairs*, Vol. 90, No. 2, March/April 2011, pp. 80–91.

40 Nancy Bernkopf Tucker and Bonnie Glaser, "Should the US Abandon Taiwan?" *The Washington Quarterly*, fall 2011, pp. 23–37.
41 Shirley Kan, *Taiwan: Major US Arms Sales Since 1990*, Washington, DC: Congressional Research Service, 3 March 2014, p. 34.
42 J. Michael Cole, "Is Taiwan's Military Becoming Too Small to Fight?" *The Diplomat*, 19 March 2014.
43 Jean-Pierre Cabestan and Tanguy Le Pesant, *L'esprit de défense de Taiwan face à la Chine. La jeunesse taiwanaise face à la tentation de la Chine (Taiwan's Will to Fight and China: The Taiwanese Youth and the Temptation of China)*, Paris: L'Harmattan, 2009, pp. 208–15; Andrew Chubb, "Propaganda, Not Policy: Explaining the PLA's 'Hawkish Faction,'" *China Brief*, Vol. 13, No. 15, 25 July 2013, pp. 6–11 and Vol. 13, No. 16, 9 August 2013, pp. 12–16.
44 Andrew Higgins, "In Taiwan Military, Chinese Spy Stirs Unease," *Washington Post*, 20 September 2011; William A. Stanton, "National Security and Taiwan's Future," Remarks made by the former head of the American Institute in Taiwan at the World Taiwanese Congress, Taipei, Taiwan, 15 March 2013.
45 Scott L. Kastner, "The Security Implications of China-Taiwan Economic Integration" in Cliff et al., *New Opportunities and Challenges for Taiwan Security*, op. cit., pp. 9–16.
46 Mainland Affairs Council, "Cross-Strait Economic Statistics Monthly," No. 250, December 2013. Available online at www.mac.gov.tw/ct.asp?xItem=107649&ctNode=5720&mp=1&xq_xCat=2013.
47 Alan D. Romberg, "From Generation to Generation: Advancing Cross-Strait Relations," *China Leadership Monitor*, No. 43, 14 March 2014, p. 5. Available online at http://media.hoover.org/sites/default/files/documents/CLM43AR.pdf.
48 Chun-yi Lee, *Taiwanese Business or Chinese Security Asset: A Changing Pattern of Interaction between Taiwanese Businesses and Chinese Governments*, London and New York: Routledge, 2011; Shu Keng and Gunter Schubert, "Agents of Unification? The Political Role of Taiwanese Businessmen in the Process of Cross-Strait Integration," *Asian Survey*, Vol. 50, No. 2, March 2010, pp. 287–310.
49 On China's use of the Taiwanese business community to influence Taiwan, cf. the interview given by Wu Jieh-min, a researcher at the Academia Sinica's Institute of Sociology, in the *Taipei Times*, 26 January 2014.
50 Andrew Higgins, "Tycoon Prods Taiwan Closer to China," *Washington Post*, 21 January 2012.
51 Zaijun Yuan, *The Failure of China's "Democratic" Reforms*, Plymouth: Lexington Books, 2012, p. 110.

Bibliography

Annual Report to Congress. *Military and Security Developments Involving the People's Republic of China 2013*, A Report to the Congress Pursuant to the FY2000 National Defense Authorization Act for Fiscal Year 2000. Washington, DC: Office of the Secretary of Defense, May 2013.
"Anti-Secession Law Adopted by NPC (full text)," 14 March 2005. Available online at www.gwytb.gov.cn/en/Special/OneChinaPrinciple/201103/t20110317_1790121.htm.
Bush, Richard C. *At Cross Purposes: US-Taiwan Relations since 1942*. Armonk, NY: M.E. Sharpe, 2004.
Bush, Richard C. *Untying the Knot: Making Peace in the Taiwan Strait*. Washington, DC: Brookings Institution, 2005.
Cabestan, Jean-Pierre. "Taiwan in 1999: A Difficult Year for the Island and the KMT." *Asian Survey*, Vol. 40, No. 1, January/February 2000, pp. 172–80.
Cabestan, Jean-Pierre. "The New Détente in the Taiwan Strait and Its Impact on Taiwan's Security and Future: More Questions than Answers." *China Perspectives*, No. 3, 2010, pp. 22–33.
Cabestan, Jean-Pierre and Le Pesant, Tanguy. *L'esprit de défense de Taiwan face à la Chine. La jeunesse taiwanaise face à la tentation de la Chine (Taiwan's Will to Fight and China: The Taiwanese Youth and the Temptation of China)*. Paris: L'Harmattan, 2009.
Cabestan, Jean-Pierre and Vermander, Benoît. *La Chine en quête de ses frontières. La confrontation Chine-Taiwan (China in Search of Its Frontiers: The Confrontation between China and Taiwan)*. Paris: Presses de Sciences Po, 2005.
Chubb, Andrew. "Propaganda, Not Policy: Explaining the PLA's 'Hawkish Faction.'" *China Brief*, Vol. 13, No. 15, 25 July 2013, pp. 6–11 and Vol. 13, No. 16, 9 August 2013, pp. 12–16.
Cliff, Roger, Saunders, Phillip C. and Harold, Scott, eds. *New Opportunities and Challenges for Taiwan's Security*. Washington, DC: RAND National Defense Research Institute, 2011. Available online at www.rand.org/content/dam/rand/pubs/conf_proceedings/2011/RAND_CF279.pdf.

Cole, J. Michael. "Is Taiwan's Military Becoming Too Small to Fight?" *The Diplomat*, 19 March 2014.
"Constitution of the People's Republic of China," enacted on 4 December 1982. Available online at www.npc.gov.cn/englishnpc/Constitution/node_2824.htm.
Cordesman, Anthony H., Hess, Ashley and Yarosh, Nicholas S. *Chinese Military Modernization and Force Development: A Western Perspective*. Washington, DC: CSIS, 23 August 2013.
Dutton, Peter, Erickson, Andrew S. and Martinson, Ryan, eds. *China's Near Seas Combat Capabilities*. Newport, RI: US Naval War College, China Maritime Studies, No. 11, February 2014.
Garver, John W. *Face Off: China, the United States and Taiwan's Democratization*. Seattle and London: University of Washington Press, 1997.
Gilley, Bruce. "Not So Dire Straits: How the Finlandization of Taiwan Benefits US Security." *Foreign Affairs*, Vol. 89, No. 1, January/February 2010, pp. 44–56, 58–60.
Glaser, Charles. "Will China's Rise Lead to War?" *Foreign Affairs*, Vol. 90, No. 2, March/April 2011, pp. 80–91.
Huang, Jing, with Li, Xiaoting. *Inseparable Separation: The Making of China's Taiwan Policy*. Singapore: World Scientific, 2010.
Information Office of the State Council. *China National Defense in 2008*, January 2009. Available online at http://english.gov.cn/official/2009-01/20/content_1210227.htm.
Information Office of the State Council. *A Diversified Employment of China's Armed Forces*, April 2013. Available online at http://news.xinhuanet.com/english/china/2013-04/16/c_132312681.htm.
"Joint Communiqué of the United States of America and the People's Republic of China," 17 August 1982. Available online at www.taiwandocuments.org/communique03.htm.
Kan, Shirley. *Taiwan: Major US Arms Sales since 1990*. Washington, DC: Congressional Research Service, 3 March 2014.
Kastner, Scott L. "The Security Implications of China-Taiwan Economic Integration" in Roger Cliff, Phillip C. Saunders and Scott Harold, eds., *New Opportunities and Challenges for Taiwan Security*. Washington, DC: RAND National Defense Research Institute, 2011, pp. 9–16.
Keng, Shu and Schubert, Gunter. "Agents of Unification? The Political Role of Taiwanese Businessmen in the Process of Cross-Strait Integration." *Asian Survey*, Vol. 50, No. 2, March 2010, pp. 287–310.
Lee, Chun-yi. *Taiwanese Business or Chinese Security Asset: A Changing Pattern of Interaction between Taiwanese Businesses and Chinese Governments*. London and New York: Routledge, 2011.
Lewis, John Wilson and Xue, Litai. *Imagined Enemies: China Prepares for Uncertain War*. Palo Alto, CA: Stanford University Press, 2006.
Office of Naval Intelligence. *The People's Liberation Army Navy: A Modern Navy with Chinese Characteristics*. Washington, DC: Navy Maritime Intelligence Center, August 2009.
Republic of China. *National Defense Report 2013*. Taipei: Ministry of National Defense, October 2013. Available online at http://report.mnd.gov.tw/m/minister.html.
Rickard, James. "Sun Tzu, Nuclear Weapons and China's Grand Strategy." Monterey: Center for Contemporary Conflict, Naval Postgraduate School, July 2008. Available online at www.au.af.mil/au/awc/awcgate/nps/rickard_chin_grand_strat_jul08.pdf.
Shichor, Yitzhak. *Missiles Myths: China's Threat to Taiwan in a Comparative Perspective*. Taipei: CAPS Papers 45, August 2008.
Shlapak, David A., Orletsky, David T., Reid, Tony I., Tanner, Murray Scot and Wilson, Barry. *A Question of Balance: Political Context and Military Aspects of the China-Taiwan Dispute*. Washington, DC: RAND, 2009.
Stanton, William A. "National Security and Taiwan's Future." Remarks made by the former head of the American Institute in Taiwan at the World Taiwanese Congress, Taipei, Taiwan, 15 March 2013.
Su Chi. *Taiwan's Relations with Mainland China: A Tail Wagging Two Dogs*. London and New York: Routledge, 2005.
Swaine, Michael D. *America's Challenge: Engaging a Rising China in the Twenty-First Century*. Washington, DC: Carnegie Endowment for International Peace, 2011.
Szonyi, Michael. *Cold War Island: Quemoy on the Front Line*. Cambridge and New York: Cambridge University Press, 2008.
Tucker, Nancy Bernkopf, ed. *Dangerous Strait: The US-Taiwan-China Crisis*. New York: Columbia University Press, 2005.
Tucker, Nancy Bernkopf. *Strait Talk: United States-Taiwan Relations and the Crisis with China*. Cambridge, MA: Harvard University Press, 2009.
Tucker, Nancy Bernkopf and Glaser, Bonnie. "Should the US Abandon Taiwan?" *The Washington Quarterly*, fall 2011, pp. 23–37.

Wachman, Alan M. *Why Taiwan? Geostrategic Rationales for China's Territorial Integrity*. Stanford, CA: Stanford University Press, 2007.
Yuan, Zaijun. *The Failure of China's "Democratic" Reforms*. Plymouth: Lexington Books, 2012.
Zhao, Quansheng, "Managing the Challenge: Power Shift in US–China Relations" in Zhao Quansheng and Liu Guoli, eds. *Managing the China Challenge: Global Perspectives*. Abingdon and New York: Routledge, 2009, pp. 230–54.
反分裂国家法, 14 March 2005. Available online at www.gwytb.gov.cn/gjstfg/xfl/201101/t20110123_1724057.htm.

Section C
Collective security

13
The United Nations in Chinese security[1]

Liselotte Odgaard

The UN plays a crucial role in Chinese security. China's growing influence in the international system after the Cold War is closely related to Beijing's recognition that the UN is the most significant global forum for obtaining legitimacy for policies of global security management. The UN has become the principal platform for China to promote its interpretation of the rules of international conduct that Beijing considers a legitimate basis for global security management after the Cold War. The principal focus for China in these efforts is the UN Security Council (UNSC) where the People's Republic of China (PRC) has had a permanent seat with veto powers since October 25, 1971. The question of the role of the UN in Chinese security is at the heart of China's attempt to influence the set-up of the current world order. For a rising great power, influencing the context of international politics is a less risky strategy than trying to change the behavior of other states directly. China's relationship with the UN is one way of influencing the context, by persuading other member states to shape the rules of international conduct as recommended by China. This type of influence limits the range of actions available to other states, and it is in this light that the UN's role in Chinese security must be assessed after the Cold War.

Two positions dominate the debate on Chinese security and the UN. One position holds that China is a reactive power or a free rider in the UN that does not take any independent initiatives.[2] According to these analyses, China concentrates on warding off proposals from the Western permanent member states of the UNSC, the US, the UK and France, that are not in agreement with central Chinese demands regarding the world order. This position varies according to whether it originates from offensive realism, defensive realism, or liberal approaches to international politics. Offensive realists argue that China uses the UN as a tool to portray itself as a relatively weak power threatened by US hegemony at a time when its focus is on building its capabilities.[3] Defensive realists argue that China's UN policy is designed to promote multipolarity so as to ameliorate adverse effects stemming from US preponderance without directly challenging Washington.[4] Liberals argue that China's UN policy is designed to ward off Western attempts to increase the role of civil and political rights in global security management.[5]

Another position sees China as a proactive power in the UN that takes initiatives founded on a concept of world order that differs from the Western liberal version of world order. According to these analyses, China has gradually developed its own interpretation of the UN principles of right and wrong conduct in global security management. China's interpretation is seen as a legitimate coherent alternative proposal for how to use the UN as a platform for global security management after the Cold War. This position also varies, depending on whether it is based on English school or constructivist approaches to international politics. The English school argues that China uses existing UN frameworks for global security management as a platform for developing and promoting its own interpretation of the principles of right and wrong conduct.[6] Constructivism argues that China's UN policy is marked by adherence to traditional norms of sovereignty and non-intervention in its pursuit of a new identity as a responsible great power based on Chinese concepts of world order.[7]

This chapter offers an assessment of the role of the UN in Chinese security after the Cold War. In the debate on China's UN multilateralism, realist and liberal analyses of China as a reactive power and a recipient of international security management in the UN were dominant until the mid-2000s. However, from this time onwards English school and constructivist analyses gradually gained more prominence, emphasizing China's role as a proactive power and a maker of international security management in the UN. The chapter substantiates this argument by, first, reviewing the literature of offensive and defensive realism and the liberal arguments on China's UN policy and their different explanations of China's position as a recipient of UN security management from 1989 to the mid-2000s. Second, the English school and constructivist literatures on the UN's role in Chinese security are reviewed with a view to demonstrating their different understandings of China's position as a maker of UN security management from the mid-2000s onwards. I argue that one element remains consistent throughout this period of change in the UN's role in Chinese security: the continued centrality of the UN as a principal arena for world order as originally argued by Samuel Kim.[8] I conclude that the centrality of the UN testifies to China's preference for revising the existing framework of global order to better accommodate Beijing's interests, as argued by the English school.

China as a taker of UN security management: 1989 to the mid-2000s

China came out of the Cold War with a security agenda in which the UN played a peripheral role. Three security concerns dominated China's relations with the outside world. First, the survival of Chinese Communist Party (CCP) rule was a principal security concern. China watched with deep concern the unravelling from within of the Soviet Union and its communist leadership in the run-up to December 25, 1991, when the remaining 12 republics emerged from the imploded Soviet Union as independent states.[9] A second central security concern was Chinese sovereignty and territorial integrity. Instability along China's borders was an immediate issue, with many neighboring states with competing claims to territory and maritime space defined by Beijing as being under Chinese sovereignty.[10] A third central security concern was to continue China's economic and social development in a new security environment without a communist bloc. Deng Xiaoping's market economic reforms begun in 1978 and China's Maoist brand of communism had already established China as a country operating independently from the bipolar Cold War East-West competition for power. The post-Cold War dominance of liberal economies in the emerging world order, the continuous challenges emerging from major domestic development issues in China, and the belief that China's economic rise was essential to maintain domestic political stability ensured that economic and social development was a top security concern for China.

The UN was not seen as a useful instrument for addressing these security concerns. Instead, it was a global multilateral forum that presented China with security challenges in areas where China already perceived itself as weak. After the Cold War, the stalemate characterizing the UNSC during the Cold War was replaced by a proactive attitude taken by the three permanent member states the US, the UK and France to reconfigure the world order according to liberal economic and political values. These powers began to use the UNSC to obtain legitimacy for undertaking Chapter VII operations without consent from target governments, provided evidence was available that a conflict produced threats to international peace and security.[11] This proactive policy flew in the face of China's concern to protect itself against outside pressures for political reform that might threaten the hold of the CCP on power, encourage separatist movements in provinces such as Tibet and Xinjiang, and derail the CCP's efforts to prioritize domestic economic and social development. As Russia became more and more estranged from the West over the course of the 1990s, China and Russia moved closer to each other as the two powers joined forces to ward off Western efforts at challenging the fundamental status in the UN system of the principles of absolute sovereignty and non-intervention. This was demonstrated in China's virulent reaction to the military actions of the North Atlantic Treaty Organization (NATO) in Kosovo and Yugoslavia in 1999–2000, which resulted in NATO missiles accidentally striking the PRC embassy in Belgrade on May 8, 1999. China saw the military actions as part of NATO's eastward expansion to the Black Sea and Caspian regions such as the Transcaucasus and Central Asia, to further weaken the influence of Russia.[12] During this honeymoon period for Western liberal world order promotion, the debate on the UN's role in Chinese security was dominated by realist and liberal analyses that capture Beijing's reactive approach to the Western challenge.

The realist approach: the UN as an arena for managing security dilemmas

Realist analyses argue that the UN is an instrument of self-reliant states used under conditions of instability for purposes of national security, which may result in the protection of the common interest in peace and stability.[13] For offensive realists, the UN is a tool that China uses for purposes of playing victim as the weaker power that is threatened by US hegemony. This portrayal of China as a victim of US containment serves to buy Beijing time to build up its economic and military resources so as to ensure its future position as a global great power. This approach would be in line with Deng Xiaoping's policy of *tao guang yang hui* (bide our time, hide your light), which means not showing off one's capabilities and keeping a low profile.[14]

According to Layne, Washington's insistence on preserving global hegemony instead of shifting the burden of balancing China to regional powers plays into China's hands because it confirms Beijing's assessment that the US is trying to compel China to accept US global leadership on US terms. US efforts to force China to adhere to US norms and values have sharpened US-Chinese tensions, as indicated by Chinese President Jiang Zemin's October 1995 remarks to the UNSC that "certain big powers, often under the cover of freedom, democracy and human rights, set out to encroach upon the sovereignty of other countries, interfere in their internal affairs and undermine their national unity and ethnic harmony."[15]

Essentially, offensive realists see the UN as an instrument without important consequences for the balance of power. Balancing dynamics will ensure that China emerges as a pole dominating the East Asian hemisphere on a par with the current US position of dominance in the Western hemisphere. However, the US has a choice of using the UN to ameliorate the transition so as to prolong its global influence or, as is the case now, use the UN to alienate China, thus increasing the element of conflict inherent in power transition. At most, the UN can be a tool used to postpone China's rise.

Defensive realists see diplomacy as a tool for moderating the effects of the security dilemma so that revisionist powers become status quo powers, even to the extent that the security dilemma may be overcome, thus altering the effects of changes in the distribution of power. The multilateral diplomacy of the UN may play a central role by influencing states' definitions of their national interests.[16]

As the weaker power compared with the US, China uses its UN diplomacy to promote multipolarity at a time when China still needs to focus on its domestic development to ensure its continued rise in terms of relative economic and military power. According to Saunders, Beijing invests resources to build diplomatic ties with small countries in regions such as the South Pacific and Africa. Their value lies in their votes in the UN General Assembly and in other international institutions. A prime example of China's efforts to build coalitions with developing countries in the UN to protect Chinese interests is the attempt to exempt developing countries from binding obligations under the Kyoto Protocol and China's success in averting criticism of its human rights record by the UN Human Rights Commission in the 1990s.[17] Pape uses the term soft balancing to describe China's response to alleged aggressive US unilateralism during the 2000s. He defines soft balancing as the use of non-military tools to delay, frustrate and undermine aggressive unilateral US policies. Soft balancing involves using China's power in the UNSC to seek peaceful resolutions, supporting the euro by diversifying China's foreign currency holdings, developing trade and security cooperation with Russia, and increasing cooperation with the EU.[18]

China's UN policy is part of a pattern whereby China seeks to ameliorate the consequences of US global dominance by promoting the non-use of force to settle security issues. China cannot match US military power and has no interest in promoting the use of force for purposes of conflict resolution. According to Swaine and Tellis, China adopts a calculative strategy towards the UN, participating fully because it enables China to shape global and regional politics. China's engagement in international institutions such as the UN has helped Beijing create a benign external environment, allowing it to focus on internal economic growth without unnerving other international actors.[19] Nathan and Ross point out that despite China's rhetorical rejection of human rights interference, it offered concessions to Western demands such as statements in the UN that China was ready to discuss and cooperate with other countries on an equal footing on the question of human rights.[20] This is demonstrated in Chinese writings on UN human rights issues. For example, Lijun Yang argues that the crimes of genocide, crimes against humanity and war crimes of the Rome Statute of the International Criminal Court (ICC) should be incorporated into China's criminal law. However, China avers that the ICC should be concerned that the provisions concerning human rights crimes do not compromise the principles of absolute sovereignty and non-intervention.[21] Avery Goldstein emphasizes that after 9/11, Beijing continued its grand strategy of reinforcing Washington's belief in the value, if not indispensability, of having China as a partner rather than an adversary. In line with this strategy, China moderated its expressions of concern about US military deployments in Central Asia during the war against Al Qaeda, voted in favor of the first UNSC resolution demanding Iraq's compliance with all disarmament requests, and did not publicly signal an intention to veto a second US-sponsored UNSC resolution on Iraq, in contrast to Russia and France. The belief in China was that restraint would further cement relations with the US and thereby serve China's national interests.[22]

In the first years after the Cold War, defensive realists pointed out that China attempted to accommodate secondary and small powers in the developing world without directly challenging the world order on which the US based its position as dominant global great power. Beijing used UN diplomacy to demonstrate that it is not planning to revolutionize the international system. Instead, it seeks to ameliorate the security dilemma by convincing other states that China's growing relative power is not accompanied by intentions to overthrow the existing global order.

The liberal approach: the UN as a forum for value-based international integration

The liberal perspective has highlighted the process by which China has moved from a position of rejecting the possibility that multilateral security frameworks such as the UN system might play a constructive role in Chinese foreign policy to one in which it has embraced the UN system. In the immediate aftermath of the Cold War, China's UN policy is a response from a non-democratic regime concerned to preserve the power of the CCP. The Western attempt to place the UNSC at the center of the efforts to enhance the role of liberal democracy and human rights in global security management called for a response from China from within the UN system. This required that China take its long-standing approach of pre-empting Western reform efforts in the UN to the next level.

In 1999, Samuel Kim noted that despite China's active participation in all UN issue areas, its substantive contribution to or impact on arms control and disarmament, economic, and environmental issues had been modest. Few UN conventions, agreements or reform proposals have been initiated or sponsored by China. Indeed, in the Human Rights Commission Beijing has successfully conducted divide-and-conquer diplomacy, pre-empting the introduction of even mild draft resolutions. One key to Beijing's success was its battle cry to developing countries that they would be next if they supported condemnation of China's human rights policies.[23] Ikenberry has pointed out that the liberal world order has sown its own seeds of discontent in the sense that the rise of non-Western states such as China is an artifact of its success. China's embrace of liberal market economic structures has ensured its rise but also allowed it to challenge US leadership. However, this challenge is not a contest about the basic rules and principles of the liberal international order. There is no competing global organizing logic to liberal internationalism. Rather, the contest is about gaining more authority and leadership within the existing order.[24] Ann Kent's analysis of China's successful revamping of the Sub-Commission on Prevention of Discrimination and Protection of Minorities and the Commission on Human Rights in the UN system reflects Ikenberry's argument. Following the sub-commission's criticism of the wide-scale abuse of human rights within Chinese territory in August 1989 in the wake of the Tiananmen crackdown in June 1989, China resurrected the non-interference argument. China positioned itself as a champion of developing countries, enabling Beijing to trade favors such as a human rights resolution on Iraq in the sub-commission for an agreement to overlook a resolution on China. Moreover, features of the sub-commission and the commission, such as the independence of experts, democratic interaction with NGOs, and an unspoken gentlemen's agreement on the allowable limits of diplomatic lobbying, have been openly challenged by China. On these grounds, China's impact on the international human rights regime is said to be potentially disruptive.[25]

Although disruptive in the intermediate term, in the liberal analysis China works within the existing regime of norms and this interaction engenders convergence between the norms of the international community and those of China in the long run. The liberal outlook gives rise to the assessment that, gradually, China is coming to recognize the importance of demonstrating consent with universal rules of conduct to enhance its claim to be a responsible power contributing to international peace and security.

Nye and Wang Jisi point out that although China's growing soft power in the form of its increasing engagement in multilateral institutions is received with mixed feelings in the US, China is using its soft power in ways that may help the US protect its overseas interests. For example, Beijing's quiet efforts to persuade the North Koreans to terminate their nuclear weapons program and to embark on an economic reform process facilitate US policy objectives on the Korean Peninsula. Likewise, Beijing's quiet diplomacy to persuade Myanmar's government to modify its behavior at home arguably paved the way for stabilizing the situation in that country. In Sudan, Western pressure for a UN presence, which was greatly resented by China, did not produce an outcome until Beijing successfully convinced Khartoum to accept such a measure.[26]

Indeed, liberal authors emphasize that in the long run Beijing will gradually adopt more and more liberal principles. One example is the calls for adjusting China's political structures that originate from demands from market economic actors for protection of property rights. Other examples include calls for the rule of law so as to offer acceptable means of handling private disputes, and compensation for expropriation of land to ensure that property ownership cannot be violated by the state. Hempton-Jones argues that liberal patterns in Beijing's foreign policy are embodied in a more relaxed attitude towards interdependence that takes two forms: an increase in cooperative behavior and a more flexible position towards external interference in state sovereignty. For example, China's attitude towards peacekeeping missions in Cambodia, Somalia and East Timor demonstrates that a hardline defense of absolute sovereignty is giving way to a more pragmatic stance that holds that sanctions and a certain level of interference in other states' internal affairs is acceptable.[27]

According to liberal analysts, China's resistance towards the liberal world order represents temporary and superficial glitches that are gradually being replaced by enhanced willingness to embrace liberal political elements. As this development crowds out Chinese resistance to liberal political principles such as the rule of law, democracy and freedom of speech, in time China will become a partner of the US in preserving the basic characteristics of the post-World War II order that preserves US global influence beyond its position of dominant global great power. Rather than an opponent to US global leadership, China will become increasingly supportive of the US as the central contributor to global security management because it serves Beijing's interests to preserve the status quo.

China as a maker of UN security management: the mid-2000s to the mid-2010s

As we reached the mid-2000s, alternative approaches to China's role in the UN, predominantly from the English school and constructivism, became more and more popular. These approaches parted company with the view that China is a reactive power whose UN policy focuses on responding to Western initiatives. A growing number of empirical developments reflected this theoretical shift that appeared to point in the direction opposite to realist and liberal analysis. China appeared to be an increasingly proactive power that might lay claim to being a status quo power with an interest in preserving existing frameworks of security management while gradually introducing elements of an alternative world order that deviates from Western demands.[28] China's security concerns—the survival of the CCP, China's sovereignty and territorial integrity, and China's continued economic and social development—remained the same. However, in contrast to the prior period, by the mid-2000s China had realized that it pays to use the UN to become a maker of world order. This change in attitude was marked by Chinese President Hu Jintao's announced Chinese vision of world order on the basis of the UN framework with his four-point plan for a harmonious world in 2005. The four points were, first, to uphold multilateralism to realize common security with the UN at the center of these efforts; second, to uphold mutually beneficial cooperation to achieve common prosperity; third, to uphold the spirit of inclusiveness to build a harmonious world based on coexistence between civilizations; and fourth, to promote UN reform so as to give the developing world a greater say in global security management.[29] Hu Jintao's UN-based vision of world order entails that for the foreseeable future, China will put a high premium on revising the existing world order to make it more amenable to Chinese interests rather than proposing an alternative founded on Chinese concepts of world order.

China's proactive UN role came on the heels of growing expectations of China's willingness to shoulder responsibility for security management by accepting more of the financial burden and by devising methods for how to address UN security issues. In the prior period, China was praised for offering assistance in times of crisis even if China's contributions were in reality negligible, such as its US$4 billion assistance to Thailand and other Asian countries in the financial crisis of 1997–8.[30] By contrast, by the mid-2000s the international community had become accustomed to China's growing influence. The attitude changed to predominantly seeing Beijing as a free rider that exercised influence on global security issues without contributing to solving them as required by a responsible great power. This attitude applies broadly, whether focusing on China's lack of support for the Philippines during the 2013 tsunami disaster or China's unwillingness in 2013 to endorse intervention in the Syrian Civil War.[31] At the 2009 UN Climate Change Conference, China insisted that economic and social development on the basis of national history and identity is a basic human right, implying rejection of binding emission standards because they will cripple industry and reduce the standard of living in the developing world. Although supported by developing countries such as Brazil, India and South Africa in its demand for revised normative foundations for climate change, China was pronounced the principal spoiler of the Copenhagen deal, which the developing countries led by the US had hoped would replace the Kyoto Protocol from 1997.[32]

China was no longer considered a new-comer that was given the benefit of the doubt when trying to demonstrate its willingness to perform as a responsible great power with obligations of global security management. On the contrary, China was seen as a power well on the way to economic and military great power status at the global level. As such, China is considered obliged to take into account the interests of other states in its pursuit of national interests. This change in attitude reflects the fact that China has become a power that actively pursues its own agenda in the UN, and this agenda is often at odds with the liberal agenda of the West.

The English school approach: the UN as a platform for two revisionist world orders

The emergence in the UN of two alternative versions of how to go about global security management, one Western-led and one Chinese-led, is reflected in the rise of the English school and constructivism as significant voices in the debate on the role of the UN in Chinese security. These perspectives provide new interpretations of China's role in the UN, reflecting that China might not be destined to either reject or embrace the existing global order, but will perhaps be somewhere in between these two extremes.

According to the English school, international anarchy engenders policy coordination between states to overcome the security dilemma with a view to protecting the common interests of states in maintaining international peace and security. The principal venue for states to coordinate policies and to establish patterns of interaction as rules of behavior that regulate right and wrong conduct is the UNSC. According to the English school, China's role in this forum has become one of taking the lead in revising the UN system according to a set of principles that differs from Western revisionist attempts without challenging the authority of the UN system as the principal forum for global security management. China goes to great lengths to ensure that its behavior and voting in the UNSC are not in breach of the basic principles of the UN system. Thereby, China demonstrates that it subscribes to a set of rules that has already been recognized by the international community as the universal framework for global security management. At the same time, Beijing promotes within-system adjustments to gradually move the UN in a direction that is more in line with its own views on how protection of the common interests of states in preserving international peace and security is best looked after.[33] This is reflected in Chinese writings on the UN, such as the analysis of China's UN diplomacy by Zhang Guihong and Feng Yuqiao. They argue that China's UN policy seeks to redress the imbalance between developed and developing countries by emphasizing the principles of sovereign equality and non-interference in internal affairs, the implementation of aid commitments by developed to developing countries, and by stressing the right to develop and exist.[34]

The current global order is not fundamentally challenged by China, but to preserve the existing global order it needs to be revised so as to accommodate Chinese interests. Clark argues that there is no prospect of China acting as a hegemon in its own right. As a consequence, at issue is whether an order can be designed by revising the existing order that also satisfies the particular preferences of both China and the US simultaneously. On the upside, China has pursued policies of regional integration and stability. However, these objectives may not be maintained in the long term, as indicated by the fact that China sees the current order as undesirably US-centric and focused on liberal-style interventionism. Instead, China privileges hyper-sovereignty values and has sought some reconfiguration of roles and responsibilities with the existing framework so as to impose greater restraints on the US and further liberate China.[35] According to Buzan, the harmonious world discourse can be seen as an attempt to package China's world view, suggesting that China has begun to take on board the common interests of states rather than merely focusing on China-specific national interests by emphasizing the value in preserving distinct civilizations, social systems and paths of development. However, this trend does not yet help China convince other international actors that its rise will be peaceful, and without peace it will be difficult for China to play a central role in global security management.[36] I argue that China's alternative world order concept is based on the common interest of developing states in peaceful coexistence. Peaceful coexistence encompasses non-interference in the internal affairs of others, mutual non-aggression, equality and mutual benefit, and mutual respect for sovereignty and territorial integrity. These principles correspond to the basic principles of the UN system, but China's interpretations of the rules differ from Western interpretations. Examples include China's veto of Western calls for intervening in Syria, and China's argument that regional and functional organizations such as the African Union (AU) and the International Atomic Energy Agency (IAEA) should play a greater role in defining when threats to international peace and security exist and in implementing security management.[37] Support for regionalization and specialization is intended to defer some of the UNSC's decision-making power to other institutions and geographical levels rather than to change existing power arrangements in a revolutionary manner. China recognizes that support for such changes might undo its growing influence in the UN system and even strengthen states that might turn out to be loyal to the Western liberal model.

A case in point is China's approach to the 2004 and 2005 proposal for changing the permanent membership of the UNSC. India, Brazil, Germany and Japan proposed that reform of the

UN system involve their admission as permanent members, arguing that the UNSC should more adequately represent the world's regions. China opposed Japanese membership, seeing Tokyo as a core member of the liberal West with designs on China, to prevent it from exercising growing power and influence in the international system. Beijing responded favorably to India's membership bid. However, China can support India at little cost as long as Washington opposes an expansion of the UNSC permanent membership. But in real terms, China provides India with little support for its demand, viewing New Delhi as an unreliable partner that has increased military and nuclear cooperation with Washington.[38]

According to English school analysts, China is concerned to maintain international peace and security to facilitate domestic social and economic development. China is not a revolutionary power, but rather a revisionist power in the sense that it intends to revise the existing world order to make it more amenable to Chinese interests and security concerns. Since China and the US have fundamental differences on how to interpret basic principles of international conduct, their agreement that the UN system is the basic political framework for world order appears less and less a solid basis for cooperation on global security management. Their different views on the interpretation of fundamental principles such as absolute sovereignty and non-interference in the internal affairs of states imply that their approaches to global security management differ too much to sustain unity on how to use the UN system for global security management in practice.

Some analysts argue that China has adopted a flexible approach to the principle of non-intervention, parting company with the demand for consent from host states.[39] However, systematic analysis of China's voting patterns and justifications for voting in specific cases reveals that Beijing has developed its own interpretation of the UN system that does not entail a flexible attitude towards absolute sovereignty or Beijing's departure from insistence on regime consent. Instead, China supports a principle of regionalization and functional specialization that seeks to defer security responsibility to regional levels and functional organizations. If calls for intervention as a result of perceived threats to international security are raised at these levels, China supports them, unless explicit demands for regime change are included. I have tested whether China has developed its own interpretation of the UN system by investigating China's response to the security issues on the UNSC agenda. In addition, I assess the voting patterns on UNSC agenda items to determine whether China has legitimacy for its interpretation of the UN system in the international community. The UNSC cases of Iran, Sudan, Myanmar, Libya and Syria are analyzed because they were on the agenda from the mid-2000s onwards when Beijing changed policy from a reactive preventive approach to a proactive revisionist policy. I conclude that China defends the old UN system of preserving the right of states to exercise authority over their external and internal policies. However, on the basis of this conservative effort, Beijing has succeeded in presenting a legitimate coexistence-style version of the UN system's principles that deviates from the interpretation of Western powers such as the US, the UK and France. In this sense, China is emerging as a maker rather than a recipient of international order. China's coexistence version of global order entails compromise because it combines Chinese interests in consent as a requirement for intervention and effective control as a basis of political authority and socio-economic development with the interests of non-Western developing countries in a regionalization of UNSC security management and in non-binding measures against severe breaches of civil and political rights. China's willingness to take into account the demands of developing countries for world order means that approximately half the UNSC member states, counting permanent as well as rotating members, adopt policies in line with Beijing's interpretation of the UN system.[40]

Liselotte Odgaard

Constructivism: the UN as a tool of identity formation

Constructivists tend to believe that China views UN policy instrumentally as an effective means of protecting China's security interests and the various elements of national identity that these encompass at a time when China is at a crossroads in defining its position in the international community. The UN sits well with China's narrative about peaceful development and the accompanying dictum that it is a status quo power with no intention of overthrowing the existing global order. At the same time, Beijing is concerned to promote the interests of developing countries so as to enhance their influence on the priorities in global security management. This fits China's identity as a non-Western developing country whose demands and interests tend to be ignored by the US and Europe. China's role as a rising developing power that is on the one hand concerned to reassure the international community of its peaceful intentions and on the other hand focused on joining forces with the developing countries because their interests are compatible with China's demands for revisions to the global order gives China an international position in between the established great powers and the developing world. This in-between position reflects the long-standing independent and alliance-free position of China from the Cold War, where China refrained from allying with the US and the Soviet Union. Instead, China carved out its own position and had its own vision of world order based on non-alignment, coexistence and socio-economic solidarity among developing countries.

Larson and Shevchenko emphasize that although China might appear to be following the prescriptions of liberal institutionalism, Beijing does not subscribe to the prevailing Western norms of individualism, human rights, transparency, democracy promotion, or humanitarian intervention. Beijing adheres to traditional norms of sovereignty and non-intervention in other states' internal affairs. For example, liberal institutionalists argue that increasing economic interdependence pressures states to adhere to international rules and norms, whereas China divides sovereignty rights into economic and political bundles, allowing intrusions into its sovereignty as embodied in the World Trade Organization's (WTO) rules and regulations while refusing to tolerate criticism of its human rights practices. China has increasingly taken on a more activist, constructivist world role that includes increased support for multilateralism, a policy that has reassured other states, enhanced China's global role, and increased its relative status. However, as mentioned above, China also has concerns that are at odds with US demands regarding world order.[41]

Richardson points out that China's involvement in UN peacekeeping enables China to frame the discourse regarding its foreign and security policy. China seeks to ensure acceptance of itself as a benign military power, countering perceptions of "the China threat" or "Chinese imperialism." To this end, peacekeeping is a low-cost, high-return activity. Instead of repeating desires for mutual peace, harmony and coexistence, peacekeepers demonstrate a commitment to world peace and development through their activities in peacekeeping missions.[42] According to Samuel Kim, China became a powerful supporter of UN peacekeeping because it had become an effective mechanism for finding political settlements for regional conflicts.[43] According to Chien-pin Li, by December 2010 over 2,000 Chinese military and police personnel participated in ten different UN peacekeeping operations, making China the top contributor among the five permanent members of the UNSC and fifteenth overall. Compared with the total of 120 personnel contributed in January 2003, the 2010 figure represents a more than 16-fold increase over an 8-year period.[44]

For some constructivists, China's shifting attitude towards UN peacekeeping indicates that the norm of human rights has been diffused into China, strengthening China's position as a responsible stakeholder of international order and consolidating its integration into the existing world order.⁴⁵ Other constructivists stress the possibility of a more Sino-centric China in future. According to these analysts, China will continue to make these contributions for as long as they are seen to assist China in demonstrating that it is a peaceful state acting responsibly in its contributions to global security management.⁴⁶ Indeed, China's current concern to demonstrate its peaceful rise holds the seeds of a Chinese-centric alternative that in time may induce Beijing to transform its revisionist within-system policy on world order to a revolutionary policy aiming at establishing a Chinese-style hegemonic world order.

In Callahan's view, the popularity of the Tianxia system as describing the Chinese vision of world order resonates with Beijing's foreign policy narrative about harmonious society. Since Chinese President Hu Jintao presented his plan for a harmonious world firmly embedded in the UN in 2005, this explanation of China's responsible engagement in the world has dominated the discourse.⁴⁷ However, Callahan argues that Tianxia is a utopia defined by order rather than freedom and it needs to be established and maintained through a world institution. In the interim, this may be the UN in a revised version as suggested by Hu Jintao, but this institution is limited by a worldview based on nation states. Ultimately, Tianxia is a proposal for a new hegemony where imperial China's hierarchical governance is up-dated for the twenty-first century.⁴⁸ Despite interesting similarities between the political vision of a harmonious society and the Tianxia concept of world order, it is difficult to establish empirically whether China's political leaders are inspired by the Tianxia ideas. The circumstantial evidence merely amounts to a temporal coincidence of the publication of Zhao Tingyang's bestselling work on Tianxia in 2005 and the announcement of political visions with compatible world views.

According to constructivist arguments, China is at a crossroads as regards its pursuit of world order. A struggle is taking place that is not merely about bureaucratic politics and organizational and personal power struggles. It is a more profound identity conflict about China's place in the world. On the one hand is the inward-looking, pluralistic tradition that calls for China to focus on its domestic development on the basis of own development path. Concomitant with this, China seeks international peace and security on the basis of multilateralism and greater influence for the developing world so as to distribute responsibility for world order to a grouping of states that has world order views that are compatible with those of China. On the other hand is the Sino-centric tradition of leader of the world that calls for China to focus on restoring the Chinese civilization as the center of governance and law. This would entail that China ultimately replaces the liberal ideal of democratic world government with a harmonious world that gives preference to a moral order based on global elite governance.

Conclusion

This chapter has argued that realists and liberalists depict the reactive part of China's UN policy that rose to prominence in the immediate aftermath of the Cold War and remained the dominant behavioral pattern until the mid-2000s. For offensive realists, this reactive role is interpreted as an appeasement policy assisting China in averting challenges to its economic and military rise to great power status. According to defensive realists, China uses the UN to ameliorate the security dilemma created by its economic and military rise by convincing other states that its growing relative power is not accompanied by intentions to overthrow the existing global order. Liberalists draw the opposite conclusion in explaining China's reactive UN policy by arguing that currently, disagreements prevail between China and the US about the direction the UN should take as the central forum for global security governance. However, these disagreements will gradually vanish as China is socialized into embracing the basic characteristics of the post-World War II order that serves to preserve US global influence beyond its superiority in economic and military capabilities. Whether the driving force behind China's reactive policy line in the UN in the immediate post-Cold War era is described as revolutionary offensive realist intentions, revisionist defensive realist motives or liberal status quo socialization, these approaches agree that China is not the mastermind of a post-Cold War UN-based order. Instead, China is jockeying for position in a UN the central characteristics of which have already been defined and which China has no interest in challenging.

The English school and constructivist approaches capture the activist Chinese UN policy that emerged from the mid-2000s onwards. For English school analysts, China's role in the UN constitutes an alternative to that of the liberal world order, but it is established on the same UN post-World War II framework. It becomes an alternative because China's prioritization and interpretation of the fundamental principles of the UN are fundamentally different. As such, it represents a different world order that changes the existing political framework from within. The constructivists take this analysis one step further by asking whether China is in the process of establishing a version of world order that is essentially Sino-centric, hence representing a new hegemonic project in which China defines the basic principles of international conduct. For the constructivists, the jury is still out as to whether China will end up traveling down the route of revisionist or revolutionary power. The answer depends on the extent to which the existing world order can accommodate China's interests and world outlook.

However convincing the arguments for the possibility of a prospective hegemonic project are, the current environment encourages China to remain on the revisionist path, promoting within-changes to the UN system for the foreseeable future. China remains by far the weaker power compared with the United States in economic and military terms. The Chinese UN engagement is based on Beijing's interest in protecting China against overseas interference and in maintaining international peace and stability while focusing on strengthening its capabilities and on maintaining coherence in a Chinese society that is increasingly marked by social and economic inequality. One reason for China's modest international ambitions is that China does not have a domestic state-society model that complements its model of international order. The harmonious society and Tianxia concepts remain rhetorical devices without much practical applicability. They have not been translated into essential political structures, such as feedback mechanisms from society to government, or into processes comparable to the use of elections to facilitate political succession. The lack of a domestic state-society model means that China has little to offer in suggesting how to solve the majority of conflicts on the UNSC agenda beyond proposing that these countries pursue their national and historic development path. Today most conflicts on the UNSC agenda concern domestic state-society relations and political structures that fail to deliver basic welfare for their citizens. China's domestic agenda and priorities makes Beijing's preference for a coexistence-style UN-based order likely to remain in place for the foreseeable future.[49]

The Chinese leader as of March 2013, President Xi Jinping, has announced that China needs to bring its own house in order first, then China needs to establish its position in its neighborhood, and only when this issue has been sorted out will China be ready to position itself at the global level.[50] Xi's priorities indicate that the inward-looking, pluralistically oriented China has priority. Hence, we should not expect any major changes to China's UN policy for the foreseeable future. Indeed, Xi's concern to bring China's own house in order may herald a return to the reactive role China played in the first decade and a half after the Cold War. However, this may just be an intermezzo where China catches its breath, preparing to determine if the world order as we know it is amenable to China's interests. The ongoing conflicts between China and its neighbors over rights and responsibilities in the South and East China Sea may be a test of the extent to which existing political frameworks remain useful for preserving international peace and security. At a more fundamental level, these conflicts may also reveal whether China continues to prioritize a coexistence-style order as suggested by the English school's community-based analysis or a revamped Sino-centric international moral hierarchy as suggested by constructivism's national-historical identity analysis.

Glossary

Beijing Consensus   China's economic development model
Bipolarity   Distribution of power with two centers of power
Chapter VII   UN Charter provision to take military and non-military action to restore international peace and security
Harmonious society   Societal balance and harmony
      héxié shèhuì 和谐社会
IAEA   International Atomic Energy Agency
Kyoto Protocol   The United Nations Framework Convention on Climate Change
Maoism   The teachings of Chinese leader Mao Zedong
      Máozédōng sīxiǎng 毛泽东思想
Multilateralism   Multiple countries working in concert on particular issues
Multipolarity   Distribution of power with more than two centers of power
Tianxia   All-under-Heaven，天下

Notes

1   The author wishes to thank the editors and Zhang Qingmin, Peter Viggo Jakobsen and Morten Hetmar Vestergaard for helpful comments. The author takes responsibility for any errors or omissions in this chapter.
2   Samuel S. Kim, "China and the United Nations," in Elizabeth Economy and Michael Oksenberg (eds), *China Joins the World: Progress and Prospects*, New York: Council on Foreign Relations Press, 1999, 42–89 has conducted a detailed analysis of China's remarkably few contributions to developing UN issue areas, often focusing instead on preventing measures such as human rights promotion from being taken.
3   Christopher Layne, "China's Role in American Grand Strategy: Partner, Regional Power, or Great Power Rival?" in Jim Rolfe (ed.), *The Asia-Pacific: A Region in Transition*, Honolulu: Asia-Pacific Center for Security Studies, 2004, 54–80 describes how China uses the UN as a tool for playing victim.
4   Robert A. Pape, "Soft Balancing against the United States," *International Security*, 30:1, 2005, 7–45 examines how China balances Washington by soft means such as trade and currency policies without directly challenging US preponderance.
5   Kim, "China and the United Nations."
6   Liselotte Odgaard, *China and Coexistence: Beijing's National Security Strategy for the Twenty-First Century*, Washington, DC: Woodrow Wilson Center Press/Johns Hopkins University Press, 2012 argues that China promotes within-system adjustments to gradually move the UN in a direction more compatible with China's demands for world order.
7   Deborah Welch Larson and Alexei Shevchenko, "Status Seekers: Chinese and Russian Responses to US Primacy," *International Security*, 34:4, 2010, 63–87 shows how China's UN policy is marked by China-centric outlooks on and models for the management of world order that are on central points in opposition to liberal institutionalism.
8   Samuel S. Kim, "China in and out of the Changing World Order," *World Order Studies Program Occasional Paper*, no. 21, Princeton: Princeton University Press, 1991, 2–3.
9   On September 6, 1991, the Soviet Union officially recognized the independence of the Baltic republics Estonia, Latvia and Lithuania. Cf. John Lewis Gaddis, *The Cold War*, London: Allen Lane, 2006, 237–57.
10 After the Cold War, China had border disputes with Tajikistan, Kyrgyzstan, Kazakhstan, Mongolia, Russia, Vietnam, Laos, India, Bhutan, South Korea, Japan and the Southeast Asian littoral states of the South China Sea. Of these, China's border disputes with Tajikistan, Kyrgyzstan, Kazakhstan, Mongolia, Russia and Laos have been resolved with permanent agreements. Some of its maritime disputes with Southeast Asian littoral states of the South China Sea have been shelved, but some of these, as well as China's boundary disputes with India, Bhutan, South Korea and Japan, remain unresolved. Cf. Odgaard, *China and Coexistence*, 87–8.

11 Chapter VII of the UN Charter provides that the UN Security Council determines the existence of any threat to the peace, breach of the peace or act of aggression and makes recommendations or decides what measures are to be taken. Under article 41, measures not involving the use of armed force, such as economic sanctions, can be taken. Under article 42, measures involving the use of armed force can be taken. Cf. Peter Malanczuk, *Akehurst's Modern Introduction to International Law*, seventh edn, London: Routledge, 1997, 388–9.
12 *Liberation Army Daily*, FBIS-CHI-1999–0609, May 26, 1999, 5.
13 Jonathan Haslam, *No Virtue Like Necessity: Realist Thought in International Relations since Machiavelli*, New Haven, CT: Yale University Press, 2002 gives an account of the central concepts and dynamics of realism.
14 Dingding Chen and Jianwei Wang, "Lying Low No More? China's New Thinking on the Tao Guang Yang Hui Strategy," *China: An International Journal*, 9:2, 2011, 195–216.
15 Layne, "China's Role in American Grand Strategy," 75–6.
16 Henry Kissinger, *A World Restored: Metternich, Castlereagh and the Problems of Peace 1812–1822*, London: Phoenix Press, 1957.
17 Philip C. Saunders, *China's Global Activism: Strategy, Drivers, and Tools*, Occasional Paper, Washington, DC: Institute for National Strategic Studies, National Defense University, 2006, 8–9, 15.
18 Pape, "Soft Balancing against the United States," 10, 42.
19 Michael D. Swaine and Ashley J. Tellis, *Interpreting China's Grand Strategy: Past, Present, and Future*, Santa Monica: RAND, 2000, 133–41.
20 Andrew J. Nathan and Robert S. Ross, *The Great Wall and the Empty Fortress: China's Search for Security*, New York: W.W. Norton, 1997, 190–1.
21 Lijun Yang, "On the Principles of Complementarity in the Rome Statute of the International Criminal Court," *Chinese Journal of International Law*, 4:1, 2005, 121–32.
22 Avery Goldstein, *Rising to the Challenge: China's Grand Strategy and International Security*, Stanford, CA: Stanford University Press, 2005, 184.
23 Kim, "China and the United Nations," 70–1.
24 G. John Ikenberry, "The Future of the Liberal World Order," *Foreign Affairs*, 90:3, 2011, 56–68.
25 Ann Kent, "China and the International Human Rights Regime: A Case Study of Multilateral Monitoring, 1989–1994," *Human Rights Quarterly*, 17:1, 1995, 1–47.
26 Joseph S. Nye Jr. and Wang Jisi, "Hard Decisions on Soft Power," *Harvard International Review*, 31:2, 2009, 21.
27 Justin S. Hempson-Jones, "The Evolution of China's Engagement with International Governmental Organizations: Toward a Liberal Foreign Policy?" *Asian Survey*, 45:5, 2005, 704.
28 This argument is made in detail in Liselotte Odgaard, "Peaceful Coexistence Strategy and China's Diplomatic Power," *The Chinese Journal of International Politics*, 6, 2013: 233–72.
29 H.E. Hu Jintao, Statement by the President of the People's Republic of China at the United Nations Summit, "Build Towards a Harmonious World of Lasting Peace and Common Prosperity" (translation), New York, 2005. Available online at www.un.org/webcast/summit2005/statements15/china050915eng.pdf (accessed January 29, 2014).
30 Ministry of Foreign Affairs of the People's Republic of China, "Pro-Active Policies by China in Response to Asian Financial Crisis," 2000. Available online at www.fmprc.gov.cn/eng/ziliao/3602/3604/t18037.htm (accessed January 24, 2014).
31 Megha Rajagopalan, "China's Meager Aid to the Philippines Could Dent Its Image," *Reuters*, 2013. Available online at www.reuters.com/article/2013/11/12/us-china-philippines-aid-idUSBRE9AB0LM20131112 (accessed January 24, 2014); Rick Gladstone, "Friction at the UN as Russia and China Veto another Resolution on Syrian Sanctions," *The New York Times*, July 19, 2012. Available online at www.nytimes.com/2012/07/20/world/middleeast/russia-and-china-veto-un-sanctions-against-syria.html?_r=0 (accessed January 24, 2014).
32 Gloria Jean Gong, "What China wants: China's Climate Change Priorities in a post-Copenhagen World," *Global Change, Peace & Security*, 23:2, 2011, 170–4.
33 Odgaard, *China and Coexistence*.
34 Zhang Guihong and Feng Yuqiao, "China's UN Diplomacy: 1971–2011," *Strategic Analysis*, 35:6, 2011, 973–81.
35 Ian Clark, "China and the United States: A Succession of Hegemonies?" *International Affairs*, 87:1, 2011, 26–7.
36 Barry Buzan, "China in International Society: Is 'Peaceful Rise' Possible?" *The Chinese Journal of International Politics*, 3, 2010, 5–36.

37 Odgaard, "Peaceful Coexistence Strategy and China's Diplomatic Power."
38 Odgaard, *China and Coexistence*, 118–9.
39 Miwa Hirono, "Using Model Cases to Guide the Chinese Courts," *China Policy Institute Blog*, April 7, 2014. Available at http://blogs.nottingham.ac.uk/chinapolicyinstitute/ (accessed April 8, 2014).
40 Ibid.
41 Larson and Alexei Shevchenko, "Status Seekers," 83–7.
42 Courtney J. Richardson, "A Responsible Power? China and the UN Peacekeeping Regime," *International Peacekeeping*, 18:3, 2011, 286–97.
43 Samuel S. Kim, "China in and out of the Changing World Order," 149.
44 Chien-pin Li, "Norm Entrepreneur or Interest Maximiser? China's Participation in UN Peacekeeping Operations, 2001–2010," *China: An International Journal*, 9:2, 2011, 313–27.
45 Jing Chen, "Explaining the Change in China's Attitude toward UN Peacekeeping: A Norm Change Perspective," *Journal of Contemporary China*, 18:58, 2009, 157–73.
46 Richardson, "A Responsible Power?"
47 Hu Jintao, "Build towards a Harmonious World of Lasting Peace and Common Prosperity," 2005.
48 William A. Callahan, "Chinese Visions of World Order: Post-hegemonic or a New Hegemony?" *International Studies Review*, 10:4, 2008, 749–61.
49 Odgaard, *China and Coexistence*, 181–202.
50 Teddy Ng, "Xi Sets Out Priorities for Foreign Policy," *South China Morning Post*, October 26, 2013. Available online at www.scmp.com/news/china/article/1340086/xi-sets-out-priorities-foreign-policy (accessed January 27, 2014).

Select bibliography

Buzan, Barry (2010) "China in International Society: Is 'Peaceful Rise' Possible?" *The Chinese Journal of International Politics*, 3

Callahan, William A. (2008) "Chinese Visions of World Order: Post-hegemonic or a New Hegemony?" *International Studies Review*, 10, no. 4

Chien-pin Li (2011) "Norm Entrepreneur or Interest Maximiser? China's Participation in UN Peacekeeping Operations, 2001–2010," *China: An International Journal*, 9, no. 2

Clark, Ian (2011) "China and the United States: A Succession of Hegemonies?" *International Affairs*, 87, no. 1

Dingding Chen and Jianwei Wang (2011) "Lying Low No More? China's New Thinking on the Tao Guang Yang Hui Strategy," *China: An International Journal*, 9, no. 2

Gaddis, John Lewis (2006) *The Cold War*, London: Allen Lane

Goldstein, Avery (2005) *Rising to the Challenge: China's Grand Strategy and International Security*, Stanford, CA: Stanford University Press

Gong, Gloria Jean (2011) "What China Wants: China's Climate Change Priorities in a post-Copenhagen World," *Global Change, Peace & Security*, 23, no. 2

Haslam, Jonathan (2002) *No Virtue Like Necessity: Realist Thought in International Relations since Machiavelli*, New Haven, CT: Yale University Press

Hempson-Jones, Justin S. (2005) "The Evolution of China's Engagement with International Governmental Organizations: Toward a Liberal Foreign Policy?" *Asian Survey*, 45, no. 5

Ikenberry, G. John (2011) "The Future of the Liberal World Order," *Foreign Affairs*, 90, no. 3

Jing Chen (2009) "Explaining the Change in China's Attitude toward UN Peacekeeping: A Norm Change Perspective," *Journal of Contemporary China*, 18, no. 58

Kent, Ann (1995) "China and the International Human Rights Regime: A Case Study of Multilateral Monitoring, 1989–1994," *Human Rights Quarterly*, 17, no. 1

Kim, Samuel S. (1991) "China in and out of the Changing World Order," *World Order Studies Program Occasional Paper*, no. 21, Princeton, NJ: Princeton University Press

Kim, Samuel S. (1999) "China and the United Nations" in Elizabeth Economy and Michael Oksenberg (eds) *China Joins the World: Progress and Prospects* (42–89), New York: Council on Foreign Relations Press

Kissinger, Henry (1957) *A World Restored: Metternich, Castlereagh and the Problems of Peace 1812–1822*, London: Phoenix Press

Larson, Deborah Welch and Alexei Shevchenko (2010) "Status Seekers: Chinese and Russian Responses to US Primacy," *International Security*, 34, no. 4

Layne, Christopher (2004) "China's Role in American Grand Strategy: Partner, Regional Power, or Great Power Rival?" in Jim Rolfe (ed.), *The Asia-Pacific: A Region in Transition* (54–80), Honolulu: Asia-Pacific Center for Security Studies

Lijun Yang (2005) "On the Principles of Complementarity in the Rome Statute of the International Criminal Court," *Chinese Journal of International Law*, 4, no. 1

Malanczuk, Peter (1997) *Akehurst's Modern Introduction to International Law*, seventh edn, London: Routledge

Nathan, Andrew J. and Robert S. Ross (1997) *The Great Wall and the Empty Fortress: China's Search for Security*, New York: W.W. Norton

Nye, Joseph S. Jr. and Wang Jisi (2009) "Hard Decisions on Soft Power," *Harvard International Review*, 31, no. 2

Odgaard, Liselotte (2012) *China and Coexistence: Beijing's National Security Strategy for the Twenty-First Century*, Washington, DC: Woodrow Wilson Center Press, Johns Hopkins University Press

Odgaard, Liselotte (2013) "Peaceful Coexistence Strategy and China's Diplomatic Power," *The Chinese Journal of International Politics*, 6

Pape, Robert A. (2005) "Soft Balancing against the United States," *International Security*, 30, no. 1

Richardson, Courtney J. (2011) "A Responsible Power? China and the UN Peacekeeping Regime," *International Peacekeeping*, 18, no. 3

Saunders, Philip C. (2006) *China's Global Activism: Strategy, Drivers, and Tools*, Occasional Paper, Washington, DC: Institute for National Strategic Studies, National Defense University

Swaine, Michael D. and Ashley J. Tellis (2000) *Interpreting China's Grand Strategy: Past, Present, and Future*, Santa Monica: RAND

Zhang Guihong and Feng Yuqiao (2011) "China's UN Diplomacy: 1971–2011," *Strategic Analysis*, 35, no. 6

14
The paper partnership
Security in Sino-European relations

Jonathan Holslag

The political dimension of the Sino-European relationship develops rapidly on paper, slowly in practice. But an interesting recent evolution is that China has become more eager to add security issues to the bilateral agenda. In 2013, for example, China conveyed to the institutions in Brussels a long note with proposals to strengthen the partnership in the next 6 years. Security figured as a top priority in that note. This chapter first evaluates to what degree Europe and China managed to cooperate on security affairs since the establishment of their strategic partnership in 2003. (For the sake of readability, I use "Europe" instead of "European Union.") While exchanges have multiplied and a few first concrete steps are evaluated positively, the overall balance remains disappointing, in Beijing's view. In spite of many common interests, there is no evidence that security is becoming a solid pillar of the partnership. The second part of the chapter discusses the prospects for closer cooperation with a particular focus on what China expects from its European partner. Beijing has many reservations about Europe as a security actor and its recent problems have only strengthened that skepticism.

This is an empirical chapter. It does not seek to contribute to the major theoretical debates about international relations. Instead, its primary goal is to add to the rich debate about the Sino-European relations and to provide some specific insights to the general observation that, for all the dialogues and exchanges, the partnership is in rather bad shape and does not weigh a great deal on the course of international events. In this way, it could also be of use to better understand how China is responding to a more challenging strategic environment and to what extent the partnership with Europe could give it more maneuverability at times of growing tensions in Asia. I will draw on a series of conversations that took place in the previous 5 years. Most of these were informal conversations with experts whom I met in Brussels or Beijing. The chapter also reviews a broad range of articles from Chinese experts. I choose articles mostly from experts with access to policy makers or published in outlets close to the government.

The state of cooperation

From a Chinese viewpoint, it is clear why Europe matters to its security. A united Europe could be a more independent Europe, less inclined to trail in the wake of the United States, and better able to help China diversify its relationships at a time of growing geopolitical claustrophobia in the Pacific. This was the calculus present in the Three Worlds Theory of Mao Zedong, the ideals of a New World Order of Deng Xiaoping, Jiang Zemin's fixation with multipolarity, and the eagerness of the following political generations to continue to invest in a strategic partnership that has had steep ups and downs. Even in the absence of strong political cooperation, Europe remained crucial to keeping China's growth on track and thus also for maintaining domestic stability and regime security. In 1990, Europe purchased about 10 percent of China's exports. By 2000, this was 16 percent.[1] In 2012, after the passing of the ravaging Eurozone Crisis, Europe still absorbed 17 percent of China's total exports. Since the turn of the century, the trade surplus with Europe has stood at about 3 percent of China's economic output.[2] Europe also remained the most important provider of technology—ranging from knowhow in the pharmaceutical and car industries to technology to build planes, turbines for ships, and satellites. This way, Europe has contributed a great deal to both China's industrial policies and its military modernization.

From a European viewpoint, it is much less obvious how China contributes to its security. Some European leaders did echo China's calls for a multipolar world, but that was at the time of America's blatant excess of unilateralism during the confusing episode of Operation Iraqi Freedom. Those noises faded soon afterward. China's rise now makes European leaders rather nervous about the reluctance of the United States to maintain its presence in the Middle East, as Washington prioritizes its Pacific security interests. This not only makes it less certain whether the comfortable security umbrella of the United States will be there when the next crisis breaks out, but also makes politicians fret about what to do in case the Pacific situation between China and the United States turns violent. The rise of China does not herald the end of the treasured transatlantic security partnership, but implies that it will come with a greater price tag. Meanwhile, China has not been very helpful in alleviating Europe's economic uncertainty, uncertainty that increasingly nourishes political fragmentation and undermines the very fundaments of the European project. The persistent trade deficit means that China is not creating external demand. Beijing's gesture of buying government debt is barely a quick fix that saddles Europe with more external debt and helps Chinese exporters more than European industries. If that were not enough, China is also seen as a spoiler of Europe's aspirations as a normative power, defying many of its norms bilaterally and in international organizations.

The result of this chasm is a kind of partnership in which Europe and China exchange more and more, but seem to become less and less able to identify which specific common security interests the partnership serves in the long run.

To be sure, talks have resulted in a series of broadly defined common interests, of the kind that one could insert in any bilateral partnership without committing oneself extensively. The best way to identify these interests is to glance through the joint statements that China and Europe customarily issue after each annual summit meeting (Table 14.1). Between 2001 and 2013, 13 such statements were released. The security concern highlighted most frequently was the nuclear program of North Korea, followed by non-proliferation and disarmament, terrorism, the situation in the Middle East, Africa, and Iran. Piracy became prominent in the statement of 2009. So far, the interests are on paper, but what does this mean in practice? In general, it implies that Chinese and European leaders often clarify their positions during summit meetings and discuss the issues during the more focused strategic dialogues, which were elevated to state counsellor and commission vice-president level in 2010. But even in that high-level strategic dialogue, most of the interaction remains limited to the clarification of interests and interpretations.[3] This is also true at the working level. Chinese officials in Brussels come to visit their counterparts much more frequently, to solicit information about the European take on security issues and to share their concerns. Yet, again, this usually has no direct consequences on the ground. Let us go through the common security priorities one by one.

Table 14.1 Overview of security priorities in the joint statements following Sino-European summits. The summit of 2011 was postponed to 2012

	2001	2002	2003	2004	2005	2006	2007	2008	2009	2010	2012	2012	2013
North Korea	1	1	1	1	1	1	1	1	1	1		1	1
Non-proliferation	1		1	1	1	1	1	1	1	1		1	1
Terrorism		1	1	1			1	1				1	1
Middle East	1	1	1				1	1				1	1
Africa						1	1	1	1	1	1	1	1
Myanmar			1	1						1		1	1
Piracy											1	1	1
Balkans	1						1						
South Asia		1							1				
Iraq				1									
Asian regional security							1						

Note: Joint statements 2001–13.

Even though North Korea is at the top of common security concerns, China hardly considers Europe an interlocutor on this matter. When North Korea withdrew from the Non-Proliferation Treaty in 2003, China briefly took an interest in European encouragement for the Six-Party Talks, but that ended when some member states, such as France and the United Kingdom, started repeating and backing American calls for more sanctions and a stronger response to new missile launches. In general, Chinese officials are appreciative of Europe's support for the Six-Party Talks, its financial contribution to the Korean Peninsula Energy Development Organization (KEDO) before that organization was shut down in 2013, its aid to the International Atomic Energy Agency (IAEA) in its efforts to verify North Korean nuclear dismantlement, and the implementation of measures decided by the six.[4] In the UN Security Council, the European permanent and temporary members hardly play a role. The bargaining on the important Resolution 1,718 (14 October 2006), which first imposed sanctions on North Korea following its first nuclear test, was a matter solely between China, the US, Russia, and Japan. The only direct attempt of the European Union to engage China occurred with regard to the situation of North Korean refugees in the border area, but it failed to get Beijing's green light for admitting the UN High Commissioner for Refugees into the area.

China and Europe have made it routine practice to flag non-proliferation and disarmament as a joint security priority. For China, Europe is a partner to strengthen multilateral cooperation on the matter and a more forthcoming interlocutor than the United States.[5] In 2004, the two sides agreed on a lengthy bilateral statement. This document was significant for China, not the least because Europe backed China's accession to the Missile Technology Control Regime, against the wishes of the United States.[6] China for its part recognized Europe's role in the Asian Regional Forum and vowed to support European initiatives within the forum in the field of non-proliferation. Europe did participate in the Inter-Sessional Meetings on Non-Proliferation of the ASEAN Regional Forum (ARF), but its role was modest at best.[7] For China, the main focus was on the competition with the United States for leadership in these meetings. Chinese officials have largely been unaware of the European Strategy against the Proliferation of Weapons of Mass Destruction of 2013 and the millions of euros of European support for non-proliferation and arms control initiatives in Southeast, South, and Central Asian countries.[8]

Since 2003, both sides have fine-tuned their positions on Iran at bilateral summits, as well as in exchanges between the Council Secretariat and the Chinese Ministry of Foreign Affairs.[9] China and the European Union recognized the double joint interest in, on the one hand, preventing Tehran from developing nuclear arms and avoiding a diplomatic collision with Washington and, on the other, continuing to trade with the Central Asian country. This fostered Chinese support for an initial strategy that was cautious about sanctions and generous with incentives. China overtly backed Europe in October 2004, when it proposed to offer Iran more economic cooperation and to deliver light-water reactors in return for the suspension of uranium enrichment and full access for the IAEA. In 2005 it also urged the Iranian government to resume the stalled talks with Europe. But within this seemingly cooperative framework, the situation was that Europe sought to work with Iran while prioritizing remaining best friends with Washington, whereas China sought to work with the EU while remaining Tehran's best friend.[10] This meant that Beijing did not refrain from resisting Europe, for instance in 2004, when it blocked a resolution requesting Iran to voluntarily cease enrichment, or in 2006, when it opposed tough sanctions in a Chapter VII-based resolution that was backed by France and the UK. Moreover, Beijing was well aware of the fact that the E3—the exchanges between France, the United Kingdom, and Germany on Iran—was often more a matter of E1+1+1, as the UK, France, and Germany did not always interpret their interests in the same way. In July 2007, China successfully reached out to Berlin to deflect new sanctions backed by the UK and the US.[11] Those sanctions did get through in 2008, though, and were followed by even tougher European measures at the beginning of 2009. China opposed both of them. "Europe's approach is not conducive to a peaceful solution," Cui Hongjian of the China Institute of International Studies wrote. "Even if its policy is not exactly the same as the American position, it tends to follow the United States on the issue of sanctions."[12] The rift remained after Catherine Ashton was appointed lead negotiator on behalf of the permanent members of the UN Security Council (P5) and Germany, which was added as an important non-Security Council stakeholder. In 2010, China disapproved of European unilateral sanctions. In 2011, it brushed aside the criticism of Catherine Ashton that Chinese companies were circumventing sanctions. In 2012, it accused Europe of intensifying confrontation when it imposed new measures. The divide only narrowed when Iran itself opted for concessions, after the elections of 2013.

Other Middle Eastern issues were also marked by frequent exchanges but limited cooperation. The region has been present on the agenda throughout almost all high-level bilateral talks. In the region itself, there are regular exchanges between embassies and delegations. In Lebanon, peacekeepers from China and European member states have worked side by side. Still, differences remained. With regard to Lebanon, China and the European permanent members of the United Nations Security Council coordinated well in the preparation of Resolution 1,701, which called on Lebanon and Israel to respect a ceasefire, and vowed to send troops to monitor the cessation of hostilities between Israel and Hezbollah. In the following years, however, a rift emerged over Hezbollah. In 1999, when the United States had already put the group on its own list of Foreign Terrorist Organizations, member states such as the United Kingdom and the Netherlands followed suit and spearheaded an internal European agreement to label Hezbollah a terrorist group. The Chinese government openly criticized this decision, with Chinese experts explaining that Hezbollah was not the root cause of the conflict and that European countries were yielding to pressure from the United States and Israel without engaging with the complexity of the situation.

Similar differences existed with regard to the conflict between Israel and Palestine. Even if China has maintained close relations with Tel Aviv, it has been a more energetic supporter of the Palestinian cause. It was one of the first to support Palestine's bid for membership of the United Nations and also resisted the calls of Israel and the United States to consider Hamas a terrorist group. Since the turn of the century, China has largely maintained its line of pragmatism and restraint. Since 2013, however, it has signaled that it wants to become more involved, by proposing its own, albeit vague, four-point proposal and requesting membership of the Middle East Quartet, formed by the United States, Russia, Europe, and the United Nations, with former British Premier Tony Blair serving as its special envoy. The four-point proposal called for an independent Palestinian state, to accelerate negotiations, to uphold the principle of land for peace, and for a greater involvement of the international community to support talks and to increase assistance to Palestine.[13] It is not clear what the intentions behind this shift are, whether it represents a genuine attempt to broker a deal, an effort to put the policy of "building new great power relations" into practice by becoming more actively engaged in world affairs, a consequence of pressure by other countries in the region, or a combination of these elements.

It is clear, though, that China does not reckon Europe to be of much importance. "The solution for the Middle East passes through Washington, no longer through the European capitals," an official stated.[14] Officials and experts point to the deep divisions between European member states. Jiaotong University's Zhang Xuekun in this regard spoke of a growing expectations-capabilities gap. "It now merely provides economic assistance to American policies in the Middle East{...}The EU can often not speak with one voice. Consider Ireland, which has a traditional fixation on the fate of the Palestinians because of its own colonial experience. The Netherlands traditionally has a pro-Israel stance, while Greece and Sweden are in the pro-Arab faction mostly because of domestic politics. Germany, Austria, and Poland too are concerned about the Palestinian question, but the legacy of World War II has made them also sensitive to the fate of the Jews."[15] Chen Shuangqing, Director of Middle East Studies at the China Institute of Contemporary International Relations, characterized Europe's policy towards the Middle East as inconsistent, sluggish, and opportunistic.[16]

Then there was Syria. Chinese officials and experts consider Europe's response to the Syrian pandemonium a mess and do not deem Europe an interlocutor of interest. "Even though the unrest in Syria directly affects the economic and security interests of Europe's southern flank, the European countries generally did not get any further than the ineffective quick fix to overthrow the Assad regime as quickly as possible."[17] Europe's impotence is attributed to a lack of interest, a lack of internal coordination, a lack of a vision for Iraq, and the absence of a solid relationship with regional powers such as Turkey.[18] The failure to broker a consensus between the member states on arming Syrian rebels in 2013 only confirmed these perceptions. Chinese officials have explained their government's four-point proposal for Syria to senior European counterparts, but this was about as far as dialogue got. At the same time, Beijing obdurately declined resolutions in the Security Council that paved the way for an armed intervention and watered down sanctions. It explained to European officials that this would aggravate regional insecurity and would make religious extremism uncontrollable.

Security in Africa was added to the agenda in 2006 primarily as a result of China's growing visibility as an investor and the crises in Darfur and Zimbabwe. While the European Union had imposed sanctions on these two countries' governments, it also sought to persuade Beijing to exert pressure. Both sides recognized the need for peace and stability. China showed itself prepared to discuss the matters with the European Commission, the Council Secretariat, the European Delegation in Beijing, and European diplomats in New York. In 2007, Special Envoy for Darfur Liu Guijin called on Brussels. He also participated in a meeting of the contact group on Darfur in Paris. But cooperation on Darfur and Zimbabwe did not take off. Even today, in the context of growing tensions in South Sudan, China does not consider Europe an important partner. China is the largest investor in the oil sector in South Sudan and relies on a pipeline to neighboring Sudan to transport its oil to the Red Sea. On the one hand, it finds that the United

States is having a much greater say in the new country: "South Sudan is America's baby," one official told me. On the other hand, it finds that Europe has no proper strategy towards the security problems in Sudan. This is somewhat different in the cases of Mali and the Central African Republic. In 2012, China took the initiative to consult with France on the problems in Mali and quickly offered to send peacekeepers. In 2014, China also maintained close contacts with France in the run-up to its intervention in the Central African Republic and also pledged peacekeepers. A senior Chinese official was very critical, though, of the fact that the rest of Europe struggled to provide the 600 promised troops in support of the French mission.[19] In general, Chinese officials and experts blamed Europe for trying to outmaneuver China, using human rights and good governance as a pretext. They insisted that Europe's formula of democracy and transparency does not work in an African context.[20] As, usual they were also well aware of the internal divisions and the tension between norms and commercial interests. More importantly, Beijing insisted that the policy proposals to promote security and peace ought to come from Africa and not from Europe. An important official said, "I think Europe should first treat Africa as an equal partner, not as its backyard. It should stop emphasizing that it contributed to Africa, and recognize what Africa contributed to Europe. This attitude prevents you from building trust in Africa. It really requires a mentality change. In the triangular relationship, your confidence in cooperation with Europe depends on the confidence that Africa has in Europe."[21]

Regarding terrorism, the European Union and China both supported the preparation of the United Nations Global Counter-Terrorism Strategy in 2006 and the United Nations Counter-Terrorism Implementation Task Force. Leaders continued to back the drafting of a Comprehensive Convention on International Terrorism and to highlight the need for multilateral cooperation in the fight against terrorism. There have been sporadic meetings with the European anti-terrorism coordinator, but without concrete outcomes. China has approached individual member states, such as France and the United Kingdom, for information about Al-Qaeda in the Islamic Maghreb (AQIM) and Al Shabaab in the Horn of Africa.

Exchanges in the field of anti-piracy were more operational. Since its arrival in the Gulf of Aden in 2008, Chinese navy officers have frequently visited European vessels and European officers Chinese vessels. For the EUNAVFOR, the European Naval Force, it was important from the start to try to engage China, but China refused to participate in the so called International Recognized Transit Corridor, a stretch of water in which merchant ships would be protected by a multilateral naval force, and the Group Transit System. Instead, and frustrating European participants, the Chinese navy chose to protect civilian ships separately by forming convoys. These were primarily meant for Chinese flagged ships, but open to others if they registered their transit with the Chinese government. Europe was also disgruntled because China initially remained reluctant to escort ships of the World Food Program and did not want to participate in Shared Awareness and Deconfliction (SHADE), an initiative to enhance coordination in anti-piracy. That changed. In 2009, a Chinese delegation was invited to discuss communication at the Operation Headquarters in Northwood, UK. A few months later, the EUNAVFOR provided support to the Chinese flotilla in the investigation of a suspicious vessel. The Chinese commander also paid several visits to the flagship of the European mission and exchanged insights with the commander of EUNAVFOR. In October, European patrol aircraft helped to track a hijacked Chinese bulk carrier that was not registered with the Maritime Security Center Horn of Africa, based at Northwood. China also accepted to communicate via MERCURY, an alert system operated by the Maritime Security Center Horn of Africa of the European Union. During one of the exchanges that year the European force commander also proposed that it would consider China as a co-chair or chair of the SHADE. In January 2010, it indeed became the SHADE's chair. In 2012, after prodding by the EU, it assumed the protection of some World Food Program shipments. To date, four such ships have been escorted between Mombasa and Somali ports.[22] Exchanges became ever more frequent. Helicopters were used to transfer officers between Chinese and European ships. Boarding teams held joint exercises.

Six years after China's first deployment in the Indian Ocean, its ships still do not participate in the Recognized Transit Corridor, but European officials and senior military officers that participated in EUNAVFOR are generally positive about the growing confidence. "It is clear that China is still testing the water, that its commanders in the Gulf of Aden have not much autonomy, and that they struggle with communication, but they are very eager to reach out to us," said one officer who was in command of the EUNAVFOR. "We were always received very well and these limited forms of cooperation have certainly allowed us to explain what Europe's role in international security is about."[23] Another commanding officer explained, "They always work very carefully and are afraid to lose face. They take time and only accept a proposal if they are sure that it will work."[24] Other European officers reported eavesdropping, ranging from radar scanning to communication taps. Chinese officials are also appreciative of Europe's willingness to reach out to China and recognize it as an important partner. Experts are more critical, though. On the one hand, they state that Europe is perhaps too eager to show its flag, but reluctant to tackle the roots of the piracy problem. "As long as the economy remains in tatters, the piracy problem will never be solved."[25] "It is the meddling of Western countries in the internal affairs of Somalia that has caused the civil war and the chaos of today," writes another academic, "sending warships can only be a temporary solution."[26] On the other hand, it is argued that some states, especially the United States and India, use the piracy problem as a pretext for strengthening their naval presence along strategic choke points. In that power play, Europe plays much less of a role.[27]

Future

The Sino-European partnership looks impressive on paper, but is modest in reality. That observation is not new. But could the two parties do better? What does China expect from its security cooperation with Europe? In 2013, the Chinese government submitted to the European Commission a long list of proposals to strengthen the partnership. That was a rather new phenomenon. Until then, it had been the European side that usually made proposals, with China being reluctant to accept them. What made this gesture even more noteworthy was the fact that Beijing put security up front. After a long period of deliberation, the result was a joint agenda with 16 pages of priorities and proposals for making strategic cooperation stronger by 2020. Again, security emerged at the beginning of the paper. Few of the 13 priorities in the security sections were anything new. They related to the strengthening of existing dialogues or the identification of shared principles: multilateralism, a rules-based global economic order, and counter-proliferation. The paragraph on cyber security did not go beyond the existing and rather unproductive dialogue. More concrete were the proposals to organize joint police training, to conduct more counter-piracy exercises, to conduct joint research in the Arctic, to share expertise in international law with regard to maritime safety, and to assist each other in providing humanitarian aid. As regards military cooperation, the only commitment was to "hold regular dialogues on defense and security policy, increase training exchanges, and gradually raise the level of EU-China dialogue and cooperation on defense and security, advancing towards more practical cooperation."[28]

This is thus an agenda of small steps. It was the result of China's wish for progress—but gradual progress—and to circumvent sensitive security issues in Asia, as well as of the reluctance of several European member states to give too much credence to China's peaceful intentions. But will that be enough to reduce mutual doubts and distrust? On China's side there remains a very pronounced lack of confidence when it comes to Europe's role as an international actor.

When the Lisbon Reform Treaty, which gave more responsibilities to the European institutions, entered into force in 2009, many Chinese officials and spectators gave it the benefit of the doubt.[29] Today, however, these doubts have only become more pronounced. There is skepticism about the sufficiency of some of the efforts to improve the governance of the internal market and the monetary union to ward off a new crisis. Zhou Hong, one of China's most prominent students of European affairs, asserted that the supranational method of decision making was again making way to intergovernmental negotiations and that this would probably not address the "lack of an effective mechanism or authority to solve new problems."[30] Others assume that Europe's economic weakness and social uncertainty will strengthen Eurosceptic and nationalist parties and make it even harder for the EU to get its act together. Professors Pang Zhongying and Bo Yongguang, for example, argue that the return to sovereign states in Europe could lead to the collapse of the Union and "a Balkanization" of the region.[31] Economic problems and debt have reduced the attention to international issues, increased the differences between the member states, and made it harder to sustain defense spending, asserted Xu Long, a Europe expert at the China Institute of International Studies, in a very incisive paper about the impact of the Eurozone Crisis on its foreign policy.[32] But there is more. Europe's economic problems have also made its leaders more concerned about the structural trade deficit with China. Trade has been the main pillar of the Sino-European relationship, but this pillar is now showing cracks. After the European Commission began to investigate alleged dumping practices of Chinese producers of solar panels and telecommunications equipment in 2012, Chinese officials accused Europe of protectionism and experts argued that more protectionism would follow if Europe remained stuck in its economic trouble.

A related question is whether the economic distress is encouraging a stronger integration of Europe's defense capabilities. Chinese experts have identified many problems with European defense cooperation. The previous enlargement has led to even more complexity in decision making and operational planning.[33] Many opportunities were missed to integrate European defense industries and to produce equipment more efficiently. It also remains difficult to overcome the different geopolitical orientations of the main member states. The Lisbon Reform Treaty has not changed that. European countries are also slow to learn from humiliating military

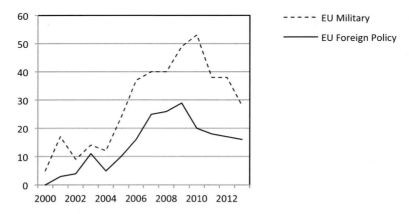

Figure 14.1 Chinese academic interest in EU military and EU foreign policy. Number of academic papers responding to "EU military" *(oumeng junshi)* and "EU foreign policy" *(oumeng waijiao zhengce)* in the largest database of Chinese papers: www.wanfangdata.com.cn

Source: Wanfang database (www.wanfangdata.com.cn).

power gaps in previous operations on the Balkans, in Libya, in Mali, and so forth. Even the measures that were prepared ahead of the European Defense Summit in December 2013 and the ones that were ultimately approved were widely considered insufficient.[34] As a commentator in a popular current affairs review writes, "The Summit did make some progress on capability, but not on mission and strategy{. . .}that leaves France often alone to secure the European periphery."[35] But even with regard to military capabilities, experts question whether Europe can fill the gaps in cyber security, in space, and in airlift.[36]

As a result, China finds it difficult to decide whom to engage. Dialogues with the European institutions are useful, but it is often hard to anticipate what they can deliver.[37] China has interacted with the European Military Staff, responsible for coordinating CFSP missions, but it is small and has limited capacity to develop cooperation. It has also interacted with the command structures of the European anti-piracy mission in the Indian Ocean, to its satisfaction, but for other operations, such as in Mali, it deems it more relevant to approach the lead nation, in this case France, or individual contributors. France has become a central and respected interlocutor for China. There are frequent exchanges on concrete hotspots in Africa between the capitals and on the ground. NATO also remains important. NATO itself has set up an outreach program to China, but Chinese officials and military officers in general are much more intrigued by NATO than by the EU's defense policy. The military section in the Chinese Mission to the European Union often spends more time following NATO than interacting with Europe. Incoming delegations of officials and think tankers are often uninterested in visiting European institutions, but very eager to call on the NATO headquarters.

This is not without reason. It is NATO that is perceived as the hard power part of Europe and it is NATO also that shows how important the United States remains in Europe's strategic orientation. China does not expect Europe to choose a more independent course from the United States. The Transatlantic Free Trade agreement is considered an indication of Europe's inclination to balance against China, at least in economic terms. Many scholars and experts have referred to it as an attempt of the United States to create a bloc to balance against China, a bloc that allows it to reindustrialize, to shape the new global economic regime, and to set the standards for new technologies.[38] Chinese experts find it unlikely that Europe will successfully develop its own, autonomous foreign and security policy. They notice how, despite the challenges in its neighborhood, European countries seem to be very keen on joining the United States in its so called pivot to Asia. In 2011, Zhao Junjie, an expert at the China Academy of Social Sciences, published a book titled *Is the Wolf Coming? The Strategic Adjustment of NATO and the EU Common Defense and Their Impact on China's Security Environment*. The monograph, with an introduction by a vice minister of the International Department of the Central Committee, argued that America was using both NATO and the European Union to prepare a containment strategy.[39] A paper written by Zhang Jian, the director of European studies at the China Institute of Contemporary International Relations, argued that Europe has no chance to play a role of importance in Asian security affairs, but that the fact that it seems to believe that it can play such role alongside the United States shows how backward its strategic thinking is. The United States' policy of entering Asia united with Europe (联欧入亚, *lan Ou ru Ya*) will end in misery, he concludes, because Europe will be completely powerless as soon as major conflicts break out in the Middle East or Russia becomes more aggressive. This was said before the annexation of the Crimea.[40] Europe's inclination to follow the United States is also mocked in the context of the arms embargo. The embargo was imposed in 1989, in the wake of the Tiananmen Crisis, and has been maintained since, even though it has been less and less clear why. Europe insists that China has to improve its human rights record, but fails to explain what exactly that entails, apart from initial statements that it related to China's signing of the UN Human and Civil Rights Convention. More recently,

Europe has informally signaled that the lifting of the arms embargo is related to transparency in military affairs and restraint in regional disputes. But China knows very well that the main stumbling block is the American veto and that several member states are willing to let the embargo go.

China's assessment of Europe's response to the recent security crises in its neighborhood is merciless. Officials just do not understand why Europe is trying to be recognized as a global actor when it cannot secure its own backyard. The response to the Arab Spring, as we have seen before, confirmed that skepticism. "In the wake of the crisis in the Middle East and Northern Africa," writes one expert, "Europe tried to show the world its hard power and its diplomatic position{. . .}but this was all bereft of any strategic vision."[41] Posited another academic, "From the current unrest in North Africa and the Middle East, we can conclude that it will take a huge cost and effort to achieve some basic goals{. . .}Europe's policy is still, to a large extent, influenced by the United States because the latter retains its traditional political and military dominance."[42] Similar comments were made on Europe's relations with Eastern Europe. In regard to the Ukrainian crisis, Chinese observers noticed that, once again, America was taking the lead in sanctions, but that Europe would face most of the consequences. "Once the situation gets out of hand," an article in *Beijing Youth Daily* argued, "Europe will bear the consequences, while the United States has no such burden."[43] A review published by the International Department of the Communist Party characterized Europe's response as embarrassing and inconsistent.[44] Europe is riding a tiger, *Xinhua News Agency* stated; its sanctions will only reduce its influence further and make Russia turn to other influential economies, perhaps Asian ones.[45] Experts trace the causes of the Ukrainian crisis to a dysfunctional neighborhood policy: too many conditions and not enough engagement.[46] The Eurozone Crisis has only made that problem worse, reducing trade and investment. "By contrast, Russia could be more generous in its economic concessions."[47]

But it is not just the negative perception of Europe's role that will limit cooperation. Chinese officials also acknowledge that their own government is not yet very keen on expanding its role in security affairs beyond its neighborhood. It is true that the leadership has acknowledged the importance of protecting overseas interest and that this is not even part of the main mission of the People's Liberation Army. Yet, by and large, the attention for the Middle East and Africa remains very limited. Officials report that the leaders tend to give the following instruction: maintain our economic presence, prevent damage to our image, and avoid casualties at the lowest cost. In practice that means evacuating expatriates whenever unrest breaks out. "At the moment there is not much of a security policy towards Africa that fills the gap between advancing our economic interests and dispatching peacekeepers," explained a senior official, "and even those peacekeepers are often sent to show the international community that we are responsible. There is no real strategy behind it."[48] The 2020 Agenda shows that there is some awareness of the common interests obtaining between Europe and China. There cannot be a new Silk Road between Europe and China without making it a secure road first. But that geopolitical interface, for now, remains thus largely a zone of oblivion, which in its turn will complicate strategic cooperation.

Conclusion

The case for a security partnership between China and Europe is strong. A strong strategic partnership would contribute to the two parties' international status and influence. With hundreds of billions of trade flowing from the one end to Eurasia to the other, there is a clear necessity to secure this geopolitical interface that stretches from the Strait of Malacca to Bab el Mandeb. This interface connects, but it also buffers. It makes it less likely that China and Europe will be drawn into a security dilemma such as pertains between China and the United States in the Pacific. The two sides are aware of all of this. They have written it down in policy papers and included it in joint statements. A new agenda was rolled out that had security at the top. Nevertheless, after about a decade of dialoguing and interacting, security cooperation remains feeble. What is more, Europe and China have not only failed to turn many of their priorities into tangible synergy; they have also competed in their geopolitical interface with irreconcilable policies. There is not much chance that this reality will change. It suffices to reconstruct China's perceptions of Europe as a security actor to understand that there is, for now, not enough trust in and appreciation of Europe's capabilities to try to build the strong security pillar that is needed to establish a true strategic partnership.

Notes

1 UNCTAD Statistical Database.
2 The accumulated trade balance (US$ 1,360 billion) divided by the accumulated GDP (US$ 46,975 billion). Period: 2000–12. Source: UNCTAD Statistical Database.
3 Conversation with two EU officials, Brussels, 12 December 2012.
4 Conversation with senior policy advisor, Beijing, 6 November 2011.
5 X. Li, "论美国和欧盟在防扩散战略上的分歧与合作 [Divergences and Cooperation of Non-Proliferation Strategy between the EU and the US]," 外交评论 [*Foreign Affairs Review*], 6, 2005, pp. 14–20.
6 European Council, *Joint Declaration of the People's Republic of China and the European Union on Non-proliferation and Arms Control*, Brussels: European Council, 8 December 2004, p. 5.
7 Conversation with EU official, Brussels, 11 July 2012.
8 European Council, *EU Strategy against the Proliferation of Weapons of Mass Destruction*, Brussels: European Council, 2 December 2003.
9 Interview with EU official, 10 March 2009.
10 Interview with Chinese official, Brussels, 7 March 2009; Interview with European official, Brussels, 10 March 2009.
11 Interview with EU official, Brussels, 4 March 2009.
12 H. Cui, "默克尔总理的合作与信心之旅 [Merkel: Journey of Cooperation and Confidence]," *Xinhua*, 4 February 2012.
13 "Chinese President Makes Four-Point Proposal for Settlement of Palestinian Question," *Xinhua*, 6 May 2013.
14 Interview with Chinese official, Brussels, 7 March 2013.
15 X. Zhang, "欧盟参与中东和平进程: 动因、角色与困境 [The EU in the Middle East Peace Process: Motivations, Roles, and Ambitions]," 欧洲研究 [*European Studies*], 4, 2009, pp. 45–59.
16 S. Chen, "叙利亚局势及其未来走向 [The Situation in Syria and its Future Direction]," 现代国际关系 [*Contemporary International Relations*], 3, 2012, pp. 1–7. Also: J. Zhang, "欧盟对北非、中东政策的走势 [Trends in the European Union's Policies Towards North Africa and the Middle East]," 现代国际关系 [*Contemporary International Relations*], 4, 2011, pp. 36–43; Z. Liu, "欧盟对北非中东政策的走势 [European Trend of North Africa Middle East Policy]," 西亚非洲 [*West Asia and Africa*], 2, 2012, pp. 11–12.
17 S. Chen, "大国势力博弈叙利亚 [Great Power Power Plays in Syria]," 当代世界 [*Contemporary World*], 3, 2012.
18 S. Zhang, "多重困境下的土耳其正义与发展党 [The Turkish Justice and Development Party under Many Difficulties]," J. Fan, "叙利亚内战的根源及其前景 [The Root Causes for the Civil War in Syria and Prospects for the Future]"; X. Zhang, "欧盟参与中东和平进程: 动因、角色与困境 [The EU In the Middle East Peace Process: Motivations, Roles, and Ambitions]"; J. Zhang, "欧盟对北非、中东政策的走势 [Trends in the European Union's Policy's Towards North Africa and the Middle East]," 当代世界 [*Contemporary World*], 3, 2014.
19 Conversation with Chinese official, Brussels, 21 March 2014.
20 J. Holslag, "China and the Coups: Coping with Political Instability in Africa," 110, 440, 2011, pp. 367–86.
21 Conversation with Chinese official, Brussels, 14 November 2012.
22 Conversation with European member state navy officer, Brussels, 24 March 2013.
23 Conversation with European member state navy officer, Den Helder, 3 June 2013.
24 Conversation with European member state navy officer, Brussels, op. cit.
25 J. Liu, "索马里海盗问题探析 [Inquiry into the Somalia Pirate Issue]," 现代国际关系 [*Contemporary International Relations*], January 2009, pp. 26–35.

26 N. Liu, "从总统辞职看索马里海盗现象的政治与社会成因 [Political and Social Causes of Resignation from the President and the Phenomenon of Somali Pirates]," 西亚非洲 [*West Asia and Africa*], January 2009, pp. 13–18.
27 See J. Holslag, "The Reluctant Pretender: China's Evolving Presence in the Indian Ocean," *Journal of the Indian Ocean Region*, 9, 1, 2013, pp. 42–52.
28 European Commission, *EU-China 2020 Strategic Agenda for Cooperation*, Brussels: European Commission, p. 4.
29 Discussion with Chinese officials from the MFA and IDCPC, Brussels, 26 May 2012.
30 H. Zhou, "统一大市场结构性顽疾中的欧洲治理转型 [The Single Market: A Structural Transformation of the Problems of European Governance]," 学术前沿 [*Academic Frontier*], 2 August 2013, pp. 21–6.
31 Z. Pang and Y. Bo, "欧盟的扩张迷思与发展模式困境 [The Difficulties of the Propagation of Europe's Development Model]," 人民论坛 [*People's Forum*], 8 August 2013. Available online at www.rmlt.com.cn/2013/0802/96969.shtml.
32 L. Xu, "主权债务危机下的欧盟外交 [The Impact of the *European Sovereign* Debt Crisis on Its Diplomacy]," 国际问题研究 [*International Studies*], 2, 2013, pp. 7–13.
33 J. Ling, "欧盟东扩对共同外交与安全政策内部决策环境的影响 [The Impact of the European Enlargement on the CFSP Decision Making Progress]," 欧洲研究 [*European Studies*], 2, 2007, pp. 44–90.
34 L. Wang and Y. Chen, "欧洲防务合作新进展及其前景 [New Progress and its for European Defence Cooperation]," 现代国际关系 [*Contemporary International Relations*], 10, 2013, pp. 17–23; H. Xie, "冷战结束以来欧洲防务一体化的进展及其面临的挑战 [Progress and Challenges Facing European Defence Integration since the End of the Cold War]," 中外企业家 [*Chinese and Foreign Entrepreneurs*], December 2013, p. 9; Y. Bi. "欧盟防务合作多轨并进 [Europe's Multi-track Defence Cooperation]," 解放军报 [*PLA Daily*], 21 December 2013.
35 G. Kong, "欧洲军离我们还有多远？ [A European Army Distant Dream?]," 世界知识 [*World of Knowledge*], 3, 2014, pp. 48–50.
36 L. Xu, "欧盟能否建立安全的通信网络？ [Could the EU Develop a Secure Communications Network?]," *China Institute of International Studies*, 23 February 2014. Available online at www.ciis.org.cn/chinese/2014–02/23/content_6689028.htm; L. Wang, "'跨过卢比孔河': 欧盟防务一体化的发展 ['Crossing the Rubicon' The Development of EU Defence Integration]," 世界知识 [*World Knowledge*], 2, 2013, pp. 44–6; H. Xie, op. cit., p. 8.
37 Conversation with Chinese official, Brussels, 21 March 2013.
38 J. Zhang, "试析欧盟在美国亚太战略中的角色 [On the EU Role in the US Strategy in the Asia-Pacific]," 现代国际关系 [*Contemporary International Relations*], 5, 2013, pp. 24–31
39 J. Zhao, 北狼动地来？ 北约战略调整与欧盟共同防务及其对中国安全环境的影响 [*NATO: Is the Wolf Coming? The Strategic Adjustment of NATO and the EU Common Defence and Its Impact on China's Security Environment*], Beijing: China Social Sciences Press, 2013.
40 J. Zhang, "试析欧盟在美国亚太战略中的角色 [On the EU Role in the US Strategy in the Asia-Pacific]."
41 C. Zhao, "欧盟的中东北非政策评析 [EU MENA Policy Review]."
42 Y. Fang, "北非中东政局对欧盟的挑战及欧盟的政策应对 [The EU's Policy Responses to the Challenges in North Africa and the Middle East]," 当代世界 [*Contemporary World*], 1, 2011.
43 W. Sun. "欧盟担忧被停供天然气在制裁俄罗斯处境尴尬 [Europe Concerned about Gas Supplies Being Stopped after Sanctions Put Russia in an Embarrassing Situation]," 北京青年报 [*Beijing Youth Daily*], 28 March 2014.
44 R. Huang, "2014年2月国际形势大事述评 [Review of the International Events in February 2014]," International Department of the Communist Party, April 2013. Available online at www.idcpc.org.cn/globalview/sjzh/1403–4.htm. Also see J. Gong, "欧盟制裁俄罗斯 意大利欢日俄游客前往旅游 [As the EU Imposes Sanctions on Russia, Italy Welcomes Russian Tourists to Travel]," 人民日报 [*People's Daily*], 28 March 2014.
45 C. Gao et al., "克里米亚能否改变国际政治生态 [The Crimea Can Change the International Outlook]," *Xinhua*, 21 March 2014.
46 J. Wang, "克里米亚大局已定，美国制裁没用 [The General Conditions of the Crimea Are Already Decided, Sanctions are Useless]," 环球时报 [*Global Times*], 15 March 2014.
47 J. Wang and W. He, "乌克兰危机的内外因素分析 [Analysis of the Internal and External Factors in the Ukrainian Crisis]," 世界知识 [*World Knowledge*], February 2014.
48 Conversation with Chinese official, Brussels, 21 March 2014.

15
Central Asia and China's security policy

Niklas Swanström

China's 'new' interest in Central Asia is rather a pivot back to Central Asia after two centuries of exclusion during the Russian and Soviet occupation of the region. With the independence of the Central Asian states in 1991 and the failure of Russia to sustain economic cooperation with the new republics, China emerged as a major player in the region, and today has arguably become the most important actor, especially in the economic realm.[1] However, Russia still retains a pre-eminent role in the region's security, even if it increasingly lacks the financial and military muscle to back its rhetoric and ambitions. While China initially largely excluded itself from the security sector for reasons that will be discussed later in this chapter, the tide has turned and today China has also emerged as a key security actor. There are still limitations to this role – to a large extent imposed by China itself to placate Russian concerns over the former's re-emergence in Central Asia – but the question is how long this will remain the case, and what China is doing and under what conditions it would need to assert its presence.

Initially, China's major concern during the first years of the Central Asian republics' independence was the potential spillover of insecurity and separatist sentiments into Xinjiang Uighur Autonomous Region, specifically among the latter's Turkic-speaking Muslim minority, the Uighurs.[2] As a result, Beijing forced the Central Asian governments, in particular Kazakhstan and Kyrgyzstan, to keep in check their own Uighur minorities. It is estimated that there are around 300,000 Uighur exiles in the region. The Chinese government initially overestimated the threat these groups posed to the security of Xinjiang, even if the Uighur question still looms large in foreign policy considerations. The focus of engagement thus shifted, with a perceived decrease of threat to China's national security, towards a more economic-driven foreign policy, one in which energy imports and securing oil and gas supplies became the overriding concern.[3]

Indeed, China has emerged as the largest economic partner of the Central Asian states, with investments from China into Central Asia having increased from US$1 billion to US$46 billion between 2000 and 2012. China now constitutes the biggest trading partner for all states with the exception of Uzbekistan. Furthermore, following President Xi Jinping's trip to Central Asia in September 2013 during which he visited four of the five regional capitals (excluding Dushanbe), and indicative of the increasing importance China attaches to the region, China signed energy deals worth a total of more than US$100 billion. With the new deals Central Asia could potentially raise its energy exports to China from 4 per cent to a significant 10 per cent of China's total imports. Moreover, Central Asia could function not only as a trade bridge between China and Europe but also as a transit route for oil and gas from Iran and the Middle East. The impact of such a bridge is highly speculative and slightly confusing but could range from, starting with China, an increase of Chinese GDP by 13 per cent to a region-wide estimate of a 50 or even 100 per cent increase in the size of the Central Asian economies over a 10-year period according to the UNDP; perhaps more realistic is the OECD estimate of a 2.3 per cent annual increase of GDP in the region.[4] Regardless of the true figures and the undoubted long-term economic boon for Europe and China – and more crucially for the Central Asian states – that would result from this transit trade, the instability of the region has decreased the potential for such a route through Central Asia.

Furthermore, it should be recognized that while Central Asia occupies a strategic position for China's foreign policy – both now and historically – the region has never been a key concern and even today is still of secondary importance compared with other states and regions such as the United States, Japan and the EU. This is not to say that Central Asia does not increasingly feature on China's agenda, however, as evidenced by the recent investments above. President Xi Jinping further placed a focus on all neighbouring states inclusive of Central Asia in a speech made on October 25, 2013, in which he reiterated the importance of China's neighbours as part of China's long-term strategy.[5]

In spite of China's predominantly economic focus, therefore, security in a broader sense has increasingly crept into the calculus of Chinese foreign policy, and for the first time it is possible to discern a more coherent and connected Chinese foreign policy towards Central Asia. In this context, at the Shanghai Cooperation Organization (SCO) summit held in Beijing in June 2012, Chinese Deputy Minister of Foreign Affairs Cheng Guoping stated that, 'the peace and stability of Central Asia relates to the core interests of China, as well as the members of the SCO. Our determination to maintain the peace and stability of Central Asia is steadfast. We will absolutely not allow the unrest that happened in West Asia and North Africa to happen in Central Asia.'[6] This raises questions of what the rationale for Chinese foreign policy in Central Asia is, what it means in terms of its security policy, and what the implications will be for both the region and other external actors. In fact there is an on-going debate as to whether economy or security is the driving factor behind China's new engagement in Central Asia.[7]

The economic and security nexus

In the Central Asian context the Chinese government has realized the importance of combining a focus on economic development with that on increased security – even though both China and the Central Asian states fall short of succeeding in many crucial aspects. With the partial exception of Kazakhstan, which has a relatively strong economy, the Central Asian states remain weak economies with low GDP, in spite of high growth rates, high levels of corruption and unequal distribution of the little resources they have. This is a fact that has served to destabilize both political and economic development. Economic factors often have a direct impact on both traditional security, such as regime survival and civil wars, and non-traditional security, such as the criminal co-option of state functions and radicalization of non-government groups due to the financial and redistributive weaknesses of states that have alienated and radicalized large groups of the populations.[8] The inability of the Central Asian states to manage growing instability and extremism will unavoidably impact on the economic calculations of Beijing or Urumqi.

The connection between stable economic development and political security is especially apparent in Xinjiang. The Chinese government, and to even a greater extent the local government in Xinjiang, has realized that the rapid and diversified development of Xinjiang, together with a more inclusive policy regarding non-Han minorities including the Uighurs, is the only path to effectively stabilizing the province, even if the relative emphasis is still on growth. The value of trade with Central Asia has grown for China at large, but there is an even larger growth for Xinjiang as it immediately neighbours Central Asia. Today the Xinjiang economy is to a great extent dependent on the stable development of trade with Central Asia. Therefore, it could be argued that the internal social stability of Xinjiang, and that of the Central Asian states, is dependent on this trade. Official statistics report that 67.7 per cent (US$7.09 billion) of Xinjiang's total foreign trade in the first 6 months of 2013 was conducted with Central Asia.[9]

Russia meanwhile is the second largest market for Xinjiang. The above figures furthermore only take into account licit trade. In fact, the illicit trade is also very significant, and ranges from the export of foodstuffs, refrigerators, and precursors for drug production to illegal workers in Central Asia and not least the bazaar trade and import of heroin. There are no good estimates of the scale of the trade but a great bulk of the bazaar trade and indeed much of the ordinary trade is, according to interviews with officials in Central Asia, not licit. What is more, the bulk of the licit trade is conducted by private enterprises, some of which the Chinese government has very little control over, while illicit narco-trafficking is run by organizations with strong networks on both sides and with a financial capacity to corrupt government structures; they are sometimes also connected to extremist organizations such as, but not limited to, the Islamic Movement of Uzbekistan, Jihadist networks in Afghanistan and the Taliban.[10] Despite this it cannot be said that the linkages between political and criminal organizations is clear. A UNODC study from 2009 estimated that US$2.2 billion of the Afghan heroin trade was organized by criminal structures with only US$55 million of the trade organized by the Taliban. It could be expected, but is not confirmed, that a similar pattern is present in Central Asia, with perhaps an even higher degree of criminal structures spreading into China rather than extremist structures. Therefore, while such trade and commerce plays a stabilizing role in Central Asia by contributing to economic development, and thus by extension the development of Xinjiang, more nefarious forms may also lead to their instability, including that of Xinjiang, if appropriate measures are not taken.

The security 'deficit' in Xinjiang and Chinese foreign policy

Despite the crucial position Central Asia has for Xinjiang in particular and China at large there has been a security 'deficit' both in real terms as well as in scholarly attention, with most of the attention, not least among Chinese scholars, having come to focus on economic interaction. Indeed, the initial issues of the border delimitations between China and Central Asian states were already largely resolved bilaterally, with only minor problems of cross-border management with Kazakhstan remaining unresolved. And while the Uighur issue is still seen as a security risk, a focus on energy has come to quickly dominate the academic debate on China's role in Central Asia.[11] Moreover, there are a number of views, especially within the PLA, that treat Central Asia as an escape route from the American containment of China. The argument is that the US has effectively encircled China and Russia and Central Asia would be the weak spot of the US containment policy. As China's military capacity increases, however, this argument diminishes in importance.

Nevertheless, this focus has changed somewhat since the end of 2013 towards a more complex view of Central Asia, not least with the imminent departure of the US-led mission in Afghanistan. Sun Zhuangzhi and Shen Shiliang, from the Chinese Academy of Science and Xinhua state news agency respectively, have pointed out that the withdrawal will create an opening, and a necessity, to improve the security ties with Central Asian states as the situation in Afghanistan has spilt over, and will continue to do so, into Central Asia.[12] A withdrawal of international troops from Afghanistan would entail both a necessity and opportunity for China to further engage

Central Asia on the issues of combating the three evils (separatism, terrorism, and religious extremism) that have been a driving force for China's international engagement. The borders between Afghanistan and the bordering Central Asian states are porous at best and in many ways Afghanistan is a part of Greater Central Asia. This is something that is manifested in Afghanistan's observer status on the SCO since 2012. China does indeed already have a growing military presence in Central Asia, as witnessed by military cooperation and military exercises conducted with the states of the region.[13] However, its level of engagement is not sufficient to increase the stability and security of Central Asia and by extension China, due not least to the current Chinese foreign policy that limits its regional engagement in security issues.

China's foreign policy since the 1950s has been based on its policy of non-intervention and the five principles of peaceful coexistence. This has been due to both a lack of ability to project force but also the likely criticism that would come from potential allies and the West were it to do so. Furthermore, implementing a more active and forceful struggle against the aforementioned "three evils" would potentially bring it into conflict with government structures in the Central Asian states. A further limitation is that the latter focus of existing security cooperation fails to take into account what could arguably be termed a fourth "evil" – that is, social instability or human insecurity as seen in the rising tension between governments and populations as well as increasing economic and social isolation for large parts of the populations. A broader human security perspective – currently not sufficiently factored into Beijing's current security concerns – will grow in importance over time.[14]

In this regard, Chinese foreign policy is still largely driven by traditional national security perceptions and the stabilization of governments in the region rather than human security, something that will create large problems for China in the future. Thus, the most immediate threats in Central Asia are today, and increasingly will be in the future, not national security in the traditional sense but rather domestic grievances, criminalization of societies, socioeconomic inequality, a lack of economic growth, as well as rampant corruption. It is increasingly evident that the destabilization of Central Asia will spill over into Xinjiang, which can be seen in the spread of radicalization, cross-border organized crime and increased migration, even if currently primarily to Russia and Kazakhstan. The new trend has so far been met with a very diversified and uncoordinated policy. The policy of non-intervention from Beijing thus clashes with a growing need for more active engagement. While the non-intervention policy is a noble one in theory, it is not necessarily to the advantage of long-term Chinese security interests or even the populations of Central Asia, who continue to endure inept and corrupt governments that are to some extent 'shielded' by the support of Moscow as well as Beijing.

The future promises difficult challenges, not least among these the continued destabilization of Central Asia, the Afghan scenario post-2014, as well as a lack of Russian cooperation on strategic issues despite annual military exercises, as there is a reluctance to fully integrate China into the military cooperation. As noted, the reduction of international forces in Afghanistan could fundamentally change the situation, making it even more unstable, something that will inevitably affect relations between Central Asia and China. The reality today is that organized crime has a virtual stranglehold over Afghanistan and some of the weaker economies in Central Asia. At least 74 per cent of the world production of opium (and by extension heroin) is produced in Afghanistan, and for the third consecutive year production has increased.[15] China accounts for around 16 per cent of the registered heroin users in the world today, a figure that is most likely much higher due to a lack of reporting; further, with a rise in Chinese affluence, more and more people have the necessary financial means to fund this form of 'recreation'.[16] Trade in the unprocessed, and more bulky, opium is also growing but has not become as important, perhaps due to the lower profit in selling opium than the processed and more addictive heroin. Producers in Afghanistan have therefore increasingly targeted the growing and increasingly affluent market in China, largely through Central Asia as the direct link through the Khyber Pass is risky and closed during the winter. The trade in precursors for heroin production from China to Afghanistan also goes through Central Asia and is increasingly lucrative as production expands in Afghanistan. This has resulted in the criminalization of the Central Asian states, in particular Tajikistan and Kyrgyzstan that have been used as transit states in the trade with Russia and China. The transit routes are ethnically based and connected to groups in Afghanistan, and less connected to terrorist groups such as Al Qaida, but the link to Xinjiang is well established through both Chinese and Central Asian networks. The economies of Tajikistan and Kyrgyzstan are virtually controlled by organized crime and the state functions are increasingly co-opted by criminal and extremist structures. This will increase the security risks for China and effectively prevent any regional effort to deal with these issues: the level of criminalization has gone too far to be easily reversed.[17] This will put even more stress on the relations with Central Asia and China's non-interventionist policy.

The Chinese leadership has claimed that China is a responsible great power (*fu zeren de daguo*) that without exception respects other countries' sovereignty. However, as stated above, there is potentially a contradiction between non-intervention and responsibility in Central Asia. As the Chinese have begun to take an interest in the external security situation the focus has been on the national security of the Central Asian states (here read: the governments) but in many cases the very governments they support are the reason for instability – both real and potential – through bad governance, corruption, and their direct co-option by criminal and extremist groups.[18] According to Andrew Stroehlein, 'embracing{. . .}[Central Asian] dictatorships is no way to bring security to Afghanistan,'[19] and this is also true in the case of China and its border security, especially as the Chinese actions are popular among the governments but not with the populations at large, who are under government pressure. In fact, many among the opposition in the Central Asian states view China as propping up the regimes as well as taking over the local economies. Anti-Chinese sentiments have become increasingly aggressive in recent years and are most often targeted at Chinese migrants, both illegal and legal. For example, the populist movements of political groups such as Protect Kyrgyzstan and the Free People grouping have targeted Chinese businesses and immigration, and in Tajikistan the Islamic Renaissance Party has also sown similar discontent.[20] This has resulted in a few unfortunate deaths of Chinese citizens – something that is only bound to increase with continuing Chinese immigration and rising anti-Chinese sentiments.[21]

The Chinese government has stated its determination not to deploy a military presence (aside from increased military-to-military cooperation) in Central Asia, regardless of the threat to Chinese citizens or investments, instead relying on local governments' protection.[22] While it is evident that this is the current position of the Chinese government, there is also a realization that China will have to engage more extensively in the region to secure itself as well as the regimes in Central Asia. Long term, it will not be enough to simply build and increase investments in infrastructure, uphold a corrupt financial system, and sustain unstable regimes; rather more intrusive measures will have to be taken that uphold long-term sustainable development and security, a realization that many in China at this stage are not yet ready to fully accept as such a development would decrease the economic impact and also force China to intervene in Central Asia's internal affairs, which it is not ready to do at this point in time. Nevertheless, scholars in China have increasingly begun to question the security implications of the current strategy towards Central Asia and speculating on what could trigger a change in the direction of the current policy, although not necessarily embracing a coercive strategy.[23] With the growing investments in Central Asia and the potentially large transit trade, instability would decrease profits and drive up transaction costs to a level investors would not accept. Like other actors, China is currently divided over how to proceed in Central Asia.

A further issue – and one that has not been sufficiently explored – is the question of different interest groups in China, such as the local and central governments, customs, police, PLA, Chinese Community Party, private businesses etc. It is clear that each has its own interests regarding China's security engagement strategy in Central Asia. The regional government in Xinjiang, for instance, depends to a large extent on the continued, licit and illicit, trade with Central Asia. This has resulted in the regional government in Xinjiang being less concerned with geo-strategic and border security than with the uninterrupted flow of trade. Furthermore, cross-border trade and energy imports have assumed such importance for Xinjiang that the Ministry of Commerce and the National Development and Reform Commission have taken a more prominent position in influencing how the region is viewed. These actors and their interests stand in sharp contrast to those with more of a focus on security interests. The PLA and the Department of Public Security are not only responsible for counter-terrorism, but the Xinjiang military region today operates the most modern fighting force in the area, which definitely frames the region in clear security terms. The realization that private business and economic profit will not continue to flourish without an increase in security is growing. In addition, corruption has become so rampant in the border region, arguably to a higher degree than most other provinces due to the illicit border trade and narcotics trade (precursors for the refinement process of opium to heroin to Central Asia and heroin to China), this is also something that has become more than a nuisance for the central government.[24] With the drawdown of troops in Afghanistan it would appear that the PLA and the Department of Public Security will take a much more active role, which will most likely have a positive impact in decreasing the rampant corruption that also feeds back into extremist and terrorist organizations.

Military cooperation between China and the Central Asian states has increased, in terms of military exercises, military aid, and modest sales of military hardware. In contrast with 1991, when there was neither cooperation nor weapons sales between Central Asia and China, by 2013 the opposite was true with the staging of the '2013 Peace Mission' and several other smaller military exercises and small, albeit growing, military aid and sales to the Central Asian states.[25] The engagement has been increasing in both quantity and, more importantly, quality, and has engaged a broader set of security structures in China. China's influence is far below that of Russian military influence but it has nonetheless significantly increased in recent years and it is evident that China will be the fastest rising military partner in the region, albeit without any actual military deployment in Central Asia, according to official Chinese sources. China has limited its permanent presence to the SCO's Regional Anti-Terrorism Structure in Tashkent, military exchanges, and the yearly military exercise, but it has not been able to establish permanent military bases in the region. However, China is careful in its military engagements in Central Asia as it does not want to upset Russia and project itself as a military competitor in the region. The usage of multilateralism through the SCO is thus an important instrument for China to engage the region militarily without incurring the displeasure of Moscow to the extent that the same operations would do if conducted on a bilateral basis.

The above notwithstanding, it remains unlikely that China would be willing to extend military-to-military cooperation significantly. The reasons for this are multiple, not least that Central Asian armed forces, being based on the same model as Russian armed forces, exhibit a very different organization, with language also being a barrier.[26] Fundamentally, there is also a lack of interest in becoming engaged in a region that could have serious military challenges and where a resolution would be difficult to find in the short to medium term. The costs would simply be too great at this moment for China to select such an option, not least politically. Therefore, at least for the time being, it is hard to imagine a threat so substantial that China would further its military engagement in Central Asia to reach the level of Russia's military presence, but it would be possible to predict such a development if Russia reduces its own military presence or if the Central Asian states feel increasingly threatened by Russia's military adventures in states such as Georgia and Ukraine.

Bilateralism versus multilateralism

Despite the noticeable exception of multilateralism with regard to the SCO, China's dialogue and engagement with Central Asia have primarily been on a bilateral level, especially in terms of economic cooperation, but there have been attempts to employ multilateral structures in dealing with security issues. Feng Zhongping argues that the SCO is a good example of an instrument in which bilateralism and multilateralism can be undertaken concurrently and in which complementarity is high.[27] This would take some of the focus away from China and the perception that it is acting inappropriately by intervening unilaterally in the internal affairs of the Central Asian states. Indeed, the sensitivity for Chinese security engagement is high, and despite its stated non-interventionist policy China's actions are often misread, which forces China increasingly to act through multilateral structures. Wu Bangguo has claimed that SCO will greatly benefit if it were to

> establish a more comprehensive security cooperation system, actively implement the Shanghai convention on fighting against the 'three forces', earnestly implement the bilateral security cooperation agreements, deepen security dialogue and consultation and information exchange, continue to hold regular joint anti-terrorism exercises, enhance security cooperation on large events, strive to increase the organizational capacity for action and rapid response capability, fiercely combat the 'three forces' and effectively curb drug trafficking, arms smuggling and other transnational organized crimes to ensure lasting peace and stability in the region.[28]

The current problems with security cooperation, despite some interesting attempts in the area of counter-terrorism (SCO Regional Anti-terrorist Structure) and tackling organized crime, are that most cooperation is embryonic and many states lack an interest in creating effective structures.[29] Despite this, the SCO has emerged as the main multilateral tool for China to deal with the three evils/three forces of separatism, terrorism and religious extremism. This said, bilateral cooperation (then primarily in the economic field) has effectively superseded multilateral cooperation, in large part due to the fact that China has realized the limitations of multilateral cooperation, as will be discussed in the following section. Nonetheless, China is rightly working to establish stronger multilateral structures through the SCO, such as an anti-terrorist centre and increased military exercises, but might have underestimated the regional problems and lack of interest in creating an effective regional organization.

One main reason to choose increased multilateralism is not that bilateralism has failed per se – it has not, which can be seen in the border delimitations between China and the Central Asian states – but rather to ease Russian uneasiness about China's presence in the security sector. By involving Russia to the extent that Russia views it as useful is a direct strategy by the Chinese, even if the limitations lie not so much in the lack of willingness of China as in the structure of SCO, such as weak institutionalism, a lack of power to act independently and insufficient resources. Moreover, Russia is not interested in strengthening the SCO as it would enable China to assert still more influence over Central Asia, a region that Russia has traditionally believed to be in its sphere of influence. In this regard, the multilateral security cooperation that Russia pushes for is in the Commonwealth of Independent States and the Collective Security Treaty Organization, organizations that exclude Chinese influence.

Overemphasis on reaching consensus and avoiding meddling in internal affairs has made it difficult to fully utilize the potential of the SCO, not least in the security domain. Moreover, all states in Central Asia but in particular Kyrgyzstan and Tajikistan are de facto influenced by organized crime and, arguably, as already mentioned, some institutions are even co-opted by criminal networks, which leads to central segments of the government institutions opposing more effective efforts to combat organized crime. This will make any external efforts to curb organized crime very difficult without changing the very institutions that comprise the Central Asian states. In any case, the leaders of Central Asia are more interested in creating an SCO that effectively supports non-intervention and lends support to their own regimes. SCO would need to 'put in place a full-fledged system for security cooperation', 'coordinate and formulate common positions on major international political, security, economic and financial issues, and become more capable and efficient in preventing and managing crises',[30] but this is unlikely to be very successful. Other Chinese leaders have also pointed out the importance of strengthening security cooperation, but the reality is that most successful cooperation is limited to bilateral engagement, despite the very high-profile multilateral military exercises and, on paper, successful action against the 'three evils' – even if the reality is that organized crime, domestic insurgency and extremism are growing in strength rather than decreasing.

Despite the limitations of the SCO, von Hauff argues that there is a basic normatively informed multilateral strategy that focuses on regional stability, something that would be acceptable in China, Russia and the Central Asian states, but the question is how deep this normative security cooperation goes.[31] It is apparent that the SCO has accepted the Chinese concept of the three evils as the foundation in practice and von Hauff also argues that organized crime is included, albeit somewhat less stringently. It is easy to see the commonalities in non-interference and securing government stability in all participating states, but the normative impact is beyond that very limited. China, and the Chinese government, has come much further in broadening the national security concept than the Central Asian states, which have both weak political and economic structures and are primarily focused on securing their regimes. I would argue that the situation is problematic, seen from a multilateral perspective, and that the normative impact is very shallow in Central Asia, and, further, that China will have major difficulties in implementing these concepts as they would threaten the governments more than the current situation of growing criminality and extremism.

The catch-22 situation for China is that the multilateral structures are virtually deadlocked but engaging unilaterally or bilaterally in the security sectors also has limitations, both from a capacity perspective and because this would fly in the face of China's desire to be seen as non-interfering and trustworthy. The focus of the Chinese government has been to introduce a 'policy of bringing harmony, security, and prosperity to neighbours{. . .}[dedicated to strengthening] mutual trust and cooperation{. . .}, easing up hot-spot tensions, and striving to maintain peace and tranquillity in Asia'.[32] There are unfortunately few possibilities to manage this division as long-term regional security is dependent on a more direct intervention that China is not willing to offer unilaterally and the SCO is unable to deliver multilaterally.

China's future engagement

Due to the relative lack of interest from the Chinese central government, as well as conflicting aims from different interest groups and individuals in China, there is no grand strategy for Central Asia on the part of Beijing and it is still debatable whether China has a real periphery strategy, even if the current policy is far more complex and mature than earlier strategies.[33] Despite this, the aggregated impact of all Chinese activities, and lack of focus from other actors, China has emerged as the single most important actor, regardless of whether China wants to be or not. Others have agreed that China's Central Asia strategy is simply a reflection of the larger strategy towards the external world, with a specific focus on the influx of natural resources into China and the large amount of trade going in the opposite direction.[34] This has changed somewhat with the peripheral (*Zhoubian*) strategy that is now putting focus on the neighbourhood; but even here there is very little focus on Central Asia. In a recent publication by the China Institute of Contemporary International Relations (CICIR) regarding the new peripheral strategy, Central Asia was notably absent and focus was instead put on Japan, the United States and, to a somewhat lesser extent, on South and Southeast Asia.[35] This relative lack of interest does not indicate a lack of geopolitical thinking or the diminished strategic importance of Central Asia but could indicate the problems China has in determining action and strategy in Central Asia.

China's role in Central Asia's security will increase exponentially over time and it will be necessary for China to step up its engagement. But even if there is a concern, and in some cases fear, of a deteriorating security situation in Central Asia with internal conflicts, spread of Islamic fundamentalism, organized crime, mass migration and a decline of the regional economies, there is currently very little willingness in Beijing to intervene, or even mediate, in regional affairs. Moreover, the obvious way for China to influence the region is through the SCO, an organization that is flawed and currently has very little impact on the regional security situation. Russia is blocking reforms of the SCO and the Central Asian states are reluctant to implement far-reaching reforms that could potentially increase focus on the their internal situation. This could change as Russia is becoming more aggressive and the Central Asian states could view China as a balancer against Russia, even if reluctantly. If there is no change, China will increasingly have to rely on external powers to stabilize the situation in Afghanistan and Central Asia, something that runs contrary to its attempt to break out of any possible containment. Indeed, dependency on US and Russian military security in the region would put China in a situation that in the long run it would be uncomfortable with.

Apart from the acrimonious relationship between the Uighur minorities in Xinjiang and the Central Asian states, Central Asia together with Pakistan forms an important part of Beijing's long-term strategy to build a strategic relationship with the Ummah (Muslim world). The continued conflict between the Chinese government and the Uighurs has complicated, and will continue to complicate, the relations with the populations of Central Asia (which tend to see the Uighur cause in the same light as their own internal situation even if it is difficult to speak of popular support), even if the government-to-government relations are strong. This is another case in which the Chinese have to change the focus from governments to people and assist in strengthening human security rather than government security.

Relations with Russia have complicated, and will continue to complicate, China's Central Asia strategy. It is evident that China's inroads in Central Asia have decreased the influence of Russia not only in economic affairs but increasingly also in the security sector.[36] While some analysts such as Lukin downplay or even dismiss Sino-Russian competition, it is evident that Russia is no longer as prominent as it once was, and that there are concerns in Russia at its increased marginalization.[37] Most visible is competition in the energy sector where Chinese involvement will effectively bypass Russian networks. This will increase the Russian reluctance to see China become a stronger actor in the security sphere, an area that Russia still controls.

In conclusion, China has emerged as the primary economic partner for Central Asia and economic interactions will continue to increase, not least due to their importance for Xinjiang. In terms of security, meanwhile, China's policy is much weaker and limited by Russian and Central Asian distrust as well as Chinese reluctance to engage in the region militarily. And while China plays the driving role in the SCO with more of an emphasis on multilateral cooperation, the organization is weak and does not have the 'teeth' that China would need it to have to satisfy its security needs in the longer run. It is clear that China will need to move away from a state-centric focus to embracing more of a human security perspective – thus recognizing that the current Central Asian governments are problems rather than solutions to the stability of the region. However, in spite of growing security cooperation, China still lags far behind Russia in terms of a military presence, a situation that is unlikely to change any time soon unless the region or even Russia experiences major instability that would force China to adopt a more assertive role.

Glossary

CAS   Chinese Academy of Science
CICIR   China Institute of Contemporary International Relations
CIS   Commonwealth of Independent States
CSTO   Collective Security Treaty Organization
Fu zeren de daguo (负责任的大国)   Responsible great power
OECD   The Organization for Economic Cooperation and Development
PLA   People's Liberation Army
SCO   Shanghai Cooperation Organization
SCO RATS   Shanghai Cooperation Organization Regional Anti-Terrorist Structure
The three evils   Separatism, terrorism and religious extremism
Uighur   Turkic ethnic group
UNDP   United Nations Development Programme
Urumqi   Capital of Xinjiang Uighur Autonomous Region
Zhoubian (周边)   Periphery

Notes

1 Central Asia was during the Soviet era fully integrated and dependent on Moscow and in practice forbidden from trading outside of the Soviet Union. Infrastructure and commercial goods came directly from Moscow and despite the exploitation of natural resources the Central Asian states were dependent on infrastructural investments and consumer goods from the rest of the Soviet Union.
2 L. Dittmer, 'Central Asia and the Regional Powers', *The China and Eurasia Forum Quarterly*, 5(4), 2007, 7–22; Y. Shichor, 'China's Central Asian Strategy and the Xinjiang Connection: Predicaments and Medicaments in a Contemporary Perspective', *The China and Eurasia Forum Quarterly*, 6(2), 2008, 55–73.
3 G. Christoffersen, 'Multiple Levels of Sino-Russian Energy Relations', in R. Bedeski and N. Swanström (eds), *Eurasia's Ascent in Energy and Geopolitics: Rivalry or Partnership for China, Russia, and Central Asia?* Abingdon: Routledge, 2012, pp. 135–53.
4 N. Swanström, 'China and Greater Central Asia: New Frontiers?' Silk Road Paper, Institute for Security and Development Policy, 2011.
5 X. Mu, 'Xi Jinping: China to Further Friendly Relations with Neighboring Countries', *Xinhuanet*, 26 October 2013. Available online at http://news.xinhuanet.com/english/china/2013–10/26/c_125601680.htm> (accessed 23 January 2014).
6 China National Radio, 'Ministry of Foreign Affairs: Unrest in West Asia and North Africa Not Allowed in Central Asia', 8 June 2012. Available online at http://news.sohu.com/20120608/n345027562.shtml (accessed 4 February 2014).
7 The debate has primarily been whether the Chinese strategy towards Central Asia has been driven by economic or security factors. After independence in 1991 most scholars argued that security concerns, not least the Uighur question, were the driving interest (Mackerras and Clarke, 2009; Allison and Jonson, 2001). This has changed to a more economically driven argument where the economic is now considered to be the driving factor, not least in terms of energy security (Petersen and Barysch, 2011; Bedeski and Swanström, 2012; Christoffersen, 1998).
8 International Crisis Group (ICG), *Central Asia: Decay and Decline*, Asia Report No. 201, 2011.
9 Global Times, *Corruption in Xinjiang*, 1 February 2013. Available online at www.globaltimes.cn/NEWS/tabid/99/ID/759545/Corruption-in-Xinjiang.aspx (accessed 3 February 2014).

10 J. Cui, 'Drug-related Crimes on the Rise in Xinjiang', *China Daily*, 21 June 2103. Available online at http://europe.chinadaily.com.cn/china/2013–06/21/content_16642101_2.htm (accessed 4 February 2014); 'Xinjiang Used by Drug Traffickers as Point of Entry to China', *China Daily*, 26 June 2010. Available online at http://news.asiaone.com/News/AsiaOne+News/Crime/Story/A1Story20100626–224019.html (accessed 4 February 2014).
11 G. Christoffersen, 2012, op. cit.; A. Itoh, 'Sino-Japanese Competition over Russian Oil', in R. Bedeski and N. Swanström (eds), *Eurasia's Ascent in Energy and Geopolitics: Rivalry or Partnership for China, Russia, and Central Asia?* Abingdon: Routledge, 2012, pp. 158–79.
12 R. Synovitz, *China's Xi Seeks Central Asian Ties For Energy, Security*, Radio Free Europe, 4 September 2013. Available online at www.rferl.org/content/central-asia-china-energy-security/25095769.html (accessed 29 January 2014).
13 S. Blank, 'The Central Asian Dimension of Chinese Military Strategy', *China Brief*, 4(10), 2004; R. Weitz, 'China's Military Goals, Policy Doctrine, and Capabilities in Central Asia', in S. Blank (ed.), *Central Asia after 2014*, Carlisle: US Army War College Press, 2013.
14 R. Bedeski, 'Reinventing Human Security: Lessons from Chinggis Khan's Biography', Stockholm Paper, Institute for Security and Development Policy, 2013.
15 United Nations Office on Drugs and Crime (UNODC), 'World Drug Report 2013', 2013. Available online at www.unodc.org/unodc/secured/wdr/wdr2013/World_Drug_Report_2013.pdf (accessed 17 February 2014), pp. x, 30.
16 UNODC, 'Transnational Organized Crime in East Asia and the Pacific: A Threat Assessment', 2013. Available online at www.unodc.org/documents/data-and-analysis/Studies/TOCTA_EAP_web.pdf (accessed 17 February 2014), p. 51.
17 ICG, op. cit.; Swanström, op. cit.
18 United Nations Office on Drugs and Crime, 'An Assessment of Transnational Organized Crime in Central Asia', 2007. Available online at www.unodc.org/documents/organized-crime/Central_Asia_Crime_Assessment.pdf (accessed 17 February 2014).
19 A. Stroehlein, *Why Uzbekistan Matters*, International Crisis Group Commentary, 18 October 2011. Available online at ww.crisis group.org/en/regions/asia/central-asia/uzbekistan/ stroehlein-why-uzbekistan-matters.aspx (accessed 22 January 2014).
20 B. Beshimov and R. Satke, 'China Extends grip in Central Asia', *Asia Times Online*, 12 November 2013. Available online at www.atimes.com/atimes/Central_Asia/CEN-01–131113.html (accessed 29 January 2014).
21 ICG, *China's Central Asia Problem*, Asia Report No. 244, 2013, pp. 15–16.
22 Ibid., pp. 13–16.
23 H. Zhao, 'China's View of and Expectations from the Shanghai Cooperation Organization', *Asian Survey*, 53(3), 2013, 436–60.
24 'Xinjiang H1 Foreign Trade Exceeds $10b, Main Partners in Central Asia', *Global Times*, 18 July 2013. Available online at ww.globaltimes.cn/content/797346.shtml#.UudrDHmCokg (accessed 28 January 2014).
25 S. Blank, 'Recent Trends in Russo-Chinese Military Relations', in R. Bedeski and N. Swanström (eds), *Eurasia's Ascent in Energy and Geopolitics: Rivalry or Partnership for China, Russia and Central Asia?* Abingdon: Routledge, 2012, pp. 108–34; N. Swanström, 'Sino-Russian Relations at the Start of the New Millennium in Central Asia and Beyond', *Journal of Contemporary China*, 23(85), 2014, 20–1; R. Weitz, 'China's Military Goals, Policy Doctrine, and Capabilities in Central Asia', in S. Blank (ed.), *Central Asia after 2014*, Carlisle: US Army War College Press, 2013.
26 R. Weitz, op. cit.
27 Z. Feng, 'Periphery Strategy Should Focus on Innovative Security Cooperation', *Contemporary International Relations*, 23(6), 2013, 52.
28 B. Wu, 'Carrying Forward Good-neighborly Friendship and Achieving Common Development', keynote speech delivered at the Supreme Assembly of Uzbekistan, 23 September 2011. Available online at www.fmprc.gov.cn/eng/wjdt/zyjh/t864104.shtml (accessed 14 February 2014).
29 C. Ziegler, 'Central Asia, the Shanghai Cooperation Organization, and American Foreign Policy: From Indifference to Engagement', *Asian Survey*, 53(3), 2013, 484–505.
30 G. Cheng, 'Immense Prospects for the Shanghai Cooperation Organization', keynote speech delivered at the Third Lanting Forum, 8 June 2011. Available online at www.fmprc.gov.cn/eng/topics/lantingluntan/t828793.shtml (accessed 3 February 2014).
31 L. von Hauff, 'A Stabilizing Neighbour?: The Impact of China's Engagement in Central Asia on Regional Security', *DGAPanalyse*, 3, 2013, p. 9; Q. Jia, 'The Shanghai Cooperation Organization: China's

Experiment in Multilateral Leadership', in A. Iwashita (ed.), *Eager Eyes Fixed on Eurasia: Russia and Its Eastern Edge*, Slavic Eurasian Studies, 16(2), Sapporo: Slavic Research Center, Hokkaido University.
32 L. von Hauff, op. cit., p. 11.
33 M. Fu, 'Reflections on China's Periphery Strategy', *Contemporary International Relations*, 23(6), 2013, 42–5; W. Callahan, 'China's Strategic Futures', *Asian Survey*, 52(4), 2012, 617–42.
34 B. Mariani, *China's Role and Interests in Central Asia*, Safer World, October 2013. Available online at ww.saferworld.org.uk/downloads/pubdocs/chinas-role-and-interests-in-central-asia.pdf (accessed 31 January 2014).
35 Z. Ji (ed.), *Contemporary International Relations*, 23(6), 2013.
36 R. Bedeski and N. Swanström (eds), *Eurasia's Ascent in Energy and Geopolitics: Rivalry or Partnership for China, Russia and Central Asia?* Abingdon: Routledge, 2012.
37 A. Lukin, 'Russian-Chinese Relations', *ISPI Analysis*, 167, April 2013, p. 5.

Select bibliography

Allison, R. and Johnson, L. (eds) (2001) *Central Asian Security: The New International Context*. Abingdon: Routledge.
Bedeski, R. (2013) 'Reinventing Human Security: Lessons from Chinggis Khan's Biography', Stockholm Paper, Institute for Security and Development Policy.
Bedeski, R. and Swanström, N. (eds) (2012) *Eurasia's Ascent in Energy and Geopolitics: Rivalry or Partnership for China, Russia and Central Asia?* Abingdon: Routledge.
Blank, S. (2012) 'Recent Trends in Russo-Chinese Military Relations', in R. Bedeski and N. Swanström (eds) *Eurasia's Ascent in Energy and Geopolitics: Rivalry or Partnership for China, Russia and Central Asia?* Abingdon: Routledge.
Christoffersen, G. (1998) *China's Intentions for Russian and Central Asian Oil and Gas*. Washington, DC: The National Bureau of Asian Research, Vol. 9, No. 2.
Dittmer, L. (2007) 'Central Asia and the Regional Powers', *The China and Eurasia Forum Quarterly*, 5(4).
International Crisis Group (2011) *Central Asia: Decay and Decline*, Asia Report No. 201.
International Crisis Group (2013) *China's Central Asia Problem*, Asia Report No. 244.
Iwashita, A. (ed) (2007) *Eager Eyes Fixed on Eurasia: Russia and its Eastern Edge*, Slavic Eurasian Studies, 16(2), Sapparo: Slavic Research Center, Hokkaido University.
Ji Zhiyue (ed.) (2013) *Contemporary International Relations*, 23(6).
Mackerras, C. and Clarke, M. (eds) (2009) *China, Xinjiang and Central Asia: History, Translation, and Crossborder Interaction into the 21st Century*. Abingdon: Routledge.
Petersen, A. and Barysch, K. (2011) *Russia, China and the Geopolitics of Energy in Central Asia*. Center for European Reform.
Shichor, Y. (2008) 'China's Central Asian Strategy and the Xinjiang Connection: Predicaments and Medicaments in a Contemporary Perspective', *The China and Eurasia Forum Quarterly*, 6(2).
Swanström, N. (2012) 'China and Greater Central Asia: New Frontiers?' Silk Road Paper, Institute for Security and Development Policy.
Swanström, N. (2014) 'Sino-Russian Relations at the Start of the New Millennium in Central Asia and Beyond', *Journal of Contemporary China*, 23(85).
United Nations Office on Drugs and Crime (2013) 'World Drug Report 2013'.
von Hauff, L. (2013) 'A Stabilizing Neighbour?: The Impact of China's Engagement in Central Asia on Regional Security', *DGAPanalyse*, 3.
Weitz, R. (2013) 'China's Military Goals, Policy Doctrine, and Capabilities in Central Asia', in S. Blank (ed.) *Central Asia after 2014*, Carlisle: US Army War College Press.
Zhao, H. (2013) 'China's View of and Expectations from the Shanghai Cooperation Organization', *Asian Survey*, 53(3).
Ziegler, C. (2013) 'Central Asia, the Shanghai Cooperation Organization, and American Foreign Policy: From Indifference to Engagement', *Asian Survey*, 53(3).

16
China's securitization of the South China Sea dispute

Daniel Lynch

Hainan Island, a province of China, is a curiously complex place. Located on the island's eastern shore is the famous resort and convention city of Bo'ao, the home, since 2004, of the Bo'ao Forum for Asia, a "non-governmental organization" (although formed by the Chinese party-state) that, every spring, hosts a cosmopolitan mega-event that attracts national leaders, business CEOs, journalists, and public intellectuals—from Asia and points beyond—to exchange ideas concerning the next phases in Asian economic integration, infrastructure improvement, security affairs, and more. The Bo'ao Forum symbolizes both Asian integration and China's centrality in the process. At the opening ceremony of the April 2014 Forum, Chinese Premier Li Keqiang gave the welcoming speech, and emphasized such platitudes as the benefits of economic integration and the need to resolve disputes using peaceful means.

But Li also managed to insert a short but sharp warning into his remarks concerning China's position on the South China Sea (SCS) dispute—a message that underscored the *other* side of Hainan: its role as the Chinese province charged with administering the entirety of the PRC's vast claim in the SCS, in addition to playing host to the "home port"—in greater Sanya, on the island's southern tip—for many of the vessels, materiel, intelligence-gathering facilities, and other assets that the People's Liberation Army Navy's (PLAN's) South Sea Fleet (headquartered at Zhanjiang, on the Chinese mainland) would deploy first in any SCS military scenario. Li's warning contained nothing substantively new, but the *People's Daily*, in reporting the premier's remarks, used the speech as a launch pad for a harsh and brittle message to Vietnam, the Philippines, other Southeast Asian claimants, and such interested third parties as the United States, Japan, and India:

> In his speech at the opening ceremony of the Bo'ao Forum for Asia, Chinese premier Li Keqiang said that China would respond decisively to any provocation on the South China Sea. Just the previous day, the Chinese defense minister Chang Wanquan had [also] expressed a firm stance on the issue. "The Chinese army comes when called upon, fights once it comes, and wins once it fights." China's firm stance has made an impact. Some say that China is making a show of its capabilities, which is quite different from its previous attitude of maintaining a low profile. Some even worry that China may resort to military action. Speculation like this adds fuel to the so called China threat theory.

But rumors that circulate are less of a problem than failing to deal with the truth. The core of China's firm stance lies in defense rather than offense. Chinese leaders have always put peaceful solutions to disputes before hard responses. The Chinese army is committed to safeguarding state sovereignty and territorial integrity and [to] dealing with threats and provocations, rather than aggression or invasion. As Premier Li Keqiang quoted, we Chinese believe in "repaying kindness with kindness and meeting wrongdoing with justice."

China's decisive stance ought to prevent neighboring countries from harboring unrealistic fantasies. China has made its position clear: we are firm in our resolve to uphold China's territorial sovereignty, we will never make any compromise, concession, or deal concerning our territorial sovereignty, and we will never permit any occupation of our territory. Only by disposing of certain countries' fantasies can we discourage further irresponsible actions.[1]

Within four weeks, however, China had launched another move of its own that many observers considered "irresponsible," the latest in a series of increasingly bold and risky steps that began in approximately 2009 and soon came to be summarized under the rubric "China's new assertiveness" or "China's new aggressiveness."[2] In early May 2014, the PRC suddenly parked a 40-story tall, US$ 1 billion oil rig in a section of the SCS also claimed by Vietnam: not far from the Paracels and a mere 120 nautical miles off the coast of the Vietnamese mainland. This gigantic operation required the assistance of 80 ships—including naval vessels, indicating that Beijing was fully aware the move would antagonize Vietnam, and probably was designed precisely for that purpose. The Vietnamese immediately dispatched vessels of their own, leading to ships ramming ships, with each side firing water cannons at the other. There were many injuries, but no deaths as of 11 May.[3] At precisely the same time, China was heaping vitriol on the Philippines for having, earlier in the week, arrested and imprisoned the crew of a Chinese fishing boat caught harvesting endangered sea turtles in a section of the SCS that the Philippines also claims. Manila vowed to prosecute the Chinese crew, whose members could face 12–20 years in prison if found guilty.[4] From the perspective of the Philippines, there was a very good chance that Beijing had dispatched the fishing boat intentionally in order to underscore China's territorial claims and to dare Manila to respond.

If China by the spring of 2014 was indeed escalating these disputes in order to provoke a decisive showdown, the move should not have come as a surprise, given the repeated, open signals from Beijing that it was determined to pursue its claims, even at the risk of inviting military conflict. In April 2013, for example—almost a year to the day before Premier Li issued his warning at Bo'ao—CCP General Secretary Xi Jinping made a highly publicized visit to the strategically critical bases of the PLAN's South Sea Fleet at Sanya and the nearby Yulin. In the event of a general war with another SCS claimant, or even more limited engagements, Yulin would serve as the primary staging point for China—a sensitive site, in any case, insofar as Yulin is also the home base for China's nuclear-armed submarine fleet, the critical third leg in the tripod of the PRC's nuclear deterrent force. The submarines shelter in caverns located underwater, not to disguise their existence—obviously, Beijing wants the US, India, and the world's other nuclear powers to know of the submarines' existence—but to protect them in the event of a war. Yulin is, therefore, both symbolically and practically important for China, and troubling and provocative for Southeast Asians. Xi Jinping's decision to visit the base could also be taken as yet another worrisome sign, depending on what he chose to say for the cameras that accompanied him throughout the visit.

At various points during his tour of Yulin, Xi issued remarks almost certainly intended to be received in Hanoi, Manila, Washington, and other capitals as yet another illustration of the PRC's iron-clad resolve in the SCS dispute. Xi instructed the young recruits he met at the base to work hard and maintain discipline, but more importantly to "nurture a fighting spirit" so that they would become "better prepared for military struggle." Clearly, the topmost CCP leader was actively pondering the possibility that a military conflict could break out. To Xi, fighting a war over the SCS was in no way "unthinkable," and he choreographed his visit and accompanying media reports in such a way as to deliver this message in elliptical, yet unmistakable, terms.[5]

Xi also took the opportunity of his Yulin visit to draw attention to some of the new military assets China could bring to the table in the event that war did break out. With the cameras rolling, the General Secretary conducted an "inspection" of several of the advanced new naval vessels recently added to the South Sea Fleet, acquisitions made possible thanks to the 175 percent increase in the PLA's budget between 2002 and 2012, the largest increase in military spending of any country during that period, which resulted in China spending twice as much as Japan and three times as much as India on defense by 2012. No other country in Asia came close.[6] One of the vessels Xi inspected was a "new type of submarine" that had recently participated in a 16-day drill and patrol mission that ventured all the way down "to the outer limits" of China's "nine-dashed line," bordering East Malaysia and Brunei. This seemed to suggest the likelihood that China did, indeed, intend to claim everything inside the line, important insofar as the PRC has still not explicitly clarified the extent of its claim. For Southeast Asians, and for those concerned about the unimpeded flow of global commerce through the region, China's drawing notice to military assets which would help it to assert control throughout the entire SCS, should it decide to make this its policy, could only be taken as another provocation—or, more positively, as fair warning to those who might object either to move out of the way or prepare for conflict.

Two days following Xi's visit to Sanya and Yulin, the PRC's State Oceanic Administration (SOA), which had just—in March 2013—been assigned the task of consolidating the enforcement activities of the several maritime agencies that had to that point separately been policing the SCS, issued an ambitious blueprint on the development of China's maritime resources through to 2020. The document appeared to be crafted carefully; it would surely play a guiding role in organizing the activities of the many different entities that would become involved in the event of a serious campaign to extract resources from the maritime regions. Indeed, it was almost certainly in line with this blueprint that the CCP decided to position the 40-story-tall oil rig just off the Vietnamese coast in May 2014, an operation that would have required many months of advance planning.[7] The SOA's blueprint made clear that resource development would certainly take place in the contested areas. Hence, the blueprint included language vowing, in the words of an outside analyst, to "expand the scope and protection of [China's] maritime rights with the purchase of new [enforcement] vessels and planes. Regular campaigns [will] be launched to protect fisheries vessels.{. . .}Beijing will step up patrols in the disputed waters."[8] In short, it seemed by May 2014 that the "new" Chinese assertiveness, by then 5 years old, had entered an even "newer," more dangerous, and potentially decisive phase.

Why, exactly, did the CCP opt for a new assertiveness?

In order to understand how the region could have arrived at the tense situation it faced by 2014, it is necessary to go back to the beginning and ask: why? What were the original motivations behind the PRC's risky moves? The reason most commonly given—not only by foreign analysts, but also by many or even most of the PRC commentators who address the issue—is that a brash and cocky new Chinese hubris suddenly appeared in the fall of 2008, as the natural and normal surge in optimism, pride, and self-confidence many Chinese people felt as a consequence of Beijing hosting the Summer Olympic Games soon degenerated, as a consequence of the global financial crisis (GFC) beginning in the United States, into a collective mentality and accompanying pose far less innocently joyous. By the end of 2008, the destruction caused by the GFC had dragged most of the world into its worst economic catastrophe since the 1930s. Tens of millions of people lost their jobs almost instantly; many of the newly unemployed would have to wait another 2 years before finding a new job; those still employed were often forced to accept pay cuts. By the middle of 2014, the US—China's putative competitor in the global power transition—was well into the sixth year of a "zero interest rate policy" and the fifth year of quantitative easing. Yet still, the US could only muster, at most, 2 percent annual increases in GDP and 2 percent annual increases in inflation. With such a devastating economic crisis striking the US in the immediate aftermath of its military debacle in Iraq, and the quagmire in Afghanistan, America appeared to many Chinese to be precariously weak and likely to grow weaker still. It certainly, or so the theory goes, would be in no position to resist effectively should China decide to become more aggressive in pursuing its interests—not only the territorial disputes in the SCS, but "China's interests" more broadly, as defined exclusively by the CCP.

The other half of the hubris argument rests on the claim that, in contrast to the US, the years 2009 and 2010 were among the most exhilarating in the PRC's history, insofar as Beijing's enormous financial stimulus package, unveiled hastily toward the end of 2008, ignited a period of unprecedentedly rapid monetary and credit growth, fueling a boom in infrastructure construction and real-estate development, in addition to an enormous housing bubble. All of this, or so it is claimed, signaled not only to the average Chinese person on the street, but even to the military and foreign policy strategists at the top of the CCP hierarchy, that, in effect, the "east wind was prevailing over the west wind," and that China could now no longer lose given that its primary globe-level competitor was reeling. This would therefore be the most logical time to launch the offensive that sooner or later would be necessary in any case: the complex mix of military, diplomatic, and economic moves that would, on launching, be pursued relentlessly until China finally achieved "reunification"—or, in other words, had secured effective control over not only Taiwan and the Senkaku/Diaoyu Islands, but also the vast stretch of water speckled with occasional islets in the SCS that the CCP insists is Chinese territory.

Beyond doubt, there was—and is—a certain mood of hubris prevailing, as recognized and criticized by the Chinese IR analysts and others who disagree with the new foreign policy assertiveness. Within the IR world, there were always a few who, evidently, were reading and taking seriously the dire warnings of countless Chinese economists, demographers, and environmental specialists who worried that the country was on the wrong track. Many or even most of these Chinese specialists had been warning of problems for years, and they seemed to become *less* optimistic in 2009 and 2010, as the global financial crisis exposed—for those paying close attention—the undeniable weaknesses and vulnerabilities in China's growth model.

While it is perhaps easy to imagine IR analysts and other social scientists whose expertise does not include economic, demographic, or environmental issues becoming filled with excessive confidence concerning China's prospects in 2008–9, is it really credible to imagine that the people at the top of the CCP hierarchy—the architects of the new assertiveness—would not have known of, or would have dismissed, the warnings of the economists and others? Could these tough-minded, no-nonsense, highly intelligent people actually have bought into the almost mystical argument of super-nationalists that the events of 2008 heralded the start of a tectonic transformation from an old world order to a new one? Or was there something quite different that convinced China's leaders to shift to a new assertiveness?

The remainder of this chapter is devoted, first, to introducing an alternative explanation for China's new assertiveness, especially in Southeast Asia, drawing on the concept of "securitization" (defined below) from the Copenhagen School of security studies; second, to outlining, in brief, how the new assertiveness unfolded in connection with the SCS dispute, consistent with the securitization argument; third, to demonstrating how unilateral Chinese securitization suddenly transformed into a "securitization dilemma" when the US decided to enter the fray in 2010; and fourth, to summarizing the situation as it stands now. To preview the conclusion: China, though facing myriad internal difficulties, continues unrelentingly to make move after provocative move, with the consequence probably being not only profound and perhaps irreparable damage to the PRC's relations with Vietnam and the Philippines, but also a wider and deeper alienation of most of the rest of Southeast Asia, reversing years of progress. The result is that most Southeast Asian states will surely continue to strengthen their relations with the US, Japan, and, to a lesser extent, India and Australia, precisely on the basis of a shared perception that China is becoming increasingly unreasonable and dangerous. The menace inherent in China's posture is, to be sure, buffered by the PRC's continued importance as an economic partner, but at the same time is intensified by a growing sense that China under the CCP, which is obviously unwilling or even unable to see the world as others see it, or to grant even the possibility that other states' distinctive views might also be legitimate, is never going to be a country that Southeast Asians can trust. Nor is it a country that responds to appeals to reason. As a result, Southeast Asian strategists seem likely to conclude that they will have little choice but to regard China with extreme wariness from this point forward, and to pursue the long-term military and diplomatic strategies necessary to meet the dangers China presents.[9]

Securitization as the source of China's new assertiveness

The first problem with using hubris as an explanation for the new assertiveness is that the two are virtually the same thing. In other words, the explanation would be circular. The behavioral patterns that, by now, more people are willing to accept as a new "aggressiveness" (controversial in the early years) are exactly the sorts of patterns one would point to as an illustration of hubris in action. On first glance, this would seem to strengthen the hubris argument, but a phenomenon can never be used to explain the phenomenon itself. If the independent variable is too strongly correlated with the dependent variable, nothing is being explained. Or, to think of it another way, when, in history, has there ever been a case of a country behaving as China has behaved in recent years and yet *not* also being regarded as intoxicated with hubris? If the two always, or nearly always, go together, then one cannot be used to explain the other. Of course there is hubris, but why?

The most common answer given to this question is, in turn, super-optimism resulting from China's claimed comparative economic success. But this then leads to the second problem with the hubris argument, as adumbrated above: China's fantastic economic successes of 2009–10, which dazzled the world—including many in China itself—were for the most part illusory, insofar as the policies used to generate the apparent successes both worsened certain harmful tendencies already present in the Chinese political-economy (e.g., an increasing over-reliance on investment to fuel growth) and planted the seeds for even greater problems down the road (the real-estate bubble, rapidly growing corporate and local government debt, decreasing efficiency of credit growth as a spur to GDP expansion, a related profusion of shadow banking activities and instruments, and more).[10] Limitations of space do not allow for a full discussion of China's myriad economic problems; the key points to stress here are that (1) the problems strike at the very roots of China's rise, its national strength, because if economic growth were to slow to a crawl (or worse), all of the other elements of what the CCP calls "comprehensive national power" would suddenly become much more difficult to attain or maintain; (2) Chinese economists, demographers, and environmental specialists were all loudly and insistently warning about these problems when the assertiveness began, and in fact had been warning about them for several years, in an increasingly urgent tone; and, most importantly, (3) China's top leaders signaled their own recognition of the country's precarious economic situation when in November 2008 they passed an enormous financial stimulus package. Controlling for GDP, if a comparably sized package had been passed in the US, it would have been valued at US$ 2 trillion. But China was said to be rising inexorably while the US was declining. Why would a super-optimistic Chinese leadership, bursting with hubris, pass a stimulus package of *any* size, let alone a package of such enormity?

Given the seriousness of the PRC's economic, demographic, and environmental problems, the only way hyper-optimism could explain the hubris, which is essentially coterminous with the new foreign policy assertiveness, is if somehow the top Chinese leadership were unaware of the problems or underestimated their significance. This, however, seems thoroughly implausible. Lower-ranking military officers and foreign policy officials might have been unaware of the problems, but not the top Party leadership, centered on Hu Jintao when the assertiveness began and Xi Jinping since 2012. The Party Center structures China's communications system to ensure that frank assessments of any problems threatening the Party's ultimate control and its other objectives will reach the top leadership. Hu and his lieutenants would have been fully aware not only of the serious economic difficulties and the dangers to China's international position these difficulties implied. They would also have known about the domestic political problems (protests, strikes, riots, and other "mass incidents") to which the economic and environmental problems were already contributing, and which threatened the power of the Chinese state from within. Indeed, anyone even casually reading the Chinese newspapers over the past 7 to 8 years will know that Hu Jintao and especially Premier Wen Jiabao demonstrated their awareness of these problems by repeatedly making statements about them in public. That, indeed, is precisely why they approved the November 2008 stimulus.

There is no denying, however, that hubris remains the dominant "explanation" for the new aggressiveness, even though it is intertwined too tightly with what it is purported to explain. There are probably two reasons for the continued popularity of hubris as the explanation. The first is simply that it is, indeed, tightly intertwined with the new aggressiveness: they go together, so it is easy to imagine the relationship must be causal. Moreover, Chinese hubris is highly visible, because below the level of the top CCP leaders there are, indeed, many public intellectuals and commentators who exude hubris in television interviews, while bloviating and boasting in blog posts, meetings with foreign groups, and on countless other occasions.

The field of security studies continues to place primary emphasis on objective material threats as the chief source of tensions in international relations—or at least the severe tensions having the potential to cause war. Although non-material factors such as perception have for two or three decades been acknowledged as significant factors, they are rarely seen as decisive other than in crisis situations, or as aggravating inter-state tensions that slowly marinate over time. Anyone assuming—whether consciously or unconsciously—that security threats, although exacerbated or ameliorated to varying degrees by factors related to perception, must ultimately be material, or "objective" or "real," would naturally be predisposed to believe that a hubris reflecting real material change must be driving the new Chinese assertiveness, particularly if the time period is 2009–10 and the analyst is not yet aware that China's dazzling growth is actually damaging the country's longer-term prospects.

In contrast, it would be difficult to conceive of the new Chinese assertiveness as arising in response to some threat, because from a materialist perspective it is unimaginable that even all of ASEAN, to say nothing of Vietnam or the Philippines alone, could pose a material threat to China; nor could Japan become a "real" threat, given China's awesome size and growing power. In other words, if mentalities must be used to explain a pattern in international behavior, the mentalities should reflect material power differentials, interests, and real threats. The only possible mentality ascribable to China under such an assumption, based on a shallow understanding of 2009–10, would be hyper-optimism, manifesting as hubris.

But from the perspective of the Copenhagen School of security studies, it is possible to put together an argument that helps to explain what the hubris theory cannot: why China's leaders, surely mindful of the PRC's actual weaknesses, and the near-certainty that economic problems, in particular, will worsen, would embark on a policy of increasing assertiveness or aggressiveness in the SCS and elsewhere, starting in about 2009.

The central insight of the Copenhagen School—whose leading figures include Barry Buzan, Ole Waever, and others based not only or even primarily in Denmark, but generally in Europe, the United Kingdom, and Australia—is that security threats are not, except in extreme cases, obvious: it can take many years of argumentation among political elites before some situation or entity comes to be accepted widely as a threat.[11] In *Security: A New Framework for Analysis* (1998), a seminal book in this school's tradition, co-authors Buzan, Waever, and Jaap de Wilde begin by positing that the range of issues, entities, or phenomena that might or might not come to be defined as security threats is extremely broad, with the result that what some states and societies define as an obvious and grave national security threat other states could not even conceive of viewing in such terms. (The authors provide as an illustration the widely varying policies among states toward immigration.) Eventually, a "securitizing actor," who might be an individual but is more likely to be a group—probably, but not necessarily, occupying offices of importance in the state—will make a "securitizing move," which simply means a public assertion (issued openly and through private networks) that some issue, entity, phenomenon, or development inside the country, outside, or both, has evolved to the point that it now poses, or very soon will pose, an *existential threat* to one of the society's most important "security referents." The critical referent concept refers to the set of core values the society is thought to hold dear, and which the securitizing actor believes (or at least claims) to be facing mortal threat: on the verge of destruction. Given that the country attaches overwhelming importance to the security referent, and is intensely committed to upholding, protecting, and nurturing this valued object (normally, a set of abstract ideals and aspirations), the securitizing actor demands that *extraordinary measures* be deployed to ward off the threat. The securitizing actor acknowledges that the measures may be costly, require sacrifices, and risk increasing internal or international tensions. But given the centrality of the values embodied in the referent and the severity of the threat to these values, extraordinary measures must be taken. If the threat—which, recall, need not refer to another country, or any organized entity—succeeds in obliterating the valued referent, the society will have suffered a profound catastrophe.

What, then, might groups at the top of the CCP regard as a high-valued referent—something that, by 2009–10, seemed to be either already in grave danger of annihilation, or else likely to face such a devastating threat in the near future? "Territorial integrity" would be an obvious candidate, given that the new assertiveness—what Buzan et al. would define as the "extraordinary measures" (and, indeed, they were experienced as extraordinary by China's neighbors and other countries, certainly in comparison with the PRC's foreign and security policies of the previous 12–13 years)—was directed most forcefully at those countries contesting Beijing's irredentist claims: Vietnam, the Philippines, and Japan. But territorial integrity as Beijing defines it did not suddenly come under grave threat in 2009, nor were there any indications that it soon would come under such threat. Indeed, the most important of China's irredentist claims, Taiwan, had just, with Ma Ying-jeou's election in 2008, *enhanced* Chinese territorial integrity, insofar as Ma pledged not to contest the CCP's insistence that Taiwan is a part of China, while hinting to Beijing that future unification was a real possibility.

The deeper, far more serious, indeed existential, threat that China began to face in approximately 2009 (though many actors had been warning of it for several years) was the threat posed by the economic, demographic, and environmental challenges, suddenly exposed as urgent, to the very "rise of China" itself. The GFC and subsequent worldwide recession exposed, for the first time, how truly vulnerable China was—and that this vulnerability seemed certain to increase given the challenges inherent in trying to implement the sort of profound economic reforms necessary to reduce the vulnerability. Even if the reforms succeeded, they would still be insufficient, because demographic trends guaranteed that the work force would certainly shrink, society would certainly grow old, and by the mid-2020s, the population itself would shrink. The population might even shrink more quickly than the demographers of 2010 were projecting, insofar as the enormity of China's pollution problems could combine with the population's rapid aging to lead to the death rate increasing (older people being more subject to illness) and life expectancy starting to fall (infants born into a highly polluted environment potentially having a shorter lifespan marred by more frequent and serious diseases). Among all the countries that had succeeded in the past in "rising," how many were shrinking in population, aging rapidly, and suffering from an increasing incidence of disease and shorter lifespans—while at the same time their economies, forced to reduce leverage and investment following years of unsustainable expansion, were mired in a long-term slump? None. So how, then, would China be able to continue rising?

The issue is even more significant than the darkly negative scenario above would indicate. The reason is that the rise of China itself is probably not the ultimate referent. The ultimate referent would be "China's salvation," "the Chinese renaissance," and related ambitions and objectives rooted deep in history, dating back at least to the early 1900s. Whatever group emerged from the violent and yet vibrant dynamism and turmoil of the first half of China's twentieth century to lead China in the decades to follow would have to be committed to realizing a Chinese renaissance. It would have been inconceivable for a government that did not act to move China in this direction to be perceived as legitimate. The renaissance and what became the rise are complex sets of goals that every patriotic Chinese person came to accept as unquestionably profoundly significant collective objectives. Failing to realize these objectives would imply the loss of everything that matters to the patriotic Chinese person. If failure were to become conclusively demonstrable in, say, the 2020s, the disappointed patriot would no longer even have the Chinese family as a unit to which to shift his or her allegiance. The extended family of decades past is now long gone, and demographic trends—utterly irreversible in the short term, no matter what the state might try—imply that the family will continue to wither in size and weaken in vitality. By 2009–10, the possibility of this complex, multifaceted, and ultimately horrific scenario unfolding must have been apparent to China's top leaders, given all the warnings being issued by specialists, in combination with what the leaders would have gleaned from the Party Center's own internal information sources. Ironically, Xi Jinping's adoption of "the China Dream" discourse and his use of it to (try to) define the meaning and purpose of his decade of leadership seems eerie in the light of the realization that this society may be in for some extremely trying circumstances in the years and decades ahead. One is almost tempted to speculate that Xi chose to promise the China Dream—which, in essence, is simply another term for the Chinese renaissance—precisely because he recognized that this deepest of all valued referents was in danger. The "middle-income trap" that Chinese economists warn about would only be the beginning.

But even though China's top leaders must have recognized these threats, they would not necessarily have seen them as unavoidable. Some of the threats may have seemed impossible to handle, but others could have been judged as threats that the CCP could, through action, tackle effectively. Rare indeed would be the national leader of any country so lacking in self-confidence that he or she decides the country's problems are insoluble. There must be a way out. And while it would be impossible to know what Hu Jintao and his lieutenants were thinking in 2009, or what Xi Jinping and the other security elites are calculating today, there is a correlation in time between the emergence of the possibility of the rise ending suddenly and the leaders' decision to become more aggressive, in the SCS and elsewhere. Could there be a causal connection? Could Hu somehow have imagined increasing aggressiveness might help to prevent or at least ameliorate all of the problems China seemed certain to face?

The one fact that might provide a clue is that it would have been blindingly obvious to Hu and other Chinese leaders that most of the rest of the world—indeed, most people in Chinese society—had no idea that China was facing such serious problems. Obviously, specialists in various areas understood, but it would not have been easy for pessimistic foreign China specialists in 2009 to convince even other China specialists, let alone government leaders, that China's rise could well be at risk. In the atmosphere of 2009, as manufactured by the media—especially the business media—China was soaring. The notion that China's rise might be just a decade or so away from ending would have seemed preposterous. As a result, the *image* of China's boundless awesomeness was a mighty tool the CCP could count on wielding for 5 to 10 more years, until the reality of China's problems slowly became increasingly apparent to more and more observers worldwide. Indeed, this process seems finally to have begun, although the possible severity and depth of the threats China faces are still not widely understood. This means that the window of opportunity during which the CCP might be able to use the image of invincibility to help pursue its "national interests" should still remain open for a few more years—and possibly longer, if the reforms the CCP suggested it might pursue at the November 2013 Third Plenum are implemented. This could well be the Party's last chance, however, to realize what it defines as "national unification," including the annexation of most of the SCS. If the CCP succeeds in what outsiders regard as a wild and unreasonable territorial grab, excitement generated in China by the development could, somehow, have a reinvigorating effect on Chinese society, which, in the CCP calculus, might then make solving some of the other problems easier—or, at least, make living with the other problems easier to accept. In point of fact, it is impossible to know what impact CCP elites imagine annexation of most of the SCS would have on the vexing internal problems. There is no question, however, that it chose to make its play before the internal problems could become highly visible. And beyond all doubt, the risks entailed in making this play—in launching the final drive for "national unification" (if, indeed, this is what is now happening)—are so enormous that whatever problems "unification" is seen as likely to help resolve must be very serious problems indeed.

The arrival of China's new assertiveness to the SCS

The new assertiveness was already widely recognized and actively being discussed when Carlyle Thayer, a former Australian diplomat with particular expertise in Vietnam, and then a full-time analyst focusing intensively on the SCS, became the first scholar to detail the key developments systematically. He pursued this task in a series of publications and presentations during 2009–10, encapsulated in an article for the journal *Security Challenges* in 2010. In the article, Thayer concentrates on what were then the dramatic new developments of 2009–10, but he notes that the groundwork for the new assertiveness was already being prepared as early as the mid-2000s, although there was no indication then (possibly the decision had not yet been made) that a new assertiveness would suddenly become apparent in 2009. The key developments in the early phases of the assertiveness included the following:

1. Satellite imagery confirmed, in 2007, that China was making rapid progress in constructing the Yulin Naval Base—the future "home port" of much of the South Sea Fleet, and the base that Xi Jinping visited in April 2013. Thayer remarks that "at the same time, China

extended an airfield on Woody Island in the Paracel Islands; consolidated its facilities at Fiery Cross Reef in the Spratly Archipelago; and maintained a continuing [since January 1995] naval presence at Mischief Reef off the west coast of the Philippines."[12] Thayer could not have known in 2010 how significant the airfield on Woody Island would soon become. In July 2012, the CCP announced that the county-level administrative entity of Sansha, adjacent to the airfield, would be elevated in status to a prefectural-level city with front-line responsibility for administering all of China's claimed land territories and their adjacent maritime zones throughout the SCS. Sansha would be garrisoned and, by means of substantial infrastructure investment, quickly transformed into an actual city.[13] The announcement of Sansha's establishment struck the Southeast Asian diplomatic community like a thunderbolt.

2. On two occasions in 2009—first in February/March, and then again in June—the PLAN dispatched ships to harass US naval intelligence-gathering vessels sent to examine the Yulin Naval Base. Thayer argues that these incidents implied the possibility China would, one day, redefine the South China Sea as no longer a "high sea," in which all manner of vessels—military as well as commercial—are legally free to operate, but instead as, in effect, an internal sea, or some other formulation in which Beijing would grant itself special rights to regulate traffic.[14] A related possibility is that the PLAN might have been probing to test whether the US economic crisis following on the debacle in Iraq had begun to affect Washington's resolve to maintain its position in the SCS. That would be a question decisively answered the following year, when Secretary of State Hillary Rodham Clinton attended the ASEAN Regional Forum in Hanoi and then unveiled "the Pivot," or US recommitment to Southeast Asia.

3. In 2009 and then again in 2010 (by now, annually), China announced a unilateral 3-month moratorium on fishing in the SCS north of the twelfth parallel, with the ban to run annually from mid-May to 1 August. Beijing insisted the ban was necessary "in order to preserve fish stocks, prevent illegal fishing, and protect Chinese fishermen," but Thayer—a specialist on Vietnam—notes that "the months of May–July are the height of the Vietnamese fishing season"; consequently, the unilateral ban was certain to be experienced as pointedly provocative by Hanoi, and was probably intended as such by Beijing.[15]

4. In 2009, "eight modern Chinese fishery administration vessels were dispatched to enforce the [fishing] ban." This led Vietnam to file a formal diplomatic protest. "The Vietnamese news media reported that China acted more aggressively [than it had done in the past]. Chinese vessels stopped, boarded, and seized the catches of Vietnamese fishing boats. They chased other Vietnamese boats out of the proscribed area." In one incident, a Chinese fishery administration vessel rammed and sank a Vietnamese boat; in another, a Chinese ship seized a Vietnamese boat and demanded that a US$ 31,700 "fine" be paid in exchange for the crew's release. (It is not clear whether the Vietnamese paid the ransom.) Similar harassment occurred in the spring of 2010 and in the following years.[16]

Consistent with Thayer, Michael Swaine and M. Taylor Fravel, assessing the situation from the vantage point of 2011 in an essay written for the *China Leadership Monitor*, agree that the new assertiveness began approximately in 2007, but for very different reasons. Whereas Thayer identifies China as the first mover, Swaine and Fravel insist that the Chinese behaviors, which soon came to anger the other SCS claimants and worry outside powers, were actually defensive moves. Swaine and Fravel readily acknowledge that, in the immediately preceding years, China had begun (1) imposing and eventually expanding the annual fishing ban referenced by Thayer; (2) conducting regular maritime security patrols, which sometimes led to the detention of Vietnamese fishermen and the cutting of cables on Vietnamese survey ships; (3) implementing various forms of political and diplomatic pressure, including the placing of markers on unoccupied reefs; and (4) conducting "scientific activities and extensive naval exercises in the vicinity." They also acknowledge that, "by and large, these activities have increased in number (or duration) and intensity over the last several years."[17]

But the reason for these, they argue, was that Beijing felt it had no choice. It was *compelled* to respond assertively because it perceived "growing and more assertive challenges to its [SCS] claims [emanating from Vietnam and the Philippines] since roughly 2007, challenges that require[d] a response in turn."[18] The authors provide as an illustration the vote by the Philippine Congress in February 2009 to approve a new archipelagic baseline law, intended (among other things) to underscore the Philippine claim. In response—but only in response (i.e., nothing would have happened if the Philippine Congress had resisted the temptation to provoke)—China issued a statement in March 2009 openly acknowledging that one of the reasons it had been dispatching maritime enforcement vessels deep into the SCS in recent years had been, as speculated, "to demonstrate [Chinese] sovereignty," an admission that irritated the other claimants.

Later in 2009, China reacted with anger when Vietnam announced a new strategy designed to elicit support for Hanoi's claims by inviting the international community to pay more attention to developments in the SCS dispute. China's longstanding position has always been—and still is—that it will only negotiate the disputes bilaterally. It flatly rejects the suggestion that the international community or international institutions (including legal institutions) should play a significant role. As a result, Swaine and Fravel conclude that when China launched a series of naval exercises in 2010, the move was designed to signal dissatisfaction with Vietnam's attempt to internationalize the dispute.[19] Had Vietnam exercised self-restraint by not involving the international community, and had instead resigned itself to dealing with China bilaterally, there would have been no need for the PRC to stage the naval exercises.

Unilateral securitization becomes a multilateral securitization dilemma

Whatever the case, by mid-2010, the situation was rapidly transforming into a multilateral imbroglio substantially more complex, fraught, dangerous, and difficult to disentangle than in the initial years. When the US decided to signal its support for the Southeast Asian claimants, even while insisting that it did not take a position on ownership of the islands themselves (it always rejected "ownership" of the high seas), Chinese securitization suddenly became a globe-level superpower securitization dilemma, but one in which the Southeast Asian claimants to the contested territories—along with other countries in ASEAN—could set the boundaries and define the role they hoped the US would be willing to play. As early as February 2009—at the beginning of the Obama Administration—Secretary of State Clinton announced that she would end the practice begun by the George W. Bush administration of dispatching only low-level officials to attend ASEAN meetings as a way of conveying disgust with the Association for granting membership to Myanmar in 1997. Clinton announced in February 2009 that she would personally attend the annual ASEAN Regional Forum (which the foreign ministers of most of the great powers routinely attend) in July 2009, and in the years to follow. In Phuket, Thailand, the city that hosted the Forum in 2009, Clinton convened a ceremony during which she formally signed the Treaty of Amity and Cooperation in Southeast Asia—a move that elicited widespread praise from Southeast Asian journalists and public intellectuals. Even in Indonesia, which had treated the Bush Administration with an icy coldness, the executive director of the influential Center for Strategic and International Studies published an op-ed in the *Jakarta Post* welcoming the US back to the region. He emphasized the significant strategic implications: "The return of the US to the region will limit the possibility, and discourage, any single major power from dominating" the increasingly integrated and institutionalized ASEAN region.[20]

The state of China-Southeast Asian security relations today

Available space does not permit a detailed discussion of all the events since 2010, during which tensions have continued to escalate. In any case, taken in isolation these events do not appear significantly different from the May 2014 oil rig episode or the fishing bans imposed in 2009. There have been far too many such events in the 2009–14 period to count, although some stand out as particularly provocative, such as the PRC move to renege on a deal brokered by the US to end a 2-month spring 2012 standoff with the Philippines over Scarborough Shoal, after which—and ever since—Chinese forces have occupied the Shoal.[21] It was about this time that the PRC's moves came more widely to be understood as stages in a long-term campaign that would end either with the PRC's eventual consolidation of control over the SCS or some sort of conflagration.[22]

Another important development in 2012 was China's successful manipulation of its client state, Cambodia—host of the July 2012 ASEAN summit—into refusing to allow wording on the SCS dispute to be included in the communiqué that would, as always, be issued at the end of the meeting. (In the event, no communiqué of any sort was issued, for the first time in ASEAN's history.) Something similar seemed to be in the works when Myanmar hosted an ASEAN summit in May 2014, at precisely the same time as the oil rig standoff between China and Vietnam. Although Myanmar had distanced itself from China beginning in 2011, and could no longer itself be considered a PRC client state, its leaders understood that they would have no choice but to rely on Chinese investment in the future in order to develop the domestic economy. They also knew that China could turn on and off the flow of arms to ethnic separatists in the mountainous northeastern part of the country at any time in order to express displeasure with Naypyidaw's moves. For these reasons, Myanmar made it clear in May 2014 that, as host of the summit, it did not wish the SCS dispute to become a major point of discussion. The potential for China to divide ASEAN was a critical factor that would help determine how the dispute would play out. Clearly, the US and Japan would be much more willing—and find it politically as well as logistically much easier—to support a united Southeast Asia than one divided. Consequently, assuming that the US and Japan are determined, for their own reasons, to resist Chinese moves to take control of the SCS, it should be expected that Washington and Tokyo will take steps to try to encourage ASEAN unity on the question.

A final point to stress: Even if the core contention of this chapter is right, and the new Chinese assertiveness was, and is, motivated not by a Chinese hyper-optimism but instead by a fear that some window of opportunity for achieving "national unification" is closing, because of the serious, and perhaps mortal, threats to China's rise as presented by a combination of almost unsolvable economic, demographic, and environmental problems, there would still be no practical or normative justification for arguing that Beijing should be accommodated and its demands met—or at least, there would be no more justification than if the demands were motivated by hyper-optimism. The Philippines, Vietnam, and other SCS claimants face their own developmental challenges; Southeast Asia as a whole has an equivalent to the "China Dream," the "ASEAN Dream," which is every bit as valid as the PRC's. There can be no justification for one country attempting to solve its internal problems by unilaterally shifting the costs onto its weaker neighbors, especially by using force to do so. China's problems are for China to solve; most, in fact, are entirely of the CCP's own making, through the dysfunctional political and economic institutions it has put into place, and as a result of the parade of irresponsible policies it has enacted in recent years, most visibly, those associated with the 2008 economic stimulus. It is inconceivable that Vietnam, the Philippines, or other countries in Southeast Asia should be expected, in a world governed by reason, to pay for these Chinese mistakes. Perhaps the many people in China who quietly understand this situation for what it is will assert themselves and demand that the Party

Center "rein its horse in at the precipice" and shelve the newly aggressive approach. If, instead, the CCP continues charging heedlessly ahead, the people of China themselves could become the greatest losers in the dangerous competition now unfolding. The historical precedents are not encouraging.

Notes

1 Li, Keqiang. "Full text of Li Keqiang's speech at opening ceremony of Boao Forum," *Xinhuanet*, 10 April 2014. Available online at http://news.xinhuanet.com/english/china/2014-04/10/c_133253231.htm (accessed 2 May 2014).
2 At least in the early years, not everyone accepted the characterization. See, for example, Swaine and Fravel (2011) and Johnston (2013). For Swaine and Fravel, the point of disagreement was not so much whether China was behaving more assertively, but why. They found many of the PRC's moves in the 2009–11 period to be actions taken in response to provocations made by Vietnam and/or the Philippines. Johnston came to a similar conclusion regarding Chinese behavior in the SCS, while rejecting entirely the notion that the PRC had become more assertive outside of Southeast Asia. Both Swaine and Fravel, on the one hand, and Johnston, on the other, criticized what they regarded as inaccuracies in media reporting and internet commentary on Chinese assertiveness, which had the effect, they said, of distorting the Chinese moves and exaggerating their seriousness. By 2013–14, however, most of the early skepticism—from these analysts and others—seemed to be fading as the number of observers alarmed by the Chinese moves continued growing rapidly.
3 Perlez, J. and Bradsher, K. "In High Seas, China Moves Unilaterally," *New York Times*, 9 May 2014. Available online at www.nytimes.com/2014/05/10/world/asia/in-high-seas-china-moves-unilaterally.html?hp (accessed 9 May 2014); Stout, D. "In the South China Sea, China Is Already Acting Like a Superpower," *Time*, 8 May 2014. Available online at http://time.com/91934/china-vietnam-south-china-sea-oil-rig-paracel/ (accessed 9 May 2014).
4 Mullany, G. "Philippines Jails Chinese Sailors in Fish Dispute," *New York Times*, 10 May 2014. Available online at www.nytimes.com/2014/05/11/world/asia/raising-stakes-in-fight-with-china-philippines-jails-fishermen.html (accessed 11 May 2014).
5 Chan, M. "Xi Jinping Calls on Navy to Be Prepared for Struggle," *South China Morning Post*, 12 April 2013. Available online at www.scmp.com/news/china/article/1212630/xi-jinping-calls-navy-be-prepared-struggle (accessed 24 April 2014).
6 Chipman, J. "Military Balance 2014 Press Statement," IISS Press Releases, 5 February 2014. Available online at www.iiss.org/en/about%20us/press%20room/press%20releases/press%20releases/archive/2014-dd03/february-0abc/military-balance-2014-press-statement-52d7 (accessed 29 April 2014).
7 Perlez, J. and Bradsher, K. "In High Seas, China Moves Unilaterally."
8 Chan, M. "Xi Jinping Calls on Navy to Be Prepared for Struggle."
9 The best single, book-length overview of China-Southeast Asia security relations is Ian Storey's outstanding *Southeast Asia and the Rise of China: The Search for Identity*, London: Routledge.
10 Lardy, N. *Sustaining China's Economic Growth after the Global Financial Crisis*. Washington, DC: The Peterson Institute, 2012.
11 The immediately following paragraphs outlining the securitization process rely extensively on Buzan et al. (1998), especially pp. 1–47. For the roots of Copenhagen School thinking, see Buzan (1991). To appreciate the School's contention that the securitization approach is not contradictory but instead complementary to materialist approaches such as realism, see Buzan and Waever (2003). For illustrations of how the approach has influenced and enriched the study of security in Asia, see Alagappa ed. (1998), and Alagappa ed. (2003).
12 Thayer, C. "The United States and Chinese Assertiveness in the South China Sea," *Security Studies*, Vol. 6, No. 2, 2010, pp. 69–84. Another scholar, Scott Bentley, also dates the start of China's new assertiveness to sometime during 2007, but for a different reason. According to Bentley, 2007 was the year Chinese maritime law enforcement agencies began—in a generally uncoordinated fashion—to conduct "what were termed 'rights protection' missions in the South China Sea"; that is, missions devoted to protecting the "rights" of Chinese fishermen by using force to drive away competitors from Vietnam, the

Philippines, and other countries. Bentley, S. "Keeping an Eye on the South China Sea," Center for International Maritime Security, 3 December 2013.
13 Heyderian, R. "Construction Tensions in the South China Sea," *Asia Times*, 26 October 2012. Available online at www.atimes.com/atimes/China/NJ26Ad02.html (accessed 18 October 2013).
14 Thayer, C. "The United States and Chinese Assertiveness in the South China Sea," pp. 74–75.
15 Ibid. p. 76.
16 Ibid. p. 77.
17 Swaine, M. and Fravel, M.T. "China's Assertive Behavior, Part Two: The Maritime Periphery," *China Leadership Monitor*, No. 35, summer 2011, p. 5. Available online at http://carnegieendowment.org/files/CLM35MS.pdf (accessed 23 October 2013).
18 Ibid. p. 7.
19 Ibid.
20 Sukma, R. "Welcoming the US Back to Southeast Asia," *Jakarta Post*, 27 July 2009. Available online at www.thejakartapost.com/news/2009/07/27/welcoming-us-back-southeast-asia.html (accessed 23 October 2013).
21 Chansoria, M. "China-Philippines Contest over Scarborough Shoal Aggravates," *Indian Review of Global Affairs*, 20 March 2014. Available online at www.irgamag.com/component/k2/item/8002-china-philippines-contest-over-scarborough-shoal-aggravates (accessed 10 May 2014).
22 For a discussion of some of the Chinese moves affecting Malaysia and Brunei, also SCS claimant states, see Storey (2011).

Select bibliography

Alagappa, M. ed. (1998) *Asian Security Practice: Material and Ideational Influences*. Stanford, CA: Stanford University Press.
Alagappa, M. ed. (2003) *Asian Security Order: Instrumental and Normative Features*. Stanford, CA: Stanford University Press.
Bentley, S. (2013) "Keeping an Eye on the South China Sea," Center for International Maritime Security, 3 December.
Buzan, B. (1991) *People, States and Fear: An Agenda for International Security Studies in the Post-Cold War Era*, second edn. Boulder, CO: Lynne Rienner Publishers.
Buzan, B. and Waever, O. (2003) *Regions and Powers: The Structure of International Security*. Cambridge, UK: Cambridge University Press.
Buzan, B., Waever, O. and de Wilde, J. (1998) *Security: A New Framework for Analysis*. Boulder, CO: Lynne Rienner Publishers.
Johnston, A. (2013) "How New and Assertive Is China's New Assertiveness?" *International Security*, Vol. 37, No. 4 (spring).
Lardy, N. (2012) *Sustaining China's Economic Growth after the Global Financial Crisis*. Washington, DC: The Peterson Institute.
Lynch, D. (2009) "China's Next Revolution," *Far Eastern Economic Review* (online edition), 1 October.
Lynch, D. (Forthcoming) *China's Futures: PRC Elites Debate the Economic, Political, Cultural, and Foreign Policy Trajectories*. Stanford, CA: Stanford University Press.
Pettis, M. (2013) *Avoiding the Fall: China's Economic Restructuring*. Washington, DC: Carnegie Endowment for International Peace.
Storey, I. (2011) *Southeast Asia and the Rise of China: The Search for Security*. London: Routledge.
Swaine, M. and Fravel, M.T. (2011) "China's Assertive Behavior, Part Two: The Maritime Periphery," *China Leadership Monitor*, No. 35 (summer).
Thayer, C. (2010) "The United States and Chinese Assertiveness in the South China Sea," *Security Studies*, Vol. 6, No. 2.

Part III
China's security forces

Section A
The PLA Army

17
The PLA Army

Dennis J. Blasko[1]

Traditionally China has been a continental power and its military primarily land-oriented. With 14 land neighbors, four of whom possess nuclear weapons, the People's Liberation Army (PLA) maintained this basic orientation until the past decade. In 2013, the Chinese government declared, "China is a major maritime as well as land country."[2] This was an expected development, foreshadowed by policy described in 2004: the PLA has shifted its priorities toward "the Navy, Air Force and Second Artillery Force, [to] strengthen its comprehensive deterrence and warfighting capabilities."[3] Nonetheless, despite the priority given to the other services, the Army has also undergone tremendous change over the past two decades.

Throughout most the 1990s, the total PLA active-duty strength was about three million personnel, with some 2.2 million in the Army. In two force reductions beginning in 1997 and 2003, 700,000 personnel were cut from the active strength, leaving 2.3 million personnel in 2005. The Army remains the largest of the services (and still the largest standing army in the world), with about 1.6 million personnel, comprising nearly 70 percent of the force.[4]

However, in November 2013 the Third Plenary Session of the Eighteenth Chinese Communist Party Central Committee decided to "optimize the size and structure of the Army, adjust and improve the proportion between various troops, and reduce non-combat institutions and personnel," adding "that joint operation command authority under the [Central Military Commission], and theater joint operation command system, will be improved."[5] At the time of this writing, details of these reforms have not been announced officially and the Ministry of National Defense has sought to downplay many rumors that have arisen. Nevertheless, it is certain that the Army will feel the majority of future force cuts and the proportion of the other services will grow even if no new billets are added to their rolls.

In early 2014, the Army is 25 percent smaller in manpower with at least 25 percent fewer units than it was in 1997. The Army has created or expanded a relatively small number of new, more technologically advanced units, called "new-type units," such as special operations (SOF), helicopter (Army aviation), and information/electronic warfare/cyber units in all military regions. It has downsized and restructured many older units, particularly infantry and tank formations, and has introduced a wide array of new equipment. But, for the most part, older weapons and equipment continue to outnumber the newer items in the inventory, though this situation is changing gradually.

The Army has become more mechanized and, as part of the "informationization" of the PLA, better equipped with modern communications and electronics. Its goal is to accomplish mechanization and make "major progress in informationization" by 2020. It is noteworthy that the goal for 2020 is to *accomplish* mechanization, but achieving full informationization is scheduled for 2049.[6]

Despite the reduction in the number of personnel and units, the Army's ability to conduct deterrence, combat, and non-traditional security missions has improved greatly since 1997. Nonetheless, many obstacles must be overcome before the Central Military Commission (CMC) is confident in the Army's ability to conduct joint and combined arms operations.

This chapter describes China's intentions for modernizing the Army, as can be learned from official sources, changes in the overall composition of the Army, and the current force structure (understanding that additional changes are imminent). Among its conclusions is that PLA Army force structure is consistent with the PLA's self-defensive doctrine and multi-dimensional deterrence strategy.[7]

China's strategic intentions in "army building"

The first defense White Paper of 1998 described the following modernization objectives:

> Reducing quantity and improving quality is a basic principle upon which the Army is to be modernized. The Chinese Army strengthens itself by relying on science and technology, and strives to make the transition from a numerically superior type to a qualitatively efficient type, and from a manpower-intensive type to a technology-intensive type. In view of the characteristics of modern wars, no effort will be spared to improve the modernization level of weaponry, reform and perfect the Army system and setup, and improve the training of troops and curricula and teaching methods of military academies.[8]

Thus the PLA's main objective is to create a smaller, more technologically advanced force. Weapons and technology (hardware) are important, but force structure, training, and education (software) are also specified. PLA leaders have consistently identified the software component of modernization to be of equal importance to upgrading hardware.

The 1998 White Paper identified the "basic objectives of China's defense policy" as "Consolidating national defense, resisting aggression, curbing armed subversion, and defending the state's sovereignty, unity, territorial integrity and security.{. . .}to avoid and curb [deter] war, and to solve international disputes and questions left over by history through peaceful means." It listed the following components of defense policy:

- "Subordinating national defense work to, and placing it in the service of, the nation's overall economic construction, and achieving the coordinated development of these two kinds of work."
- "Implementing the military strategy of active defense. Strategically China pursues the defensive policy featuring self-defense and gaining mastery by striking only after the enemy has struck . . . China upholds the principle of self-defense by the whole people and the strategic concept of people's war . . . On the basis of its existing weaponry, China carries forward and develops its fine traditions."
- "China does not seek hegemonism, nor does it seek military blocs or military expansion. China does not station any troops or set up any military bases in any foreign country. China opposes the arms race."

Subsequent White Papers have shifted priorities slightly or modified some terminology, but the basic principles and objectives of PLA modernization continue even as the announced defense budget has grown from about US$10 billion (81.257 billion yuan at an 8.29 exchange rate) in 1997 to roughly US$132 billion (808 billion yuan at a 6.12 exchange rate) in 2014.[9] Unfortunately, the Chinese government has not explained how the budget is divided among the services; therefore, it is not possible to determine whether funding has actually followed the priorities identified in 2004, "Navy, Air Force and Second Artillery," with the Army assumed to be bringing up the rear.

The 2010 White Paper added "maintaining social harmony and stability" as a "critical task" for the armed forces (which include the PLA, People's Armed Police [PAP], and militia) and reiterated that "accomplishing mechanization and attaining major progress in informationization by 2020" was the PLA's primary near-term goal.[10] However, it does not specify any particular warfighting objective to be accomplished by that date. In 2013, the White Paper stated that the Army is accelerating

> the development of army aviation troops, light mechanized units and special operations forces, and enhancing building of digitalized units, gradually making its units small, modular and multi-functional in organization so as to enhance their capabilities for air-ground integrated operations, long-distance maneuvers, rapid assaults and special operations.[11]

These changes seek to reorient the Army from "theater defense to trans-theater mobility." For the PLA, "trans-theater [or trans-regional] mobility" means the ability to deploy forces from one military region to another and along China's coast, not (yet) to project force far beyond China's borders. Since 2006, the PLA has undertaken a series of trans-regional exercises experimenting particularly with the command and control of these complex joint operations supported by civilian capabilities.

Army force structure changes

Prior to the 1997 force reduction, Army "mobile operational units" were assigned to 24 group armies or were under the command of military region or military district headquarters as "independent" forces. Maneuver forces (infantry and armored units) numbered about 73 infantry divisions (though some were not at full strength), 11 tank divisions, and 13 tank brigades, plus seven helicopter regiments (no SOF units were identified).

Total infantry and armored divisions in 2014 were about 23 (and probably decreasing to around 20), along with about 58 (or more) infantry and armored brigades. (These numbers do not include border and coastal defense units.) Most of the reduction in the number of divisions comes from the infantry force; only one armored division remains. Mechanized infantry units now are found in all military regions, including about eight divisions and 21 brigades, amounting to half of the infantry force, up from only about 5 percent of infantry divisions before reductions started. The Army Aviation Corps has also expanded in number and size of units as well as total aircraft. Army special operations forces (SOF) have expanded, with six former SOF groups being upgraded to brigades and at least two new brigades added. These changes are summarized in Table 17.1.

The 2013 White Paper stated that the forces known as "mobile operational [or combat] units" number 850,000 personnel.[12] Since 1997, they have been reduced in number and size, but upgraded in firepower and mobility. However, the number of static Army border and coastal defense units does not appear to have changed significantly since 1997. This force is estimated to include approximately 56 border defense regiments, nine border defense battalions, five patrol craft units, two coastal defense divisions, three coastal defense brigades, 32 coastal defense and artillery regiments, and four

Dennis J. Blasko

Table 17.1 Army maneuver (infantry, armored, helicopter, and SOF) units[i]

	1997	2014
Group armies	24	18
Infantry divisions	90	22 (probably decreasing)
Armored divisions	12	1
Infantry brigades	7	41 (probably increasing)
Armored brigades	13	17
Brigade equivalents (infantry and armor)*	224	104
Army aviation regiments/brigades	7/0	7/6
SOF groups/regiments/brigades	7/0/0	2/1/8

Notes: * Brigade equivalent = 5 battalions; 1 division = 2 brigade equivalents.
[i] *The Military Balance 1996/97*, London: The International Institute for Strategic Studies, 1996, p. 179 and *The Military Balance 2014*, p. 232.

coastal defense battalions.[13] Approximately 200,000 or more active-duty PLA ground force personnel are estimated to be assigned to this mission (over 12 percent of all Army personnel).[14]

Changes to the Army's force structure have occurred through a variety of means.

- Entire headquarters and units were disbanded.
- Some units previously assigned to headquarters that were disbanded were transferred to headquarters that remained.
- Many divisions were downsized to brigades. This mostly happened to infantry divisions, but since late 2011 all armored divisions but one were transformed into a mechanized infantry brigade and an armored brigade.
- Infantry and armored divisions were restructured to have only three maneuver regiments instead of the four regiments previously found in a full-strength, Soviet-model division.
- Divisions and brigades were reorganized to become different types of units, such as amphibious mechanized infantry divisions and light mechanized infantry divisions and brigades.
- Some units were transferred to other services or the PAP. In the late 1990s, an infantry division was transferred to the Navy to become the second Marine brigade. At about the same time, 14 Army divisions were transferred to the PAP and reorganized to become "mobile divisions" responsible for domestic security. At the end of 2010, two short-range ballistic missile brigades, which had been created earlier in the decade as Army units, were reflagged as Second Artillery brigades.[15]
- Some units were transferred from active-duty into the PLA reserves.
- New units were added to the force and a few were expanded in size and organizational level. But the number of new and expanded units is much smaller than the number of units that were eliminated or downsized.

Over the past 15 years, the PLA has introduced a number of different types of unmanned aerial vehicles (UAVs) into the force. Some of them are short-range, hand-held models, while others are larger with longer ranges and flight duration. Artillery, reconnaissance, SOF, electronic warfare,

The PLA Army

and communications units have experimented with using UAVs mostly for reconnaissance and communications relay purposes.[16] So far, no armed UAVs are reported in the Army's inventory.

As part of the development of the PLA's electronic warfare and cyber warfare capabilities, over the past decade foreign analysis has revealed ten Technical Reconnaissance Bureaus assigned to the military regions. These units are part of the system overseen by the General Staff Department Third Department (Technical Reconnaissance). They conduct "communications intelligence, direction finding, traffic analysis, translation, cryptology, computer network defense, and computer network exploitation" in support of military region operations.[17] Additionally, several electronic countermeasure brigades or regiments are found in the military regions. Some reserve and militia forces also have cyber and electronic warfare missions.

New equipment of all types has been added to the inventory as many older pieces have been retired. Simultaneously, many existing models of weapons and equipment have been upgraded with more advanced communications, computers, and subcomponents. Because the overall size of the force is smaller, not as much new equipment is now required as would have been prior to the force reductions and restructuring.

Nonetheless, most units still are composed of a mix of older and newer equipment. A review of numbers found in *The Military Balance* for the various types of equipment in the Army indicates that only about 30 to 40 percent of all ground force major equipment would be considered "new" or "modern." For example, out of a total of 6,840 main battle tanks, 4,200 are based on the Type 59-series with only 2,640 newer Type 96/98/99 series.[18]

Current Army force structure

The four General Departments (General Staff, Political, Logistics, and Armament Departments) serve as the national-level headquarters for the Army as well as organizing and directing the other services.[19] Most Army units come under the command of headquarters at the military region (MR), provincial military district (MD)/garrison level, and military sub-district (MSD)/garrison levels. People's Armed Forces Departments (PAFD) headquarters are found at county and grassroots (township or sub-district) levels. MD, MSD, and PAFD are considered local headquarters.

Military regions – regional headquarters

The Chinese mainland is divided into seven military regions each covering two or more provinces, autonomous regions, or centrally administered cities. Military regions are military region leader level organizations and are named after the city in which their headquarters are located. In early 2014 the seven MRs (in protocol order) are structured as follows:

- Shenyang MR, consisting of the Liaoning, Jilin, and Heilongjiang MDs and the northeastern part of Inner Mongolia
- Beijing MR, consisting of the Beijing and Tianjin Garrisons and the Hebei, Shanxi, and Inner Mongolia MDs
- Lanzhou MR, consisting of the Shaanxi, Gansu, Qinghai, Ningxia, Xinjiang, Nanjiang (southern Xinjiang, actually the northwest part of Tibet) MDs and the western part of Inner Mongolia
- Jinan MR, consisting of the Shandong and Henan MDs
- Nanjing MR, consisting of the Shanghai Garrison and the Jiangsu, Zhejiang, Anhui, Fujian, and Jiangxi MDs

- Guangzhou MR, consisting of the Hunan, Guangdong, Guangxi, Hainan, and Hubei MDs
- Chengdu MR, consisting of the Chongqing Garrison and the Sichuan, Xizang (Tibet), Guizhou, and Yunnan MDs

Each MR commander shares responsibility with a political commissar, both of whom are assisted by several Army deputy commanders and deputy political commissars, the regional Air Force commander, and a naval fleet commander in the Jinan, Nanjing, and Guangzhou MRs. Army deputy commanders are assigned individual portfolios, such as operations, logistics, or armament. These personnel form the nucleus of the MR-level party committee with the political commissar acting as first secretary.

MR staffs parallel, but are smaller than, the organization of the four General Departments. Each MR has a headquarters department (consisting of operations, intelligence, informationization, etc.) overseen by a chief of staff, political department, joint logistics department (JLD), and armament department. In addition to supervising the work of the headquarters department, the chief of staff oversees the directors of the JLD and armament department.

Subordinate to MR headquarters are (see Figure 17.1):

1) "mobile operational units" organized into group armies or independent units
2) logistics units organized into joint logistics sub-departments and armament support (repair/maintenance) units

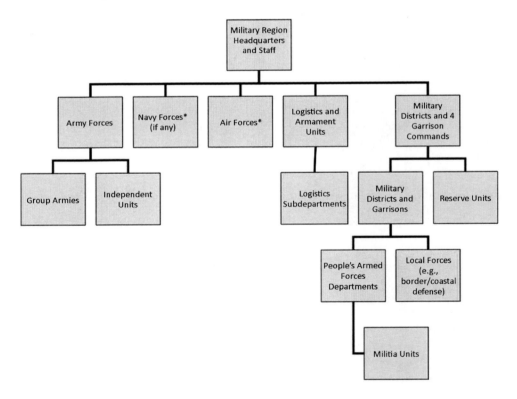

Figure 17.1 Military region structure

Note: * In peacetime, the chain of command for Navy and Air Force units located in an MR also runs to service headquarters in Beijing. In time of war, they may be assigned to war zone headquarters to take part in military operations.

3) provincial Military Districts and Garrison Commands for the four centrally administered cities of Beijing, Tianjin, Shanghai, and Chongqing

Navy and Air Force units in the region have a dual chain of command, reporting directly to service headquarters in Beijing in peacetime, but may come under direct MR (or theater/war zone) command during war. Second Artillery units located in the MR report directly to Second Artillery headquarters in Beijing; conventional Second Artillery units may be assigned to support war zone operations in time of war. During peacetime, MR headquarters are administrative organizations charged to prepare the forces in their regions to accomplish the specific missions assigned to each MR.

In time of emergency, MR headquarters are likely to be formed into temporary operational war zone headquarters to conduct military or non-traditional security operations. These *ad hoc* wartime headquarters would be formed around the structure of an MR headquarters, but could be augmented, and perhaps commanded, by officers from higher headquarters in Beijing. The boundaries of a war zone will not necessarily correspond directly with the pre-existing MR boundaries, but will vary according to the operational objectives assigned to the war zone.

Local headquarters

Each Military District headquarters is responsible for a single province or autonomous region and bears its province or region's name, and is a corps leader grade organization (with one exception). The garrison headquarters in Beijing, Tianjin, Shanghai, and Chongqing share the same corps leader organizational grade level and have similar responsibilities as MD headquarters. The Beijing Garrison is called a *weishuqu*, while the other garrisons are *jingbeiqu*.

MD commanders and political commissars are responsible for local and reserve forces (both reserve units and militia units) in their province and for mobilization preparations. MD commanders and political commissars are assisted by deputies and staffs similar to, but smaller than, MR headquarters.

Active-duty local forces under MD command may include coastal and border defense units, as well as infantry, armor, or artillery units. MD headquarters also oversee logistics depots and bases and armament units, such as repair and maintenance depots, in their province. MD headquarters command PLA reserve units in their province or autonomous region.

Each MD is divided into military sub-districts (MSDs) and garrisons (*jingbeiqu*), which are division leader grade organizations. MSDs are found in prefectures or cities and counties and take the name of their prefecture, city, or county. Since 2003, MSDs in provincial capital cities and some other important cities have been designated as "garrisons." The most recently formed garrison is the Sansha Garrison Command, part of Hainan MD, on the Paracel Islands in the South China Sea, established in July 2012.[20]

In 2014, there were approximately 296 MSD and 39 garrison headquarters at the division leader grade. Two "fort district" headquarters are at this level of command: Waichangshan in Shenyang MR and Neichangshan in Jinan MR. Both MSD and these garrison headquarters are responsible for formulating mobilization plans, organizing conscription/demobilization, supporting reserve and militia training, and supervising the activities of PAFDs in their areas. In border regions, MSD/garrison headquarters command PLA border/coastal defense troops and their operations.[21]

In addition to the duties described above, garrison units guard military facilities, maintain order among the troops and perform duties similar to military police functions in other armies. According to the 1998 White Paper, it is the responsibility of garrison units in large- and medium-sized cities to "check, inspect and handle cases of infringements of military discipline by military personnel as well as cases of violations of relevant rules by military vehicles."[22] These soldiers have authority only over PLA personnel and are not involved in the law enforcement activities of the local public security apparatus.

People's Armed Forces Departments (PAFD) are found at county, city, district, township (town) or sub-district levels, and sometimes at work unit level, such as large factories. PAFDs are primarily responsible for meeting local conscription quotas for the active force and the militia as determined by MSD and MD headquarters. They also assist in logistics support for units in their area and are involved with supporting demobilized soldiers and organizing reserve and militia training. Grassroots PAFDs provide peacetime command for militia units in their areas of responsibility.

County, city, and municipal district PAFD headquarters are led by active-duty PLA officers and are regiment leader grade organizations. Below them, grassroots PAFD headquarters at township or sub-district levels are non-active-duty organizations.[23] Grassroots PAFD headquarters are manned by local civilian cadre who wear PLA uniforms but have distinctive insignia and rank epaulets. These local civilian PAFD cadre are called *zhuanzhi renminwuzhuang ganbu*, often shortened to *zhuanwu ganbu*. The number of civilian *zhuanwu ganbu* supporting the Chinese armed forces is not known and probably is counted among the total number of militia personnel.

In addition to falling under the MR chain of command, all local headquarters from MD to PAFD levels are departments of the corresponding Communist Party committees and serve as local government organizations responsible for military work.[24] In order to maintain party supervision of military affairs, the local civilian party secretary is dual-hatted as the first secretary of the party committee of the corresponding PLA headquarters. Local party committees are required to have at least two meetings a year on military affairs and local government and party leaders should also spend at least 2 days a year studying military knowledge.[25] Based on individual personalities, the relationship between military officers and local party secretaries and other party officials probably varies from place to place.

Operational and tactical units

PLA Army operational and tactical units are organized as

- Group armies (corps leader grade organizations)
- Divisions and joint logistics sub-departments (division leader grade organizations)
- Brigades (division deputy leader grade organizations)
- Regiments or groups (regiment leader grade organizations)
- Battalions or squadrons (battalion leader grade organizations)
- Companies (company leader grade organizations)
- Platoons (platoon leader grade organizations)
- Squads or weapons crews (commanded by non-commissioned officers, they have no grade level)

Organizations from group army to regiment level are known as *budui*, usually translated as "unit." Organizations from battalion to squad level are known as *fendui*, "small units," or grassroots level units.

The PLA Army

Group armies

Group armies are composed of combinations of divisions, brigades, and regiments. The total number of personnel assigned to group armies probably varies from roughly 30,000 to about 50,000 depending on specific composition.

After the reductions of the late 1990s, the variation in group army structure has increased considerably from previous years. The majority of group armies contain a mix of three to six maneuver divisions and brigades. Maneuver units are supported by an artillery brigade, an air defense brigade, an engineer regiment, a communications regiment, a chemical defense regiment or battalion, a reconnaissance battalion, an army aviation brigade or regiment (in some group armies), an SOF brigade or group (in some group armies) and logistics and armament support units (see Figure 17.2).

Though group armies often are considered to be corps-sized units, in reality they control many fewer personnel and units than do corps in the US military. A group army with an all

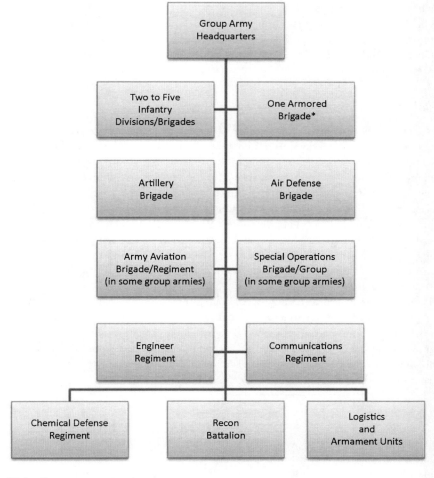

Figure 17.2 Group army structure

Note: * The Thirty-eighth Group Army has an armored division.

brigade maneuver force would be more comparable to a US division than a corps. Likewise, PLA divisions are much smaller than US Army and Marine Corps divisions.

The 2013 White Paper enumerated the numeric designators for the 18 group armies for the first time:

- Shenyang MR: Sixteenth Group Army, Changchun, Jilin; Thirty-ninth Mechanized Group Army, Liaoyang, Liaoning; Fortieth Group Army, Jinzhou, Liaoning
- Beijing MR: Twenty-seventh Group Army, Shijiazhuang, Hebei; Thirty-eighth Mechanized Group Army, Baoding, Hebei; Sixty-fifth Group Army, Zhangjiakou, Hebei; plus two guard divisions in Beijing
- Lanzhou MR: Twenty-first Group Army, Baoji, Shaanxi; Forty-seventh Group Army, Lintong, Shaanxi; plus four independent infantry divisions in Xinjiang/Nanjiang MDs
- Jinan MR: Twentieth Group Army, Kaifeng, Henan; Twenty-sixth Group Army, Weifang, Shandong; Fifty-forth Group Army, Xinxiang, Henan
- Nanjing MR: First Group Army, Huzhou, Zhejiang; Twelfth Group Army, Xuzhou, Jiangsu; Thirty-first Group Army, Xiamen, Fujian
- Guangzhou MR: Forty-first Group Army, Liuzhou, Guangxi; Forty-second Group Army, Huizhou, Guangdong; plus independent infantry brigades in Hainan and Hong Kong
- Chengdu MR: Thirteenth Group Army, Chongqing; Fourteenth Group Army, Kunming, Yunnan; plus three independent infantry brigades in Tibet[26]

Divisions

PLA divisions are structured with regiments as their next lower organizational level. Unlike some other militaries, PLA division headquarters *do not* command brigades. PLA infantry units are categorized as motorized, heavy or light mechanized, amphibious mechanized, or mountain.

Infantry divisions now command two infantry regiments, an armored regiment, an artillery regiment, and an air defense regiment, plus reconnaissance, chemical defense, engineer, communications, and logistics (medical, supply, maintenance, repair, etc.) battalions or companies. An infantry division's manpower strength is about 10,000 personnel. Divisions often are characterized as having "a thousand" vehicles, which include tanks, armored personnel carriers/infantry fighting vehicles, artillery, trucks, and smaller vehicles. The transformation of six motorized infantry divisions into two brigades each was reported in early 2014, but the transformation of all six has not yet been confirmed.

The one remaining armored division commands three armored regiments (each with a mechanized infantry battalion), an artillery regiment, and an air defense regiment, plus similar support units as found in an infantry division, with about 8,000 personnel and 300 tanks and armored personnel carriers.[27] In late 2011, the internet in China carried reports of armored divisions transforming to become an armored brigade and a mechanized infantry brigade. This process occurred in all other armored divisions by the end of 2013.

Brigades

Operationally, brigades appear to have become equivalent to divisions now that many former divisions have been transformed into brigades. However, brigades have a division deputy leader organizational grade. In the active-duty force, infantry, armor, artillery, air defense, army aviation, SOF, engineer, and electronic countermeasure units all may be organized as brigades. Depending on the type, brigades probably range from 2,000 to 6,000 personnel, with numbers and types of vehicles assigned varying greatly (often characterized as in the hundreds). Infantry and armored brigades appear generally to command four or five combat battalions; an artillery regiment, which is smaller than a division artillery regiment; an air defense battalion; and logistics and armament support units.[28]

Regiments and groups

Regiments are composed of numbered companies (identified by numbers 1 to 12) of their basic type (infantry, armored, etc.), which usually are assigned under the command of three battalion headquarters. In addition to maneuver battalions, combat regiments have artillery or mortar and anti-aircraft units permanently assigned. Regimental headquarters may also command engineer, chemical defense, and logistics and armament support units, usually of company size. Depending on the type of unit, regiments may have from about 1,000 to over 2,500 personnel, with over 100 armored vehicles in armored and mechanized units.

Under the Soviet system of organization, the combined arms regiment was the basic combat maneuver unit in the PLA Army. Regiment headquarters commanded and supported operations directly down to individual companies, with the battalion level headquarters having little actual planning and logistics responsibility (unlike the US and many other foreign armies). Over the past decade, PLA doctrine has attempted to shift the focus of the basic combat maneuver unit down to the battalion level, emphasizing the temporary formation of "modular" combined arms battalions for specific missions and tasks, using a process similar to what is known in the West as "task organization."

The Army has approximately 15 ship groups, including about 250 landing craft, to perform a variety of functions.[29] Approximately 12 ship transport groups are assigned to joint logistics sub-departments and border defense units. Some units also have reconnaissance missions in addition to their transport mission to supply coastal defense units stationed on small islands. One unique ship group in the Nanjing MR is stationed at the Dongshan Island amphibious training area to provide operational support to amphibious training.[30] At least four patrol craft groups and one battalion level unit are assigned to border defense units to conduct patrol missions on rivers and inland lakes.

Battalions

Battalions are generally composed of three to five companies under the command of a battalion commander and political instructor and a small staff consisting of deputy battalion commander(s), deputy political instructors(s), and the director of a battalion medical clinic. The size of the battalion staff indicates that many command and staff functions traditionally have been conducted at regiment or brigade headquarters and not in the battalion headquarters. The total number of personnel in a battalion varies according to unit type, but probably ranges from about 200 to 700, with around 30 armored vehicles (or 18 to 24 artillery or anti-aircraft weapons) with additional trucks and light vehicles in support.

Currently units are experimenting with how to augment battalion staffs with personnel to perform the coordination and planning work required when additional units are assigned to form a combined arms battalion. In some cases junior officers from subordinate companies have been brought up to battalion level; in other cases a few NCOs have been assigned to battalion headquarters. Eventually, it is likely that the table of organization and equipment for battalion headquarters will be adjusted by permanently assigning more personnel to the headquarters staff. This process could take several years before it is implemented throughout the entire Army.

Border and coastal defense units

Army border defense and coastal defense units are commanded by military sub-district headquarters. Border defense units are mostly organized into light infantry regiments that man fixed observation posts and patrol the borders on foot and by various other methods (horses, snowmobiles, etc.) depending on the terrain in their area of responsibility. A few patrol craft units, two horse cavalry battalions, and several cavalry companies augment the infantry units.[31] Coastal defense units may be infantry or artillery and often are stationed on small islands.

Border and coastal defense regiments probably are manned by about 2,000 personnel each and have limited mobility for offensive maneuvering during combat situations. These are purely defensive and early warning units. Army coastal defense units may be equipped with artillery, but are not known to employ anti-ship cruise missiles (unlike Navy coastal defense units).

Logistics sub-departments

Joint logistics sub-departments (JLSDs) consist of fixed supply and repair depots/bases as well as the support units assigned to these bases and depots. JLSDs are division leader grade headquarters that manage support units such as material and fuel depots, hospitals, transportation units, maintenance, and repair units. JLSDs also run large farms for sideline production.

Approximately 27 JLSDs are distributed among the seven military regions and are under the supervision of the MR headquarters JLD.[32] Each has a unique structure usually consisting of roughly 10 to 15 subordinate regiment leader grade units. While some JLSDs command units in only one province, others have subordinate units stationed in multiple provincial-level jurisdictions. In order to support field operations, JLSDs form temporary emergency support brigades from their subordinate elements. The composition of emergency support brigades varies according to the mission and units being supported.

At least two ship transport groups, used for river and coastal transport, are assigned to Nanjing MR JLSDs (in Shanghai and Nanjing). Mobile fuel pipeline units have been identified in the Lanzhou, Nanjing, Guangzhou, and Chengdu MRs.

Reserve units

The reserve force (consisting of PLA reserve units and the militia) has been reorganized along with the modernization of the active-duty force since 1997. PLA reserve units were reported to number about 510,000 personnel in 2009, but this figure is probably increasing as the Navy, Air Force, and Second Artillery add reserve units.[33]

The bulk of the PLA reserve unit strength still supports the Army. Reserve units are organized in divisions, brigades, and regiments based on provincial boundaries and are commanded by their respective MD headquarters. In total, the Army reserve force consists of approximately 38 divisions, 28 brigades, and several regiments. Over one-third of Army reserve units are dedicated to local air defense and are equipped mostly with anti-aircraft guns. A reserve logistics support brigade has been created in each military region since 1997.[34]

Conclusions

The Chinese government has presented a general outline of how the PLA Army will modernize. Analysis of publicly available data provides evidence to support the implementation of China's officially stated intentions. There is no doubt the PLA is smaller but more technologically advanced than it was 15 years ago. The Army is estimated to be at least 25 percent smaller in personnel with a similar reduction in the number of mobile combat units. More personnel and force structure reductions appear imminent.

PLA equipment has been upgraded through the introduction of new technology on new platforms and new technologies added to older weapons. Nonetheless, less than half the equipment in the Army can now be considered modern and the modernization of the full force is still many years away. Even the 2020 goal calls only for "accomplishing mechanization and *attaining major progress* in informationization." Achieving full informationization will probably come decades later. Impending personnel and force structure cuts could speed up this process by requiring fewer items of new equipment to be issued to a smaller, but better trained force.

Command structures focus on mainland defense

When future cuts are made, multiple Army headquarters and combat and support units will probably be either eliminated or downsized. Major reductions in officer billets could be achieved by restructuring the local headquarters chain of command. Abolishing or adjusting the size of MD/MSD/PAFD headquarters and redistributing their responsibilities could save the PLA money, which could then be put to other uses or services. Such a restructuring, however, would almost certainly encounter significant bureaucratic opposition, but could be justified by advances in communications and organizational effectiveness that allow fewer headquarters to control more units.

Even if potential future personnel cuts of several hundred thousand active-duty PLA personnel were to be borne primarily by the Army, the Army would still remain the largest service. Its officers will probably continue to dominate headquarters from Beijing to county-level through the local headquarters chain of command. This command system reflects a traditional continental, defensive orientation, which is only gradually being expanded beyond China's borders and coastal waters. Despite the low probability of a major land invasion of the mainland, the PLA currently is structured mainly to cope with such a threat by implementing defense mobilization at the regional or national level. No matter what future reforms are made, continental defense will remain a major PLA mission.

The existing chain of command also is structured to react to (and in some cases deter) a variety of domestic non-traditional security challenges, such as internal stability, terrorism, disaster relief, medical emergencies, etc. For these missions, PLA reserve and militia units, commanded by local headquarters, often are the first-responders providing manpower and equipment support until out-of-area forces arrive.

PLA doctrine envisions many forms of joint campaigns executed beyond the Chinese mainland that could put naval, Air Force, or missile units in the lead role. Currently the existing peacetime chain of command must shift to an *ad hoc* wartime war zone command structure to accommodate the operational changes necessary to execute long-distance joint missions. More efficient command structures are expected to be a major part of future structural reforms. It is possible that in the future naval or Air Force officers will command at least some military regions (or whatever new headquarters replace MRs) because of the potential requirement to conduct sea and air campaigns beyond China's borders.

Chinese military planners see potential military threats originating from both its land and maritime borders. *The Science of Military Strategy*, written in 2001, states, "we may face two kinds of war in the foreseeable future. One is to fight against local invasion by outside hostile forces; the other is to fight for the reunification of our country.{. . .}But even if the direct enemy is inferior to us, it is still possible that powerful enemies may intervene."[35] Details of the PLA's contingency planning are not known by the general public, but clearly campaigns against possible military challenges from Taiwan, Japan, or other Asian neighbors, many of whom could be supported by the US, are foreseen in PLA doctrine. If China's deterrence posture fails and the PLA is forced to fight, it will seek early victory, but be prepared for protracted war: "Under high-tech conditions, it is the target of both sides to fight a quick battle and force a quick decision. But it doesn't remove the possibility to achieve the military object through enduring operations if it is necessary."[36]

Force structure reflects strategically defensive orientation

Over the past 15 years downsizing has occurred in all military regions. While Army units have become more mechanized and informationized, their deployments continue to reflect a strategically defensive posture, emphasizing the Army's mission to deter aggression against the Chinese mainland. Group armies and independent units have both offensive and defensive capabilities at the operational and tactical levels. The manner in which they operate (offensively or defensively) depends on the military situation and the tasks assigned them, not the location of their home garrisons. With only a few exceptions, large formations of ground troops are stationed at considerable distances from borders and would require long-distance movements to get into assembly areas and offensive positions. In nearly all cases, Army units would be required to move significant distances using land (road and rail), air, and water (sea or river) means of transportation. In the era of satellite reconnaissance and social media, such movements are unlikely to be made in secret, reducing the chances that ground forces will attain strategic surprise. Achieving operational and tactical surprise, however, could be possible through the use of deception and concealment measures.

Further reflecting the PLA's strategically defensive and deterrence posture is the limited long-distance airlift capacity in the Air Force, the limited number of medium and large amphibious ships in the Navy, and the relatively small size of the Army's helicopter force. The PLA's logistics infrastructure remains focused on interior lines of communications, with minimal capacity to project and sustain forces on exterior lines. In order to conduct long-distance movements for large units, the use of civilian transportation and logistics/maintenance support is essential. PLA doctrine calls for the mobilization of civilian forces to support military campaigns. Such mobilization is also likely to compromise strategic surprise in the modern era. Mobilization could, however, be used to signal China's intentions as part of its deterrence posture.

As the Army continues to be reduced in size a major development to watch will be whether the PLA's long-range sea and airlift capabilities are built up using some of the manpower billets and funds saved by shrinking the size of the Army. A more mechanized Army requires much greater rail, sea, and air transport capacity and has much larger fuel and repair requirements than the forces of the past. The Army's amphibious units outnumber the Navy's Marine force by two to one (two Army amphibious mechanized infantry divisions and one amphibious armored brigade to two Marine brigades). Yet most Navy amphibious ships (including the three large Type 071 amphibious assault ships) are assigned to the South Sea Fleet and provide support mainly to the two Marine brigades. Army ship transport units provide transport, logistics, and reconnaissance support mostly to coastal operations and would be of little help in moving large formations over long distances (over a few hundred miles) at sea. Thus, the PLA's potential for long-range, relatively rapid amphibious operations appears for now to be found in the Marine brigades and not the Army. Likewise, except for some Army reconnaissance and SOF parachute capabilities, the vast majority of the PLA's airborne (parachute) assault capability is found in the Air Force's three airborne divisions.

Army aviation (helicopter) and special operations forces represent the Army's main potential for putting boots on the ground in distant operational areas. The two forces frequently train together. However, even with the expansion of these units over the past decade, they still remain a relatively small segment of the ground force. Unlike SOF units in the United States military, PLA SOF units are not supported by a similar array of special mission fixed wing and rotary wing aircraft and other enabling units to provide stealthy transport, firepower, logistics, and intelligence support. PLA SOF units will probably continue to grow and improve with their focus mostly on commando-type and long-range reconnaissance missions.

Currently the Army only has about 760 helicopters of all types to support its "mobile operational units."[37] Attack helicopters have been introduced only in the last decade. Helicopter forces will probably continue to expand and diversify their mission capabilities. The creation of an airmobile force of brigade or multi-brigade size is possible, but would probably require the addition of at least a hundred more helicopters in one region for such a force to be capable of operating on its own along with a dedicated infantry force of appropriate size. An integrated PLA airmobile force would take several years to develop doctrine and train to attain the proficiency necessary for PLA leaders to have confidence in its employment.

A final element indicating the PLA's strategically defensive posture is the fulltime commitment of about 200,000 Army personnel to border and coastal defense. These units are located immediately on China's borders and have defensive, early warning missions. They are not suited for cross-border offensive operations, nor are they likely to be moved from one region to another during times of emergency. The transformation of the Xi'an Army Academy to the Border Defense Academy, as well as numerous senior officer visits to border units and the media attention given the force suggest that border defense units will continue to be an important part of the Army force structure.

Smaller forces require higher readiness and training levels

A smaller Army means that all units must maintain high levels of operational readiness. The emphasis on preparing all units for "diversified" missions is seen by the fact that units from all military regions take part in training with foreign militaries, are assigned UN peacekeeping missions, and respond to disaster relief and other emergencies as necessary.

Major training themes observed in all military regions include experimentation with command and control structures for joint operations, how to conduct combined arms operations at battalion level, testing trans-regional deployments within China, improving land-air integration, and conducting operations in complex electromagnetic environments on widely dispersed battlefields linked by improved communications and computer networks. However, these experiments have revealed that battalion headquarters are not staffed adequately to control combined arms operations and that "some" battalion commanders are not prepared for their new responsibilities.

Since 2006, the Army has conducted a series of trans-regional operations within China incorporating Navy, Air Force, Second Artillery, and civilian support. The largest trans-regional exercises were "Stride 2009" and "Mission Action 2013," reportedly involving 50,000 and 40,000 personnel respectively, conducted by multiple divisions and brigades. The PLA is also seeking to improve the integration of SOF, helicopter, UAV, and electronic/cyber warfare units into its maneuver and firepower capabilities. In 2013 Nanjing and Guangzhou MRs held two large airmobile operations with 70 to 100 helicopters of various types.

Beginning in 2002, the PLA Army has conducted over 40 combined exercises with foreign troops from over 20 countries, some in China, others outside the country. Most of these exercises have been relatively small in scale, ranging from a few dozen to a couple hundred personnel, often including SOF personnel, and usually emphasizing non-traditional security missions, such as anti-terrorism and disaster relief. Larger exercises have been conducted with Russia and the Shanghai Cooperation Organization nations, again usually focusing on non-traditional security missions. The largest of these exercises was the first bilateral China-Russia "Peace Mission-2005," which included approximately 10,000 troops. Since 2003, the PLA has also occasionally invited foreign observers to watch full divisions and brigades exercising in the field in China.[38]

Senior PLA leaders are well aware of the capabilities of their force. They have made realistic evaluations of the many obstacles to modernization yet to be overcome and acknowledge the large gap between PLA capabilities and those of other advanced militaries. Realistic evaluations of personnel qualities, force structure, training, logistics, and technological shortcomings are common in the PLA's own internal writings. Such assessments are found much less frequently in the English-language sources, but one recent example may be found in a statement by Professor Yang Shuqi of the National Defense University: "it must be clear that the overall military training level of the PLA is still not high as compared with that of the armies of the world's military powers, the training system is not yet perfect, and the means and conditions for the close-to-actual-combat training are not complete."[39]

As can be seen from the official Chinese statements above, the general directions and trends in the modernization of the PLA Army have been outlined publicly in broad terms for more than 15 years. Evidence of these trends can thus be found in a large body of Chinese military writing, much of it available on the internet and Chinese television, but with many details found only in Chinese. However, despite a relative degree of transparency at the strategic level, many questions remain at the operational and tactical levels of the force. Some of these questions can be answered through close attention to official Chinese sources, but many remain unaddressed mostly for reasons of operational security. The PLA now constantly reminds its troops to be careful what they say while on the phone and to others over the internet. A number of "military enthusiasts," empowered by Chinese social media, add to the conversation on the internet; however, though some of their insights prove to be valid, others must be treated with caution. In any case, there is so much change underway within the PLA and so much information available, it is difficult to maintain accurate, up-to-date databases. Finally, the PLA is an organization unique among militaries; attempting to understand what is going on in the PLA by mirror-imaging developments in the US or Soviet (now Russian) militaries is a sure path to misperceptions.

The PLA leadership understands that it has a difficult road ahead as the force seeks to achieve the capabilities of an advanced military. Though it is bound to become smaller, the Army remains an integral element of the PLA. Its progress in building capabilities "commensurate with China's international standing" deserves continued comprehensive and objective analysis.[40]

Notes

1 This chapter draws on and updates information found in the second edition of the author's book, *The Chinese Army Today: Tradition and Transformation for the Twenty-first Century*, London: Routledge, 2012. It updates and revises portions of a longer paper on the same subject presented at the "PLA as Organization" conference held June 13–14, 2012 in Vienna, VA.
2 Information Office of the State Council, The Diversified Employment of China's Armed Forces, 2013. All of China's white papers can be found at http://english.gov.cn/official/2005–08/17/content_24165.htm (accessed 13 March 2014), and will be cited hereafter by their title and year.
3 China's National Defense in 2004.
4 J. Hackett (ed.), *The Military Balance 2014*, London: The International Institute for Strategic Studies, 2014, p. 232.

5 "China to Optimize Army Size, Structure: CPC Decision," *PLA Daily*, 16 November 2013. Available online at http://eng.chinamil.com.cn/news-channels/china-military-news/2013–11/16/content_5651458.htm (accessed 13 March 2014).
6 China's National Defense in 2006 and China's National Defense in 2008.
7 China's concept of deterrence is explained in G. Peng and Y. Yao (eds), *The Science of Military Strategy*, Beijing: Military Science Publishing House, 2005, pp. 213–29. The original Chinese text was written in 2001.
8 China's National Defense, July 1998.
9 Ibid. and "China Defense Budget to Increase 12.2 pct in 2014: Report," *Xinhua*, 5 March 2014. Available online at http://news.xinhuanet.com/english/special/2014–03/05/c_133161044.htm (accessed 13 March 2014). While the dollar amount of the officially announced Chinese defense budget has grown by a factor of about 13 since 1997, the amount of renminbi growth is 10 times the 1997 budget reflecting the difference in exchange rates. Foreign analysts generally agree that the *announced* defense budget does not include all defense-related streams of income. The PLA budget may be augmented by additional central funding (for example, foreign arms purchases), local funding (to support mobilization and demobilization), and by efforts generated by the PLA itself (such as food grown on its own farms). However, these income streams vary in number and amount from year to year and no consistent source of data is available to capture these variable sources of funds. Moreover, among the numerous organizations and individuals who attempt to estimate actual defense-related spending, there is no consensus on which additional sources of income should be included (for example, should the PAP budget be included as military spending?). Thus, these estimates vary greatly and rarely does any organization itemize exactly what they have included in their calculation. Currently, estimates are found in the range of 40 to 50 percent more than the officially announced figure to roughly double the announced numbers. Nonetheless, it is likely that "in recent years an increasing percentage of 'actual' PLA funding has been placed 'on the books'; that is, officially reported figures increasingly reflect actual spending." See Adam P. Liff and Andrew S. Erickson, "Demystifying China's Defence Spending: Less Mysterious in the Aggregate," *The China Quarterly*, 2013. Available on CJO 2013 doi:10.1017/S0305741013000295.
10 China's National Defense in 2010.
11 The Diversified Employment of China's Armed Forces, 2013.
12 Ibid.
13 The order-of-battle list for border and coastal defense units is derived primarily from a 2009 Chinese list, "Chinese PLA Border and Coastal Defense Units [中国人民解放军边防海防部队]." Available online at http://bbs.junhunw.cn/forum.php?mod=viewthread&tid=626 (accessed 15 March 2014). The information in this list was crossed-checked with other sources.
14 D. Blasko, "PLA Ground Force Modernization and Mission Diversification: Underway in All Military Regions," in R. Kamphausen and A. Scobell (eds), *Right-Sizing the People's Liberation Army: Exploring the Contours of China's Military*, Carlisle, PA: US Army War College, 2007, p. 309.
15 M. Stokes, "Expansion of China's Ballistic Missile Infrastructure Opposite Taiwan," *AsiaEye*, 18 April 2011. Available online at http://blog.project2049.net/2011/04/expansion-of-chinas-ballistic-missile.html (accessed 15 March 2014).
16 CCTV-7, Military Report, 25 December 2010, 26 July 2011, 17 September 2011, 9 October 2011, and 29 October 2011.
17 M. Stokes, J. Lin and L. C. R. Hsiao, "The Chinese People's Liberation Army Signals Intelligence and Cyber Reconnaissance Infrastructure," Project 2049 Institute, 11 November 2011, pp. 11–13. Available online at http://project2049.net/documents/pla_third_department_sigint_cyber_stokes_lin_hsiao.pdf (accessed 15 March 2014).
18 The Military Balance 2014, p. 232.
19 China's National Defense in 2006.
20 "China to Deploy Military Garrison in South China Sea," *China Daily*, 20 July 2012. Available online at www.chinadaily.com.cn/xinhua/2012–07–20/content_6499218.html (accessed 15 March 2014).
21 China's National Defense in 2004 and China's National Defense in 2006.
22 China's National Defense, July 1998.
23 China's National Defense in 2006.
24 Ibid.
25 Z. Bo, "The PLA and the Provinces," in D. Finkelstein and K. Gunness (eds), *Civil-Military Relations in Today's China Swimming in a New Sea*, Armonk: M. E. Sharpe, 2007, p. 96–130.
26 The Diversified Employment of China's Armed Forces, 2013; locations and independent units from Blasko, *The Chinese Army Today*, updated by Chinese media reporting.

27 For a description of the Sixth Armored Division's organization, see "China to Honor Commitment to Olympic 'Zero Defect' Attitude [特稿：中国兑现奥"采访"零拒绝"承诺新姿态]," *Xinhua*, 1 August 2008. Available online at http://news.xinhuanet.com/newscenter/2008–08/01/content_8898068.htm (accessed 15 March 2014).
28 *The Military Balance 2011*, London: The International Institute for Strategic Studies, 2011, p. 199.
29 Blasko, *The Chinese Army Today*, p. 189.
30 "Speaking with Nanjing MR Ship Group Commander Fang Rongsong [对话南京军区某船艇大队大队长方荣松]," *PLA Daily*, 30 March 2010. Available online at http://chn.chinamil.com.cn/2006jswy/2010–03/30/content_4168117.htm (accessed 15 March 2014).
31 "Cavalry Style Remains in Border Area," *PLA Daily*, 18 April 2012. Available online at http://eng.chinamil.com.cn/news-channels/china-military-news/2012–04/18/content_4838835.htm (accessed 15 March 2014).
32 Blasko, *The Chinese Army Today*, pp. 52 and 85.
33 "National Defense Reserve Strength [国防后备力量]," *Xinhua*, 22 September 2009. Available online at http://news.xinhuanet.com/mil/2009–09/22/content_12098695.htm (accessed 15 March 2014).
34 *The Military Balance 2014*, p. 232.
35 Peng and Yao, *The Science of Military Strategy*, pp. 448 and 451.
36 Ibid., p. 428.
37 *The Military Balance 2014*, p. 233.
38 Blasko, *The Chinese Army Today*, pp. 206–9 and "China Stresses Its Defensive Military Policy," *Global Times*, 2 August 2013. Available online at www.globaltimes.cn/content/801085.shtml#.U0gcLsYZIYV (accessed 11 April 2014).
39 "PLA's Military Training in 2014 Focuses on Upgrading Actual-Combat Level," *PLA Daily*, 12 February 2014. Available online at http://eng.chinamil.com.cn/news-channels/china-military-news/2014–02/12/content_5767261.htm (accessed 16 March 2015). See also D. Blasko, "The 'Two Incompatibles' and PLA Assessments of Military Capability," in *The Jamestown Foundation China Brief*, 9 May 2013. Available online at www.jamestown.org/programs/chinabrief/single/?tx_ttnews%5Btt_news%5D=40860&tx_ttnews%5BbackPid%5D=25&cHash=496c5a633f18729a58f908301c557db1 (accessed 16 March 2014).
40 The term in quotes is found in The Diversified Employment of China's Armed Forces, 2013.

Suggested further reading

D. Blasko, *The Chinese Army Today: Tradition and Transformation for the Twenty-first Century*, London: Routledge, 2012

R. Kamphausen, D. Lai, and A. Scobell (eds), *The PLA at Home and Abroad,* Strategic Studies Institute, US Army War College, June 2010

R. Kamphausen, D. Lai, and T. Tanner (eds), *The "People" in The PLA: Recruitment, Training, and Education in China's Military*, Strategic Studies Institute, US Army War College, September 2008

R. Kamphausen, D. Lai, and T. Tanner (eds), *Learning by Doing: The PLA Trains at Home and Abroad*, Strategic Studies Institute, US Army War College, 2012

R. Kamphausen, D. Lai, and T. Tanner (eds), *Assessing the People's Liberation Army in the Hu Jintao Era*, Strategic Studies Institute, US Army War College, 2014

18

The Chinese Air Force and Chinese security

Kenneth Allen and Jana Allen

This chapter provides an overview of China's People's Liberation Army Air Force (PLAAF) and its role in China's security.[1] We begin by providing a historical perspective on the PLAAF's role in China's security, followed by seven sections that examine its organizational structure; leadership, missions, responsibilities and strategy; weapons and equipment; officer corps recruitment and education; enlisted force recruitment and education; unit training; and foreign relations.

The PLAAF is clearly moving forward in many areas, including deploying and training with more advanced aircraft and air defense (surface-to-air missiles, anti-aircraft artillery, and radar) systems; however, other areas, such as recruitment, education, training, and career progression of personnel have proven more difficult to modernize. As long as these challenges persist, personnel will be a weak link and will impact the PLAAF's ability to utilize its increasingly high-tech weapons systems and equipment to the full capability, particularly in a more complex environment.

The PLAAF's role in China's security

Since its founding in 1949, the PLAAF has never had to engage an enemy inside China's borders other than individual shootdowns of manned and unmanned reconnaissance aircraft that were near or inadvertently crossed the border (*PLAAF 2010*). The only times the PLAAF has engaged in any sustained air-to-air combat were during the Korean War (1950 to 1953) and the 1958 Taiwan Strait Crisis, which lasted only a few days; however, its surface-to-air missile (SAM) and anti-aircraft artillery (AAA) units shot down almost 600 American aircraft while stationed in Vietnam (1965 to 1969) and Laos (1970 to 1973). During the 1979 border conflict with Vietnam, the PLAAF did not enter Vietnamese airspace or engage Vietnamese air defense assets near the border. The last shootdown by a PLAAF SAM occurred against a Vietnamese aircraft that inadvertently crossed the border in October 1987. To put this in perspective, however, none of China's neighbors have engaged in any sustained air-to-air combat since the end of the Vietnam War in 1975. As a result, none of them have any wartime experience.

Until the late 1990s, the PLAAF's doctrine, equipment, organizational structure, and training focused on point and area defense, which limited its capabilities to engage in defensive or offensive operations beyond China's borders. During that time, Naval Aviation was responsible for engaging all foreign aircraft beyond China's maritime borders from the Korean Peninsula to Vietnam. It was not until 1996, when Beijing reacted to Taiwan's first presidential elections, that the PLAAF flew its first flights out over the Taiwan Strait.[2] Even so, the PLAAF did not fly its first flights to the centerline of the Strait until Beijing reacted to President Lee Teng-hui's "two states" comments in July 1999 (Allen and Allen, *China Brief*, 2011).[3] Since then, however, the PLAAF has shared the responsibility of maritime air defense along the entire coast with Naval Aviation.

In terms of equipment, training, and organizational structure, the PLAAF began to receive more capable fighters and SAMs in the late 1990s, the greater range and lethality of which have allowed the PLAAF to project its defensive and potentially offensive curtain further beyond the coast. Its bombers and reconnaissance aircraft have also begun flying more and longer sorties over the entire maritime domain. Engagement by the PLAAF's airborne troops has been hindered by a lack of airlift; however, according to the 2013 US Department of Defense (DOD) report on China's military, "In an effort to address its strategic airlift deficiency, China is also developing a heavy lift transport aircraft, possibly identified as the Y-20."[4] Even its small number of heavy airlift IL-76s are predominantly being used for supporting military operations other than war (MOOTW), such as evacuating Chinese civilians from Libya and providing humanitarian assistance and disaster relief (HA/DR) supplies to neighboring countries.

Although the PLAAF was created in 1949, it was not until 2004 that the Chinese Communist Party's (CCP) Central Military Commission (CMC) (or "Central Committee's Military Commission") authorized it to have its own component of the PLA's "Active Defense" strategy, which coincided with the CMC's implementation of the goal of "integrated joint operations" and with the appointment of the PLAAF, PLAN, and PLASAF commanders as CMC members. This was almost 20 years after the CMC in 1986 authorized the PLAN to have its own component, known as "Offshore Defense." The PLAAF's new strategy is known as "Integrated Air and Space, Simultaneous Offensive and Defensive Operations." Although the concept of "Integrated Air and Space" is new to the PLAAF, it began working on the concept of "Simultaneous Offensive and Defensive Operations" in the late 1980s.[5] Because the PLA's General Armament Department (GAD), not the PLAAF, manages China's military space program, "Integrated Air and Space" refers only to the PLAAF utilizing the information technology (IT) component of space-based platforms for command and control purposes. In contrast, the US Air Force (USAF) has been integrating air and space capability since the first Gulf War and as of 2000 controlled almost 90 percent of DOD space-related resources.[6]

On 23 November 2013, China implemented its first ever air defense identification zone (ADIZ), which covers the East China Sea and overlaps Japan's ADIZ and the Senkaku/Diaoyu Islands. It also overlaps the Republic of Korea's ADIZ (KADIZ), which includes Ieodo Rock.[7] China is also considering creating an ADIZ in the South China Sea and perhaps elsewhere. The PLAAF, along with Naval Aviation, will have the primary responsibility of enforcing the ADIZ, which sees an average of more than 1,000 commercial flights daily.[8] In just the first few days after it was implemented, the United States (B-52s), Japan (F-15s), and South Korea flew several military aircraft sorties in the declared ADIZ, and China responded by scrambling S-30 aircraft (these were not identified as PLAAF or Naval Aviation) to "conduct routine patrols and monitor targets in the zone."[9] In response, South Korea has also expanded its own ADIZ southward, thus encompassing submerged rocks within the overlapping exclusive economic zones (EEZ) of China and South Korea.[10] To further complicate the situation, within a week, Taiwan's Air Force dispatched more than 30 fighter jet sorties to the part of Taiwan's ADIZ that intersects with China's newly designated ADIZ and part of Japan's ADIZ.[11]

What does all of this mean for the future? As the PLAAF moves forward over the next decade, it will continue to receive better equipment with longer legs and greater lethality. It will also expand its training to match its strategic, campaign, and tactical doctrine, which will help it meet more challenging tasks from China's leadership to support additional demands to protect China's territory, national interests, and people outside China's immediate perimeter. There is no doubt that the PLAAF is gradually accomplishing these tasks; however, other challenges remain, such as recruitment, education, training, and career progression for professional military personnel, which also affect the PLAAF's operational capability. In addition, China has not fought a war inside its borders since the Civil War in the 1940s, at which time the PLAAF did not even exist. During the 1979 border conflict with Vietnam, not a single aircraft flew across the border or engaged the Vietnamese Air Force. Improvements in PLA capabilities over the past decade are undeniably tied to improvements in weapon systems.[12] The PLA can now boast fourth-generation fighters equipped with modern jammers, communications systems, and weapons. However, improvements in military capabilities should also be credited to advances in other key areas. Since the late 1990s, the PLA has implemented new doctrine and strategies more suitable to twenty-first century warfare. It has placed a greater emphasis on training and operationalizing its military forces. Lastly, the PLA has developed a clear sense of mission and purpose. These factors all contribute to a greatly improved and more capable PLA, which shows every sign of becoming a truly modern military with a small but growing ability to influence global events. On the positive side, the PLAAF's strengths include more modern fighters and air defense systems, and willingness to accept extreme losses and be critical of shortcomings in order to improve capabilities. On the negative side, it is difficult for the PLAAF to recruit and retain the number of technologically proficient officers and enlisted personnel. In addition, pilot training, experience, and development of tactics still fall short of the best Western militaries and the PLAAF lacks cooperative experience with modern combat, and, although it appears proficient in conducting detailed planning, there is significant uncertainty about its ability to react effectively to a very fluid, dynamic military situation. Meanwhile, whereas the USAF has the same basic aircraft with updated versions of the same sensors, avionics, and missiles over the past decade, the PLAAF has added more types of aircraft to its inventory, and these are comparable in performance to the fourth-generation USAF aircraft (Shlapak 2014). The Chinese pilots would likewise have at their disposal weapons and other equipment that reflect parity with those found on a typical US fighter. Finally, in the authors' opinion, if, for whatever reason, China were to engage in full-scale combat, it remains to be seen whether the PLAAF could sustain a high level of offensive and defensive operations for any length of time, especially if their airfields, air defense systems, and command facilities came under attack.

Organizational structure

Branches and specialty units[13]

The PLAAF, which is one of three PLA services, consists of the following five branches/arms and five specialty units and subunits.[14] In the PLA, units include operational and support corps-, division-, brigade-, and regiment-level organizations. For example, aviation, SAM, logistics, and communications regiments are considered units. Other than flight colleges, no other academic institutions are considered units. The PLA defines subunits, which are sometimes translated as elements or detachments, as organizations at the battalion, company, and platoon level. Some definitions include squads as subunits. Subunits can be either permanent, or they can be *ad hoc* organizations, such as communications, radar, vehicle, maintenance, or launch/firing subunits. Subunits are also identified as the "grassroots" level.

- Five branches
    - Aviation
    - Surface-to-air missile
    - Anti-aircraft artillery
    - Radar
    - Airborne
- Five specialty units
    - Communications, which was previously a branch
    - Radar, which is also a branch
    - Electronic countermeasures (ECM)
    - Chemical defense, which includes nuclear and biological
    - Technical reconnaissance.

The PLA's organizational and officer corps structure is based on a 15-grade system, which has existed since 1988.[15] Although the PLAAF has added new weapons and equipment throughout the force over the past decade, the only significant changes to its organizational structure have occurred in the aviation branch. Figure 18.1 shows the basic organizational structure of the five branches and the different types of highest-level unit headquarters down to the regiment level. Each type of unit headquarters is either directly subordinate to a higher level headquarters, which include bases (corps deputy leader grade), command posts (corps deputy leader grade or division leader grade), Military Region Air Forces (MRAF) Headquarters (military region deputy leader grade), or PLAAF Headquarters (military region leader grade). Each type of unit headquarters has subordinate units or subunits (see Figure 18.1).

In the PLAAF, divisions, brigades, and regiments can each serve as the highest-level headquarters below the PLAAF Headquarters, MRAF Headquarters, base, or command post levels. Divisions can have subordinate regiments, battalions (flight and maintenance groups), and/or companies (flight and maintenance squadrons). Brigades, which are never subordinate to a division and do

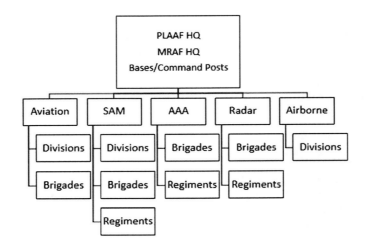

Figure 18.1 PLAAF branches and subordinate units

not have subordinate regiments, can have subordinate battalions and/or companies. Whereas air divisions have subordinate regiments, flight groups (battalion), and flight squadrons (company), air brigades only have subordinate flight groups and squadrons. Meanwhile, the SAM branch can have division, brigade, or regiment headquarters with subordinate battalions and/or companies, and the AAA branch can have brigade or regiment headquarters with subordinate battalions and/or companies. Since 1992, the Fifteenth Airborne Corps has been organized into three airborne divisions with subordinate regiments, battalions, and companies; however, it may also transition back to a brigade structure.

Leadership

The PLAAF's leadership structure is usually discussed in terms of its Party Congress, Party Committees, leaders, and four departments.[16] However, as the PLA attempts to implement "joint integrated operations," there has been greater interest in how the PLAAF is, or is not, being integrated into a joint command structure, including the CCP CMC's four General Departments, which consist of the General Staff Department (GSD), General Political Department (GPD), General Logistics Department (GLD), and General Armament Department (GAD), as well as the seven Military Region (MR) Headquarters, Academy of Military Science (AMS), and National Defense University (NDU).

Party congresses and Party committees

According to the *China Air Force Encyclopedia*, PLAAF Party members elect members of the PLAAF Party Congress (about 280–300 members), and, once elected, the Party Congress members are responsible for discussing and deciding key PLAAF issues. The Party Congress is also responsible for electing the members of the PLAAF Party Committee, which consists of about 40–45 members.[17] The Party Committee then elects a Standing Committee, which consists of about 10–12 members, and a Discipline Inspection Commission, which consists of about 11 members.[18] In most cases, the political commissar (PC) serves as the party secretary and the commander serves as the deputy secretary. However, three PLAAF commanders—Wu Faxian, Zhang Tingfa, and Qiao Qingchen—were also the Party secretary as a result of having previously served as the PLAAF PC.[19]

While the PLAAF Party Congress meets only once every 5 to 6 years, the Party Committee meets about twice a year to review the Standing Committee's actions and to decide important PLAAF issues. Meanwhile, the Party Committee's Standing Committee is responsible for making the daily decisions concerning the PLAAF, but is accountable to the Party Committee for its decisions. The PLAAF Party Congress does not typically coincide with the National Party Congress. For example, the Eighth, Ninth, and Tenth PLAAD Party Congresses were respectively held in December 1993, February 1999, and May 2004.

PLAAF leadership

In the PLA, the term "leaders" refers to the commander, PC, deputy commanders, and deputy PCs. Depending on the circumstances, it can also include the director of the four departments— Headquarters Department, Political Department, Logistics Department, and Equipment Department. It is important to note that each organization down to the regiment level has multiple deputy commanders and one or more deputy PCs. For example, the PLAAF currently has five deputy commanders and three deputy PCs. Each of the seven MRAF Headquarters has at least two deputy commanders and one to two deputy PCs.[20] Together with the director of each of the four departments, these officers comprise the headquarters' Standing Committee.

Joint leadership and the four General Departments

One of the biggest issues that helps define the PLAAF's role in joint integrated operations today concerns how it is, or is not, integrated into the PLA's "joint" leadership structure, which consists of the CCP's CMC, the four General Departments (which serve concurrently as the Army/Ground Force Headquarters), AMS, NDU, and seven MR headquarters.[21]

Starting in 2003, PLAAF officers began filling the key CMC member- and MR leader-grade billets shown below. Equally important, they were allowed to wear their Air Force uniform.[22]

- CMC Member: Prior to 2004, only three of the PLAAF's eight commanders—Liu Yalou, Wu Faxian, and Zhang Tingfa—had served as a member of the CMC. In September 2004, the CMC added the commander of the PLAN, PLAAF, and PLASAF as permanent members. Since then, PLAAF commanders Qiao Qingchen, Xu Qiliang, and Ma Xiaotian have served in this position. In October 2012, for the first time, a PLAAF officer, General Xu Qiliang, became one of two vice chairmen of the CMC, who are essentially the highest ranking professional military personnel in China.
- Deputy Chief of the General Staff (DCOGS): In July 2004, Lieutenant General Xu Qiliang was appointed as the first PLAAF officer to serve as one of the DCOGSs. When he became the PLAAF commander in September 2007, he was replaced by Lieutenant General Ma Xiaotian. Ma received his third star in 2009. Although it appeared that at least one of the DCOGS billets was designated as a permanent PLAAF billet, Ma was not replaced by a PLAAF officer when he became the PLAAF commander in November 2012, which implies that this is not the case.
- Deputy Director of the GPD: In 2005, Lieutenant General Liu Zhenqi was appointed as the first PLAAF officer to serve as a deputy director of the GPD. He received his third star in 2008. He retired in 2011 and was not replaced by a PLAAF officer.
- Deputy Director of the GLD: In 2005, Lieutenant General Li Maifu was appointed as the first PLAAF officer to serve as a deputy director in the GLD. He retired in 2010 and was not replaced by a PLAAF officer.
- Deputy Director of the GAD: The GAD has never had a non-Army officer serve as a deputy director.
- Academy of Military Science: In 2003, PLAAF Lieutenant General Zheng Shenxia became the first Air Force officer to be selected as head of the prestigious AMS. His successor in 2007, Lieutenant General Liu Chengjun, is also a PLAAF officer and will most likely remain in that billet until his mandatory retirement age of 65 in 2015.[23] Both of them received their third star.
- National Defense University: In August 2006, PLAAF Lieutenant General Ma Xiaotian was appointed as the first PLAAF officer to serve as Commandant of NDU. In December 2009, Lieutenant Liu Yazhou became the first PLAAF officer appointed as NDU's PC, where he will most likely remain until his mandatory retirement age of 65 in 2017, which will coincide with the Nineteenth Party Congress.[24]

PLAAF leadership changes at the Eighteenth Party Congress

The CCP's Eighteenth Party Congress in November 2012 saw a major change in the PLA's leadership. The key PLAAF leadership changes that occurred during the congress were as follows:[25]

- General Xu Qiliang, who became the PLAAF commander in 2007, was promoted to become one of the two CMC vice chairmen and a concurrent CCP Politburo member. Xu is the first PLAAF officer to become a CMC vice chairman. In terms of protocol order, Xu is listed behind

the other vice chairman, General Fan Changlong, who had never served in a CMC member-grade billet and, as such, skipped a grade to become a vice chairman. Of particular significance is that Xu is identified as an Air Force general and continues to wear an Air Force uniform.
- General Ma Xiaotian, who had served as a DCOGS since 2007 and received his third star in 2009, replaced Xu as the eleventh PLAAF commander, party deputy secretary, and CMC member. While serving as a DCOGS, Ma received his third star in 2009 and had the intelligence and foreign affairs portfolios. Ma is currently listed seventh out of eight in protocol order among the CMC members. Given his age, Ma will most likely serve as the commander only until the Nineteenth Party Congress in 2017.
- General Tian Xiusi replaced General Deng Changyou as the PLAAF's twelfth political commissar and party secretary. Tian, who received his third star in July 2012, never served in the Air Force and was the Chengdu MR political commissar since 2010. Tian was born in 1950 and will have to retire at age 65 in 2015.[26] According to *PLAAF 2010*, the PLAAF has had 11 previous PCs from 1949 until Tian was selected, and, as shown below, there is no discernible pattern in selecting them. Although it was surprising that a non-PLAAF officer was selected as the PC in 2012, his primary role is to oversee all party-related work, including party discipline. Since assuming office, Tian has traveled extensively to PLAAF units and has spoken at high-level meetings on party-related aspects of the PLAAF. Other than the fact that it continues to show that the Army-dominated CMC has an impact on the PLAAF, especially concerning personnel issues, there do not appear to be any political or military-strategic implications of these moves.
  - The first eight PCs began their careers in the Army and then transferred to the PLAAF. The next three served their entire careers in the PLAAF.
  - Two alternated between PLAAF and GPD political officer billets. The other nine PCs served only in PLAAF billets once they joined or transferred to the PLAAF.
  - Only four deputy PLAAF PCs have become the PLAAF PC.

The seven military regions

Each MR headquarters, which "exercises direct leadership over the Army units within its area of responsibility," has an average of five deputy commanders.[27] In 1988, the practice of concurrently "dual-hatting" each MRAF commander and PLAN Fleet commander as one of the MR deputy commanders was institutionalized as a result of adjusting the PLA's grade structure.[28] However, the other MR deputy commanders, who serve full-time on the staff, are Army officers. Furthermore, like the four General Departments, no PLAAF officers have served as the director of an MR first-level department and only a few PLAAF personnel apparently hold positions in any of the departments. Of note, only some of the seven MRAF PCs serve as concurrent MR deputy PCs. According to the *PLA Air Force Officer Handbook* and a search of the internet, only the PCs for the Guangzhou, Lanzhou, Nanjing, and Shenyang MRAFs are concurrently serving as MR deputy PCs. It is not clear why the Beijing, Chengdu, and Jinan MRAF PCs are not.[29]

PLAAF missions, responsibilities, and strategy

PLAAF missions and responsibilities

In the mid-1990s, the PLAAF's primary air defense responsibilities were to protect China's airfields, principal political and economic centers, heavy troop concentrations, and major military facilities and transportation systems (Allen, Pollack, and Krumel 1995). As a result, most fighter airfields, which were equipped primarily with J-6 aircraft, and virtually all of the SAMs were concentrated around China's large cities; however, given the short ranges of most Chinese fighters, the lack of an appreciable aerial refueling capability, and the inability to fly at night, the PLAAF's ability to mount an effective air defense of China against a strong adversary, such as the United States, remained questionable. In addition, the number of PLAAF bomber and attack aircraft units were limited in quantity and quality. The PLAAF described its secondary mission as support for the PLAA and PLAN but emphasized that this must be indirect support only (i.e., airlift and interdiction), because it was largely incapable of providing direct fire support to the ground forces. Moreover, only a small portion of the overall force structure had the capability to deliver air-to-surface ordnance and the PLAAF did not possess any precision-guided weapons. Furthermore, coordination among the three services and joint training remained extremely limited.

During the 2000s, as a result of acquiring a vast array of new weapon systems with longer ranges, including aircraft and missiles (SAMs, air-to-air missiles, and air-to-surface missiles), which are capable of operating in all-weather conditions and at night, the PLAAF has been able to expand its defensive capabilities from point defense to area defense and, in conjunction with its new strategy in 2004, to begin transitioning toward the ability to conduct simultaneous offensive and defensive operations.

A summary of the PLAAF's missions and responsibilities, which was published in the 2002 to 2012 versions of *China National Defense*, states that the PLAAF is a strategic service and the main force for carrying out air operations.[30] The PLAAF's primary mission is to organize homeland air defense to protect territorial air, with an emphasis on "defending the capital as the center" and "defending coastal and border areas as the key." Should China perceive a threat to its territorial air, the PLAAF will likely be tasked with organizing air offensive operations independently or jointly with the PLAA, PLAN, and/or PLASAF, engaging in joint operations against enemy invasion from the air, and conducting air strikes against the enemy. To satisfy the strategic requirements of conducting both offensive and defensive operations, the PLAAF is working to ensure the development of a combat force structure that focuses on air strikes, air and missile defense, and strategic projection, to improve its leadership and command system and build up an informatized, networked support system. It conducts training on confrontation in complex electromagnetic environments (CEME), and carries out maneuvers, drills, and combat training in various tactical situations. Additionally, the PLAAF has carried out MOOTW, such as providing air security for major national events, emergency rescue and disaster relief, international rescue, and emergency airlift.

Unfortunately, a review of available PLA sources did not find any statements concerning the role of PLAAF Headquarters and the MRAF Headquarters and their relationship to the four General Departments, seven MRs or theaters. Although the PLAAF most likely has a document, such as a *gangyao*, that clearly lays out these relationships, the only information found was in *China's National Defense 2008*. According to this document, in peacetime, the PLAAF practices a leadership system that combines operational command with administrative organizations in order to build all components of the Air Force. To accomplish this, the Air Force consists of a headquarters, seven MRAFs, corps- and division-level command posts, divisions, brigades, and regiments.[31]

PLAAF strategy

In 2004, the CMC approved the PLAAF, for the first time in its history, to implement a service-specific aerospace strategy known as "Integrated Air and Space Operations, Being Prepared for Simultaneous Offensive and Defensive Operations" to complement the overall PLA's "Active

Defense Strategy."[32] Bureaucratically, this was a big moment for the PLAAF. The CMC authorized the PLAN to have its own service strategy in 1986 ("Offshore Defense") and the PLAAF had lobbied unsuccessfully since 1987 to follow suit. In 2004, that battle was finally won.

According to Hong Kong press reports, the CMC's approval of the new strategy was timed to coincide with the PLAAF's Tenth Party Congress in May 2004 and represented a major milestone in China's efforts to build a strategic Air Force, which has not only strategic missions and long-range weapon systems, but also its own service-specific strategy.[33] The approval also signaled a fundamental shift in how the PLAAF was to be viewed. The article stated that this change was encapsulated in three new assertions on the strategic positioning of the PLAAF:

- First, the PLAAF is a national Air Force led by the CCP.
- Second, a modern Air Force must be built to unify aviation and spaceflight, combine defense and offense, and unify information and firepower.
- Third, the PLAAF should be a strategic Air Force standing side by side with the Army and Navy to achieve command of the air, ground, and sea.

China's 2004 to 2012 versions of *China's National Defense* clearly show the growing importance of the PLAAF and its missions.[34] However, although each white paper describes the PLAAF's transition to simultaneous offensive and defensive operations, none of them reference integrated air and space.

Even though the white papers have not referred to this component, the PLAAF has apparently thrown its hat into the space ring, having indicated its desire to become actively involved in managing China's military space program with an emphasis on the informatization aspects. Specifically, in March 2004, the PLAAF published *Air and Space Battlefield and China's Air Force*, following in August 2006 with *The Science of Integrated Air and Space Operations*.[35] Although the first doctrinal book did not provide linkage between space and the PLAAF, the last chapter of the second book, which contains forewords by the PLAAF's commander General Qiao Qingchen and political commissar General Deng Changyou, lays out six steps for China in establishing a model in which "the PLAAF is the leading organization for 'integrated air and space,' the PLAAF is{. . .}the leading organization to manage China's military space force, and the PLAAF is the primary force for [air and space] combat."[36] Though the book focuses on managing the "informatization" aspects of the space program, it does not indicate that the PLAAF wants to manage the launch sites, satellite development, and missile program. The six proposed steps are as follows:

- Determine a scientific development model for creating a sound process for employing air and space power.
- Establish an Air Force Space organization to use as the base for organizing integrated air and space operations.
- Establish PLAAF space units.
- Establish information links that provide technology for integrated air and space operations.
- Nurture Air Force space personnel with a knowledge of space.
- Expand the PLAAF's overall scope of warfighting power, increasing the PLAAF's air offense capabilities, air defense counter-missile capabilities, and airborne troop combat capabilities.

In July 2009, the PLAAF published *Strategic Air Force*, which contained about 50 articles on the subject by various authors.[37] Several articles mentioned "integrated air and space" but provided absolutely no substance to the discussion. However, the introduction to the first section started by stating that no country today that has space power has a space force, nor does any country have or is preparing to have its space troops reside in a service outside of its Air Force. This is the crux of the PLAAF's argument that it should "manage" the PLA's space program. While the Second Artillery Force is also advocating management of the space program, it is highly unlikely that the GAD, which serves primarily as the Army's equipment department, will give up this mission.

Responding to Hu Jintao's historic missions

Also in 2004, the CMC directed the PLA to develop high-tech conventional warfighting capabilities as well as prepare for nontraditional security operations. "The Historic Missions of Our Military in the New Period of the New Century," articulated by PRC President and CCP leader Hu Jintao in 2004, provided the PLA with a mandate to think beyond conventional warfighting scenarios.

The PLAAF definitely demonstrated progress in this area in February to March 2011, when it sent four IL-76s to evacuate Chinese civilians from Libya. Altogether, the aircraft flew 1,655 Chinese from Libya to Khartoum, Sudan, and then brought 287 back to China.[38]

PLAAF campaigns

The PLAAF has traditionally focused its airpower theory on campaign and tactical combat operations as a series of air campaigns within the PLA's overall campaign. The PLAAF has been very methodical in the way it has defined its campaign theory and used it to provide operational guidance for its forces. PLAAF campaign theory can be categorized into campaign theory for aviation (aircraft), air defense (SAM, AAA, and radar troops), and airborne troops.[39] Not surprisingly, these three categories reflect the way the PLAAF is organized administratively and operationally in terms of its five branches (aviation, surface-to-air missiles, anti-aircraft artillery, radar, and airborne troops) and supporting elements (political structure, logistics, maintenance, communications, etc.).

At the operational/campaign level, 1999 was a watershed year (*PLAAF 2010*). In 1999, the PLA made major revisions to its long-standing doctrinal concepts and guidance for combat at the operational level of war (campaigns). It did so in order to prepare to fight the type of future conflicts it assessed as most likely. The *New-Generation Operations Regulations* issued to all of the services were intended to redirect PLA thinking about the operational art into the age of high-tech warfare. In short order, the PLAAF followed suit with the publication of *The Outline of Campaigns of the Chinese People's Liberation Army Air Force*. While not publicly available, this document most likely reflected those new aerospace operational concepts and principles, as well as command and control arrangements, the PLAAF intended to introduce in order to comport with the new trend toward high ops-tempo joint operations. In short, operationally, the PLAAF began to make its leap from a doctrinal mindset of single-service combined-arms operations to the more complex and coordination-intensive realm of joint operations and from a previous focus on the tactical to an added dimension of operational-level awareness.

The PLAAF's campaign theory can also be categorized according to the campaign's characteristics, objectives, form, operational scale, command relationships, and the services and branches that participate. In May 2000, the PLA's NDU Press published *Science of Campaigns*, which categorized military operations into 22 distinct types of campaigns. For the first time, the PLA identified joint campaigns, which were listed last after the Army, Navy, Air Force, and Second Artillery campaigns. Of the 22 campaigns, air offensive, air defense, and air blockade campaigns were specifically designated Air Force campaigns. The PLAAF's airborne forces were designated as a joint airborne campaign, and PLAAF AAA and SAM forces were expected to play a major role in the PLA's joint anti-air strike campaign.[40]

In May 2006, NDU Press published a revised version of *Science of Campaigns*, which had only 17 types of campaigns and focused more on jointness. For example, joint campaigns were listed first. The revised version allowed the PLAAF to retain its offense campaigns and defense campaigns; however, because the airborne troops belong to the PLAAF, airborne campaigns were re-designated as PLAAF campaigns, and air blockade campaigns were incorporated into joint blockade campaigns.[41]

PLAAF weapons and equipment

This section provides information on the PLAAF from DOD's 2013 Report to Congress on China's military.[42] According to the report, China continues to field increasingly modern fourth-generation aircraft, but the force still consists mostly of older second- and third-generation aircraft, or upgraded variants of those aircraft. Since the flight of the first J-20 stealth fighter prototype in January 2011, China has tested at least two more prototypes. The prototype, referred to as the "J-31," is similar in size to a US F-35 fighter and appears to incorporate design characteristics similar to the J-20. It conducted its first flight on 31 October 2012.

China continues upgrading its H-6 bomber fleet (originally adapted from the late 1950s Soviet Tu-16 design) with a new variant that possesses greater range and will be armed with a long-range cruise missile. China also uses a modified version of the H-6 aircraft to conduct aerial refueling operations for many of its indigenous aircraft, increasing their combat range.

The PLA Air Force possesses one of the largest forces of advanced SAM systems in the world, consisting of a combination of Russian-sourced SA-20 battalions and domestically produced HQ-9 battalions.

China's aviation industry is developing a large transport aircraft (likely referred to as the Y-20) to supplement China's small fleet of strategic airlift assets, which currently consists of a limited number of Russian-made IL-76 aircraft. These heavy lift transports are needed to support airborne command and control (C2), logistics, paradrop, aerial refueling, and reconnaissance operations, as well as humanitarian assistance and disaster relief missions.

Developments in China's commercial and military aviation industry indicate improved aircraft manufacturing, associated technology, and systems development capabilities. Some of these advances have been made possible by business partnerships with Western aviation and aerospace firms (including cleared US defense contractors), which provide overall benefit to China's military aerospace industry. China will continue to seek advancement in aerospace technology, capability, and proficiency to rival Western capabilities.

China's future air force anti-access/area-denial (A2/AD) capabilities will be bolstered by the development of a fifth-generation fighter force, which is not likely to be fielded before 2018. Key characteristics of fifth-generation fighters include high maneuverability, lack of visibility on radar due to very low-observable stealth shaping, and an internal weapons bay. Other key features of these aircraft are modern avionics and sensors that offer more timely situational awareness for operations in network-centric combat environments, radars with advanced targeting capabilities and protection against enemy electronic countermeasures, and integrated electronic warfare systems with advanced communication and global positioning system (GPS) navigation functions. These next generation aircraft will improve China's existing fleet of fourth-generation aircraft (Russian built Su-27/Su-30 and indigenous J-10 and J-11B fighters) by utilizing low-observable platforms to support regional air superiority and strike operations. Additionally, China's continuing upgrades to its bomber fleet may provide the capability to carry new, longer-range cruise missiles. Similarly, the acquisition and development of longer-range unmanned aerial vehicles (UAV), including the BZK-005, and unmanned combat aerial vehicles (UCAV), will increase China's ability to conduct long-range reconnaissance and strike operations. The PLAAF has approximately 100 helicopters, including primarily the Z-8 and Z-9 airframes. In 2009, the PLAAF assumed full responsibility for training all of its helicopter crew members, which includes the first female aviators (Blasko 2014).[43]

China's ground-based air defense A2/AD capabilities will likely be focused on countering long-range airborne strike platforms with increasing numbers of advanced, long-range SAMs. China's current air and air defense A2/AD components include a combination of advanced long-range SAMs—its indigenous HQ-9 and Russian SA-10 and SA-20 PMU1/PMU2, which have the advertised capability to protect against both aircraft and low-flying cruise missiles. China continues to pursue the acquisition of the Russian extremely long-range S-400 SAM system (400 km), and is also expected to continue research and development to extend the range of the domestic HQ-9 SAM to beyond 200 km.

As explained above, since 2004 the PLAAF has had its own strategy (simultaneous offensive and defensive operations) and has been acquiring weapons with longer ranges and greater lethality to be able to extend its air defense capabilities, which is its primary mission. These weapons are being integrated into a smaller PLAAF and are being used to implement the PLAAF's three campaigns: air offense, air defense, and airborne. Although it is important to pay attention to the PLAAF's acquisition of new equipment and increased capabilities, the ultimate question is whether the PLAAF can effectively operate them in combat in a sustained manner.

PLAAF force size

Until 2013, the PLAAF had not provided official public information about the current number of personnel, including the number and percentage of officers and enlisted personnel by rank. Although no official figures had been published before 2013, Xu Guangyu, a retired PLA major general from the GSD, published an article in July 2010 that stated that the PLAAF constituted about 12 percent of the 2.3 million-man PLA, which equates to 276,000 personnel.[44] On the other hand, however, the PRC's *China's National Defense* 2012 stated that the PLAAF currently has 398,000 personnel, which is 17 percent of the total.[45]

Since 1949, the PLAAF has implemented ten force reductions, all of which were part of larger PLA force reductions. While some of the reductions affected the entire force, others focused strictly on certain levels of headquarters. Although the figures available in different PLA sources are often inconsistent, it appears that in September 1953, the PLAAF increased its personnel from the existing 210,000 to 257,000. PLAAF reporting states that it had its highest number of personnel in 1972, but the number was not specified. By the end of 1976, the force was somewhere between 16 and 27 percent less than 1972.[46] Since then, the PLAAF has averaged force reductions of 10 to 20 percent each time the PLA has instituted a force reduction.[47] Again, according to Xu Guangyu, the PLA will reduce its force in stages over the next 20 years to about one and a half million, which will result in a reduction in the Army's percentage and an increase in the PLAAF's percentage of the total number of personnel; however, no numbers were given.[48]

Officer corps recruitment and education

Historically, PLAAF officer corps recruits consisted of high school graduates and outstanding enlisted members, but, over the past decade, the PLAAF has made a concerted effort to attract more students and new graduates from civilian science, technology, and engineering academic institutions. This trend reflects a greater effort by the PLA to create a more professional, educated military force capable of meeting the challenges of modern "informatized" warfare. The PLAAF's officer cadets can be divided into three basic groups: aviation cadets (male and female), non-aviation cadets, and students in the National Defense Student Program.

Male aviation cadets

The PLAAF is still searching for the best way to recruit, educate, and train its male aviation cadets.[49] After graduation, they serve as aviators, which include fighter, attack, helicopter, bomber, and transport pilots, as well as bomber and transport navigation and communications officers. Historically, the PLAAF recruited high school graduates and outstanding enlisted members, but it has gradually increased the recruitment of college students and graduates. For education and political reliability reasons, recruiting targets Han Chinese from specific provinces and municipalities. In addition, most Han Chinese live in rural areas, where the education levels are lower. Until recently, the PLAAF has always separated male and female aviators during training and, with only a few exceptions, at their operational units.

Male aviation cadet recruitment

The PLAAF Headquarters Department's Aviator Recruiting Bureau, which has a regional selection center and multiple selection sites subordinate to each of the seven MRAFs, is responsible for all aviation cadet recruiting activities.

In the early 2000s, the PLAAF progressively introduced new programs to recruit graduates from PLA colleges and students and graduates from civilian colleges with a science and engineering background. The programs are listed below:

- 2000 (4+2+1 program): PLA college graduates with a 3-year senior technical or 4-year bachelor's degree in missiles or telecommunications receive a second (2-year) bachelor's in military science plus 1 year of transition training.
- 2003 (4+2+1 program): Civilian college graduates with a 3-year senior technical or 4-year bachelor's degree in science or engineering receive a second (2-year) bachelor's in military science plus 1 year of transition training. In late 2013, however, the PLAAF stopped recruiting civilian college graduates in favor of recruiting college students who are enrolled in the Defense Student Programs discussed below.[50]
- 2006 (2+2+1 program): Civilian college students in their second or third year with a major in science or engineering receive 2 years of basic aviation theory along with basic and advanced flight training, after which they receive a bachelor's in military science followed by 1 year of transition training.
- 2010: The PLAAF selected the first group of 12 new enlisted members (24 years old or younger) from PLAAF units and a Beijing Military Region group army who already had a college degree. The goal was to assign them to PLAN, PLAAF, and Army units and treat them as equals to officers. They spent 2 years receiving their basic aviation education at the Air Force Aviation University as well as flight training in a CJ-6 and K-8. In June 2012, only two of the original 12 (16 percent) completed the training and received a bachelor's in military science.[51]
- 2011: The PLAAF's Political Department launched a new aviation cadet program in the PLAAF's National Defense Student Program at Tsinghua University, whereby 32 students will receive 3 years of education at Tsinghua followed by 1 year of education at the Air Force

Aviation University in Changchun.[52] On graduation, they will then be assigned to a flight college for their flight training. In 2013, the PLAAF initiated similar programs for National Defense Program students at Beijing University (25 students) and Beijing University of Aeronautics and Astronautics (30 students).[53]

Information from 2010 provides a good overview of the number of cadets recruited. In early 2010, the PLAAF dispatched about 400 recruiters to 170 locations in 30 of China's provinces, autonomous regions, and municipalities. In the end, the new class consisted of 1,100 cadets, including 836 high school graduates, 200 college students/graduates and 64 enlisted members already enrolled in PLAAF officer colleges.

To meet its goals of recruiting better educated members as aviation cadets, the PLAAF has had to adjust the maximum age for recruits. The maximum age for aviation cadets is 20 years old for high school graduates, 22 years old for second-year college students, and 24 years old for military or civilian college graduates.

Female aviation cadets

In March 2012, the PLAAF celebrated the sixtieth anniversary of the first female aviators joining an operational unit, thus becoming one of 16 countries with female air force pilots today.[54] Although their numbers have been small, women are playing an increasingly important role as evidenced by the selection of China's first female astronaut for its first (and successful) manned space docking mission. Since the early 1980s, the PLAAF has averaged a new group of about 30 to 40 female cadets every 3 years; however, as a result of the PLAAF's consolidation of its flight colleges in 2011 and the shift to a "4+1" program for the ninth group that began in 2008, the tenth group did not begin training until 2013.[55] Historically, female aviators have been separated from their male counterparts throughout their cadet education and training, as well as in their operational units. The majority have been assigned to all-female crews in a single flight group in the Thirteenth Air Division's Thirty-eighth Regiment, where they conduct charter flights, disaster relief, and research-oriented trial flights, as well as reforestation and cloud seeding. However, this pattern has been slowly changing since 2000, including mixed IL-76 crews, one transport division commander, and a new group of J-10 pilots, JH-7 weapon systems officers (WSOs), and MI-17 helicopter pilots.[56] Of note, the PLAAF did not begin specialized training for WSOs in two-seat multirole aircraft (JH-7) in operational units until early 2011. Previously, pilots merely switched between the front and rear seats.

Aviation cadet and post-graduate education and training

As of 2012, the PLAAF completely revised its education and training curriculum for new pilots.[57] The new program is called the "Four Phase" system, also known as the "4+1+1 model." It includes a 4-year academic education phase, 1-year professional education phase, 6-month combat aircraft transition training, and 6-month combat application training phase. These phases are discussed in more detail below.

From 1950 to 2004, basic education for all new PLAAF pilot cadets was conducted at the Changchun Flight School/College. While some cadets remained in Changchun, the remaining cadets transferred to another flight school/college to receive their flight training. In May 2004, the PLAAF created the Air Force Aviation University in Changchun, Jilin Province, to replace the Changchun Flight College. The university is composed of the following two division leader-grade bases:

- Flight Basic Training Base
- Flight Training Base

As of 2012, the university has been responsible for providing 4 years of basic education and 6 months of basic flight training for all male and female high school graduates and outstanding enlisted personnel selected as aviation cadets. It also has special programs for the remaining aviation cadets. As explained above, the new program is called the "Four Phase" system, or the 4+1+1 model, and includes the following four phases:

- Phase 1: Academic education, which all male and female high school graduates and outstanding enlisted personnel selected as aviation cadets receive for 4 years at the Air Force Aviation University, and which includes aviation theory, 70 flight hours in the CJ-6 basic trainer at the university's Flight Basic Training Base, parachute training, and survival training. The graduates receive a bachelor's of engineering degree.
- Phase 2: Professional education, which takes place for 2 years at one of the PLAAF's three flight colleges and is organized according to the final operational aircraft the new pilots will fly—fighter, ground attack, bomber, or transport. On completion of the program, each pilot receives a bachelor's in military science degree.
- Phase 3: Combat aircraft transition training in an advanced trainer, which now occurs during the first 6 months at an operational base and includes flight techniques and basic tactic training.
- Phase 4: Combat application training, which takes 6 months in the unit's operational aircraft and includes basic tactics, tactics application, combined-arms combat, and joint combat training.

Cadet washout rate

Normally, the PLAAF has not published information about the washout rate for its male aviation cadets, which includes pilots and crew members; however, according to a PLAAF book published in 2010, the washout rate for male cadets has been 50 percent.[58] In addition, analysis of information concerning female aviation cadets has indicated a washout rate of at least 50 percent.

Pilot PME and graduate degrees

All aviators are considered military-track officers and move up the promotion ladder in this career field. It does not appear that pilots receive any basic-level professional military education (PME) after they are assigned to their permanent unit. Furthermore, unless pilots are a staff officer or commanding officer in a regiment, brigade, or division headquarters, it does not appear that they receive any mid-level PME. However, commanding and staff officers attend their intermediate (battalion/major and regiment/colonel) and advanced (division/senior colonel) PME for one year at the Air Force Command College in Beijing, where they receive a certificate.[59]

During the 2000s, the PLAAF began providing the opportunity for certain pilots to receive a master's degree. For example, in October 2009, eight test pilots at the PLAAF's Xi'an Yanliang Flight Test and Training Group were the first pilots in the unit to receive a 2-year master's degree at Northwestern Polytechnical University.[60] In January 2003, Jin Wenya, who was a member of the sixth female pilot class, became the first female in the PLAAF to receive a master's degree, which she began in 2000.[61]

Non-aviation cadet recruitment, education, and training

PLAAF non-aviation officers come from military academic institutions, a National Defense Student (Reserve Officer) Program, and direct recruitment of civilian graduates.[62] The PLAAF, which has multiple officer academic institutions, separates its education and training system at each level (cadet, basic, intermediate, and advanced) on the basis of the five officer career tracks: military/command, political, logistics, equipment, and special technical. Whereas all PLAAF academic institution graduates receive their specialty training as a cadet, defense students and directly recruited graduates must receive their specialty training after graduation. In addition, almost all new officers serve a 1-year probationary period and must serve at least 8 years before leaving the military.

PLAAF academic institutions

Although the PLAAF directly recruits its pilot cadets, it selects its non-aviation cadets for PLAAF academic institutions on the basis of how well they score on the National Unified College Entrance Examination, as well as the results of a political reliability review. These personnel come from among high school graduates, 2-year enlistees who have served 1 year, noncommissioned officers (NCOs) who have served 2 to 3 years, as well as the children of military officers who have served on the border for 20 years, and pilots and crew members who have served a full career.[63]

The PLAAF's non-aviation cadets can attend one of the following academic institutions:[64]

- PLAAF Command College, Beijing
- Air Force Engineering University, which has six subordinate colleges (Natural Science College, Aerospace Engineering College, Air Defense Missile College, Information and Navigation College, Air Traffic Control and Navigation College, and Equipment Management and Security College), Xi'an, Shaanxi Province[65]
- Air Force Logistics College, Xuzhou, Jiangsu Province
- Air Force Airborne Troop College (in Guilin, Guangxi Province, previously known as the Guilin Air Force College)
- Air Force Early Warning College in Wuhan, Hubei Province (previously known as the Radar College)
- Air Force First Aviation (Technical/Aircraft Maintenance) College, Xinyang, Henan Province

Although most cadets receive a 4-year bachelor's degree, some technical track cadets receive only a 3-year senior technical (associate's) degree. Currently, it is estimated that only 60 to 75 percent of cadets receive a bachelor's degree, while the remaining cadets receive a senior technical degree.[66] Although the PLAAF is aiming to have all cadets receive a bachelor's degree, no information is available about when this will happen. PLAAF non-aviation officers receive their education and specialty training as cadets and are then assigned directly to their operational unit. Cadets also receive a small monthly stipend for living expenses.[67]

PLAAF's National Defense Student (Reserve Officer) Program

In 1998, the PLA initiated a National Defense Student Program, which is also called the Reserve Officer Program, in a few civilian universities.[68] In May 2000, the State Council and CMC issued the "Decision Concerning Establishing a System for Civilian Colleges to Educate and Train Military Officers." To date, the PLA has created programs in 118 civilian universities, including 19 PLAAF programs.

In September 2006, the PLAAF stated that its goal for 2010 was to have 60 percent of its officers come from civilian college graduates, but two-thirds of this 60 percent (40 percent of all officers) was to come from the Defense Student Program and one-third (20 percent of all officers) from direct recruitment of civilian college graduates. As of September 2011, the PLAAF had recruited 21,000 Defense Students, of which 13,000 had graduated. Accounting for approximately 6,000 students still in the program, this equates to a graduation rate of 90 percent. Unfortunately, the PLAAF does not publish figures for the total number of new officers who have graduated from military and civilian academic institutions, so the percentage of defense students within this total is not known.

Although the regulations state that at least 70 percent of the graduates must earn a science and engineering degree, it appears that closer to 100 percent achieve this. Yet another goal is to have at least 70 percent of the graduates assigned to division and lower units. Finally, the number of female students is limited to a maximum of 5 percent. On graduation, the defense students are assigned to an operational unit, a PLAAF academic institution, or a training unit where they receive their specialty training. In addition, about 40 percent of defense students move directly to graduate school.

Direct recruitment of civilian graduates

The PLAAF's goal in 2010 was to recruit 20 percent of its new officers from civilian college graduates with bachelor's, master's, or doctorate degrees, but it is not clear if it met this goal. Since 1998, more than 5,000 civilian graduates have joined the PLAAF.[69] Many of these students participated in the "211 Project," which is a civilian education reform program that was initiated during China's Ninth Five-Year Plan (1996–2000). The program's stated goal is to raise the research standards of high-level universities and cultivate strategies for socio-economic development.

The Political Department accepts applications by all direct recruits in late August. In addition, individual units are allowed to recruit personnel to meet their requirements. Depending on their career track and specialty, graduates must receive basic military-political and pre-billet specialty training, which includes 3 to 12 months of military-political training at a PLAAF academic institution followed by 2 to 3 months of probation, which includes basic specialty and on-the-job training (OJT) in the billet at their new unit.

In addition, if the wife of a pilot has an appropriate college degree, she can be directly recruited as an officer. Most of these spouses serve in support billets, such as logistics, meteorology, and administration.

Enlisted force recruitment and education

In essence, from 1949 to 1999, the PLAAF's enlisted force consisted primarily of an undereducated or illiterate force of conscripts who served for 4 years and could then remain on active duty for a total of 16 years before being demobilized and sent home.[70] In 1999, however, the PLA created a 30-year enlisted career program consisting of 2 years as a conscript/volunteer and up to 28 years as an NCO. This new program has resulted in the recruitment of an increasing number of educated high school graduates, college students, and college graduates into the NCO corps. Today, the size of the PLAAF's NCO corps is growing and currently accounts for 60 percent of the entire enlisted force and about 80 percent in the aviation branch. In contrast, 2-year enlistees account for the majority of enlisted personnel in the airborne, SAM, and AAA branches.

Since 2009, the PLAAF has implemented significant reforms to bring in more college students and graduates as 2-year enlistees and to recruit some directly as NCOs, but it is facing certain problems in retaining them after their first tour of duty, including utilizing their skills, salary, marriage and family, housing, and respect. Additionally, the PLAAF enlisted career track is still evolving, unlike in the US Air Force, where enlisted personnel have clearly established career paths and are given the opportunity for leadership roles up to the highest level. Even though the PLA/PLAAF began reforming its enlisted force in 1999, major adjustments were implemented in 2009 and 2011. As a result, given that an enlisted career program did not exist prior to 1999, it will be 2029 before any enlisted personnel who joined in 1999 (2039 for those who joined in 2009) complete a 30-year career under the new structure.

As a technical service, the PLAAF has always had a greater need than the Army for more technically qualified enlisted personnel. As such, it has been the responsibility of the local People's Armed Forces Department (PAFD) to select the proper personnel for the PLAAF. The major problem, however, has been that, by law until 2011, two-thirds of all new enlisted personnel were required to come from rural areas, where they would be lucky to have received a ninth-grade education. As such, the PLAAF still had to start from scratch with their technical education. During the early 2000s, the PLAAF took the lead in directly recruiting civilian college students and graduates as new 2-year enlistees and NCOs. Even so, given the reduction from 4 years to 2 years as a new enlistee, personnel who deal with equipment maintenance receive only basic technical training before being assigned to their permanent billets. Once they complete this training, they often have only about 15 months of active duty left before they are either demobilized or promoted to an NCO billet.

In addition, not every NCO billet allows for in-residence technical PME as they move up the career ladder. For example, the PLAAF has only one formal NCO school, which is the Dalian Air Force Communications NCO school. Some NCOs are allowed to attend a 2- or 3-year degree program for NCOs at one of seven officer academic institutions, or return to a technical training base for a few months.

Still another issue the PLAAF is facing is what to do with the growing number of NCOs who have replaced junior officers in technical leadership billets since the 2003–4 force reduction. To date, they are filling officer billets but are still called "acting" leaders because the PLA officers' 15-grade system does not allow NCOs to be given an officer grade.

Conscript training

Because the PLAAF does not have a single training base for new conscripts, such as the USAF's Lackland Air Force Base, PLAAF conscripts are assigned to either an operational unit or a technical training base to receive basic training. At either assignment, the duration of basic training lasts about 2 months and ends sometime in late January or February. Once they complete basic training, conscripts assigned to an operational unit are then reassigned within the same unit, where they receive individual and unit training. New conscripts initially assigned to a technical training base for basic training remain there for technical training as well. After completing their technical training, they are reassigned to an operational unit located elsewhere.

Basic training

All incoming PLAAF conscripts arrive at either an operational unit or a technical training unit in mid-December for about 2 to 3 months of basic training. The actual length of time for basic training varies, depending on one's branch, but it usually ends around the Chinese New Year (Spring Festival), which occurs sometime between late January and mid-February. However, some training continues until late February or early March. Basic training instructors are junior officers or junior NCOs assigned on a temporary basis from an operational unit. After basic training is completed, the instructors return to their unit.

Operational unit OJT

Conscripts who complete their basic training at an operational unit are then assigned to a company within that operational unit, where they learn how to function in squads and platoons. After being assigned to their billets, they receive OJT, individual training, and unit training to learn their specialty. The PLA expects that, after the first 6 months of their 2-year conscription period, conscripts will be sufficiently proficient in their job to take part in training at a larger training organization.[71]

Within the operational unit, an organization called a training unit oversees basic training and OJT for the new conscripts.[72] From December through February, these training units provide conscript basic training. Once basic training is over, the training units transition to providing short-term training courses for NCO squad leaders and officers.

Technical training units

As noted above, some new conscripts are assigned directly to a technical training unit, where they receive basic training followed by technical training. The PLAAF has numerous training bases, regiments, and groups. Most, if not all, of these training units appear to be co-located with an operational unit.[73] The duration of technical training depends on the type of specialty learned.

NCO selection, retention, and evaluation process

Conscripts who remain on active duty at the end of their conscription period do so by becoming NCOs or attending one of the PLAAF colleges to become officers. Conscripts who desire to become NCOs can either be selected on the basis of merit or pass an exam for entrance into an NCO program of study at a PLAAF officer college or NCO school. In both cases, the process is highly competitive and selection is by no means guaranteed.

Unit training

An assessment of individual and unit training is essential to understanding how the PLAAF's capabilities have progressed over the past 20 years and what they might be in the future. Unfortunately, no such assessment by the US Government is publicly available.[74]

There is no question that all of the PLAAF's branches and specialty units have increased their combat capabilities during scripted exercises over the past decade. However, since the PLAAF has not fought in any aerial combat since 1958, it is unclear exactly how effective it would be during actual combat against a battle-tested opponent, and whether it can sustain operations for any length of time beyond its borders, especially if its airfields and air defense sites come under attack.

Unit training

The PLAAF is gradually moving from single unit to combined-arms (two or more branches) training, to joint (two or more services or with a foreign country) training, and from point and area defense to long-range simultaneous offensive and defensive operations. In addition, pilots are in the process of transitioning from similar to dissimilar aircraft training under all types of conditions. One of the most significant reforms in PLAAF pilot training began in early 2012, when pilots were finally allowed autonomy to develop their own flight plan and then conduct "unrestricted air combat" that involves air intercept training in designated airspaces without strict control from the ground.[75] Additionally, in late 2012, the PLAAF began allowing controllers on the KJ-200 and KJ-2000 airborne early warning aircraft to interact directly with combat pilots in the air.[76]

According to *PLAAF 2010*, all of the PLAAF's branches have clearly increased the types of training they conduct, including training at night, in all-weather conditions, and deploying long distances, including flying over water at minimum altitudes, as well as conducting combined-arms training with other PLAAF branches and joint training with other services and countries (*PLAAF 2010*). Although the annual DOD report on the PLA provides general statements about the PLAAF's training and exercises, such as conducting training in complex electromagnetic and joint environments, Congress does not require the report to include a detailed assessment.[77] China's biennial *China's National Defense* provides an overview of the PLAAF, including its training, but also lacks details.[78] For example, *China's National Defense 2008* states that the Air Force "stresses technical and tactical training in complex environments, combined training of different arms and aircraft types, and joint training{. . .}and intensifying the training of aviation units in counter-air operations, air-to-ground attacks and joint operations."[79]

While *PLAAF 2010*, DOD annual reports, and the biennial *China's National Defense* do not provide assessments of the PLAAF's training, Lt Col Michael Flaherty states, "PLAAF training now includes aerial combat training between dissimilar aircraft, long-range offensive air missions, surface task force protection missions, and live munitions delivery," but it still has "deficits in training." For example, he states, "in-flight refueling training is still limited by the small number of aerial tankers and refueling configured combat aircraft," and "while the scope for pilot initiative has improved with more modern systems and somewhat less rigid training scenarios, air intercept training still relies heavily on ground control." In addition, "while some new beyond visual range (BVR) tactics and doctrine have been observed, these remain immature and limited."[80]

Ultimately, the effectiveness of PLAAF training depends heavily on how far from China's border and from the PLAAF's command post the air combat occurs and how well the PLAAF's aircraft and SAMs can coordinate with each other, so that the SAMs do not shoot down their own aircraft in the engagement zone. Furthermore, PLAAF bases may be destroyed by long-range missiles during an actual conflict, thus forcing aircraft to return to another base further away without refueling en route.

Air defense zone coordination

One of the PLAAF's biggest challenges is to be able to conduct tactical coordination between its combat aircraft and Air Force, Navy, and Army air defense forces (SAM, AAA, and radar) within the same airspace. According to various PLA publications:

- A defense zone is an area where aviation and air defense forces with defensive combat missions are responsible for safeguarding against or resisting enemy offensives.[81]

- Air force combined-arms tactical coordination consists of separating airspace, targets, altitude, directions, and time. Airspace separation is the primary means, with the others serving as secondary means. Air force joint tactical coordination with the Navy and Army consists of establishing a joint command organization and separating forces by combat phases, combat missions or tasks, and combat direction or area.[82]

As early as 1986, the PLAAF began creating tactical training coordination zones to conduct combined-arms training between PLAAF aircraft and air defense forces, as well as joint training with naval vessels and ground force air defense units.[83] Although the PLAAF has created these training zones, it appears that most of the training is opposition force, where aircraft and SAMs oppose each other rather than working together against incoming aircraft.[84]

Foreign relations

The PLAAF's foreign relations program is an increasingly important component of China's overall foreign relations program.[85] It has gradually expanded from merely exchanging delegations to conducting combined exercises with individual countries and the Shanghai Cooperation Organization (SCO).[86] In 2001, the PLAAF Command College created a program for foreign officers that, since 2009, has included PLAAF officers. In addition, the PLAAF has begun to perform MOOTW abroad to support national goals. In September 2013, the USAF's Chief of Staff visited China for the first time since 1998. Although the PLAAF commander was invited to pay a reciprocal visit to the United States in 2014 for the first time since 1995, he has declined the invitation.

Combined exercises

Since the mid-2000s, the PLAAF has increasingly become involved in combined exercises with foreign air forces. These exercises have allowed the PLAAF to demonstrate its improving capabilities to the international community, observe and learn from foreign militaries in an operational environment, and build trust and solidify security cooperation with select countries.

The combined exercises can be divided into two categories: those with the SCO and those with individual, non-SCO countries. The following bullets provide a brief overview of the key exercises. Of note, all of the deployments have been supported by IL-76 transports, and some have involved aerial and/or ground refueling en route:

- Peace Mission 2007: JH-7s and Airborne forces to Russia
- Peace Mission 2010: H-6s, escorted by J-10s, flew into and out of Kazakhstan, where they dropped bombs
- Peace Mission 2013: JH-7s[87]
- Turkey (Anatolian Eagle 2010): Su-27s
- Pakistan (Shaheen 2011): J-11s
- Belarus (2011) and Venezuela (2011): Airborne forces

Shaheen 2011 was conducted in six steps, including "intelligence and information exchange, long-range maneuver, establishment of a joint command structure, adaptability training, comprehensive training and theoretical discussions." It should be noted, however, that all of these exercises are highly scripted and the PLAAF trains on the individual components of each exercise for months in advance.

Functional exchanges

The PLAAF has been sending delegations abroad led by senior colonels or major generals since the late 1980s. These exchanges typically include discussions on personnel, training, logistics, and maintenance issues.

Since the media generally covers only high-level PLAAF visits, little information is available about the types and total number of functional exchanges. A few articles, however, provide a glimpse at the program. In January 2007, *PLA Daily* reported, "In recent years, the PLAAF organized a total of 13 groups of senior- and mid-level officers to visit other countries. It also received air force delegations from 43 foreign countries." Unfortunately, no figures are available for the exchanges since that time.

These visits offer most PLAAF officers their only chance to travel abroad. PLAAF functional delegations visit the host country's air force headquarters, academic institutions and operational units, where they receive briefings, ask questions, view equipment and sometimes see live demonstrations. In July 2003, Senior Colonel Guo Chengliang, who was the Director of the PLAAF's Military Affairs Department, led a delegation to France to discuss pilot recruitment and NCO selection. His delegation visited eight organizations, including the Air Force Schools Command, 721st Base, 217th Base, and personnel center.

From 2002 through 2010, the PLAAF's monthly journal, *China Air Force*, published about 20 articles written by PLAAF delegation members who visited foreign countries or by officers who studied abroad, including in France, Italy, Pakistan, Britain, Australia, and Russia. The delegations visited flight schools and operational units, where they focused on pilot recruitment, education, and training, including simulators. The articles noted that pilots visited France in 2004 and 2011 and flew in the back seat of a Mirage-2000. In June 2011, another pilot visited Norway, Finland, and Sweden, where he flew in a Swedish L-39 trainer.

Conclusions

While much analysis of the PLAAF focuses on the hardware only, it is important to factor in every component of the PLAAF. Specifically, in order to better understand the PLAAF's historical and future role in China's security, one must examine its combat history, of which there has been none since the 1950s, as well as its evolving doctrine, organizational structure, personnel, logistics, maintenance, education, and training. It is clear that the PLAAF is moving forward in many areas, including deploying and training with more advanced aircraft and air defense weapon systems (SAMs, AAA, and radar); however, the PLAAF's ability to conduct sustained combat and support operations has not been tested in decades. Should a future conflict occur, it remains unclear whether the PLAAF can execute a high level of simultaneous offensive and defensive operations for any length of time, especially if its command centers, airfields, SAMs, AAA, radar, and logistics hubs suffer significant losses. In fact, even the threat of sustained missile strikes would probably negatively impact the PLAAF's readiness level, forcing repeated relocation of aircraft and air defense assets to avoid destruction. Furthermore, PLAAF operations would be only one piece of any Chinese military campaign, and it remains to be seen how well China's civilian and military leadership can integrate PLAAF operations with the other components of the PLA, including the Army, Navy, and Second Artillery, during a major military conflict.

Additionally, other areas, such as personnel, have proven more difficult to modernize than weapon systems and equipment. The PLAAF has taken significant strides in recent years toward reforming the recruitment, education, training, and career progression, but the issue of personnel continues to be a weak link. While it is difficult to determine the extent of this, it impacts the

PLAAF's ability to utilize its increasingly high-tech weapon systems and equipment to its full capability, especially in a more complex environment.

Glossary

Academy of Military Science　军事科学院
Administrative and functional departments　机关
Air and Space Battlefield and China's Air Force　空天战场与中国空军
Air Defense Identification Zone　防空识别区
Air Defense Zone　防空区
Air Force Dictionary　空军大辞典
Air Force Engineering University　空军工程大学
Air Force First Aviation College　空军第一航空学院
Air Force Logistics College　空军勤务学院
Air Force Military Thought 空军军事思想概论
Air Force Strategy Transformation and Flight Personnel Education Innovation　空军战略转型与人才教育创新
Airborne　空降兵
An Introduction to Air Force Military Thought　空军军事思想概论
Anti-aircraft artillery　高射炮兵
Aviation　航空兵
Bingtuan leader　正兵团
Branch/arm　兵种
CCP Central Committee's Military Commission/Central Military Commission　中央军委
Chemical defense　防化
China Air Force Encyclopedia　中国空军百科全书
China Air Force magazine　中国空军
China's National Defense　中国的国防
Communications　通信
Comparison of Chinese and Foreign Military Flight Education　中外军事飞行教育比较研究
Contemporary Military Organizational Reform Research　当代军事体制变革研究
Coordination zones　战术训练协作区
Discipline Inspection Commission　纪律检查委员会
Electronic countermeasures　电子对抗
Four General Departments　四总部
Gangyao　纲要
General Armament Department　总装北部
General Logistics Department　总后勤部
General Political Department　总政治部
General Staff Department　总参谋部
Grassroots level　基层
Kongjun Bao　空军报, identified on the cover in English as *Air Force News*
Leaders　领导首长
Ma Xiaotian　马晓天
Military Region　军区
Modern Military Organizational Reform Research　当代军事体制变革研究
National Defense Student　国防生
National Defense University　国防大学

Party Committee　党委
Party Congress　党代表大会
People's Liberation Army Air Force Officer's Handbook　中国人民解放军空军军官手册
PLA Air Force Female Pilots　中国人民解放军空军女飞行员
PLA Press　解放军出版社
PLAAF Command College　空军指挥学院
Political commissar　政治委员
Qiao Qingchen　乔清晨
Radar　雷达
Reserve Officer　后备军官
Science of PLA Political Work　中国人民解放军政治工作学
Service　军种
Specialty units and subunits　专业部分队
Standing Committee　党委常委
Strategic Air Force　战略空军论
Subunit　分队
Surface-to-air missile　地空导弹兵
Technical reconnaissance　技术侦察
World Military Yearbook　世界军事年鉴
Wu Faxian　吴法宪
Xu Qiliang　许其亮
Zhang Tingfa　张廷发

Notes

1 The report uses the following documents as a base and updates the information accordingly: Kenneth Allen, *The Ten Pillars of the People's Liberation Army Air Force: An Assessment*, The Jamestown Foundation, April 2011; Kenneth Allen, "PLA Air Force Organizational Reforms: 2000–2012" in Kevin Pollpeter and Kenneth W. Allen, eds, *The PLA as Organization v2.0*, which will be published in 2014, and is hereafter identified as *PLAAF Organization*; Kenneth Allen, "Chinese Air Force Officer Recruitment, Education and Training," *China Brief*, volume 11, issue 22, 30 November 2011; Kenneth Allen, "PLA Air Force Male Aviation Cadet Recruitment, Education and Training," *China Brief*, volume 12, issue 5, 2 March 2012; Kenneth Allen and Emma Kelly, "China's Air Force Female Aviators: 60 Years of Excellence (1952–2012)," *China Brief*, volume 12, issue 12, 22 June 2012; *People's Liberation Army Air Force 2010* (Dayton, OH: National Air and Space Intelligence Agency, 1 August 2010), hereafter identified as *PLAAF 2010*; and Kenneth W. Allen, "The Organizational Structure of the PLAAF" in Richard P. Hallion, Roger Cliff, and Phillip C. Saunders, eds, *The Chinese Air Force: Evolving Concepts, Roles and Capabilities* (Washington, DC: National Defense University, 2012), hereafter identified as *PLAAF Structure*.
2 According to a Taiwan MND spokesman on 4 August 1999, "Following Beijing's 1996 military exercise to threaten Taiwan, Communist Chinese airplanes began flying over the Taiwan Strait." State Department Briefing with James Rubin, *Federal Information Systems Corporation, Federal News Service*, 3 August 1999.
3 US State Department Briefing with James Rubin, *Federal Information Systems Corporation, Federal News Service*, 3 August 1999.
4 2013 *Annual Report to Congress on Military and Security Developments Involving the People's Republic of China*, 2013. Available online at www.defense.gov/pubs/2013_china_report_final.pdf (accessed 1 January 2014).
5 Two PLAAF books published in 2006 provide some initial insight into these concepts: Cai Fengzhen and Tian Anping, eds, *The Science of Integrated Air and Space Operations* (Beijing: PLA Press, August 2006); Min Zengfu, ed., *An Introduction to Air Force Military Thought* (Beijing: PLA Press, January 2006). The latter book was published as part of the PLAAF's Military Theory Research Tenth 5-Year Plan. In 1998, PLAAF Headquarters approved the basic concept of the book so that research could begin. Both

books have an introduction by the PLAAF commander and CMC member at the time, General Qiao Qingchen. For further information on the PLAAF's doctrine see Kevin M. Lanzit and Kenneth Allen, "Right-Sizing the PLA Air Force: New Operational Concepts Define a Smaller, More Operational Force" in Roy Kamphausen and Andrew Scobell, eds, *Right-Sizing the People's Liberation Army: Exploring the Contours of China's Military* (Carlisle, PA: US Army War College Strategic Studies Institute, September 2007), Chapter 9, pp. 437–78.

6   John A. Tirpak, *The Integration of Air and Space*, Air Force Magazine, vol. 83, No. 7, July 2000. Available online at www.airforcemag.com/MagazineArchive/Pages/2000/July%202000/0700airandspace.aspx (accessed 1 January 2014).

7   Zachary Keck, "South Korea to Expand Its Air Defense Identification Zone," *The Diplomat*, 2 December 2013.

8   Peter Nicholas, Jeremy Page, and Yuka Hayashi, "US, China Signal Retreat from Standoff Over Air-Defense Zone," *Wall Street Journal*, 5 December 2013.

9   Aaron Mehta, "USAF Chief: Chinese Air Defense ID Zone Shows Need for Communication," defensenews.com, 11 December 2013; Ben Blanchard and Roberta Rampton, "China Scrambles Jets to New Defense Zone, Eyes US, Japan Flights," Reuters, 29 November 2013.

10 "South Korea Expands Air Defense Zone Southward," *Xinhua*, 8 December 2013.

11 Joseph Yeh, "Aircraft Intercepted by Japanese Military," *The China Post*, 3 December 2013.

12 Wayne A. Ulman, "China's Military Aviation Forces" in Andrew S. Erickson and Lyle J. Goldstein, eds, *Chinese Aerospace Power: Evolving Maritime Roles* (Newport, RI: China Maritime Studies Institute and the Naval Institute Press, 2011).

13 Unless noted, the information in this section comes from *PLAAF 2010*, *PLAAF Structure*, and *PLAAF Organization*.

14 The three services are Army, Navy, and Air Force. Second Artillery is an independent branch, not a service. Since 1985, the *World Military Yearbook*, which is published annually or biennially by *PLA Press*, has listed the five PLAAF branches in order as aviation, SAM, AAA, radar, and airborne. Until 2007, they did not identify the specialized units and subunits. Beginning with the 2007 edition, the yearbook has added the five specialty units and subunits in the order of communications, radar, ECM, chemical defense, and technical reconnaissance. As for the biennial *China's National Defense*, only the 2002 and 2008 editions identify the branches. The 2002 edition confused the issue by identifying only four branches (aviation, SAM, AAA, and airborne) and listed the five specialty units and subunits as communications, radar, ECM, chemical defense, and special technical. The 2008 edition listed eight branches in the following order: aviation, air defense (SAM and AAA), airborne, communications, radar, ECM, technical reconnaissance, and chemical defense. It did not mention specialty units and subunits. Meanwhile, the Ministry of National Defense's website states that the PLAAF has five branches (aviation, SAM, AAA, radar, and airborne) and other specialized units and subunits.

15 For an overview of the 15-grade structure see Kenneth Allen, "Introduction to the PLA's Organizational Reforms: 2000–2012" in Pollpeter and Allen, eds, *The PLA as Organization v2.0*.

16 Unless noted, the information in this section comes from *PLAAF 2010*, *PLAAF Structure*, *PLAAF Organization*, and Kenneth Allen, *The Ten Pillars of the People's Liberation Army Air Force: An Assessment*.

17 Liu Feng'an, "Chinese Communist Party Congresses at Various Levels of the CPLA Air Force" in Yao Wei, ed., *China Air Force Encyclopedia* (Beijing: Aviation Industry Press, November 2005), p. 361.

18 Regulations state that, depending on the level in the chain of command, the number of Standing Committee members ranges from seven to 15. *Science of PLA Political Work* (Beijing: NDU Press, May 2006), pp. 170–1. The PLAAF's Standing Committee most likely consists of the commander, PC, some (if not all) of the deputy commanders and deputy PCs, and the directors of the Headquarters, Political, Logistics, and Equipment Departments. It does not appear that the PC of the Logistics Department and Equipment Department are on the Standing Committee.

19 The fourth commander to serve as the Party secretary was Liu Yalou, *Dictionary of China's Communist Party Central Committee Members for 1921–2003* (Beijing: Chinese Communist Party History Press, 2004), pp. 465–6, 587–8, 824–5, and 1052–3.

20 Unless noted, the information in this subsection comes from *PLAAF Organization*. For the list of all PLAAF leaders at the end of 2012 see the blog at http://club.xilu.com/xinguancha/msgview-950389-104372.html?PHPSESSID=a78cb23ead24848375566c5fb016e7db (accessed 1 January 2014).

21 See Kenneth W. Allen, "Assessing the PLA's Promotion Ladder to CMC Member Based on Grades vs. Ranks," *China Brief*, volume 10, issue 15, 22 July 2010 (Part 1) and volume 10, issue 16, 5 August 2010 (Part 2). Available online at www.jamestown.org/programs/chinabrief/archivescb/cb2009/?tx_

22 Prior to 1998, Air Force and Navy personnel serving in any type of joint organization were required to wear an Army uniform.
23 Liu Chengjun's biography, available online at http://baike.baidu.com/view/1141118.htm (accessed 1 January 2014).
24 Liu Yazhou's biography, available online at http://baike.baidu.com/view/270429.htm (accessed 1 January 2014). Although Liu has been identified as a PLAAF officer, he shifted between Air Force and Army political officer billets throughout his career. Most importantly, however, he currently wears an Air Force uniform as the NDU PC. For an assessment of the PLA's political officer system, see Kenneth Allen et al., "China's Military Political Commissar System in Comparative Perspective" and Category: China Brief, Elite, Military/Security, China and the Asia-Pacific, Russia "Assessing PLA Navy and Air Force Political Commissar Career Paths," *China Brief*, volume 13, issue 5, 4 March 2013.
25 Unless noted, the information in this subsection comes from *PLAAF Organization*.
26 "Tian Xiusi Becomes the PLA Air Force Political Commissar and Has Real War Experience," *caixin.co*, 30 October 2012. Available online at http://china.caixin.com/2012-10-30/100454054.html (accessed 1 January 2014). His biography is available at http://baike.baidu.com/view/585708.htm.
27 Hu Guangzheng, ed., *Modern Military Organizational Reform Research* (Beijing: Military Science Publishing House, October 2007), p. 96.
28 The reason why MRAF commanders were not concurrent MR deputy commanders prior to 1988 is because, from 1979 to 1988, the PLA had 18 grades instead of 15. Prior to 1988, MRAF Headquarters had the grade of *bingtuan* leader, which was between the corps leader and MR deputy leader grade. In 1988, the PLA abolished the *bingtuan* level and upgraded all of the *bingtuan* leader-grade organizations, including the MRAF Headquarters, to MR deputy-leader grade organizations and downgraded all of the *bingtuan* deputy leader-grade organizations to corps leader. As a result, the MRAF commanders were concurrently made MR deputy commanders to match their new grade.
29 According to the *People's Liberation Army Air Force Officer's Handbook* (Beijing: Lantian Press, November 2006), p. 35, only the Guangzhou and Nanjing MRAF PCs are authorized to be concurrent MR deputy PCs; however, based on a search of the Internet in early 2012, the PCs for the Lanzhou and Shenyang MRAFs have apparently been added to the list. Hereafter, this book is identified as *Air Force Officer Handbook*.
30 The information in this paragraph is compiled from the information about the PLAAF in the PRC's eighth biennial *China's National Defense* since 1998. *China's National Defense*, Information Office of the State Council of the People's Republic of China. The reports are commonly referred to as China's Defense White Papers.
31 *China's National Defense 2008*.
32 Qiao Qingchen, "Air Force Strategy" in *China Air Force Encyclopedia*, pp. 55–7. At the same meeting, Jiang Zemin stepped down as the chairman and the CMC approved elevating the commanders of the PLAN, PLAAF, and PLASAF as CMC members.
33 "From Supportive Service to Strategic Air Force: Major Change in China's Air Force Buildup Thinking," *Hong Kong Feng Huang Wang*, 28 June 2004.
34 *China's National Defense* 2004 to 2012.
35 Cai Fengzhen and Tian Anping, eds, *Air and Space Battlefield and China's Air Force* (PLA Press, March 2004); Fengzhen and Anping, eds, *The Science of Integrated Air and Space Operations*. Of note, neither of these books were published as part of a specific plan, nor did they have an editorial committee to oversee the publication. The only authority for the books comes from the fact that the PLAAF commander and PC each wrote a foreword. At the time of the first book (2004), Cai was the commandant of the PLAAF Engineering University in Xi'an. At the time of the second book (2006), he had moved up to be one of the deputy chiefs of staff in the Headquarters Department at PLAAF Headquarters. Tian is an instructor at the PLAAF Engineering University.
36 Cai and Tian, eds, *The Science of Integrated Air and Space Operations*, pp. 299–301.
37 Zhu Hui, ed., *Strategic Air Force* (Beijing: Lantian Press, July 2009).
38 "Hu, Wen Orders 'All-out Efforts' to Secure Life of Nationals," *Xinhua*, 22 February 2011. Available online at http://english.sina.com/china/2011/0222/361035.html (accessed 1 January 2014). Additional information obtained from www.chinadaily.com.cn/china/2011-03/02/content_12103843.htm, www.chinadaily.com.cn/china/2011-03/05/content_12121535.htm, and http://english.peopledaily.com.cn/90001/90776/90883/7308966.html (accessed 1 January 2014).

39 Teng Lianfu and Jiang Fusheng, eds, *Air Force Combat Research* (Beijing: National Defense University Publishers, May 1990), p. 155.
40 Wang Houqing and Zhang Xingye, eds, *Science of Campaigns* (Beijing: National Defense University Press, May 2000). The remaining nineteen campaigns are as follows: ground force campaigns—mobile warfare, positional offensive, urban offensive, positional defensive, and urban defensive; naval forces campaigns—sea blockade, sea lines of communications (SLOC) destruction, coastal raid, anti-ship, SLOC defense, naval base defense; Second Artillery campaigns—nuclear counterattack, conventional ballistic missile campaigns; and joint service campaigns—blockade, landing, anti-air raid, airborne, and anti-landing.
41 Zhang Yuliang, ed., *Science of Campaigns* (Beijing: National Defense University Press, May 2006).
42 *Annual Report to Congress on Military and Security Developments Involving the People's Republic of China 2013*.
43 "Female Helicopter Pilots," *Kongjun Bao*, 21 March 2011, p. 1.
44 Major General Xu Guangyu, "Evolution of China's Military over the Next 20 Years," *Chinese Academy of Social Sciences Journal*, 27 July 2010. Available online at http://theory.people.com.cn/GB/12365190.html (accessed 1 January 2014). A review of The International Institute for Strategic Studies' (IISS) *Military Balance* shows the following figures for a total force of 2.3 million: 2004 to 2007 was 400,000, which equates to 17.3 percent; 2008 was 250,000, which equates to 10.9 percent; and 2010 to 2013 was 300,000 to 330,000, which equates to 13.0–14.3 percent. James Hackett, ed., *The Military Balance* (London: Routledge Journals for The International Institute for Strategic Studies (IISS)).
45 *China's National Defense 2012*.
46 For 1975, one source (*Air Force Dictionary*) cited a 100,000-man reduction, which equated to a 16.4 percent reduction; a second source (*Contemporary Military Organizational Reform Research*) cited a 190,000-man reduction; and a third source (*China Air Force Encyclopedia*) reported a 26.9 percent reduction. The information can be found at Chronology of Events Appendix in Zhu Rongchang, ed., *Air Force Dictionary* (Shanghai: Shanghai Dictionary Press, September 1996), p. 977; Hu Guangzheng, ed., *Contemporary Military Organizational Reform Research* (Beijing: Military Science Publishing House, October 2007), p. 465; and Qiao Qingchen, "Air Force of the CPLA" in *China Air Force Encyclopedia*, pp. 1233–4.
47 See the Chronology of Events Appendix in the *Air Force Dictionary*, pp. 973, 977, 980 and 982; *Contemporary Military Organizational Reform Research*, p. 465; Jiang Yanyu, *60 Years of New China's National Defense and Military Building* (Beijing: Party-founded Reading Material Press, September 2009), p. 25, 37, 43 and 55; Qiao Qingchen, "Air Force of the CPLA" in *China Air Force Encyclopedia*, pp. 1233–4.
48 Xu Guangyu, "Evolution of China's Military over the Next 20 Years."
49 Unless noted, the information on male aviation cadets comes from Kenneth Allen, "PLA Air Force Male Aviation Cadet Recruitment, Education and Training," *China Brief*, volume 12, issue 5, 2 March 2012.
50 "PLA Air Force Stop Recruiting Pilots from Civilian College Grads," *Xinhua*, 25 September 2013. Available online at http://news.xinhuanet.com/english/china/2013-09/25/c_132749622.htm.
51 The PLAAF's monthly journal *China Air Force*, issue 2011-4, p. 8.
52 Shen Jinke, Yang Zhen and Zhang Zimian, "Visiting the First Group of Air Force and Qinghua University Joint Education of Flight Cadets," *China Air Force*, issue 2011-10, pp. 20–2.
53 "General Regulations for Air Force Pilot Recruitment in 2013," *233 Net*, 22 August 2013. Available online at www.233.com/gaokao/zhaosheng/Cadet/20120822/081947480-7.html (accessed 1 January 2014).
54 Unless otherwise noted, the information on female aviators comes from Kenneth Allen and Emma Kelly, "China's Air Force Female Aviators: 60 Years of Excellence (1952–2012)," *China Brief*, volume 12, issue 12, 22 June 2012. In September 2012, the PLAAF also published a detailed history of the female aviation program in *PLA Air Force Female Pilots* (Beijing: Lantian Press, September 2012).
55 Wei Changchun, "The Air Force Recruited 40 Female Pilots This Year," *Air Force Net*, 12 April 2013. Available online at www.kjzfw.net/Item/244.aspx (accessed 17 March 2014).
56 According to one article, the females in the JH-7 are assigned as WSO; however, the only photos of them standing near a JH-7 shows only females, which implies they are both pilots and WSOs. Xie Hong, "Training and Education of PLA Air Force Pilots in Reform," *Trainer*, number 3, 19 September 2012, pp. 3–6.
57 The information in this section comes from Fu Guoqiang, ed., *Comparison of Chinese and Foreign Military Flight Education* (Beijing: Military Science Press, January 2013), and Bai Chongming and Ji Changguo, eds, *Air Force Strategy Transformation and Flight Personnel Education Innovation* (Beijing: Lantian Press, May 2010).
58 *Air Force Strategy Transformation and Flight Personnel Education Innovation*, p. 70.

59 *Comparison of Chinese and Foreign Military Flight Education* and *Air Force Strategy Transformation and Flight Personnel Education Innovation.*
60 Information obtained from http://blog.sina.com.cn/s/blog_4dacb4240100g2is.html (accessed 1 January 2014).
61 *PLA Air Force Female Pilots*, p. 167.
62 Unless otherwise noted, the information in this subsection comes from Allen, "Chinese Air Force Officer Recruitment, Education and Training."
63 *PLAAF Officers Handbook.*
64 Ibid.
65 During 2012 and 2013, the Air Force Engineering University (AFEU) made some significant reforms to its organizational structure. Information obtained from www.afeu.cn/web/kgdd/yxsz/ (accessed 1 January 2014).
66 Interviews and analysis of multiple articles.
67 *PLAAF Officers Handbook.*
68 Unless otherwise noted, the information in this subsection comes from Allen, "Chinese Air Force Officer Recruitment, Education and Training."
69 Ibid.
70 Unless otherwise noted, the information in this section comes from: analysis of multiple years of the PLAAF's newspaper *Kongjun Bao*; four special reports on the history of the enlisted force in *China Armed Forces*, number 12, volume 4, 2011 (Beijing: Xinhua News Agency Military Department), pp. 22–43; *PLA Air Force Enlisted Force Handbook* (Beijing: Lantian Press, November 2006); and Dennis J. Blasko, *The Chinese Army Today: Tradition and Transformation for the Twenty-first Century* (London: Routledge, 2006).
71 *The Chinese Army Today: Tradition and Transformation for the Twenty-first Century*, p. 51.
72 Song Shilun and Xiao Ke, eds, *Chinese Military Encyclopedia* volume 2 (Beijing: Academy of Military Science Publishers, July 1997), p. 300.
73 Interviews with PLA officers.
74 Unless otherwise noted, the information in the Training section comes from Allen, *The Ten Pillars of the People's Liberation Army Air Force.*
75 Xu Tongyuan, "Unrestricted Air Combat: The Second Golden Helmet Awards," *China Armed Forces*, number 19, volume 1, 2013, pp. 28–31.
76 Cheng Fuming, Fu Xuecheng and Guo Huarong, "Airborne 'Command Post,'" *China Air Force*, 2013-01, pp. 39–43.
77 Office of the Secretary of Defense, *Annual Report to Congress Military and Security Developments Involving the People's Republic of China: 2010.*
78 *China's National Defense* 1998 to 2012.
79 *China's National Defense* 2008.
80 Michael P. Flaherty, "Red Wings Ascendant: The Chinese Air Force Contribution to Antiaccess," *Joint Forces Quarterly*, issue 60, first quarter 2011, pp. 96–100.
81 Li Chao, "Air Defense Zone" in *China Air Force Encyclopedia*, p. 173.
82 Du Jinwang, "Air Force Tactical Coordination" in *China Air Force Encyclopedia*, p. 116.
83 Zhang Qin and Chen Taisheng, "A Certain Air Division Creates a Tactics Training Coordination Zone," *Jiefangjun Bao*, 17 June 1986. Gong Heping, "Air Force Universally Creates Tactics Training Coordination Zones," *Jiefangjun Bao*, 9 January 1987. Additional information was obtained from http://dlib.eastview.com/browse/doc/14267128 and http://dlib.eastview.com/browse/doc/14279734 (accessed 1 January 2014).
84 Li Haiyuan, "Nanjing MRAF Air Division Organizes Multi-Branch Opposition Force Training Event under Information Technology Conditions," *Jiefangjun Bao*, 30 July 2004. Available online at http://people.com.cn/GB/ junshi/1076/2676207.html (accessed 1 January 2014); Guo Weihu, "A Certain SAM Regiment vs an Air Force Air Regiment," Chinamil.com, 4 June 2010. Available online at http://tp.chinamil.com.cn/news/2010-06/04/content_4232603.htm (accessed 1 January 2014).
85 Unless otherwise noted, the information in this section comes from Kenneth Allen and Emma Kelly, "Assessing the Growing PLA Air Force Foreign Relations Program," *China Brief*, volume 12, issue 9, 26 April 2012.
86 The SCO initially formed in 1996 as the Shanghai Five, including China, Russia, Kazakhstan, Kyrgyzstan, and Tajikistan. In 2001 Uzbekistan joined and the group was renamed as the SCO. Originally intended to provide a mechanism to resolve border disputes, over time the SCO's activities expanded to include increased military cooperation, intelligence sharing, and counterterrorism drills. Andrew Scheineson, "The Shanghai Cooperation Organization," 24 March 2009. Available online at http://www.cfr.org/china/shanghai-cooperation-organization/p10883 (accessed 23 March 2014).

87 "Chinese Air Forces Combat Group Organizes Actual-Combat Training," *People's Daily Online*, 12 August 2013.

Suggested further reading

English sources

Allen, K. (1991) *People's Republic of China People's Liberation Army Air Force*, Washington, DC: Defense Intelligence Agency.

―――― (1997) "PLAAF Modernization: An Assessment" in Lilley, J. R., and Downs, C. (eds), *Crisis in the Taiwan Strait*, Washington, DC: NDU Press.

―――― (1999) "PLA Air Force Logistics and Maintenance—What Has Changed?" in Mulvenon, J. and Yang, A. (eds), *The People's Liberation Army in the Information Age*, Santa Monica, CA: RAND.

―――― (2000) "PLA Air Force Operations and Modernization" in Puska, S. M. (ed.), *The People's Liberation Army after Next*, Carlisle, PA: Strategic Studies Institute.

―――― (2002) "Introduction to the PLA's Administrative and Operational Structure" and "PLA Air Force Organization" in Mulvenon, J. and Yang, A. (eds), *The People's Liberation Army as Organization*, Santa Monica, CA: RAND.

―――― (2002) "Logistics Support for PLA Air Force Campaigns" in Scobell, A. and Wortzel L. M. (eds), *China's Growing Military Power: Perspectives on Security, Ballistic Missiles, and Conventional Capabilities*, Carlisle, PA: Strategic Studies Institute.

―――― (2002) "PLA Air Force Organization" in Mulvenon, J. and Yang, A. (eds), *The People's Liberation Army as Organization*, Santa Monica, CA: RAND.

―――― (2003) "PLA Air Force Overview," *Chinese Military Update*, RUSI, vol. 1, no. 4.

―――― (2003) "PLA Air Force: Lessons Learned 1949–2002" in Burkitt, L., Scobell, A. and Wortzel, L. (eds), *The Lessons of History: The Chinese People's Liberation Army at 75*, Carlisle, PA: Strategic Studies Institute.

―――― (2003) "The PLA Air Force's Mobile Offensive Operations" in Edmonds, M. (ed.), *Taiwan's Security and Air Power: Taiwan's Defence against the Air Threat from Mainland China*, London: RoutledgeCurzon.

―――― (2005) "PLA Air Force Foreign Relations," *Chinese Military Update*, London: RUSI, vol. 3, no. 1.

―――― (2005) "Reforms in the PLA Air Force," *China Brief*, vol. 5, iss. 15.

―――― (2007) "Air Force Deterrence and Escalation Calculations for a Taiwan Strait Conflict: China, Taiwan, and the United States," in Swaine, M. D., Yang, A. N. D. and Medeiros, E. S. (eds), *Assessing the Threat: The Chinese Military and Taiwan's Security*, Washington, DC: CEIP.

―――― (2010) "Assessing the PLA's Promotion Ladder to CMC Member Based on Grades vs. Ranks," *China Brief*, vol. 10, iss. 15 (Part 1) and vol. 10, iss. 16 (Part 2).

―――― (2011) "Assessing the PLA Air Force's Ten Pillars," *China Brief*, vol. 11, iss. 3.

―――― (2011) "Chinese Air Force Officer Cadet Recruitment, Education, and Training," *China Brief*, vol. 11, iss. 22.

―――― (2011), *The Ten Pillars of the People's Liberation Army Air Force: An Assessment*, Washington, DC: Jamestown Foundation special report.

―――― (2012) "China's Air Force Male Aviation Cadet Recruitment, Education and Training," *China Brief*, vol. 12, iss. 5.

―――― (2012) "The Organizational Structure of the PLAAF" in Hallion, R. P., Cliff, R. and Saunders, P. C. (eds), *The Chinese Air Force: Evolving Concepts, Roles and Capabilities*, Washington, DC: National Defense University.

―――― (2014) "Trends in PLA International Initiatives under Hu Jintao," Carlisle, PA: Strategic Studies Institute, to be published in 2014.

―――― (2015) "PLA Air Force Organizational Reforms: 2000–2012" in Pollpeter, K. and Allen, K. (eds), *The PLA as Organization v2.0*, Washington, DC: Defense Group Inc., to be published in 2014.

Allen, K. and Allen, J. (2005) "Controlling the Airspace Over the Taiwan Strait" in Tsang, S. (ed.), *If China Attacks Taiwan: Military Strategy, Politics and Economics*, London: Routledge.

―――― (2011) "Assessing China's Response to US Reconnaissance Flights," *China Brief*, vol. 11, iss. 16.

Allen, K. and Kelly, E. (2012) "Assessing the Growing PLA Air Force Foreign Relations Program," *China Brief*, vol. 12, iss. 9.

―――― (2012) "China's Air Force Female Aviators: 60 Years of Excellence (1952–2012)," *China Brief*, vol. 12, issue 12.

Allen, K. and Latham, R. (1991) "Defense Reform in China—The PLA Air Force," *Problems of Communism*, May.

Allen, K., Chao, B. and Kinsella, R. (2013) "China's Military Political Commissar System in Comparative Perspective," *China Brief*, vol. 13, iss. 5.

Allen, K., Clemens, M., Glinert, S. and Yoon, D. (2013) "Assessing PLA Navy and Air Force Political Commissar Career Paths," *China Brief*, vol. 13, iss. 5.

Allen, K., Pollack, J. and Krumel, G. (1995) *China's Air Force Enters the Twenty-first Century*, Santa Monica, CA: RAND.

Blasko, D. J. (2014) "Chinese Helicopter Development: Missions, Roles, and Maritime Implications" in Dutton, P., Erickson, A. S. and Martinson, R. (eds), *China's Near Seas Combat Capabilities*, Newport, RI: Chinese Maritime Studies Institute.

Cliff, R., Fei, J., Hagen, J., Hague, E., Heginbotham, E. and Stillion, J. (2011) *Shaking the Heavens and Splitting the Earth: China's Air Force Employment Concepts in the Twenty-first Century*, Santa Monica: CA, RAND.

Erickson, A. S. and Goldstein, L. J. (2011) *Chinese Aerospace Power: Evolving Maritime Roles*, Newport, RI: China Maritime Studies Institute and the Naval Institute Press.

Fisher, R. D. (2003) "PLA Air Force Equipment Trends" in Flanagan, S. J. and Marti, M. M. (eds), *The People's Liberation Army and China in Transition*, Washington, DC: National Defense University Press.

Lanzit, K. M. and Allen, K. (2007) "Right-Sizing the PLA Air Force: New Operational Concepts Define a Smaller, More Capable Force" in Scobell, A. and Kamphausen, R. (eds), *Right-Sizing the People's Liberation Army: Exploring the Contours of China's Military*, Carlisle, PA: Strategic Studies Institute.

Lewis, J. W. and Xue, L. (1999) "China's Search for a Modern Air Force," *International Security*, vol. 24, no. 1.

National Air and Space Intelligence Center (2010) *People's Liberation Army Air Force 2010*, Wright-Patterson AFB, OH: Author.

Shlapak, D. (2014) "Chinese Air Superiority in the Near Seas" in Dutton, P., Erickson, A. S. and Martinson, R. (eds), *China's Near Seas Combat Capabilities*, Newport, RI: Chinese Maritime Studies Institute.

Zhang, X. (2003) "Air Combat for the People's Republic: The People's Liberation Army Air Force in Action, 1949–1969" in Ryan, M. A., Finkelstein, D. M. and McDevitt, M. (eds), *Chinese Warfighting: The PLA Experience Since 1949*, Armonk, NY: M. E. Sharpe.

Chinese sources

Academy of Military Science (September 2011) *Military Terminology of the Chinese People's Liberation Army* [中国人民解放军军语], Beijing: Academy of Military Science Press.

—— (2005) 《中国空军百科全书》 [*China Air Force Encyclopedia*], Beijing: 航空工业 出版社 [Aviation Industry Press].

Bai Chongming and Ji Changguo (eds) (May 2010) *Air Force Strategy Transformation and Flight Personnel Education Innovation*, Beijing: Blue Sky Press [蓝天出版社].

Cai Fengzhen [蔡凤震] and Tian Anping [田安平] (eds) (2004) 《空天战场与中国空军》 [*Air and Space Battlefield and China's Air Force*], Beijing: 解放军出版社 [Liberation Army Press].

—— (eds) (March 2004) *Air and Space Battlefield and China's Air Force*, Beijing: PLA Press.

—— (eds) (August 2006) *The Science of Integrated Air and Space Operations*, Beijing: PLA Press.

Cai Fengzhen, Tian Anping, Chen Jiesheng [陈杰生], Cheng Jian [程建], Zheng Dongliang [郑东良], Liang Xiaoan [梁小安], Deng Pan [邓攀] and Guan Hua [管桦] (eds) (2006) 《空天一体作战学》 [*The Study of Integrated Air and Space Operations*], Beijing: 解放军出版社 [Liberation Army Press].

Chen Daojin [陈道金] and Liu Yuan [刘媛] (2009) 〈飞行院校跨越发展的战略定位与告素质飞行学员培养〉 ["Flight Academic Institutions Leap Ahead in Developing the Strategic Position and High Quality of Educating and Training Aviation Cadets"] in Li Chunjian [李纯剑] (ed.), *Research on New Century New Period Air Force Academic Institution Transformation Building and Personnel Education and Culture* [新世纪新阶段空军院校转型建设与人才培养研究], Beijing: Blue Sky Press [蓝天出版社], pp. 55–66.

He Weirong (ed.) (2006) *Science of Air Force Training*, Beijing: Academy of Military Science Press.

Li Daguang [李大光] (2001) 《太空战》 [*Space War*], Beijing: 军事科学出版社 [Military Science Press].

Li Rongchang [李荣常] and Cheng Jian [程建] (2003) 《空天一体信息作战》 [*Integrated Air and Space Information Warfare*], Beijing: 军事科学出版社 [Military Science Press].

Liu Yazhou [刘亚洲], Qiao Liang [乔良] and Wang Xiangsui [王湘穗] (2003) 〈战争空中化与中国空军〉 ["Combat in the Air and China's Air Force"], in Shen Weiguang [沈伟光] (ed.), Xie Xizhang [解玺璋] and

Ma Yaxi [马亚西] (assoc. eds), 《中国军事变革》 [*China's Military Transformation*], 新华出版社 [Xinhua Press], pp. 79–104.

Liu Yazhou and Yao Jun (eds) (August 2007) *A History of China's Aviation*, second edn (中国航空史 [第二版]), Hunan: Hunan Science and Technology Press.

People's Liberation Army Air Force [中国人民解放军空军] (1994) 《空军战术学》 [*Study of Air Force Tactics*], Beijing: 解放军出版社 [Liberation Army Press].

——— (November 2006) *People's Liberation Army Air Force Officer's Handbook* [中国人民解放军空军军官手册], Beijing: Blue Sky Press [蓝天出版社].

——— (November 2006) *PLA Air Force Enlisted Force Handbook* [中国人民解放军空军士兵手册], Beijing: Blue Sky Press [蓝天出版社].

PRC State Council's Information Office (1998–2012) *China's National Defense* [中国的国防].

Wang Houqing [王厚卿] and Zhang Xingye [张兴业] (eds) (2000) 《战役学》 [*Study of Campaigns*], Beijing: 国防大学出版社 [National Defense University Press].

Yao Wei (ed.) (November 2005) *China Air Force Encyclopedia* [中国空军百科全书], Beijing: Aviation Industry Press.

Yu Daqing (ed.) (December 2011) *PLA Officer Handbook*, Beijing: PLA General Political Department Cadre Department.

Zhang Yuliang [张玉良] (ed.) (2006) 《战役学》 [*Study of Campaigns*], Beijing: 国防大学出版社 [National Defense University Press].

Zhang Zhiwei [张志伟] and Feng Chuanjiang [冯传奖] (2006) 〈试析未来空天一体作战〉 ["Thoughts on Future Integrated Air–Space Operations"], 《军事科学》 [*Military Science*], vol. 2, pp. 52–9.

Zhao Yiping (ed.) (2007) *People's Liberation Army Military History* [中国人民解放军军史] volume III in *China Military Encyclopedia*, second edn [中国军事百科全书第二版], Beijing: Encyclopedia of China Publishing House.

Zhu Rongchang (ed.) (September 1996) *Air Force Dictionary* [空军大辞典], Shanghai: Shanghai Dictionary Press.

19
China's "fortress fleet" comes of age

James R. Holmes[1]

China is constructing what *fin de siècle* historian Alfred Thayer Mahan might have styled a "fortress fleet." This was a naval contingent that seldom if ever ventured beyond protective fire from gunners ashore. Practitioners of the fortress fleet viewed land-based fire support as the great equalizer between a lesser regional navy and stronger opponents operating in the coastal state's geographic environs. For Mahan, who lived in an age of rudimentary technology, "fortress fleet" was a term of opprobrium—a rebuke to commanders who embraced this defensive-minded approach. A century hence, however, naval technology may make this a workable strategy for any coastal state that confines its seaward ambitions to within range of shore-based weaponry. China appears to be just such a great power.

Mahan disliked fortress-fleet strategies for a simple reason: because guns' range was too short to make the approach viable. To shelter under the fort's guns, a navy had to stay within small sea areas, and thus remained perpetually on the tactical defensive. That prospect repelled Mahan, who preached the gospel of offensive sea control. Now that the ranges of land-based armaments—tactical aircraft, anti-ship missiles, short-range submarines and patrol craft—are measured in hundreds of miles, a navy can prosecute highly offensive operations and tactics while remaining under this protective aegis. Technology has liberated the fortress fleet from coastal waters—freeing it to prosecute intensely offensive tactics and operations while remaining on the strategic defensive.

This approach conforms ideally to "active defense," an offensive form of strategic defense prescribed not just by Mao Zedong, the Chinese Communist Party's founding chairman, but also by sea-power theorists such as Sir Julian Corbett. Offshore active defense is the approach the People's Liberation Army (PLA) has made the core of its maritime strategy. The fortress fleet is a method for putting active defense into effect. Strategies and forces exist to give decision-makers options.

Holding opponents at bay with shore-based firepower opens up new vistas for the PLA Navy. Adding shore-based tactical aircraft, cruise and ballistic missiles, submarines, and missile-armed patrol craft to the fleet's striking power could provide a great equalizer for China's navy while it remains weaker than that of the United States. Indeed, such an approach would spare Beijing from constructing a navy as large as—and symmetrical to—the US Navy.

In operational terms, the capacity for land-based sea denial would grant the fleet a measure of liberty to venture beyond East Asia should the leadership see the need. Whether Beijing contents itself with managing events in the China seas or opts for a broader geographic footprint, land-based sea power promises to constitute a major part of the force mix.

How does a fortress fleet win?

Active defense is a strategy of the temporarily weaker power. It balks a superior opponent's strategy until such time as the lesser power can shift the balance of forces, seize the counteroffensive, and win. The weak have to conscript all instruments at their disposal, and fight smart, to pull off a victory over dominant foes. Accordingly, it seemingly comes as second nature to Chinese strategists to combine shore-based and seagoing implements into a unified, highly joint maritime strategy. The distinction between *maritime* and *naval* is a distinction with a difference. Naval strategy refers to the use of a single instrument of power, the navy, to accomplish strategic goals. Maritime strategy is grand strategy. Writes Mahan, it means integrating all tools able to shape events in the nautical domain—naval, military, non-military—into an instrument by which seafaring states open up commercial and political access to important theaters.[2] Such ideas may help explain the allure Mahan's writings exert in contemporary China.

The distinction between naval and maritime strategy often escapes notice among even learned commentators in the West. Not so in China. While it is a relative newcomer to maritime enterprises, China arguably entertains a more mature, thoughtful, all-encompassing concept of sea power than does the United States, the predominant seafaring state of the day. Sea power, then, is about more than fleets—and indeed about more than navies. Long-range aircraft and missiles based on land, and operated by armies and air forces, are implements of sea power as surely as destroyers or aircraft carriers plying the briny main. Beijing is pursuing warships and naval aircraft, to be sure.[3] Its naval buildup over the past two decades has been impressive by any standard. But it has fielded land-based hardware with equal aplomb. Its aim, apparently, is to hold up a defensive, "access-denial" shield behind which a blue-water PLA Navy can execute offensive or defensive missions China's leadership deems wise. Alternatively, Beijing could dispatch the fleet beyond reach of access-denial weaponry, trusting to land-based armaments to hold adversaries at bay in the fleet's absence.

Strategist Carl von Clausewitz helps clarify the logic behind fortress-fleet strategies. This is a strategy of the weak, but the weak sometimes win. Writes Clausewitz, "wars have in fact been fought between states of *very unequal strength*," and the lesser combatant can prevail if it arranges matters astutely. Why? Because one belligerent need not overthrow the other to prevail. It can manipulate calculations among the stronger antagonist's leadership, dissuading that antagonist from fighting to the finish. "Inability to carry on the struggle," continues Clausewitz, "can, in practice, be replaced by two other grounds for making peace: the first is the improbability of victory; the second is its unacceptable cost."[4] In other words, one opponent can crush its opponent and impose its will. Failing that, it can convince that opponent that it is unlikely to win, or that the costs of winning are greater than the value of the victory itself.

Now map this to maritime Asia. Fortress-fleet logic demarcates a zone on the map where a stronger navy operating far from home will find it hard, if not impossible, to prevail. It may risk prohibitive losses even if the leadership deems the cause worthwhile. It may even lose in the contested theater, depending on how large a naval contingent it hazards in battle against a coastal state fighting close to home—where defenders can concentrate their entire strength against a fraction of the enemy's. The outer limits of this zone are traced by the maximum effective firing range of shore-based weaponry—of the latter-day counterparts to the fort's guns, in Mahanian parlance. The China seas, much of the Western Pacific, the Bay of Bengal, and part of the Arabian Sea now lie within reach of missiles based on Chinese territory, according to the Pentagon's annual reports on Chinese military power (see Figure 19.1 below[5]).

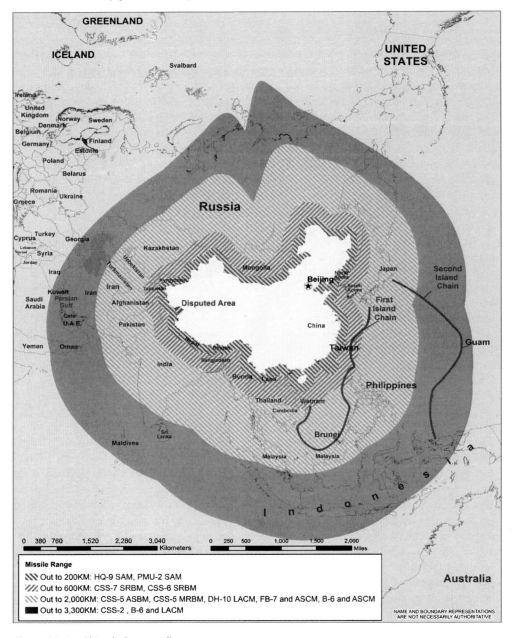

Figure 19.1 China's fortress-fleet zone

Source: US Defense Department, *Annual Report to Congress: Military and Security Developments Involving the People's Republic of China, 2010*, p. 32.

China's "fortress fleet" comes of age

The graphic depicts the striking ranges of various missiles positioned around the Chinese periphery. Ships operating within the cross-hatched central zone will be able to count on fire support from anti-ship ballistic missiles should that system live up to its billing.

Access denial, then, is at once a threat and a bargain. Defenders who possess integrated land/sea forces can threaten to exact frightful costs even on stronger outsiders. If they display sufficient capability and the resolve to use it, they may make believers of their adversaries—and thus achieve a measure of deterrence. Disheartening adversaries is preferable to waging a dangerous, unpredictable struggle to defeat them. In return, savvy defenders may offer not to interfere with the outside power's most critical interests in the contested zone. Chinese officials and spokesmen, for instance, take pains to point out that Beijing has no desire to interfere with freedom of navigation in Asia—Washington's stated interest—in China's backyard. Cost/benefit logic could prompt the United States to stand down rather than risk its Pacific Fleet—the strut on which its strategic position in Asia rests—in combat against this rising challenger. At a minimum Washington will think twice before gambling its status as the regional hegemon on such an uncertain enterprise. Indecision grants Beijing time, and thus opens up strategic vistas.

In short, a successful fortress-fleet strategy may grant Beijing the potential to weave anti-ship cruise and ballistic missiles, niche capabilities such as diesel-electric submarines and fast patrol boats, and non-military measures into an intricate coercive diplomacy that transforms maritime Asia into no-go territory for the US Navy, the force on which the US strategic position in Asia rests. Indeed, astute maritime strategy could give Beijing the dominant say in regional affairs.

The Mahanian critique

So much for the strategic logic impelling fortress-fleet strategy. Let's investigate the operational and force-structure dimension of this phenomenon. The development of such a maritime strategy cuts against the dominant trend of recent decades, when battle fleets sporting high-tech defenses—most famously the Aegis combat system installed aboard US *Ticonderoga-* and *Arleigh Burke*-class vessels—have sailed the world's oceans with few worries about access to important maritime theaters. Coastal defenses remained immature while coastal defense fleets hugged the shorelines, posing few dangers to oceangoing fleets.

In short, local defenders had few options against dominant navies such as that of the United States or Japan, its closest Asian ally. Unable to do much, they went into a defensive crouch. The Soviet Union, for instance, deployed its ballistic-missile submarine fleet in near-shore "bastions" under protective cover of its surface fleet and land-based tactical aviation. (The modern PLA Navy may have imported this defensive outlook via Admiral Liu Huaqing, its commander during the 1980s and its de facto founder. Liu was an avid student of Fleet Admiral Sergei Gorshkov's writings.[6] Or, more accurately, Soviet strategic preferences may have reinforced those already in place among Chinese strategists.) Mahan condemned this defensive outlook roughly a century ago, in his commentary on the Russo-Japanese War of 1904–5. This mentality mainly gripped continental nations. Even great land powers like *fin de siècle* Russia were prone to it. Russian commanders and statesmen considered the navy a short-range extension of shore defenses and thought little about the decisive fleet actions that captivated naval thinkers such as Mahan.

It was natural for strategists reared on land warfare to think in terms of defending fixed fortifications. But this flouted the Mahanian vision of marine combat, a vision reliant on firepower and mobility.[7] For Mahan, moreover, naval strategy was about offense. It was about amassing "overbearing power" that drove an enemy's flag from important waters and allowed the victor to blockade the coasts of the vanquished afterward.[8] To exercise "command of the sea," or "sea control" in today's parlance, a navy had to roam the high seas far beyond the range of shore-based gunnery, taking its chances in encounters with hostile battle fleets.[9]

With his offensive mindset, it comes as no surprise that Mahan reviewed the Russian Navy's performance against the Imperial Japanese Navy scathingly. Russian strategy was strongly defensive in character during that conflict. Russian commanders went on the defensive from the outset and stayed there. Squadrons remained close to port while shunning a battle that might have advanced their strategic aims. Formations based at Port Arthur and Vladivostok seldom conducted sorties beyond range of shore-based fire support, mainly heavy artillery installed at the two coastal strongholds. Admiral Heihachirō Tōgō's Combined Fleet exacted a heavy toll in lives and ships during the Russians' rare forays onto the high seas.

By war's end, in fact, wreckage from Russian fleets littered the bottoms of the Yellow Sea and the Tsushima Strait.[10] Russian sea power had come to grief. Aghast at this, Mahan branded the fortress fleet a "radically erroneous" concept of naval warfare, lamenting the defensive instincts and habits Russia's land-warfare traditions had instilled in Russian mariners.[11] He reproached Russian commanders for inverting the relationship between the port and the fleet.[12] The Port Arthur fleet was ostensibly there to protect the port. In reality it took refuge under the port's guns for defense. In so doing, the Russian Navy conserved warships St. Petersburg should have risked in combat with Japan's navy.

Broadly, Mahan castigated the fortress-fleet strategy for three ill effects. One, it encouraged defensive-mindedness. Mahan, the prophet of offensive sea power, urged seagoing nations to amass bases and ships to carry on commerce overseas. The fortress–fleet concept not only arose from longstanding Russian strategic preferences but reinforced them, enervating Russian sea power over the long term. He found Russian strategic culture repellent because it ceded the initiative to prospective foes. Two, it instilled an unhealthy obsession with coastal defense. Continental nations tend to think in terms of land defense against predatory neighbors that might invade and occupy the homeland, much as Napoleon pierced the Russian heartland in 1812. Russians fretted about protecting geographic features and fixed sites from attack.

Ranging across the seas to protect trade and commerce or duel enemy men-of-war was a concept foreign to many Russian strategists. And three, defensive-mindedness inclined Russian strategists to disperse the fleet, exposing any given detachment to destruction. Because the Russians were obsessed with protecting coastal sites, their navy tended to scatter detachments about in an effort to defend important harbors and "narrow seas," meaning straits and other maritime passages. Each detachment was inferior to an opponent that could mass its entire fleet for battle. Defeat was foreseeable under such circumstances, insisted Mahan. Piecemeal Japanese naval victories cost Russia its navy, and thus its standing as an Asian sea power.[13]

This indictment arguably applied not only to Russia but to China's Qing Dynasty, whose navy had fallen prey to the Imperial Japanese Navy a decade before the Russo-Japanese War. The relevance of this critique to modern-day China, however, is questionable. Twenty-first-century China is not a decaying dynastic power forced into a defensive position at sea. Mahan's critique, furthermore, is largely a function of technology. Radical scientific and technical progress coupled with Chinese strategic traditions may help Beijing refute the objections he raised. The fortress fleet may become not only an option for China, but its seagoing weapon of choice.

A strategy predicated on managing events at sea from shore fits the strategic and operational proclivities of China, a determinedly land-centric power, just as it did for Imperial Russia. In contrast to Imperial Russia, however, China has the technology and resources to make such a strategy work. Andrew Erickson and David Yang observe that "the idea of striking a ship from land is not new and{. . .}the idea of 'using the land to control the sea' (以陆制海) in this way is very appealing to China, given its geostrategic situation."[14] This would be a fortress fleet "with Chinese characteristics," to borrow the ubiquitous Chinese phrase.

A key feature of this strategy is that high technology promises to liberate the PLA Navy from coastal waters. In the age of Mahan, the fortress could provide covering fire for the fleet within an arc the radius of which equaled the maximum effective range of gunfire. Thus, for example, the Russian fleet had to remain within a few miles of Port Arthur for protection against Japan's Combined Fleet. No more. Today the reach of land-based naval weaponry could extend well beyond the "near seas" shoreward of the "first island chain" that roughly parallels the Chinese coastline, running from the Japanese Archipelago through Taiwan and along the Philippine Archipelago. The island chain lies from 100 to 500 miles offshore, depending on the latitude. The breadth of this protective aegis will depend on how well China's scientific and engineering communities master anti-ship technology. Some weapon systems under development boast the potential to deliver payloads of enormous destructive power against moving targets at sea hundreds of miles distant. The "fortress," then, now holds the potential to create a defensive bastion encompassing the China seas if not beyond.

This technology-driven strategy is also a cost-effective strategy. Even the latest anti-ship wizardry is cheap by comparison with warships built to slug it out with enemy fleets on the high seas. Fire support thus eases the demands on the Chinese Navy to construct ships able to go toe-to-toe with their American counterparts. Even a modest PLA Navy blue-water fleet could accomplish Beijing's goals so long as it remains within reach of fortress China. Such cover would keep the US fleet at a safe distance. A fortress fleet, then, represents a relatively low-cost way to fulfill Beijing's aims at sea while sparing China an expensive, escalatory, ship-for-ship arms race with the US Navy. Pursuing enabling technologies to build such a fleet only makes sense for China's political leadership. Indeed, other regional powers may replicate this approach as low-cost precision weaponry proliferates.

Chinese defenders think offensively

Nor is China as defensively minded as Imperial Russia. Mahan considered the fortress fleet "a dominant conception in Russian military and naval thought."[15] More than that, he discerns a "*national prepossession* in favor of a Fortress Fleet" that shaped Russian officers' handling of operations and tactics during the struggle with Imperial Japan (emphasis original). The term had not yet been invented, but Mahan saw Russian "strategic culture" acting on multiple levels to stifle the offensive spirit in the Russian Navy. RAND analyst Jack Snyder coined the term in the 1970s, defining strategic culture as "the body of attitudes and beliefs that guides and circumscribes thought on strategic questions, influences the way strategic issues are formulated, and sets the vocabulary and perceptual parameters of strategic debate."[16] It is a kind of national strategic personality, or way of doing things.

Colin Gray expands on Snyder's concept. For Gray, strategic culture works on three levels: "public culture," strategic culture proper, and the organizational cultures of individual military institutions.[17] Public culture is high culture that pervades an entire society, molding habits of mind. Strategic culture is that subset of attitudes and beliefs that bears directly on the process of matching ways and means with political ends. That culture is a dual-edged sword becomes obvious on the organizational level. An institution blessed with a healthy, innovative culture can thrive under stressful conditions. Should bad habits become embedded in the organizational culture and incorporated into bureaucratic routine, on the other hand, they can be exceedingly difficult to break. An agile, adaptive institution modifies or sheds elements of its routine as needed to keep apace of changes to the strategic setting.

Fortunately for Beijing, contemporary China—unlike tsarist Russia—is heir to a strategic culture that equips the PLA to wield a modern fortress fleet to good effect. Admittedly, many China scholars portray Chinese public culture as innately defensive in outlook. China scholar John King Fairbank noted that war was historically a "disesteemed" element of China's Confucian orthodoxy, "and the disesteem was given an ethical basis that has colored Chinese thinking ever since."[18] Chinese statesmen "consistently put less stress on the glory of fighting" than their counterparts in Islam and Christendom owing to the "pacifist bias of the Chinese tradition."[19]

This is true, but it overlooks the radical changes in Chinese society since the dynastic era. On the strategic and operational levels, contemporary China departs from Fairbank's account of a society predisposed to pacifism. The epic events of Communist China's founding—the Long March (1933–5), the Sino-Japanese War (1937–45), the Chinese Civil War (1945–9)—all prime Chinese commanders to deploy offensive operations and tactics for strategically defensive purposes within geographically circumscribed areas. These are precisely the conditions they confront offshore today, where the US Navy rules China's historic maritime periphery and the PLA Navy is just starting to assert itself.

Beijing draws its vocabulary of strategy and operations in large part from Mao. From his experiences battling the Japanese and Nationalist armies, Mao assumed that communist forces would start off fighting from a position of weakness. But he also insisted they could reverse the unfavorable military balance given time and smart, offensively minded strategy. He insisted, for instance, that the Japanese invaders had "advantages only in one respect," namely military hardware and efficiency.[20] They suffered from shortcomings in all other respects: lacking sufficient resources, secure communications with the Japanese home islands, and clear war aims and strategy. These deficiencies would worsen over time, weakening the occupying force.

Mao's Red Army could hasten this process, deliberately exacerbating Japanese shortcomings while correcting its own. China boasted such inherent advantages as vast strategic depth, complex terrain, and nearly limitless manpower reserves. The Red Army could overcome its relative military weakness by tapping such resources. Even inferior CCP forces, furthermore, could concentrate against small or isolated Japanese formations, achieving local superiority for small battles. Such engagements would yield cumulative effects. By taking the offensive on the micro-level, and even within a macro-level strategic defensive, Chinese forces could wear down their enemies, level the balance of forces, and ultimately take the offensive. "Only a complete fool or a madman," accordingly, "would cherish passive defense as a talisman."[21] Active measures, insisted Mao, constituted sound strategy even for the lesser army.

Mao's concept of active defense—a concept the PLA Navy has transposed to the sea under the guise of offshore active defense[22]—referred to the art of creating conditions for a strategic counteroffensive that yields a decisive victory.[23] Along these lines, from its inception the PLA Navy employed a force of small combatants—fast patrol boats, coastal submarines, and small frigates—to defend Chinese coastlines. With few vital interests at stake offshore, Maoist China contented itself with a "sea-denial" strategy. A navy prosecuting a sea-denial strategy sees little need to control the seas itself; it merely wants to bar a superior foe from critical expanses for a finite interval. Putting a Maoist spin on the concept, Admiral Stansfield Turner notes that sea denial is essentially "guerrilla warfare at sea." A lesser navy, says Turner, "hits and runs" at a time of its own choosing. If successful, this ratchets up the costs of forcing entry into vital waters to unbearable levels, even for a stronger adversary.[24]

Maoist China, then, considered the PLA Navy a force for waging "people's war at sea." This remained the standard wisdom about naval strategy until Deng Xiaoping commenced opening China to the world in the late 1970s. Then, because economic reform demanded overseas trade, it became necessary to construct a more robust, oceangoing navy to protect that trade. As a result, bigger, more capable, longer-range platforms started appearing by the 1990s, supplemented by purchases from post-Soviet Russia. Yet strikingly, the PLA Navy continued investing heavily in near-seas platforms such as fast patrol boats even as it began assembling the rudiments of a sea-control fleet.[25] Old technology and strategy remained useful in Beijing's eyes.

Operating in conjunction with the submarine fleet, land-based anti-ship missiles, and mine-layers, small craft seek to convert offshore waters into a Chinese preserve. If they display the capacity to mete out punishment, they can hope to dissuade opponents such as the US Pacific Fleet or the Japan Maritime Self-Defense Force (JMSDF) from operating there in wartime despite those fleets' overall superiority to the PLA Navy. People's war at sea, then, involves fusing sea- and land-based armaments into a highly offensive strategy designed to punish enemy forces along Chinese coasts. If executed adeptly, such a strategy will dissuade hostile forces from ever attempting hostile entry into Asian seas.

Despite its continental outlook and the lingering influence of Russian naval traditions—a bequest dating from China's Cold War alliance with the Soviet Union—China will likely prove a more determined, more formidable sea power than tsarist Russia ever was. Offensive sea denial represents the modern-day equivalent to gunfire from Port Arthur or Vladivostok during the Russo-Japanese War. As land-based fire expands its reach, China's sea-control fleet will see its freedom of action expand commensurately.

Coastal defense ventures offshore

As technology progresses, coastal defense is coming to be recognized as feasible. Mahan castigates proponents of the fortress-fleet philosophy for placing "all stress on the fortress, making the fleet so far subsidiary as to have no reason for existence save to help the fortress."[26] This was faulty thinking because the Russian fleet "was kept tied to the fortress, a vague possible shadow of help to it{. . .}apparently without a thought of offensive action" against the Imperial Japanese Navy.[27] Disgraceful defeat ensued. Today, however, Chinese naval development promises to liberate the fleet from close-in defense, letting PLA Navy surface action groups and, ultimately, aircraft-carrier task forces prowl the China seas at will. (In 2009, after years of dissembling, Beijing more or less confirmed plans to build a carrier fleet, although it specified no particular timetable.[28]) No longer must the sea-control navy shelter close to Chinese coastlines for protection.

The ideas of Clausewitz also illuminate the dynamics at work along the Asian seaboard. The Clausewitzian concept of the "culminating point of the attack," for example, is acutely relevant to maritime Asia. A veteran of the Napoleonic Wars, he thought in land-warfare terms. He postulated that if an army invades a neighboring state, it starts off at a sizable military advantage. (If not, its commander is foolish to undertake the offensive.) As an army pushes deeper into enemy territory, however, its margin of superiority begins to narrow. In a sense, the invaders then become the victim of their own success. Their advance stretches their lines of communication, making resupply and reinforcement a challenge. Because they operate within easy reach of their own bases, by contrast, the defenders accumulate reciprocal advantages such as nearby manpower and bases and familiarity with the physical and cultural terrain. Familiar surroundings, in short, bestow a home-turf advantage on defending forces.

Unless the commanders of the invading army can summon up the resources, the will, and the creativity to push through to victory, the attack will reach a crossover point beyond which the defender holds the upper hand.[29] Once the attack culminates, the ability to attain strategic goals ranges from difficult to impossible, leaving the would-be conqueror demanding terms from a position of weakness. The same holds true for naval strategy. Sir Julian Corbett, Mahan's contemporary and intellectual rival, applied Clausewitz's logic to the sea. For Corbett, the disadvantages of the offensive were as follows: "It grows weaker as it advances, by prolonging its communications, and that it tends to operations on unfamiliar ground. The advantages of the Defensive are chiefly: Proximity to the base of supply and repair stations, familiar ground, facility for arranging surprise by counter attack, and power of organizing in advance."[30] Following this logic, the defender can blunt attacks by a superior adversary along multiple axes provided it holds an "interior" position. The stronger force normally converges on the weaker along "exterior lines." The interior position, however, provides the defender the luxury of nimbly shifting forces from place to place. This helps offset the advantages that go to the superior belligerent.

In maritime East Asia, China occupies the interior position against a US Navy steaming westward across the Pacific on exterior lines. War, however, is an intensely interactive process that Clausewitz likened to a "collision of two living forces."[31] As the PLA extends the range of land-based weaponry, upgrades its sea-denial fleet, and continues building a blue-water fleet, Beijing will push the culminating point of the attack outward from Chinese coasts. By doing so, it may well realize its aim of sea denial, deterring the US fleet from attempting forcible entry into Asian waterways. More broadly, the PLA Navy may ultimately contend for sea control should Beijing choose to do so.

Scientific and technological progress will play its part. Over the past few years, reports that the PLA is poised to field an "anti-ship ballistic missile" (ASBM) capable of striking ships underway in the Pacific have excited anxiety in the West. In 2010, Admiral Robert Willard, commander of the US Pacific Command, informed the US House and Senate that China is "developing and testing a conventional anti-ship ballistic missile based on the DF-21/CSS-5 MRBM designed specifically to target aircraft carriers," the core of the US Navy fleet.[32] Even the American arsenal features no such capability. Mastering such a technology would represent an impressive feat of weapons engineering, not only because the payload must maneuver to strike a moving target but because finding, tracking, and targeting ships in the vast emptiness of the Pacific Ocean poses a daunting challenge.

If the PLA can strike at high-value units such as aircraft carriers or amphibious landing ships at long range—reportedly up to 2,500 km for the PLA's Dong Feng-21C missiles, which are fired from mobile launchers—it can start whittling down advancing US forces around the time they pass through the second island chain, which runs roughly from northern Japan through the US island stronghold at Guam before terminating at New Guinea. The Pentagon takes a more modest estimate of ASBM range, pegging it at around 1,500 km. Even this more limited hitting range spans all of the China seas and well out into the Western Pacific and Indian Ocean—as Figure 19.1 illustrates.

A China able to strike effectively within the second island chain with sufficient numbers of rounds could hope to replicate Imperial Japanese strategy for World War II—but without seizing island bases far from Asian coastlines. Interwar strategists in Tokyo envisioned depleting the US Pacific Fleet through "interceptive operations," namely air and submarine attacks from Japanese-held islands. Such attacks would attenuate US strength as a precursor to a decisive fleet engagement.[33] Against the Chinese, similarly, US naval forces would near the culminating point once they entered the ASBM threat envelope, the missile's maximum effective firing range.[34]

Once coupled with stealthy submarines, mine warfare, and the panoply of capabilities already in place for sea denial, this would represent coastal defense on a truly grand scale. Second Artillery missile forces would confer impressive strategic depth on mainland coasts, largely freeing the PLA Navy to pursue other political aims such as recovering Taiwan or upholding Beijing's maritime-territorial claims in the South and East China seas. In an era of mobile missile batteries—short-range ballistic missiles positioned opposite Taiwan have attracted the most attention—a "fortress" has become a more flexible concept than it was during the age of Mahan. Shore-based fire support could be positioned virtually anywhere along the seacoast to support the fleet, depending on the contingency.

Coastal defense, in short, need no longer rely on fixed, passive defenses stationed at a few sites. In effect the entire distended Chinese coastline is a fortress bristling with anti-ship armaments.

Numbers matter less

Finally, Mahan faulted Russian commanders for their defensive mentality and fixation on protecting critical nodes, an outlook that he insisted had goaded them into ill-conceived fleet dispositions. Mahan upbraided fortress-fleet strategists for dividing the fleet into detachments "characteristically defensive in numbers" in hopes of "supporting thus a cherished fortress."[35] By dividing the Russian Navy into Baltic Sea, Black Sea, and Pacific fleets, and further subdividing the Pacific Fleet into Vladivostok and Port Arthur squadrons, St. Petersburg exposed each contingent to resounding defeat at the hands of an enemy such as Japan, which could concentrate the bulk of its navy against a detachment. Much like Mao's outmanned, outgunned Red Army, the Japanese fleet could hurl itself against part of an enemy force, attaining local preponderance in combat. It could achieve victory in stepwise fashion.

Beijing has less to fear in this regard. If successful, a Chinese sea-denial strategy would shut the US Navy out of Asian waters west of Guam, some 900–1,500 miles from the mainland coast. Behind this protective screen, PLA Navy flotillas could execute their missions without hazarding pitched sea battles against superior enemy forces. The corollary is that Beijing need not construct a navy that matches the US Navy in numbers or even in capability. To date China has taken a leisurely approach to naval development, building small ship classes and evaluating their performance in order to improve on their design in subsequent classes. No surface combatant has yet gone into serial production. This unhurried approach to fleet experimentation betokens growing confidence on political leaders' part in the capacity of the PLA Navy for sea denial. If China's strategic frontier now lies between the first and second island chains, Chinese fleet experimentation will likely continue in this manner.

The upshot could be a PLA Navy configured far differently from the US Navy. For instance, Beijing may not need aircraft carriers comparable to the US Navy's *Nimitz-* or *Ford-*class nuclear-powered flattops to accomplish its goals at sea. Regional navies such as the JMSDF constitute a better benchmark for the PLA Navy's sea-control fleet, including its carriers. Outbuilding the JMSDF, which has put to sea a light aircraft carrier known as a "helicopter destroyer" or DDH, constitutes a more manageable task for the immediate future. A modest carrier would offer a technological springboard to vessels comparable to the *Nimitz* over the longer term, should Beijing choose to invest in such behemoths. In all likelihood the first indigenous Chinese flattops will be improved versions of *Liaoning*, a retired Soviet-era flattop refitted for service in the PLA Navy. Over time, as Chinese shipbuilders amass the expertise needed to build such large, complex vessels, more ambitious carriers may lie in store.

A new kind of navy

It appears, then, that technology is helping China answer the objections Alfred Thayer Mahan raised about fortress fleets a century ago. Chinese strategic culture is predicated on offensive defense, and the Chinese Navy increasingly possesses the implements to make a fortress-fleet strategy—the embodiment of this outlook—work. In an epoch of anti-ship weaponry delivered from land and sea, a coastal state like China that merely covets a measure of control over its offshore environs may be able to mount a stout defense without risking a major fleet engagement.

It can also enlist guidance from Corbett. Whereas titanic fleet-on-fleet battles were the *sine qua non* of offensive Mahanian strategy, Corbett maintained that a lesser fleet—a "fleet in being"—could assume the defensive temporarily until the opportunity arose to retake the offensive. Chinese commanders could regain the upper hand through reinforcement, or they could let land-based systems pummel an enemy fleet before accepting battle with its battered remnants on favorable terms. In short, Beijing can now harness a hybrid fortress-fleet/fleet-in-being strategy for strategically defensive aims.[36] Here's why:

- Defense dominance: By the 1970s, advances in Warsaw Pact shore-fired weapons threw the US Navy onto the defensive at sea. Starting in the 1980s, the navy restored maneuverability to its maritime strategy. Technological means such as the Aegis combat system—a composite phased-array radar, computer, and fire-control system that enables cruisers and destroyers to safeguard high-value units—allowed the fleet to defend itself against land-based weaponry such as anti-ship missiles and manned bombers. But as detailed here, the ensuing cycle of interaction and innovation has produced lethal, low-cost anti-ship weaponry that could negate US forces' access to the Asian maritime commons. Washington can no longer take access to these waters for granted. Whether future technical and operational developments can again return the offensive element to strategy remains to be seen.
- A different kind of navy: A latter-day fortress-fleet strategy would not only reflect but reinforce Chinese land-power preferences, allowing Beijing to pacify its maritime flank while it tends to economic development and other pressing interests ashore. It will also grant the navy leadership greater latitude to design a fleet around Asian rivals such as Japan or Australia rather than the capabilities of the dominant sea power, the United States. While the PLA Navy and US Navy force structures may converge over the long term, simply because the United States represents the gold standard for seafaring excellence, Beijing can probably get by with a more modest, less costly force for some time to come. A strategy that permits China to control the sea from the land looks like an economical way to uphold Chinese interests on the high seas.[37]
- Conventional deterrence: Technology will bolster conventional deterrence *vis-à-vis* Washington if the ASBM and other sea-denial capabilities pan out. No longer will US presidents blithely order expeditionary forces into the Asian littoral, as the Clinton Administration did when it dispatched two carrier battle groups to the vicinity of Taiwan in 1995–6, after the mainland conducted "missile tests" to influence the island's presidential election. The ensuing debacle has propelled Beijing's strategy and force development ever since. The PLA was unable to detect the US flattops, much less threaten them. If China can mount a deterrent to similar deployments, the credibility of US security guarantees in the region will suffer. In particular, forward bases in Japan anchor the US presence in Asia. Should Tokyo come to doubt that Washington can keep its commitments, it may resign itself to conciliating Beijing. If denied access to Okinawa and other facilities, the United States would find itself falling back to Guam, its remote base in the second island chain.
- A risk-taking fleet: Mahan reproached Russian commanders for neglecting to concentrate the Pacific Fleet and risk a decisive engagement with Japan at the outset of the war. As a result, the outcome of the conflict depended on what happened in a ground theater, Manchuria. Blocking the sea lanes connecting Japanese expeditionary forces in Manchuria with the Japanese home islands—their chief source of supplies and reinforcements—represented the best use of Russian naval might. As a land power, Russia had little to lose by hazarding

combat that might cost it the fleet. Accustomed to thinking about defending fortifications and reluctant to risk pricey warships, however, St. Petersburg balked at such a daring course of action. For China, however, mobile "fortresses," or missile batteries able to strike distant targets, will ease such misgivings on Beijing's part. Fire support from land sites will reduce the risk to the Chinese fleet. Battle will become conceivable.

Politics is acting in Beijing's favor as well. During the Russo-Japanese War, Tokyo could bombard Port Arthur, a Russian seaport wrested from a foreign country, without fear of rousing the Russian populace for a fight to the finish and resuscitating the tsar's tottering rule. The prospect of losing Port Arthur meant little to ordinary Russians. By contrast, carrying the war onto Russian soil would have enraged them. US leaders have no such freedom to strike at PLA bases. Hitting these sites—sites within the Chinese homeland—would inflame an already nationalist Chinese populace. Indeed, much of the commentary on the US military's "AirSea Battle" concept centers on the fact that its framers evidently contemplate launching a "blinding" campaign against the PLA at the very beginning of a conflict.[38]

This would be a highly escalatory gambit, needless to say. No American president would order such strikes lightly. Recognizing this, Beijing can in effect dare Washington to strike China and risk escalating the war into an all-out conflict the costs and perils of which would outweigh the presumably modest political objectives at stake for the United States. And even if the PLA Navy did suffer a fiasco of Tsushima Strait dimensions, China would retain considerable control over the China seas by virtue of ASBMs and the array of sea-denial weaponry that would remain to it after a defeat. Beijing, in short, enjoys options and fallbacks tsarist Russia never did, from both material and diplomatic standpoints.

In closing, it is worth pointing out that a fortress-fleet strategy cannot work as well in remote theaters. Revolutionary shore-fired weaponry used in concert with sea-denial assets may enable Beijing to manage events along the Chinese maritime perimeter—that is, close to home—with great confidence. But at the same time, urgent interests are beckoning Chinese leaders' attention southward toward the Indian Ocean, the Persian Gulf, and Africa. Indeed, the Chinese Communist regime has bet its survival on economic development, which in turn depends on ready supplies of seaborne oil, natural gas, and other raw materials that transit the Indian Ocean.

The PLA Navy must venture into South Asia to protect the shipping lanes and other Chinese geopolitical interests there. As the Chinese fleet establishes a presence in the Indian Ocean, however, it will find itself far from Chinese shores, in waters that lie mostly beyond the range of ASBMs, diesel submarines, and fast patrol craft. Fortress-fleet logic avails Beijing little there. It only extends as far as anti-ship technology can take it.

Complicating matters further, the PLA Navy will find itself on Indian home turf, where New Delhi openly avows its ambitions for naval primacy.[39] What if the Indian Ocean strategic environment becomes competitive? If it does, the PLA Navy will be forced to match an ambitious Indian Navy, ship for ship and plane for plane. And this leaves aside the US Navy, which has vowed to preserve its own supremacy in the Indian Ocean.[40] However impressive new technologies may be, consequently, they cannot exempt Beijing from high-end naval development altogether. As Alfred Thayer Mahan might counsel: the ASBM represents a potent capability for China, but it is no panacea.

James R. Holmes

Fortress fleets, present and future

Based on sea-power theory and the Chinese example, what is a fortress fleet? We can detect four determinants. From narrow to broad, these include geography, technology, strategy, and politics. An interior power that wants to secure its maritime perimeter while projecting limited force out to sea is ideally suited to this approach. It can hope to hold stronger yet exterior-line competitors at bay while pursuing the goals it considers worthwhile. It can attempt sea denial on a grand scale. Cheap weapons technology, in particular mobile anti-ship missiles, allows defenders in effect to station sentinels along its coast in support of a strategically defensive posture. It can shift defensive firepower around to critical theaters along the periphery, mounting layered anti-ship defenses at points of impact with rivals. Maritime weaponry presents commanders far more options than the fleet would in isolation.

A fortress fleet is the working component of an active strategic defense prosecuted through offensive methods. Active defense does erect a suit of armor around important sea areas. In metaphorical terms, it puts a sumo suit in place to deter opponents from military action in these areas, and to cushion blows from adversaries who persevere in the face of deterrent measures. In Clausewitzian parlance, a fortress-fleet strategy positions a lesser defender to win outright if it cannot impress on the opponent that the costs and dangers of war should rule it out. And finally, fortress-fleet arrangements work best for political leaders who keep their ambitions in check. Deploying the navy beyond range of shore-based fire support exposes the fleet to the uncertainties and hazards that befall all oceangoing fleets. Maritime strategists should track signs that regional powers' aspirations are beginning to outrun their strategic capacity.

The strategic competition in Asia, then, is important not just because it illuminates how China may transact business in the maritime realm, but because it provides a means to test the possibilities of maritime strategies that fully incorporate the terrestrial component of sea power. China's maritime strategy is worth monitoring not just for its practical implications but to inform the theory underlying nautical endeavors.

Notes

1 James R. Holmes is Professor of Strategy at the US Naval War College and co-author of *Red Star over the Pacific* (Naval Institute Press, 2013). The views expressed here are his alone.
2 For more, see James R. Holmes and Toshi Yoshihara, "Mahan's Lingering Ghost," Naval Institute *Proceedings* 135, no. 12 (December 2009). Available online at www.usni.org/magazines/proceedings/2009-12/mahans-lingering-ghost.
3 In 2015, estimates the authoritative website GlobalSecurity.org, China will field 71 submarines of various types, 1 aircraft carrier, 27 destroyers, 45 frigates, 94 missile-armed fast patrol boats, 52 amphibious-warfare ships, and assorted support craft. The complexion of the navy is changing as it retires old, less capable vessels in favor of newer vessels more in keeping with modern navies. While raw numbers of hulls will not grow rapidly for the time being, then, the fleet's combat power is making substantial progress. Tracking the performance not just of the ships themselves but of their sensors, fire control, and weaponry is thus a matter of some urgency for US and allied analysts. "Chinese Warships," *GlobalSecurity.org*, April 4, 2014. Available online at www.globalsecurity.org/military/world/china/navy.htm.
4 Carl von Clausewitz, *On War*, ed. and trans. Michael Howard and Peter Paret (Princeton: Princeton University Press, 1976), pp. 90–1.
5 US Department of Defense, *Military and Security Developments Involving the People's Republic of China*, 2013, p. 81. Available online at www.defense.gov/pubs/2013_china_report_final.pdf.
6 See for instance Bernard Cole, *The Great Wall at Sea*, second edn (Annapolis: Naval Institute Press, 2010), p. 178.

7 Julian S. Corbett, *Some Principles of Maritime Strategy*, intro. Eric J. Grove (repr. 1911; Annapolis: Naval Institute Press, 1988), p. 211.
8 Alfred Thayer Mahan, *The Influence of Sea Power upon History, 1660–1783* (repr. 1890; New York: Dover, 1987), p. 138.
9 Geoffrey Till, *Seapower*, second edn (London and New York: Routledge, 2009), pp. 145–56.
10 Denis Warner and Peggy Warner, *The Tide at Sunrise: A History of the Russo-Japanese War, 1904–1905* (repr. 1974; London: Frank Cass, 2002), pp. 324–38, 494–520.
11 Alfred Thayer Mahan, "Retrospect upon the War between Japan and Russia," in Mahan, *Naval Administration and Warfare* (Boston: Little, Brown, 1918), p. 155.
12 Mahan, "Retrospect upon the War between Japan and Russia," pp. 133–73.
13 The Russian Black Sea Fleet remained intact following the conflict, but it was a wasting asset. Turkey, perennially at odds with Russia, refused to permit the fleet to exit the Black Sea through the Bosporus and Dardanelles.
14 Andrew S. Erickson and David D. Yang, "Using the Land to Control the Sea? Chinese Analysts Consider the Anti-ship Ballistic Missile," *Naval War College Review* 62, no. 4 (autumn 2009): pp. 53–86.
15 Alfred Thayer Mahan, *Naval Strategy* (Boston: Little, Brown, 1911), p. 391.
16 Jack Snyder, *The Soviet Strategic Culture: Implications for Nuclear Options* (Santa Monica: RAND, 1977), p. 9. As it happens, Snyder was also analyzing Russia. In his case, the challenge was to determine whether the Soviet leadership accepted the Western logic of nuclear deterrence.
17 Colin S. Gray, "Out of the Wilderness: Prime Time for Strategic Culture," *Comparative Strategy* 26, no. 1 (January 2007): pp. 7–9.
18 Gray, "Out of the Wilderness," p. 7.
19 Gray, "Out of the Wilderness," pp. 7–9.
20 Mao Zedong, "On Protracted War," in *Selected Writings of Mao Tse-Tung*, vol. 2 (Beijing: Foreign Languages Press, 1965), p. 134.
21 Mao Zedong, "Strategy in China's Revolutionary War," in *Selected Writings of Mao Tse-Tung*, vol. 1 (Beijing: Foreign Languages Press, 1966), pp. 207, 224.
22 Alexander Chieh-cheng Huang, "The Chinese Navy's Offshore Active Defense Strategy," *Naval War College Review* 47, no. 3 (summer 1994): pp. 9–18; Jun Zhan, "China Goes to the Blue Waters: The Navy, Sea Power Mentality, and the South China Sea," *Journal of Strategic Studies* 17, no. 3 (September 1994): pp. 180–208.
23 Mao, "Strategy in China's Revolutionary War," pp. 207, 224.
24 Stansfield Turner, in Till, *Seapower*, p. 153.
25 Nan Li, "All at Sea: China's Navy Develops Fast Attack Craft," *Jane's Intelligence Review*, September 2009: pp. 2–3.
26 Mahan, *Naval Strategy*, p. 385.
27 Mahan, *Naval Strategy*, p. 404.
28 Greg Torode, "At Arm's Length," *South China Morning Post*, April 2, 2010.
29 Contends Clausewitz, "The attacker is purchasing advantages that may become valuable at the peace table, but he must pay for them on the spot with his fighting forces. If the superior strength of the attack—which diminishes day by day—leads to peace, the object will have been attained. There are strategic attacks that lead up to the point where their remaining strength is just enough to maintain a defense and wait for peace. Beyond that point the scale turns and the reaction follows with a force that is much stronger than that of the original attack. This is what we mean by the culminating point of the attack." Clausewitz, *On War*, p. 528.
30 Corbett, *Some Principles of Maritime Strategy*, p. 329. Unlike Mahan, Corbett explicitly looked to Clausewitz to inspire his sea-power theories.
31 Clausewitz, *On War*, p. 77.
32 "Statement of Admiral Robert F. Willard, US Navy, Commander, US Pacific Command, before the House Armed Services Committee on US Pacific Command Posture," March 23, 2010. Available online at http://armedservices.house.gov/pdfs/FC032510/Willard_Testimony032510.pdf.
33 Wendell Minnick, "Chinese Anti-ship Missile Could Alter US Power," *Defense News*, April 5, 2010, p. 6; Wendell Minnick, "China Developing Anti-Ship Ballistic Missiles," *Defense News*, January 14, 2008. Available online at www.defensenews.com/story.php?i=3307277.

34 Whether the ASBM will prove viable, and how manageable a threat it will pose, are matters of often vehement debate in US naval circles. For example, the US Naval Institute *Proceedings*, the navy's professional journal, has published several articles arguing the point. See Andrew S. Erickson and David D. Yang, "On the Verge of a Game-Changer," *Proceedings* 135, no. 5 (May 2009): pp. 26–32; Sam J. Tangredi, "No Game Changer for China," *Proceedings* 136, no. 2 (February 2010): pp. 24–9; Craig Hooper and Christopher Albon, "Get Off the Fainting Couch," *Proceedings* 136, no. 4 (April 2010): pp. 42–7.
35 Mahan, *Naval Strategy*, p. 396.
36 Corbett, *Some Principles of Maritime Strategy*, pp. 209–16.
37 Erickson and Yang, "Using the Land to Control the Sea?" p. 77.
38 Jan van Tol, Mark Gunzinger, Andrew F. Krepinevich, and Jim Thomas, *AirSea Battle: A Point-of-Departure Operational Concept* (Washington, DC: Center for Strategic and Budgetary Assessments, May 2010). The Pentagon has released no formal statement of how it intends to prosecute AirSea Battle—compelling analysts to rely on think-tank studies and expert commentary.
39 For one among many statements of Indian maritime ambitions, see Rajat Pandit, "'Blue-water Navy Is the Aim," *Times of India*, November 1, 2006. Available online at http://timesofindia.indiatimes.com/articleshow/263611.cms.
40 US Navy, Marine Corps, and Coast Guard, *A Cooperative Strategy for Twenty-first Century Seapower*, 2007. Available online at www.navy.mil/maritime/Maritimestrategy.pdf.

20
The Second Artillery and nuclear forces in 2014

Richard D. Fisher, Jr.

Introduction

In a rare semi-official acknowledgement of its two most modern active intercontinental missile programs, on 15 February 2014 the newspaper *Space News*, published by the China Aerospace Science and Industry Corporation (CASIC), acknowledged "sensational" Western reports of tests of the "DF-41" mobile intercontinental ballistic missile (ICBM) and the "JL-2" submarine launched ballistic missile (SLBM). The article then assured that China's defense construction would not upset the "strategic balance" and only promote "stability" in the Asian region.[1] But after years of development, it appears that these two most modern Chinese intercontinental-range nuclear missiles may enter service in the People's Liberation Army Navy (PLAN) in 2014 and then in the Second Artillery Corp (SAC) by 2015 or 2016. Inasmuch as both missiles have the potential to be armed with multiple independently targeted nuclear warheads, their deployment is one major factor contributing to disagreement over the size of China's nuclear forces and concern that China's nuclear missile forces may be starting a period of more rapid growth.

Established on 1 July 1966, the Second Artillery Corp was created to build up and control China's new nuclear-armed missile forces, which had been developed at great speed and expense to compensate for China's lack of an aerospace sector to develop modern bombers. Under the direct control of the Central Military Commission, the Second Artillery Corps has been China's primary nuclear deterrent and warfighting force, though it gained a non-nuclear warfighting mission in the 1990s.

Along with the introduction of new intercontinental-range missiles, it is also clear that the Second Artillery will soon introduce new intermediate and medium range ballistic missiles (IRBM, MRBM) and may also be in the process of adding a new type of short-range ballistic missile (SRBM), in addition to new longer range land-based land attack cruise missiles (LACMs). While ICBMs are primarily nuclear armed, IRBMs, MRBMs, SRBMs and LACMs can be either nuclear or conventionally armed. In addition to its mission of deterring strategic strikes against China, the Second Artillery is also able to contribute to new joint-force strategies against land and naval targets. There are also indications that the Second Artillery in the future may be able to contribute to space launch, missile defense and anti-satellite missions.

Relatively less attention is paid to the potential nuclear capabilities of other branches of the PLA. The PLAN receives the most attention due to its pending deployment of the second-generation Type 094 nuclear ballistic missile submarine (SSBN) and development of a third-generation Type 096 SSBN. But the PLAN may also have a significant tactical nuclear weapon delivery capability in the form of its land-based strike aircraft and soon-to-be deployed LACMs. The People's Liberation Army Air Force (PLAAF) has long had a strategic nuclear capability in its Xian Aircraft Corp (XAC) H-6 medium bombers, which have been modernized and may be supplemented by two new strategic bombers. The PLA Army or Ground Forces may also have some number of tactical artillery-delivered nuclear weapons.

In addition, having long criticized the United States for pursuing missile defense, it is clear that China is doing the same, for strategic, theater and tactical missile defense. Early missile defense initiatives are tied to China's anti-satellite space warfare programs but it appears that later programs will be spread among the Second Artillery, the PLAAF and the PLAN. The PLA has yet to decide which service will lead space warfare efforts, but these could also involve nuclear attack missions.

Broader nuclear strategy

China's nuclear strategy, or "nuclear policy" remains clouded in ambiguity and insufficient transparency—which is desired by China's leadership in order to gain advantage over potential adversaries. The Chinese government has never made public a set of central government or military documents that describe China's nuclear strategy/policy and explain the deployment, systems and modernization plans for its nuclear and missile forces. Furthermore, the Chinese government has refused multiple US requests for meetings with the PLA to discuss nuclear issues. Instead, foreign analysts are left to speculate about China's nuclear strategy based on some government statements, a larger body of "grey" literature such as academic writings and what can be inferred from what is known about strategic weapons and their deployment.

Among analysts, one pole of the debate is represented by those who view China's nuclear strategy objective as seeking "assured" but "minimum" deterrence.[2] China's nuclear arsenal will remain smaller than that of the US and Russia, but sufficient to deter attack, and secure enough to assure retaliation. It will also be kept in a low state of alert, warheads separate from missiles.[3] One well known Chinese nuclear analyst/strategist described China's objective thus: "to make this small arsenal a credible deterrent, China has to make it survivable to a first nuclear strike, even if that strike is overwhelming and devastating. In Chinese literature, 'few but effective' (*jinggan youxiao*) are the words most frequently used to describe its necessary arsenal."[4]

Toward the other end of the spectrum, some, such as former US Army attaché to Beijing Dr. Larry Wortzel, suggest that China cultivates disinformation regarding its real nuclear strategy and intentions.[5] Other analysts point to China's increasing nuclear and conventional missile forces, requirements for future military campaigns such as conquering Taiwan, and the contradictions in its vaunted "No First Use" of nuclear weapons pledges to argue that China is moving toward an "active defense" posture that could include nuclear warfighting operations.[6] There is also wide variance in estimates of the size of the Chinese nuclear arsenal. Some arms control advocates estimate that China only had 250 nuclear warheads in 2013,[7] while on 9 August 2012, General Robert Kehler, commander of the US Strategic Command (STRATCOM), said that China's nuclear arsenal numbered "several hundred."[8]

General Kelher was defending US intelligence community estimates of a smaller number in the face of much larger estimates of China's nuclear arsenal, such as was offered in 2012 by retired Russian Colonel General Viktor I. Esin, former Chief of Staff of the Russian Strategic Rocket

Forces. In a rare Russian-source statement of concern regarding China's nuclear developments, Esin estimated that in 2011, China's production of 40 tons of nuclear material could enable China to build 3,600 nuclear weapons. Of these, Esin estimated that there could be 1,600–1,800 warheads, with 800–900 "deployed."[9] As Esin spent his career in the Strategic Rocket Forces it has to be considered that he has had access to unique Russian intelligence on China's nuclear posture.

Underground Great Wall

General Esin's estimates followed the remarkable late 2011 assessment by the Georgetown University Asian Arms Control Project, led by Dr. Phillip Karber, of China's Underground Great Wall. While not loudly proclaimed by the Chinese government, Karber and his students were able to assemble a large database of literature, video data and satellite imagery to describe China's recent program that started in the 1970s, but became more intense in the 1990s, to build an estimated 5,000 km of tunnels that could be used to base or store nuclear weapons.[10] In the main this vast tunnel system reflects the Chinese government's explicit desire that its nuclear forces remain viable. But the vastness of this system logically raises questions regarding the real size of China's nuclear forces. In addition, some new base structures such as those in the Delingha region suggest an "active defense," or offensive nuclear posture. In this area, new mobile ICBMs can emerge from underground tunnels and quickly target the US ICBM bases in North Dakota and Minnesota.

Second strike

China is also changing its nuclear posture through the development of sea and airborne "second strike" systems. After decades of development China's second-generation nuclear ballistic missile submarine is expected to start deterrence patrols in 2014. These submarines will increase China's nuclear missile inventory, initially by 60 missiles with multiple warhead versions likely to follow. When deployed, these missiles will probably have their warheads "mated," a significant change of their "alert" status. China's expected development of a new strategic bomber and new nuclear-armed cruise missiles means that air-delivered strategic and tactical nuclear weapons may be increasing.

Tactical nuclear weapons

Very little has been stated about China's tactical nuclear arsenal. Some analysts claim that the PLA does not currently employ tactical nuclear weapons.[11] However, retired Russian General Victor Esin has provided a startling estimate that China may have up to 650 tactical nuclear weapons. These are distributed as follows: 440 for aircraft; 150 for DF-11 SRBMs and CJ-10 LACMs; and 30–60 for the DF-15 SRBM.[12] If Esin's estimate is valid, this would be more than the estimated US tactical nuclear arsenal of about 500 weapons.

Intercontinental missiles

According to the 2014 issue of the International Institute for Strategic Studies' (IISS) *Military Balance*, the Second Artillery Corp controls up to seven brigades or about 20 silo-based and 46 mobile intercontinental ballistic missiles (ICBMs).[13] Asian military sources, however, assess that the Second Artillery has at least one reload for mobile ICBMs, meaning that total numbers may be as high as 112.[14] In addition, the 2012 US Department of Defense report on Chinese military modernization, the last to offer ICBM numbers, lists "50–75" missiles and "50–75" launchers, indicating variance in estimates.[15] Some are stationary liquid-fueled missiles based in silos and others, both liquid- and solid-fueled, are mobile missiles based in caves or underground tunnel complexes. Their most recent important development has been the recent or imminent introduction of independently targeted multiple-warhead (MIRVed) ICBMs. In addition, the PLA Navy has three or four[16] new Type 094 nuclear-powered ballistic missile submarines (SSBNs), with 12 JL-2 submarine launched ballistic missiles each, with estimates that five more may be built,[17] meaning a potential total of 60 JL-2s.

ICBMs

The Second Artillery deploys two types of liquid-fueled intercontinental-range missiles, the Dongfeng-4 (DF-4, East Wind-4, and US designator CSS-3) and the DF-5 (CSS-4), both from the "first generation" of long-range missile development dating back to a March 1965 research program.[18] Based on the earlier DF-3 medium range ballistic missile (MRBM), the DF-4 became operational in 1980 as the PLA's first two-stage missile with a range of 5,400 km, sufficient to put a 1–3 megaton (MT) warhead on Moscow. While 20–35 may have been delivered,[19] only about ten, or enough for one brigade, were believed to be operational in 2013.[20] DF-4s are stored horizontally in caves and towed out to nearby launch pads for fueling and launch. They have been upgraded regularly, especially in their electronic command, control and logistics systems.

The dominant Second Artillery liquid-fueled ICBM is the DF-5, the latest version of which may be the DF-5A or the multiple-warhead armed DF-5B. The 12,000 km range DF-5 entered service in 1981 and the improved 13,000 km range DF-5A entered service in 1986. The Pentagon had noted that it expected the DF-5 to be replaced with a "longer range CSS-4 Mod 2" by 2006.[21] While the DF-5 and DF-5A are reported to have one 1–3 MT warhead, Asian military sources have spoken about a "DF-5B" with five to eight multiple warheads,[22] but such a version has not been mentioned in open US reports. The longstanding open number estimate for the DF-5 has been "about 20," based in stationary silos. However, this missile has been seen in horizontal tunnel storage, raising questions whether the Second Artillery has a greater number of DF-5s. There was a program to develop a "second generation" liquid-fueled ICBM, first called the DF-14 and later renamed DF-22, that would have featured better engines and road-mobility, but this program was cancelled in January 1985.[23]

Following significant advances in fabricating large 2-meter diameter solid-fuel rocket motors, it was also decided in January 1985 that the PLA would instead develop the solid-fueled DF-31 (CSS-10 Mod 1), with later development of a sea-based variant called the JL-2. From the DF-22 program, the early DF-31 inherited its three-stage concept, diameter, stainless steel structure, guidance systems and the goal of mobility.[24] First tested successfully in May 1995, the DF-31 is reported to be able to loft a 700 kg warhead up to 8,000 km.[25] In contrast to Russian mobile ICBMs that use a heavy off-road capable transporter-erector-launcher (TEL), the DF-31 uses a simpler Taian Corporation tractor-trailer truck that requires paved roads. The missile is "cold launched" or forced out of a tube before engine ignition. So far it is assessed that only one brigade of DF-31 ICBMs have been deployed. Instead, the Second Artillery has so far deployed at least two brigades[26] of the 11,200+ km range DF-31A (CSS-10 Mod 2). This missile's greater performance was made possible by the development of weight saving fiber-composite structures. Both the DF-31 and DF-31A are assessed to carry one 1 MT warhead plus penetration aids, which was confirmed by a 2008 partial image of the DF-31A warhead bus.

The first images of the DF-41 appeared in 2007 and 2008, showing a much larger launch tube atop a large 16-wheel TEL closer in concept to modern Russian mobile ICBM TELs. This was later identified as being based on the Taian HFT 5980A 16-wheel vehicle.[27] Additional images from 2013 and 2014 show that this missile may be near to beginning production and deployment and that there may also be a specialized missile reload carrying vehicle. Test flights of the DF-41 were revealed by US sources to have taken place on 24 July 2012 and 13 December 2013.[28] Then in late December 2014, US government sources revealed that on 13 December 2014, the DF-41 was tested lofting an unspecified number of MIRV warheads.[29] The DF-41 is reported to have a 2.25 meter diameter motor, three stages and a range of 15,000 km. But the DF-41's most notable feature is that it may carry up to ten multiple independently targetable reentry vehicles (MIRVs).[30] Assuming a total missile load-out of 12 missiles, including one reload per launcher, one DF-41 brigade could have up to 120 warheads.

SLBMs

After a protracted development dating back to the 1960s, US Defense and Navy officials estimate that the new PLA Navy Type 094 SSBN will begin its first deterrence patrols in 2014.[31] This will mark the first such naval nuclear deployment by China and the beginning of its "second strike" nuclear deterrent capability. Development of the 8,000 km range JL-2 SLBM started in 1976 though its first land-based test was not until 1999. Deployment would not follow until 15 years later, as its development faced reported difficulties. The JL-2 was test launched successfully from a Type 094 SSBN on 22 December 2013.[32] Based on the DF-31, the JL-2 has three solid-fuel stages and reportedly just one 1–3 MT warhead.[33] However, there are Chinese-source rumors that a 10,000 km JL-2A may be in development. Inasmuch as the successor Type 096 SSBN is expected in the 2020s,[34] there may also be a larger "JL-3" under development, most likely to be MIRV equipped.

Theater missiles

While its inventory of ICBMs may for now be smaller than that of Russia and the US, it is also the case that China has the largest and most sophisticated inventory of theater range missiles. These are produced in IRBM, MRBM, SRBM and land attack cruise missile (LACM) varieties and most feature multiple types of warheads. In the 1990s such missiles compensated for the PLAAF's insufficient strike aircraft, but in recent years these missiles complement more powerful air and naval strike forces in new joint-forces strategies. The 2014 *Military Balance* credits the Second Artillery with 9 MRBM brigades with 134 missiles, 8 SRBM brigades with 252 missiles and 2 LACM brigades with about 54 missiles.[35] However, the Pentagon reported that in December 2012 the PLA had 1,100 SRBMs[36] and in 2011 reported the PLA had "200–500" Ground Launched Cruise Missiles.[37] A May 2011 report citing Taiwan "intelligence sources" said that by 2012 the PLA could be aiming 1,800 missiles at Taiwan.[38]

IRBMs

In early 2011 signals appeared that the PLA was developing a new class of mobile Intermediate Range Ballistic Missile, in the form of a CASIC official being quoted saying that a new 4,000 km range Intermediate Range Ballistic Missile could emerge by 2015.[39] Then in early 2012 a new 14-wheel TEL from CASIC's Sanjiang Corporation emerged, adding to speculation about a new IRBM.[40] A January 2014 story on the Sina.com website also reported that China was developing new IRBMs to target US forces in Guam.[41] In March 2014 a US government source "confirmed China's development" of the "DF-26C," a 2,200 mile (3,500 km) range IRBM.[42] The designator "DF-26C" implies there may be a DF-26A and DF-26B. A Chinese article noted that the DF-26 could carry multiple payloads: nuclear warhead; anti-ship ballistic missile (ASBM); anti-satellite; satellite; and hypersonic maneuvering warheads.[43] Another Chinese source suggests that the DF-26 uses a new 12-wheel Taian TEL, which would indicate that this missile is a product of the China Aerospace Science and Technology Corporation (CASC).[44]

The previously cited Sina.com article suggests that there may also be a "DF-27" under development, a possible 8,000 km range missile intended to be armed with a new Hypersonic Glide Vehicle (HGV) based warhead.[45] This source suggests that the DF-27 may be an early Chinese attempt to assemble a capability similar to the proposed US "Prompt Global Strike" system of intercontinental non-nuclear strike systems. A US government source revealed that on 9 January 2014 China conducted a test of an HGV,[46] which has the potential to increase a missile's range by 50 percent.

MRBMs

The most numerous type of MRBM deployed by the Second Artillery is the CASIC DF-21 (CSS-5) family. Emerging from late 1970s' requirements to develop missiles capable of waging "guerilla warfare," the DF-21 is the more successful land-based variant of the naval JL-1, China's first long-range solid-fuel missile. Becoming operational in 1991, the DF-21, like the JL-1, is "cold launched" from a tube, but is towed as part of a Hanyang truck-based TEL. It is stored in cave or tunnel bases. Credited with a 2,150 km range, it was supplemented by the 2,500 km range DF-21A in 1996; both can be armed with nuclear or high-explosive warheads.[47] IISS reports for 2013 indicate that there was one brigade of the early DF-21 and six brigades of the DF-21A.[48]

In mid-2007 images began appearing on Chinese websites of a new MRBM on a ten-wheel Sanjiang TEL, later assessed to a new version of the DF-21.[49] Early images appeared to show two variants, one with a sharper cold-launch tube cover and one with a rounder tube cover, with the latter possibly indicating a multiple warhead carrying capability. The former is called the "DF-21C" and is probably equipped with a maneuvering precision-guided warhead based on technology from the US *Pershing II* MRBM, probably obtained by China in the early 1990s.[50] As such, it in all likelihood uses a nose-mounted radar for precision attacks against fixed targets with nuclear and non-nuclear warheads. It is credited with a range of 1,750 km[51] and IISS reports that in 2013 the Second Artillery had two brigades of the DF-21C.[52]

IISS also noted that one brigade of the DF-21D ASBM is "forming."[53] This missile is believed to utilize multiple sensors in its warhead stage, which when combined with maneuvers to decrease warhead speed allow the warhead to locate a moving target for final guidance cues moments before impact. Initial targeting cues can be supplied by Over the Horizon (OTH) radar, surveillance and electronic intelligence (ELINT) satellites and aircraft, unmanned aircraft or other ships and submarines. The DF-21D has generated great concern in the US Navy because it is difficult to intercept and is intended to target large US capitol ships such as aircraft carriers.[54] The ASBM, when combined with other aircraft-, submarine- and ship-launched strike missiles, could threaten to overwhelm US Navy defenses.

The Second Artillery has also deployed one brigade of the 800–1,000 km range DF-16 missile that was revealed in March 2011 by Taiwan National Security Bureau Director Tsai Der Sheng.[55] Later in 2011 and then in 2012, images of the DF-16 showed that it was a CASIC program using a new Sanjiang ten-wheel TEL. Later images indicated that the DF-16 consists of a new larger diameter first stage but uses the warhead stage of the DF-11 SRBM. This means it could employ multiple payloads, to include nuclear, high explosive, electromagnetic pulse and submunitions.

The Second Artillery and nuclear forces

In the DF-16 the Second Artillery has a system better able to defeat Taiwan's new anti-missile interceptors by virtue of higher speed or longer range "depressed trajectory" flights.[56]

SRBMs

The Second Artillery's solid-fuel, mobile, short-range ballistic missile (SRBM) force grew out of an initiative of the CASIC in the early 1980s to develop for export what became the DF-11 (CSS-7) family of SRBMs. Critical to the success of this missile was CASIC's early cooperation with its subsidiary Sanjiang and the MAZ bureau in Belarus, to develop new TELs, following Sanjiang's acquisition of a MAZ 543 truck from Egypt. The early DF-11 had a range of only 280–300 km and payload of 500 kg. But China's decision, following the 1989 Tiananmen Massacre, to prepare for militarily conquering Taiwan spurred development of the DF-11A (CSS-7 Mod 2) that appeared in 1998. It has a reported range of 350 km and introduced variable warheads: high explosive, fuel-air explosive; electromagnetic pulse; submunition and nuclear.[57] Chinese sources indicate that the warhead stage separates from the missile in part to help confuse defensive systems. IISS reports that the Second Artillery Corp had four brigades of DF-11s in 2013.

The CASC produces the DF-15 (CSS-6) family of SRBMs, perhaps starting as a competitive response to the DF-11, and entering PLA service in 1990. The DF-15 has a range of 600 km, though a DF-15A is said to have a range of 900 km, and they are reported to be equipped to carry high-explosive, electromagnetic pulse and nuclear warheads.[58] The early DF-15 was used during coercive military exercises directed at Taiwan in July 1995 and March 1996. In 2007 images emerged of two new DF-15 variants. The first, called DF-15B with a reported 800 km range,[59] carried a warhead similar to that used by the US *Pershing II* MRBM and probably has a similar radar-guided precision attack capability. The DF-15C has an elongated warhead section consistent with that required for a "deep penetration" capability to attack underground targets. IISS reports that the Second Artillery had four DF-15 brigades in 2013.

Since the early 2000s China has been developing a new class of shorter-range but highly accurate and maneuverable SRBMs, primarily to compete for export sales. They may also be cheaper to produce to replace older SRBMs. They also give the Second Artillery the option of saturating a target, such as Taiwan, with missiles attacking from multiple trajectories, which can overwhelm defensive systems. The first of these new SRBMs reportedly to be adopted by the Second Artillery is a product of CASC, called M-20 for export, or DF-12 in PLA service.[60] In early 2013 a Chinese official also stated that the M-20 had been purchased by the Chinese government.[61] Smaller than the DF-11 and DF-15, the DF-12 may have a range of 280 km or 300–420 km.[62] CASIC markets the 150 km range B-611 and the 260 km range B-611M. These are also maneuverable SRBMs equipped with high-explosive, fuel-air explosive or submunition warheads. TELs for the DF-12 and B-611 are able to carry two missiles, versus one for the DF-11 and DF-15.

LACMs

The PLA's program to develop modern land attack cruise missiles extends back to the 1970s, aspiring to follow US and Soviet LACM programs. While subsonic in speed, cruise missiles are also far less expensive than ballistic missiles and numbers can be increased rapidly. Ironically, China would obtain pieces of the US *Tomahawk* cruise missile via the former Taliban government in Afghanistan and obtain a small number of Soviet/Russian Kh-55 LACMs via the Ukraine. But it would require success in developing a small efficient turbojet engine before a *Tomahawk*/Kh-55-class cruise missile could emerge in about 2007, the CJ-10 (CJ, *Changjian*, long sword). Displayed prominently in the October 2009 Communist Party anniversary parade in Beijing, three CJ-10 launch/storage boxes are carried on what appears to be a Sanjiang TEL. This LACM is thought to have a 1,500–2,000 km range. IISS reports that the Second Artillery had two brigades of CJ-10 LACMs in 2013. In May 2013 a US Air Force official identified a "CJ-20" that may be a nuclear-armed air-launched version of the CJ-10.[63] Informal Chinese sources have mentioned a possible larger 3,000 km range LACM program.

Air and naval theater nuclear systems

While there may be some disagreement over whether China employs significant numbers of tactical nuclear weapons, it does maintain a growing number of delivery systems for these weapons. In response to its worsening relations with the Soviet Union in the mid-1960s China developed its first tactical nuclear weapons, tested in 1972, which then equipped a small number of Nanchang Aircraft Corporation Q-5A tactical nuclear strike fighters. The tactical nuclear delivery mission is probably carried out by the Xian Aircraft Corporation JH-7 and JH-7A strike fighter, 120 of which equip five regiments of the PLA Naval Air Force (PLANAF) and 120 equip four regiments in the PLA Air Force (PLAAF).[64] Inasmuch as they are assigned this mission in the Russian Air Force, the PLAAF's 73 Russian-built Sukhoi Su-30MKK and the PLANAF's 24 Su-30MKK2 strike fighters could also perform this mission.

It is also becoming increasingly clear that the PLA is reviving a strategic bomber force. The PLAAF's 90 or so XAC H-6 bombers include about 20 new-production H-6K versions.[65] First seen in 2005, the H-6K features new Russian D-30KP turbofans that extend its radius to about 3,000 km, new radar and optical targeting systems, and the ability to carry six to eight new CJ-10K land attack cruise missiles—which could be nuclear armed. The H-6K, similarly to the much modified US Boeing B-52 bomber (both of which are early 1950s designs), will also perform precision conventional strikes. But XAC is estimated to be developing one or two new bombers. One design is believed to be a stealthy subsonic-speed "flying wing" design similar to the US Northrop-Grumman B-2.[66] In April 2014, Asian military sources relayed to the author that by 2025, XAC is expected to field its next generation bomber called "H-20." This "flying wing" design is expected at about the same time as next-generation Russian and US flying wing bombers.[67] The other design may be a smaller but supersonic-speed medium bomber, a model of which appeared in early 2013. However, another source notes that this project may have been cancelled in deference to the larger new strategic bomber, and that the revealed model was a Shenyang Aircraft Corporation concept.[68]

Less is known about the possibility of existing tactical nuclear weapons in the PLA Navy, but this has to be considered, as versions of the CJ-10 LACM may in the future equip PLAN ships and submarines. In 2012 and 2013 images of the PLAN weapons test ship No. 892 featured box-launchers similar to that of the land-based CJ-10 LACM, indicating that a naval version of the LACM may soon equip PLAN ships. In addition, in early 2014 images of a submarine vertical launch tube configured to carry seven LACMs emerged from a Chinese academic engineering article, similar to the US concept for carriage on some of its nuclear cruise missile submarines. It is not clear whether the new submarine vertical LACM tubes will equip an upgraded version of the current Type 093 nuclear attack submarine, or the expected next-generation Type 095.

Strategic defenses

Despite China's at times virulent opposition to American missile defense initiatives, China has also had longstanding interest in developing its own missile defense. In 1963 Mao Zedong ordered Qian Xuesen to begin the "640 Program" to develop China's first missile interceptors, which had developed an interceptor prototype and a targeting radar but no deployed system when cancelled by Deng Xiaoping in 1980. It appears that since the early 1990s China's strategic defense and anti-satellite programs have advanced cooperatively. In 2004 a PLA Senior Colonel explained to the author that the PLA had not decided who would lead the PLA's military space effort: the Second Artillery, PLAAF or General Armaments Department (GAD). It is possible that, with no single lead service, the PLAAF, Second Artillery and even the GAD may produce various strategic defense programs.

Already, there may be a pattern of Second Artillery-GAD cooperation in strategic defense. The SC-19 ASAT interceptor, believed to have been derived from the KT-1 solid-fuel space launch vehicle, probably a GAD program, was ultimately derived from the Second Artillery's DF-21 MRBM. The SC-19 may also have formed the bases for missile interception exercises in 2008 and 2013. One possible future Second Artillery contribution to strategic defense may be the previously mentioned DF-26 IRBM program, which may have an ASAT mission. There is also the *Kuaizhou* mobile space launch system tested on 25 Septermber 2013, possibly derived from the DF-31,[69] and which may use a new Sanjiang 14-wheel TEL. A second *Kuaizhou* was launched on 21 November 2014, and was likely revealed as CASIC's civilian truck-mobile FT-1 space launch vehicle at the November 2014 Zhuhai Airshow.[70] It is not known if *Kuaizhou* is a GAD or Second Artillery controlled program, but such a space launch vehicle could also launch ASAT payloads.

Conclusion

While China's nuclear warfighting mission will increasingly include the use of the PLA Air Force and the PLA Navy, it can be expected that the majority of this mission will remain with the Second Artillery Corps. China's recent investment in its "Underground Great Wall" is intended to preserve the viability of its decision to rely primarily on land-based nuclear missile forces. While there is great doubt by some analysts that China will "sprint to parity" with US or Russian nuclear forces, China's development of MIRV warheads will allow it to rapidly increase its warhead numbers and will give it the option to seek parity. Nevertheless, a significantly larger Chinese nuclear force will bolster the confidence of China's leadership to pursue near-term strategic goals as it will decrease their fear of US and Russian nuclear forces. This means that China will continue to seek the conquest of Taiwan, and press territorial disputes with Japan, the Philippines, Vietnam and India. Into the 2020s, a much larger Second Artillery Corp will also give China's leadership greater confidence to project China's growing conventional military power into other regions of the globe.

Notes

1 "官媒首证实东风41和巨浪2洲际导弹试射消息 [First Official Media Confirmation that the Dong Feng-41 Intercontinental Missile and JL-2 Were Test Fired]," *Jagged Military Network Web Page*, 15 February 2014. Available online at http://bbs.tiexue.net/post2_7068162_1.html.
2 For a recent affirmation of this view, see, M. Taylor Fravel and Evan S. Mederios, "China's Search for Assured Retaliation, The Evolution of Chinese Nuclear Strategy and Force Structure," *International Security*, fall 2010; also see Jeffrey Lewis, *The Minimum Means of Reprisal: China's Search for Security in the Nuclear Age*, Cambridge, MA: MIT Press, 2007.
3 Mark A. Stokes, "China's Nuclear Warhead Storage and Handling System," *Project2049 Web Site*, 12 March 2010. Available online at http://project2049.net/documents/chinas_nuclear_warhead_storage_and_handling_system.pdf.
4 Yao Yunzhu, "Chinese Nuclear Policy and the Future of Minimum Deterrence," in *Perspectives on Sino-American Strategic Nuclear Issues: Strategic Insights*, September 2005. Available online at www.hsdl.org/?view&did=457629. Major General Yao Yunzhu, who is currently director of the Center for

China-America Defense Relations at the People's Liberation Army's Academy of Military Science, is well known as a Chinese strategic issues expert with extensive experience in international policy and academic circles.

5 Larry M. Wortzel, "China's Nuclear Leakage," *The Diplomat*, 7 August 2012. Available online at http://thediplomat.com/2012/08/chinas-nuclear-leakage/.

6 Mark Schneider, "The Nuclear Doctrine and Forces of the People's Republic of China," *Comparative Strategy*, July/August 2009.

7 "Status of World Nuclear Forces," *Federation of American Scientists Web Page*. Available online at www.fas.org/programs/ssp/nukes/nuclearweapons/nukestatus.html.

8 Hans M. Kristensen, "STRATCOM Commander Rejects High Estimates for Chinese Nuclear Arsenal," *FAS Strategic Security Blog*, 22 August 2012. Available online at http://blogs.fas.org/security/2012/08/china-nukes/.

9 Colonel General (ret.) Victor Yesin, "Third after the United States and Russia, on China's Nuclear Potential Without Underestimation or Exaggeration," originally published in *Voenno-promyshlenyi Kur'er (VPK)*, No. 17, 2 May 2012, translated by Anna Tsipokina for The Potomac Foundation, with assistance from Dr. Hung Nyugen, p. 2.

10 William Wan, "Digging Up China's Nuclear Secrets," *The Washington Post*, 30 November 2011, p. 1.

11 See Hui Zhang, "China's Nuclear Weapons Modernization: Intentions, Drivers and Trends," Belfer Center, Harvard University. Available online at http://belfercenter.hks.harvard.edu/files/China NuclearModernization-hzhang.pdf; Gregory Kulacki has asserted, "US observations of China's military facilities, equipment, and training suggest China does not maintain a stockpile of tactical nuclear weapons"; see "China's Nuclear Arsenal: Status and Evolution," *Union of Concerned Scientists Web Page*, October 2011. Available online at www.ucsusa.org/assets/documents/nwgs/UCS-Chinese-nuclear-modernization.pdf.

12 Yesin, pp. 5–7.

13 International Institute of Strategic Studies, *The Military Balance, 2014*, London: Routledge, 2014, p. 231.

14 Author interview, November 2013.

15 Office of the Secretary of Defense, *Annual Report to Congress, Military and Security Developments Involving The People's Republic of China, 2012*, Washington, DC: Department of Defense, p. 29. These annual reports mandated by the US Congress are not obliged to provide all known data about the PLA, in order to conceal intelligence sources and methods. A classified version is also made available to members of Congress.

16 The estimate of four Type 094 SSBNs is offered by *IHS Jane's*; see Ridzwan Rahmat, "PACOM Chief Says China Will Deploy Long-Range Nuclear Missiles on Subs This Year," *IHS Jane's Navy International*, 25 March 2014. Available online at www.janes.com/article/35965/pacom-chief-says-china-will-deploy-long-range-nuclear-missiles-on-subs-this-year.

17 Office of the Secretary of Defense, *Annual Report to Congress, Military and Security Developments Involving The People's Republic of China, 2013*, Washington, DC: Department of Defense, p. 6.

18 John Wilson Lewis and Hua Di, "China's Ballistic Missile Programs, Technologies, Strategies, Goals," *International Security*, Vol. 17, No. 2 (fall 1992), p. 10.

19 "DF-4," *IHS Jane's Strategic Weapon Systems*, online edition, accessed on 18 December 2013.

20 *Military Balance, 2014*, op. cit.

21 Office of the Secretary of Defense, *Report to the Congress Pursuant to the FY2000 Defense Authorization Act, Annual Report on the Military Power of the People's Republic of China*, Washington, DC: Department of Defense, 28 July 2003, p. 31.

22 Interview with author, June 2007.

23 Lewis and Hua Di, pp. 25–6; also see 中国第二代战略武器研制简史 [A Brief History of China's Development of Second Generation Strategic Weapons]," *KKTT blog*, 30 July 2009. Available online at http://liuqiankktt.blog.163.com/blog/static/121264211200963034727830/?suggestedreading&wumii; The *KKTT blog* has proven to be one of the most reliable Chinese open-source forums for analysis of Chinese missiles and strategic systems.

24 Ibid.

25 "DF-31," *IHS Jane's Strategic Weapons Systems*, online edition, accessed on 18 December 2013.

26 *Military Balance, 2014*, op. cit.

27 "DF-41猜想 [DF-41 Suspect]," *KKTT blog*, 21 December 2013. Available online at http://liuqiankktt.blog.163.com/blog/static/1212642112013111945054350/.

28 Bill Gertz, "China Conducts Second Flight Test of New Long-Range Missile," *The Washington Free Beacon*, 17 December 2013. Available online at http://freebeacon.com/china-conducts-second-flight-test-of-new-long-range-missile/.

29 Bill Gertz, "China Tests ICBM with Multiple Warheads," *The Washington Free Beacon*, 18 December 2014. Available online at http://freebeacon.com/national-security/china-tests-icbm-with-multiple-warheads/.
30 "DF-41," *IHS Jane's Strategic Weapon Systems*, online edition, accessed on 18 December 2013.
31 Bill Gertz, "PLA Navy to Begin First Strategic Missile Submarine Patrols Next Year," *The Washington Free Beacon*, 23 July 2013. Available online at http://freebeacon.com/national-security/pla-navy-to-begin-first-strategic-missile-submarine-patrols-next-year/; Ridzwan, op. cit.
32 "JL-2猜想 [JL-2 Speculation]," *KKTT blog*, 1 January 2014. Available online at http://liuqiankktt.blog.163.com/blog/static/121264211201311314191377/.
33 "JL-2," *IHS Jane's Strategic Weapons Systems*, online edition, accessed on 18 December 2013.
34 *Annual Report to the Congress{...}2013*, p. 6.
35 *Military Balance, 2014*, op. cit. The IISS numbers for SRBM and LACM missiles are more comparable with US numbers for their respective launchers.
36 *Annual Report to the Congress{...}2013*, p. 5.
37 Office of the Secretary of Defense, *Annual Report to Congress, Military and Security Developments Involving The People's Republic of China, 2011*, Washington, DC: Department of Defense, p. 78.
38 "China to Target 1,800 Missiles at Taiwan in 2012," *Agence France Presse*, 20 May 2011. Available online at www.defensenews.com/article/20110520/DEFSECT04/105200307/China-Target-1-800-Missiles-Taiwan-2012-.
39 Zhang Han and Huang Jingjing, "New Missile 'Ready by 2015,'" *Global Times*, 18 February 2011. Available online at http://military.globaltimes.cn/china/2011–02/624275.html.
40 In early 2012 it was thought this was a 12-wheel TEL, but in early 2014 it was revealed to be a 14-wheel TEL. For early reporting, see Bill Gertz, "China Unveils New Nuke Missile, Fresh Challenge to US Pacific Forces," *The Washington Free Beacon*, 7 March 2012. Available online at http://freebeacon.com/china-unveils-new-nuke-missile/.
41 "深度：揭秘二炮3款新型中程导弹 可歼灭关岛美军 [Insight: Secret of Three New Second Artillery Medium Range Missile That Can Wipe Out the US Military Base in Guam]," Sina.com Web Page, 23 January 2014. Available online at http://mil.news.sina.com.cn/2014–01–23/1154761435.html.
42 Bill Gertz, "China Fields New Intermediate-Range Nuclear Missile," *The Washington Free Beacon*, 3 March 2014. Available online at http://freebeacon.com/china-fields-new-intermediate-range-nuclear-missile/.
43 "Insight{...}," op. cit.
44 "DF-26猜想 [Suspected DF-26]," *KKTT blog*, 6 March 2014. Available online at http://liuqiankktt.blog.163.com/blog/static/1212642112014252284269/.
45 "Insight{...}," op. cit.
46 Bill Gertz, "China Conducts First Test of Ultra High-Speed Missile Vehicle," *The Washington Free Beacon*, 13 January 2014. Available online at http://freebeacon.com/china-conducts-first-test-of-new-ultra-high-speed-missile-vehicle/.
47 "DF-21," *IHS Jane's Strategic Weapons Systems*, online edition, accessed on 18 December 2013.
48 *The Military Balance, 2014*, op. cit.
49 Richard Fisher, "New Chinese Missiles Target the Greater Asian Region," *International Assessment and Strategy Center Web Page*, 24 July 2007. Available online at www.strategycenter.net/research/pubid.165/pub_detail.asp.
50 Matthew Robertson, "Chinese Carrier-killer Based on US Technology," *The Epoch Times*, 21 June 2011. Available online at www.theepochtimes.com/n2/china-news/chinese-carrier-killer-based-on-us-technology-57974.html.
51 "DF-21," op. cit.
52 *The Military Balance, 2014*, op. cit.
53 There has been some variance of opinion over whether the DF-21D has been "deployed" inasmuch as it has not been publicly reported to have conducted an "operational" test against a moving ship at sea. A counterargument has been that it has probably been tested against ship-sized stationary targets on land and that the PLA does not want to allow the US to observe how it employs this missile.
54 For an excellent analysis of the DF-21D ASBM, see Andrew S. Erickson, *Chinese Anti-Ship Ballistic Missile (ASBM) Development: Drivers, Trajectories and Strategic Implications*, Washington, DC: The Jamestown Foundation, May 2013.
55 Michael Cole, "PRC Missile Could Render PAC-3 Obsolete," *The Taipei Times*, 18 March 2011. Available online at www.taipeitimes.com/News/front/archives/2011/03/18/2003498473/1 (accessed 26 February 2014).

56 Richard Fisher, in Sean Meade, "China's DF-16 Medium Range Ballistic Missile," *ARES Blog, Aviation Week and Space Technology*, 14 September 2012. Available online at www.aviationweek.com/Blogs.aspx?plckBlogId=blog:27ec4a53-dcc8-42d0-bd3a-01329aef79a7&plckPostId=Blog:27ec4a53-dcc8-42d0-bd3a-01329aef79a7Post:6978292b-4cb6-4b72-ac44-be024a73d061.
57 "DF-11 (CSS-7/M-11)," *IHS Jane's Strategic Weapons Systems*, online edition, accessed on 18 December 2013.
58 "DF-15," *IHS Jane's Strategic Weapon Systems*, online edition, accessed on 18 December 2013.
59 Ibid.
60 "东风12射程世界第一 落选型号出口土耳其 [Dongfeng 12{...}]," *Global Times,* mil.huanqiu.com, 30 July 2013. Available online at http://mil.huanqiu.com/mlitaryvision/2013-07/2702528.html.
61 Richard Fisher, "Report Suggests China Could Be Adopting New SRBM," *IHS Jane's Defence Weekly*, 5 August 2013.
62 "Dongfeng 12{...}," op. cit.
63 "Cruise Missile Threat in Asia," *The Defence Journal*, 20 September 2013. Available online at http://thedefencejournal.blogspot.com/2013/09/cruise-missile-threat-in-asia.html.
64 *The Military Balance, 2014*, pp. 235, 236.
65 Ibid., p. 236.
66 Hui Tong, "H-20," *Chinese Military Aviation web page*, last modified on 15 July 2013. Available online at http://chinese-military-aviation.blogspot.com/p/attack-aircraft-ii.html.
67 Bill Sweetman and Richard D. Fisher, Jr., "Future Bombers under Study in China and Russia," *Aviation Week and Space Technology*, 18 September 2014. Available online at www.strategycenter.net/research/pubID.339/pub_detail.asp.
68 Andreas Rupprecht, "A Glimpse of China's Future Bomber?" *Air Combat Magazine*, September 2013, p. 33.
69 Richard Fisher, "China Launches Fast-Response SLV," *IHS Jane's Defence Weekly*, 25 September 2013.
70 Richard D. Fisher, Jr., "China Launches Second Kuaizhou Mobile SLV," *Jane's Defence Weekly*, 26 November 2014. Available online at www.janes.com/article/46360/china-launches-second-kuaizhou-mobile-slv.

Section B
China's evolving space capabilities

21
China's evolving space capabilities
Implications for US interests

Mark Stokes and Ian Easton

Introduction

The PRC is emerging as a world leader in space. Managed by a diverse set of military and civilian organizations, Chinese political authorities view space power as one element of a broader international competition in comprehensive strength and science and technology (S&T). With preservation of its monopoly on power as an overriding goal, the CCP consolidates its legitimacy through achievements in space. Adopting an integrated civilian and military perspective in its plans and programs, PRC investment in space technology supports economic development and advances national defense modernization. Successes in space symbolize the emergence of the PRC as a world power. How China intends to leverage its newfound power remains uncertain.

The PRC's programmatic successes in space are significant. Notable achievements include manned space platforms, reliable space launch vehicles, and satellites. China has made substantial progress in developing peaceful and practical uses of space technology. In addition to supplying cost-effective international commercial launch services, the PRC's space program supports economic development through subsidized modernization of China's high technology industries, contributing to natural disaster warning and response, and developing commercial applications of space technology.

China's space ambitions are in part peaceful in nature. Yet technologies can also be weaponized, and military applications of dual-use space technology are a principal concern: space technology increases the capacity of the PLA to project military power vertically into space and horizontally beyond its immediate periphery. Freedom of action in space offers the PLA potential military advantages on land, at sea, and in the air. At present, PLA space and counterspace programs do not appear integrated from an organizational, operational planning, or acquisition perspective. Yet the PLA is rapidly improving its space and counterspace capabilities in order to support CCP interests and defend against perceived challenges to sovereignty and territorial integrity.

The US remains the principal illustrative scenario guiding the PLA's military ambitions in space and the trigger issue is Taiwan. Beijing seeks the military capacity to coerce Taiwan's democratically elected government into a political settlement on PRC terms. Success may require a credible ability to deter, delay, or deny possible intervention of US forces in a cross-Strait conflict. Space assets enable extended range precision strike operations intended to deny US access to or an ability to operate within a contentious area in the Asia-Pacific region.[1] Sophisticated conventional ballistic and ground-launched cruise missiles may be an effective means of suppressing regional air defenses and military operations from airbases and carriers at sea. Barring effective countermeasures, the PLA's ability to complicate US access to space assets is likely to grow over the next 10–15 years.

This chapter examines China's national and military space program. The report first addresses civilian oversight and support of China's space program, including political drivers and budgetary support under national-level science and technology programs. The analysis then details how the General Armaments Department (GAD) is organized to manage space systems acquisition, transport payloads, and maintain space systems in orbit. Discussion then turns to China's space R&D and industrial base, and an overview of selected national and military programs. The report next outlines the role of the General Staff Department (GSD) in developing space requirements and leveraging space assets for integrated joint operations.

Civilian support for China's space program

With the preservation of its political system as an overriding goal, the CCP prioritizes investments into space technology for a number of reasons, including the establishment of the PRC as an equal among world powers, i.e., prestige. Space is an arena for both international competition and cooperation. Successes in manned spaceflight foster national pride and enhance the domestic and international legitimacy of the CCP. Indeed, since the Cold War, space technology has been viewed as a metric of political legitimacy, national power, and status within the international community.

Senior civilian leaders within the party and government view space as a national priority and therefore direct significant resources toward the country's space-related technology base. However, space policy, planning, and program management appear fragmented and loosely coordinated among a range of military and civilian players. At an early point in China's space program (August 1989), State Council authorities directed the establishment of a State Space Leading Group to coordinate bureaucracy and determine priorities. Its status today is unknown, although a similar leading group exists for China's lunar exploration program. Without an empowered civilian space policy organization such as NASA, executive authority defaults to the PLA GAD for coordinating the R&D and manufacturing of space systems, and commercial and military space launches. As the national executive authority for civil and military space by default, GAD adopts an integrated civil and military approach to managing space programs. In other words, Chinese space systems support both civilian and military users. Development of space technology supports the vision outlined by President Hu Jintao and his predecessor, Jiang Zemin, for the PLA to adopt "new historic missions" to sustain the CCP, safeguard national development, and contribute to global peace and stability.[2]

Beyond supporting political and military purposes, investments into space systems support PRC economic development goals, including transformation of China into an "informatized" society. China's commercial satellite launch business is a source of revenue for the defense industry, and China's remote sensing community may eventually market commercial space imagery to international customers. Remote sensing data can be leveraged for land planning, disaster warning, recovery and response, and weather forecasting.

The State Council establishes general priorities in policy and planning documents, such as the National Long-Term Science and Technology Development Plan for 2006–20, five year plans, the State High Technology Research and Development Program (e.g., the "863" program), and occasional White Papers on space.

Organizations within the space bureaucracy, including the Chinese Academy of Sciences (CAS), the PLA, and defense industry, seek senior party and government support for national-level programs. While a rough counterpart to NASA, the China National Space Administration (CNSA) functions in large part to facilitate international exchanges and cooperative programs with other space-faring nations.

Since the beginning of its space program in the 1950s, the PRC has prioritized international space-related interactions in order to further national political, scientific, technological, and economic goals. Focusing on space-related S&T, as well as the application of space systems, CNSA has formed multilateral and bilateral partnerships with a wide range of international partners. Funded in part by 863 Program grants, China's university system plays a prominent role in space-related R&D.

The PRC government subsidizes technology development, R&D, manufacturing, and launching of satellites and other space systems. Like other countries, the risk and expense associated with the development and manufacturing of space systems require party and government support. China's space and missile industry relies on central government subsidies, although the subsidized proportion of the space industry's budget is unknown.

Exchanges include cooperative relationships between civilian universities and subordinate research centers with counterparts in the United States, Taiwan, Europe, Russia, and the Ukraine.

In short, senior PRC civilian leaders provide policy guidance and authorize resources for the country's space-related technology base. However, civilian oversight appears to be fragmented, and space programs are loosely coordinated among a range of military and civilian players. National technology plans, such as the 863 Program, are an important subsidy for space technology development. However, in the absence of an empowered civilian space policy organization, GAD integrates civil and military uses of space, and coordinates R&D, manufacturing, and launch of space systems.

The role of the PLA General Armaments Department in China's space program

The CCP Central Committee, CMC, and State Council rely on the PLA GAD for successful execution of national and military space acquisition policies. The GAD is answerable to the CMC for establishing defense and space acquisition policies, managing China's space program, developing technical solutions to satisfy operational requirements, and overseeing defense industrial research, development, and manufacturing.

Over the past two decades, the GAD and China's defense R&D establishment have been breaking down barriers that have hampered the country's ability to field complex space-related systems. In order to address shortcomings in defense and space technology development, the CMC directed a reorganization of the GAD's predecessor, the Commission of Science, Technology, and Industry for National Defense (COSTIND) in 1998. Part of COSTIND was renamed the State Administration for Science, Technology and Industry for National Defense (SASTIND) and spun off into the civilian Ministry of Industry and Information Technology (MIIT). The remaining elements of COSTIND were merged with the GSD Equipment Department to form the GAD. Today, the GAD oversees a national-level S&T advisory committee, a number of administrative departments, and operational space units.

GAD S&T Committee

The GAD S&T Committee consists of expert working groups that advise CMC members and civilian authorities on long-term technology acquisition planning and space policy and operations. At least 20 national-level technology working groups, supported by defense R&D laboratories around the country, leverage and pool resources to review progress, advise national leaders on resource allocation, and focus resources to overcome technological bottlenecks.

GAD Administrative Departments

Beyond the S&T Committee, the GAD consists of as many as 10 second-level departments responsible for various facets of force modernization, space planning and programming, and space operations. A GAD Space Equipment R&D Center appears to serve as an interface with space system users.[3] The Comprehensive Planning Department appears responsible for overall space-related modernization planning and policy. Space architecture development appears to fall within the purview of the GAD Electronic and Information Infrastructure Department, which is China's leading authority for planning, programming, and budgeting for PLA "informatization" development. It establishes general R&D investment priorities and standards. The GAD Electronic and Information Infrastructure Department consists of at least four bureaus and one program office. The Aerospace Equipment Bureau is responsible for charting the PLA's future space-based communications and surveillance architecture and may manage R&D and manufacturing contracts with the space and missile industry. The department also has program management functions, such as the Beidou Program Office, also known as the China Satellite Navigation System Management Office.

China's space command

The GAD Headquarters Department probably functions as an operational command responsible for space launch, tracking, and control. Managed by the GAD Chief of Staff and operating as the China Satellite Launch and Tracking Systems Department (CLTC), the Headquarters Department oversees China's space launch operations, including Jiuquan, Xichang, and Taiyuan satellite launch centers, and a new space launch center under construction on Hainan Island. Between 1970 and early 2012, CLTC had launched 157 satellites for domestic and international customers.

- *Jiuquan*: Jiuquan Satellite Launch Center, under GAD Base 20 (63600 Unit), supports LM-2C, LM-2D, and LM-4 launch of satellites into low-earth orbit, as well as manned space missions on the LM-2F. Base 20 is also a key facility for ballistic and land attack cruise missile testing.
- *Taiyuan*: Taiyuan Satellite Launch Center, under GAD Base 25 (63710 Unit), functions as China's primary platform for satellite launches into sun-synchronous orbit. Situated in Kelan County (Shanxi Province), Base 25 is also a key facility for testing of medium and intermediate range ballistic missiles.
- *Xichang*: Xichang Satellite Launch Center, under Base 27 (63790 Unit), is China's primary platform for launch of satellites into geosynchronous orbit (GEO). Xichang reportedly has capacity to launch between eight and ten satellites a year. Base 27 was the launch point of the PLA's January 2007 test of a kinetic kill vehicle against an aging Chinese weather satellite.[4]
- *Wenchang*: On completion, Wenchang Space Launch Center on Hainan Island will serve as a base for launches of heavy payloads associated with the manned space program. The launch vehicle will be transported to Hainan via ship from new manufacturing facilities in Tianjin, rather than rail.

The GAD has a well established infrastructure for space tracking, control, and surveillance. In order to accommodate its growing space-based infrastructure, China's space surveillance system is gradually expanding in scope and sophistication. Headquartered in Weinan (Shaanxi Province), Base 26 likely functions as a space and missile surveillance center, and plays a role in monitoring and identifying debris and other objects in space. The GAD's space tracking network consists of a center in Xian, fixed land-based sites, at least one mobile system, and four Yuanwang tracking ships capable of operating throughout the Pacific, Atlantic, and Indian Oceans. The GAD also operates a number of foreign tracking and control locations.

The Base 26 space surveillance system may fuse data from other sources. One organization possibly supporting the GAD's space tracking network is the China Academy of Science's Space Target and Debris Observation and Research Center, under the purview of the Purple Mountain Observatory in Nanjing. The GSD First Department Survey and Mapping Bureau works in partnership with CAS to operate a very long baseline interferometer (VLBI) network of radio telescopes that support China's space tracking system. Passive satellite surveillance information may be provided by GSD Third and Fourth Departments. China's R&D community also has been exploring options for basing space surveillance platforms in space. During peacetime, the GAD Headquarters Department likely directs space operations from the Beijing Space Command and Control Center.

Launch vehicles

The GAD's space transportation infrastructure depends on a well established and increasingly reliable family of launch systems to deploy payloads into space for military and civilian users. To date, four basic series of Long March (LM) liquid-fueled launch vehicles deliver payloads to orbits at varying altitudes and inclinations around the earth. The LM launch vehicle family has roots in the country's ballistic missile program, specifically the Dongfeng-4 (DF-4) and Dongfeng-5 (DF-5) intercontinental ballistic missile (ICBM) systems. Based on a March 1965 CMC decision, formal design work on the two missile systems commenced in May 1966. By 1970, initial technical designs were completed. The first DF-5 prototype was assembled in May 1971, and tested from Base 20 on September 10, 1971. Its design was certified in 1973. Both the 211 and 7102 Factory in Sichuan assembled prototypes for testing. The warhead design, however, was not completed until July 1986.[5]

The LM-1, a derivative of the DF-4, successfully sent a satellite into low-earth orbit in April 1970, but the program was canceled the following year. The LM-2 series has been used for delivering both remote sensing and communications satellites from Jiuquan and Xichang Space Launch Centers. The LM-2F is China's most powerful launch vehicle to date, able to boost more than 8,000 kg into low-earth orbit. Sharing the same first and second stage as the LM-2C, the LM-3 series integrates a cryogenic third stage that has been used for boosting heavier payloads into space from Xichang Space Launch Center.

Other launch vehicles include the LM-2D and LM-4 series, which have transported remote sensing, weather, and other payloads in sun-synchronous orbit from Taiyuan Space Launch Center. The LM-2D has launched payloads into both low-earth orbit and sun-synchronous orbit from Jiuquan Space Launch Center.[6] Originally a backup to the LM-3 for launch of communications satellite, preliminary research on the LM-4 series began in 1982, with formal R&D commencing the following year. After the successful launch of China's first Dongfanghong-2 (DFH-2) communications satellites on the LM-3, the main mission of LM-4 shifted to sun-synchronous orbit satellite launches.

Since 2008, China has been investing resources in a new generation of launch vehicles, including the LM-5, LM-6, and LM-7. The LM-5 is said to be designed to lift a 25-ton payload to low-earth orbit (LEO), or a 14-ton payload into geostationary transfer orbit (GTO). With R&D beginning in September 2009, the Shanghai Academy of Space Technology's (SAST) LM-6 is expected to be a smaller launch vehicle capable of boosting 500 kg into orbit. The LM-7 is designed to place a 5.5-ton payload into a sun-synchronous orbit at an altitude of 700 km. China's space and missile industry also is developing large high-thrust solid rocket motors for delivering large payloads.

China's space industrial infrastructure

Senior civilian and military leaders and the GAD rely on state-owned defense industrial establishments for research, development, and manufacturing of space systems. Administrative oversight of China's defense industry is exercised by the MIIT. Formed in summer 2008, the MIIT oversees a restructured and downgraded COSTIND, which had been a PLA organization that previously reported to the State Council.

MIIT's SASTIND is administratively in charge of defense industrial enterprises that support military-related R&D, manufacturing, and follow-on support. SASTIND seeks to foster greater competition within the defense industry in order to better meet the requirements of the PLA, as well as encourage greater civil-military integration (CMI). SASTIND provides policy guidance to 11 state-owned defense industrial enterprise groups responsible for space and missiles, electronics, aviation, nuclear-related products, shipbuilding, and other sectors. A key guiding principle is CMI, the process of combining the defense and civilian industrial bases so that common technologies, manufacturing processes and equipment, personnel, and facilities can be used to meet both defense and commercial needs.

The two industrial groups that make up the space and missile industry include China Aerospace Science and Technology Corporation (CASC) and China Aerospace Science and Industry Corporation (CASIC). As state-owned enterprises, CASC and CASIC receive government subsidies, although efforts have been made to introduce market-based incentives. Led by a group of senior-level executives well under the age of 50, the most extensive shifts in China's research, development, and industrial capacity have taken place within its space and missile (aerospace) industry. The aerospace industry enjoys a historical legacy with a proven record of success, well established channels and methods for overcoming technological bottlenecks, and the prestige needed to recruit some of China's best and brightest.

Both CASC and CASIC are organized in a manner similar to US defense corporations, with a corporate-level structure and various business divisions, referred to as academies. Like US defense industrial business divisions, each academy focuses on a core competency, such as medium-range ballistic missiles, short range ballistic missiles, ICBMs and satellite launch vehicles, cruise missiles, and satellites. While US defense companies tend to specialize further within a business division, CASC/CASIC academies are organized into R&D and/or design departments, research institutes focusing on specific sub-systems, sub-assemblies, components, or materials; and then testing and manufacturing facilities. Each academy is accountable for profit and loss, and includes an information collection and dissemination institute that diffuses technical information obtained from abroad and within China.[7]

China Aerospace Science and Technology Corporation (CASC)

CASC develops and manufactures space launch vehicles, strategic ballistic missiles, satellites, and other space flight vehicles. CASC employs more than 100,000 engineers, technicians, and workers. Its functional business divisions specialize in ballistic missiles and space launch vehicles, large solid rocket motors, liquid-fueled engines, satellites, and related sub-assemblies and components. CASC's dedicated export management and international contracting entity is the China Great Wall International Corporation (CGWIC).

- *China Academy of Launch Technology (CASC First Academy)*: The CASC First Academy, also known as the China Academy of Launch Technology (CALT), is China's largest entity involved in the development and manufacturing of space launch vehicles and related ballistic missile systems. Among its products are China's entire inventory of liquid-fueled ballistic missiles and selected solid-fueled systems. The CASC First Academy is also a leading organization in China's manned space program. Subordinate research institutes specialize in guidance, navigation, and control sub-systems, re-entry vehicles, and launchers.
- *Academy of Aerospace Solid Propulsion Technology (CASC Fourth Academy)*: With over 7,000 employees and also known as the Academy of Aerospace Solid Propulsion Technology, the CASC Fourth Academy is the key business division responsible for development and manufacturing of solid rocket motors with diameters of 2 meters or more. The CASC Fourth Academy is centered on its design department and has five research institutes and three production facilities involved in all aspects of large, high-thrust solid rocket motor development.
- *Academy of Space Propellant Technology (CASC Sixth Academy)*: With roots dating back to 1965 and established in its current form on April 26, 2002, the CASC Sixth Academy, also known as the Academy of Space Propellant Technology (or 067 Base), is China's primary organization engaged in research, development, and production of liquid-fueled propulsion systems. Originally centered in the Qinling Mountain range west of Xian, the 067 Base employs around 10,000 people in four research institutes and one factory, and is now headquartered in Xian.
- *Shanghai Academy of Space Technology (CASC Eighth Academy)*: The CASC Eighth Academy, also known as the SAST, designs, develops, and manufactures specialized launch vehicles, satellites, and other aerospace systems. Established in August 1961, the CASC Eighth Academy is the aerospace industry's largest and most diverse business division. SAST oversees a dedicated design department—the 509th Research Institute—that focuses on weather, synthetic aperture radar, and electronic reconnaissance satellites.
- *China Academy of Space Technology (Fifth Academy)*: Established in February 1968, the CASC Fifth Academy, or China Academy of Space Technology (CAST), is China's primary organization engaged in satellite design, development, and manufacturing. Based in Beijing's northwestern suburbs, CAST institutes, factories, and other enterprises are centered on the 501st Design Department, which functions as CAST's overall systems engineering organization.

China Aerospace Science and Industry Corporation (CASIC)

The second major industrial enterprise engaged in space-related R&D and production is the CASIC, which employs more than 100,000 engineers, technicians, and workers. The enterprise specializes in conventional defense and aerospace systems, including tactical ballistic missiles, antiship and land attack cruise missiles, air defense missile systems, direct ascent anti-satellite interceptors, operationally responsive tactical microsatellites, and associated tactical satellite launch vehicles. CASIC's principle export management enterprise is the China Precision Machinery Import-Export Company (CPMIEC).

- *Academy of Information Technology (CASIC First Academy)*: CASIC's First Academy, also known as the Academy of Information Technology, has designed and fielded microsatellites. Work-

ing with the academic community, the CASIC First Academy is one of a number of entities within China focused on operationally responsive tactical microsatellites that ostensibly could be launched on solid-fueled launch vehicles. It also is engaged in R&D satellite applications and GPS/inertial guidance units.
- *CASIC Second Academy*: CASIC's Second Academy is the principal industrial group responsible for kinetic kill counterspace systems, and is China's largest producer of air defense missile systems. Established in 1961, and with a growing emphasis on integrated air and space defense, it consists of a design department, ten specialized research institutes, a simulation center, three factories, and nine independent commercial enterprises.
- *CASIC Third Academy*: CASIC's Third Academy, established in 1961, is China's premier enterprise engaged in design, development and production of cruise missiles, other aerodynamic vehicles and propulsion systems, and associated launchers. Centered in the Third Design Department, the Third Academy has ten research institutes and two factories, with over 13,000 employees.
- *CASIC Fourth Academy*: CASIC's Fourth Academy was established in 2002 and specializes in design, development, and manufacture of the DF-21 medium-range ballistic missile and associated variants.
- *CASIC Sixth Academy*: CASIC's Sixth Academy is responsible for advanced tactical solid fuel propulsion systems, as well as restartable hybrid liquid-solid engines. The CASIC Sixth Academy manages smaller diameter motors, including kick motors designed to boost communications satellites to geosynchronous orbit.
- *CASIC Ninth Academy (066 Base)*: The second CASIC producer of ballistic missile systems is the Ninth Academy. Also known as 066 Base, the Ninth Academy was created in August 1969 as a third line industry, specifically supplying cruise missile components to the Third Academy. Its most prominent product is the DF-11 short range ballistic missile.
- *Jiangnan Aerospace Group (061 Base)*: Founded in 1964, Jiangnan Aerospace Group, also known as 061 Base, employs more than 6,000 personnel, of which 650 are technicians. Headquartered in Guizhou and with subordinate entities in Suzhou, 061 Base is a primary supplier of specialized missile components and software.
- *Hunan Space Bureau (068 Base)*: The 068 Base was established in 1970 in Hunan's Shaoyang area as a third line production complex. Currently centered in Changsha, its core competencies include special materials and components, such as magnets, diamond coatings, and antennas. More recently, the base has become a key center for R&D and production of reconnaissance platforms operating in near space.

In summary, two large state-owned defense industrial establishments are responsible for the research, development, and manufacture of China's space systems. CASC and CASIC are at the forefront of Chinese spacecraft and space transportation development, and play a key role in delivering space systems to civilian and military customers.

Selected space programs

Leveraging the talent in the space and missile industry, the PLA GAD and State Council authorities oversee a range of space programs. Relying on a strategy of incremental modifications to proven designs, China is gradually improving its ability to overcome complex systems engineering challenges and field reliable and cost-effective space systems. The GAD and space industry manage R&D and production associated with individual programs through a dual chain of command that divides administrative and technical responsibilities. Limited available information

Shenzhou manned space program

China has made considerable efforts over the past two decades to send humans into space as a powerful icon of international prestige and national pride. Based on CCP Central Committee guidance, program management of the manned space program was centralized within the GAD's China Manned Space Engineering Office (also known as the 921 Engineering Office). The CASC Fifth Academy plays a leading role in design, development, and manufacturing of orbital modules.

Also known as Project 921, Shenzhou is the nation's largest space program in terms of scope and breadth of participation by defense industries. The origins of China's current manned space program can be traced to the late 1980s when Chinese leaders convened a series of conferences to discuss the optimal design for a manned spacecraft. The decision was ultimately made to develop a space capsule, rather than a space plane or space shuttle design, which eventually became the Shenzhou spacecraft. The Politburo, on September 12, 1992, directed investment of resources to support this effort. The Shenzhou program began with a series of unmanned launches. The most momentous event in the history of China's space program took place in October 2003, when China sent then-Lieutenant Colonel Yang Liwei of the PLA Air Force (PLAAF) into space.[8]

Lunar exploration program

Building on the successes of its manned space program, China's lunar exploration program represents an empowerment of the CNSA as a national space program manager. Based on recommendations from the China Academy of Sciences, and backed by the CNSA, China's senior leadership began consideration of a lunar exploration program in 1995 as a focus area under the 863 Program. The GAD's predecessor, the COSTIND, began detailed planning in 1998. By 2004, the State Council and CCP Central Committee directed the formation of a Lunar Orbit Exploration Project Leading Small Group to coordinate efforts across the bureaucracy. The lunar exploration program differs from the manned space program in that it is managed at the national level rather than falling under direct military purview.

The program has been structured into three phases.[9] Phase I was designed to be a technology demonstration, involving the launch of lunar orbiters Chang'e-1 in 2007 and Chang'e-2 in 2010. Launched in October 2010, Chang'e-2 is said to focus on future lunar rover landing zones, surveying of Lagrangian points, and testing of upgrades to the Chinese space tracking and control network. Phase II of the lunar exploration program began in 2013 and is believed to include docking, controlling, and mapping missions. Phase III is slated for 2017 with the launch of Chang'e-5 on the LM-5E heavy launch vehicle for collecting samples from the lunar surface. The program has its sights set on a manned lunar landing for sometime after 2025.[10]

Space station program

Ostensibly supporting the lunar program, China plans to put a space station into orbit by 2020.[11] Tiangong, or the "Heavenly Palace," is alleged to consist of a main module with two detachable modules on either side. Tiangong-1 conducted docking missions with the unmanned Shenzhou-8 spacecraft in November 2011. Two follow-on Tiangong spacecraft are planned. The Tiangong-2 space laboratory is scheduled to be launched by 2015, and designed to test technologies for larger space stations, including long-term living conditions for astronauts. The Tiangong-2 will be able to accommodate three astronauts for about 20 days at a time. Tiangong-3 is projected to allow astronauts to remain onboard for 40 days while studying regenerative life-support technology and methods for replenishing fuel and air during missions. The Shenzhou-9 and -10 are scheduled to dock with Tiangong-1 in 2012.[12]

Space-based intelligence, surveillance, and reconnaissance

Increasing spatial resolution and an ability to monitor US activity in the Asia-Pacific region (including the locations of US aircraft carrier battle groups) in all weather conditions are likely to enhance China's capacity for power projection.[13] Over the years, the PLA and Chinese aerospace industry have fielded electro-optical, radar, and other space-based sensor platforms that can transmit images of the earth's surface to ground stations in near-real time. Satellite communications offer a survivable means of communication that will become particularly important as the PLA operates further from China's borders.

A regional strike capability would rely in part on high resolution, dual-use space-based synthetic aperture radar (SAR), electro-optical (EO), and possibly electronic intelligence (ELINT) satellites for surveillance and targeting. China's space industry is reportedly nearing completion of its second generation SAR satellite, and its EO capabilities have been progressing steadily. While information is sparse, there are indications that at least some funding has been dedicated toward developing a space-based ELINT capability. Existing and future data relay satellites and other beyond line of sight communications systems could relay targeting data to and from the theater and/or Second Artillery's operational-level command center. GAD engineers have published detailed research on a satellite sensor architecture for targeting of ships at sea. China is also deploying a robust weather satellite capability, oceanography satellites, specialized satellites for survey and mapping, and possibly space-based sensors capable of providing early warning of ballistic missile launches.

Electro-optical satellites

The PLA and China's defense R&D community are seeking to field an EO satellite system with increasingly high resolution. China's first experimental imagery system was launched in November 1975. With at least 13 launched since April 2006, Yaogan remote sensing satellites appear to be military space platforms designed for EO and SAR imaging missions. The PLA's first EO satellite is said to be the Yaogan-2, launched on May 25, 2007. The Yaogan-5, probably carrying another EO payload, was launched from Taiyuan on December 15, 2008 on an LM-4B. As of November 2011, at least four systems exhibiting characteristics similar to the Yaogan-2 and Yaogan-5 satellites have been launched into orbit.

The Shijian-11 series was also developed by CAST's DFH. The specific nature of the vehicle has yet to be determined. The first was launched on November 12, 2009 on an LM-2C from Jiuquan Satellite Launch Center into a roughly 700 km x 98 degree orbit. Among many visions shared by senior engineers within China's space establishment, one is developing an electro-optical camera able to image ground targets with a 0.1 meter spatial resolution. Current state of the art is 0.25 meter.

Synthetic aperture radar satellites

SAR satellites are a core component of militarily relevant surveillance architecture supporting over-the-horizon (OTH) targeting of surface assets. SAR satellites use a microwave transmission to create an image of maritime and ground-based targets. They can operate night or day and in all weather conditions, and are therefore well suited for detection of ships in a wide area. Processed

SAR imagery may depict a ship in various ways, depending on weather conditions, ship orientation and construction, and beam focus. An SAR satellite is also able to image ship wakes, from which information on ship speed and heading can be deduced.

China is expected to have multiple types of space-based SAR systems in orbit over the coming years that cater to various users. Preliminary research on space-based SAR systems began in the 1980s. China's initial space-based SAR system—the Huanjing series—was planned as part of a small disaster-monitoring satellite constellation. The PLA's first dedicated military SAR satellite in the Yaogan series was probably deployed in 2006. The CASC Eighth Academy appears to have been the satellite's lead systems integrator, and also produced the launch vehicle (LM-4B) on which the satellites have been launched. More than a dozen of these systems have been launched to date.

Electronic reconnaissance satellites

To augment its SAR and EO systems, the PLA has probably fielded a rudimentary electronic reconnaissance architecture. Chinese military analysts view electronic reconnaissance as necessary to accurately track and target US carrier strike groups in near-real time from lower earth orbit as part of China's long-range precision strike capability, including its anti-ship ballistic missile (ASBM) system. Major surface vessels, such as aircraft carriers, have prominent electromagnetic, acoustic, and infrared signatures and large radar cross section. Although controlling emissions from carriers is feasible for limited periods of time, air operations depend on electromagnetic radiation.

The PLA experimented with electronic reconnaissance satellites in the mid-1970s. Design studies on an electronic reconnaissance satellite constellation for geolocation of surface targets began in the mid-1990s. Chinese writings have indicated that while the numbers of electronic reconnaissance satellites are increasing, they have been unable to meet the demands placed on them by various intelligence consumers. Electronic reconnaissance satellites appear to have been launched in pairs.

Oceanographic satellites

Oceanographic satellites are useful for disaster warning, recovery, and response, support for fishing, exploitation of maritime resources, as well as for military (especially naval) operations. Multispectral sensors may be able to detect ships at sea. China launched initial variants in May 2002 and April 2007. The satellites, integrating electro-optical and other sensors, are mainly used for monitoring water color, water environment, and temperatures. An initial follow-on variant, the HY-2, was launched in 2009, with subsequent launches expected in 2012, 2015, and 2019.[14]

Meteorological satellites

Since its inception in 1988, China's Fengyun (FY) weather satellite program has been another reflection of China's ambitions in space. Fengyun satellites collect and provide strategic weather reconnaissance data for civilian and military purposes. China's meteorological satellite program began with Chinese Premier Zhou Enlai's 1970 approval of a CMC proposal to initiate R&D on weather satellites. With the launch of the first FY-1A in 1988, China became the third nation to launch its own meteorological satellites. Since then, the PRC has launched four FY-1 weather satellites into polar orbit, five FY-2 geosynchronous weather satellites, and two FY-3 satellites that were boosted into polar orbits on Long March-4 launch vehicles. A follow-on generation geosynchronous weather satellite, the FY-4, was expected to enter service in 2014.[15]

Ballistic missile warning infrared satellites

Space-based assets with infrared sensors are utilized to detect hot plumes from ballistic missiles, and other heat sources. The first US missile early warning system, MIDAS, was launched in the early 1960s and was followed by Defense Support Program (DSP) satellites in the early 1970s. Chinese engineers have indicated interest in ballistic missile early warning satellites, at least in part for purposes of countermeasures against US DSP and space tracking and surveillance system (SBIRS). Detection of ballistic missile launches while in the boost phase could facilitate cueing of missile defense radar systems. There is no firm evidence that China has deployed a space-based ballistic missile early warning capability. However, there is a technical foundation: for example, with infrared sensors associated with the FY weather satellite program.

Survey and mapping satellites

Military geodesy has long been important for determining precise positions of points on the earth's surface for mapping and to support ballistic missile operations. Scientific applications, such as determining the precise size and shape of the earth, have become increasingly important for satellite tracking, global navigation, and missile defense operations. China's first digital imaging system capable of stereo earth-terrain mapping was the Shiyan-1, also referred to as Tansuo-1, which was launched in 2004 on an LM-2C. With R&D beginning in March 2008, a dedicated survey and mapping satellite—the ZY-3—was launched on an LM-4B from Taiyuan in January 2012. Presumably, the satellite would be capable of three-dimensional digital terrain imaging.[16]

Space-based communications and navigation satellite systems

Space-based platforms are a critical means of communicating over the horizon. The PLA appears to be applying principles of network-centric warfare to communicate and correlate data from increasingly sophisticated sensor architecture. Network-centric warfare equips soldiers, airmen, and soldiers with a common operational picture that significantly increases situational awareness. As a result, individuals and units equipped to participate in the network are able to synchronize action without necessarily having to wait for orders, which in turn reduces their reaction time. In addition, the network allows for dispersed and flexible operations at lower cost. Therefore, the introduction of a networked common tactical picture based on an advanced tactical data link program is a paradigm shift that could gradually break down the PLA's traditionally stovepiped, service-oriented approach to defense.

Communications satellites

China has long had an interest in communications satellites, with one initial motivation being to raise the level of education for China's masses. Since the launch of its first experimental communications satellite in January 1984 and the first operational system in March 1988, China's communications satellite capacity has grown in sophistication. As many as nine commercial communications satellites are owned or operated by organizations in China. Before the development and launch of dedicated military communications satellites, the PLA most likely leased civilian transponders operating in the C- and Ku-bands, such as SinoSat and ChinaSat.

The CASC Fifth Academy (CAST) is the industrial lead systems integrator for major communications satellite programs. The CAST's latest generation communications satellite, the DFH-4, is a larger, heavier payload. Leveraging successes with the DFH-4 telecommunications satellite, the PLA appears to have invested in dedicated military communication satellites, including the Fenghuo-1 and Shentong systems. Fenghuo-1, also known as ChinaSat-22, was launched in January 2000 and functioned as the PLA's first dedicated military communications satellite. Weighing 2,300 kg and designed to operate for 8 years, Fenghuo-2 (Chinasat-22A) was launched in September 2006. Shentong-1, also known as ChinaSat-20, was launched in November 2003, and is said to incorporate steerable spot beams operating in the Ku Band. Shentong-2 (ChinaSat-20A) was launched on November 25, 2010.

Data relay satellites

To expand the scope of its communications satellite architecture, China has been developing a data relay capability. China's first generation data relay satellite, the Tianlian-1, was launched in April 2008 and a second in July 2011. Theoretically, the satellites, using a basic DFH-3 bus, support the manned space program. The satellites could also allow sensors to operate beyond line of sight of ground stations in China. Engineers have developed concepts for an even more sophisticated data relay architecture in the future.[17]

Navigation satellites

Navigation satellites are another important aspect of China's space development. China's first generation navigation satellite system, the Beidou-1, consisted of two geosynchronous satellites (plus spares) for civil and military purposes and was limited to coverage within the Asia-Pacific region. This was an active location system, with a signal from a handheld unit transmitted to the two geosynchronous satellites, which then transmitted the signal to an earth station. The earth station measured the differential in the two signals (one per satellite), determined the location that fit, and then transmitted that data back to the handheld unit.

Planning for a second generation of navigation satellites, the Beidou-2 (Compass) program began in April 1999 under sponsorship of GSD First Department and with participation from civilian entities. This system was closer to the GPS and the Russian GLONASS system, with passive receivers receiving signals from an array of medium earth orbit satellites. The eighth Beidou-2 satellite was launched from Xichang Satellite Launch Center in April 2011, with another 24 satellites expected.

The Beidou system was initially associated with the European Union (EU) on the Galileo navigation satellite system, an alternative to the GPS. The Chinese, however, were apparently excluded from various aspects of the program, including key software components, and were given only limited workshare. Consequently, the Beidou-2 system may be seen as the Chinese answer to the now delayed European program. The GSD First Department Survey and Mapping Bureau is the primary military organization responsible for the ground segment of China's satellite navigation system.

Microsatellite programs

In a crisis situation, China may have the option of augmenting existing space-based assets with microsatellites launched on solid-fueled launch vehicles. Weighing between 10 and 100 kilograms, microsatellite programs to date appear experimental in nature, but competency and experience could translate into a lower-cost, operationally responsive space capability. Microsatellites also serve as experimental technology test beds for MEMS, and formational flight as an integrated constellation that could offer greater survivability due to numbers and potentially reduced radar cross section. Microsatellites have also been viewed as technology demonstrations for counterspace operations, including ASAT kinetic kill vehicles. A number of R&D organizations in China have entered the microsatellite field, including CAS, CASIC First, CASC Fifth, and CASC Eighth Academies, Nanjing University of Aeronautics and Astronautics (NUAA), Harbin Institute of Technology (HIT), and Qinghua and Zhejiang Universities.

Chinese entities have also been investing resources in placing microsatellites into orbit with operationally responsive solid-fueled systems. Development of an operationally responsive launch vehicle appears to be one of the most ambitious efforts by China's aerospace industry to field a product through privately raised funds, at least in its initial phase. The CASIC Fourth Academy developed the Kaituozhe (KT) small launch vehicle in order to serve the domestic and foreign market for boosting small and microsatellites with weights of less than 100 kilograms into low-earth orbit. The status of these programs is unclear.

In summary, military and civilian authorities are leveraging the talent that exists within the space industry to field a wide range of increasingly advanced space capabilities. China is gradually improving in its ability to overcome complex systems engineering challenges and field reliable and cost-effective space systems. National-level space programs are examples of progress that is being made. Other programs, including space-based sensors, communications systems, operationally responsive microsatellites, and near space platforms support a PLA that is able to conduct an increasingly diverse range of military operations.

Space support for PLA integrated joint operations

Senior PRC civilian leaders within the party and government view space as a national priority and direct significant resources toward the country's space-related R&D and technology base. Effective utilization of the space domain, and ability to deny others the use of space, is also central to PRC defense modernization goals. The operational demands of "informatized" warfare and integrated joint operations, or the ability of individual services to coordinate operations, drive investment in space technologies. Space systems enable long-range precision strike operations during campaigns to enforce territorial claims and resolve sovereignty disputes.

Space systems, including remote sensing, navigation, communications, weather, and survey and mapping satellites, enable the delivery of conventional payloads at increasingly long distances.[18] An assured ability to penetrate air and missile defenses and neutralize targets with precision strikes enables sustained dominance over the skies of a particular region. The integrated application of space systems, long-range precision assets such as ballistic missiles, and manned air combat platforms creates synergies that could allow the attainment of air superiority in regional conflicts.

Looking horizontally beyond its immediate periphery and vertically into space, Chinese analysts view disruption of the US ability to project conventional power as a legitimate force modernization goal. The ability to operate freely in space and deny others freedom of operation facilitates defense against advanced US long-range precision strike capabilities expected to be in place by 2025.[19] Promoting the merging of air and space into a single integrated aerospace domain, Chinese writings stress the importance of space technology in a broader "national aerospace security system."[20] Space systems also help reduce vulnerability to first strikes against China's nuclear deterrent, and help assure the ability to carry out a retaliatory response.

Role of the General Staff Department in space operations

The General Staff Department (GSD) oversees a broad and diffuse organizational infrastructure for developing requirements and operating portions of the ground segment supporting space operations. Entities within the GSD, the Air Force, the Navy, and the Second Artillery appear to play a key role in developing operational requirements for surveillance and other space systems applications. GSD, GAD, and Service missions could evolve as Chinese competencies in space expand. While previous studies have addressed GSD organizational issues, the process for how GSD develops operational requirements remains opaque.

First Department (Operations Department)

The GSD Operations Department develops requirements for and manages joint military use of navigation, geodetic, metrological, and oceanographic space systems. The Survey and Mapping Bureau manages the ground segment of the Beidou satellite positioning system. The bureau leverages a national satellite laser ranging (SLR) network for precise determination of satellites, a capability critical for ensuring precision of the Beidou navigation satellite system. The Survey and Mapping Bureau is also believed to operate a VLBI network of radio telescopes that support China's space tracking system. The First Department's Weather and Hydrological Bureau manages military meteorological satellite data and also oversees a specialized unit responsible for space weather analysis and forecasting.

Second Department (Intelligence Department)

The GSD Second Department appears to play a role in the development of space-based reconnaissance operational requirements and operation of ground receiving stations. More specifically, the key organization is the GSD Second Department Technology Bureau, also known as the Beijing Institute of Remote Sensing Information or GSD Space Technology Reconnaissance Bureau.

Third Department (Technical Reconnaissance Department)

The GSD Third Department functions as China's primary signals intelligence (SIGINT) collection and analysis entity. Organized into 12 regional and functional bureaus, the GSD Third Department manages a large bureaucracy for communications intelligence (COMINT) collection, translation, and analysis. The Third Department's Twelfth Bureau may intercept satellite communications from sites throughout China and possibly from space-based collection assets. It also appears to play a role in the PLA's space tracking network.

Informatization Department

The GSD Informatization Department (formerly the Communications Department) develops operational requirements for and oversees use of dedicated military communications satellites, such as the Fenghuo and Shentong systems (ChinaSat-22 and ChinaSat-20). Key organizations within the Informatization Department responsible for developing operational and technical requirements include the Equipment Bureau and S&T Bureau Sixty-first Research Institute.

Fourth Department (Radar and Electronic Countermeasures Department)

The GSD Fourth Department is responsible for radar and electronic countermeasures and appears capable of disrupting adversary use of communications, navigation, synthetic aperture radar and other satellites. The Fourth Department may oversee one or possibly two satellite jamming regiments. The Fourth Department may operate electronic reconnaissance satellite ground receiving stations to support joint targeting.

PLA counterspace development

Freedom of action in space, and an ability to deny an adversary access to its space assets, offer military advantages in land, air, maritime, and information domains. The United States and other powers are dependent on space assets for military operations and to ensure an advantage over potential adversaries. The US relies on space-based assets for communications, navigation, missile warning, environmental monitoring, and reconnaissance. Given vulnerabilities in space infrastructure, a potential adversary could target US space capabilities and seek to deny advantages gained through the leveraging of space capabilities. Space superiority is characterized by the freedom to operate in space while denying the same to an adversary.[21]

The PRC has been investing in a range of passive and active counterspace technologies, and has demonstrated a rudimentary capability to track and intercept satellites orbiting around the earth's poles in the lower reaches of outer space. Chinese pundits highlight trends toward the militarization of space and outline requirements for counterspace operations in future conflicts. However, non-destructive means of denying an enemy use of satellites and mitigating threats from space debris may be a more urgent priority than fielding kinetic kill vehicles. China is also investing in the means to deny an adversary effective use of space surveillance assets through concealment, camouflage, and deception. Elements of a viable counterspace program include an architecture that fuses multiple sources of data in order to detect, identify, and track satellites and other space objects; development and production of technologies that neutralize threats; and a clearly defined and well trained organization able to coordinate and execute counterspace operations.

Space surveillance network

Counterspace operations depend on a survivable space surveillance network, and China is gradually developing a supporting infrastructure. China's ability to track and mitigate space debris could serve as a metric for the amount of progress that is being made. In 2003, CNSA initiated a long-term action plan (2006–20) for detecting and mitigating space debris. The program includes a planned space-based surveillance system for tracking debris, satellites, and other objects in space.[22]

The CAS Space Target and Debris Observation and Research Center provides early warning of small debris threatening manned orbital vehicles, a role that was highlighted during the Shenzhou-7 mission. In October 2009, Chinese media described the nation's first satellite maneuver to avoid a collision. The satellite may have been one of the Yaogan series. The PLA and civilian counterparts have also been enhancing national satellite laser range finding capabilities, and investing in radar systems for satellite surveillance and tracking.

Kinetic kill vehicle development

China's "national aerospace security system" calls for an ability to track and engage foreign flight vehicles transiting space, including ballistic missiles. China's space and missile industry conducted successful tests of a KKV in January 2007 and January 2010, thus demonstrating an ability to intercept polar orbiting satellites and rudimentary medium-range ballistic missiles during the mid-course of flight. At least one KKV funding source during the late 1990s and earlier this decade appears to be the 863–409 program (and possibly the 863–706 program).

Counterspace organization

The lead organization within the PLA for counterspace operations remains an open question, as does the relationship between national space and counterspace policies and programs. GAD-affiliated organizations have produced assessments of space strategy, characterizing space power and advocating prioritization of space technology in order to further PLA warfighting under conditions of "informatization," including counterspace operations and "space superiority." Analysts differentiate between "hard" and "soft" counterspace measures, and relevance of an independent "space force" that would centralize space operations under a unified command.

Discussion of an independent space force has been underway since the 1990s, and resolution of the issue has yet to be achieved. Regardless, uncertainty surrounds the role of the GAD, PLAAF, Second Artillery, or other entities in managing space operations, including planning, programming, and budgeting functions; satellite launch, tracking, and control; ground processing; and counterspace operations. Another possible contentious issue could be ownership over future flight vehicles that operate in or transit all domains of space, near space, and the terrestrial atmosphere. With the concept of counterspace operations still in its infancy, observers note that technological and legal issues constrain the pace of development. Nevertheless, as one senior PLAAF official noted, "space control is a reasonable extension of air control."[23]

In summary, the PLA is improving its ability to monitor events in the Asia-Pacific region through an expanded system of space-based remote sensing, communications, and navigation satellites. China's space program is intimately connected with the country's ballistic missile programs. In addition to common technologies, synergies are created through integration of space, air, and long-range precision strike operations that exemplify the PLA's evolving concept of air and space (aerospace) power. Aerospace power is the key to gaining strategic advantages by application of military force via platforms operating in or passing through air and space. As its persistent sensor and command and control architecture increases in sophistication and range,

Table 21.1 Known or suspected Chinese ground-launched ASAT tests

Date	ASAT variant	Target	Altitude	Result
07/07/2005	SC-19	None known	Unknown	Rocket test
02/06/2006	SC-19	Unknown satellite	Unknown	Target flyby
01/11/2007	SC-19	FY-1C satellite	865km	Target destruction
01/11/2010	SC-19	CSS-X-11 ballistic missile	250km	Target destruction
01/27/2013	Possibly SC-19	Unknown ballistic missile	Unknown	Target destruction
05/13/2013	Possibly DN-2	None known	10,000 to 30,000km	Rocket test

Source: Adapted from Brian Weeden, "Anti-Satellite Tests in Space: The Case of China," SWF, August 29, 2013, p. 3.

the PLA's ability to hold at risk an expanding number of targets throughout the western Pacific Ocean, South China Sea, and elsewhere around its periphery is expected to grow.

Conclusion

The PRC has made significant advances in its space program and is emerging as a space power. In addition to bolstering the political prestige of the CCP, advances in space will enable more effective military operations at increasingly greater distances from Chinese shores. Over the next 10–15 years, more advanced precision strike assets, integrated with persistent space-based surveillance, a single integrated air and space picture, and survivable communications architecture, could enhance greater confidence in enforcing a broader range of territorial claims around China's periphery.

The PLA oversees a broad and diffuse organizational infrastructure for developing requirements and overseeing R&D, manufacturing, and operation of space systems. As access to foreign technology grows, bridges between various bureaucracies established through initiatives such as the 863 Program appear to facilitate more efficient diffusion of technology within China's civilian and military sectors. The overlap between civilian and military applications of space technology is considerable, and it is often difficult to draw a clear line of separation between them.

Aerospace power has been one of the most effective tools of PRC political and military coercion. Although other interests compete for attention and resources, the Taiwan scenario remains the principle strategic direction of PRC national security policy makers, defense planners, and acquisition authorities.

While the overall level of its space technology may not match that of the United States and other space-faring nations, China's relative advances are significant. Given asymmetries in reliance on space systems, even relative increases in Chinese space capabilities could present challenges for the United States. A survivable space-based sensor architecture, able to transmit reconnaissance data to ground sites in China in near-real time, facilitates the PLA's ability to project firepower at greater distances and with growing lethality and speed. Trends indicate that China's basic satellite coverage of waters and land within the Asia-Pacific region could, over time, approach that of the United States. The range of China's precision strike assets is expanding out to Guam, Australia, Southeast Asia, and India. Space assets could provide deployed ASBM assets under the Second Artillery with highly accurate geo-locational data on intervening US forces.

China is also pressing forward with an ambitious counterspace program, including ground- and space-based space surveillance systems, electronic warfare capabilities, and KKVs. A space surveillance system capable of detecting and tracking objects with low radar cross sections is a fundamental prerequisite for effective and precise counterspace operations. The PLA service assigned the operational counterspace mission remains an open question.

Space technology will also continue to be an important driver for economic growth. Satellite sales and launch services offer China's defense industrial complex with an expanding source of revenue. Technology spin-offs may offer competitive advantages in certain sectors, such as satellite navigation products. Exports of space technology sales pose challenges to the United States not only because of China's non-market-based economy, but also because of military and security concerns.

China's interaction with other space-faring powers furthers national political, scientific, technological, and economic goals. Space is a significant metric of national power, and the United States remains a world leader within this domain. However, China is emerging as a relative competitor in selected areas of space technology. While collaboration in space may benefit both the United States and China, Beijing's lack of transparency over budgets and potential risks associated with military applications of space technology remain major causes for concern.

Notes

1 Wayne A. Ulman, "China's Emergent Military Aerospace and Commercial Aviation Capabilities," Testimony before the US-China Economic and Security Review Commission, May 20, 2010. Available online at www.uscc.gov/hearings/2010hearings/written_testimonies/10_05_20_wrt/10_05_20_ulman_statement.php.
2 See, for example, Dean Cheng, "China's Space Program: A Growing Factor in US Security Planning," *Heritage Backgrounder*, August 16, 2011. Available online at www.heritage.org/Research/Reports/2011/08/Chinas-Space-Program-A-Growing-Factor-in-US-Security-Planning.
3 The Space Equipment Integrated R&D Center [航天装备总体研究发展中心] Senior Engineer is Yang Qiangwen [杨强文].
4 Craig Covault, "Chinese Test Anti-Satellite Weapon," *Aviation Week & Space Technology*, January 17, 2007. Available online at www.aviationweek.com/aw/generic/story_channel.jsp?channel=space&id=news/CHI01177.xml.
5 For the most comprehensive background on China's ballistic missile program, see John Lewis Wilson and Hua Di, "China's Ballistic Missile Programs: Technologies, Strategies, Goals," *International Security*, Vol. 17, No. 2, fall 1992.
6 "The LM-2D," China Great Wall Industry Corporation website, April 1, 2010. Available online at www.cgwic.com/LaunchServices/LaunchVehicle/LM2D.html.
7 See, for example, Mark Stokes, Appendix One and Appendix Two, "China's Evolving Conventional Strategic Strike Capability: The Anti-Ship Ballistic Missile Challenge to US Maritime Operations in the Western Pacific and Beyond," Project 2049 Occasional Paper, September 2009. Available online at http://project2049.net/documents/chinese_anti_ship_ballistic_missile_asbm.pdf.
8 Stephanie Lieggi and Leigh Aldrich, "China's Manned Space Program: Trajectory and Motivations," James Martin Center for Nonproliferation Studies, October 6, 2003. Available online at http://cns.miis.edu/stories/031006.htm.
9 "China's Space Program: Civilian, Commercial, and Military Aspects." Available online at www.highfrontier.org/Archive/hf/Finkelstein%20China's%20Space%20Program.pdf.
10 Bruce Sterling, "Chinese Manned Moon Landing, 2025," Wired.com, September 19, 2010. Available online at www.wired.com/beyond_the_beyond/2010/09/chinese-manned-moon-landing-2025/.
11 David Leonard, "China's First Space Station: A New Foothold in Earth Orbit," Space.com, May 6, 2011, May 27, 2011. Available online at www.space.com/11592-china-space-station-tiangong-details.html.
12 "Launch of China's Manned Spacecraft Shenzhou-9 Scheduled," Xinhua, February 17, 2012. Available online at http://english.cntv.cn/20120217/115356.shtml.
13 For a summary of militarily relevant aspects of space-based sensors, see Andrew S. Erickson, "Satellites Support Growing PLA Maritime Monitoring and Targeting Capabilities," *Jamestown China Brief*, Vol. 11, Issue 3, February 10, 2011. Available online at www.jamestown.org/single/?no_cache=1&tx_ttnews%5Btt_news%5D=37490&tx_ttnews%5BbackPid%5D=7&cHash=20e0b222a8c961508f37fa5b72ad1925.
14 Jiang Xingwei, Lin Mingsen, and Tang Junwu, "The Programs of China Ocean Observation Satellites and Applications," National Satellite Ocean Application Service briefing, February 26, 2008 (in English).
15 "The First Satellite in Fengyun-3 Series to Be Launched in 2006 [风云三号系列的第一颗卫星将于2006年发射]," *Xinhua*, March 23, 2004. Available online at http://news.qq.com/a/20040323/000009.htm.
16 See "LM-4B Successfully Launches ZY-3 and VesselSat-2 Satellites," CGWIC News Release, January 2012. Available online at www.cgwic.com/news/2012/0110_VesselSat-2_%E5%8D%A2%E6%A3%AE%E5%A0%A1_%E6%90%AD%E8%BD%BD.html.
17 Wu Ting-yong, Wu Shi-qi, and Ling Xiang, "A MEO Tracking and Data Relay Satellite System Constellation Scheme for China," *Journal of Electronic Science and Technology of China*, December 2005.
18 See China's Defense White Paper (*China's National Defense in 2008*), January 20, 2009. Available online at http://news.xinhuanet.com/english/2009–01/20/content_10688124_1.htm (accessed August 29, 2009).

19 For a detailed assessment of US programs, see Xie Wu, "Four Major Challenges Facing an Accelerated US 'Prompt Global Strike' Program [美"快速全球打击"难获快速发展 面临四大难题]," *China Daily*, June 11, 2010. Available online at www.chinadaily.com.cn/hqjs/jsyw/2010–06–11/content_446614_2.html.
20 "Establishing a National Aerospace Security System [建立我国的空天安全体系]," *Science News* [科学时报], February 24, 2002. Available online at www.cas.cn/xw/zjsd/200202/t20020224_1683499.shtml.
21 For a primer, see *Counterspace Operations*, Air Force Doctrine Document 2–2.1, August 2, 2004. Available online at www.dtic.mil/doctrine/jel/service_pubs/afdd2_2_1.pdf.
22 For reference to the action plan and space-based surveillance system, see "China Decides on Three Major Engineering Programs for 2006–2020 Space Debris Action Plan [中国确定2006至2020年空间碎片行动计划三大工程]," CNSA, December 25, 2003. Available online at www.cnsa.gov.cn/n615708/n676979/n676983/n886611/66292.html.
23 See Liu Yazhou Wenzhai at http://wenku.baidu.com/view/ce7fa62458fb770bf78a5534.html, p. 8.

Section C
China's security in the information age

22
China's security in the information age

Greg Austin

On 27 February 2014, Xi Jinping became the first General Secretary of the Chinese Communist Party (CCP) to head the Leading Group[1] on Cyber Security and Informatization.[2] In his first meeting as chair, he told the group that China would do what was required to become a "cyber power" (*wǎngluò dàguó*). The security motivations of the decision have three main sources: acceptance that informatization is a major currency of international power; an understanding that the United States enjoys dominance in military uses of cyber space; and fears of the use of internet means by critics and enemies of the CCP to undermine its legitimacy at home. In addition, there were two organizational drivers of the new leadership arrangements. First, Xi distrusts the internal security forces, which had become far too powerful, having dared to use cyber assets against the leadership.[3] They are also riddled with corruption. Second, the leaders are not satisfied with progress under previous arrangements in the development of China's capabilities in either cyber security or informatization.

This chapter offers a broad overview of how China's leaders see the main strands of their security policy in the information age. It situates the highly publicized topics of cyber espionage and the Great Firewall (political surveillance and control of the internet) against the background of a much bigger canvas of policy, especially cyber war-fighting capability on the one hand and, on the other, the development pathway and needs of national economic security.[4] This chapter suggests that China's behavior in domestic cyber surveillance and international cyber espionage, though each in a certain sense fundamental to the character of the current political and economic system in China, can be interpreted differently from certain prominent views[5] if one looks carefully at existing scholarly analysis and if one takes account of the Chinese leaders' view at a strategic level. The leaders' view is situated against the background of global cyber space development and the international distribution of military power. It is a view that is both comprehensive (multi-sector) and long term (future looking). In that connection, it could be observed at the outset that the overwhelming share of scholarly and public analysis in the United States on military and espionage aspects of cyber policy in China has been about the operational or tactical level, not the strategic level. There is no book length study that looks in depth at both China's military cyber strategies and its capabilities. One simple reason is that there are no comprehensive public sources available. The shorter analyses provide excellent insights into particular aspects but do not provide a comprehensive picture.[6] By contrast, on internal security policy, there are many excellent detailed studies on the leadership's strategic level approach to the impact of the information age and on the sorts of capabilities they have assembled to protect their interests.[7] Yet even on that subject, much of the information is secret in China and our picture is far from complete.

China and cyber warfare

In cyber warfare, China is coming from behind. It started late and it is still catching up, especially to the United States.[8] An accessible reference point for the time lag is to compare, on the one hand, a 1996 article by Nye and Owens in *Foreign Affairs* on "America's Information Edge,"[9] in which US capability and ambition are made plain in general but impressive terms, and, on the other hand, an authoritative assessment that by 1999, China's leaders had not even committed to a concept of information war.[10] The imbalance in open source reporting in recent years on Chinese cyber capability against the United States compared with that in the reverse direction[11] should not obscure the reality, discussed further below, that China is not only in catch up mode but still lags badly.

What is cyber war? Official US documents, such as the Top Secret Presidential Policy Directive (PPD) 20[12] of October 2012 and the Joint Force doctrine manual on information operations[13] of November 2012 make plain the extent of modern information warfare as the United States would conduct it. These documents therefore define the extent of their needs for defense or offense against countries that might be adversaries of the United States, such as China. In defining cyber space, PPD20 refers not just to the internet, computers and networks, but also to telecommunications networks and processors and controllers in any automated system that can be operated remotely.[14] Cyber operations in wartime seek to impair the confidentiality, integrity or availability of not just the machines but the data contained therein. This can include penetrating enemy intelligence systems and altering the information about one's own forces. PPD20 states that the United States will seek to apply "cyber effect operations" (COE) in all spheres of national activity affecting war, diplomacy and law enforcement. It says that offensive COE (OCOE) "can offer unique and unconventional capabilities to advance US national objectives around the world with little or no warning to the adversary or target and with potential effects ranging from subtle to severely damaging." An authoritative US think tank study embraced an even broader definition: cyber conflict is "broader than cyber warfare, including all conflicts and coercion between nations and groups for strategic purposes utilizing cyberspace where software, computers, and networks are both the means and the targets."[15] In the above discussion, the reference to attack with little or no warning has serious consequences for previous approaches to military strategy that depend on various degrees of warning, from years or months to days, depending on the scenario. If the United States seeks a military cyber capability "in all spheres of national activity affecting war, diplomacy and law enforcement," then—as its leaders believe—China must be able to combat that.

The recognition by China's leaders of these considerations can be seen in their public speeches and in policy changes after the issue of cyber attacks came to prominence in 1999 during the NATO military campaign against the former Yugoslavia. In 2000, Jiang Zemin, then General Secretary of the CCP and Chairman of its Central Military Commission (CMC), made several speeches laying out the idea that new developments in information technologies had transformed global strategic realities in all domains: political, economic, social and military.[16] In 2001, the country upgraded its leadership structure in this policy domain. The State Informatization Leading Group (SILG) remained the main body, but it was brought more fully under the CCP apparatus, and leadership of it was entrusted to the premier, instead of one of the vice premiers. In 2003, the CMC approved a major change in military doctrine to narrow the focus, away from "winning a local war under high tech conditions" to one of "winning a local war under conditions of informatization." That year, the first major and long running cyber espionage operation attributed to China, Titan Rain, was launched. In 2005, former prime minister Wen Jiabao described informatization as a "mega-trend for world development."[17] In 2006, China issued a National Informatization Plan 2006–2020 addressing a wide range of policy domains. A 2011 report by the Chinese Academy of Sciences assessed that these technologies "will profoundly affect the structure, organization and activity patterns of future society."[18]

The 2003 commitment by the CMC to a military strategy that placed advanced cyber warfare capabilities and tactics at the heart of all military planning and operational development has intensified in the decade since, with each biannual defense White Paper showing an evolution in what this would mean.[19] By 2006, the CMC had approved training regulations for cyber combat operations. In 2007, the PLA made an explicit shift from a narrow view of informatized wars that focused on computers, networks and the transmission of code to a more comprehensive view that saw IW as involving the entire electromagnetic spectrum. The 2008 White Paper set a new mission in informatized wars of ensuring China's "electromagnetic space security." To this end, the PLA would henceforth devote far more effort to training its personnel for combat in complex electromagnetic environments. This White Paper summarized some of the other achievements in informatization across all military areas, including strategy, training and education. Thus, the broader conceptualization of cyber war as understood in US doctrinal statements has been well articulated in Chinese sources, including in a brief mention in the 2008 White Paper on National Defense (published in 2009).[20]

But the development of the capability by China has been lagging well behind the articulation of the need for it. There are three organizational or structural issues that affect the pace of China's military informatization. First, the armed forces provide much of the technical infrastructure and some personnel for the internal security cyber missions. Many PLA cyber staff have internal security missions. Second, the decision by the CMC to proceed with informatization was part of a double-barrelled commitment to "mechanization and informatization," meaning that the armed forces would still need to complete mechanization while gearing up for cyber war. Third, there is recognition in the PLA that China will never be able to match the United States in what it spends on national defense, including narrowly on cyber assets.

By 2014, in announcing the intention to become a "cyber power," China was committing to an international security strategy (not just a military strategy) that placed cyber capabilities and the cyber environment, including the global balance of power in cyber space, at the center of everything, including diplomacy and development of the national industrial base. In March 2014, China announced yet another double-digit increase in its public defense budget, having announced in November 2013 that it would increase its spending on cyber warfare.

In respect of the global balance of cyber power, China has consistently assessed that the "United States has established the leading position in the military realm" of the information age because of its overall scientific and technological lead.[21] China's 2010 White Paper also gives an insight into how good its leaders think their joint operations capability (needed for advanced information warfare) is. It notes that China has obtained only a "preliminary level" of interoperability between different elements of its armed forces within this sphere. A Chinese military observer writing in 2012 commented that "all core technologies are basically in the hands of US companies, and this provides perfect conditions for the US military to carry out cyber warfare and cyber deterrence."[22]

The United States government and the best-informed American analysts (from the intelligence community) think much the same. The US analysts are relatively unanimous in asserting that the United States has an unmatched military cyber power, for several reasons.[23] First, it has been able to build off its undisputed pre-eminence in the civilian information technology sector. It has been able to provide appropriate incentive mechanisms to the private sector to have them allocate R&D resources to military applications. Second, China lacks the necessary testing ground for strong military cyber capabilities, especially the capacity for integrated command and control of joint operations. The analysts cite in the US case a strong tradition of such operations, refined in combat around the globe almost non-stop since the Goldwater Nichols Act of 1986. They link this then to a US history of offensive cyber operations beginning at least as early as the 1999 campaign against the former Yugoslavia. Third, and most importantly, the United States has unmatched human and technical intelligence collection capabilities needed for effective cyber offensive operations against military targets and for achieving information dominance, its declared military strategy. (China now has the same strategy of trying to achieve information dominance at the beginning of a conflict.)

There is a distinction to be made between, on the one hand, comprehensive cyber military power, based on joint operations across the entire electromagnetic spectrum, including reliance on space based assets, and on the other hand capability in niche areas, such as some areas of cyber espionage. China's armed forces are well short of where they want to be in cyber warfare capability. China may have closed the gap in conventional military armaments between it and the United States in some areas of capability, but one might imagine that the gap in cyber warfare capability has probably widened. We don't, however, really know, needing much more information than is available now to reach a confident assessment. On the basis of available evidence, it has been argued that China's military leaders must be in a state of "despair at the breadth and depth of modern digital information and communications systems and technical expertise available to their adversaries."[24] In the civil sector, China's leaders bemoan slow progress in technological innovation, as universities remain only weak contributors to commercial R&D, and as the brain drain from the country shows no signs of slowing.[25] China remains only an average performer in global comparisons, having actually lost ground for the last 3 consecutive years in the World Economic Forum's annual network readiness index, to slip from thirty-sixth in 2011 to sixty-second in 2014.[26] Indexes can only provide a rough indication and depending on their methodology can often be challenged in numerous ways. Yet a closer look at most sectors of the Chinese economy bears out the view that informatization has penetrated in a stop-start fashion, and in all cases has been limited by the general S&T levels in the Chinese economy and industry as a whole.

China has to take into account not only US strategies and capabilities, but also those of key US cyber allies, such as Taiwan, Japan, Australia, the United Kingdom, France and Germany. China has no such allies, a fact that exacerbates its already disadvantageous position from the technological point of view. According to Charles Krauthammer, the originator in 1990 of the term "unipolar moment," the Western alliances were then a primary foundation of American pre-eminence.[27] At that time, the allies included 16 NATO members, Japan and Australia. Today, NATO, with 28 members, is actively co-operating with 20 additional countries on cyber defense. By comparison, in the cyber world, China has no real allies in military uses of cyber space, except potentially Russia, which is anyway as untrusting of China in military and espionage aspects of cyber space as the United States is.[28]

Since China's armed forces remain weak relative to those of the United States, a circumstance of strategic military inferiority, Chinese strategists have in their discussions seized on the idea that cyber assets can nonetheless provide capabilities for attack against a superior enemy.[29] For example, the strategists have argued that Chinese military planners should look for cyber means to blunt the US capability to mobilize a large naval and air force in the vicinity of Taiwan. This argument about the asymmetrical potential of cyber weapons has also been extended with some justification to what might be termed exclusively cyber operations, where one side uses cyber means to attack the cyber assets of the enemy. The argument is that in cyber space, the offense has the advantage: one side can execute a disabling pre-emptive attack that can deliver a huge advantage through strategic surprise in such a way as to disable superior forces for sufficient time to achieve a politically significant military outcome.

There is no strong consensus in specialist circles about the viability of such operational strategies if China were to attempt them. They would have a certain appeal to Chinese decision-makers, since China is in almost every other sense clearly inferior in military capability to the United States, a degree of inferiority only magnified by the US alliances. According to US intelligence sources, there is some evidence that China has developed operational plans in this direction. But in terms of overall strategy (the conduct of an entire war as opposed to discrete combat operations in a war), the arguments do not stand up all that well once we consider the full extent of modern information warfare, especially potential cyber impacts across the full spectrum of operations, from conventional to nuclear. In particular, once we consider the impact of pre-emptive cyber strikes on command and control of strategic nuclear missile forces, we quickly realize that this is a domain where the idea of a disabling first strike by cyber means could have serious escalatory potential, even if it were feasible.

The Great Firewall

China's leaders see their political system and security as dependent on tight controls on freedom of speech, assembly, association and even of conscience. They remain committed to the concept of dictatorship, albeit an increasingly consultative one. Against this background, they have decided that the internet and mass communications capability of mobile computing and mobile telephony must be tightly controlled. In 2007, the general secretary, Hu Jintao, told a meeting of the Politburo that, "Whether we can cope with the internet is a matter that affects the development of socialist culture, the security of information, and the stability of the state."[30] This has been the consistent view of the leadership since at least the late 1990s.[31] As technologies improved and became available on larger scales between 1995 and 2000, so too did the size and capability of China's control apparatus. Given the distributed nature of the internet, and mobile telephony, the leaders decided around 2001 that the old methods of monitoring and censorship would no longer work by themselves, and that they needed a policy of social control, where security and propaganda officials would work with internet service providers, Party members, and volunteers to monitor and report on unacceptable activities. In 2001, the newly established Internet Society of China began co-opting private internet service providers to monitor traffic. In 2004, the government set up the China Internet Illegal Information Reporting Center (CIIRC), supported by the MPS and other agencies. This was part of the Communist Party's reliance on social control. It uses the CIIRC to enable public supervision of all internet activity. But in opting for social control, China was not reducing its commitment to censorship and physical controls. In 2004, China almost doubled its intake of students in bachelor's courses for public security technology (meaning mostly cyber surveillance technology) compared with the previous year.[32] This commitment to train large numbers of IT specialists for control of the internet has delivered amazing capabilities, well documented in studies of the high speed with which unacceptable material is removed from the internet.[33]

There have been several discreet fields of concern in internal security: use of the internet to challenge CCP rule; use of advanced IT capabilities to organize public protests on livelihood, environmental or social issues; and cyber crime. While all of these concerns can be addressed by the development of a common public security apparatus, each has required tailored approaches that have increased the costs of government efforts. The rapid evolution of threats has brought visible evolution in policy.³⁴ By 2011, the annual budgets for the central government departments working on public security began to climb dramatically, with the announced spend for central departments in 2013 standing at 31 percent higher than in 2010 (in current prices not adjusted for inflation)—193 billion RMB compared with 147 billion RMB.³⁵ The 2014 projected spend was 205 billion RMB, an increase of 6.1 percent on the previous year.³⁶

In the 60-point policy reform agenda released after the Third Plenum of the CCP in November 2013, the leaders committed yet again to "expand forces to manage the network according to the law, accelerate the perfection of leading structures for internet management, guarantee the security of the national network and of information." By February 2014, as mentioned above, the leaders had elevated information security to an even higher priority by assigning it to the leadership of Xi Jinping. He already had responsibility as chair of three other leadership groups highly relevant to cyber security and informatization: the new National Security Committee, the Leading Group on the comprehensive deepening of reform, and the CMC. The 60-point reform agenda had announced the establishment of the National Security Committee, with a mission to "perfect national security structures and national security strategies, and guarantee national security." The establishment within the framework of public security of yet another high-level committee is a reliable indicator of deepening concerns on the part of leadership about their ability to control security in the internet age. Every few years, beginning in 1993/1994, they have created some new mechanism like this as an add-on to pre-existing committees or leading groups on internal security.

China's cyber intelligence apparatus is, in terms of manpower, probably the biggest ever assembled in human history. It requires the nationwide mobilization of censors, propagandists, monitors, private corporations, universities, schools, work places and IT specialists to collect information. After that, it requires armies of internet police, internal security forces, lawyers, courts and prisons to conduct operations to enforce discipline as the CCP sees it. It requires real time intelligence collection and delivery by technical and human means across the country's entire population of 1.3 billion people, and among the diaspora communities in another 20 or more countries. Yet, if we are relying on public sources, we have no precise detail on the total numbers of Chinese officials, uniformed personnel, contractors, co-opted private sector workers and volunteers who are engaged in cyber surveillance domestically. We have only a few foundations on which to base an assessment of the technical qualification and political effectiveness of this massive surveillance force.

There have been repeated and high profile intelligence failures in internal security surveillance in China in spite of massive capabilities. For example, security agents were unable to prevent the short-lived defection of Wang Liqun to the US embassy in Chengdu in February 2012 or the April 2012 flight from house arrest in Shandong province of a blind activist, Cheng Guangcheng, to arrive undetected inside the US embassy in Beijing, a journey of almost 500 kilometers. In both cases, cyber surveillance assets would have been deployed and should have helped prevent the occurrences. Moreover, one of the highest priorities of internal cyber surveillance is the prevention of public demonstrations, but these occur in the hundreds of thousands each year. Publications such as the *China Digital Times* report regularly on the breaches of China's digital security and its weaknesses in stopping discussion. In fact, China has reached the situation where it has become more tolerant of "online activism" is if it can ensure "offline obedience."³⁷ But even the latter is challenged on a daily basis around the country in spite of the Great Firewall. Many ordinary people in China know how to access banned websites. The leaders' faith in their new "great wall" as a viable defense in cyber space may be as misplaced as the faith of earlier rulers in the various versions of the classic forerunner built from stone and earth. There is no questioning the engineering ambition and initial psychological impact of the wall, but for how long and against which enemies can it serve its purpose?

Cyber espionage

The information age has levied massive new intelligence requirements on China. Simultaneously, the new technologies have brought with them unprecedented opportunities for remote access to information of intelligence interest, and all major countries are exploiting that. But, in the security sphere, as discussed above, advanced information technologies are not exclusively used for surveillance and espionage. They have also become primary weapons of war. Moreover, warfighting strategies of major powers (the United States, Russia and China included) now assign information dominance at a strategic level as the necessary condition for victory. Thus mapping the entire information warfare capability of all China's potential adversaries, and monitoring changes in them on a daily basis, have become additional requirements for its espionage services. The same agencies are tasked with collection internationally of technical and economic intelligence to support China's economic strategies, including scientific and technological development. Its technical capabilities for cyber intelligence collection put it among the major actors: the United States, Russia, the United Kingdom, France and Israel. But that is a fairly simplistic assessment that does not take into account a whole host of non-technical considerations and that probably overstates China's capability relative to that of the United States.[38]

The available academic literature and open source information on the activities of China's international intelligence agencies provide rich detail on the scope of collection, but little information on the analysis or the subsequent uses to which information is put. We can name the agencies involved, and we can estimate the number of people working in them, and there are descriptions of a number of operations (though even most of these accounts are patchy).[39] We can see the Chinese policies in practice but we have only a mixed picture of the degree to which these policies are intelligence-based. We know what information is being scooped up by the collectors but not exactly how much of it is being translated into or summarized in Chinese and to whom it is then transferred.

The 2013 Mandiant report on China's cyber espionage assessed that the country's main signals intelligence and cyber espionage organization—the Third Department of the General Staff Department People's Liberation Army (PLA)—may have "130,000 personnel divided between 12 bureaus, three research institutes, and 16 regional and functional bureaus."[40] This may give a reasonable upper limit to the cyber espionage capability of China in terms of total manpower, but many of these would not be front line collectors, monitors or analysts. The proportion of skilled manpower to task (graduates in information technology and hackers involved in cyber espionage) is probably relatively low compared with the proportion in comparable US agencies.

Institutional settings for cyber surveillance and espionage

For China, the challenges of controlling the political effects of the information revolution at home and those of collecting foreign intelligence by cyber means are at first glance problems of a different order. The former, captured in the metaphor of the Great Firewall, is a strategic level objective that involves massive human and financial resources and activities throughout the entire country; while cyber espionage is far more contained activity limited to a relatively small number of people in specialized agencies. Yet for China these are not such distinctly segregated activities as in other countries. The apparently neat separation in the United States between the foreign focus of the Central Intelligence Agency (CIA), the domestic law enforcement focus of the Federal Bureau of Investigation (FBI), and the domestic legal constraints on the cyber espionage of the National Security Agency have arisen because of the country's particular political system. Yet, as recent decades have shown, there are operational needs where the agencies have to cross some of those boundaries. Moreover, as President Obama said on 17 January 2014, history has shown that governments, even good ones, can't be trusted when it comes to the boundaries of intelligence collection.[41] What then might China's unique political system mean for the issue of boundaries and the cross-over between functions?

An overview of the development of how these issues have played out in China (mostly in the pre-cyber era) can be found in Guo's impressive study, *China's Security State*, which recounts the complex interplay between military and civilian agencies in an environment where (historically at least) China's intelligence and security concerns "have been primarily domestic."[42] Of special note, as Guo observes, the "military and civilian domestic security functions are interwoven in complicated ways that are different from those of most regimes."

Inside the Chinese government, there are at least two senior political figures responsible for cyber espionage. The first at the time of writing is Meng Jianzhu, a Politburo member and the Secretary of the Central Political and Legal Commission (CPLC), a Party body that is arguably the single most powerful institution in the entire country. It controls all police, all courts, all judges, and all draft legislation, as well as non-military espionage for internal and international security. It controls all encryption and technical standards for China's governmental apparatus, including the armed forces. The CPLC runs a variety of intelligence agencies of which the two most powerful are found within the Ministry of Public Security and the Ministry of State Security. The second intelligence leader is General Fang Fenghui, the Head of the General Staff Department (GSD) of the PLA and a member of the Central Military Commission. He is responsible for military espionage and cyber operations by three separate departments of the People's Liberation Army (Second, Third and Fourth). These two men have significant other duties (accountabilities) apart from intelligence collection, most notably operations and policy planning.

Inter-agency relations between the various intelligence bodies are almost certainly subject to the same pressures as those in other countries. General Fang is not a member of the Politburo, but Meng Jianzhu is. Nevertheless both are very powerful. Inside China, there is no predictable or reliable legal regime that offers consistent redress for or protection against unlawful electronic surveillance. There have been only a few cases in the courts, so few in number as to represent what can only be the tip of an iceberg. There is no judicial review of electronic surveillance actions by the intelligence and security apparatus comparable to the sort undertaken in the United States by the court set up by the Foreign Intelligence Surveillance Act (FISA). This absence of judicial review guarantees that the procedures followed by China's agencies inside their own country are probably even more random and unchecked than similar activities were in the United States before the FISA court was set up in 1978. Moreover, there is no well developed legal regime of privacy in China, with new regulations on this being passed only late in 2012 after the leadership change at the Party Congress in November that year. There is only a weak freedom of information regime, and a well-entrenched social disposition to discretion and confidentiality. In this environment, and given the history of China's domestic politics, Xi Jinping and other members of the Standing Committee of the Politburo would find it very difficult to go past these two senior leaders to look into the day to day surveillance activities of the intelligence agencies in the interests of correcting some policy path, such as theft of intellectual property, even if they were of a mind to do so. The preoccupation of the Chinese leadership with the internal security dimensions of cyber space has trumped all other concerns, such as innovation in the universities, the informatization of agriculture, or faster informatization in the armed forces. It is therefore unlikely that the leaders would burn political capital with the leaders of the front line surveillance and intelligence agencies to investigate them for industrial espionage (for commercial benefit rather than national security purposes) even if they felt they needed to.

The bigger picture

The announcement on 27 February 2014 of China becoming a cyber power was steeped in the idea of a competitive international system that is the hallmark both of the realist vision in international relations theory and of classic Chinese communist framings of world order. Yet in China's march toward becoming an advanced information economy and society, a process that was launched in embryonic form in 1983, there has been from the outset a persistent recognition that the development of China's capabilities would be heavily dependent on foreign technologies, foreign specialists and foreign investors. This had a dual aspect: on the one hand China needed massive inputs from the outside world, and on the other it needed the outside world to buy its related industrial production. This reliance on the outside world has had a profound impact on China's security policies, both in classic military terms and in internal security terms.

Over the last three decades, the balance between domestic and foreign assets in China's information society development has changed dramatically in the detail, but the interdependence is still a very powerful force at a general level. Thus, in spite of China's seemingly natural disposition to a realist framing of its cyber ambitions, it has had to operate in a deeply internationalist process of exchange that forces it to accommodate the outside world. China wants to be a cyber power in a realist sense but finds itself very much mired in a liberal internationalist world.

There are leading scholars of the information society outside China who take this reality one step further. They see the new age of advanced information and communications technologies as sufficiently pervasive and transformative to call into question old notions of state sovereignty, national power and frontier defense. The new vision is one of a borderless world where information utilities (such as Microsoft, Apple and Huawei) and venture capital have acquired such power that they redefine the contours of the global and national political economy, and of social loyalty.[43] This vision also includes an appreciation of new forms of distributed moral and political power arising directly from the mass availability of cheap and uncontrollable forms of social media. This school of thought comes close to the concept of common security, the idea that a state imagines its national security as indistinguishable from the security of the larger international society. The idea of common security is only weakly articulated in China but it fits very closely with the notion of a transformational cyber reality and the borderless world of cyber space that does have a bigger following in China than the idea of common security.

All three mindsets mentioned above (realist, liberal internationalist, and transformative information society) can be found in official Chinese rhetoric about the country's national security. The locus of the type of discussion or emphasis given to each idea depends largely on the functional responsibilities of the government departments. The armed forces and security agencies give primary authority to a realist vision, the economic and technology ministries and the foreign ministry pay most attention to internationalist interpretations, while the third view (the transformational and borderless world) has an eclectic following. One finds its adherents in the Chinese Academy of Sciences, the Advisory Committee for State Informatization and the emerging school of information ethics in China. One of President Xi's main economic advisers, Liu He, had experience working among this third group around the turn of the century.

There is a fourth constituency that is highly influential in policy for cyber space that pays little attention to any school of thought, but which unconsciously drags China away from realist impulses toward co-operative or common security. This is the private sector which in China is, in nationality terms, very much a hybrid—what Stalin would have called a form of cosmopolitanism (people with non-national loyalties in contrast to those with visible patriotism). A number of significant Chinese information technology and related services firms are listed on foreign stock exchanges, many others are part-owned by Taiwanese, Americans, Japanese, Koreans or

Europeans. Three examples of this interest group at work may be worth mentioning. First, based on patent data, the main sources of IT innovation in China today apart from Huawei, ZTE and Hon Hai remain foreign-invested firms, working through the large number of research laboratories they have set up in China.[44] Second, there is an organization called the United States Information Technology Office (USITO), constituted as a non-profit organization and located in Beijing, which represents the interests of several peak industry bodies from the United States inside China. It is regularly consulted by or offers self-initiated advice to the Chinese government on new legislation or regulations in the IT sector. It has occasional discussions with Chinese authorities about cryptography involved in imported products, even as cryptography remains one of the more sensitive national security technologies. Third, elites in China regard foreign higher education as superior to that available in China, with President Xi's daughter having enrolled at Harvard University in 2010, where according to newspaper reports she studied until 2012.[45] Over 290,000 Chinese students, most privately funded, were studying in the United States on 1 April 2014,[46] and most of these end up staying there. While these factors generate a relatively formless and apolitical influence on foreign policy, a form of unstructured cosmopolitanism, they do reinforce the otherwise weak tendency toward common security ideals.

As a result of the small number of common security advocates in China, the main contest is between realism and liberal internationalism, and it has been widely studied.[47] There has been no decisive victory for one mindset over the other. In particular, there appears to be a pervasive contradiction between a bristling "great power" mentality, associated with acquiring progressively greater military capability (the realist view), and an integrationist, economics-based approach in which national prosperity separate from a peaceful global economy is simply not imagined (the liberal internationalist view). For a number of reasons, China's leaders have tolerated this pervasive contradiction without forcing any sort of resolution. Fundamentally, if asked, they would say that the two streams of thought and policy are not incompatible. They would say that this is how the world operates and they could point to the United States as the best exemplar. They would say that even though a state must keep its national defenses in order, this in no way obviates the pursuit of mutual self-interest either in economics or in security policy. Henry Kissinger has articulated this in respect of the United States.[48]

Emergence of cyber diplomacy

As China participated in the internationalized system of exchange in IT products and related services, as it adapted to the opportunities and threats from the militarization of cyber space, and as it grappled with international pressure over domestic censorship of the internet, it has been forced like other states to gradually ramp up its capabilities for cyber diplomacy. Before 2000, China's first forays in the area of international governance of the IT sector and related communications policy were practical, case specific and low key. This was quite well illustrated by a low level of engagement with the International Telecommunications Union (ITU) around the turn of the century.[49] China did support related resolutions in the UNGA beginning in 1998. Its participation in the preparation for the World Summit for an Information Society in 2002 and 2003 marked the first significant effort by it to match its foreign policy to the new diplomatic challenges of the information age.

In a 2011 speech to the UN, China's ambassador Wang Qun acknowledged the seriousness of the impact of the information age on security: "information and cyberspace security represents a major non-traditional security challenge confronting the international community. Effective response to this challenge has become an important element of international security."[50] The ambassador went on to say that the international community should view this issue from the new perspective of "a community of common destiny" and "work together toward a peaceful, secure and equitable information and cyber space." This approach contrasts quite strongly with that of mainstream military strategists in China. Wang advocated five principles that together represent a comprehensive statement of the country's view on the diplomatic aspects of international security in the information age, but as sketched in more detail, the vision is a mix of co-operative security concepts and competitive realism. He set out five goals:

1. Peace (or war avoidance), including prevention of a cyber arms race and non-proliferation of cyber weapons, and retention of the right of self-defense against cyber attack or sabotage.
2. Sovereignty and territorial integrity will remain basic norms, with states being the main actor in governance of information and cyber space and with states being obliged to refrain from using cyber tools to interfere in the domestic affairs of others.
3. Balancing between freedom and security, both on the domestic stage (uphold the rule of law to keep order in cyber space) and in international affairs (practicing power politics in cyber space in the name of cyber freedom is untenable).
4. Co-operation: the interdependence of cyber networks means that "no country is able to manage only its own information and cyber business" or "ensure its information and cyber security by itself"; all countries need to work together.
5. Equitable development: developed countries have an obligation "to help developing countries enhance capacity in information and cyber technology and narrow the digital divide."

One of the major vectors of China's cyber diplomacy impacting security has been the battle over internet governance. In September 2011, China, Russia and two other countries brought forward a proposal at the UN called an "International Code of Conduct for Information Security."[51] The content is wide ranging and seeks to prohibit non-peaceful uses of the internet as well as to internationalize internet governance.[52] On face value, the proposals might seem relatively common sense, but in favoring a more powerful voice for governments in international management and oversight of the internet they carry the risk of being used to support repression of free speech, freedom of association and freedom of conscience. The Chinese approaches have been vigorously opposed by liberal democracies.

In this environment, the goal of co-operation on cyber space issues between China on the one hand and the United States and its allies on the other may seem remote. But the confrontation in the political domain is in strong contrast with the situation in other areas of policy, especially economic and social. The gathering momentum in these areas has been captured in a series of UNGA agreements and resolutions, especially the December 2011 Resolution adopted by the General Assembly on the report of the Second Committee (UN Docs A/66/437) on Information and Communications Technologies for Development, and an associated General Assembly resolution (UN Docs A/Res/66/184). In other areas, some headway has been made. For example, by the end of 2013, the annual Sino-US Internet Forum has been convened seven times. The US-China Joint Law Enforcement Liaison Group, though set up in 1998, became progressively more active and effective after 2005, including in fighting cyber crime. In August 2011, it succeeded in a joint operation against a global child pornography network, shutting down 18 websites after years of unsuccessful bilateral talks. Its meeting in late 2013 involved some 80 participants meeting over 2 days. In one Chinese view, there are several areas for relatively easy progress in multilateral diplomacy: emergency response to cyber security, supply chain security, undersea cable protection and action against groups such as WikiLeaks, Anonymous, LulzSec and AntiSec.[53] Moreover, there is now some expectation in government circles in the West that the hard edges of the ideological battle with China over internet governance may be honed down, in part because of pressing mutual concerns over the cyber security of critical international infrastructure, and in part because Western diplomats are now beginning to realize that the sharp battle lines drawn by them have been counter-productive. Yet these developments constitute a snail's pace of movement toward any concept of common security.

It is China's weakness in the broader vision of cyber conflict that determines its military strategy of disabling critical infrastructure in the United States in the event of an imminent war with it. As President Barack Obama observed in his State of the Union Address, in a clear allusion to China, "our enemies are also seeking the ability to sabotage our power grid, our financial institutions, and our air traffic control systems."[54] Yet both countries want stability in cyber space in order to foster continuing economic and technological exchange, and an end to current destabilizing cyber practices. The overarching policy question then becomes one of comparing national insecurities and vulnerabilities, and then eventually addressing them. The two countries appear to need a diplomatic strategy for managing a very big asymmetry of power in cyber space. US Defense Secretary, Chuck Hagel, put this on the table before a visit to China in April 2014.[55] He said that the Department of Defense "will maintain an approach of restraint to any cyber operations outside of US government networks. We are urging other nations to do the same." This is noteworthy not simply because the Pentagon is recognizing for the first time how its immense cyber power is aggravating its own security dilemma, but also because it is a recognition that US military strategy has to address the basic reality that cyber space is a global commons on which the prosperity of all major economies now depend. The United States expects China to respond positively with a commitment to similar restraint.

Prospects

China wants to be a cyber power. It is determined to maximize its military capabilities in cyber space and its capabilities to control domestic uses of the internet. It is making steady progress in that direction. Yet Chinese leaders see the country as non-competitive in war-fighting uses of cyber space compared with the United States and its global web of alliances. It is in part this weakness that drives China's cyber space policy, but in any case its leaders still tend, viscerally it seems, much more toward a classic vision of great power rivalry than to a liberal internationalist view. In spite of acceptance by the leaders of large doses of co-operative behavior, they see themselves in a combative world, and in a cyber arms race with the United States. This is most likely where they will stay—at least until there is some sort of crisis. China is finding new grounds for a bristling military posture as a result of its maritime disputes with neighbors, such as Japan, Vietnam and the Philippines, and because of United States strategies in the Western Pacific.

The overall weak state of China's cyber warfare capability stands in stark contrast to its cyber capabilities for internal security surveillance and foreign espionage. Even so, while China has demonstrated massive capability in these areas, the discussion above has suggested that there is room to question the measure of China's hard power that results from the capability.

As China has pursued high technology development, it has deepened its integration in the process of international exchange. In addition, the information age has brought with it certain social and economic forces that have been weakening both the realist disposition and the CCP hold on power. In the 20 years since the internet was introduced to the public in China, the CCP has consistently been forced to adjust its strategies to accommodate more pluralism. The relaxation of tension between China and Taiwan in recent years may also contribute to a softening of China's realist disposition. As the state-owned economy shrinks to 25 percent of GDP by the year 2020, as business people begin to exert their influence in the CCP, and as the ICT sector becomes increasingly dominant in the scenarios for sustaining economic growth, the leaders may be increasingly obliged to conform more strongly to the liberal international view. They may even begin to edge toward the more radical idea of common security that is inherent in the unstructured cosmopolitanism of the global market, a disposition that many in China's information technology community, especially its entrepreneurs and scientists, already exhibit.

Notes

1. In China's political system, a Leading Group is a small number of political leaders who function as a sub-committee of the Politburo and/or the State Council. Such groups are the place where policies are developed, executed and monitored in line with previous (often quite broad) decisions of the higher bodies. Their membership usually cuts across functional bureaucratic lines of individual portfolios.
2. Between 2001 and 2014, this group was led by the premier. Before that, from 1993 to 2001, it was led by a vice premier. Until the 2014 announcement, the group's remit was simply "informatization." This means the application in all walks of society and the economy of advanced information and communications technology. Cyber security had been part of this brief, but not such a publicly prominent part. The word informatization is hardly used in English, probably because we take the phenomenon for granted. It is widely used (in local rendering) in other major languages. It is often used in Chinese, as in other languages, in comparison with "industrialization" to describe a period in economic and social development or a process of fundamental transformation of the society and economy in ways that realign social relationships and political power.
3. Reporting on this is mixed. A credible report has surfaced claiming that the now convicted former leader Bo Xilai was involved in tapping telephone calls made between Communist Party Secretary General Hu Jintao and the investigator sent to Chongqing to look into the Bo case while he was still party secretary of the provincial level city. Reports of electronic surveillance of leaders take on more significance in the context of stories covered in the American press in 2012, which detailed the personal wealth of the immediate families of then prime minister Wen Jiabao and the extended family of Xi Jinping, general secretary in-waiting at the time. The extensive detail of the news stories appears to have been drawn from a level of knowledge of the leaders' families that would normally be available only to an insider. According to the Bloomberg story, "Assets were traced using public and business records, interviews with acquaintances and Hong Kong and Chinese identity-card numbers." Some of this information was obtained online. There have been subsequent revelations, through the leak of a massive database on offshore bank accounts in the British Virgin Islands and the Cook Islands, about a number of people in China in senior positions. See Greg Austin, "Terabyte Leaks and Political Legitimacy in the United States and China," *The Globalist*, 24 January 2014. Available online at www.theglobalist.com/terabyte-leaks-political-legitimacy-u-s-china/.
4. In a 2014 book, *Cyber Policy in China*, Polity Press: Cambridge, UK, I lay out the prospects for the country to achieve its ambition of becoming an advanced information society. It gives a broad overview of the evolution of China's policies from 1983 onwards, when China adopted the goal of making its electronics industry grow twice as fast as the rest of the economy. The book addresses the political, economic and military aspects of China's ambition.
5. For example, the claims by some leading US figures and analysts that Chinese cyber espionage represents the greatest illicit transfer of wealth in history or that it is a strategy to undermine US economic security are not, in this author's view, proven in the public record by their advocates. For a lengthy exposition supporting the claims, see William C. Hannas, James Mulvenon, and Anna B. Puglisi, *Chinese Industrial Espionage: Technology Acquisition and Military Modernisation*, Routledge, New York (Asian Security Studies), 2013.
6. An excellent overview of Chinese strategic ideas for cyber war can be found in Timothy L. Thomas, *Decoding the Virtual Dragon*, Foreign Military Studies Office, Fort Leavenworth KS, 2007; Hwang Ji-jen, *China's Cyber Warfare: The Strategic Value of Cyberspace and the Legacy of People's War*, PhD thesis, Newcastle University, 2012; and Dennis F. Poindexter, *The Chinese Information War: Espionage, Cyberwar, Communications Control and Related Threats to United States Interests*, McFarland Inc., Jefferson NC, 2013. Some of the best articles are the following: Desmond Ball, "China's cyber warfare capabilities," *Security Challenges*, 7(2), 2011, 81–103; Magnus Hjortdal, "China's use of cyber warfare: Espionage meets strategic deterrence," *Journal of Strategic Security*, 4(2), 2011, 1–24; Christopher R. Hughes, "Fighting the smokeless war," in Hughes and Gudrun Wacker (eds), *China and the Internet: Politics of the Digital Leap Forward*, Routledge, London, 2003, 139–61; David Lai, "Introduction," in R. Kamphausen, D. Lai, and A. Scobell (eds), *The*

PLA at Home and Abroad: Assessing the Operational Capabilities of China's Military, US Army War College Press, Carlisle PA, 2010; Kevin Polpetter, "Towards an integrative C4ISR system: Informationization and joint operations in the People's Liberation Army," in Kamphausen, Lai, and Scobell (eds), op. cit., 193–236; Andrew Scobell, "Discourse in 3-D: The PLA's evolving doctrine, circa 2009," in Kamphausen, Lai, and Scobell (eds), op. cit. 99–134; James Mulvenon, "'True is false, false is true, virtual is reality, reality is virtual': Technology and simulation in the Chinese military training revolution," in R. Kamphausen, A. Scobell, and T. Tanner, T. (eds), *The "People" in the PLA: Recruitment, Training, and Education in China's Military*, United States Army Strategic Studies Institute, Carlisle PA, 2008, 49–98; James Mulvenon, "The PLA and information warfare," in James C. Mulvenon and Richard H. Yang (eds), *The People's Liberation Army in the Information Age*, RAND, Santa Monica CA, 1999. Short insights can be found in several other sources, such as Richard A. Clarke and Robert K. Knake, *Cyber War: The Next Threat to National Security and What to Do About It*, HarperCollins, New York, 2010; Roger Cliff, John F. Fei, Jeff Hagen, Elizabeth Hague, Eric Heginbotham, and John Stillion, *Shaking the Heavens and Splitting the Earth: Chinese Air Force Employment Concepts in the Twenty-first Century*, RAND, Santa Monica CA, 2011; annual reports by the US Department of Defense to Congress on *Military and Security Developments Involving the People's Republic of China* (various years), United States Dept of Defense, Washington, DC; Bryan Krekel, Patton Adams, and George Bakos, "Occupying the information high ground: Chinese capabilities for computer network operations and cyber espionage," Prepared for the US–China Economic and Security Review Commission by Northrop Grumman Corp., 2012. Available online at www.gwu.edu/~nsarchiv/NSAEBB/NSAEBB424/docs/Cyber-066.pdf.

7 Zhang Junhua and Martin Woesler (eds), *China's Digital Dream—The Impact of the Internet on Chinese Society*, London, European University Press, 2003; Hughes and Wacker (eds), op. cit., 139–61; Tai Zixue, *The Internet in China: Cyberspace and Civil Society*, Routledge, New York, 2006; Jens Damm and Simona Thomas (eds), *Chinese Cyberspaces: Technological Changes and Political Effects*, Routledge, London and New York, 2006; Johan Lagerkvist, *The Internet in China: Unlocking and Containing the Public Sphere*, Lund, Lund University, 2006; Wu Xu, *Chinese Cyber Nationalism: Evolution, Characteristics, and Implications*, Lexington Books, Lanham MD, 2007; Zhao Yuezhi, *Communication in China: Political Economy, Power, and Conflict*, Rowman and Littlefield, Lanham MD, 2008; Zheng Yongnian, *Technological Empowerment: The Internet, State, and Society in China*, Stanford University Press, Stanford CA, 2008; Zhang Xiaoliang and Yongnian Zheng, *China's Information and Communications Technology Revolution: Social Changes and State Responses*, Taylor & Francis, London, 2009; Yang Guobin, *The Power of the Internet in China: Citizen Activism Online*, Columbia University Press, New York, Paperback Edition, 2011, First Edition 2009; David Kurt Herold and Peter Marolt (eds), *Online Society in China: Creating, Celebrating, Instrumentalising the Online Carnival*, Routledge, London and New York, 2011.
8 A fuller account of this is available in Austin, op. cit., 130–45.
9 Joseph F. Nye Jr and William A. Owens, "America's information edge," *Foreign Affairs*, 1996 (March/April). Available online at www.foreignaffairs.com/articles/51840/joseph-s-nye-jr-and-william-a-owens/americas-information-edge.
10 Mulvenon, "The PLA and information warfare," op. cit.
11 The revelations by Edward Snowden beginning in June 2013 remain one of the few public sources of information on US cyber operations of any kind against China.
12 Available at www.fas.org/irp/offdocs/ppd/ppd-20.pdf.
13 Joint Chiefs of Staff, *Information Operations*, Joint Publication 3–13, 27 November 2012. Available online at http://www.dtic.mil/doctrine/new_pubs/jp3_13.pdf.
14 The document is available at www.fas.org/irp/offdocs/ppd/ppd-20.pdf.
15 James C. Mulvenon and Gregory J. Rattray (eds), *Addressing Cyber Instability*, Cyber Conflict Studies Association, 2012, x. The Executive Summary can be accessed at www.cyberconflict.org/storage/CCSA%20-%20Addressing%20Cyber%20Instability.pdf.
16 See Jiang Zemin, *On the Development of China's Information Technology Industry*, Central Party Literature Press and Shanghai Jiatong University Press, 2009, published in translation by Elsevier, Oxford UK, 2010. The book is a collection of speeches and articles.
17 Gov.cn, "Govt OKs informatization development plan," 4 November 200. Available online at www.gov.cn/english/2005–11/04/content_91435.htm.
18 Li Guojie (ed.), *Information Science and Technology in China: A Roadmap to 2050*, Chinese Academy of Social Sciences, Science Press, Beijing; Springer, Heidelberg, 2011.
19 For an overview, see Austin, op. cit., 132–6.

20 Information Office of the State Council, "China's National Defense in 2008," January 2009. Available online at www.china.org.cn/government/whitepaper/node_7060059.htm.
21 Qu Weizhi, *China's Path to Informatization*, Cengage Learning Asia, Hong Kong, 2010, English Kindle Edition, loc. 426. See also various speeches to the Central Military Committee between 2000 and 2005 by Jiang Zemin, Jiang, op. cit. 2010, Kindle Edition, locs. 4953, 4977–8, 5010.
22 See Adam Segal, citing the military newspaper *China Defense*, "The cyber trade war," *Foreign Policy*, 25 October 2012. Available online at www.foreignpolicy.com/articles/2012/10/25/the_cyber_trade_war.
23 See Austin, op. cit., 133–4.
24 Desmond Ball, "China's Cyber Warfare Capabilities," *Security Challenges*, 7(2) (winter 2011), 81–103.
25 See Austin, op. cit., 121–3. The international migration of labor and entrepreneurship is a normal phenomenon, and can flow both ways. In the case of China's scientific and technical elites, the character of the flow has been unbalanced—more outward than inward. China has moved to overcome this imbalance but not adequately, as far as the leaders are concerned. National talent management is now one of the highest priorities of the CCP, rather than the government.
26 See annual editions of World Economic Forum and ISEAD, Global Information Technology Report, available at WEF, Geneva, www.weforum.org/reports/global-information-technology-report-2013, and similar addresses by year.
27 Charles Krauthammer, "The unipolar moment," *Foreign Affairs*, 70(1), America and the World (1990/1991), 23–33. He said in the second paragraph that there is one pole: "The center of world power is the unchallenged superpower, the United States, attended by its Western allies."
28 China and Russia are both members of the Shanghai Cooperation Organization whose members signed a treaty for co-operation on information security in 2006, but the main focus of this collaboration is internal security. The treaty is in the form of a "Statement of Heads of State of Member States of Shanghai Cooperation Organization on International Information Security."
29 See Thomas, op. cit., 267–70 for an overview.
30 *China Daily*, 25 January 2007. Available online at http://english.peopledaily.com.cn/200701/24/eng20070124_344445.html.
31 For a more detailed analysis, see Austin, *Cyber Policy in China*, 62–74.
32 For details, see Austin, op. cit., 64.
33 See for example Zhu Tao, David Phipps, Adam Pridgen, Jedidiah R. Crandall, and Dan S. Wallach, "The velocity of censorship: High-fidelity detection of microblog post deletions," Cornell University Library. Submitted 4 March 2013, arXiv:1303.0597v1 [cs.IR]. Available online at http://arxiv.org/abs/1303.0597; and Zhu Tao, David Phipps, Adam Pridgen, Jedidiah R. Crandall, and Dan S. Wallach, "Tracking and quantifying censorship on a Chinese microblogging site," Cornell University Library. Submitted 26 November 2012, arXiv:1211.6166v1. Available online at http://arxiv.org/ftp/arxiv/papers/1211/1211.6166.pdf.
34 For an overview, see Austin, op. cit., 62–74.
35 For 2013 figure, see China National People's Congress, "Full text: Report on China's central, local budgets (2014)." Available online at www.npc.gov.cn/englishnpc/Speeches/2014–03/18/content_1856702.htm. For 2010 figure, see Ministry of Finance, "*Guānyú 2010 nián zhōngyāng hé dìfāng yùsuàn zhí háng qíngkuàng uǔ 2011 nián zhōngyāng hé dìfāng yùsuàn cǎo'àn de bàogào* [Report on the Implementation of the Central and Local Budgets for 2010 and on the Draft Central and Local Budgets for 2011]," Fourth Session of the Eleventh National People's Congress, 5 March 2011. Available online at http://online.wsj.com/public/resources/documents/2011NPCBudgetReportZhFull.pdf.
36 See Ministry of Finance, "Report on the Implementation of the Central and Local Budgets for 2010 and on the Draft Central and Local Budgets For 2011, Second Session of the Twelfth National People's Congress." Available online at http://online.wsj.com/public/resources/documents/2014Budget_Eng.pdf.
37 See David Kurt Herold, "Introduction: Noise, spectacle, politics: Carnival in Chinese cyberspace," in Herold and Marolt, op. cit., 1–19, p. 12.
38 Senior US officials with detailed knowledge of China's intelligence capabilities interviewed by the author believe US capability to be far superior to that of China.
39 Sources include Mandiant, "APT1: Exposing one of China's cyber espionage units," 2013. Available online at http://intelreport.mandiant.com/; Krekel et al., op. cit.
40 Mandiant, op. cit.
41 Remarks by the President on the Review of Signals Intelligence, 17 January 2014. Available online at www.whitehouse.gov/the-press-office/2014/01/17/remarks-president-review-signals-intelligence.

42 Xuezhi Guo, *China's Security State: Philosophy, Evolution and Politics*, Cambridge University Press, Cambridge UK, 2012, 445.
43 An insight into how loyalty is being transformed can be found in the account of the way US citizens working for Symantec who were trying to decipher the Stuxnet worm reacted to their realization that they could be interfering with live feeds to a US-initiated covert intelligence operation against Iran. They decided to persist, believing that their duty to their corporation's mission and clients demanded it: "How digital detectives deciphered Stuxnet, the most menacing malware in history," *Wired*, 11 July 2011. Available online at www.wired.com/2011/07/how-digital-detectives-deciphered-stuxnet/. An insight can also be gleaned from the public positioning of US-based corporations, such as Microsoft, on their dealings with China, as articulated regularly by leading representatives who consistently say: "They are all our customers," meaning no distinction is to be made in political loyalty between China and the United States. Leading US IT corporations have counted Chinese security agencies among their customers and leading US corporations have been prepared to change their privacy standards and intellectual property rights regimes to satisfy Chinese regulatory demands. For its part, Huawei has declared publicly that it does not owe any patriotic allegiance to China that might compel it to undertake cyber espionage. All of these statements can be taken with a grain of salt.
44 See Huang Lucheng, Wang Kangkang, Wu Feifei, Lou Yan, Miao Hong, and Xu Yanmei, "SWOT analysis of information technology industry in Beijing, China using patent data," in B. Murgante et al. (eds), *ICCSA 2012*, part 1, 447–61, 457–8. The authors cite patent data from 2010 for all of China that shows that of the top ten patent assignees, the top two were Chinese (Huawei and ZTE) and the other eight were foreign (Samsung, Sony, Panasonic, IBM, Canon, Intel, Sharp and LG).
45 See http://chinese-leaders.org/xi-jinping/ (accessed 18 May 2014).
46 Student and Exchange Visitor Program (United States Department of Immigration and Customs Enforcement], "Sevis by the Numbers," General Summary and Quarterly Review, 14 April 2014. Available online at www.ice.gov/doclib/sevis/pdf/by-the-numbers1.pdf. See also Kelly Chung Dawson, "Chinese immigration to US still rising," *China Daily*, 17 September 2013. Available online at http://usa.chinadaily.com.cn/epaper/2013–09/17/content_16975662.htm.
47 A useful summary of the main arguments and the principal studies up to 2010 can be found in Barry Buzan, "China in international society: Is peaceful rise possible?" *Chinese Journal of International Politics*, 3(1) (2010), 5–36.
48 Henry Kissinger, *Diplomacy*, Simon & Schuster, New York, 1995, 29–55.
49 That low level of interest contrasts with the current situation where a Chinese national is expected to move from being deputy secretary general to become secretary general of the ITU in an election for the post in late 2014.
50 Wang Qun, Speech by H. E. Ambassador Wang Qun at the First Committee of the Sixty-sixth Session of the GA on Information and Cyberspace Security, 20 October 2011. Available online at www.fmprc.gov.cn/eng/wjdt/zyjh/t869580.htm (last accessed 28 August 2012).
51 See www.fmprc.gov.cn/eng/zxxx/t858978.htm.
52 For an overview of China's position, see a statement prepared for a conference in Geneva in 2014 hosted by the United Nations Institute for Disarmament Research: "An International Code of Conduct for Information Security: China's perspective on building a peaceful, secure, open and cooperative cyberspace," 10 February 2014. Available online at www.unidir.ch/files/conferences/pdfs/a-cyber-code-of-conduct-the-best-vehicle-for-progress-en-1–963.pdf.
53 Yi Wenli, "Divergence and co-operation between China and the US on the cyberspace issue," *Contemporary International Relations*, 4 (2012), 124–41, 138.
54 State of the Union Address, 12 February 2013. Available online at www.whitehouse.gov/the-press-office/2013/02/12/remarks-president-state-union-address.
55 David Alexander, "Hagel, ahead of China trip, urges military restraint in cyberspace," Reuters, 28 March 2014. Available online at www.reuters.com/article/2014/03/28/us-usa-defense-cybersecurity-idUSBREA2R1ZH20140328.

Index

Abe, Shinzo 86, 92, 117, 177
Ahn Joong Geun 177
Air Defense Identification Zone (ADIZ) 86, 117, 276; air defense zone coordination 294–5
anti-access/area denial (A2/AD) 12, 87, 188, 285, 307, 319, 315
anti-imperialism 35, 41, 139–40, 149–51; south-south cooperation 142; *see also* Mao Zedong: house-cleaning policy; Third World
Arab Spring 65, 72, 153, 226
Arctic Ocean: Arctic Council 160–2; China's economic presence in 59; China's projects 159–60; China's trips to the Arctic 156; China's views on 156–7; donut hole 162; melting ice caps 10, 155; new sea lanes 155; Northern Sea Route 155, 159; strategic implications 156–7; *Xuelong* (Sea Dragon) polar icebreaker 156
ASEAN 14, 67–8; ASEAN Dream 252; ASEAN Plus Three 144; ASEAN Regional Forum 67; ASEAN Way 68
Asian 1997 financial crisis 10, 51, 67, 69–70, 142–3, 207
Asian Monetary Fund (AMF) proposal 143

balance of power 25, 98, 139, 203, 357; in the Taiwan Strait 83, 187
Beijing Consensus 53
bilateralism 7, 82; China's stance towards 231, 235–36, 251
BRICs 53, 128, 152–3, 174
Burma 9, 36, 252; conflict with ethnic Kachin rebel groups 127; relations with China 206, 252

Cambodia 145; hosting of 2012 ASEAN Summit 252
campaign-style policing 69
Central Military Commission (CMC) 258, 276, 282–3, 356–7
Central Party School 65
Central Political-Legal Committee 69, 71
Central Political and Legal Commission (CPLC) 362
Chen Shui-bian 60, 184–5, 194; independence-leaning initiatives 185

Chiang Ching-kuo 183
Chiang Kai-Shek 37, 105, 192; attempts to recover mainland 29, 182; policy towards Japan 149–50
China: culture of harmony 2–3, 16, 30, 259; Ministry of Commerce 167; population size 49; rise of 173, 218, 248
China, cybersecurity 16, 72–3, 88; aspirations to be a cyber-power 355; asymmetric potential of 358–9; cyberespionage 361; cyberintelligence 360; cyberwarfare 261, 356–9; diplomacy of 364–6; Five Principles of Cyber Diplomacy 365; institutional settings of 361–2; internet governance 365; military strategy 356–7; role of private sector 363–4; The Great Firewall 359–60
China, economy: access to raw materials 56; charm offensive 52; commercial diplomacy 59; confiscation of foreign owned enterprises 37; economic growth 49, 53, 175–6; economic interdependence 54; economic security 4–5, 50–1, 247–9; economic statecraft 5–6, 14; economic stimulus 245–46; environmental effects 50; fears of Western encirclement 55–6, 111; Modern Silk Road 58; preferential trade agreements (PTAs) 58–9; Regional Comprehensive Economic Partnership (RCEP) 60; resource diplomacy 56–7; state-owned enterprises 54, 145, 147–9, 152; Trans-Pacific Partnership (TPP) 56, 60; World Trade Organization (WTO) 52, 59; *see also* energy security; maritime trade routes
China, foreign policy: Angola Model 148; core national interests 125–6, 173, 181–2, 188, 249; grand strategy 26–7; international organizations 12, 67, 128, 138, 143–4, 160; non-interference 66–8, 131, 183, 208–9, 232; pragmatism 21, 26, 221; relations with Africa 10, 42, 57, 144, 147–9, 154; relations with Brazil 152–3; relations with Latin America 151–3; relations with Middle East 220–1; soft power 52; strategic culture 25–7, 30–1, 74, 311–12; use of deception 27–8; views on international order 201–2, 206; White Paper on Peaceful Development 123, 126; *see also* Beijing Consensus; BRICs; United Nations

Index

China, nuclear forces 15–16; air and naval theater nuclear systems 328; deterrence 322; ICBMs 321, 324–5; intercontinental missiles 324–5; IRBMs 325–6; LACMs 327–8; missile defense 328–9; MRBMs 326–7; No First Use pledge 322; nuclear policy 322–3, 328–9; Second Artillery Corp (SAC) 321; second-strike systems 323; size of arsenal 322–3; SLBMs 321, 325; SRBMs 327; tactical nuclear weapons 328; theater missiles 325–8; Underground Great Wall 323

China, relations with Central Asia: bilateralism or multilateralism 235–6; economic relations 229–30; illicit trade 231–3; military cooperation 234–5; relationship between development and political security 230–1; security deficit 231; spillover effects into Tibet and Xinjiang 229, 237

China, relations with Europe 13, 153; Albania military aid 42; anti-piracy cooperation 222–3; conflict over Africa 148, 221–2, 226; economic relations 218, 224; European arms embargo 225–6; joint statements 219; nuclear non-proliferation 219; positions on Iran 220; preferential trade talks 59; security relations 217–18; terrorism cooperation 222; view of Europe of not much importance 221; *see also* NATO

China, relations with India 9, 127–8, 138, 144–5; border clashes 12, 25, 40, 127; cooperation within BRICs 152; support for India Security Council bid 208–9; trade relations 128; *see also* India

China, relations with Japan 8–9; anti-Japanese protests 113–14; Chinese nationalism 109, 117; cooperative development 107, 114–17; Diaoyu/Senkaku island dispute 57, 84, 107, 113–18; 126, 178, 244, 276; during the Cold War 104–8; effect on Sino-American relations 83–4, 105, 107–8; First Sino-Japanese War 168; General Tojo's Japan's exploitation of resources of Northeast China 138; history tensions 105; maritime threats 108; Mukden Incident 116; remilitarization debate 106, 112–14; Tripartite Environment Ministers Meeting (TEMM) 68; *see also* ADIZ, Japan

China, relations with Korea 11, 22–3; during the Cold War 169; economic relations with North Korea 169–71; economic relations with South Korea 167; effect on Sino-American relations 84–5, 172–3; human resources exchange between China and South Korea 171; Korean War 38, 168; Mutual Aid and Cooperation Friendship Treaty 168; North Korea nuclear program 11, 167, 172, 174–8, 219, strategic cooperative partnership between China and South Korea 171; strategic value of North Korea 167, 172–3, 178; Tripartite Environment Ministers Meeting (TEMM) 68; *see also* North Korea; South Korea

China, relations with less-developed countries (LDC) 10, 41–2; economic aid 142; LDC support for China's nuclear test 141; post-1989 PRC shift in support for 141; pro-LDC policies 142; relationship with anti-imperialist policy 139–40; security agenda 141; support for anti-Soviet forces 139 *see also* anti-imperialism; Third World

China, relations with Russia 7–8, 14, 36–41, 139–40, 161, 203, 234–7; arms sales 96–8; border disputes 93–4; Chinese response to Crimea crisis 57–8, 93, 99; competition in Central Asia 229; energy cooperation 94–6; post-Soviet collapse rapprochement 90–1; Sino-Soviet split 39–40, 90, 168–9; soft balancing against West 91, 93, 97–9; strategic partnership 91, 98; Treaty of Good-Neighborly and Friendly Cooperation 93; Yellow Peril 94; *see also* Russia

China, relations with South Asia: arms transfers to Pakistan 129; counterbalance to India in region 123–4, 127; economic investment in 124–5; relations with Bangladesh 130–1; relations with Nepal and Bhutan 132–4; relations with Pakistan 124–5, 128–30; relations with Sri Lanka 131–2; role as offshore balancer 127, 134; strategic engagement in 127–8; trade relations 125, 129; *see also* China, relations with India; string of pearls

China, relations with Southeast Asia 6, 14, 146–7; Joint Declaration of ASEAN and China on Cooperation in the Field of Non-Traditional Security 68–9; relations with Vietnam 42, 57; Sino-Vietnamese War 275, 277; *see also* South China Sea dispute

China, relations with Taiwan 11–12; 92 consensus [*jiu-er gongshi*] 184, 193; Anti-Secession Law 185–7; armed liberation 181; Beijing's state constitution 182; China ambiguity about possible use of force 187; China policy towards 38, 43–4; China strategy to achieve unification 12, 183, 194, 334–5; Cross-Strait Service Trade Agreement (CSSTA) 60, 192; cross-strait trade 60, 167, 191–2; democratic influence on the PRC 193–4; dollar diplomacy 124; Economic Cooperation Framework Agreement (ECFA) 59–60, 185, 192; effect on Sino-American relations 83, 183, 185, 188; espionage 190; military objectives 187–8; One-China Policy 12, 181, 183–4, 190, 192, 194; peaceful unification 181, 185, political objectives of 190–1; PLA battle plan for 10, 188–9; Second Taiwan Strait Crisis 275; security policy 186; Strait Exchange Foundation (SEF) 183; symbolic dependence of 195; *Taishang* 191–3; Third Taiwan Strait Crisis 8, 110–11, 184; Taiwanese concerns about increasing dependence on China 191–2; United Front 3, 191–3; *see also* Taiwan

Index

China, relations with USA 7, 36, 45–6, 151, 178, 204; American forces in Japan 83–4; arms race 87, 311, 314; Asia pivot 7, 86, 92, 126, 173, 188; China Threat theory 55, 126, 210, 241; common interests 81–2; constructive engagement 45; currency manipulation 55; cyberwarfare 356–9; global commons 82, hegemony 13, 23, 98–9, 107, 128, 134, 201–3; holdings of US dollars 55; military competition 87, 349, 351; missile defense systems 87, 328; nuclear proliferation concerns 82, 84, 219; re-establishment of relations 169; strategic encirclement 56, 86; Taiwan arms sales 82–3, 189

China, security 1, 232; Defense White Paper 258; Great Wall security orientation 4; influenced by Marxism/Leninism 34, 40; response to color revolutions 72; role of morality and ideology in policy 2, 23; security state apparatus 74; *see also* collective security; domestic security; energy security; food security; human security

China, space capabilities 16; achievements 334; anti-satellite weaponry 87; China Aerospace Science and Technology Corporation (CASC) 339–40; China Aerospace Science and Industry Corporation (CASIC) 321, 339–41; civilian support for 335–6; counterspace organization 350; General Armaments Department 336–7; industrial infrastructure 339; integrated joint operations 347; launch vehicles 338–9; Lunar exploration program 342; personnel 348; relation with science and technology 334, 351; Shenzhou manned space program 342; space-based surveillance systems 343–5, 349; space-based communications systems 345–7; space command 337–8; space station program 342–3

China Dream 30, 34, 55–6, 161, 248

Chinese Consultative People's Political Conference (CCPPC) 192–3

Chinese nationalism: 4, 43, 57, 116, 146; during the late Qing 140, 149–51; government encouragement of 109

class struggle 3, 150

climate change 9, 59, 75, 152, 174; China's response to 207; effects on security 118, 158–9

Clausewitz, Carl von 307, 313–4

Clinton, Hillary 173, 251

collective security 12–13; *see also* Shanghai Cooperation Organization

Confucianism 2, 34, 312; Confucian pacifism 23–5; morality 3; relation with Legalism 26; views on international order 24–5, 211–13

constructivism 202, 206–7, 210–13

Copenhagen School of Security Studies 247–9

cult of the defense 2

Deng Xiaoping 44–5, 140, 150, 312; emphasis on economics over revolution 44, 140; foreign policy 8, 12, 182–3, 203; policy towards Japan 107–9; reform and opening up 52, 169; response to Tiananmen Square protests 140–1

Democratic Progressive Party (DPP) 60, 83, 193; stance towards China 184–6; *see also* China, relations with Taiwan

Department of Public Security 71, 234; *see also* public security

domestic security, of China 16–17; preservation of CCP rule 153, 202

economics *see* China, economy

energy security 56–8, 96, 145, 159, 229–30; Chinese dependence on foreign oil 54–5, 145; Chinese energy cooperation with Russia 94–6; Chinese trade with Africa 147; Chinese trade with Central Asia 229–30

English School 202, 207–9; *see also* constructivism

European Union 28, 52, 87, 114; defense capabilities 224–5; dependence on NATO 225; *see also* China, relations with Europe

Exclusive Economic Zones (EEZ) 7, 276; in the Arctic 156, 159, 163

Falun Dafa/Gong 70–1; Zhongnanhai demonstrations 71

food security 155–8, 163

foreign aid, Chinese 4, 10, 140, 147–8

geography: relationship with security 28–30

global 2009 financial crisis 51–3; 55, 175, 243–44

Gou Haibo 160

guerrilla warfare 3

Hainan 241; Bo'ao Forum 241

Hatoyama, Yukio 115–16

Ho Chi Minh 38, 41

Hong Kong 12, 51; Communist agreement not to re-take 43

Hu Jintao 72, 185; foreign policy 45; Great Firewall 359; harmonious society 12–13, 56, 206–7; 211–12; historic missions for the PLA 284; policy towards Japan 115; policy towards Taiwan 185

human security 66, 232, 237–8

India 97; hegemony in South Asia 123–4; post-colonial passions 144–5; *see also* China, relations with India; China, relations with South Asia

Indian Ocean 58, 123, 144–5, 152, 225, 314, 338; PLA Navy presence in 223, 317

interest groups 234, 364; *see also* Regulations on the Registration and Management of Social Organizations

island chains 8, 15, 86, 187, 190, 311, 314–16

373

Index

Japan: 2+2 Meeting 175; Article Nine 104–5; colonial administration over Korea 168; concert of democracies 86; defense budget 108, 117; nuclear weapons ban 112; post-war economic miracle 105; relations with South Korea 177; relations with USA 110–12, 117–18; Russo-Japanese War 168; Self-Defense Force 106, 110; *see also* China, relations with Japan

Jang Sung Taek: execution of 167, 175–6

Jiang Zemin 45, 52, 64; information technologies 356; policy towards Taiwan 183–4; strengthening ruling capacity of the Party 71; United Nations 203

Jong-Il, Kim 169–70

Jong-un, Kim 175–6

juche 168

just wars 2, 4, 24–6

Kan, Naoto 115–17

Khrushchev, Nikita 39–40; peaceful coexistence 4, 40, 169

Koizumi, Junichiro 8, 112–13, 115, 178

Kuomintang (KMT) 12, 60, 83, 149, 193; Chinese Civil War 90; espionage 182; modern policy towards the PRC 181–2, 185; support for by the Taiwan military 189

Leading Small Groups: chaired by Xi Jinping 73; cybersecurity 16; Lunar Orbit Exploration Project 342; National Security 64; Stability Maintenance Work 71; to defeat 2008 Olympics criticism 147

Leaning Towards One Side Theory [*yibiandao*] 36; *see also* Mao Zedong Thought

Lee Teng-hui 183–4, 276

Legalism 26

liberalism 205–6, 363–4

Li Keqiang 53; on the South China Sea 241–2; war against pollution 50

Lin Biao 41

Lisbon Reform Treaty 224; *see also* European Union

Ma Ying-jeou 60, 185–6, 247; relations with the PRC 83, 193

Mahan, Alfred Thayer 306–11, 315; critique of Russian naval strategy 309–10; distinction between maritime and naval 307

Manchus 29; territorial conquests 29–30, 140, 149–50

Mao Zedong 3, 35–46; borrowing of China's martial subculture 3; contradiction 3; diplomacy 36; house-cleaning policy 35–6; influence on naval strategic culture 312; Mao Zedong Thought 3; missile policy 328–29; nuclear policy 40; policy towards Japan 149–50, 312; policy towards Taiwan 182

maritime trade routes 58; Malacca Dilemma 58, 145–6, 159; sea lanes of communication (SLoCs) 58

Marxism-Leninism 34–5

mass incidents 69

Meng Jianzhu 362

Ming Dynasty 24, 29–31; territorial expansion 149

multilateralism 14, 86, 130, 251; China's stance towards 12, 143, 169, 202–7, 211, 219, 234–37

Myanmar *see* Burma

National Security Committee 64; scope of responsibilities 64–5

new security concept (NSC) 67

Nicaragua Canal 152

non-aligned movement 138

non-traditional security 6, 65–6, 74, 269–70; China's security predicament 69–70; interest of Chinese scholars and policymakers in 67; international cooperation on 67–9; lack of distinction from traditional threats 65; regulation of 70–1; relationship with domestic stability 69; *see also* Tibet; Xinjiang

North American Treaty Organization (NATO) 8, 14; bombing of PRC's embassy in Belgrade 91, 203; campaign against Yugoslavia 356; relationship with China 225, 358; relationship with Russia 90–2, 99

North Korea: August Factional Strife 168; Chosun Trade Bank 167; economic dependence on China 167; foreign aid from the US 169–70; Korean War 168; third nuclear test 110–11, 167, 172; paradox of self-determination 176; possible collapse of 172

nuclear non-proliferation Iran – European Union nuclear talks 220

Obama, Barack 45, 92, 184, 362, 366; *see also* China, relations with USA: Asia pivot

Park Geun-hye 175, 177–8

Party Congress: 11th Party Congress 4; 15th Party Congress 69; 18th Party Congress 64, 280–1

peaceful coexistence 4, 7, 169, 208; Five Principles of Peaceful Coexistence 10, 23, 127–8, 232

People's Armed Police (PAP) 69

People's Liberation Army (PLA) 4, 15, 271; amount of active personnel 257, 260; battalions 267; border and coastal defense units 268; brigades 266–7; chain of command 269; defensive orientation 270–1; divisions 266; group armies 265–6; impact of force cuts 257–61, 269–72; logistics sub-departments 268; military budget 5, 14, 243, 259; military modernization 7, 268–9, 272; military regions and structure 261–4, 281; operational and tactical units 264; order of priorities 181; organizational structure 259–61;

regiments and groups 267; reserve units 268; strategy 25, 258–9; ties to Huawei 16; *see also* anti-access/area denial

People's Liberation Army Air Force (PLAAF) 15; academic institutions 290; aircraft 276–7, 285–6; branches and subordinate units **278**; campaign theory 284–5; education 290–2; force size 286; foreign relations 295–6; leadership 279–80; missions and responsibilities 277, 281–2; organizational structure 277–9; Party Congress 279, recruitment 288; role in Chinese security 275–7; strategy 282–4; unit training 292–4

People's Liberation Army Navy (PLAN) 58; active defense strategy 15, 276, 283, 306–7, 312, 318; anti-ship ballistic missiles (ASBM) 314; coastal defense 313–15; fortress fleet strategy 307–11, 316–18; in remote theaters 317; missile strike range 308–9; possible conflict with the USA 317; strategic culture 312; strategically defensive aims 316–17; *see also* anti-access/area denial

people's war 3–4, 41, 72, 258, 312–13
permanent revolution 3–4, 35, 41
political commissars (PCs) 262–3
power transition theory 5, 7, 204, 244
public security 69, 264, 359–60
Putin, Vladimir 58, 92, 95–7

Qian Qichen 67
Qing Dynasty 93, 310; choice between frontier and maritime defense 29; legacy of territorial expansion 1, 30, 140, 149–50

realism/realpolitik 201, 363–5; Chinese realism 26–7, 151, 203–5
Regulations on the Registration and Management of Social Organizations 71–2
Rise of China *see* China; rise of
Roh Moo-hyun 171, 178
Romance of the Three Kingdoms 28
Russia: annexation of Crimea 93, 99; de-Stalinization 39; economy 96–7; relations with the USA 92; Russo-Georgian War 95; Russo-Japanese War 168; *see also* China, relations with Russia

Scarborough Shoal 85, 252
September 11 73, 112, 204
Seven Military Classics 26
Severe Acute Respiratory Syndrome (SARS) outbreak 6, 65, 71–2
Shanghai Convention on Combating Terrorism, Separatism, and Extremism 67
Shanghai Cooperation Organization (SCO) 8–9, 68–9, 145–6; 230, 235–6; reasons for creation 13–14
Sinocentrism 21–3, 211
Six-Party Talks 174

small states and the balance of power 124
South Asian Association for Regional Cooperation (SAARC) 9, 130 –1, 134
South China Sea dispute 85–6, 145–7; Chinese strategic thinking in 250–1; effect on Sino-American relations 85–6, hubris argument 243–6; militarized conflict over 85; oil rig in the Paracels 242; resource development 243; satellite imagery 249–50; South Sea Fleet 243, 249; Xi Jinping's remarks on 242–3; Yulin military base 242
South Korea: economic relations with China 167; Korean War 168; relations with Japan 177; trust-building on Korean Peninsula 175
Stalin, Joseph 11, 37–8
State Oceanic Administration 58, 243
string of pearls 123, 152
Sun Yat-Sen 189, 194
Sun Zi 2, 21, 26–8, 187; influence on foreign policy 188

Taiwan 11; Japanese invasion of 29; relations with the US 83; social identity 83; US arms sales to 189; *see also* China, relations with Taiwan
territorial boundaries, China: 1, 15, 202
territorial disputes: relation with economic security 61; *see also* China, relations with Japan; China, relations with Southeast Asia
terrorism 6, 14, 65, 218; Chinese anti-terrorism efforts 64, 68, 92, 222, 234–5
Third World 10, 124, 141, 144–5
three evils 6, 14, 68, 232, 235–6
Three Principles of the People 189
Tiananmen 1989 protests 44, 108, 140–1, 205, 327
Tibet 30; effect on Sino-Indian relations 9, 127–8; policies towards 133, 150–1; protests in 2008 73; Qinghai-Tibet railway line 133, separatism 64–5, 203
Treaty of Amity and Cooperation in Southeast Asia 251
tribute system 22, 25
Two Middle Areas [*liangge zhongjian didai*] 41; *see also* Mao Zedong Thought

United Communist Party of Nepal (UCPN-M): influence of Maoism 133
United Nations 67, 107, 114; Chinese policy towards 107, 114, 201–4; Chinese voting patterns 209; Economic Commission for Asia and the Far East (ECAFE) study of continental shelf between Japan and Taiwan 107; peacekeeping operations 57–8, 207, 210–11; Security Council 58, 113, 130, 160; Security Council membership reform 113, 208–9; soft balancing 204; UN Security Council Resolution 2094 167; *see also* constructivism; English School; liberalism; realism

Index

United Nations Conventions on the Law of the Sea (UNCLOS) 85, 156, 160, 162
United Nations Human Rights Commission 121, 141–2, 147, 204–5

warfare: China's number of 2, 26
Wen Jiabao 71, 128, 246, 357
Westphalian system 22–3, 71
World Health Organization 71, 186
world revolution *see* permanent revolution
Wu Bangguo 69, 235

Xi Jinping 7, 45–6, 64–5, 96, 132, 242–3; Chinese dream 4, 34, 55, 248; foreign policy 212–13; influenced by Mao Zedong 45; on cybersecurity 16, 355; policy towards Taiwan 186; proposal of New Pattern of Great Power Relations 174–5; support of Korean unification 177
Xinjiang 6, 30, 73–4, 82, 95; economic development and political security 230–1; illicit trade 234; policy towards 150–1; security importance of 30, 231–2; separatism 13, 229; Urumqi protests 65, 73

Yasukuni Shrine 8, 92, 112–15, 118, 177
Yeltsin, Boris 90–2; foreign policy 91, 95

Zhou Enlai 8, 38–9, 182, 344; policy towards Japan 107–9; visits to the Third World 41
Zhou Yongkang 71